Computational and Mathematical Methods in Information Science and Engineering

Computational and Mathematical Methods in Information Science and Engineering

Editors

Wen Zhang
Xiaofeng Xu
Jun Wu
Kaijian He

Basel • Beijing • Wuhan • Barcelona • Belgrade • Novi Sad • Cluj • Manchester

Editors

Wen Zhang
Beijing University of
Technology
Beijing, China

Xiaofeng Xu
China University of
Petroleum
Qingdao, China

Jun Wu
Beijing University of
Chemical Technology
Beijing, China

Kaijian He
Hunan Normal University
Changsha, China

Editorial Office
MDPI
St. Alban-Anlage 66
4052 Basel, Switzerland

This is a reprint of articles from the Special Issue published online in the open access journal *Mathematics* (ISSN 2227-7390) (available at: https://www.mdpi.com/si/mathematics/Comput_Math_Methods_Inf_Sci_Eng).

For citation purposes, cite each article independently as indicated on the article page online and as indicated below:

Lastname, A.A.; Lastname, B.B. Article Title. *Journal Name* **Year**, *Volume Number*, Page Range.

ISBN 978-3-0365-8470-6 (Hbk)
ISBN 978-3-0365-8471-3 (PDF)
doi.org/10.3390/books978-3-0365-8471-3

© 2023 by the authors. Articles in this book are Open Access and distributed under the Creative Commons Attribution (CC BY) license. The book as a whole is distributed by MDPI under the terms and conditions of the Creative Commons Attribution-NonCommercial-NoDerivs (CC BY-NC-ND) license.

Contents

About the Editors vii

Wen Zhang, Xiaofeng Xu, Jun Wu and Kaijian He
Preface to the Special Issue on "Computational and Mathematical Methods in Information Science and Engineering"
Reprinted from: *Mathematics* 2023, 11, 3187, doi:10.3390/math11143187 1

Hong-Ding Yang, Yun-Huan Lee and Che-Yang Lin
On Study of the Occurrence of Earth-Size Planets in Kepler Mission Using Spatial Poisson Model
Reprinted from: *Mathematics* 2023, 11, 2508, doi:10.3390/math11112508 5

Maryam Cheema, Muhammad Amin, Tahir Mahmood, Muhammad Faisal, Kamel Brahim and Ahmed Elhassanein
Deviance and Pearson Residuals-Based Control Charts with Different Link Functions for Monitoring Logistic Regression Profiles: An Application to COVID-19 Data
Reprinted from: *Mathematics* 2023, 11, 1113, doi:10.3390/math11051113 19

Xian Shan, Zheshuo Zhang, Xiaoying Li, Yu Xie and Jinyu You
Robust Online Support Vector Regression with Truncated ε-Insensitive Pinball Loss
Reprinted from: *Mathematics* 2023, 11, 709, doi:10.3390/math11030709 33

Chengliang Wang, Feifei Yang and Quan-Lin Li
Optimal Decision of Dynamic Bed Allocation and Patient Admission with Buffer Wards During an Epidemic
Reprinted from: *Mathematics* 2023, 11, 687, doi:10.3390/math11030687 55

Chun-Yao Lee, Nando Purba and Guang-Lin Zhuo
Defects Classification of Hydro Generators in Indonesia by Phase-Resolved Partial Discharge
Reprinted from: *Mathematics* 2022, 10, 3659, doi:10.3390/math10193659 79

Xin Cao, Qin Luo and Peng Wu
Filter-GAN: Imbalanced Malicious Traffic Classification Based on Generative Adversarial Networks with Filter
Reprinted from: *Mathematics* 2022, 10, 3482, doi:10.3390/math10193482 107

Erjiang E, Ming Yu, Xin Tian and Ye Tao
Dynamic Model Selection Based on Demand Pattern Classification in Retail Sales Forecasting
Reprinted from: *Mathematics* 2022, 10, 3179, doi:10.3390/math10173179 125

Kaijian He, Don Wu, and Yingchao Zou
Tourist Arrival Forecasting Using Multiscale Mode Learning Model
Reprinted from: *Mathematics* 2022, 10, 2999, doi:10.3390/math10162999 141

Jiekun Song, Zeguo He, Lina Jiang, Zhicheng Liu and Xueli Leng
Research on Hybrid Multi-Attribute Three-Way Group Decision Making Based on Improved VIKOR Model
Reprinted from: *Mathematics* 2022, 10, 2783, doi:10.3390/math10152783 153

Jun Wu, Xin Liu, Yuanyuan Li, Liping Yang, Wenyan Yuan and Yile Ba
A Two-Stage Model with an Improved Clustering Algorithm for a Distribution Center Location Problem under Uncertainty
Reprinted from: *Mathematics* 2022, 10, 2519, doi:10.3390/math10142519 175

Yifei Zhao, Jianhong Chen, Shan Yang and Yi Chen
Mining Plan Optimization of Multi-Metal Underground Mine Based on Adaptive Hybrid Mutation PSO Algorithm
Reprinted from: *Mathematics* **2022**, *10*, 2418, doi:10.3390/math10142418 . . . . **193**

Bai Liu, Xiangyi Zhang, Runhua Shi, Mingwu Zhang and Guoxing Zhang
SEPSI: A Secure and Efficient Privacy-Preserving Set Intersection with Identity Authentication in IoT
Reprinted from: *Mathematics* **2022**, *10*, 2120, doi:10.3390/math10122120 . . . . **213**

K. Jeganathan, M. Abdul Reiyas, S. Selvakumar, N. Anbazhagan, S. Amutha, Gyanendra Prasad Joshi and et al.
Markovian Demands on Two Commodity Inventory System with Queue-Dependent Services and an Optional Retrial Facility
Reprinted from: *Mathematics* **2022**, *10*, 2046, doi:10.3390/math10122046 . . . . **233**

Yu-Kai Weng, Cheng-Han Li, Chia-Chun Lai and Ching-Wei Cheng
Equation for Egg Volume Calculation Based on Smart's Model
Reprinted from: *Mathematics* **2022**, *10*, 1661, doi:10.3390/math10101661 . . . . **255**

Yunqi Jiang, Huaqing Zhang, Kai Zhang, Jian Wang, Shiti Cui, Jianfa Han and et al.
Reservoir Characterization and Productivity Forecast Based on Knowledge Interaction Neural Network
Reprinted from: *Mathematics* **2022**, *10*, 1614, doi:10.3390/math10091614 . . . . **265**

Zhenpeng Li, Ling Ma, Simn Chi and Xu Qian
Structural Balance under Weight Evolution of Dynamic Signed Network
Reprinted from: *Mathematics* **2022**, *10*, 1441, doi:10.3390/math10091441 . . . . **287**

Peiyue Cheng, Guitao Zhang and Hao Sun
The Sustainable Supply Chain Network Competition Based on Non-Cooperative Equilibrium under Carbon Emission Permits
Reprinted from: *Mathematics* **2022**, *10*, 1364, doi:10.3390/math10091364 . . . . **309**

Yuan Wang, Liping Yang, Jun Wu, Zisheng Song and Li Shi
Mining Campus Big Data: Prediction of Career Choice Using Interpretable Machine Learning Method
Reprinted from: *Mathematics* **2022**, *10*, 1289, doi:10.3390/math10081289 . . . . **341**

Mengli Fan, Yi Huang and Wei Xing
Information Acquisition for Product Design in a Green Supply Chain
Reprinted from: *Mathematics* **2022**, *10*, 1160, doi:10.3390/math10071160 . . . . **359**

Zhiqing Meng, Jing Zhang, Xiangjun Li and Lingyin Zhang
Lightweight Image Super-Resolution Based on Local Interaction of Multi-Scale Features and Global Fusion
Reprinted from: *Mathematics* **2022**, *10*, 1096, doi:10.3390/math10071096 . . . . **375**

About the Editors

Wen Zhang

Wen Zhang currently works as a professor and Ph.D. supervisor at the Beijing University of Technology, Beijing, China. He is also the Deputy Director of the Blockchain Research Center of Beijing University of Technology, Beijing, China. He received a Ph.D. degree from the School of Knowledge Science of Japan Advanced Institute of Science and Technology (JAIST), Nomi, Japan. Prof. Zhang is currently a member of the Technical Committee of Security and Emergency Management of the Chinese Institute of Command and Control (CICC), a member of the Systems Engineering Society of China (SESC) and a part-time researcher at China Europe International Business School (CEIBS). He also previously worked as a program member at the PRICAI International Conference and the IEEE SMC International Conference. Prof. Zhang has published nearly 80 papers in international academic journals and conference proceedings. His research mainly focuses on data mining, big data analytics, machine learning and business intelligence.

Xiaofeng Xu

Xiaofeng Xu currently works as a professor and Ph.D. supervisor at the China University of Petroleum, China. He received a Ph.D. degree in Management Science and Engineering from Harbin Engineering University, Harbin, China. Professor Xu studies operations management and smart logistics systems, as well as their applications. He currently serves as a council member at the Chinese Society of Optimization, Overall Planning and Economic Mathematics (SCOPE), Secretary-General of the Technical Committee of Marine System Engineering of the Systems Engineering Society of China (SESC), Deputy Secretary-General of the Youth Committee of the Chinese Academy of Management Science (CAMS) and Director of the Decision Science Branch of the Operations Research Society of China (ORSC).

Jun Wu

Jun Wu currently works as a professor and Ph.D. supervisor at the Beijing University of Chemical Technology, Beijing, China. He received a Ph.D. in Management Science and Engineering from Xi'an Jiaotong University, Xi'an, China. He is currently the Deputy Director of the Laboratory of Transportation and Logistics with Big Data. He was selected into the "Program for New Century Excellent Talents in University" of the Ministry of Education in 2008. Professor Wu currently serves as an executive council member at the Decision Science Branch of the Operations Research Society of China (ORSC), a member of the Technical Committee of Emergency Management of the Systems Engineering Society of China (SESC), as well as a member of the Cold Chain Logistics Sub-Technical Committee of National Logistics Standardization Technical Committee. His research interests include big data analytics, intelligent algorithms, intelligent logistics, supply chain management, risk assessment and emergency management.

Kaijian He

Kaijian He currently works as a professor and Ph.D. supervisor at Hunan Normal University, Changsha, China. He received a Ph.D. in Management Science from City University of Hong Kong, Hong Kong SAR, China. He is the Deputy Secretary-General of the Decision Science Branch of the Operations Research Society of China (ORSC) and a member of the Technical Committee of Security and Emergency Management of the Chinese Institute of Command and Control (CICC). He specializes in economic forecasting, risk forecasting, big data analysis and deep learning and has published nearly 80 papers in international and domestic academic journals.

Editorial

Preface to the Special Issue on "Computational and Mathematical Methods in Information Science and Engineering"

Wen Zhang [1,*], Xiaofeng Xu [2], Jun Wu [3] and Kaijian He [4]

1. College of Economics and Management, Beijing University of Technology, Beijing 100124, China
2. College of Economics and Management, China University of Petroleum, Qingdao 266580, China; xuxiaofeng@upc.edu.cn
3. College of Economics and Management, Beijing University of Chemical Technology, Beijing 100013, China; wujun@mail.buct.edu.cn
4. College of Tourism, Hunan Normal University, Changsha 410081, China; paulhekj@hunnu.edu.cn
* Correspondence: zhangwen@bjut.edu.cn

With the emergence of big data and the resulting information explosion, computational and mathematical methods provide effective tools to handle the vast amounts of data and information used in big data analytics, knowledge discovery and distillation, and decision-making for solving complex problems in the world. The objective of this Special Issue titled "Computational and Mathematical Methods in Information Science and Engineering" is to provide the scientific community a channel to exchange their recent advances in computational and mathematical methods encountered in information science and engineering to address the real problems that occur in practice, including the theory and potential applications. The response of the scientific community has been significant, with nearly sixty papers being submitted for consideration, and finally, twenty papers were accepted following a rigorous peer-review process based on quality and novelty criteria.

The paper authored by Yang et al. [1] proposes a methodology based on a spatial Poisson regression model with model parameters being inferred by the Bayesian framework to investigate the occurrence rate for Earth-sized planets orbiting Sun-like stars. They analyze an exoplanet sample and its corresponding survey completeness data by using computational and mathematical methods.

The paper authored by Cheema et al. [2] studies GLM-based control charts using different link functions (i.e., logit, probit, c-log-log, and cauchit) with the binary response variable. The Pearson residuals (PR)- and deviance residuals (DR)-based control charts for logistic regression are proposed under different link functions.

The paper authored by Shan et al. [3] develops a robust online support vector regression algorithm based on a non-convex asymmetric loss function to handle the regression of noisy dynamic data streams. Inspired by pinball loss, a truncated-insensitive pinball loss (TIPL) is proposed to solve the problems caused by heavy noise and outliers.

The paper authored by Wang et al. [4] considers two control mechanisms for three types of wards and patients to prevent patients from nosocomial cross-infection and secondary infections of COVID-19: one is the dynamic bed allocation to balance the resource utilization among isolation, buffer, and general wards; the other is to effectively control the admission of arriving patients according to the evolution process of the epidemic.

The paper authored by Lee et al. [5] proposes a phase-resolved partial discharge (PRPD) shape method to classify different types of defect generator units by using offline partial discharge (PD) measurement instruments. The experimental measurement was applied to two generators in the Inalum hydropower plant, located in North Sumatera, Indonesia.

Citation: Zhang, W.; Xu, X.; Wu, J.; He, K. Preface to the Special Issue on "Computational and Mathematical Methods in Information Science and Engineering". *Mathematics* **2023**, *11*, 3187. https://doi.org/10.3390/math11143187

Received: 17 July 2023
Accepted: 19 July 2023
Published: 20 July 2023

Copyright: © 2023 by the authors. Licensee MDPI, Basel, Switzerland. This article is an open access article distributed under the terms and conditions of the Creative Commons Attribution (CC BY) license (https://creativecommons.org/licenses/by/4.0/).

The paper authored by Cao et al. [6] proposes a feature image representation method and Adversarial Generative Network with Filter (Filter-GAN) to solve the problem of imbalanced data in malicious traffic classification. The results show that the feature image representation method can effectively characterize the original session traffic, and Filter-GAN can generate more efficient samples.

The paper authored by E et al. [7] aims to propose a dynamic model selection approach that combines individual selection and combination forecasts based on both the demand patterns and the out-of-sample performance for each item for sales forecasting in the retail industry.

The paper authored by He et al. [8] exploits different multiscale data features in tourist arrival movement. Two popular Mode Decomposition models (MD) and the convolutional neural network (CNN) model are introduced to model the multiscale data features in the tourist arrival data. The data patterns at different scales are extracted using these two different MD models which dynamically decompose tourist arrival into the distinctive intrinsic mode function (IMF) data components.

The paper authored by Song et al. [9] proposes a hybrid multi-attribute three-way group decision-making method and provides detailed steps. The authors transform all attribute values of each expert into IVIFNs. Then, they determine expert weights based on interval-valued intuitionistic fuzzy entropy and cross-entropy and use interval-valued intuitionistic fuzzy weighted average operator to obtain a group comprehensive evaluation matrix.

The paper authored by Wu et al. [10] proposes a two-stage model based on an improved clustering algorithm and the center of gravity to deal with the multi-facility location problem arising from a real-world case. First, a distance function used in clustering is redefined to include both the spatial indicator and the socio-economic indicator. Then, an improved clustering algorithm is used to determine the optimal number of distribution centers needed and the coverage of each center.

In mine extraction planning, the paper authored by Zhao et al. [11] establishes a multi-objective planning model with the objective of obtaining the best economic efficiency, grade, and ore quantity, taking into account the constraints of ore grade fluctuation, ore output from the mine, production capacity of mining enterprises, and mineral resources utilization.

The paper authored by Liu et al. [12] proposes a quantum privacy-preserving set intersection protocol for IoT scenarios, which has higher security and linear communication efficiency. This protocol can protect identity anonymity while protecting private data.

The paper authored by Jeganathan et al. [13] examines the demand for two commodities in a Markovian inventory system, one of which is designated as a major item (Commodity-I) and the other as a complimentary item (Commodity-II). Demand arrives according to a Poisson process, and service time is exponential at a queue-dependent rate.

The paper authored by Weng et al. [14] proposes an innovative idea to derive the mathematical model and volume equation of an egg's shape, calculate its volume, and verify the accuracy of the mathematical equation using the volume displacement method. Using the proposed equation, the minimum error between the calculated egg volume and actual egg volume is 0.01%.

The paper authored by Jiang et al. [15] proposes a knowledge interaction neural network (KINN) to solve the issue of reservoir characterization in production management by integrating the physical principle of the waterflooding process (material balance equation) with an artificial neural network (ANN).

The paper authored by Li et al. [16] propose an opinion–edges co-evolution model on a weighted signed network. By incorporating different social factors, five evolutionary scenarios were simulated to investigate the feedback effects. The scenarios included the variations in edges and signed weights and the variations in the proportions of positive and negative opinions.

The paper authored by Cheng et al. [17] examines multi-tiered closed-loop supply chain network competition under carbon emission permits and discusses how stringent carbon regulations influence the network performance.

The paper authored by Wang et al. [18] uses eXtreme Gradient Boosting (XGBoost), a machine learning (ML) technique, to predict the career choice of college students using a real-world dataset collected in a specific college. In addition, SHAP (Shapley Additive exPlanation) was employed to interpret the results and analyze the importance of individual features.

The paper authored by Fan et al. [19] studies the interaction between the product development mode and the acquisition of consumers' environmental awareness (CEA) information in a two-echelon green supply chain.

The paper authored by Meng et al. [20] proposes a lightweight image reconstruction network (MSFN) for multi-scale local feature interaction based on a global connection of the local feature channel for real-time interactive devices with a fast response.

As the Guest Editors of the Special Issue, we greatly appreciate all authors who submitted their articles for consideration. We would also like to express our gratitude to all the reviewers for their valuable comments and suggestions to improve the submitted papers. The goal of this Special Issue was to attract high-quality and novel papers in the field of "Computational and Mathematical Methods in Information Science and Engineering". We hope that these accepted and published papers will be considered impactful by the international scientific community and that these papers will motivate further research on computational and mathematical methods for solving complex problems in various fields, disciplines, and applications.

Funding: This research was supported in part by the National Natural Science Foundation of China under Grant Nos. 71932002 and 72174018; the Beijing Natural Science Foundation under Grant No. 9222001; the Philosophy and Sociology Science Fund from Beijing Municipal Education Commission (SZ202110005001).

Conflicts of Interest: The authors declare no conflict of interest.

References

1. Yang, H.-D.; Lee, Y.-H.; Lin, C.-Y. On Study of the Occurrence of Earth-Size Planets in Kepler Mission Using Spatial Poisson Model. *Mathematics* **2023**, *11*, 2508. [CrossRef]
2. Cheema, M.; Amin, M.; Mahmood, T.; Faisal, M.; Brahim, K.; Elhassanein, A. Deviance and Pearson Residuals-Based Control Charts with Different Link Functions for Monitoring Logistic Regression Profiles: An Application to COVID-19 Data. *Mathematics* **2023**, *11*, 1113. [CrossRef]
3. Shan, X.; Zhang, Z.; Li, X.; Xie, Y.; You, J. Robust Online Support Vector Regression with Truncated ε-Insensitive Pinball Loss. *Mathematics* **2023**, *11*, 709. [CrossRef]
4. Wang, C.; Yang, F.; Li, Q.-L. Optimal Decision of Dynamic Bed Allocation and Patient Admission with Buffer Wards during an Epidemic. *Mathematics* **2023**, *11*, 687. [CrossRef]
5. Lee, C.-Y.; Purba, N.; Zhuo, G.-L. Defects Classification of Hydro Generators in Indonesia by Phase-Resolved Partial Discharge. *Mathematics* **2022**, *10*, 3659. [CrossRef]
6. Cao, X.; Luo, Q.; Wu, P. Filter-GAN: Imbalanced Malicious Traffic Classification Based on Generative Adversarial Networks with Filter. *Mathematics* **2022**, *10*, 3482. [CrossRef]
7. Yu, M.; Tian, X.; Tao, Y. Dynamic Model Selection Based on Demand Pattern Classification in Retail Sales Forecasting. *Mathematics* **2022**, *10*, 3179. [CrossRef]
8. He, K.; Wu, D.; Zou, Y. Tourist Arrival Forecasting Using Multiscale Mode Learning Model. *Mathematics* **2022**, *10*, 2999. [CrossRef]
9. Song, J.; He, Z.; Jiang, L.; Liu, Z.; Leng, X. Research on Hybrid Multi-Attribute Three-Way Group Decision Making Based on Improved VIKOR Model. *Mathematics* **2022**, *10*, 2783. [CrossRef]
10. Wu, J.; Liu, X.; Li, Y.; Yang, L.; Yuan, W.; Ba, Y. A Two-Stage Model with an Improved Clustering Algorithm for a Distribution Center Location Problem under Uncertainty. *Mathematics* **2022**, *10*, 2519. [CrossRef]
11. Zhao, Y.; Chen, J.; Yang, S.; Chen, Y. Mining Plan Optimization of Multi-Metal Underground Mine Based on Adaptive Hybrid Mutation PSO Algorithm. *Mathematics* **2022**, *10*, 2418. [CrossRef]
12. Liu, B.; Zhang, X.; Shi, R.; Zhang, M.; Zhang, G. SEPSI: A Secure and Efficient Privacy-Preserving Set Intersection with Identity Authentication in IoT. *Mathematics* **2022**, *10*, 2120. [CrossRef]

13. Jeganathan, K.; Reiyas, M.A.; Selvakumar, S.; Anbazhagan, N.; Amutha, S.; Joshi, G.P.; Jeon, D.; Seo, C. Markovian Demands on Two Commodity Inventory System with Queue-Dependent Services and an Optional Retrial Facility. *Mathematics* **2022**, *10*, 2046. [CrossRef]
14. Weng, Y.-K.; Li, C.-H.; Lai, C.-C.; Cheng, C.-W. Equation for Egg Volume Calculation Based on Smart's Model. *Mathematics* **2022**, *10*, 1661. [CrossRef]
15. Jiang, Y.; Zhang, H.; Zhang, K.; Wang, J.; Cui, S.; Han, J.; Zhang, L.; Yao, J. Reservoir Characterization and Productivity Forecast Based on Knowledge Interaction Neural Network. *Mathematics* **2022**, *10*, 1614. [CrossRef]
16. Li, Z.; Ma, L.; Chi, S.; Qian, X. Structural Balance under Weight Evolution of Dynamic Signed Network. *Mathematics* **2022**, *10*, 1441. [CrossRef]
17. Cheng, P.; Zhang, G.; Sun, H. The Sustainable Supply Chain Network Competition Based on Non-Cooperative Equilibrium under Carbon Emission Permits. *Mathematics* **2022**, *10*, 1364. [CrossRef]
18. Wang, Y.; Yang, L.; Wu, J.; Song, Z.; Shi, L. Mining Campus Big Data: Prediction of Career Choice Using Interpretable Machine Learning Method. *Mathematics* **2022**, *10*, 1289. [CrossRef]
19. Fan, M.; Huang, Y.; Xing, W. Information Acquisition for Product Design in a Green Supply Chain. *Mathematics* **2022**, *10*, 1160. [CrossRef]
20. Meng, Z.; Zhang, J.; Li, X.; Zhang, L. Lightweight Image Super-Resolution Based on Local Interaction of Multi-Scale Features and Global Fusion. *Mathematics* **2022**, *10*, 1096. [CrossRef]

Disclaimer/Publisher's Note: The statements, opinions and data contained in all publications are solely those of the individual author(s) and contributor(s) and not of MDPI and/or the editor(s). MDPI and/or the editor(s) disclaim responsibility for any injury to people or property resulting from any ideas, methods, instructions or products referred to in the content.

Article

On Study of the Occurrence of Earth-Size Planets in Kepler Mission Using Spatial Poisson Model

Hong-Ding Yang [1,*], Yun-Huan Lee [2] and Che-Yang Lin [3]

[1] Institute of Statistics, National University of Kaohsiung, Kaohsiung 81148, Taiwan
[2] Department of Finance, Ming Chuan University, Taipei 11103, Taiwan
[3] Department of Business Administration, Yuanpei University of Medical Technology, Hsinchu 30015, Taiwan
* Correspondence: hongdingyang0111@gmail.com

Abstract: The problem of determining the occurrence rate for Earth-size planets orbiting Sun-like stars is emerging in the universe. We propose a methodology based on a spatial Poisson regression model with model parameters being inferred by the Bayesian framework to investigate this occurrence rate. We analyzed an exoplanet sample and its corresponding survey completeness data. Our results suggest that 46% of Sun-like stars have an Earth-size (i.e., 1–2 times Earth radii) planet with an orbital period of 5–100 days. Furthermore, we are also interested in the occurrence rate of Earth analogs hosted by GK dwarf stars (i.e., orbital period of 200–400 days and size 1–2 times Earth radii). After completeness correction, we obtained an occurrence rate of 0.18% based on the proposed methodology.

Keywords: conditional autoregressive model; Markov chain Monte Carlo; occurrence rate; spatial Poisson model

MSC: 62J05; 62J12; 62J20; 85-10; 85A35

1. Introduction

In spatial epidemiology, the spatial distribution of diseases is used to construct disease maps for finding the complex spatial patterns of interesting diseases. When Bayesian hierarchical models are used to investigate the disease mapping, various spatially structured random effects can be considered in models. Recently, we have been witnessing a resurgence of interest in disease mapping, and many efficient methods have been proposed in the literature (see Moraga and Lawson 2012 [1]; Duncan et al., 2017 [2]; Lawson 2018 [3]; Baer and Lawson 2019 [4]). To the best of our knowledge, the application of disease mapping concepts to explore related issues in astronomy within the context of spatial regression remains unaddressed. This knowledge gap is the driving force behind our investigation into whether spatial disease mapping techniques can be utilized to examine the occurrence of Earth-size planets in the Kepler survey. Disease mapping leverages neighboring region information for parameter estimation in epidemiology, leading to more accurate spatial predictions. In this study, we extended this approach by incorporating spatial random effects to capture the spatial correlation in the data. Interestingly, the incorporation of neighboring region information is still relatively unexplored in astronomy (e.g., Petigura et al., 2018 [5]).

To the best of our knowledge, however, how to apply the concepts of disease mapping to discuss the related issues in astronomy has not been adequately addressed under the spatial regression settings. This motivates us to explore whether the techniques of spatial disease mapping can be applied to investigate the occurrence of Earth-size planets in the Kepler survey.

The Kepler mission aims to explore the diversity of planets and planetary systems. The discovery of thousands of transiting planets and planet candidates by the Kepler mission drastically broadens our knowledge of exoplanets, especially in the category of close-in ($\lesssim 1$ AU) and small ($\lesssim 4$ earth radii) planets around main-sequence dwarf stars (see Batalha 2014 [6]; Burke et al., 2014 [7]; Mullally et al., 2015 [8]). The inference of the occurrence of Earth-size planets is an interesting problem that has attracted the attention of astronomers because of the important theories regarding planet formation and evolution models (see Benz et al., 2014 [9]). Owing to the low false positive rate of the survey (see Fressin et al., 2013 [10]; Lissauer et al., 2014 [11]) while seeing different results from Santerne et al. (2016) [12] for giant-planet candidates, numerous works offered a window into the statistical studies of planet occurrence rates in terms of orbital periods and planet radius (see Dong and Zhu 2013 [13]; Fressin et al., 2013 [10]; Petigura et al., 2013 [5]; Burke 2015 [14]; Dressing and Charbonneau 2015 [15]; Silburt et al., 2015 [16]; Morton et al., 2016 [17]).

In this paper, we took the exoplanet sample and its corresponding survey completeness from Petigura et al., 2013 [5]. In the proposed methodology, we defined the planet occurrence to be based on the detection of a planet within a specified range of orbital period and orbital radius. To consider the spatial dependences of the data, we applied a spatial Poisson regression model (e.g., Besag et al., 1991 [18]; Chen and Yang 2011 [19]; Cressie 2015 [20]) to model the detection probability of an exoplanet. Further, to infer the posterior probability of detecting an exoplanet, a stochastic algorithm based on Markov chain Monte Carlo (MCMC) under the Bayesian framework was designed. Finally, the posterior inferences can simultaneously describe the number of exoplanets and the corresponding occurrence rate in the study region.

The remainder of this paper is organized as follows. In Section 2, we introduce a joint modeling methodology and present how to estimate parameters in the proposed model. Section 3 applies the proposed model to determine the occurrence rate of the Kepler planet. We conclude the paper with a discussion in Section 4.

2. Methodology

Let D be a bounded continuous random field in the $\Re^2$, which is partitioned into $n = n_1 \times n_2$ regular grids $D_1, \ldots, D_n$ with $D = \bigcup_{i=1}^{n} D_i$ and $D_i \cap D_j = \emptyset$ for $i \neq j$. Let Y_i, $i = 1, \ldots, n$, be a random variable that counts the number of exoplanets in grid D_i. For grid D_i, the expected number, E, of exoplanets can be easily evaluated by:

$$E = \frac{1}{n}\sum_{i=1}^{n} Y_i.$$

Motivated by the concept of a standardized mortality ratio in epidemiology (see Kelsall and Wakefield 2002 [21]; Lawson 2018 [3]), a standardized occurrence ratio of exoplanets for the grid D_i is defined by

$$r_i = \frac{Y_i}{E}, \; i = 1, \ldots, n.$$

In general, one can simply use r_i as the occurrence rate of exoplanets in grid D_i. Here, one potential influential factor is that a large amount of gravity generally exists among planets, and the correlation of the data set among grids should be considered in estimating such an occurrence rate. Obviously, the quantity r_i does not take into account the dependence among $\{Y_1, \ldots, Y_n\}$. Thus, using r_i to estimate the occurrence rate of exoplanets of the grid D_i may yield inaccurate results. Motivated from existing works (see Kelsall and Wakefield 2002 [21]; Chen and Yang 2011 [19]; Moraga and Lawson 2012 [1]; Lawson 2018 [3]; Baer and Lawson 2019 [4]), a spatial conditional autoregressive (CAR) model (see Moraga and Lawson 2012 [1]; Cressie 2015 [20]; Lawson 2018 [3]; Baer and Lawson 2019 [4]) was applied, which was used to describe possible spatial correlations among $\{Y_1, \ldots, Y_n\}$. The estimates of the occurrence rate of exoplanets in the grid D_i, $i = 1, \cdots, n$, were then proposed.

2.1. Spatial Poisson Regression Model

For $i = 1, \ldots, n$, let R_i be the occurrence rate of exoplanets in grid D_i. Then, an intuitive model for Y_i given R_i; $i = 1, \ldots, n$, is a Poisson distribution as follows:

$$Y_i \mid R_i \sim \text{Poi}(R_i E). \tag{1}$$

In Equation (1), $R_i E$ represents the intensity rate of the Poisson process and $R_i > 0$ is the main parameter of interest in this research. In this paper, our goal was to incorporate the spatial dependence of $Y_1, \ldots, Y_n$ to estimate the unobserved variables $R_1, \ldots, R_n$. Suppose that there are p grid-level covariates observed in grid D_i denoted together with 1 for the intercept by $x_i = (1, x_{i1}, \ldots, x_{ip})'$. As suggested in Basag et al. (1991) [18], the occurrence rate R_i of interest can be modeled in the following manner:

$$\ln(R_i) = x_i'\beta + \delta_i; \; i = 1, \ldots, n, \tag{2}$$

where $\beta = (\beta_0, \beta_1, \ldots, \beta_p)'$ is the vector of regression coefficients and δ_i is a spatial random error process. In spatial statistics, the spatial random errors $\delta = (\delta_1, \ldots, \delta_n)'$ capture the spatial variation and can offer a local adjustment to the mean trend due to unobserved covariates. In general, we assume that δ follows a multivariate Gaussian process as follows:

$$\delta \mid \sigma^2, \phi \sim N\left(0, \sigma^2 V(\phi)\right), \tag{3}$$

where the $n \times n$ matrix $V(\phi)$ is a spatial correlation matrix, ϕ is an unknown parameter, and σ^2 is a variance component. According to the CAR model, $\sigma^2 V(\phi)$ given in Equation (3) can be further decomposed as

$$\sigma^2 V(\phi) = (I - \phi C)^{-1} M,$$

where $C = (c_{ij})$ is an $n \times n$ spatial association matrix, I is an identity matrix, and $M = \sigma^2 I$. Under these settings, we have the following facts: (i) $(I - \phi C)$ is nonsingular; (ii) when $\phi \in (\phi_{\min}, \phi_{\max})$, $(I - \phi C)^{-1} M$ is symmetric and positive-definite, where the upper and lower limits of ϕ are evaluated by the inverses of the smallest and the largest eigenvalues of the spatial association matrix. For the sake of simplicity, in this paper, we constructed C according to the rook contiguity structure; that is, the (i, j)th element of C is of the following form:

$$c_{ij} = \begin{cases} 1, & i \sim j; \\ 0, & \text{otherwise.} \end{cases} \tag{4}$$

Note that $i \sim j$ in Equation (4) represents that D_i and D_j are neighbors with a common boundary.

We define $N_i \equiv \{j \mid j \sim i\}$ to be the neighborhood set of grid D_i and $\delta_{-i} \equiv (\delta_1, \ldots, \delta_{i-1}, \delta_{i+1}, \ldots, \delta_n)'$; then, the conditional distribution of δ_i conditioned on δ_{-i} is given by

$$\delta_i \mid \sigma^2, \phi, \delta_{-i} \sim N\left(\phi \sum_{j \in N_i} c_{ij} \delta_j, \sigma^2\right), \tag{5}$$

for $i = 1, \ldots, n$. Note that the joint distribution of $\delta_i \mid \sigma^2, \phi, \delta_{-i}, i = 1, \ldots, n$ can be shown to be a multivariate Gaussian distribution as in Equation (3) based on the factorization theorem of Besag (1974) [22] and the properties of multivariate Gaussian distributions. Readers can better understand the correctness of Equation (5) by referring to De Oliveira (2012) [23] for a comprehensive and systematic introduction to the CAR model. It is obvious from Equation (5) that the spatial dependence is considered through the information derived from neighbors. Notice that the spatial Poisson regression model offers the advantage of incorporating information from neighboring regions to enhance parameter estimation and prediction. Additionally, it is worth noting that the consideration of data correlation in recent literature is still relatively uncommon, as observed in studies such as Petigura et al. (2018) [24].

2.2. Prior Specifications and Posterior Distribution

Using the Bayesian approach, we set mutually independent prior distributions on parameters β, σ^2, and ϕ as shown in Table 1. For β and σ^2, the hyper-parameters are pre-specified constants such that the corresponding priors are nearly flat. Based on the CAR model, the spatial dependence parameter ϕ must fall within (ϕ_{min}, ϕ_{max}) to ensure that $(I - \phi C)^{-1}$ is a positive-definite matrix. However, ϕ_{min} can be less than zero, leading to a negative spatial correlation, which is rare in practice. Hence, we further restricted the spatial correlation parameter ϕ domain to $(0, \phi_{max})$, ensuring positive spatial correlation. This modification ensures that the model captures the desired spatial dependence structure and aligns with common practices in the field. According to the priors in Table 1, the joint prior distribution of β, σ^2, and ϕ, denoted as $\pi(\beta, \sigma^2, \phi)$, is given by

$$\pi(\beta, \sigma^2, \phi) = \pi(\beta)\pi(\sigma^2)\pi(\phi) \propto \sigma^{-2(a+1)} \exp\left(-\frac{1}{b\sigma^2}\right); \quad \sigma > 0, \ \phi \in (0, \phi_{max}). \tag{6}$$

Combining Equations (1)–(3) and Equation (6), the joint posterior distribution of σ^2, ϕ, β, and δ conditioned on observed data $Y = (Y_1, \ldots, Y_n)'$ satisfies:

$$\begin{aligned}
p(\sigma^2, \phi, \beta, \delta \mid Y) &= \frac{p(\sigma^2, \phi, \beta, \delta, Y)}{p(Y)} \\
&\propto \prod_{i=1}^n p(Y_i \mid R_i) p(\delta \mid \sigma^2, \phi) \pi(\beta, \sigma^2, \phi) \\
&\propto \exp\left(\sum_{i=1}^n Y_i(x_i'\beta + \delta_i) - E\sum_{i=1}^n \exp(x_i'\beta + \delta_i)\right) \\
&\quad \times \left(\det\left(\sigma^2 V(\phi)\right)\right)^{-1/2} \exp\left(-\frac{1}{2\sigma^2}\delta' V(\phi)^{-1}\delta\right) \\
&\quad \times \sigma^{-2(a+1)} \exp\left(-\frac{1}{b\sigma^2}\right).
\end{aligned} \tag{7}$$

Because the joint posterior distribution in Equation (7) cannot be applied directly to generate posterior samples of model parameters, an alternative method called a Markov chain Monte Carlo (MCMC) method will be introduced in the following to generate posterior samples of model parameters.

Table 1. Priors for model parameters β, σ^2, and ϕ.

Parameter	Prior Distribution	Support of Hyper-Parameter
β	Non-informative prior	
σ^2	Inverse gamma (a, b)	$a, b > 0$
ϕ	Uniform $(0, \phi_{max})$	$\phi_{max} > 0$

2.3. Posterior Inferences of Model Parameters

To generate posterior samples of σ^2, ϕ, β, and δ, the conditional posterior distributions of each parameter given all of the others are needed. One can then successively sample these conditional posterior distributions and obtain Markov chains in the parameter spaces that will converge to the joint posterior distribution of Equation (7) under Tierney's conditions (1994) [25].

Next, we summarize all necessary conditional posterior distributions for σ^2, ϕ, β, and δ_i, $i = 1, \ldots, n$, based on Equations (1)–(7) as follows:

$$
\begin{aligned}
p(\sigma^2 \mid \phi, \beta, \delta, Y) &\propto p(\delta \mid \sigma^2, \phi) \pi(\sigma^2) \\
&\propto \sigma^{-2(n/2+a+1)} \exp\left(-\frac{1}{\sigma^2}\left(\frac{1}{b} + \frac{1}{2}\delta'(I - \phi C)\delta\right)\right) \\
p(\phi \mid \sigma^2, \beta, \delta, Y) &\propto p(\delta \mid \sigma^2, \phi) \pi(\phi) \\
&\propto (\det(V(\phi)))^{-1/2} \exp\left(\frac{\phi}{2\sigma^2} \delta' C \delta\right) \\
p(\beta \mid \sigma^2, \phi, \delta, Y) &\propto \prod_{i=1}^n p(Y_i \mid R_i) \pi(\beta) \\
&\propto \exp\left(\sum_{i=1}^n Y_i x_i' \beta - E \sum_{i=1}^n \exp(x_i' \beta + \delta_i)\right) \\
p(\delta_i \mid \sigma^2, \phi, \beta, \delta_{-i}, Y) &\propto p(Y_i \mid R_i) p(\delta_i \mid \sigma^2, \phi, \delta_{-i}) \\
&\propto \exp\left(Y_i \delta_i - E \exp(x_i' \beta + \delta_i) - \frac{1}{2\sigma^2}\left(\delta_i^2 - 2\delta_i \phi \sum_{j \in N_i} c_{ij} \delta_j\right)\right)
\end{aligned}
$$

We notice that $p(\sigma^2 \mid \phi, \beta, \delta, Y)$ is an inverse gamma distribution; that is, $\sigma^2 \mid \phi, \beta, \delta, Y \sim IG(n/2 + a, (1/b + \delta'(I - \phi C)\delta/2)^{-1})$. Therefore, a Gibbs sampling algorithm (see Geman and Geman 1984 [26]) can be used to generate the posterior samples of σ^2. However, $p(\phi \mid \sigma^2, \beta, \delta, Y)$, $p(\beta \mid \sigma^2, \phi, \delta, Y)$, and $p(\delta_i \mid \sigma^2, \phi, \beta, \delta_{-i}, Y)$, $i = 1, \ldots, n$, are not all standard distributions; hence, a Metropolis–Hastings algorithm (see Chib and Greenberg 1995 [27]) can be applied to ϕ, β, and δ_i, respectively, to iteratively generate an ergodic Markov chain that yields the corresponding posterior samples. In particular, generating the posterior samples of ϕ is relatively difficult because ϕ appears in the covariance matrix $V(\phi)$. In this paper, we treated ϕ as a discrete random variable that is defined on finite grid points from 0 to ϕ_{max}; hence, the values of matrix $V(\phi)$ on these finite grid points can be computed in advance. For each step, the posterior sample of ϕ is generated from a probability mass function, which is based on the values of $(\det(V(\phi)))^{-1/2} \exp\left(\frac{\phi}{2\sigma^2} \delta' C \delta\right)$ evaluated on the finite grid points of $\phi \in (0, \phi_{max})$.

Based on the posterior samples of σ^2, ϕ, β, and δ_i, $i = 1, \ldots, n$, the inferences of model parameters and the occurrence rate of exoplanets in grid D_i, $i = 1, \ldots, n$, can be obtained.

3. Application of the Proposed Methodology

To model the occurrence distribution of planets as a function of the planet period and radius, Petigura et al. (2013) [5] considered transiting planets that are all hosted by GK-type stars. They defined GK-type stars as those with surface temperatures of 4100 K $\leq T_{eff} \leq$ 6100 K and gravities of 4.0 cm/s$^2 \leq \log g \leq$ 4.9 cm/s^2. Furthermore, these planets are restricted to the brightest GK-type stars observed by *Kepler* ($Kp = 10$–15 mag). These 42,557 stars have the lowest photometric noise in the Kepler survey, thereby maximizing the detectability of Earth-size planets. In the present work, we mainly studied the occurrence rate of planets based on the catalog by Petigura et al. (2013) [5], which can compare our findings with their seminal work by adopting the same study region. Figure 1 shows the scatter plot of the data. Let x_1 be the orbital period (days), x_2 be the planet size (Earth radii), and $D = [6.25, 400] \times [1, 16]$ be the region of interest for this work; it is divided into the 6×4 grids shown in Figure 2. Let Y_i record the number of events in grid D_i for $i = 1, \ldots, 24$. Please note that the region D is the same as in Petigura et al. (2013) [5].

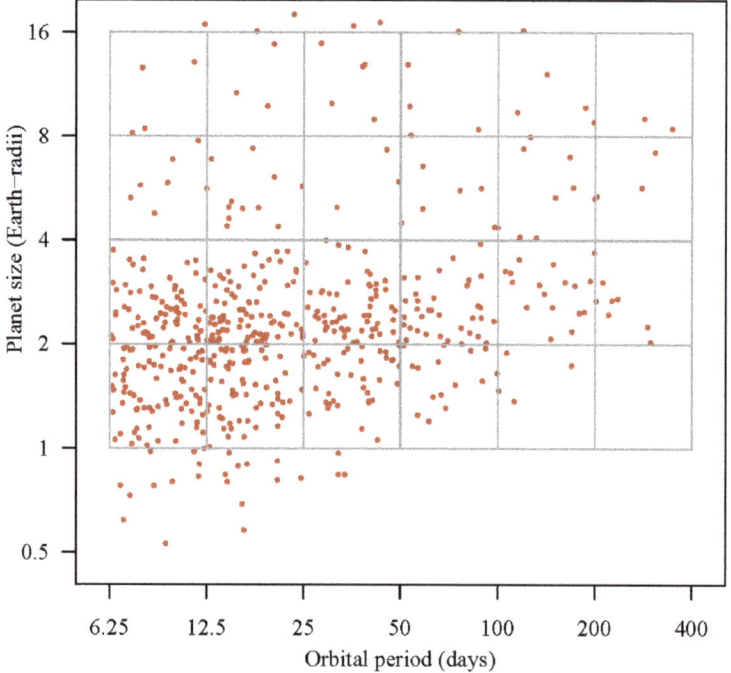

Figure 1. The scatterplot of exoplanets in the x_1–x_2 space and the 24 subregions D_i, $i = 1, \cdots, 24$.

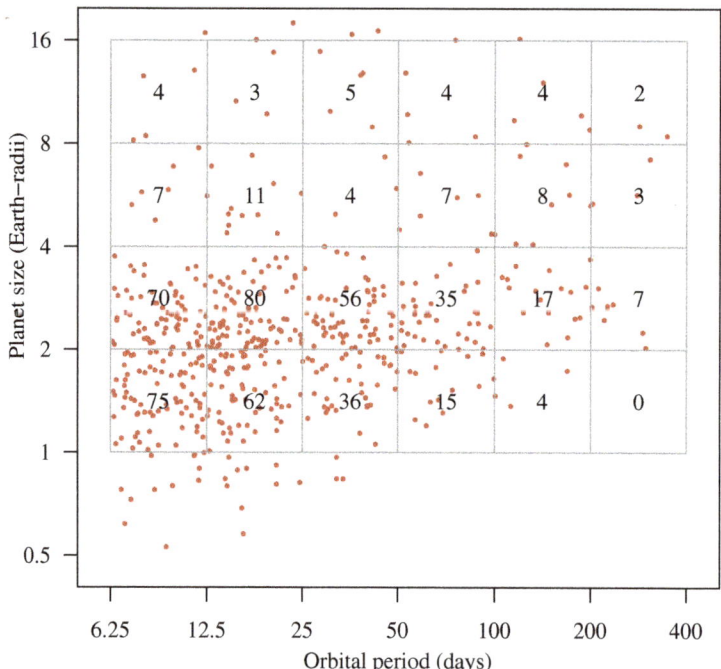

Figure 2. The values of Y_i for $i = 1, \cdots, 24$.

We applied the linear regression model illustrated in Equation (2) of Section 2.1 to model the occurrence rate R_i and considered two grid-level covariates, x_{i1} and x_{i2}, in the model, where x_{i1} and x_{i2} are, respectively, defined by the central points of the orbital period (days) and planet size (earth radii) of the grid D_i (i.e., the central coordinate of the grid D_i) for $i = 1, \ldots, 24$. As a result, the used model, called Model 1, is given by

$$\ln(R_i) = \beta_0 + \beta_1 x_{1,i} + \beta_2 x_{2,i} + \delta_i; \; i = 1, \ldots, 24, \tag{8}$$

where β_0, β_1, and β_2 are unknown regression coefficients, and δ_i is a spatial random error process. Based on the Bayesian approach in Section 2.3, prior distributions of parameters in $\theta = (\sigma^2, \phi, \beta_0, \beta_1, \beta_2)'$ are, respectively, set as follows:

$$\begin{aligned}
\sigma^2 &\sim IG(3, 0.001) \\
\phi &\sim U(0, \phi_{\max}) \\
\beta_0 &\sim U(-20, 20) \\
\beta_1 &\sim U(-20, 20) \\
\beta_2 &\sim U(-20, 20)
\end{aligned}$$

Note that $\phi_{\max}$ is 0.29 because the smallest eigenvalue of C is 3.42. Since we lacked additional information about the central tendencies of the parameters, we selected the hyper-parameter values for the prior distributions based on the preference for larger variances. Although larger variances may result in a slower convergence, the MCMC algorithm can still converge. Additionally, the larger variances allow for more flexibility and variation in the MCMC updates, enhancing the parameter space exploration.

Next, we first examined the hypothesized model (i.e., Equations (1)–(3)) that is suitable for analyzing the occurrence rate of Earth-size planets in the Kepler survey. In this paper, we conducted a simulation study based on the Pearson chi-squared test to illustrate the goodness of fit of the used model (i.e., Equation (8)); Model 1). In addition, as listed in the bottom of Table 2, a model (i.e., Model 2) with only the regressors and a model (i.e., Model 3) with only the spatial random error process were also used for comparison. Let $Y_i^{*(t)}; i = 1, \ldots, 24$, be independently generated from $\mathrm{Poi}\big(R_i^{*(t)} E\big)$, with E being the expected number of exoplanets evaluated according to the observed data Y, where $R_i^{*(t)}$ is an estimate of the occurrence rate R_i based on the posterior medians of θ under the used model (i.e., Model 1, Model 2, or Model 3) and $t = 1, \ldots, 5$, represents the t-th simulation. For each simulation replicate, the goodness-of-fit test statistic is computed in the following manner:

$$\chi^{2(t)} \equiv \sum_{i=1}^{24} \frac{\left(Y_i^{*(t)} - R_i^{*(t)} E^{*(t)}\right)^2}{R_i^{*(t)} E^{*(t)}}$$

where $E^{*(t)}$ is the expected number of exoplanets evaluated based on the t-th simulated data $Y_i^{*(t)}; i = 1, \ldots, 24$. The simulation results are displayed in Table 2. First, we notice that Model 2 with only the regressors has a large $\chi^{2(t)}$ value for each simulation replicate. This indicates that Model 2 without considering the spatial correlation of the data is very inappropriate. Comparing the proposed model (i.e., Model 1) versus Model 3, they have relatively small $\chi^{2(t)}$ values and hence Model 1 and Model 3 are both appropriate for the analysis of the occurrence rate of Earth-size planets. Overall, the $\chi^{2(t)}$ values of Model 1 are slightly smaller than those of Model 3, which further suggests to us to use Model 1 (i.e., Equation (8)) to analyze the data set. Even if all the estimated regression coefficients are not significant (see Table 3), in general, the regressors should slightly contribute to evaluating the occurrence rate. Moreover, Figure 3 shows 95% credible intervals of Y_i; $i = 1, \ldots, 24$, for Model 1, Model 2, and Model 3. The results are in accord with Table 2; that is, Figure 3 reveals that Model 2 performs poorly and that Model 1 and Model 3 are fairly comparable. On the other hand, we notice that the data may contain potential biases that may arise from observational precision that results in inaccurate estimates of the underlying occurrence rates. In our proposed methodology, the random effects describe the spatial correlation in the data and are a suitable remedy for missing explanatory variables, addressing the limitations caused by uncollected vital variables. The simulation results indicate the effectiveness of our approach in mitigating potential biases and enhancing the model's explanatory power. Based on the results in Table 2 and Figure 3, Model 1 in Equation (8) is acceptable and hence we used it to analyze the occurrence rate of Earth-size planets in the next content.

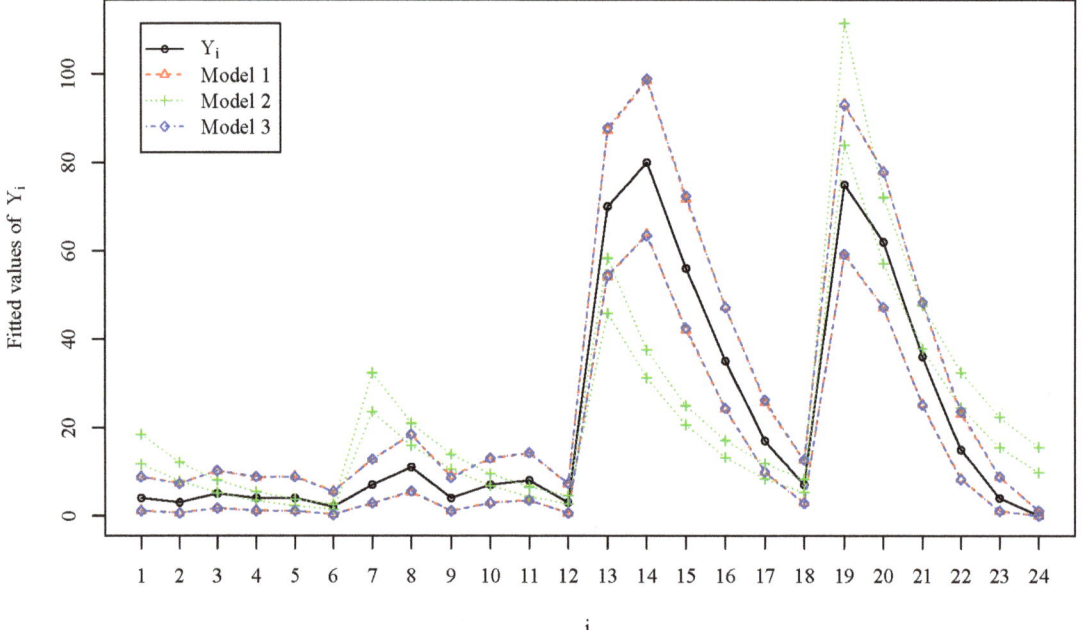

Figure 3. The 95% credible intervals for Models 1–3. Model 1: a model with the regressors and the spatial component; Model 2: a model with only the regressors; Model 3: a model with only the spatial component.

Table 2. The expected numbers and the values of chi-squared test statistics for Model 1, Model 2, and Model 3 based on the observed data Y and the simulated data $Y^{*(t)} = \left(Y_1^{*(t)}, \ldots, Y_{24}^{*(t)}\right)'$, where t represents the t-th simulation with $t = 1, \ldots, 5$.

		$Y^{*(t)}$					Y
		1	2	3	4	5	
Model 1	$E^{*(t)}$	23.167	24.958	22.917	22.917	23.500	23.000
	$\chi^{2(t)}$	0.665	0.389	0.560	0.680	0.580	0.129
Model 2	$E^{*(t)}$	23.083	23.000	22.125	22.917	23.125	23.000
	$\chi^{2(t)}$	29.606	19.295	13.640	26.167	10.892	222.619
Model 3	$E^{*(t)}$	22.000	21.042	21.958	21.125	24.333	23.000
	$\chi^{2(t)}$	0.823	0.769	0.803	0.809	0.774	0.140

Note: Model 1: $\ln(R_i) = \beta_0 + \beta_1 x_{1,i} + \beta_2 x_{2,i} + \delta_i$; Model 2: $\ln(R_i) = \beta_0 + \beta_1 x_{1,i} + \beta_2 x_{2,i}$; Model 3: $\ln(R_i) = \beta_0 + \delta_i$; $i = 1, \ldots, 24$.

Table 3. Summary of posterior inferences for model parameters.

Parameter	2.5%	5%	Median	95%	97.5%	Mean	S.D.
β_0	−6.052	−5.673	−0.283	2.852	3.128	−0.85	2.739
β_1	−0.957	−0.893	0.066	0.593	0.664	−0.021	0.453
β_2	−1.987	−1.696	0.444	1.935	2.222	0.332	1.097
σ^2	45.641	49.314	74.668	119.905	132.288	78.394	22.407
ϕ	0.029	0.029	0.116	0.232	0.261	0.122	0.068

Note: S.D. represents the standard deviations for each model parameter.

We implemented 200,000 iterations for the posterior calculations to obtain a convergent sequence and approximately independent posterior samples. The first 100,000 iterations were discarded as burn-in. Then, one has an approximately independent joint posterior sample size of 100,000 by subsampling every 10th scan. The execution time for 200,000 MCMC iterations was 56.26471 s on an i7-12700 2.10 GHz PC. The system environment was R language version 4.2.3 lined to Intel's Math Kernal Library (MKL) on Windows 11. The core codes of the MCMC process were implemented using custom-written code without relying on external packages. The trace plot in Figure 4 displays the logarithm values of Equation (7) for the 200,000 MCMC iterations. Given that the proposed model incorporates multiple parameters and random effect terms, we assessed the overall convergence of the MCMC process using these logarithm values. Notably, the trace plot reveals that it belongs to an interval within the 200,000 iterations, implying that the MCMC process has reached convergence. Table 3 presents posterior inferences based on 10,000 posterior samples for model parameters. Furthermore, the posterior means of $R_i = \exp(x_i'\beta + \delta_i)$ for $i = 1, \ldots, 24$, are shown in Figure 5. Figure 6 displays the results with estimated occurrence rates P_i, $i = 1, \ldots, 24$ in each grid.

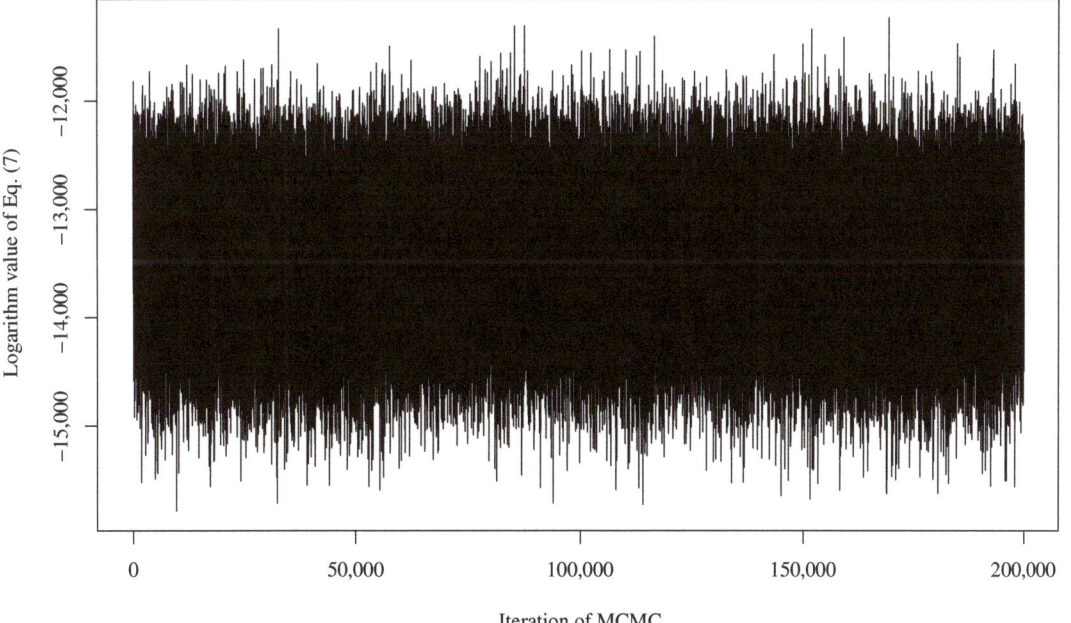

Figure 4. The logarithm trace plot of Equation (7) for the 200,000 MCMC iterations.

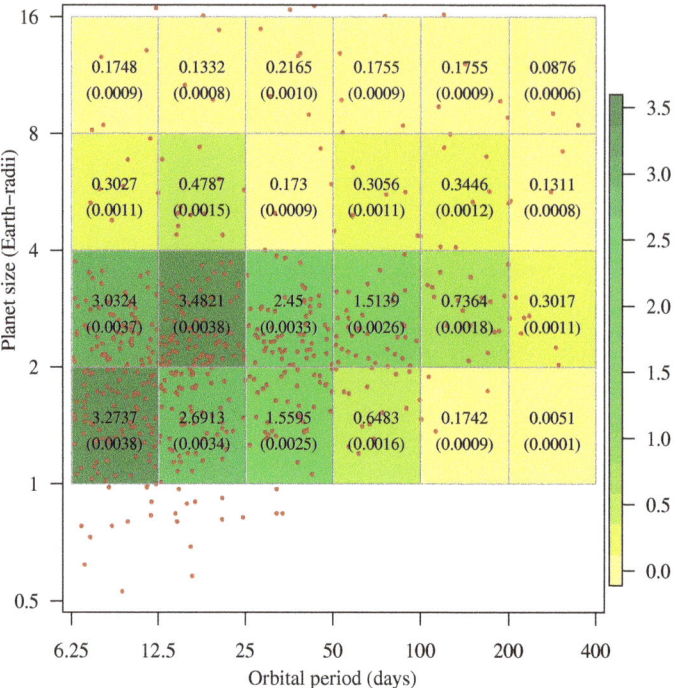

Figure 5. The posterior means of $R_i = \exp(x_i'\beta + \delta_i)$ for $i = 1, \cdots, 24$.

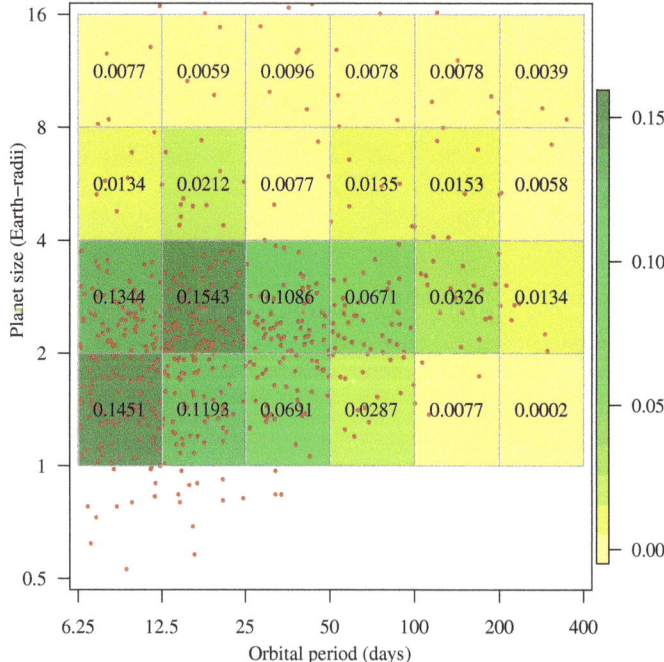

Figure 6. The estimated occurrence rates $P_i = R_i / \sum_{j=1}^{24} R_j$ for $i = 1, \cdots, 24$ without using completeness.

Next, we considered the variable detection efficiency (or completeness) in order to identify realistic occurrence rates. After obtaining the estimated occurrence rates in each cell shown in Figure 6, we further considered the survey completeness in order to identify realistic occurrence rates. The values of completeness function used here were constructed by Foreman-Mackey et al. (2014) [28]. We can thus obtain the true occurrence rates P_i^{tr}, $i = 1, \ldots, 24$ in each cell, as shown in Figure 7. Because the method proposed in this paper is presented as a totally different approach to that of Petigura et al. (2013) [5], we need to make a comparison with Petigura et al.'s method (2013) [5]. We computed realistic occurrence rates with different values of orbital period (P) and planet radius (R) and the corresponding realistic occurrence rates, as shown in Table 4. Note that case (i) in Table 4 corresponds to Jupiter-size planets.

From Table 4, we find that (1) for cases (ii), (iii), (iv), (vii), and (ix), the occurrence rates obtained from the proposed method are larger than those of Petigura et al. (2013) [5] by approximately a factor of two; (2) for cases (i), (v), and (vi), the occurrence rates obtained the proposed method are almost the same as Petigura et al.'s (2013) [5]; and (3) for cases (viii) and (x), the occurrence rates obtained by Petigura et al. (2013) [5] are larger than the proposed method herein. Because the proposed model considers the information of neighbors, the grid density is high, which will produce higher occurrence rates. On the contrary, if the grid density is low, lower rates will occur. Furthermore, both methods confirm the occurrence rates of planets with (i) $P = 5$–100 d and size 8–16 $R_\oplus$; (ii) $P = 25$–50 d and size 1–16 $R_\oplus$; and (iii) $P = 50$–100 d and size 1–16 $R_\oplus$.

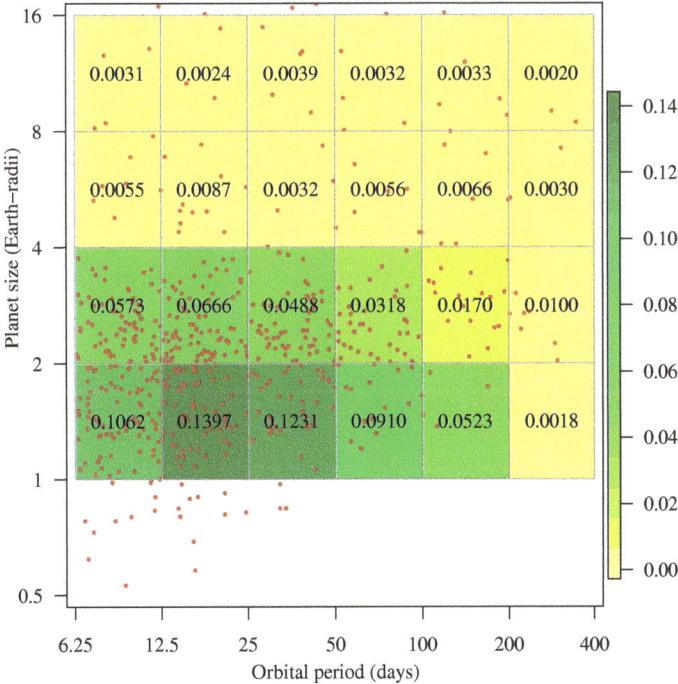

Figure 7. The true occurrence rates P_i^{tr} for $i = 1, \cdots, 24$.

Furthermore, we are interested in the occurrence rate of Earth analogs hosted by GK dwarf stars, i.e., $P = 200$–400 d and size 1–2 $R_\oplus$. From the scatter plot shown in Figure 1, there are no planets in this grid, and there are few planets in the neighborhood of this grid. Thus, it is reasonable that the occurrence rate of this grid is very small. After completeness correction, we find the occurrence rate to be 0.18% (please see case (viii) in

Table 4), whereas the values obtained by Petigura et al. (2013) [5], Foreman-Mackey et al. (2014) [28], and Chen and Hung (2019) [29] are 5.7%, 1.9%, and 2.5%, respectively. The proposed method indicates that 46% of Sun-like stars have an Earth-size (1–2 $R_\oplus$) planet with $P = 5$–100 d. This value is higher than Petigura et al.'s (2013) [5] due to the spatial model considering the information of neighbors. We further conducted an additional extrapolation of the hot Jupiter occurrence rate (i.e., the occurrence rate of 1–10 days and 8–24 $R_\oplus$) and compared it to the findings of Petigura et al. (2018) [24]. Their study reported a hot Jupiter occurrence rate of 0.57%, whereas our extrapolated estimate stands at 4.17%. According to the scalability of our proposed model, it provides an extrapolation with new data. To the best of our knowledge, utilizing neighboring data information for occurrence rate estimation in astronomy is a novel approach that has not been previously observed. According to the inference of Petigura et al. (2013) [5], we may imply that the nearest Earth-size planets in habitable zones of Sun-like stars are expected to orbit a star further than 12 light-years from Earth because we adopted the 46% occurrence rate.

Table 4. Comparison of realistic occurrence rates with different values of orbital period (P) and planet radius (R).

Case	Period (P)	Radius (R)	Petigura et al. (2013) [5]	The Proposed
(i)	5–100 d	8–16 $R_\oplus$	1.6%	1.26%
(ii)	5–100 d	1–2 $R_\oplus$	26%	46% *
(iii)	6.25–12.5 d	1–16 $R_\oplus$	8.9%	17.21% *
(iv)	12.5–25 d	1–16 $R_\oplus$	13.7%	21.74% *
(v)	25–50 d	1–16 $R_\oplus$	15.7%	17.9%
(vi)	50–100 d	1–16 $R_\oplus$	15.2%	13.16%
(vii)	6.25–25 d	1–2 $R_\oplus$	11.5%	24.59% *
(viii)	200–400 d	1–2 $R_\oplus$	5.7%	0.18%
(ix)	<50 d	1–2 $R_\oplus$	19.2%	36.9% *
(x)	200–400 d	2–4 $R_\oplus$	5%	1%

* represents the occurrence rates obtained by the proposed method are larger than Petigura et al. (2013) by approximately a factor of 2.

4. Discussion

Motivated by the study of Petigura et al. (2013) [5] on the prevalence of Earth-size planets orbiting Sun-like stars, we adopted a joint modeling approach to investigate the occurrence rates of planets around GK dwarfs. The inferred occurrence rate of Earth analogs around GK dwarfs increases to 46%. Compared with that of Petigura et al. (2013) [5], our approach increases the occurrence rate of Earth analogs by approximately a factor of two. Nevertheless, our model suggests that the occurrence rate for Kepler planets with radii between 1 and 2 earth radii and orbital periods between 50 and 400 days is 0.1451. Similar to most of the results in the literature, our occurrence rate of 0.1451 is also larger than the results computed by Petigura et al. (2013) [5], Dong and Zhu (2013) [13], and Foreman-MacKey et al. (2014) [28]. We cautiously contend that our proposed model exhibits a higher occurrence rate compared to other methods, attributed to the incorporation of spatial random effects. These effects effectively capture the spatial correlation in the data and moderately compensate for any missing explanatory variables. Applying our analysis to the entire Kepler planet sample ($Q1 - Q16$) will be left to future work. On the other hand, the current approach does not consider the influence of time on occurrence rates. All the data are treated as being from the same time point. Given the flexible nature of the proposed model, we plan to incorporate the effect of time using a Poisson process in future expansions. The expanded model will allow for dynamic predictions of variables over time.

Taking into account the survey incompleteness, we confirm the study of Petigura et al. (2013) [5]: the occurrence rates of planets with (i) $P = 5$–100 d and size 8–16 $R_\oplus$; (ii) $P = 25$–50 d and size 1–16 $R_\oplus$; and (iii) $P = 50$–100 d and size 1–16 $R_\oplus$. The inferred occurrence rates of Kepler planets suffer severely from systematic uncertainties (see Burke 2015 [14]). Follow-up spectroscopic observations of host stars will refine some of these uncertainties, providing a planet sample with better stellar parameters and pipeline completeness for our model and others to revise the proposed model, and thus present better constraining theories of planet formation and evolution.

Author Contributions: Methodology, H.-D.Y.; software, H.-D.Y.; formal analysis, Y.-H.L. and C.-Y.L.; resources, H.-D.Y.; writing—original draft, H.-D.Y., Y.-H.L. and C.-Y.L.; writing—review and editing, Y.-H.L. and C.-Y.L. All authors have read and agreed to the published version of the manuscript.

Funding: The research was funded by the National Science and Technology Council, R.O.C., grant number MOST 109-2118-M-390-001, and MOST 111-2118-M-390-003.

Institutional Review Board Statement: Not applicable.

Data Availability Statement: Not applicable.

Conflicts of Interest: The authors declare no conflict of interest.

References

1. Moraga, P.; Lawson, A.B. Gaussian component mixtures and CAR models in Bayesian disease mapping. *Comput. Stat. Data Anal.* **2012**, *56*, 1417–1433. [CrossRef]
2. Duncan, E.W.; White, N.M.; Mengersen, K. Spatial smoothing in Bayesian models: A comparison of weights matrix specifications and their impact on inference. *Int. J. Health Geogr.* **2017**, *16*, 47. [CrossRef]
3. Lawson, A.B. *Bayesian Disease Mapping: Hierarchical Modeling in Spatial Epidemiology*; Chapman and Hall: London, UK; CRC: Boca Raton, FL, USA, 2018.
4. Baer, D.R.; Lawson, A.B. Evaluation of Bayesian multiple stage estimation under spatial CAR model variants. *J. Stat. Comput. Simul.* **2019**, *89*, 98–144. [CrossRef]
5. Petigura, E.A.; Howard, A.W.; Marcy, G.W. Prevalence of Earth-size planets orbiting Sun-like stars. *Proc. Natl. Acad. Sci. USA* **2013**, *110*, 19273–19278. [CrossRef] [PubMed]
6. Batalha, N.M. Exploring exoplanet populations with NASA's Kepler Mission. *Proc. Natl. Acad. Sci. USA* **2014**, *111*, 12647–12654. [CrossRef]
7. Burke, C.J.; Inglis, A.J.; Perisic, O.; Masson, G.R.; McLaughlin, S.H.; Rutaganira, F.; Shokat, K.M.; Williams, R.L. Structures of PI4KIIIβ complexes show simultaneous recruitment of Rab11 and its effectors. *Science* **2014**, *344*, 1035–1038. [CrossRef] [PubMed]
8. Mullally, F.; Coughlin, J.L.; Thompson, S.E.; Rowe, J.; Burke, C.; Latham, D.W.; Batalha, N.M.; Bryson, S.T.; Christiansen, J.; Henze, C.E.; et al. Planetary candidates observed by Kepler. VI. Planet sample from Q1–Q16 (47 months). *Astrophys. J. Suppl. Ser.* **2015**, *217*, 31. [CrossRef]
9. Benz, W.; Ida, S.; Alibert, Y.; Lin, D.; Mordasini, C. Planet population synthesis. *arXiv* **2014**, arXiv:1402.7086.
10. Fressin, F.; Torres, G.; Charbonneau, D.; Bryson, S.T.; Christiansen, J.; Dressing, C.D.; Jenkins, J.M.; Walkowicz, L.M.; Batalha, N.M. The false positive rate of Kepler and the occurrence of planets. *Astrophys. J.* **2013**, *766*, 81. [CrossRef]
11. Lissauer, J.J.; Marcy, G.W.; Bryson, S.T.; Rowe, J.F.; Jontof-Hutter, D.; Agol, E.; Borucki, W.J.; Carter, J.A.; Ford, E.B.; Gilliland, R.L.; et al. Validation of Kepler's multiple planet candidates. II. Refined statistical framework and descriptions of systems of special interest. *Astrophys. J.* **2014**, *784*, 44. [CrossRef]
12. Santerne, A.; Moutou, C.; Tsantaki, M.; Bouchy, F.; Hébrard, G.; Adibekyan, V.; Almenara, J.M.; Amard, L.; Barros, S.; Boisse, I.; et al. SOPHIE velocimetry of Kepler transit candidates-XVII. The physical properties of giant exoplanets within 400 days of period. *Astron. Astrophys.* **2016**, *587*, A64. [CrossRef]
13. Dong, S.; Zhu, Z. Fast Rise of "Neptune-Size" Planets (4–8 $R_\oplus$) from P 10 to 250 days—Statistics of Kepler Planet Candidates up to 0.75 AU. *Astrophys. J.* **2013**, *778*, 53. [CrossRef]
14. Burke, C.J.; Christiansen, J.L.; Mullally, F.; Seader, S.; Huber, D.; Rowe, J.F.; Coughlin, J.L.; Thompson, S.E.; Catanzarite, J.; Clarke, B.D.; et al. Terrestrial planet occurrence rates for the Kepler GK dwarf sample. *Astrophys. J.* **2015**, *809*, 8. [CrossRef]
15. Dressing, C.D.; Charbonneau, D. The occurrence of potentially habitable planets orbiting M dwarfs estimated from the full Kepler dataset and an empirical measurement of the detection sensitivity. *Astrophys. J.* **2015**, *807*, 45. [CrossRef]
16. Silburt, A.; Gaidos, E.; Wu, Y. A statistical reconstruction of the planet population around Kepler solar-type stars. *Astrophys. J.* **2015**, *799*, 180. [CrossRef]
17. Morton, R.; Verth, G.; Fedun, V.; Shelyag, S.; Erdélyi, R. Evidence for the photospheric excitation of incompressible chromospheric waves. *Astrophys. J.* **2013**, *768*, 17. [CrossRef]
18. Besag, J.; York, J.; Mollié, A. Bayesian image restoration, with two applications in spatial statistics. *Ann. Inst. Stat. Math.* **1991**, *43*, 1–20. [CrossRef]
19. Chen, C.S.; Yang, H.D. A joint modeling approach for spatial earthquake risk variations. *J. Appl. Stat.* **2011**, *38*, 1733–1741. [CrossRef]
20. Cressie, N. *Statistics for Spatial Data*; John Wiley & Sons: Hoboken, NJ, USA, 2015.
21. Kelsall, J.; Wakefield, J. Modeling spatial variation in disease risk: A geostatistical approach. *J. Am. Stat. Assoc.* **2002**, *97*, 692–701. [CrossRef]

22. Besag, J. Spatial interaction and the statistical analysis of lattice systems. *J. R. Stat. Soc. Ser. B Methodol.* **1974**, *36*, 192–225. [CrossRef]
23. De Oliveira, V. Bayesian analysis of conditional autoregressive models. *Ann. Inst. Stat. Math.* **2012**, *64*, 107–133. [CrossRef]
24. Petigura, E.A.; Marcy, G.W.; Winn, J.N.; Weiss, L.M.; Fulton, B.J.; Howard, A.W.; Sinukoff, E.; Isaacson, H.; Morton, T.D.; Johnson, J.A. The California-Kepler survey. IV. Metal-rich stars host a greater diversity of planets. *Astron. J.* **2018**, *155*, 89. [CrossRef]
25. Tierney, L. Markov chains for exploring posterior distributions. *Ann. Stat.* **1994**, *22*, 1701–1728. [CrossRef]
26. Geman, S.; Geman, D. Stochastic relaxation, Gibbs distributions, and the Bayesian restoration of images. *IEEE Trans. Pattern Anal. Mach. Intell.* **1984**, *6*, 721–741. [CrossRef] [PubMed]
27. Chib, S.; Greenberg, E. Understanding the metropolis-hastings algorithm. *Am. Stat.* **1995**, *49*, 327–335.
28. Foreman-Mackey, D.; Hogg, D.W.; Morton, T.D. Exoplanet population inference and the abundance of Earth analogs from noisy, incomplete catalogs. *Astrophys. J.* **2014**, *795*, 64. [CrossRef]
29. Chen, J.H.; Hung, W.L. Parametrizing the Kepler exoplanet period-radius distribution with the bivariate normal inverse Gaussian distribution. *J. Appl. Stat.* **2019**, *46*, 725–736. [CrossRef]

Disclaimer/Publisher's Note: The statements, opinions and data contained in all publications are solely those of the individual author(s) and contributor(s) and not of MDPI and/or the editor(s). MDPI and/or the editor(s) disclaim responsibility for any injury to people or property resulting from any ideas, methods, instructions or products referred to in the content.

Article

Deviance and Pearson Residuals-Based Control Charts with Different Link Functions for Monitoring Logistic Regression Profiles: An Application to COVID-19 Data

Maryam Cheema [1], Muhammad Amin [1], Tahir Mahmood [2,3], Muhammad Faisal [4], Kamel Brahim [5] and Ahmed Elhassanein [5,*]

1. Department of Statistics, University of Sargodha, Sargodha 40100, Pakistan
2. Industrial and Systems Engineering Department, College of Computing and Mathematics, King Fahd University of Petroleum and Minerals, Dhahran 31261, Saudi Arabia
3. Interdisciplinary Research Centre for Smart Mobility and Logistics, King Fahd University of Petroleum and Minerals, Dhahran 31261, Saudi Arabia
4. Faculty of Health Studies, University of Bradford, Bradford BD7 1DP, UK
5. Department of Mathematics, College of Science, University of Bisha, P.O. Box 551, Bisha 61922, Saudi Arabia
* Correspondence: el_hassanein@yahoo.com

Abstract: In statistical process control, the control charts are an effective tool to monitor the process. When the process is examined based on an exponential family distributed response variable along with a single explanatory variable, the generalized linear model (GLM) provides better estimates and GLM-based charts are preferred. This study is designed to propose GLM-based control charts using different link functions (i.e., logit, probit, c-log-log, and cauchit) with the binary response variable. The Pearson residuals (PR)- and deviance residuals (DR)-based control charts for logistic regression are proposed under different link functions. For evaluation purposes, a simulation study is designed to evaluate the performance of the proposed control charts. The results are compared based on the average run length (ARL). Moreover, the proposed charts are implemented on a real application for COVID-19 death monitoring. The Monte Carlo simulation study and real applications show that the performance of the model-based control charts with the c-log-log link function gives a better performance as compared to model-based control charts with other link functions.

Keywords: ARL; control charts; COVID-19 data; deviance residuals; link functions; logistic profiling; Pearson residuals

MSC: 62P30; 62J02; 62J12; 62J20

1. Introduction

Quality is one of the main requirements of any organization's product and service goodwill. The control charts are the main tools of statistical process control (SPC) for monitoring the quality of products to improve the process capability [1]. In the last few decades, different control charts have been introduced and implemented in various industries to monitor the online process. These control charts include the Shewhart control chart [2], the cumulative sum (CUSUM) control chart [3] and the exponential weighted moving average (EWMA) control chart [4]. The Shewhart-type control chart is the memoryless control chart and is applied to detect the large shift in the mean and standard deviation of the process. However, EWMA and CUSUM are memory-type structures used to monitor small changes in the process parameters.

A single quality characteristic of a process is monitored by control charts, which may be quantitative or qualitative. Sometimes, the quality characteristic depends upon the explanatory variable(s). When the quality characteristic follows a normal distribution and is linearly associated with the explanatory variable, it is termed a simple linear profile. In linear profiling, one may want to monitor the intercept, slope, and error variance [5].

In profiling, if the normality assumption is violated, we move towards the generalized linear model (GLM)based profiling. The term GLM refers to a large class of models popularized by Nelder and Wedderburn [6]. In the literature, several monitoring studies were designed based on the GLM approach, and such charts are termed model-based control charts. Skinner et al. [7] proposed a model-based control chart using deviance residuals while the response variable follows a Poisson distribution, and they used the square root link function. Jearkpaporn et al. [8] proposed a model-based scheme based on the deviance residual for the system in which the response variable follows a Gamma distribution, and they used the log link function. In addition, Skinner et al. [9] studied the effectiveness of GLM-based control charts on the semiconductor process data based on the deviance residuals. Koosha and Amiri [10] considered the effect of autocorrelation presence between the observations in different levels of the independent variable in a logistic regression profile on the monitoring procedure (T^2 control chart) and proposed two remedies to account for the autocorrelation within logistic profiles. Shu et al. [11] reviewed the literature on regression control charts based on their importance and practical applications. Asgari et al. [12] proposed the GLM-based control chart to monitor a two-stage procedure under Poisson distribution. Amiri et al. [13] investigated the profiles with binomial and Poisson responses in phase I and monitored them using three methods, namely Hoteling T^2 statistic, the F method, and the likelihood ratio test (LRT). Amiri et al. [14] concentrated on Phase II monitoring and proposed procedures for monitoring multivariate linear and GLM regression profiles. Qi et al. [15] developed a control chart to monitor GLM profiles using the weighted likelihood ratio tests. Moheghi et al. [16] studied the robust estimation and monitoring of parameters in GLM profiles in the presence of outliers. Recently, Kinat et al. [17] proposed the Pearson and deviance residuals-based control charts for the inverse gaussian response. Moreover, recent studies on GLM-based control charts and their applications can be found in the literature [18–23].

One of the most important members of the GLM family is the logistic regression profile. When the quality characteristics follow the Bernoulli distribution, we use the logistic regression profile. Different link functions can be used for logistic regression profiling. These link functions include the logit, probit, log-log, complementary log-log (c-log-log), and cauchit link function. Koosha et al. [10] studied the effect of applying different link functions on the performance of the T^2 control chart in monitoring the parameters of logistic regression profiles, and they found that the logit link function is best for logistic regression. Yu et al. [24] analyzed the performance of the LRProb chart under the assumption that only a small number of predictable abnormal patterns are available. Hakimi et al. [19] proposed some robust approaches to estimate the logistic regression profile parameters to decrease the effects of outliers on the performance of the T^2 control chart. Khosravi et al. [25] proposed three self-starting control charts to monitor a logistic regression profile that models the relationship between a binomial response variable and explanatory variables. Alevizakos [26] proposed two indices, cp and Spmk, for logistic regression profiles using different link functions: the logit, probit, and the c-log-log. The value of each index is approximately the same regardless of the used link functions. Jahani et al. [27] developed two control charts based on Wald and Rao score test (RST) to monitor nominal logistic regression profiles in Phase II.

The available literature showed that most researchers focused on deviance residuals-based control charts with probit and logit link functions. In this study, we evaluate the performance of various link functions in logistic regression profiling based on Pearson and deviance residuals, and find out which one of the link functions shows better performance. The outline of the research work is described as: Section 2 involves the methodology. Section 3 presents the structure of the proposed control charts based on Pearson and deviance residuals. Section 4 consists of numerical evaluations, which include the simulation study of the proposed control charts. Section 5 describes a real-life application, and finally, Section 6 consists of the conclusion and future recommendations.

2. The GLM-Based Control Charts

The GLM-based control chart is used to enhance the ability of linear profile when the variable of interest follows an exponential family distribution. In this study, GLM-based control charts are designed based on deviance residuals (DR) and Pearson residuals (PR) of the logistic regression. Figure 1 shows all the steps of our proposed approach.

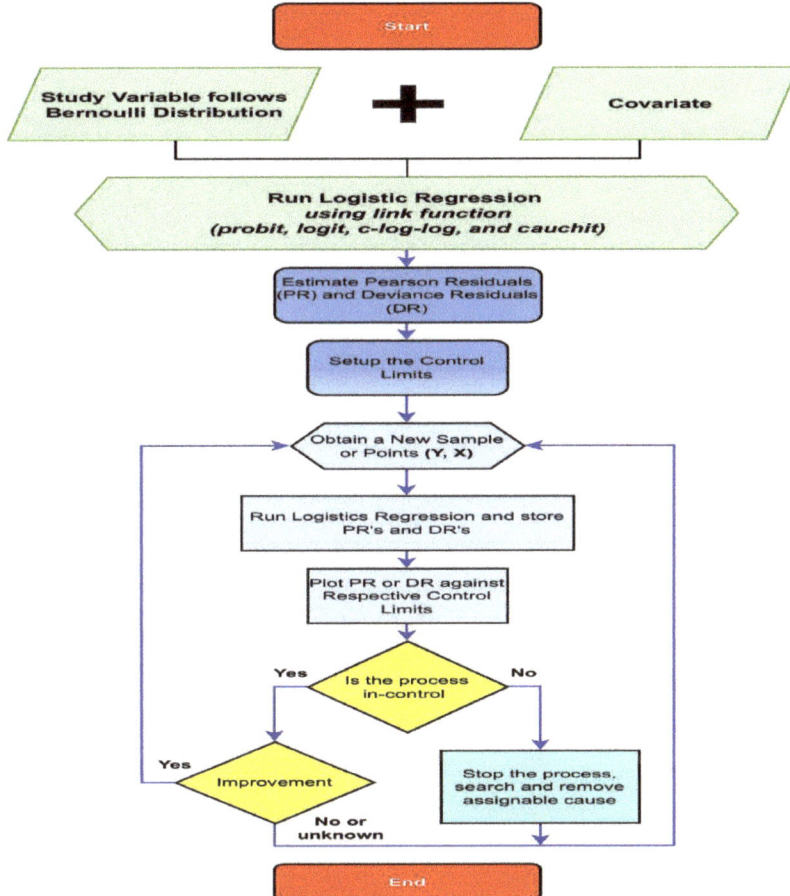

Figure 1. Follow chart of the process.

Suppose that our variable of interest (y) follows the Bernoulli distribution with probability mass function given by:

$$p(y_i|\pi_i) = \pi_i^{y_i}(1-\pi_i)^{1-y_i} \; ; \; y = 0, 1 \tag{1}$$

where π_i is the probability of success. The logistic regression model is a subset of the binomial regression model. When the response variable (y) of a regression model belongs to the Bernoulli distribution, the logistic regression model is the most commonly used statistical model; i.e., $y_i \sim Be(\pi_i)$, where the probability π_i is a function of X_i and is defined by:

$$\pi_i = \frac{\exp(x_i'\beta)}{1+\exp(x_i'\beta)}, \qquad (2)$$

where x_i is the ith row of X, which is an $n \times (p+1)$ data matrix with p explanatory variables, and β is a $(p+1) \times 1$ vector of regression coefficients. The mean and variance of Bernoulli distribution are, respectively. given by $E(y_i) = \pi_i$ and $var(y_i) = \pi_i(1-\pi_i)$.

To convert Equation (1) into an exponential format, we rewrite it as:

$$f(y|\pi_i) = exp\left[log\left(\pi_i^{y_i}(1-\pi_i)^{1-y_i}\right)\right] \qquad (3)$$

$$= exp(y_i log \pi_i + (1-y_i)\log(1-\pi_i)) \qquad (4)$$

$$= exp(y_i log \pi_i + \log(1-\pi_i) - y_i \log(1-\pi_i)) \qquad (5)$$

$$= exp(y_i log\left(\frac{\pi_i}{1-\pi_i}\right) - y_i \log(1-\pi_i)) \qquad (6)$$

The logit link function is suitable for linking π_i and X_i in the logistic regression profiles denoted by $g(\pi_i)$, which is defined by:

$$g(\pi_i) = log\left(\frac{\pi_i}{1-\pi_i}\right) = \beta_0 + \beta_1 x_{i1} + \beta_2 x_{i2} + \ldots + \beta_p x_{ip}, \qquad (7)$$

We also assume some other link functions such as the probit, c-log-log, and the cauchit to fit the logistic regression model. These link functions are given below:

$$\text{probit} \quad g(\pi_i) = \phi^{-1}(\pi_i)$$

$$\text{c-log-log} \quad g(\pi_i) = \ln(-ln(1-\pi_i))$$

$$\text{cauchit} \quad g(\pi_i) = \tan(\pi(\pi_i - 0.5))$$

The maximum likelihood estimator (MLE), based on the iterative reweighted least square technique (IRLS), is the most often used approach for estimating the parameter β, where the following log-likelihood of Equation (5) should be maximized.

$$l = \sum_{i=1}^{n}[y_i \log(\pi_i) + (1-y_i)\log(1-\pi_i)]$$

$$l = \sum_{i=1}^{n}[y_i \log(\pi_i) + \log(1-\pi_i) - y_i \log(1-\pi_i)]$$

$$l = \sum_{i=1}^{n}[\log(1-\pi_i)] + \sum_{i=1}^{n}y_i[\log \pi_i - log(1-\pi_i)]$$

$$l = \sum_{i=1}^{n}[\log(1-\pi_i)] + \sum_{i=1}^{n}y_i\left[\log\left(\frac{\pi_i}{1-\pi_i}\right)\right]$$

Substituting Equations (1) and (7) in the above expression, we have:

$$l = \sum_{i=1}^{n}\left[\log\left(1 - \frac{\exp(x_i'\beta)}{1+\exp(x_i'\beta)}\right)\right] + \sum_{i=1}^{n}y_i x_i'\beta$$

After some simplifications, the result is as follows:

$$l = -\sum_{i=1}^{n}[\log(1+\exp(x_i\beta))] + \sum_{i=1}^{n}y_i x_i'\beta \qquad (8)$$

Differentiating Equation (3) with respect to β and equating to zero yield:

$$\frac{\partial l}{\partial \beta} = \sum_{i=1}^{n}(y_i - \pi_i)x'_i = 0 \qquad (9)$$

Equation (4) is solved using the IRLS algorithm and obtained:

$$\hat{\beta}_{MLE} = \left(X'\hat{W}X\right)^{-1}X'\hat{W}\hat{z}, \qquad (10)$$

where

$$\hat{W} = diag(\hat{\pi}_i(1-\hat{\pi}_i)), \text{ and } \hat{z}_i = \log(\hat{\pi}_i) + \frac{y_i - \hat{\pi}_i}{\hat{\pi}_i(1-\hat{\pi}_i)}, \qquad (11)$$

where $\hat{\pi}_i = \frac{\exp(x'_i\hat{\beta}_{MLE})}{1+\exp(x'_i\hat{\beta}_{MLE})}$. The general form of the DR for the logistic regression model has the following form:

$$r_i^D = sign(y_i - \hat{\pi}_i)\sqrt{|2\{y_i \log \hat{\pi}_i + (1-y_i)\log(1-\hat{\pi}_i)\}|},$$

However, the PR for the logistic regression is defined as:

$$r_i^P = \frac{y_i - \hat{\pi}_i}{\sqrt{\hat{\pi}_i(1-\hat{\pi}_i)}}$$

3. Structure of the Control Charts

The Shewhart control chart includes a baseline as well as an upper control limit (UCL) and lower control limit (LCL), which are represented as dashed lines that are symmetric around the baseline. Measurements are plotted against a timeline on the chart. Measurements that exceed the limits are considered out of control (OOC). The control chart's central line (CL) is the acceptable value, which is an average of the historical check standard values. If our interest is to plot or monitor the $\hat{\theta}$ statistic, then the UCL, CL, and LCL for $\hat{\theta}$ are, respectively, given by:

$$UCL = E(\hat{\theta}) + kSD(\hat{\theta})$$

$$CL = E(\hat{\theta})$$

$$LCL = E(\hat{\theta}) - kSD(\hat{\theta}),$$

where E is the expectation of $\hat{\theta}$, k is the charting constant, and SD is the standard deviation of $\hat{\theta}$.

3.1. Logistic Regression Model-Based Control Chart Based on PR

In the model-based control chart, control limits of the PR are obtained as:

$$UCL = E\left(r_i^P\right) + k_1\sqrt{Var\left(r_i^P\right)}$$

$$CL = E\left(r_i^P\right)$$

$$LCL = E\left(r_i^P\right) - k_1\sqrt{Var\left(r_i^P\right)},$$

where k_1 is a constant that defines the size of control limits and is selected based on the fixed in-control (IC) average run length (ARL_0). When any PR crosses the control limits, then the PR-logistic chart indicates the process is OOC otherwise, in IC condition.

3.2. Logistic Regression Model-Based Control Chart Based on DR

In the model-based control chart, control limits of DR are obtained by the following expressions:

$$\text{UCL} = \text{E}\left(r_i^D\right) + k_2\sqrt{\text{Var}\left(r_i^D\right)}$$

$$\text{CL} = \text{E}\left(r_i^D\right)$$

$$\text{LCL} = \text{E}\left(r_i^D\right) - k_2\sqrt{\text{Var}\left(r_i^D\right)},$$

where k_2 is a constant that defines the size of control limits and is obtained against the fixed ARL_0. When any DR crosses the control limits, the DR-logistic chart indicates that the process is OOC otherwise, in IC condition.

4. Monte Carlo Simulation Study

In this section, we evaluate the performance of the proposed control charts under different link functions with the help of a simulation study.

4.1. Performance Measures

The performance of the proposed control charts is evaluated using average run length (ARL) (cf. [17,28]). The run length (RL) is described as the number of points till a signal is indicated, and ARL is the average of the RL. The ARL is divided into two categories: IC (ARL_0) and OOC (ARL_1). When the control chart is in a stable state, we use ARL_0 as the chart's performance measure, but when the process is in an unstable state, we use ARL_1. A chart is considered to be the best among those under discussion if, on the fixed ARL_0, it has the smallest ARL_1. Hence, in this study, we focused on the ARL to evaluate the performance of the control charts under different link functions.

4.2. Data Generation

For the simulation purpose, firstly, we generate the response variable from the Bernoulli distribution with parameter π_i i.e., $y_i \sim Be(\pi_i)$, where $\pi = \frac{e^{(\beta_0 + \beta_1 x)}}{1 + e^{(\beta_0 + \beta_1 x)}}$, $x \sim uniform(0, 100)$. The true values of β_0 and β_1 are set to be 0.05 and 0.06, respectively. These variables are generated for a fixed sample size $n = 1000$.

4.3. Algorithm for Charting Constants

The following algorithm is used to find out charting constants.

i Set the arbitrary value as a charting constant and set regression coefficients as $\beta_0 = 0.05$ and $\beta_1 = 0.06$;
ii Generate 1000 observations of the input variable (x) from the uniform distribution;
iii The mean of the logistic response variable (π_i) is determined for each observation using Equation (2);
iv The response variable is generated from the Bernoulli distribution with parameter π_i defined in step ii;
v Fit the logistic regression model and obtain the residuals DR and PR;
vi For the control charts based on PR and DR, calculate the mean and standard error of DR and PR, respectively;
vii Determine the UCL and LCL of each proposed control chart using steps (i) and (viii). Plot the PR and DR against their respective limits;
vii To obtain specified ARL_0, repeat steps i–vii, 10,000 times.

If specified ARL_0 does not achieve, then adjust the previous arbitrary value and repeat steps i–viii until specified ARL_0 is obtained. By using the above-stated algorithm, the control charting constants are reported in Table 1.

Table 1. Constants for the logistic regression profiling with $ARL_0 = 200$ under various link functions.

PR				DR			
logit	probit	c-log-log	cauchit	logit	probit	c-log-log	cauchit
1.045	1.0443	1.0462	1.0443	1.045	1.0443	1.0456	1.0457

4.4. Results and Discussion

This section discusses the simulated results of the logistic model-based control charts with different link functions. Furthermore, we evaluate the performance of control charts by inserting the additive shifts in parameters of the model, such as β_0, β_1, and μ_x.

Monitoring β_0, β_1 and μ_x in Terms of ARL

In this section, we evaluate the simulation results of the control charts based on PR and DR in terms of ARL. For the out-of-control scenario, we considered the shifts in the μ_i by changing the β_0 into $\beta_0 + \eta$, β_1 into $\beta_1 + \theta$, and by changing the μ_x into $\mu_x + \delta$. The OOC results in terms of ARL are reported in Tables 2–4.

Table 2. Performance of $ARL_0 = 200$ with shift in β_0 under considered link functions.

	PR				DR			
η	logit	probit	c-log-log	cauchit	logit	probit	c-log-log	cauchit
0	201.56	199.99	200.97	200.92	200.24	199.68	199.13	199.49
0.04	117.87	121.46	129.14	121.95	119.01	124.69	111.15	125.00
0.08	53.93	56.15	62.80	61.25	55.93	55.25	55.08	66.47
0.12	24.00	23.96	26.20	22.28	21.57	22.76	20.85	21.42
0.16	7.67	7.56	9.29	7.96	8.59	7.33	10.29	8.10
0.2	4.07	4.21	3.75	3.75	3.38	3.83	3.67	3.81
0.24	2.53	2.71	2.62	2.50	2.50	2.94	3.09	2.55
0.28	2.58	2.42	2.41	2.49	2.48	2.44	2.41	2.44

Table 3. Performance of $ARL_0 = 200$ with shift in β_1 under considered link functions.

	PR				DR			
θ	logit	probit	c-log-log	cauchit	logit	probit	c-log-log	cauchit
0	201.09	201.69	199.03	199.27	200.86	200.36	200.31	199.38
0.04	188.83	152.21	162.73	153.03	190.78	149.65	177.08	153.47
0.08	121.46	127.65	137.29	117.82	122.48	110.83	123.97	122.37
0.12	84.68	77.35	68.47	89.39	85.48	77.45	89.37	79.77
0.16	55.09	44.39	56.99	45.46	55.61	48.50	47.45	54.95
0.2	31.51	29.45	32.36	36.05	31.61	30.97	37.22	27.83
0.24	15.24	14.28	20.94	16.72	15.37	13.17	13.21	15.89
0.28	10.47	10.13	9.99	10.81	10.67	8.03	11.10	12.70

In Table 2, we evaluate the performance of the proposed control charts for monitoring β_0 in terms of ARL_1 under various link functions. The outcomes revealed that raising shifts minimizes the ARL_1 values for control charts based on DR and PR by using considered link functions. The estimated ARL_1 values at maximum shift ($\eta = 0.28$) for the logit, probit, c-log-log, and the cauchit link functions are 2.58, 2.42, 2.41, and 2.49, respectively. On comparing the performance of link functions in the PR-based control charts, we found that the c-log-log link function outperforms other link functions. The estimated ARL_1 of the DR-based control chart at the maximum shift ($\eta = 0.28$) for the logit, probit, c-log-log, and the cauchit link functions are 2.48, 2.44, 2.41, and 2.44, respectively. It is clear from the results that the c-log-log link function performs better than the other link functions. Finally, it is also observed that the DR-based control chart with the c-log-log link function outperformed the PR-based control chart with the c-log-log link function.

Table 4. Performance of $ARL_0 = 200$ with shift in μ_x under considered link functions.

	PR				DR			
δ	logit	probit	c-log-log	cauchit	logit	probit	c-log-log	cauchit
0	199.28	201.73	199.61	201.54	199.68	199.49	200.05	199.36
0.04	52.19	59.56	51.04	58.92	63.32	62.33	60.67	64.53
0.08	8.29	8.20	8.47	6.99	8.58	8.31	8.72	9.16
0.12	2.81	2.60	2.88	2.54	2.40	2.50	2.58	2.75
0.16	2.48	2.47	2.51	2.49	2.53	2.52	2.53	2.50
0.2	2.63	2.61	2.64	2.59	2.61	2.62	2.62	2.65
0.24	2.80	2.79	2.77	2.82	2.76	2.78	2.71	2.70
0.28	2.95	2.89	2.95	2.95	2.84	2.94	2.94	2.93

In Table 3, we evaluate the performance of the proposed control charts for monitoring β_1 in terms of ARL_1 under various link functions. The outcomes revealed that an increase in shift minimizes the ARL_1 values for control charts. The estimated ARL_1 values at maximum shift ($\theta = 0.28$) for the logit, probit, c-log-log, and the cauchit link functions are 10.47, 10.13, 9.99, and 10.81, respectively. On comparing the performance of link functions in PR-based control charts, we found that the c-log-log link function outperforms other link functions. The estimated ARL_1 of the DR-based control chart at the maximum shift ($\theta = 0.28$) for the logit, probit, c-log-log, and the cauchit link functions are 10.67, 8.03, 11.10, and 12.70, respectively, which reveals that the probit link function performs better than the other link functions. On comparing the performance of the DR- and the PR-based control charts in monitoring β_1 under different link functions, we observed that the DR-based control charts with probit link function perform better than the PR-based control charts with other link functions.

In Table 4, we evaluate the performance of the proposed control charts for the shifts in μ_x in terms of ARL'_1s under various link functions. The outcomes revealed that raising shifts minimizes the ARL'_1s values for control charts based on DR and PR by using considered link functions. Table 4 presents the estimated ARL'_1 values of the PR-based control charts under different link functions. The estimated ARL'_1 values report at maximum shift ($\delta = 0.28$) for the logit, probit, c-log-log, and the cauchit link functions are 2.95, 2.89, 2.95, and 2.95, respectively. On comparing the performance of link functions in PR-based control charts, we found that the probit link function outperforms other link functions. Further, the estimated ARL'_1 of the DR-based control chart at the maximum shift ($\delta = 0.28$) for the logit, probit, c-log-log, and the cauchit link functions are 2.84, 2.94, 2.94, and 2.93, respectively. It is clear from the results that the logit link function performs better than the other link functions. Finally, on comparing the performance of DR- and PR-based control charts in monitoring μ_x under different link functions, we observe that the DR-based control charts with the logit link function perform better than PR-based control charts as compared to the other link functions.

5. Application: COVID-19 Deaths Profile Monitoring

In this modern era, COVID-19 affects different people in different ways. Here, we monitor the mortality status of COVID-19 patients who were admitted to Benazir Bhutto Shaheed Hospital, Rawalpindi, Pakistan. This data had been already collected by Akhtar et al. [29], where they collected this data from three hospitals, and we are considering one of these hospital data sets. In this application, our response variable (Y) is binary ($y = 1$, if the COVID patient is discharged deceased; otherwise, $y = 0$). Therefore, we consider this application for the evaluation of our proposed control charts. The data about the demographic and vital signs of all adult COVID-19 patients who were discharged from Benazir Bhutto Shaheed Hospital, Rawalpindi, during the first wave of COVID-19 (February to August 2020) were retrospectively collected. The National Early Warning Score (NEWS) was calculated by following the work of the Royal College of Physicians (RCP) (2012, page 14), and considered an independent variable in this study. The NEWS is based on a simple aggregate scoring system, which is computed based on vital signs (see Table 5 [30]).

Table 5. The strategy to estimate national early warning score (NEWS).

Physiological Parameters	3	2	1	0	1	2	3
Respiration Rate	≤8		9–11	12–20		21–24	≥25
Oxygen Saturations	≤91	92–93	94–95	≥96			
Any Supplemental Oxygen		Yes		No			
Temperature	≤35.0		35.1–36.0	36.1–38.0	38.1–39.0	≥39.1	
Systolic Blood Pressure	≤90	91–100	101–110	111–219			≥220
Heart Rate	≤40		41–50	51–90	91–110	111–130	≥131
Level of Consciousness				Alert			Voice, Pain, or Unconscious

We had data of a total of 916 COVID-19 patients, consisting of mortality status (y) and NEWS (x). Based on the available data, we run logistic regression by setting logit, probit, c-log-log, and cauchit link functions. The Pearson (PR) and deviance (DR) residuals were obtained for estimated logistic regression models under each link function, and their means and standard deviations (SD) are reported in Table 6. Further, we set $ARL_0 = 200$ and obtained the limits of PR and DR-based control charts, which are also given in Table 6. To make the OOC dataset, we have estimated a new response variable (Y_1) by using $\mu_Y - uniform(0, 0.2)$. Similarly, we estimated logistic regression models and obtained shifted PR's and DR's. The PR- and DR-based control charts under different link functions are presented in Figures 2–5. The points under the pink and white shaded areas belong to the IC and OOC situation, respectively. The blue color points indicate the IC PR's and DR's, while the red color shows the OOC points. The PR- and DR-based control charts under the logit function are presented in Figure 2, while proposed control charts based on the probit function are portrayed in Figure 3. Figures 4 and 5 consist of PR and DR-based control charts under c-log-log and cauchit link functions, respectively. The out-of-control points are counted for each chart and reported in Table 6. It is revealed that the PR- and DR-based control charts under the cauchit link function have captured a large number of OOC signals. The second largest OOC points were detected by the PR- and DR-based control charts for the c-log-log link function. Hence, PR- and DR-based control charts under cauchit link and c-log-log link functions outperform all their counterparts.

Table 6. For the COVID-19 data, the mean and standard deviation of logistic regression residuals, control limits and OOC signals under different link functions.

Link Functions	logit		probit		c-log-log		cauchit	
Residuals	PR	DR	PR	DR	PR	DR	PR	DR
Mean	−0.0019	−0.1476	−0.0011	−0.1468	−0.0015	−0.1473	−0.0078	−0.1529
SD	0.9971	1.0337	0.9979	1.034	0.9964	1.0345	0.9916	1.0352
LCL	−1.0234	−1.1939	−1.0152	−1.1873	−1.0375	−1.2051	−1.0591	−1.2222
UCL	2.256	1.899	2.277	1.9071	2.2192	1.8847	2.1154	1.8429
OOC Signals	83	97	83	83	97	97	144	144

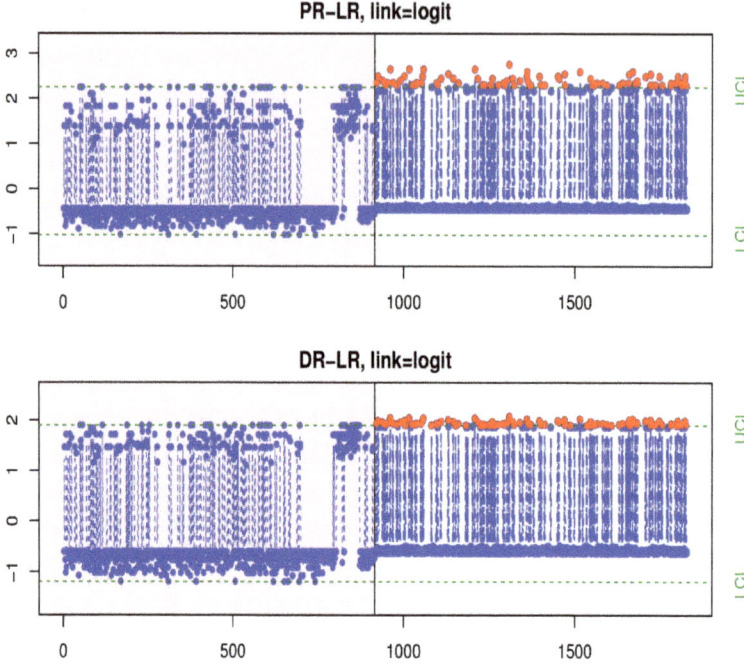

Figure 2. Control chart based on PR and DR with the logit link function.

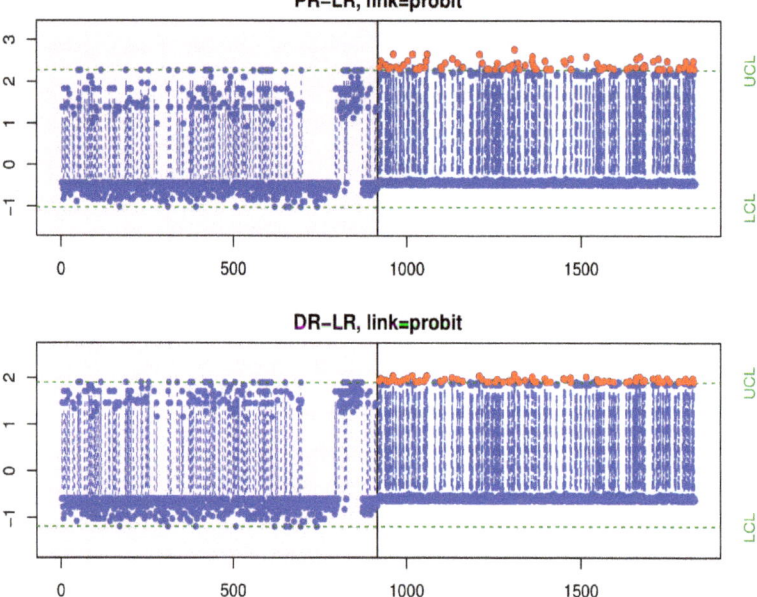

Figure 3. Control chart based on PR and DR with the probit link function.

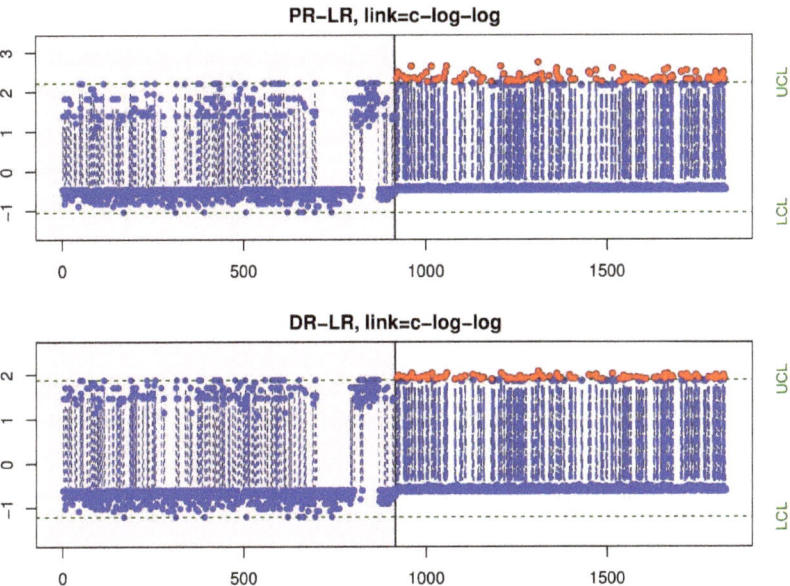

Figure 4. Control chart based on PR and DR with the c-log-log link function.

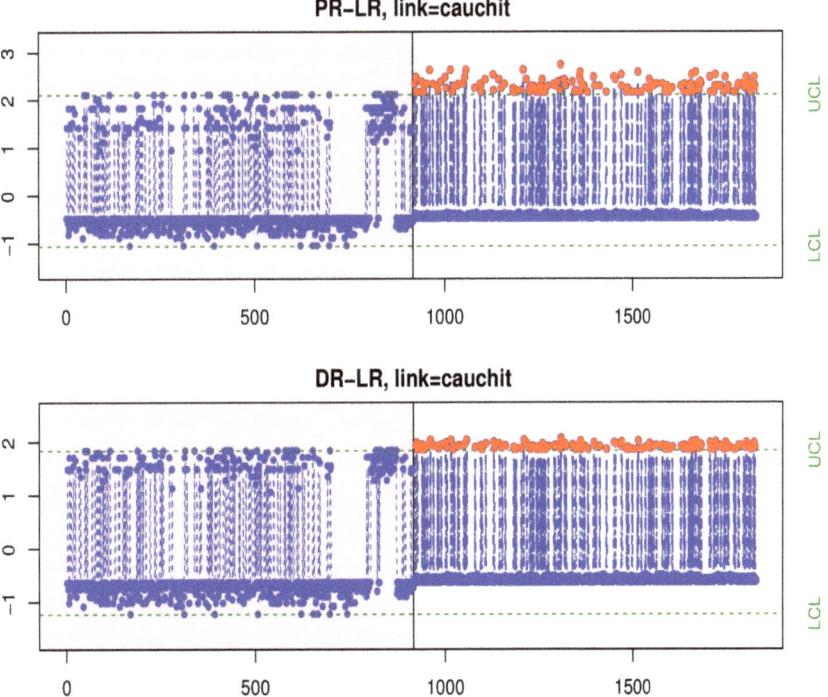

Figure 5. Control chart based on PR and Dr with the cauchit link function.

6. Conclusions

In this study, the control charts are constructed based on the LR residuals (Pearson residuals (PR) and deviance residuals (DR)) with different link functions (the logit, probit, c-log-log, and cauchit). We evaluate the performance of the control charts with the help of a simulation study, where ARL is considered as the evaluation criterion. The simulation study shows that in monitoring β_0, the c-log-log link function showed good performance for both PR and DR control charts as compared to the other link functions. While monitoring β_1, the DR-based control chart with the probit link function performs better as compared to the PR-based control charts and with other link functions due to its minimum ARL. We also conclude that in monitoring μ_x, the logit link function gives a better performance for the DR-based control chart as compared to the PR-based control charts with other link functions. For the COVID-19 death data, the PR- and DR-based control charts were implemented and showed that charts based on the cauchit link function indicated a large number of signals. The 2nd link function which gives the 2nd largest OOC is the c-log-log link function. Therefore, it is concluded from the results that mostly the DR-based control charts with the c-log-log link function give a better performance as compared to the other link functions.

Author Contributions: Methodology, M.C., M.A., T.M., M.F., K.B. and A.E.; Formal analysis, M.C., M.A., T.M., M.F., K.B. and A.E.; Writing—original draft, M.C.; Writing—review & editing, M.A., T.M., M.F., K.B. and A.E. All authors have read and agreed to the published version of the manuscript.

Funding: This research was funded by the Deanship of Scientific Research at University of Bisha, grant number UB-GRP-42-1444.

Data Availability Statement: Not Applicable.

Acknowledgments: The authors extend their appreciation to the Deanship of Scientific Research at University of Bisha for funding this research through the general research project under grant number (UB-GRP-42-1444).

Conflicts of Interest: The authors declare no conflict of interest.

References

1. Mahmood, T.; Xie, M. Models and monitoring of zero-inflated processes: The past and current trends. *Qual. Reliab. Eng. Int.* **2019**, *35*, 2540–2557. [CrossRef]
2. Shewhart, W.A. *Economic Control of Quality of Manufactured Product*; Macmillan And Co., Ltd.: London, UK, 1931.
3. Page, E.S. Continuous inspection schemes. *Biometrika* **1954**, *41*, 100–115. [CrossRef]
4. Roberts, S.W. Control chart tests based on geometric moving averages. *Technometrics* **2000**, *42*, 97–101. [CrossRef]
5. Zhu, J.; Lin, D.K. Monitoring the slopes of linear profiles. *Qual. Eng.* **2009**, *22*, 1–12. [CrossRef]
6. Nelder, J.A.; Weddernburn, R.W.M. Generalized linear models. *J. R. Stat. Soc. Ser. A* **1972**, *135*, 370–384. [CrossRef]
7. Skinner, K.R.; Montgomery, D.C.; Runger, G.C. Process monitoring for multiple count data using generalized linear model-based control charts. *Int. J. Prod. Res.* **2003**, *41*, 1167–1180. [CrossRef]
8. Jearkpaporn, D.; Montgomery, D.C.; Runger, G.C.; Borror, C.M. Process monitoring for correlated gamma-distributed data using generalized-linear-model-based control charts. *Qual. Reliab. Eng. Int.* **2003**, *19*, 477–491. [CrossRef]
9. Skinner, K.R.; Montgomery, D.C.; Runger, G.C. Generalized linear model-based control charts for discrete semiconductor process data. *Qual. Reliab. Eng. Int.* **2004**, *20*, 777–786. [CrossRef]
10. Koosha, M.; Amiri, A. The effect of link function on the monitoring of logistic regression profiles. In Proceedings of the World Congress on Engineering 2011, London, UK, 6–8 July 2011.
11. Shu, L.; Tsui, K.L.; Tsung, F. Regression Control Charts. Encyclopedia of Statistics in Quality and Reliability. 2008. Available online: https://onlinelibrary.wiley.com/doi/abs/10.1002/9780470061572.eqr260 (accessed on 15 January 2023).
12. Asgari, A.; Amiri, A.; Niaki, S.T.A. A new link function in GLM-based control charts to improve monitoring of two-stage processes with Poisson response. *Int. J. Adv. Manuf. Technol.* **2014**, *72*, 1243–1256. [CrossRef]
13. Amiri, A.; Koosha, M.; Azhdari, A.; Wang, G. Phase I monitoring of generalized linear model-based regression profiles. *J. Stat. Comput. Simul.* **2015**, *85*, 2839–2859. [CrossRef]
14. Amiri, A.; Yeh, A.B.; Asgari, A. Monitoring two-stage processes with binomial data using generalized linear model-based control charts. *Qual. Technol. Quant. Manag.* **2016**, *13*, 241–262. [CrossRef]
15. Qi, D.; Wang, Z.; Zi, X.; Li, Z. Phase II monitoring of generalized linear profiles using weighted likelihood ratio charts. *Comput. Ind. Eng.* **2016**, *94*, 178–187. [CrossRef]

16. Moheghi, H.R.; Noorossana, R.; Ahmadi, O. GLM profile monitoring using robust estimators. *Qual. Reliab. Eng. Int.* **2021**, *37*, 664–680. [CrossRef]
17. Kinat, S.; Amin, M.; Mahmood, T. GLM-based control charts for the inverse Gaussian distributed response variable. *Qual. Reliab. Eng. Int.* **2020**, *36*, 765–783. [CrossRef]
18. García-Bustos, S.; Zambrano, G. Control charts for health surveillance based on residuals of negative binomial regression. *Qual. Reliab. Eng. Int.* **2022**, *38*, 2521–2532. [CrossRef]
19. Hakimi, A.; Amiri, A.; Kamranrad, R. Robust approaches for monitoring logistic regression profiles under outliers. *Int. J. Qual. Reliab. Manag.* **2017**, *34*, 494–507. [CrossRef]
20. Kim, J.-M.; Ha, I.D. Deep learning-based residual control chart for count data. *Qual. Eng.* **2022**, *34*, 370–381. [CrossRef]
21. Mahmood, T.; Iqbal, A.; Abbasi, S.A.; Amin, M. Efficient GLM-based control charts for Poisson processes. *Qual. Reliab. Eng. Int.* **2022**, *38*, 389–404. [CrossRef]
22. Soleimani, P.; Asadzadeh, S. Effect of non-normality on the monitoring of simple linear profiles in two-stage processes: A remedial measure for gamma-distributed responses. *J. Appl. Stat.* **2022**, *49*, 2870–2890. [CrossRef]
23. Yeganeh Chukhrova, N.; Johannssen, A.; Fotuhi, H. A network surveillance approach using machine learning based control charts. *Expert Syst. Appl.* **2023**, *219*, 119660. [CrossRef]
24. Yu, J.; Liu, J. LRProb control chart based on logistic regression for monitoring mean shifts of auto-correlated manufacturing processes. *Int. J. Prod. Res.* **2011**, *49*, 2301–2326. [CrossRef]
25. Khosravi, P.; Amiri, A. Self-Starting control charts for monitoring logistic regression profiles. *Commun. Stat.-Simul. Comput.* **2019**, *48*, 1860–1871. [CrossRef]
26. Alevizakos, V.; Koukouvinos, C.; Lappa, A. Comparative study of the Cp and Spmk indices for logistic regression profile using different link functions. *Qual. Eng.* **2019**, *31*, 453–462. [CrossRef]
27. Jahani, K.; Feili, H.; Ohadi, F. Phase II monitoring of the nominal logistic regression profiles based on Wald and Rao score test statistics (a case study in healthcare: Diabetic patients). *Int. J. Product. Qual. Manag.* **2019**, *27*, 161–176. [CrossRef]
28. Amin, M.; Mahmood, T.; Kinat, S. Memory type control charts with inverse-Gaussian response: An application to yarn manufacturing industry. *Trans. Inst. Meas. Control* **2021**, *43*, 656–678. [CrossRef]
29. Akhtar, H.; Akhtar, S.; Rahman, F.U.; Afridi, M.; Khalid, S.; Ali, S.; Akhtar, N.; Khader, Y.S.; Ahmad, H.; Khan, M.M. An overview of the treatment options used for the management of COVID-19 in Pakistan: Retrospective Observational Study. *JMIR Public Health Surve.* **2021**, *7*, e28594. [CrossRef]
30. Royal College of Physicians. *National Early Warning Score (NEWS): Standardising the Assessment of Acute Illness Severity in the NHS*; Report of a Working Party; RCP: London, UK, 2012.

Disclaimer/Publisher's Note: The statements, opinions and data contained in all publications are solely those of the individual author(s) and contributor(s) and not of MDPI and/or the editor(s). MDPI and/or the editor(s) disclaim responsibility for any injury to people or property resulting from any ideas, methods, instructions or products referred to in the content.

Article

Robust Online Support Vector Regression with Truncated ε-Insensitive Pinball Loss

Xian Shan *, Zheshuo Zhang, Xiaoying Li, Yu Xie and Jinyu You

College of Science, China University of Petroleum, Qingdao 266580, China
* Correspondence: 20120029@upc.edu.cn

Abstract: Advances in information technology have led to the proliferation of data in the fields of finance, energy, and economics. Unforeseen elements can cause data to be contaminated by noise and outliers. In this study, a robust online support vector regression algorithm based on a non-convex asymmetric loss function is developed to handle the regression of noisy dynamic data streams. Inspired by pinball loss, a truncated ε-insensitive pinball loss (TIPL) is proposed to solve the problems caused by heavy noise and outliers. A TIPL-based online support vector regression algorithm (TIPOSVR) is constructed under the regularization framework, and the online gradient descent algorithm is implemented to execute it. Experiments are performed using synthetic datasets, UCI datasets, and real datasets. The results of the investigation show that in the majority of cases, the proposed algorithm is comparable, or even superior, to the comparison algorithms in terms of accuracy and robustness on datasets with different types of noise.

Keywords: regression; data stream; non-convex loss function; noise-resilient; online-learning

MSC: 68T09; 62R07

1. Introduction

Machine learning-based techniques attempt to investigate the patterns in the data and the reasoning behind it. Researchers in the field of machine learning field have shown significant interest in support vector regression (SVR) algorithms owing to the strong theoretical basis and excellent generalization ability. SVR has proven to be a reliable method for regression and has been widely used in several applications, such as wind speed forecasting [1,2], solar radiation forecasting [3], financial time series forecasting [4,5], travel time forecasting [6], among others.

Classic SVR is a powerful regression method. It works by minimizing the empirical risk loss and the structural risk, which are defined by the loss function and the regularization term, respectively. Given a training dataset $T = \{(\mathbf{X}_i, y_i) \mid \mathbf{X}_i \in \mathbf{R}^m, y_i \in \mathbf{R}, i = 1, 2, \ldots, N\}$, SVR aims to find a linear function $f(\mathbf{X}) = \mathbf{W}^T\mathbf{X} + b, \mathbf{W} \in \mathbf{R}^m, b \in \mathbf{R}$ or a nonlinear function $f(\mathbf{X}) = \mathbf{W}^T\phi(\mathbf{X}) + b$ in feature space, to reveal the patterns and trends in the data. The minimal problem is described as follows:

$$\min \quad \frac{1}{2}\|f\|_{\mathcal{H}}^2 + C\sum_{i=1}^{N} L(f(\mathbf{X}_i) - y_i) \tag{1}$$

C is the regularization parameter used to adjust the model complexity and training error. The loss function $L(\cdot)$ measures the difference between the predicted and observed values, which is used to define empirical risk loss. The regularization term makes $f(x)$ as flat as possible to avoid overfitting. The regression estimator is obtained by solving a convex optimization problem where all the local minima are also global.

The loss function is of significant importance for SVR. It should accurately reflect the noise characteristics present in the training data. In recent years, researchers have

---

Citation: Shan, X.; Zhang, Z.; Li, X.; Xie, Y.; You, J. Robust Online Support Vector Regression with Truncated ε-Insensitive Pinball Loss. *Mathematics* **2023**, *11*, 709. https://doi.org/10.3390/math11030709

Academic Editors: Wen Zhang, Xiaofeng Xu, Jun Wu and Kaijian He

Received: 13 December 2022
Revised: 22 January 2023
Accepted: 27 January 2023
Published: 30 January 2023

Copyright: © 2023 by the authors. Licensee MDPI, Basel, Switzerland. This article is an open access article distributed under the terms and conditions of the Creative Commons Attribution (CC BY) license (https://creativecommons.org/licenses/by/4.0/).

developed various loss functions. The most commonly used loss functions are the squared loss, linear loss, Huber loss, and ε-insensitive loss [7]. Squared loss [8,9] is a metric that assesses the discrepancy between the predicted and actual values by calculating the mean squared error. It is a smooth function which can be solved quickly and accurately by convex optimization methods. However, it is sensitive to large errors, making it less robust than other techniques. Linear loss [10,11] is a general loss function applicable to several problems. It is less sensitive to large errors than the squared loss because it is designed by absolute errors. Huber loss [12] is a combination of linear and squared losses and is designed to simultaneously provide robustness and smoothness by using squared loss for the smaller errors and linear loss for the larger errors. The combination of the two loss functions allows for a more sophisticated understanding of the data. The ε-insensitive loss [10,11] augments the linear loss by introducing an insensitive band to the data, which promotes sparsity.

In the current era of data abundance, accurately analyzing dynamic data with noise and outliers using SVR is a challenging but essential task.

One of the problems is that the loss function is not sufficiently resilient to general noise in the data and can be adversely affected by outliers. Data collection processes are influenced by various external factors, resulting in noise and outliers in the data. Across numerous fields, including finance, economy, and energy, data are regularly accompanied by a considerable amount of asymmetric noise. Further, noise has several forms and is difficult to identify and remove. For example, asymmetric heavy-tailed noise that is predominantly positive is typically found in automobile insurance claims [13]. The energy-load data contain non-Gaussian noise with a heavy-tailed distribution [14]. The popular loss functions mentioned above are usually symmetric, which means that the loss incurred is the same degree regardless of the direction of the prediction error. They have proven themselves in situations where the noise is symmetric, such as the Gaussian noise and Uniform noise. However, they are not as robust as dealing with asymmetric noise, including heavy-tailed noise and outliers. This was demonstrated in a previous study [7,15,16]. In addition, comparing the predicted value to the target value, there may be different impacts of over-estimation and under-estimation [7,14]. Take the energy market as an example, hedging contracts between retailers and suppliers are commonly used to stabilize the cost of goods in short term, thus reducing economic risk. Over-prediction and under-prediction both result in economic losses, albeit of different magnitudes. Over-forecasting may incur the cost of disposing of unused orders, while under-forecasting may cause retailers to pay a higher price for energy loads than the contract price. Developing a more accurate regression model requires consideration of the various penalties for over-estimation and under-estimation.

To handle the asymmetric noise while considering the distinct effects of positive and negative errors, two asymmetric loss functions have been proposed: quantile loss and pinball loss [15,17,18]. These loss functions differ in terms of different penalty weights for positive and negative errors, thus making them more robust to asymmetric noise.

Moreover, outliers have a severe impact on the accuracy of the model. The presence of outliers skews the data and causes large deviations from the expected results. It is crucial to consider the presence of outlier when constructing and evaluating a model. Given the under-forecasting in dealing with general noise and outliers, there is a need for designing a broader range of loss functions to address these issues. Researchers have developed non-convex loss functions to handle outliers, such as correlated entropy loss [16,19] and truncated loss functions [8,18,20,21]. These two strategies limit the outlier loss to a specific range, thereby reducing the impact of outliers on the regression function. The asymmetric loss function and the truncated loss functions have proven to be viable strategies for improving the robustness of regression models.

Another problem is that the batch learning framework used by a typical SVR is unsuitable for the data flow environment. Traditional SVRs involve batch learning, which can be challenging when dealing with large datasets owing to the increased storage requirements and computational complexity. Researchers have proposed various solutions to address this problem, such as the convex optimization technique outlined in [9,15] and online learning algorithms based on the stochastic approximation theory [22–24]. The online SVR presented in [9] and the Canal loss-based online regression algorithm described in [22] are used as examples. Therefore, despite the efficiency of the proposed online learning algorithms for handling regression problems in data streams, other solutions may be required when noise and outliers are present.

The current study aims to present an online learning regression algorithm based on truncated asymmetric loss functions, which can effectively address the regression problem in noisy data streams. We propose a novel online SVR, termed TIPOSVR, established within the regularization framework of SVR and solved by the online gradient descent (OGD) algorithm. TIPOSVR uses an innovative loss function. The main contributions of this study are as follows:

(1) TIPL function proposed is a bounded, non-convex and asymmetric loss function. Asymmetricity helps in dealing with problems arising due to the presence of asymmetric noise, and truncation is used to reduce the effect of outliers. Additionally, the inclusion of an insensitive band increases the sparsity of the model. It is possible to effectively deal with the general noise and reduce the sensitivity to outliers.
(2) An online SVR (TIPOSVR), based on the TIPL function, is developed to address the issue of the data dynamics problem. The algorithm is solved using the OGD approach.
(3) Computational experiments are performed on the synthetic, benchmark, and real datasets. Results of the experiments indicate that TIPOSVR proposed in this study is more accurate than the comparison algorithms in most scenarios. It has been shown that the TIPOSVR has a high degree of robustness and generalizability.

The remainder of this paper is organized as follows. Section 2 of this paper provides a literature review, while Section 3 presents the regularization framework and the robust loss function of SVR. Section 4 proposes an online SVR based on the TIPL function. To validate the performance of the proposed algorithm, Section 5 presents numerical experiments on the synthetic, UCI benchmark, and real datasets which compare TIPOSVR with some classical and advanced SVRs. Finally, Section 6 summarizes the main findings, limitations, and prospects for future work of this paper.

2. Literature Review

SVR has been widely used and implemented in various fields as a powerful machine learning algorithm. This section provides an overview of the recent advances in robust loss functions and online learning algorithms.

2.1. Robust Loss Function

Noise is generally classified into two categories: characteristic noise and outliers. It has been reported [21,25] that the ε-insensitive loss function is more effective for dealing with uniform noise datasets, whereas the squared loss function is more effective in dealing with Gaussian noise datasets. Aside from Gaussian and Uniform noise, asymmetric noise, especially heavy-tail noise, also significantly affects the accuracy of a regression model. Studies have shown that an asymmetric loss function can be used to solve the asymmetric noise problem [15,17,18]. The quantile regression theory provides the basis for deriving an asymmetric loss function [15]. Assigning different penalty weights to positive and negative errors allows for a wider range of noise distributions. Quantile regression has been increasingly used since the 1970s. Refs. [26,27] have adopted the quantile loss function, incorporating an adjustment term $\nu\varepsilon$ and $C(\nu\tau(1-\tau)\varepsilon)$, to adjust the asymmetric insensitive region within the regularization framework, as expressed in optimization problem Equation (1). The introduction of the parameter ν to control the width of the asymmetric ε-insensitive area ensures that a certain percentage of the samples are situated in this area and classified as support vectors. Consequently, an insensitive band that can accommodate the necessary amount of samples is outputted to address the sampling issue, thereby facilitating the automated control of accuracy. The pinball loss is developed based on quantile regression [15,18]. Extensive research on pinball loss has been conducted, leading to the development and application of the sparse ε-insensitive pinball loss [16] and the twin pinball SVR [28].

Several studies have been conducted to address the outlier problem, with a focus on developing a non-convex loss function. The correlation entropy loss [16,19] is a loss function derived from the correlation entropy theory based on the Gaussian or Laplacian kernel. As the error moves away from zero in either direction, the loss value eventually increases to a constant. Another type of non-convex loss function is horizontal truncated loss. In this case, the loss value of the outlier is a constant. As described in [22], Canal loss is a ε-insensitive loss with horizontal truncation. Ref. [29] construct a non-convex loss function by subtracting two ε-insensitive loss functions, which yield a linear loss with horizontal truncation. A non-convex least square loss function, proposed in [8], is based on the horizontal truncation and squared loss. Experimental evidence suggests that these loss functions successfully reduce the impact of outliers. The aforementioned methods produce bounded loss functions that help reduce the sensitivity of the model to outliers by maintaining the loss of outliers within a certain limit.

For a dataset containing noise and outliers, a combination of the asymmetric loss function and truncated loss function is proposed to improve the robustness of the regression model, because such a combination covers a more comprehensive range of noise distributions.

Most of the analysis uses batch learning SVR. Batch algorithms assume that data can be collected and used via a single step process, ignoring any changes that may occur over time. This is not the case in today's era of the Big Data age, where the data are constantly in flux [23,30,31]. Batch algorithms are faced with memory and computational problems because of the considerable amount of data needed by these algorithms. Researchers have now focused on investigating online learning algorithms to improve the performance of regression strategies in the face of data flow.

2.2. Online Learning Algorithm

A regression algorithm should be designed to easily integrate new data into the existing model to address the storage and computational issues caused by a large amount of data. Online learning algorithms have been discussed and implemented in previous studies [23,24,32,33]. A kernel-based online extreme learning machine is proposed by [34]. An online sparse SVR method is introduced in [35].

Nevertheless, these techniques are formulated in the context of convex optimization, which is unsuitable for non-convex optimization problems. The online learning approach is further improved according to the theory of pseudo-convex function optimization theory [33]. Studies on online learning algorithms for non-convex loss functions have been performed, including the online SVR [22] and a variable selection [36] based on Canal loss.

This study presents an online SVR that contains a bounded and non-convex loss function. The algorithm is designed to be noise-resilient and sparse while being capable of capturing the various data characteristics.

3. Related Work

3.1. Robust Loss Function

The loss function plays a key role in any regression model. The sensitivity of a model to asymmetric noise is reduced using the pinball loss function, which is an asymmetric loss function. Further, the truncated loss function reduces the effect of outliers.

3.1.1. Pinball Loss

The pinball loss is derived from quantile regression, which is more effective for dealing with different forms of noise than linear loss. Pinball loss is defined as follows:

$$L_\tau(u) = \begin{cases} u, & u > 0 \\ -\tau u, & u \leq 0 \end{cases} \tag{2}$$

where τ is an asymmetry parameter. By adjusting the value of τ, we can address the problems of over and under-prediction to different degrees, making it suitable for datasets with different noise distributions. Cross-validation is the preferred method to determine the best value of τ. When $\tau = 1$, the pinball loss is equivalent to a linear loss.

Incorporating a ε-insensitive band into the pinball loss enables the pinball loss to be sparser and resilient to minor errors. ε-insensitive pinball loss is defined as:

$$L_{\varepsilon,\tau}(u) = \begin{cases} u - \varepsilon & u > \varepsilon \\ 0 & -\varepsilon/\tau \leq u \leq \varepsilon \\ -\tau u - \varepsilon & u < -\varepsilon/\tau \end{cases} \tag{3}$$

Pinball loss and ε-insensitive pinball loss present a potential solution to counteract the asymmetric distribution of noise. These two convex loss functions are particularly susceptible to severe noise and outliers owing to the lack of an upper bound.

3.1.2. Truncated ε-Insensitive Loss

The horizontal truncation technique provides an efficient approach to dealing with outliers. The truncated ε-insensitive loss is a variant of the ε-insensitive loss that includes a horizontal truncation, as shown in Figure 1. As suggested by [22], the truncated ε-insensitive loss known as Canal loss promotes sparsity and robustness. It is defined as follows:

$$L_{\text{Canal}}(u) = \begin{cases} |u| - \varepsilon, & \varepsilon < |u| < \delta \\ 0, & |u| \leq \varepsilon \\ \delta - \varepsilon, & |u| \geq \delta \end{cases} \tag{4}$$

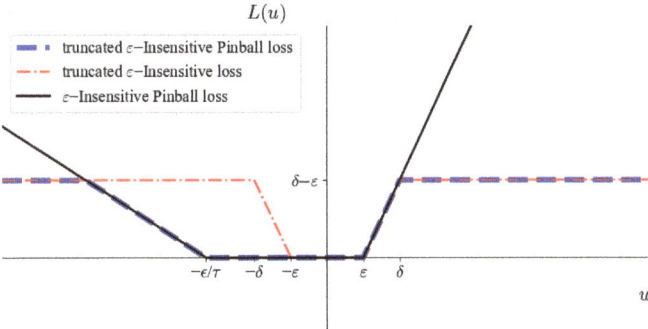

Figure 1. Loss functions.

By limiting the loss of outliers to a predetermined value $\delta - \varepsilon$, the impact of outliers on the model is limited, thereby increasing the robustness of the model. The ε-insensitive band and the area $|u| \geq \delta$ contribute to the sparse solution of the algorithm.

3.2. Online SVR

Online learning algorithms integrate new arrival data into the historical model and adjust the model through the parameter update strategy. When constructing a model, the instantaneous risk is used instead of empirical risk. Online SVR is expressed as an instantaneous risk minimization problem under the regularization framework. It is defined as follows:

$$\min \quad R_{inst}[f, \mathbf{X}_i, y_i] = \frac{1}{2}\|f\|_{\mathcal{H}}^2 + C \cdot L(f(\mathbf{X}_i - y_i)) \tag{5}$$

The objective function consists of two components: a regularization term $\frac{1}{2}\|f\|_{\mathcal{H}}^2$ and a loss function $L(\cdot)$ representing the instantaneous risk. The regularization parameter C is typically set by cross-validation. The model can be updated using the latest information and previous support vector data patterns by incorporating the instantaneous risk. Consequently, the memory requirements and the number of calculations are lower than those of the batch algorithm.

4. Online SVR Based on Truncated ε-Insensitive Pinball Loss Function

In this section, we present a modified version of the pinball loss function, called TIPL, which is a non-convex and asymmetric loss function. In addition, an online SVR for the TIPL is designed and solved using the OGD.

4.1. Truncated ε-Insensitive Pinball Loss Function (TIPL) and Its Properties

4.1.1. Truncated ε-Insensitive Pinball Loss Function

Inspired by the pinball loss function, TIPL is developed, which is defined as follows:

$$L_{\text{TIP}}(u) = \begin{cases} \delta - \varepsilon, & u \geq \delta \\ u - \varepsilon, & \varepsilon \leq u < \delta \\ 0, & -\varepsilon/\tau \leq u < \varepsilon \\ -\tau u - \varepsilon, & -\delta/\tau \leq u < -\varepsilon/\tau \\ \delta - \varepsilon, & u < -\delta/\tau \end{cases} \quad (6)$$

where τ is an asymmetric parameter, ε is an insensitive parameter, and δ is the truncation parameter. TIPL is divided into five parts, as shown in Figure 1. If the error u is within the specified tolerance range $[-\varepsilon/\tau, \varepsilon]$ as ε-insensitive area, the loss is zero. The loss is $u - \varepsilon$ for $u \in [\varepsilon, \delta)$, and $-\tau u - \varepsilon$ for $u \in [-\delta/\tau, -\varepsilon/\tau)$. Except in the above cases, when $u \in (-\infty, -\delta/\tau)$ or $u \in [\delta, \infty)$, the loss is fixed as a constant $\delta - \varepsilon$.

TIPL is an improved version of the pinball loss that offers improved resistance to noise and outliers, and produces a sparser representation of the solution. The ε-insensitive band promotes sparsity and thus saves computing resources. Applying horizontal truncation limits the impact of outliers on the loss value and increases the algorithm's robustness to large disturbances and outliers. The asymmetric feature makes the model more versatile and applicable to a wide range of noise types.

TIPL is expressed in an equivalent form:

$$\min\{\delta - \varepsilon, \max\{-\tau u - \varepsilon, u - \varepsilon, 0\}\} \quad (7)$$

4.1.2. Properties of the TIPL Function

Property 1. $L_{TIP}(u)$ *is a non-negative, asymmetric, and bounded function.*

Proof. (1) For $\forall u \in R$, $L_{TIP}(u) \geq 0$. TIPL is non-negative.

(2) From Equation (6), $L_{TIP}(u) = -\tau u - \varepsilon$ if $u \in [-\delta/\tau, -\varepsilon/\tau)$. $L_{TIP}(u) = u - \varepsilon$, if the error $u \in [\varepsilon, \delta)$. Obviously, $L_{TIP}(u) \neq L_{TIP}(-u)$ if $\tau \neq 1$. $L_{TIP}(u)$ is not symmetrical.

(3) From Equation (6), $L_{TIP}(u) \leq \delta - \varepsilon$, so $L_{TIP}(u)$ is bounded. □

Property 2. $L_{TIP}(u)$ *includes and extends both ε-insensitive loss function and truncated ε-insensitive loss function.*

Proof. From Equation (6),

When $\delta = \infty$, $L_{TIP}(u)$ reduces to the ε-insensitive pinball loss function.

When $\tau = 1$, $L_{TIP}(u)$ is equivalent to the truncated ε-insensitive loss function.

By inheriting the asymmetry of pinball losses and the immunity to outliers of truncated ε-insensitive loss, TIPL achieves a higher level of resilience. TIPL differs from the ε-insensitive pinball loss in that the former incorporates horizontal truncation, which limits the loss of outliers to some extent and makes the model more robust. Unlike truncated ε-insensitive loss, TIPL loss takes advantage of asymmetric functions. It assigns different penalty weights to positive and negative errors, enabling it to deal with general noise distributions. δ and τ are determined using a data-driven process. □

Property 3. *The derivative of $L_{TIP}(u)$ is discontinuous.*

Proof.

$$L'_{TIP}(u) = \begin{cases} -\tau, & -\delta/\tau \leq u < -\varepsilon/\tau \\ 0, & \text{otherwise} \\ 1, & \varepsilon \leq u < \delta \end{cases} \tag{8}$$

As can be seen from Equation (8),
$$\lim_{u \to -\varepsilon/\tau^-} L'_{TIP}(u) = -\tau \neq \lim_{u \to -\varepsilon/\tau^+} L'_{TIPL}(u) = 0,$$
$$\lim_{u \to -\delta/\tau^-} L'_{TIP}(u) = 0 \neq \lim_{u \to -\delta/\tau^+} L'_{TIP}(u) = -\tau,$$
$$\lim_{u \to \varepsilon^-} L'_{TIP}(u) = 0 \neq \lim_{u \to \varepsilon^+} L'_{TIP}(u) = 1,$$
$$\lim_{u \to \delta^-} L'_{TIP}(u) = 1 \neq \lim_{u \to \delta^+} L'_{TIP}(u) = 0.$$

The derivative of $L_{TIP}(u)$ is discontinuous, which precludes using a convex optimization to solve it. □

4.2. Online SVR Based on the Truncated ε-Insensitive Pinball Loss Function

Within the regularization framework of SVR, the online SVR model with TIPL is derived by incorporating the loss function $L_{TIP}(\cdot)$ into Equation (5), which is defined as:

$$\min \quad \frac{1}{2}\|f\|_{\mathcal{H}}^2 + C \cdot L_{TIP}(f^{k-1}(\mathbf{X}_k) - y_k) \tag{9}$$

We chose the OGD to solve the non-convex optimization problem presented by the TIPL loss function. The online algorithm updates the regression function by incorporating the initial decision function f^k and the new sample $(\mathbf{X}_k, y_k)$.

The learning process involves generating a series of decision functions $(f^0, f^1, \ldots, f^N)$, with the initial hypothesis f^0 and the updated regression function f^k. When a new sample $(\mathbf{X}_k, y_k)$ arrives, the predicted value $f^{k-1}(X_k)$ is calculated by the historical decision function f^{k-1}, and the loss value $L_{TIP}(f^{k-1}(\mathbf{X}_k) - y_k)$ is determined by combining $f^{k-1}(X_k)$ with the actual label y_k.

The update process of f^k is defined as follows:

$$f^k = f^{k-1} - \gamma_k \cdot z_k \tag{10}$$

where $\gamma_k > 0$ is the learning rate; $z_k = C \cdot \partial_f L_{TIP}(f^{k-1}(X_k) - y_k)|_{f=f^{k-1}} + f^{k-1}$. $\partial_f L_{TIP}(f^{k-1}(\mathbf{X}_k) - y_k)$ is determined by the renewable nucleus, i.e., $\partial_f L_{TIP}(f^{k-1}(\mathbf{X}_k) - y_k) = L'_{TIP}(f^{k-1}(\mathbf{X}_k) - y_k) \cdot \kappa(\mathbf{X}_k, \cdot)$. With $u_k = (f^{k-1}(\mathbf{X}_k) - y_k)$, z_k is expressed as follows:

$$z^k = \begin{cases} C \cdot k(\mathbf{X}_k, \cdot) + f^{k-1} & \varepsilon \leq u_k < \delta \\ f^{k-1} & \text{otherwise} \\ -C \cdot \tau k(\mathbf{X}_k, \cdot) + f^{k-1} & -\delta/\tau \leq u_k < -\varepsilon/\tau \end{cases} \tag{11}$$

Combining Equations (10) and (11), the iterations for the decision function is defined as:

$$z^k = \begin{cases} (1 - \gamma_k)f^{k-1} - \gamma_k C \cdot k(\mathbf{X}_k, \cdot) & \varepsilon \leq u_k < \delta \\ (1 - \gamma_k)f^{k-1} & \text{otherwise} \\ (1 - \gamma_k)f^{k-1} + \gamma_k C \cdot \tau k(\mathbf{X}_k, \cdot) & -\delta/\tau \leq u_k < -\varepsilon/\tau \end{cases} \tag{12}$$

The sample is not a support vector if $u_k \in [-\varepsilon/\tau, \varepsilon]$ or $(-\infty, -\delta/\tau) \cup [\delta, +\infty)$. The two regions are ε-insensitive or outlier regions, in which the samples from these regions are not considered during the update process. The proposed SVR model not only preserves the sparsity of ε-insensitive loss but also increases the sparsity by eliminating outliers.

Algorithm 1 details the proposed TIPOSVR algorithm.

Algorithm 1: Online support vector regression algorithm based on the truncated ε-insensitive Pinball loss function.

Input: Initial assumption (decision function) f^0, hyperparameter $\gamma > 0, \lambda > 0$, $\tau > 0, \varepsilon > 0, \delta > 0, C > 0, k > 0$. Data sample $(\mathbf{X}_i, y_i), i = 1, 2, \cdots\cdots$,

Output: sequence of decision functions $(f^0, f^1, \cdots\cdots, f^N)$

1: **for** $k = 1, 2, \cdots\cdots$ **do**
2:     Receive data $\mathbf{X}_k$
3:     Predict $f^{k-1}(\mathbf{X}_k)$
4:     Receive true label y_k
5:     Compute $u_k = f^{k-1}(\mathbf{X}_k) - y_k$
6:     **if** $\varepsilon \leq u_k < \delta$
7:         $f_k \leftarrow (1 - \gamma_k)f^{k-1} - \gamma_k C \cdot k(\mathbf{X}_k, \cdot)$
8:     **elif** $-\delta/\tau \leq u_k < -\varepsilon/\tau$
9:         $f_k \leftarrow (1 - \gamma_k)f^{k-1} + \gamma_k C \cdot \tau \cdot k(\mathbf{X}_k, \cdot)$
10:    **else**
11:        $f_k \leftarrow (1 - \gamma_k)f^{k-1}$
12:    **end if**
13: **end for**

4.3. Convergence of TIPOSVR

In the research of the regularized instantaneous risk minimization with Canal loss, Ref. [22] reveals that the regularized Canal loss satisfies an inequality analogous to that of a convex function on **R**, apart from two small, unidentifiable intervals. Strong pseudo-convexity is defined based on this representation, and the convergence performance of NROR is analyzed using online convex optimization theory. It has been demonstrated that if the prediction deviation sequence does not fall into the unrecognizable region of Canal loss, the average instantaneous risk will converge to the minimum regularization risk at a rate of $o\left(T^{-1/2}\right)$.

Drawing inspiration from [22], this section illustrates the strong pseudo-convexity of the regularization TIPL loss, and concludes TIPOSVR's convergence rate of the average instantaneous risk to the minimum regularization risk. Definitions and propositions of strong pseudo-convexity in this section are taken from [22].

Definition 1 ([22] Strong pseudo-convexity). *A function $f : \chi \to \mathbf{R}$ is said to be strongly pseudo-convex (SPC) on $\chi_1 \subset \chi$ with respect to $\bar{x} \in \chi$, if*

$$f(x) - f(\bar{x}) \leq K\langle f'(x), x - \bar{x}\rangle \tag{13}$$

holds for all $x \in \chi_1$, with $f'(x)$ a Clarke subgradient of f at x, $K > 0$ is a conatant. If the Inequality Equation (13) holds with respect to any $\bar{x} \in \chi_1$, f is called SPC on $\chi_1 \subset \chi$. The collection of SPC functions on χ_1 with $K > 0$ are denoted as $\mathcal{W}_K(\chi_1)$.

When $k = 1$, a strongly pseudo-convex function is equivalent to a convex function. In order to understand the strong pseudo-convexity of the regularized TIPL's loss, which is a piecewise convex function, further analysis is required. Propositions 1 and Propositions 2 [22] enable us to verify the strong pseudo-convexity of TIPL loss.

Proposition 1 ([22]). *Let $f : \mathbf{R} \to \mathbf{R}$ be a univariate continuous function. Assume that on each interval of $(-\infty, a], (a, b), [b, \infty)$, $f(x)$ is convex, and $f'_-(a) < 0, f'_+(b) > 0, f'_+(a) \neq 0, f'_-(b) \neq 0$. Then we have that the Inequality (13) holds for any fixed $\bar{x} \in R$ and $x \in R$ with*

$$K = \max\left\{1, \frac{f'_-(a)}{f'_+(a)}, \frac{f'_+(a)}{f'_-(a)}, \frac{f'_-(b)}{f'_+(b)}, \frac{f'_+(b)}{f'_-(b)}, \frac{f'_-(a)}{f'_+(b)}, \frac{f'_+(b)}{f'_-(a)}\right\} \quad (14)$$

Proposition 2 ([22]). *Let $f : \mathbf{R} \to \mathbf{R}$ be a univariate continuous function. Let $a_0 < a_1 < \cdots < a_m$ be the real numbers, $a_0 = -\infty$ and $a_m = +\infty$. On each interval of $[a_i, a_{i+1}], f(x)$ is convex, and $i = 0, 1, ..., m - 1$. Let S be the set of the minimum points of f on R. Suppose that the optimal solution set $S \in [a_q, a_{q+1}]$. With $q \in [0, \cdots, m-1]$. Moreover, suppose that $f(x)$ is strictly decreasing when $X \leq \mathrm{Inf}S$ and strictly increasing when $X \geq \mathrm{Sup}S$. Then, for any fixed $\bar{x} \in [a_0, a_m]$ and $x \in [a_0, a_m]$. Inequality (13) holds with*

$$K = \max\left\{1, \frac{f'_+(a_\mu)}{f'_-(a_{v+1})}, \frac{f'_-(a_i)}{f'_+(a_j)} \mid q \in [0,..,m-1], \mu \in [v+1,..,q]\right.$$
$$\left. v \in [0,..,q-1], i \in [q+1,..,j], j \in [q+1,..,m-1]\right\} \quad (15)$$

It is evident from Proposition 1 and Proposition 2 that the parameter K of strong pseudo-convexity is associated with the directional derivatives at the end of the intervals. The strong pseudo-convexity of regularized TIPL loss is obtained from Lemma 1 and Lemma 2. The proof of lemmas and theorems can be found in the supplementary material.

Lemma 1. *Denote $\Omega_0 = [t_0 - \delta/\tau - C|\beta|, t_0 - \delta/\tau] \cup [t_0 + \delta, t_0 + \delta + C|\beta|]$, suppose $0 \notin \Omega_0$, $f(t) = \frac{1}{2}t^2 + C \cdot L_{TIP}(\beta(t - t_0))$ is SPC with $K = \max\left\{2, 1 + \frac{C \cdot \tau^2 X^2}{\delta}, 1 + \frac{C \cdot \tau X^2}{\delta \cdot \tau - \varepsilon}\right\}$ on $R \backslash \Omega_0$.*

Lemma 2. *Let the sequence instance (X_t, y_t) satisfy $k(X_t, X_t) \leq X^2$. For a fixed $g \in \mathcal{H}$*

$$u^t = (f^t - g)/\|f^t - g\|, t_0 = y_t - g(X_t) + u^t(X_t) \cdot \langle u^t, g \rangle,$$

$$\Omega_0 = \left[-\delta/\tau - (u^t(X_t))^2, -\delta/\tau\right] \cup \left[\delta, \delta + (u^t(X_t))^2\right]$$

Assuming $t_0 \notin \Omega_0, \xi_t = f^t(X_t) - y_t \notin \Omega_0$, we have

$$R_{inst}[f^t, X_t, y_t] - R_{inst}[g, X_t, y_t] \leq K \cdot \left\langle \partial_f R_{inst}[f^t, X_t, y_t]\Big|_{f=f^t}, f^t - g \right\rangle_{\mathcal{H}} \text{ with}$$

$$K = \max\left\{2, 1 + \frac{C \cdot \tau^2 X^2}{\delta}, 1 + \frac{C \cdot \tau X^2}{\delta \cdot \tau - \varepsilon}\right\}. \quad (16)$$

Lemma 2 demonstrates that, under the given assumptions, f and g of instantaneous loss satisfy the inequality of strong pseudo-convexity. Subsequently, we can employ online convex optimization technology to analyze the convergence performance of TIPOSVR. The theorem provides the rate measure of TIPOSVR convergence to minimize risk.

Theorem 1. *Set example sequence $S = \{(X_t, y_t)\}_{t=0}^T$ be $k(X_t, X_t) \leq X^2$ holds for all t. $(f^0, \cdots, f^T)$ represents a hypothetical sequence produced by TIPOSVR, $R_{inst}[g, S] = \frac{1}{T}\sum_{t=1}^T R_{inst}[g, X_t, y_t]$, and $\hat{g} = \arg\min_{g \in \mathcal{H}} R_{inst}[g, S]$. Fix $C, \varepsilon > 0, 0 < \eta < C$ and set the learning rate $\eta_t = \eta \cdot t^{-1/2}$. We assume that each hypothesis f^t generated by TIPOSVR satisfies the hypothesis stated in Lemma 2, for $t = 0, 1, 2 \cdots T$, and then we have the following expression*

$$\frac{1}{T}\sum_{t=1}^T R_{inst}[f^t, X_t, y_t] \leq R_{inst}[\hat{g}, S] + \alpha T^{-1/2} + o\left(T^{-1/2}\right) \quad (17)$$

Among them, $\alpha = \frac{2KX^2}{\eta} + 4KX^2\eta$, $K = \max\left\{2, 1 + \frac{C \cdot \tau^2 X^2}{\delta}, 1 + \frac{C \cdot \tau X^2}{\delta \cdot \tau - \varepsilon}\right\}$.

In Theorem 1, we get an $o\left(T^{-1/2}\right)$ regret boundary. For each t, $f^{t-1}(\mathbf{X}_t) - y_t \notin \Omega_0$, Ω_0 is the union of two intervals with length $u^2(\mathbf{X}_t) \leq X^2$. For f^t exceeding this hypothesis in practice, the prediction error $f^t(\mathbf{X}_t) - y_t$ may fall within the zone Ω_0, where losses are flat. In this case, sample $(\mathbf{X}_t, y_t)$ is identified as a non support vector by TIPOSVR.

5. Numerical Experiments

We performed experiments on multiple datasets with noise and outliers to evaluate the effectiveness of the TIPOSVR. The performance of our model is then compared with those of other online SVR models. The datasets adopted consist of synthetic datasets, benchmark datasets, and real datasets. The artificial dataset evaluates performance under specific fluctuations, while the benchmark and real-world datasets allow for assessing performance in realistic environments. In the experimental part, three comparison algorithms are used in the experiment: ε-SVR (SVR with ε-insensitive loss), SVQR (SVR with ε-insensitive pinball loss), and NROR (SVR with truncated ε-insensitive loss), as shown in Table 1. Batch algorithms are not included in the comparison algorithms because they are inappropriate for training with large datasets.

Table 1. Loss functions.

Loss Function	Definition
Linear ε-Insensitive loss	$\max\{0, |u| - \varepsilon\}$
ε-Insensitive Pinball loss	$\max\{-\tau u - \varepsilon, u - \varepsilon, 0\}$
Canal loss	$\min\{\delta - \varepsilon, \max\{0, |u| - \varepsilon\}\}$

Experiments are carried out using Python 3.8 on a PC with an Intel i7-5500U CPU 2.40 GHz.

To ensure the accuracy and effectiveness of the assessment, we chose absolute mean error (MAE), root mean square error (RMSE), and time to run (TIME) as the assessment metrics. Details of the evaluation criteria are presented in Table 2.

Table 2. Table of evaluation criteria.

Evaluation Criteria	Definition
MAE	$\frac{1}{n}\sum_{t=1}^{n}\left|\hat{f}^{t-1}(x_t) - y_t\right|$
RMSE	$\sqrt{\frac{1}{n}\sum_{t=1}^{n}\left(\hat{f}^{t-1}(x_t) - y_t\right)^2}$

MAE is the average of the absolute errors. RMSE is the square root of the mean square error, which provides the standard deviation of the errors. MAE is not as sensitive to outliers as RMSE, which puts more emphasis on large error values.

Samples from the dataset are randomly selected to form the training and test sets, with outliers and noise added to the training set. A grid search method was used to identify the optimal values of the parameters. The Gaussian kernel $k(x, x') = exp(-\kappa\|x - x'\|^2)$ was selected as the kernel in the work. TIPOSVR includes hyperparameters such as the insensitivity coefficient ε, the asymmetry parameter τ, the truncation parameter δ, the regularization parameter C, the learning rate γ and the kernel parameter κ. To negate the effects of the kernel and regularization parameters, the most effective values of C and κ were identified through ε-SVR, and the same values were then used for the other three models. Grid search and five-fold cross-validation were performed on the training set for each dataset to obtain the highest accuracy. C was taken from $\{0.1, 0.5\}$ while κ choosen from $\{0.5, 1, 2, 4, 8, 16\}$. The NROR algorithm was employed to determine the truncation parameter δ from $\{0.4, 0.8, 1.6\}$. Cross-validation and grid search methods in TIPOSVR were used to select the asymmetric parameter τ from $\{0.4, 0.8, 1, 1.2, 1.4\}$. The insensitivity parameter was set to 0.04 for simplicity.

5.1. Synthetic Datasets

The synthetic dataset is generated by a bivariate function defined as follows:

$$f(x_1, x_2) = \frac{(5 - x_2)^2 + (6 - x_1)^2}{(5 - x_1)^2 + (5 - x_2)^2} \tag{18}$$

where x_1 and x_2 are input features of the sample with uniform distribution $U[0, 10]$, $x_1 \in [0, 10]$, $x_2 \in [0, 10]$ and $(x_1, x_2) \neq (5, 5)$. The output features are generated by Equation (18), which is shown in Figure 2.

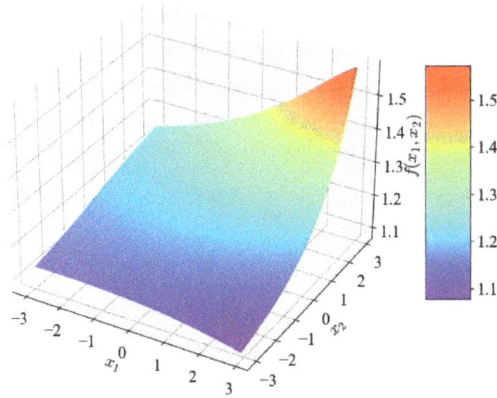

Figure 2. Function for synthetic dataset.

Different types of noises are added to the dataset to evaluate the effectiveness of the proposed algorithm. Consider the label of the training sample $\tilde{y}_i$ to be of the form $\tilde{y}_i = y_i + \zeta_i$, where ζ_i is noise sampled according to the noise distribution. The synthetic dataset is affected by five different types of noise: symmetric homoscedastic noise, symmetric heteroscedastic noise, asymmetric homoscedastic noise, asymmetric and heteroscedastic, and asymmetric heteroscedastic noise that varies with the independent variable. Samples generated by the bivariate function are polluted with noise. Five noisy training datasets are generated as follows:

Type I.
$$\tilde{y}_i^{(1)} = y_i + \zeta_i^{(1)} \tag{19}$$

$\zeta_i^{(1)}$ is the Gaussian noise with a normal distribution $N(0, 2)$, whereas $\tilde{y}_i^{(1)}$ is the data label that contains symmetric homoscedastic noise.

Type II.
$$\tilde{y}_i^{(2)} = y_i + \zeta_i^{(2)} \tag{20}$$

$\zeta_i^{(2)}$ is the Gaussian noise whose distribution obeys $N(0, 2)$, where σ^2 is a random number on the interval $[0, 6]$, $\tilde{y}_i^{(2)}$ is the data label containing symmetric heteroscedastic noise.

Type III.
$$\tilde{y}_i^{(3)} = y_i + \zeta_i^{(3)} \tag{21}$$

$\zeta_i^{(3)}$ is the Chi square noise whose distribution obeys $\chi^2(1)$. $\tilde{y}_i^{(3)}$ is the data label containing asymmetric and homoscedastic noise.

Type IV.
$$\tilde{y}_i^{(4)} = y_i + \zeta_i^{(4)} \tag{22}$$

$\zeta_i^{(4)}$ is the Chi square noise with a Chi square distribution $\chi^2(n)$, where n is the random number on the interval $[1,4]$. $\tilde{y}_i^{(4)}$ is the data label containing asymmetric and heteroscedastic noise.

Type V.
$$\tilde{y}_i^{(5)} = y_i + x_i \cdot \zeta_i^{(1)} \tag{23}$$

$\tilde{y}_i^{(5)}$ is the data label containing asymmetric and heteroscedastic noise where the noise varies $x_i \cdot \zeta_i^{(1)}$ significantly with the independent variable x.

The probability density function of Gaussian distribution $N(0,2)$ is shown in Figure 3. The mean is zero and the variance is 2. The skewness of Gaussian distribution $N(0,2)$ is 0. This distribution is symmetric.

The probability density function of $\delta_{\chi^2} - 4$ is shown in Figure 4. The mean of $\delta_{\chi^2} - 4$ is zero and the variance of $\delta_{\chi^2} - 4$ is 8. The skewness of $\delta_{\chi^2} - 4$ is $\sqrt{2}$. This distribution is asymmetric.

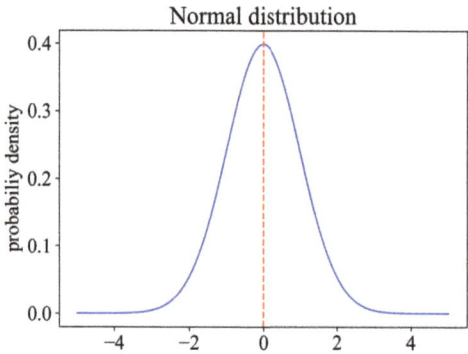

Figure 3. The probability density function of Gaussian distribution $N(0,2)$.

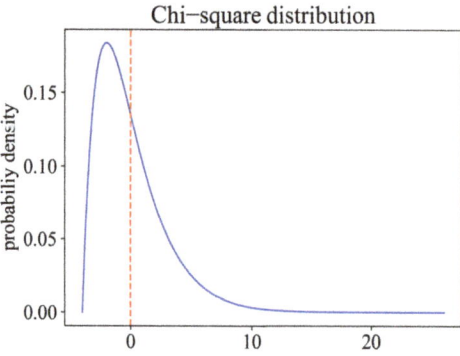

Figure 4. The probability density function of Chi square distribution $\delta_{\chi^2} - 4$.

The noise level is determined by the ratio of noisy data in the training set, which are set to 0%, 5%, 20%, 40%, 50%, or 60%. The training set consists of 5000 samples with noise, and the test set consists of 5000 samples without noise. The experimental results are listed in Tables 3–7. The performance of TIPOSVR demonstrates its effectiveness in making accurate predictions across diverse datasets.

Table 3 lists the accuracy and learning time of algorithms for the symmetric homovariance noise dataset. The most outstanding results of each indicator are in bold font. At a low noise level, the performance of the various algorithms is comparable, yet TIPOSVR's running time is significantly longer than the other comparison algorithms. The benefits of TIPOSVR are not particularly noticeable in datasets that are symmetric and have a low level of noise. However, when the noise level is high, TIPOSVR outperforms the comparison algorithm.

Table 3. Operation results of algorithms under the influence of noise type I for synthetic dataset.

Noise Rate	Loss Function	MAE	RMSE	TIME (S)
0	NROR	0.081	0.136	**7.70**
	ε-SVR	0.073	0.116	8.41
	SVQR	0.098	0.134	8.49
	TIPOSVR	**0.071**	**0.098**	8.53
0.05	NROR	0.083	0.140	**7.36**
	ε-SVR	0.084	0.145	7.69
	SVQR	0.077	0.106	8.18
	TIPOSVR	**0.073**	**0.105**	8.25
0.2	NROR	0.091	0.158	6.56
	ε-SVR	0.115	0.171	8.60
	SVQR	0.087	0.122	7.24
	TIPOSVR	**0.084**	**0.116**	**6.21**
0.4	NROR	0.094	0.155	5.54
	ε-SVR	0.150	0.208	8.97
	SVQR	0.095	0.124	5.98
	TIPOSVR	**0.086**	**0.120**	**3.94**
0.5	NROR	0.103	0.164	**4.42**
	ε-SVR	0.159	0.209	8.92
	SVQR	**0.079**	**0.135**	4.95
	TIPOSVR	0.091	0.145	5.17
0.6	NROR	0.193	0.280	3.82
	ε-SVR	0.195	0.247	8.92
	SVQR	0.146	0.219	3.68
	TIPOSVR	**0.096**	**0.131**	**2.85**

The accuracy and learning time of various algorithms for symmetric heteroscedastic noise datasets are summarized in Table 4. The MAE and RMSE of the TIPOSVR are lowest when the noise rate is 5%, 40%, 50%, and 60%, showing that the TIPOSVR has achieved an excellent matching effect. TIPOSVR is trained with the minimum time when the noise rates are 50% and 60%, indicating that it provides accurate predictions while saving computational resources. TIPOSVR shows the best accuracy and is followed by NROR and SVQR. ε-insensitive loss provides the worst accuracy for datasets corrupted by heteroscedastic noise. The performance of asymmetric ε-insensitive loss and truncated asymmetric ε-insensitive loss is superior to that of symmetric loss, indicating that the ability to deal with heteroscedastic noise can be significantly enhanced by adjusting the asymmetric parameters.

Table 4. Operation results of algorithms under the influence of noise typeII for synthetic dataset.

Noise Rate	Loss Function	MAE	RMSE	TIME (S)
0	NROR	0.080	0.125	8.90
	ε-SVR	**0.060**	0.099	**7.88**
	SVQR	0.074	**0.098**	8.21
	TIPOSVR	0.082	0.119	7.95
0.05	NROR	0.081	0.136	**7.70**
	ε-SVR	0.093	0.139	8.04
	SVQR	0.076	0.104	7.69
	TIPOSVR	**0.070**	**0.101**	7.71
0.2	NROR	0.074	0.115	**6.00**
	ε-SVR	0.089	0.120	8.16
	SVQR	**0.081**	**0.111**	6.69
	TIPOSVR	0.082	0.117	6.97
0.4	NROR	0.076	0.131	5.35
	ε-SVR	0.136	0.177	8.38
	SVQR	0.092	0.134	**5.09**
	TIPOSVR	**0.073**	**0.113**	5.62
0.5	NROR	0.095	0.148	5.35
	ε-SVR	0.132	0.172	8.38
	SVQR	0.094	0.122	4.49
	TIPOSVR	**0.069**	**0.111**	**3.52**
0.6	NROR	0.160	0.272	5.28
	ε-SVR	0.180	0.250	8.15
	SVQR	0.104	0.153	4.06
	TIPOSVR	**0.096**	**0.142**	**3.39**

Results of different algorithms on asymmetric homoscedastic noise are tabulated in Table 5. In the absence of noise, the time and accuracy performance of SVQR is clearly superior to other methods. The evidence indicates that truncation has no effect on data regression when there is no noise, however, it will cause a longer running time. As the noise rate increases, the superiority of TIPOSVR becomes more and more apparent, especially when the noise rate is 40%, 50%, and 60%, where it attains the best accuracy. The results show that TIPOSVR can achieve the highest accuracy in a relatively short time for asymmetric noise.

Simulation results of algorithms for asymmetric heteroscedastic noise datasets are presented in Table 6. The experimental results show that TIPOSVR achieves the best MAE performance at overall noise levels. It yields the lowest RMSE when the noise rate is 0%, 20%, 50%, and 60%. TIPOSVR performs better than NROR. The comparison between NROR and TIPOSVR, in terms of both truncated losses, reveals that asymmetric truncated loss is more effective than symmetric loss for heteroscedastic noise. The asymmetric feature diminishes the influence of asymmetric noise on the regression function. The results confirm the theoretical analysis.

The test accuracy and learning time of different algorithms, as the noise value varies with the independent variable, are shown in Table 7. This dataset presents a more intricate situation. The noise in the dataset depends on the independent variable. More noise and outliers are likely to appear. The results show that all algorithms are sensitive to noise level. TIPOSVR is still significantly more accurate than the comparison algorithms and shows its proficiency in dealing with general noise and outliers.

Table 5. Operation results of algorithms under the influence of noise type III for synthetic dataset.

Noise Rate	Loss Function	MAE	RMSE	TIME (S)
0	NROR	0.075	0.107	**8.55**
	ε-SVR	0.076	0.111	8.61
	SVQR	**0.068**	**0.095**	8.84
	TIPOSVR	0.072	0.103	9.02
0.05	NROR	0.068	0.105	8.55
	ε-SVR	**0.065**	0.102	8.82
	SVQR	0.071	0.118	8.12
	TIPOSVR	**0.065**	**0.096**	**6.96**
0.2	NROR	**0.077**	0.134	**7.60**
	ε-SVR	0.087	0.125	9.09
	SVQR	0.088	0.139	7.79
	TIPOSVR	**0.077**	**0.118**	7.79
0.4	NROR	0.083	0.143	7.60
	ε-SVR	0.124	0.151	9.22
	SVQR	0.088	0.119	7.55
	TIPOSVR	**0.075**	**0.118**	**7.22**
0.5	NROR	0.103	0.159	6.46
	ε-SVR	0.125	0.185	8.67
	SVQR	0.111	0.174	6.87
	TIPOSVR	**0.098**	**0.164**	**5.62**
0.6	NROR	0.099	0.143	5.29
	ε-SVR	0.129	0.188	8.23
	SVQR	0.234	0.351	5.75
	TIPOSVR	**0.087**	**0.112**	**4.47**

Table 6. Operation results of algorithms under the influence of noise typeIV for synthetic dataset.

Noise Rate	Loss Function	MAE	RMSE	TIME (S)
0	NROR	0.077	0.115	8.28
	ε-SVR	0.089	0.118	**7.83**
	SVQR	0.084	0.129	7.94
	TIPOSVR	**0.072**	**0.101**	8.12
0.05	NROR	0.074	0.107	**6.23**
	ε-SVR	0.074	**0.106**	7.97
	SVQR	0.080	0.120	7.86
	TIPOSVR	**0.070**	0111	8.13
0.2	NROR	0.078	0.148	7.04
	ε-SVR	0.092	0.120	8.09
	SVQR	0.081	0.109	6.46
	TIPOSVR	**0.071**	**0.097**	**6.41**
0.4	NROR	0.174	0.285	7.04
	ε-SVR	0.094	0.149	7.81
	SVQR	0.083	**0.113**	4.67
	TIPOSVR	**0.077**	0.134	**4.30**
0.5	NROR	0.133	0.237	**3.42**
	ε-SVR	0.249	0.366	7.19
	SVQR	0.174	0.225	7.24
	TIPOSVR	**0.107**	**0.152**	7.75
0.6	NROR	0.220	0.286	**3.84**
	ε-SVR	0.232	0.288	9.01
	SVQR	0.230	0.277	7.96
	TIPOSVR	**0.126**	**0.165**	5.00

Table 7. Operation results of algorithms under the influence of noise type V for synthetic dataset.

Noise Rate	Loss Function	MAE	RMSE	TIME (S)
0	NROR	0.081	0.124	8.61
	ε-SVR	0.086	0.118	8.05
	SVQR	0.078	0.113	8.19
	TIPOSVR	**0.069**	**0.100**	**7.94**
0.05	NROR	0.088	0.118	8.28
	ε-SVR	0.077	0.113	8.31
	SVQR	0.086	0.120	**8.11**
	TIPOSVR	**0.069**	**0.101**	8.17
0.2	NROR	0.089	0.127	7.78
	ε-SVR	0.101	0.134	8.44
	SVQR	0.087	0.127	7.71
	TIPOSVR	**0.079**	**0.113**	**7.68**
0.4	NROR	0.102	0.148	7.11
	ε-SVR	0.107	0.160	8.43
	SVQR	0.101	0.138	6.79
	TIPOSVR	**0.083**	**0.124**	**6.39**
0.5	NROR	0.101	0.141	7.11
	ε-SVR	0.166	0.228	8.45
	SVQR	0.099	0.145	5.87
	TIPOSVR	**0.090**	**0.130**	**5.59**
0.6	NROR	0.147	0.233	**3.71**
	ε-SVR	0.127	0.194	8.64
	SVQR	0.172	0.265	6.41
	TIPOSVR	**0.085**	**0.115**	6.76

In summary, the study indicates that TIPOSVR is effective when applied to datasets with different types of noise. In particular, at high noise levels (when the noise rate reaches 50% and 60%), TIPOSVR provides accurate predictions in a timely manner. This algorithm shows excellent robustness and generalizability.

5.2. Benchmark Datasets

In this section, four datasets are selected from the UCI benchmark dataset, including the Dry Bean dataset (DB), the Grid Stability Simulation dataset (EGSSD), the Abalone dataset, and the Gas Turbine Generation (CCPP). To evaluate the results, three benchmark algorithms are employed: ε-SVR, NROR, and SVQR. Table 8 provides an overview of the attributes and sample numbers of the UCI benchmark datasets.

Table 8. Benchmark datasets description.

Tag	Dataset	Samples	Attributes
A	CCPP	9568	4
B	DB	13,611	17
C	EGSSD	10,000	12
D	Abalone	4177	8

The data from the datasets are normalized and split equally into training and test datasets. Research is conducted using datasets with symmetric noise characterized by homogeneous and heteroscedastic variances. The performance of TIPOSVR is evaluated and compared with that of the comparison algorithms on the four benchmark datasets. The selection of the hyperparameters follows the same approach as that used for the synthetic datasets.

Figures 5 and 6 shows the MAE and RMSE values obtained from TIPOSVR and the comparison algorithms for the UCI benchmark datasets with homogeneous Gaussian noise added. No remarkable disparity is observed in the performance of the four methods without noise when analyzing the A dataset. The performance of ε-SVR and SVQR vary significantly as the noise rate increases. When the noise rate reaches 40%, 50% and 60%, TIPOSVR and NROR demonstrate superior performance compared to the other two methods. In the majority of cases, TIPOSVR has been found to be the most effective. When the noise rate reaches 60%, it is only inferior to NROR. On dataset B, TIPOSVR, NROR and ε-SVR demonstrate the same level of performance with no noise present. As the noise rate increases, both ε-SVR and SVQR display more variations. The variation of both TIPOSVR and NROR are less than that of the two methods mentioned above. At noise rates of 40% and 50%, TIPOSVR proves to be more effective than NROR. At a noise rate of 60%, TIPOSVR and NROR demonstrate comparable results. In comparison to SVQR, the performance of TIPOSVR, NROR and ε-SVR on the C dataset are superior when the noise level is 0, 5%, 20% and 40%. At noise rates of 50% and 60%, NROR and TIPOSVR show superior performance compared to the other two methods, with TIPOSVR exhibiting the best results. For the D dataset, NROR and TIPOSVR demonstrate the same level of performance, regardless of the noise rate, which is superior to the other two methods. In terms of noise, the RMSE of TIPOSVR is smaller than that of NROR.

The data indicate that TIPOSVR does not excel in symmetric homogeneity datasets at low noise rate, and may even be inferior to NROR. At a high noise rate, TIPOSVR's performance is equivalent to NROR, surpassing the other two comparison algorithms, and even surpassing NROR in some cases. TIPOSVR has been found to be successful in dealing with regression problems that have a high noise level.

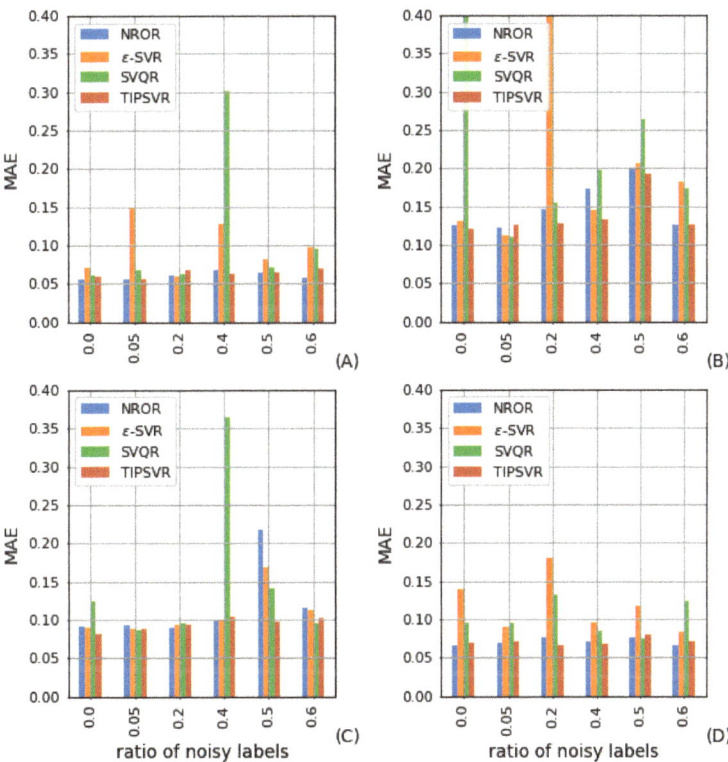

Figure 5. MAE for Gaussian noise of homogeneity on (**A**) CCPP, (**B**) DB, (**C**) EGSSD, (**D**) Abalone.

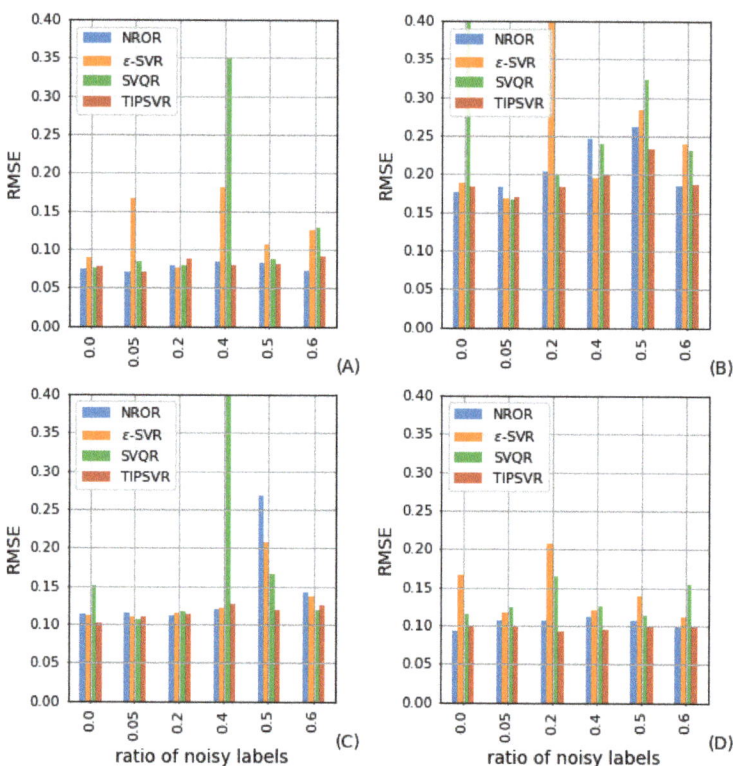

Figure 6. RMSE for noise of homogeneity on (**A**) CCPP, (**B**) DB, (**C**) EGSSD, (**D**) Abalone.

The bar graph in Figures 7 and 8 illustrate the MAE and RMSE of each algorithm for the benchmark datasets with heteroscedastic noise added. If the noise rate is not more than 40% for datasets A and C, there is no significant distinction between the four methods. At noise rates of 40%, 50% and 60%, NROR and TIPOSVR demonstrate superior performance compared to ε-SVR and SVQR, with TIPOSVR displaying the best results at 60%. At a noise rate of 20%, NROR and TIPOSVR prove to be more effective than SVQR and ε-SVR when applied to dataset B. Furthermore, when the noise rate increases to 50% and 60%, TIPOSVR outperforms NROR. In the D dataset, TIPOSVR and NROR have consistently demonstrated better performance than SVQR and ε-SVR. TIPOSVR and NROR demonstrated an equivalent level of performance.

It is observable that in the dataset with heteroscedasticity noise, when the noise rate is high, TIPOSVR and NROR have comparable performance, and TIPOSVR are usually more effective than NROR. The loss function that accounts for asymmetry exhibits improved performance.

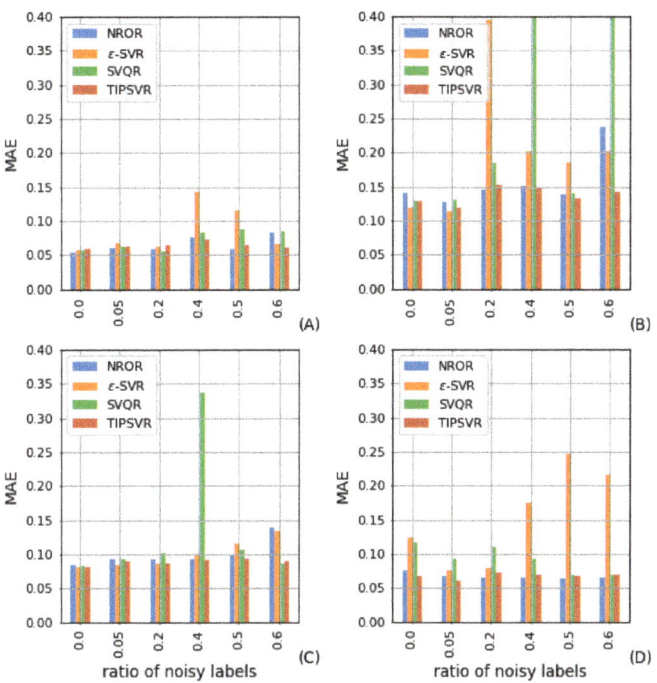

Figure 7. MAE for noise of heteroscedasticity on (**A**) CCPP, (**B**) DB, (**C**) EGSSD, (**D**) Abalone.

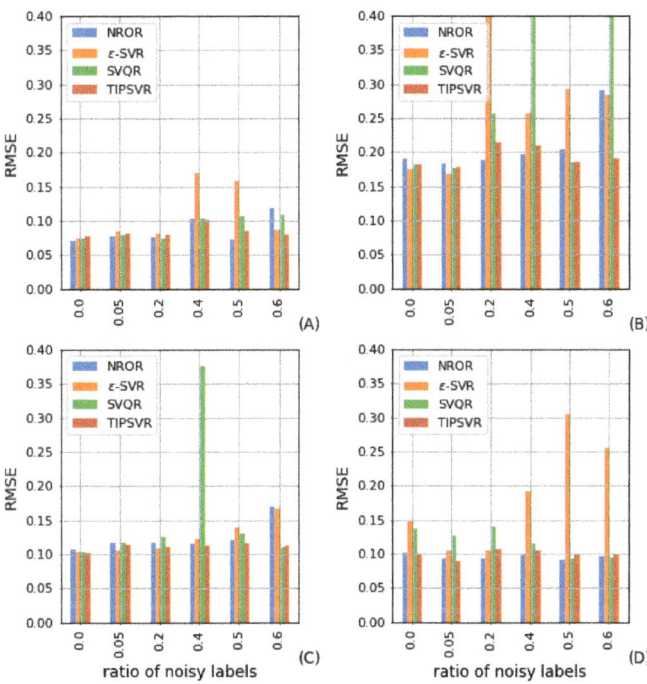

Figure 8. RMSE for noise of heteroscedasticity on (**A**) CCPP, (**B**) DB, (**C**) EGSSD, (**D**) Abalone.

5.3. Real Datasets

We perform an experiment using actual data from the gas consumption dataset [37]. The dataset consists of 18 features: minimum temperature (minT), average temperature (aveT), maximum temperature (maxT), minimum dew point (minD), average dew point (aveD), maximum dew point (maxD), minimum humidity (minH), average humidity (aveH), maximum humidity (maxH), minimum visibility (minV), average visibility (aveV), maximum visibility (maxV), minimum air pressure (minA), average air pressure (aveA), maximum air pressure (maxA), minimum wind speed (minW), average wind speed (aveW) and maximum wind speed (maxW), and the prediction label is Natural Gas Consumption (NGC).

No noise is added to the data labels on the real datasets. The training set and the test set are divided into equal parts. The parameters and comparison algorithms settings remain the same as before, and the calculation results are presented in Table 9.

Table 9. Evaluation table based on real dataset experimental result.

Loss Function	MAE	RMSE	TIME (S)
NROR	0.066	0.103	**2.11**
ε–SVR	0.096	0.121	2.30
SVQR	0.094	0.130	2.30
TIPOSVR	**0.059**	**0.102**	2.14

Table 9 illustrates the performance of various algorithms on an actual dataset. In Table 9, TIPOSVR is shown to perform optimally with an MAE of 0.059 and an RMSE of 0.102, indicating its ability to provide a reliable estimate of the real datasets. TIPOSVR remains a viable option compared to other algorithms when dealing with real-world problems.

In summary, all datasets show the effectiveness of TIPOSVR. It is still possible to accurately represent the data distribution even though it is corrupted by noise or outliers. This indicates that the algorithm is advantageous in handling noisy data and lends itself to regression in the data flow.

6. Conclusions

In this paper, we review the progress of SVR and find that the existing regression algorithms are insufficient to effectively predict dynamic data streams containing noise and outliers effectively.

This study introduces TIPL to assess instantaneous risk in the SVR model. This new loss function is a combination of asymmetry loss and truncated non-convex loss function that offers a variety of advantages. TIPL adjusts the weights of the penalties for both positive and negative errors using asymmetric parameters τ. τ allows us to partition the fixed width of the ε-insensitive area without sacrificing its sparsity. Horizontal truncation is used to deal with large noise and outliers. TIPL incorporates and extends the pinball loss, ε-insensitive loss, and truncated ε-insensitive loss.

Within the regularization framework, a TIPL-based online SVR algorithm is developed to perform robust regression in a data flow context. Given the non-convexity of the proposed model, an online gradient descent algorithm is chosen to solve the problem.

Experiments are performed on synthetic datasets, UCI datasets, and real datasets corrupted by Gaussian, heteroscedastic, asymmetric, and outlier noise. Our model has been found to be more resilient to noise and outliers than some classical and advanced methods. It also has better prediction performance and faster learning speed. The proposed model is therefore expected to provide more accurate predictions in the dynamic flow of data while consuming fewer computational resources than the batch learning approach.

The main disadvantage of this model lies in the use of multiple hyperparameters. Choosing the appropriate parameter values is essential for the algorithm to achieve optimal performance. In our ongoing research, we aim to develop techniques for determining the optimal hyperparameters for a given training set.

Supplementary Materials: The following supporting information can be downloaded at: https://www.mdpi.com/article/10.3390/math11030709/s1.

Author Contributions: Conceptualization, X.S. and Z.Z.; methodology, X.S., J.Y. and Z.Z.; software, Y.X.; writing—original draft preparation, X.S., X.L. and Z.Z. All authors have read and agreed to the published version of the manuscript.

Funding: This research was partially supported by the National Natural Science Foundation of China under Grant No. 71901219.

Institutional Review Board Statement: Not applicable.

Informed Consent Statement: Not applicable.

Data Availability Statement: The datasets used in this paper are all available at the following links: 1. http://archive.ics.uci.edu/ml/ (accessed on 12 December 2022); 2. http://www.csie.ntu.edu.tw/~cjlin/libsvmtools/datasets/ (accessed on 12 December 2022).

Acknowledgments: This work is supported by National Natural Science Foundation of China (Grant No. 71901219).

Conflicts of Interest: The authors declare no conflict of interest.

Abbreviations

The following abbreviations are used in this manuscript:

SVR	Support Vector Regression
TIPL	Truncated ε-insensitive pinball loss function
TIPOSVR	Support Vector Regression based on Truncated ε-insensitive pinball loss function

References

1. Hu, Q.; Zhang, S.; Xie, Z.; Mi, J.S.; Wan, J. Noise model based ε-support vector regression with its application to short-term wind speed forecasting. *Neural Netw.* **2014**, *57*, 1–11. [CrossRef] [PubMed]
2. Hu, Q.; Zhang, S.; Yu, M.; Xie, Z. Short-Term Wind Speed or Power Forecasting With Heteroscedastic Support Vector Regression. *IEEE Trans. Sustain. Energy* **2015**, *7*, 1–9. [CrossRef]
3. Ramedani, Z.; Omid, M.; Keyhani, A.; Band, S.; Khoshnevisan, B. Potential of radial basis function based support vector regression for global solar radiation prediction. *Renew. Sust. Energ. Rev.* **2014**, *39*, 1005–1011. [CrossRef]
4. Khemchandani, R.; Dr, J.; Chandra, S. Regularized least squares fuzzy support vector regression for financial time series forecasting. *Expert Syst. Appl.* **2009**, *36*, 132–138. [CrossRef]
5. Lu, C.J.; Lee, T.S.; Chiu, C.C. Financial time series forecasting using independent component analysis and support vector regression. *Decis. Support Syst.* **2009**, *47*, 115–125. [CrossRef]
6. Philip, A.; Ramadurai, G.; Vanajakshi, L. Urban Arterial Travel Time Prediction Using Support Vector Regression. *Transp. Dev. Econ.* **2018**, *4*, 7. [CrossRef]
7. Awad, M.; Khanna, R. Support Vector Regression. In *Efficient Learning Machines: Theories, Concepts, and Applications for Engineers and System Designers*; Apress: Berkeley, CA, USA, 2015; pp. 67–80. [CrossRef]
8. Wang, K.; Zhong, P. Robust non-convex least squares loss function for regression with outliers. *Knowl.-Based Syst.* **2014**, *71*, 290–302. [CrossRef]
9. Zhang, H.C.; Wu, Q.; Li, F.Y. Application of online multitask learning based on least squares support vector regression in the financial market. *Appl. Soft. Comput.* **2022**, *121*, 108754. [CrossRef]
10. Vapnik, V. *The Nature of Statistical Learning Theory*; Springer: New York, NY, USA, 2000; Volume 8, pp. 1–15. [CrossRef]
11. Vapnik, V. *Statistical Learning Theory*; Springer: New York, NY, USA, 1998.
12. Balasundaram, S.; Prasad, S. On pairing Huber support vector regression. *Appl. Soft. Comput.* **2020**, *97*, 106708. [CrossRef]
13. Balasundaram, S.; Meena, Y. Robust Support Vector Regression in Primal with Asymmetric Huber Loss. *Neural Process. Lett.* **2019**, *49*, 1399–1431. [CrossRef]
14. Wu, J.; Wang, Y.G.; Tian, Y.C.; Burrage, K.; Cao, T. Support vector regression with asymmetric loss for optimal electric load forecasting. *Energy* **2021**, *2021*, 119369. [CrossRef]
15. Ye, Y.; Shao, Y.; Li, C.; Hua, X.; Guo, Y. Online support vector quantile regression for the dynamic time series with heavy-tailed noise. *Appl. Soft. Comput.* **2021**, *110*, 107560. [CrossRef]
16. Yang, L.; Dong, H. Robust support vector machine with generalized quantile loss for classification and regression. *Appl. Soft. Comput.* **2019**, *81*, 105483. [CrossRef]
17. Koenker, R.; D'Orey, V. Algorithm AS 229: Computing Regression Quantiles. *Appl. Stat.* **1987**, *36*, 383. [CrossRef]

18. Yang, L.; Dong, H. Support vector machine with truncated pinball loss and its application in pattern recognition. *Chemom. Intell. Lab. Syst.* **2018**, *177*, 89–99. [CrossRef]
19. Singla, M.; Ghosh, D.; Shukla, K.; Pedrycz, W. Robust Twin Support Vector Regression Based on Rescaled Hinge Loss. *Pattern Recognit.* **2020**, *105*, 107395. [CrossRef]
20. Tang, L.; Tian, Y.; Li, W.; Pardalos, P. Valley-loss regular simplex support vector machine for robust multiclass classification. *Knowl.-Based Syst.* **2021**, *216*, 106801. [CrossRef]
21. Safari, A. An e-E-insensitive support vector regression machine. *Comput. Stat.* **2014**, *29*, 6. [CrossRef]
22. Liang, X.; Zhipeng, Z.; Song, Y.; Jian, L. Kernel-based Online Regression with Canal Loss. *Eur. J. Oper. Res.* **2021**, *297*, 268–279. [CrossRef]
23. Jian, L.; Gao, F.; Ren, P.; Song, Y.; Luo, S. A Noise-Resilient Online Learning Algorithm for Scene Classification. *Remote Sens.* **2018**, *10*, 1836. [CrossRef]
24. Zinkevich, M. Online Convex Programming and Generalized Infinitesimal Gradient Ascent. In Proceedings of the International Conference on Machine Learning, Los Angeles, CA, USA, 23–24 June 2003.
25. Karal, O. Maximum likelihood optimal and robust Support Vector Regression with lncosh loss function. *Neural Netw.* **2017**, *94*, 1–12. [CrossRef] [PubMed]
26. Huang, X.; Shi, L.; Pelckmans, K.; Suykens, J. Asymmetric -tube support vector regression. *Comput. Stat. Data Anal.* **2014**, *77*, 371–382. [CrossRef]
27. Anand, P.; Khemchandani, R.; Chandra, S. A v-Support Vector Quantile Regression Model with Automatic Accuracy Control. *Res. Rep. Comput. Sci.* **2022**, 113–135. [CrossRef]
28. Tanveer, M.; Tiwari, A.; Choudhary, R.; Jalan, S. Sparse pinball twin support vector machines. *Appl. Soft. Comput.* **2019**, *78*. [CrossRef]
29. Zhao, Y.P.; Sun, J.G. Robust truncated support vector regression. *Expert Syst. Appl.* **2010**, *37*, 5126–5133. [CrossRef]
30. Li, X.; Xu, X. Optimization and decision-making with big data. *Soft Comput.* **2018**, *22*, 5197–5199. [CrossRef]
31. Xu, X.; Liu, W.; Yu, L. Trajectory prediction for heterogeneous traffic-agents using knowledge correction data-driven model. *Inf. Sci.* **2022**, *608*, 375–391. [CrossRef]
32. Chen, L.; Zhang, J.; Ning, H. Robust large-scale online kernel learning. *Neural Comput. Appl.* **2022**, *34*, 1–21. [CrossRef]
33. Shalev-Shwartz, S.; Singer, Y.; Srebro, N.; Cotter, A. Pegasos: Primal estimated sub-gradient solver for SVM. *Math. Program.* **2011**, *127*, 3–30. [CrossRef]
34. Wang, X.; Han, M. Online sequential extreme learning machine with kernels for nonstationary time series prediction. *Neurocomputing* **2014**, *145*, 90–97. [CrossRef]
35. Santos, J.; Barreto, G. A Regularized Estimation Framework for Online Sparse LSSVR Models. *Neurocomputing* **2017**, *238*, 114–125. [CrossRef]
36. Lei, H.; Chen, X.; Jian, L. Canal-LASSO: A sparse noise-resilient online linear regression model. *Intell. Data Anal.* **2020**, *24*, 993–1010. [CrossRef]
37. Wei, N.; Yin, L.; Li, C.; Li, C.; Chan, C.; Zeng, F. Forecasting the daily natural gas consumption with an accurate white-box model. *Energy* **2021**, *232*, 121036. [CrossRef]

Disclaimer/Publisher's Note: The statements, opinions and data contained in all publications are solely those of the individual author(s) and contributor(s) and not of MDPI and/or the editor(s). MDPI and/or the editor(s) disclaim responsibility for any injury to people or property resulting from any ideas, methods, instructions or products referred to in the content.

Article

Optimal Decision of Dynamic Bed Allocation and Patient Admission with Buffer Wards During an Epidemic

Chengliang Wang, Feifei Yang * and Quan-Lin Li

School of Economics and Management, Beijing University of Technology, Beijing 100124, China
* Correspondence: yangfeifei@bjut.edu.cn

Abstract: To effectively prevent patients from nosocomial cross-infection and secondary infections, buffer wards for screening infectious patients who cannot be detected due to the incubation period are established in public hospitals in addition to isolation wards and general wards. In this paper, we consider two control mechanisms for three types of wards and patients: one is the dynamic bed allocation to balance the resource utilization among isolation, buffer, and general wards; the other is to effectively control the admission of arriving patients according to the evolution process of the epidemic to reduce mortality for COVID-19, emergency, and elective patients. Taking the COVID-19 pandemic as an example, we first develop a mixed-integer programming (MIP) model to study the joint optimization problem for dynamic bed allocation and patient admission control. Then, we propose a biogeography-based optimization for dynamic bed and patient admission (BBO-DBPA) algorithm to obtain the optimal decision scheme. Furthermore, some numerical experiments are presented to discuss the optimal decision scheme and provide some sensitivity analysis. Finally, the performance of the proposed optimal policy is discussed in comparison with the other different benchmark policies. The results show that adopting the dynamic bed allocation and admission control policy could significantly reduce the total operating cost during an epidemic. The findings can give some decision support for hospital managers in avoiding nosocomial cross-infection, improving bed utilization, and overall patient survival during an epidemic.

Keywords: buffer wards; mixed-integer programming; dynamic bed allocation; patient admission control; COVID-19 pandemic

MSC: 90B50

1. Introduction

In recent years, the outbreaks of major infectious diseases have posed a significant threat to human health, life security, and economic development worldwide. For example, coronavirus disease 2019 (COVID-19) is sweeping the world rapidly, with over 500 million confirmed cases and over 6 million deaths globally reported by the World Health Organization as of 17 April 2022 (https://covid19.who.int/ (accessed on 17 April 2022)). The U.S. Department of Health and Human Services report showed that the average daily admissions peaked at 145,000 during the week in mid-January 2022 due to the impact of the Omicron variant (https://protect-public.hhs.gov/pages/hospital-utilization (accessed on 1 April 2022)). The extreme shortage of hospital beds has resulted in COVID-19 patients not being rationally scheduled and non-COVID-19 patients not receiving urgent care, which significantly increases the risk of virus transmission and patient death.

As we all know, inpatient beds are one of the critical resources in the daily operation of hospitals, and their effective dispatch directly affects the operation efficiency and service level of the whole hospital [1]. Rapid and reasonable decision-making in limited bed allocation is crucial for preventing and controlling epidemics. Hospitals must simultaneously face the following challenges: (1) First, hospitals must urgently allocate a certain number of isolation beds at negative pressure for the treatment of COVID-19 patients. (2) Then, hospitals must guarantee necessary daily medical needs and provide essential medical services for non-COVID-19 patients with different degrees of emergency, especially those with high emergency health conditions (The U.S. Centers for Disease Control and Prevention, 2020; https://www.cdc.gov/coronavirus/2019-ncov/hcp/relief-healthcare-facilities.html (accessed on 1 April 2022)). (3) Last, to avoid cross-infection within the hospitals and to ensure the normal operation of medical facilities simultaneously, hospitals must develop relevant screening policies to screen newly arrived inpatients, especially those who have the risk of the incubation period of COVID-19 but are excluded temporarily (which we call "at-risk-of-COVID-19" patients) [2,3]. Therefore, it is an urgent problem to make a reasonable decision on bed allocation and patient admission control under limited resources during an epidemic.

At present, research on cross-infection prevention in hospitalization for infectious diseases mainly focuses on three classes: (1) Put at-risk-of-COVID-19 patients into isolation beds for separating inpatient management, for example, in Singapore and Italy [4,5]. (2) The hospitals provide each inpatient with the necessary personal protective equipment and then place them in the general wards [6]. (3) Many hospitals have set up buffer wards in emergency rooms, operating rooms, or general wards to pay close attention to new inpatients at a certain period to screen COVID-19 patients, just as in Egypt and China [3,7]. However, the first way can cause an extreme shortage of isolation beds, and in the second way, nosocomial infections may still appear despite the provision of additional personal protective equipment for inpatients. In contrast, inpatient observation in the buffer wards (a separate area for a single person in a single room) can effectively identify asymptomatic and incubated COVID-19 patients. Additionally, patients requiring acute or emergency treatment are attended to promptly in buffer wards even when nucleic acid test results are unknown, thus relieving the pressure of medical treatment for non-COVID-19 patients during a pandemic.

Our work is motivated by the need for hospital managers to rationalize bed allocation and patient admissions during the evolution of the COVID-19 pandemic so hospitals can take on the dual obligation of admitting patients and screening for latent COVID-19 patients to prevent cross-infection and improve overall patient survival. At the same time, hospital administrators face the challenge of balancing limited resources in different types of wards and patients caused by the time-varying nature and high uncertainty of hospital resource requirements. In this paper, we study the problem of dynamic bed allocation and patient admission control in a hospital with three types of wards in the COVID-19 epidemic. The bed manager faces trade-offs: (1) From the perspective of dynamic bed allocation, the arrival rate of COVID-19 patients directly leads the isolation beds to be insufficient or empty due to the fluctuations of the epidemic. In this context, balancing the allocation of beds among different types of wards is critical to improving bed utilization. (2) From the perspective of patient admission control, admitting too many elective patients will delay the treatment of emergency and COVID-19 patients in the future while admitting too few elective patients may result in a waste of medical resources. To solve the above problems, we propose an MIP model to jointly optimize bed resource allocation and patient admission. Specifically, the bed manager should make the bed allocation decisions on the isolation, buffer, and general wards and how many elective patients should be admitted in each period. Considering the stochastic arrivals, the uncertainty of the length of stay, and the preference of hospital administrators, we propose a dynamic bed allocation and patient admission control problem with the objective of minimizing the total operating cost reflecting multiple criteria. The total operating cost is composed of the bed retrofitting cost, the empty cost, the waiting cost, the rejection cost, and the delayed transfer cost.

Based on the above analysis, the main contributions to this study are:

(1) Considering buffer wards established to prevent cross-infection and secondary infection of COVID-19 inside the hospital, we study the dynamic bed allocation and patient admission control problem with three different types of wards during an epidemic, isolation

wards for admission of COVID-19 patients, buffer wards to screen the incubation risk of COVID-19, and general wards to admit emergency and elective patients who have excluded the risk of the incubation period of COVID-19.

(2) We formulate a MIP model that considers three different types of wards and patients for dynamic joint optimization of bed allocation and patient admission decisions. In addition, we propose a BBO-DBPA algorithm to solve this joint optimization problem and obtain an optimal decision scheme that minimizes the total operating cost of the hospital.

(3) Numerical experiments are conducted to investigate how the optimal decision scheme depends on some key parameters. Furthermore, we evaluate the performance of the optimal decision scheme by comparing it with some benchmark policies which are executable and have significant practical implications.

The remainder of this paper is organized as follows. In Section 2, we briefly review the relevant literature. Section 3 presents the problem description and symbol introduction. Section 4 gives the basic optimization formula for the programming problems. Section 5 describes the proposed BBO-DBPA algorithm. In Section 6, we analyze the numerical results and evaluate the performance of the optimal policy with benchmark policies. Section 7 makes conclusions and presents future research.

2. Literature Review

This paper focuses on the impact of dynamic bed allocation and patient admission control policies during the COVID-19 pandemic. So, the following three streams of literature contribute to this research: the inpatient management of epidemics, bed planning, and patient admission scheduling.

For the inpatient management of epidemics, hospitals tend to adopt three ways of admission to arrange newly arrived patients during the pandemic. The first is to place both confirmed, and unconfirmed patients in isolation wards [5,8]. Heins et al. [9] forecasted the short-term bed occupancy of patients with confirmed and suspected COVID-19 by Monte Carlo simulation and used the predictions to guide bed allocation. The second way for hospitals is to admit patients who cannot be confirmed for COVID-19 to the general wards with additional personal protection [6]. A cross-sectional study by Liu et al. [10] found that this could somewhat free up isolation beds. Unfortunately, unexpected infections still occur. In order to prevent and control the epidemic more strictly, the last method is to set up buffer wards to provide timely treatment to critically ill patients in some hospitals [3,7,11,12]. In terms of the operation management of hospitals with buffer wards during a pandemic, Liu et al. [13] built the infinite- and finite-horizon Markov decision process (MDP) models and proposed various iteration algorithms to obtain the optimal policy.

The bed planning problem concerns how many beds should be allocated among multiple patient classes. From the perspective of bed types, scholars have studied single and multiple types of beds. For the single type of beds, some researchers have focused on solving different specific problems and developed integer programming models. Pishnamazzadeh et al. [14] studied the bed planning problem by considering elastic management, developed an integer planning model and solved it using a simulated annealing algorithm. Lei et al. [15] considered the bed planning problem for both deterministic and stochastic length of stay and constructed an integer planning model by solving it using the CPLEX solver. Research on the multi-type bed planning problem mainly focuses on two classes: how to assign beds with specific features to a set of patients with specific requirements and how many beds are configured in the various departments considering different goals. Most papers construct integer programming models for the first class and solve them using heuristic algorithms [16,17]. For the second class, Mathematical programming models and simulation models are the most commonly used methods to deal with this problem [18–21]. In terms of dynamic bed management in a pandemic, Ma et al. [22] developed a dynamic programming model to study the allocation of two types of beds (isolation beds and ordinary beds) and the effect of the subsidy policy on serving three types of patients (COVID-19, emergency, and elective patients). The study shows that the dynamic allocation between isolation and ordinary beds can provide better utilization of bed resources.

The patient admission scheduling problem (PAS problem) is first studied by Demeester et al. [23]. It refers to assigning patients to appropriate beds within the planning horizon to maximize treatment efficiency, patient comfort, and medical resource utilization while considering patients' preferences and meeting necessary medical restrictions. From a strategic point of view, patient admission scheduling is a kind of resource planning. To solve this kind of problem, scholars have built integer programming optimization models and put forward effective search algorithms to solve the specific problem. Relevant studies can be divided into two streams according to whether the research needs are random or not. Some scholars have studied the needs of deterministic patients and constructed integer programming models, which have solved these models using a tabu search algorithm [24], general low-level heuristics algorithm [25], column generation algorithm [26], biogeography-based optimization algorithm [27,28], Fix-and-Relax and fix-and-optimization method [29], exact solution method [30] and so on. Another kind of literature has studied the dynamic situation of the PAS problem, that is, the patient demand is random. They built the integer programming models and solved them by using the simulated annealing algorithm [31], late acceptance hill-climbing algorithm [32], and column generation algorithm [33].

Although the current research on optimizing bed allocation and patient admission control has achieved initial results, it still faces challenges. In terms of the research on bed allocation decisions, most researchers have studied the problems of hospital bed configuration in different departments [34,35]. Specifically, Broek d'Obrenan et al. [36] considered the bed allocation for multi-types of patient flow among different departments. However, the above study only considered the allocation of hospital beds for ordinary patients and ignored the allocation of isolation beds for infectious patients during the COVID-19 pandemic. Studies on patient admission scheduling have considered the problem that different types of patients are assigned to different types of wards according to their preferences [22,30]. However, few studies consider bed retrofitting between different types of wards. For the optimal decision under the pandemic, some papers noted the optimization of inpatient admission only in buffer wards (e.g., Liu et al. [13]) but did not consider the reality that different types of patient flows need to be placed in different types of wards. To our knowledge, almost no one has studied the dynamic bed allocation and patient admission control problem considering the buffer wards during the pandemic. In this study, we study the dynamic bed allocation and patient admission control problem in a hospital with three different types of wards during an epidemic. Furthermore, we propose a mix-integer programming approach to obtain optimal dynamic bed allocation and patient admission control policies.

3. Problem Statement

In this section, we describe the problem of dynamic bed allocation and patient admission control, considering three different types of wards in a hospital during a pandemic. Additionally, we present the system structure and mathematical notations.

3.1. Problem Description

To illustrate our problem more clearly, Figure 1 illustrates this problem of dynamic bed allocation and patient admission decisions for one hospital. Inpatients are divided into three types after the initial screening at the triage table: confirmed COVID-19 patients, at-risk-of-COVID-19 emergency patients, and at-risk-of-COVID-19 elective patients. To ease analysis, patients with positive COVID-19 nucleic acid we considered are unvaccinated and are infected for the first time. Additionally, at-risk-of-COVID-19 patients refer to those who have not confirmed COVID-19 temporarily but have the incubation risk of COVID-19. For simplicity, we define these three types of patients as COVID-19, emergency, and elective patients in the remainder of the paper. During the regular management of the COVID-19 epidemic, the hospital has three types of wards: isolation wards, buffer wards, and general wards. If there are empty beds in the isolation wards, COVID-19 patients are admitted and occupy an empty bed directly upon arrival. As introduced above, emergency and elective patients should be sent to the buffer wards for COVID-19 screening. Similar to COVID-19 patients, emergency patients are directly admitted once they arrive. Unlike the first two, the bed managers perform admission control for elective patients: admit them to the buffer wards directly or let them join the waiting queue. In the buffer wards, once an inpatient has been diagnosed with COVID-19, this patient should be immediately moved to the isolation wards; otherwise, the patient will be excluded from COVID-19 risk and discharged or transferred to the general wards. The maximum duration of patient observation in the buffer wards is usually between 3 and 6 days. To make reasonable and efficient use of bed resources, hospitals adopt a dynamic bed allocation policy, that is, retrofitting some empty beds in one type of ward into beds in other types of wards. Note that the number of empty beds reserved in different types of wards differs at the beginning of the planning horizon. Based on the process described above, bed managers need to decide the number of retrofitted beds among different types of wards and the number of elective patients admitted to buffer wards in each planning period.

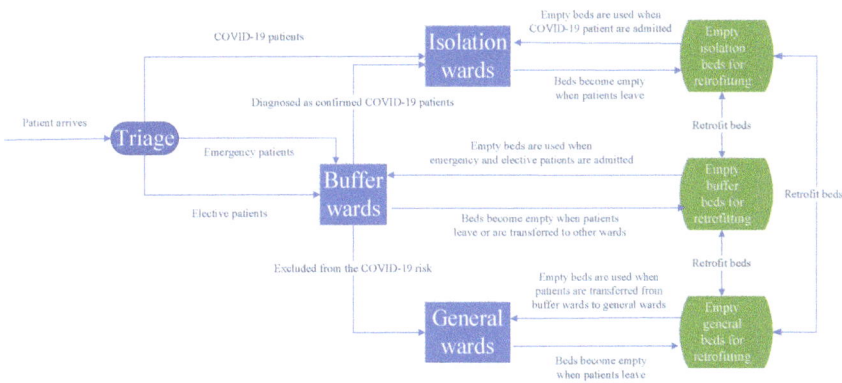

Figure 1. The illustration of patient flow and bed allocation considering buffer wards.

According to the epidemiological characteristics, the epidemic shows a fluctuating trend. To cover the entire epidemic trend, we assume that the arrival process of COVID-19 patients shows the characteristics of first increasing and then decreasing. Additionally, we assume that inpatients are not allowed direct access to the general wards during an epidemic to prevent nosocomial infections, which is in line with the literature, for example, He et al. [7]. For ease of understanding, we give the sequence of events in any period as follows.

1. At the beginning of period t, the hospital manager ascertains the number of beds occupied by different types of patients and the total number of beds in each type of ward, respectively. In addition, the number of elective patients in the waiting queue is obtained.
2. The hospital manager retrofits some beds in each type of ward.
3. Patients in buffer wards are transferred to isolation wards or general wards. The hospital manager obtains the number of patients requiring to be transferred and actually transferred from buffer wards to other types of wards according to the bed information of the wards, respectively.
4. Newly arrived patients are admitted. The COVID-19 patients must be admitted immediately using the reserved empty isolation beds. Additionally, the hospital should admit emergency patients upon arrival to the buffer wards due to the greater urgency level than elective patients. Moreover, new incoming elective patients join

the waiting list if they are not admitted. Elective patients who cannot be admitted in this period will be evaluated as to whether they will be admitted in the later periods.
5. At the end of period t, the cured patients are discharged from the designated inpatient wards. At the same time, empty beds are cleaned following cleaning and disinfecting procedures before admitting new patients or retrofitting other types of wards. This is a common setting in the literature, e.g., Liu et al. [13] and Ma et al. [22].

3.2. Definition of Parameters and Variables

We introduce a summary of the notations defined and additional parameters and variables in Table 1. Note that, for notational and model simplicity, the bed retrofit between the general and isolation beds can be carried out with the intermediate medium of buffer beds.

Table 1. Notations of the model.

Sets	Definitions
I	The set of patient types, indexed by i. $i \in I = \{1,2,3\}$, where type 1, type 2, and type 3 represent the COVID-19 patients, the emergency patients, and elective patients, respectively
J	The set of ward types, indexed by j. $j \in J = \{1,2,3\}$, where type 1, type 2, and type 3 denote the isolation wards, buffer wards, and general wards, respectively
L	The set of bed retrofit policies, indexed by l. The bed retrofit policies includes four types: $l = 1$ represents the retrofit from buffer beds to isolation beds and $l = 3$ for reverse conversion; $l = 2$ represents the retrofit from general beds to buffer beds and $l = 4$ for reverse conversion
T	The set of time periods, indexed by t
Parameters	**Definitions**
N	The total number of beds in the hospital
$\lambda_{i,j,t}$	The number of patient arrivals in type $i \in I$ in ward type $j \in J$ in period $t \in T$
$d_{i,j,t}$	The number of type $i \in I$ patients who need to transfer from buffer wards to ward type $j \in J$ in period $t \in T$
$\mu_{i,j,t}$	The number of patients' discharge in type $i \in I$ in ward type $j \in J$ in period $t \in T$
c_l	The unit retrofitting cost of adopting the bed retrofit policy $l \in L$
δ_j	The opportunity cost of an empty bed in ward type $j \in J$
σ	The waiting cost of an elective patient in the waiting queue per unit time
h_i	The rejection cost of a type $i \in I$ patient
$\sigma_{i,j}$	The delaying cost of a type $i \in I$ patient that needs to be transferred but is delayed
Variables	**Definitions**
$n_{l,t}$	The number of beds retrofitted by policies $l \in L$ in period $t \in T$
x_t	The number of elective patients admitted to the buffer wards in period $t \in T$
$X_{i,j,t}$	The number of inpatients in type $i \in I$ in ward type $j \in J$ in period $t \in T+1$
$Y_{j,t}$	The number of beds in ward type $j \in J$ in period $t \in T+1$, including occupied and empty beds
$D_{i,j,t}$	The number of patients in type $i \in I$ transferred from the buffer wards to ward type $j \in J$ in period $t \in T$
W_t	The number of patients in the waiting queue in period $t \in T+1$ (i.e., the length of waiting queue)

4. Mathematical Formulation

In this section, we consider a finite planning horizon of T periods and give a mathematical formulation of the dynamic bed allocation and patient admission control problem by developing a MIP model. The objective of our problem is to minimize the total operating cost, including the bed retrofitting cost, the empty cost, the waiting cost of elective patients, the rejection cost of COVID-19 patients and emergency patients, and the delayed transfer cost of patients who should be transferred but were not. The decision variables are $n_{i,t}$ and x_t. Based on the above analysis, this problem can be formulated as follows:

$$\min \ Z = \sum_{t \in T} \sum_{l \in L} n_{l,t} c_l + \sum_{t \in T} w W_t + \sum_{t \in T} \sum_{j \in J} \delta_j (Y_{j,t+1} - \sum_{i \in I} (X_{i,j,t+1} + \mu_{i,j,t})) + \\ \sum_{t \in T} \sum_{j \in J} \sum_{i \in I} \sigma_{i,j} (d_{i,j,t} - D_{i,j,t}) + \sum_{t \in T} h_1 [\lambda_{1,1,t} - (Y_{1,t+1} - \sum_{i \in I} X_{i,1,t} - \\ \sum_{i \in I} D_{i,1,t})] + h_2 [\lambda_{2,1,t} - (Y_{2,t+1} - \sum_{i \in I} X_{i,2,t} + \sum_{j \in J} \sum_{i \in I} D_{i,1,t})] \quad (1)$$

Subject to

$$n_{1,t} \leq Y_{2,t} - \sum_{i \in I} X_{i,2,t} \quad \forall t \in T \quad (2)$$

$$n_{2,t} \leq Y_{3,t} - \sum_{i \in I} X_{i,3,t} \quad \forall t \in T \quad (3)$$

$$n_{3,t} \leq Y_{1,t} - \sum_{i \in I} X_{i,1,t} \quad \forall t \in T \quad (4)$$

$$n_{4,t} \leq Y_{2,t} - \sum_{i \in I} X_{i,2,t} - n_{1,t} \quad \forall t \in T \quad (5)$$

$$n_{1,t} n_{3,t} = 0 \quad \forall t \in T \quad (6)$$

$$n_{2,t} n_{4,t} = 0 \quad \forall t \in T \quad (7)$$

$$Y_{1,t+1} = Y_{1,t} + n_{1,t} - n_{3,t} \quad \forall t \in T \quad (8)$$

$$Y_{2,t+1} = Y_{2,t} + n_{2,t} + n_{3,t} - n_{1,t} - n_{4,t} \quad \forall t \in T \quad (9)$$

$$Y_{3,t+1} = Y_{3,t} + n_{4,t} - n_{2,t} \quad \forall t \in T \quad (10)$$

$$D_{2,j,t} = \min\{Y_{j,t+1} - \sum_{i \in I} X_{i,j,t}, d_{2,j,t}\} \quad \forall j \in J, \forall t \in T \quad (11)$$

$$D_{3,j,t} = \min\{Y_{j,t+1} - \sum_{i \in I} X_{i,j,t} - D_{2,j,t}, d_{3,j,t}\} \quad \forall j \in J, \forall t \in T \quad (12)$$

$$x_t \leq \lambda_{3,2,t} + W_t \quad \forall t \in T \quad (13)$$

$$x_t \leq \max\{Y_{2,t+1} - \sum_{i \in I} X_{i,2,t} + \sum_{i \in I} D_{i,1,t} + \sum_{i \in I} D_{i,3,t} - \lambda_{2,2,t}, 0\} \quad \forall t \in T \quad (14)$$

$$X_{i,1,t+1} = X_{i,1,t} + D_{i,1,t} + \min\{\lambda_{i,1,t}, Y_{1,t+1} - \sum_{i \in I} (X_{i,1,t} + D_{i,1,t})\} - \\ \mu_{i,1,t} \quad \forall t \in T \quad (15)$$

$$X_{2,2,t+1} = X_{2,2,t} - D_{2,1,t} - D_{2,3,t} + \min\{\lambda_{2,2,t}, Y_{2,t+1} - \\ \sum_{i \in I} (X_{i,2,t} - D_{i,1,t} - D_{i,3,t})\} - \mu_{2,2,t} \quad \forall t \in T \quad (16)$$

$$X_{3,2,t+1} = X_{3,2,t} - D_{3,1,t} - D_{3,3,t} + x_t - \mu_{3,2,t} \quad \forall t \in T \quad (17)$$

$$W_{t+1} = W_t + \lambda_{3,2,t} - x_t \quad \forall t \in T \quad (18)$$

$$X_{i,3,t+1} = X_{i,3,t} + D_{i,3,t} - \mu_{i,3,t} \quad \forall i \in I, \forall t \in T \quad (19)$$

Equation (1) is the objective function by minimizing hospital operating costs, including five parts. The first term refers to the bed retrofitting cost. The second term is associated with the waiting cost. The third term indicates the empty cost of the bed, where $\sum_{i \in I} (X_{i,j,t+1} + \mu_{i,j,t})$ represents the maximum number of patients before discharge in wards j at period t. The fourth term represents the delayed transfer cost. The last two items express the rejection costs of COVID-19 patients and emergency patients, where $Y_{1,t+1} - \sum_{i \in I} X_{i,1,t} - \sum_{i \in I} D_{i,1,t}$

represents the number of beds that can receive COVID-19 patients, and $Y_{2,t+1} - \sum_{i \in I} X_{i,2,t} + \sum_{j \in J} \sum_{i \in I} D_{i,1,t}$ represents the number of beds that can receive emergency patients.

Constraints (2)–(5) ensure that the number of retrofitted beds is no more than the number of empty beds in different types of wards. Note that the empty beds in the buffer wards should be the first ones retrofitted to isolation beds and then the general beds, considering the pandemic control. Constraints (6) and (7) guarantee that no bed is repeatedly retrofitted between any two types of beds in any period t. Constraints (8)–(10) are bed conservation. Constraints (11)–(12) represent the patient transfer relationship, where $Y_{j,t+1} - \sum_{i \in I} X_{i,j,t}$ and $Y_{j,t+1} - \sum_{i \in I} X_{i,j,t} - D_{2,j,t}$ show the number of empty beds in type 2 and type 3 wards before the patients were transferred, respectively. Constraint (13) ensures that the number of elective patients admitted to buffer wards does not exceed the sum of newly arrived patients and patients waiting in the queue in period t. Constraint (14) ensures that the number of elective patients admitted is no more than the number of empty beds in the buffer wards after admitting emergency patients. Constraints (15)–(19) are the patient flow conservation where a and b represent the number of empty beds before patients are admitted to type 1 and type 2 wards, respectively.

5. The Solution Method

In this section, we propose a BBO-DBPA algorithm to solve the dynamic bed allocation and patient admission control problem. Biogeography-based optimization (BBO) is a new effective evolutionary algorithm that is often used for solving NP-hard problems, and it is proven to have a better performance compared to some other evolutionary algorithms [37]. To ensure that all solutions in the operation of the BBO-DBPA algorithm meet the model constraints, we first provide the solution representation in the following.

5.1. Solution Representation and Decoding

In this research, we consider some constraints when representing the solutions so that the solutions will always be feasible in the following optimization operations. In order to represent all decision variables conveniently, we present each feasible solution in a three-part vector. The first part, $rd\_n_{1,3,t}$, shows the retrofitting between buffer wards and isolation wards. The second part, $rd\_n_{2,4,t}$, represents the retrofitting between buffer wards and general wards. The third part, rd_x_t, indicates the number of elective patients admitted. These three parts have T cells, and each cell is a real number between 0 and 1.

Equations (20) and (21) describe the decoding process for $rd\_n_{a,a+2,t}$, $a = 1, 2$.

$$tmp_{a,t} = \lceil rd\_n_{a,a+2,t}(freebed_{a,t} + freebed_{a+1,t}) - 0.5 \rceil - freebed_{a+1,t} \qquad (20)$$

$$\begin{cases} n_{a,t} = -tmp_{a,t} & \text{if } tmp_{a,t} < 0 \\ n_{a+2,t} = tmp_{a,t} & \text{if } tmp_{a,t} \geq 0 \end{cases} \qquad (21)$$

where $tmp_{a,t}$ is an intermediate variable, $freebed_{j,t}$ represents the number of empty beds in wards j in period t, and

$$freebed_{j,t} = Y_{j,t} - \sum_{i \in I} X_{i,j,t} \qquad (22)$$

Equation (23) describes the decoding process rd_x_t.

$$x_t = \begin{cases} rd\_x_t(freebed_{2,t} - \lambda_{2,2,t}) & \text{if } 0 \leq freebed_{2,t} - \lambda_{2,2,t}) < \lambda_{3,2,t} + W_t \\ rd\_x_t(\lambda_{3,2,t} + W_t) & \text{if } \lambda_{3,2,t} + W_t \leq freebed_{2,t} - \lambda_{2,2,t}) \end{cases} \qquad (23)$$

This solution representation method can ensure that the solution in the optimization operation always meets constraints (2)–(7) and (13)–(14).

5.2. Creating Initial Solutions

In the BBO-DBPA algorithm, the diversity of initially generated solutions can significantly affect the effectiveness of the optimization process. We use generating solutions twice to increase the diversity of the initial generation solutions. In the first step, some solutions are randomly generated. In the second step, if there are duplicates among these solutions, this number of solutions is randomly generated to replace these duplicates. This operation ensures that the generated solutions are likely to be different.

5.3. Migration

The BBO-DBPA algorithm uses migration operation to share the features from good solutions to poor solutions effectively. The migration operation can preserve good solutions and further expand the search scope of the solutions. Each solution will be migrated in the algorithm based on the value of the immigration rate ($\lambda(s)$) and the emigration rate (μ_s), which is calculated as in Equations (24) and (25), respectively. According to (24) and (25), the good solution has a larger emigration rate and a lower immigration rate than the poor solution.

$$\lambda(s) = I(1 - \text{HSI}_s/\text{HSI}_{\max}), \tag{24}$$

$$\mu(s) = E\text{HSI}_s/\text{HSI}_{\max}, \tag{25}$$

where I is the maximum immigration rate; E is the maximum emigration rate; HSI_s is the fitness value of solution s. The better the solution, the smaller the total cost and the larger the fitness value. $\text{HSI}_{\max}$ is the maximum fitness value. Algorithm 1 shows the migration operation of the BBO-DBPA algorithm.

Algorithm 1 The pseudo-code of the migration operation.

1: $s \Leftarrow$ the solution s
2: length $(s) \Leftarrow$ the size of the solution
3: $\lambda(s) \Leftarrow$ calculate the migration rate of all solutions according to Equation (24)
4: $\mu(s) \Leftarrow$ calculate the migration rate of all solutions according to Equation (25)
5: **For** i from 1 to length(s) **do**
6:     NOC $\Leftarrow$ the number of codes, the value of NOC is $3T$
7:     **For** j from 1 to NOC **do**
8:         $r_1 \Leftarrow$ random value between 0 and I
9:         **If** $r_1 < \lambda(s)$ **then**
10:             $s_k \Leftarrow$ random solution with a probability proportional to $\mu(s)$
11:             $s_i(j) = s_k(j)$
12:         **End if**
13:     **End for**
14: **End for**

5.4. Mutation

In the BBO-DBPA algorithm, a mutation operation is performed to increase the variety of solutions and to escape from the local optimality trap. Different solutions have different mutation rates. The mutation rate of the solution s is related to the prior probability of existence s (P_s). In general, high and low HSI solutions are less likely to exist than medium HSI solutions. The relationship between P_s and HSI is shown in Figure 2.

The mutation rate $m(s)$ is calculated as in Equation (26).

$$m(s) = m_{\max}(1 - P_s/P_{s_k}), \tag{26}$$

where $m_{\max}$ is the maximum mutation probability; P_{s_k} is the maximum prior probability of existence.

If only the mutation operation described above is performed, the mutation probability of the good solutions and the poor solutions is relatively large. This way allows the poor solutions to improve but also makes the good solutions likely to worsen. To keep the good solutions, we add the elite strategy to the mutation operation of the BBO-DBPA algorithm. We only perform the mutation operation on the poor half of all solutions. Algorithm 2 shows the mutation operation of the BBO-DBPA algorithm.

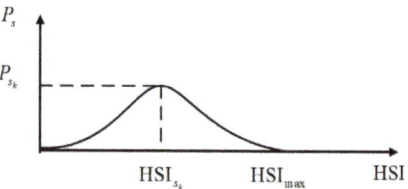

Figure 2. The relationship between P_s and HSI.

Algorithm 2 The pseudo-code of the migration operation.

1: $s \Leftarrow$ the solution s
2: **For** i from 1 to length(s)/2 **do**
3:     $m(s) \Leftarrow$ the mutation probability of solution s
4:     **For** j from 1 to NOC **do**
5:         $r_2 \Leftarrow$ random value between 0 and E
6:         **If** $r_2 < m(s)$ **then**
7:             $s_i(j) = s_i^{'}(j)$ random solution with a probability proportional
8:             to $\mu(s)$
9:         **End if**
10:    **End for**
11: **End for**

5.5. The Structure of the BBO-DBPA Algorithm

The general framework of the BBO-DBPA algorithm is shown in Figure 3. Specifically, the experiment is conducted in the following steps:

Step 1: Setting the parameters of the algorithm, including the maximum number of iterations (maxGeneration), the size of the initially generated solutions (N), the maximum immigration rate (I), the maximum emigration rate (E), and the maximum prior probability of existence (P_{s_k}), the maximum mutation probability (m_{max}).

Step 2: Initiating solutions. The BBO-DBPA algorithm generates the initial solutions as described in Section 5.2 and starts the improvement loop after generating the initial solutions.

Step 3: Sorting of solutions. The costs of the decision options represented by those solutions are calculated as described in Section 5.1, and the fitness values are given to these solutions. Based on it, all solutions are sorted from largest to smallest.

Step 4: Migration operation. Execute the migration operation as described in Section 5.3.

Step 5: Mutation operation. Execute the mutation operation as described in Section 5.4.

Step 6: If the number of iterations is greater than maxGeneration, stop the iteration and output the optimal solution; otherwise, proceed to Step 3.

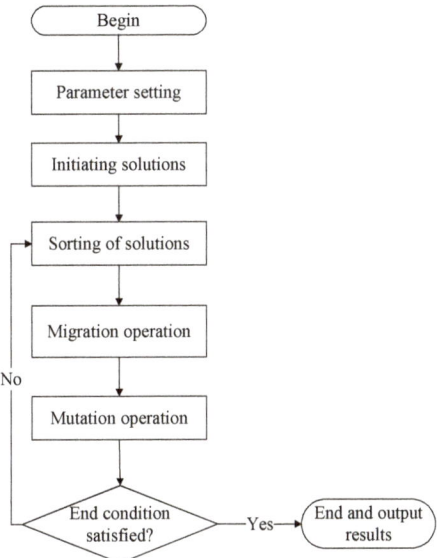

Figure 3. The flow chart of the BBO-DBPA algorithm.

6. Computational Experiments

In this section, we first analyze the base case by implementing the BBO-DBPA algorithm with a large finite iteration to find the optimal policy. Then, we present a sensitivity analysis to discuss how the optimal policy depends on some key parameters. Finally, the performance advantages are examined by comparison with some benchmark policies. All the experiments are performed in MATLAB R2019b software. The experiments were run on a computer with Windows 10 and an Intel Core i5-11400H processor with a 2.70 GHz frequency and 16 GB of RAM.

6.1. Data Setting

The main data source is obtained from the public data website, which provides relevant hospitalization data for the benchmark example in Demeester et al. [24] (https://people.cs.kuleuven.be/wim.vancroonenburg/pas/, accessed on 17 April 2022). Specifically, we set N = 286, T = 14, $X_{2,3,1}$ = 15, $X_{3,3,1}$ = 168. In addition, the information on arrival and discharge for ED and elective patients is given in Appendix A1. Because there is no benchmark dataset available for the problem formulated in this study, we refer to the real data of reported COVID-19 from March 1 to March 7 and 27 April to 3 May 2022, in Jilin province in China. It has raised the government's concerns due to the sudden outbreak of the regional epidemic (please see Appendix A2 for specific data). This number of reported COVID-19 was chosen as a benchmark for simulating the volatility of the pandemic and effectively operating our proposed model at a given scale (i.e., 286 total beds). According to Pollock and Lancaster [38], for the patient transfer in the buffer wards, we consider that 80% of the number of reported COVID-19 (as type i = 1 patient) enter the isolation wards directly, and 20% of the number of reported COVID-19 (as type i = 2 or 3 patients) enter the buffer wards to spend the observation period. We assume that COVID-19 patients in the incubation period will be detected during the observation period in the buffer wards. Thus, we set the observation period as three days based on COVID-19 evolution characteristics [39,40]. The computer randomly generates the detection time of confirmed COVID-19 patients in the buffer wards. In addition, the computer randomly generates the discharge times based on the average length of stay of 7 days for COVID-19 patients [41]. To ease understanding, we show all the hospitalization information of the three types of patients in the base case in Appendix A3. Based on Ma et al. [22] and communication with medical staff in real hospitals, we set the unit retrofitting cost: $c_l = 10$ for $\forall l \in L$; the opportunity cost of an empty bed: $\delta_1 = 3$; $\delta_2 = \delta_3 = 2$; the waiting cost of an elective patient in the waiting queue per unit time: $w = 11$; the rejection cost: $h_1 = 500$, $h_2 = 150$, $h_3 = 0$; and the delaying cost of a type-i patient that requires to be transferred but is delayed: $\sigma_{i,j} = 1$, $\forall i \in I$, $\forall j \in I$.

Furthermore, we modify the values of some parameters to investigate their impact on the sensitivity analysis. Table 2 shows the sensitivity analysis numerical cases we considered. About the parameters of the BBO-DBPA algorithm, we set the number of initial solutions at 2000, the number of iterations at 150, the maximum immigration rate at 1, the maximum emigration rate at 1, and the maximum mutation rate at 0.02.

Table 2. Information on sensitivity analysis of numerical cases.

Case	Modified Parameter	Values
1	The total number of beds (N)	206, 246, **286** [1], 326, 366
2	The number of COVID-19 patients' arrival ($\lambda_{1,1,t}$)	Multiple 0.5, 0.75, **1**, 1.25, 1.5 of base case's arrival rate of COVID-19 patients
3	The number of COVID-19 patients' arrival ($\lambda_{3,2,t}$)	Multiple 0.8, 0.9, **1**, 1.1, and 1.2 of base case's arrival rate of elective patients

[1] The bolded numbers are the same as the values in the base case.

6.2. Base Case Study

We use the BBO-DBPA algorithm with a large finite space. After 992 s of running time and 150 iterations, we obtain the optimal policy with the minimum total operating cost of 22,672 in this hospital system. We present the results in Table 3. The results show that the number of buffer beds retrofitted to isolation beds first increases and then decreases. That is because the demand for isolation beds increases as more and more new COVID-19 patients arrive, then decreases in the planning horizon. Intuitively, there is no retrofit of buffer beds to general beds because the demand for isolation beds is higher than that for buffer beds or general beds during the pandemic.

Table 3. Hospital optimal decision scheme for dynamic bed allocation and admission control.

Decision	$t=1$	$t=2$	$t=3$	$t=4$	$t=5$	$t=6$	$t=7$	$t=8$	$t=9$	$t=10$	$t=11$	$t=12$	$t=13$	$t=14$
$n_{1,t}$	4	0	13	20	14	35	46	48	35	15	15	13	2	0
$n_{2,t}$	56	51	53	12	11	7	0	22	19	29	2	3	0	2
$n_{3,t}$	0	1	0	0	0	0	0	0	0	0	0	0	3	0
$n_{4,t}$	0	0	0	0	0	0	0	0	0	0	0	0	0	0
x_t	60	51	50	25	28	20	8	8	20	28	15	6	9	11

The number of general beds retrofitted to buffer beds shows two peaks respectively on days 1–3 and days 8–10, and the number is higher during days 1–3 than days 8–10. That is because buffer beds are in short supply when faced with a demand from non-COVID-19 patients in the early periods. After the incubation period (3 days), the number of general beds retrofitted to buffer beds decreases to ensure the needs of the general wards as patients in the buffer wards start to move to the general wards. The reason for the peak on days 8–10 is that the decrease in the number of patients admitted to the buffer wards on days 4–7 leads to the decrease in the number of patients transferred to the general wards on days 8–10, which leads to more empty beds to retrofit. In addition, three isolation beds are retrofitted to buffer beds on day 13. The reason is that with fewer COVID-19 patients arriving in the latter periods, the empty isolation beds can be retrofitted into buffer beds to admit more non-COVID-19 patients.

Figures 4 and 5 give the total number of beds in different types of wards and the number of patients in the waiting queue. In Figure 4, the blue line indicates the number of beds in the isolation wards, the red line represents the number of beds in the buffer wards, and the green line shows the number of beds in the general wards. Figure 4 shows that the number of isolation beds increases rapidly in the first seven days, then the increasing trends are moderate in the latter periods. Moreover, the number of buffer beds increases rapidly from day 1 to 4 and decreases gradually after day 5. Furthermore, the number of general beds shows an overall downward trend. The reason for the above trend corresponds to the decision variables, which are shown in Table 3. Figure 5 shows that the number of patients in the waiting queue gradually increases over time. Intuitively, as the number of COVID-19 arrivals increases, some buffer beds are retrofitted to isolation beds, the buffer beds are in short supply, and more and more elective patients are joining the waiting queue to wait for inpatient services. The optimized results can provide decision support for hospital administrators. During a pandemic, hospitals should make some beds empty to admit future arrivals of COVID-19 patients and emergency patients by controlling the admission of elective patients and retrofitting beds, which can help improve bed utilization and overall patient survival.

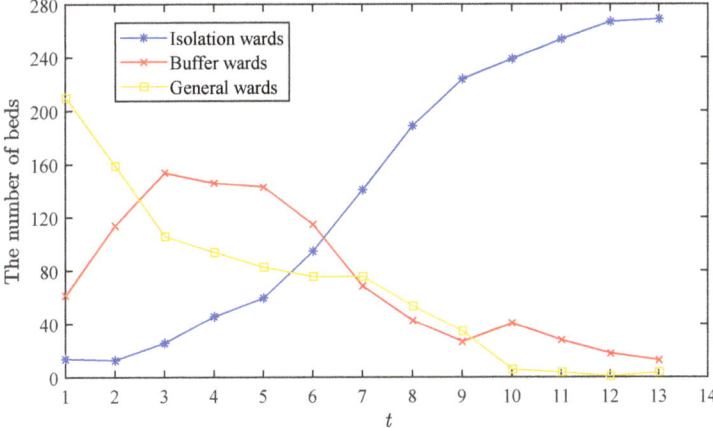

Figure 4. The number of beds in different types of wards.

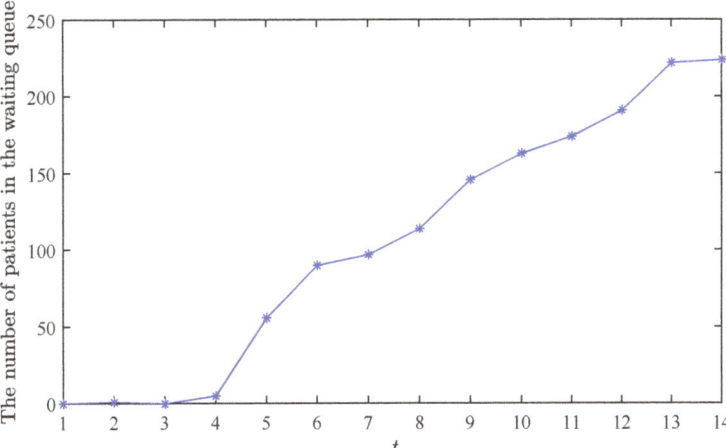

Figure 5. The number of patients in the waiting queue in base case.

6.3. Sensitivity Analysis

In this section, a sensitivity analysis is used to verify the effectiveness of the proposed model in dealing with different situations. We first conduct the experiments with some variations in the total number of beds, the arrival rate of COVID-19 patients, and the arrival rate of elective patients to explore the impact of the pandemic outbreak on hospital operations. Then, we compare our optimal policy with some benchmarks. Note that all the other parameters we do not mention are the same as the baseline values.

6.3.1. Impact of the Total Number of Beds

We first consider the impact of the total number of beds by varying N from 206 to 366 with a difference of 40. Table 4 shows the execution time of the BBO-DBPA algorithm in seconds and the total operating cost depending on the number of beds. Moreover, we investigate the impact of the total number of beds on the optimal dynamic policy in Table 5. We can see that the trend of each decision variable is roughly the same as the base case when we change the total number of beds. The larger the number of beds, the larger the number of general beds retrofitted to buffer beds, the larger the number of buffer beds retrofitted to isolation beds, and the larger the number of elective patients admitted.

Table 4. The execution time and optimization results in case 1.

N	206	246	286	326	366
The execution time	1013	996	992	991	1004
The total operating cost	48,958	28,546	22,672	18,603	14,946

In the first periods, the number of general beds retrofitted to buffer beds and the number of elective patients admitted when $N = 206$ and 246 are smaller than those when $N = 286, 326,$ and 366. The reason is that the empty beds are insufficient to retrofit from general wards to buffer wards. On days 9 to 14, the number of admitted elective patients when $N = 326$ and 366 is more than when $N = 206, 246,$ and 286. The reason is that the supply of buffer beds when $N = 326$ and 366 is more abundant than when $N = 206, 246,$ and 286, so more elective patients can be admitted.

Figures 6–9 show the number of beds in each type of ward and the number of patients in the waiting queue under the different total numbers of beds, respectively. In Figures 6–9, the blue, red, green, black, and mauve lines indicate the corresponding indicator values when the total number of beds is 206, 246, 286, 326, and 366, respectively. As the total number of beds increases, the number of beds in each type of ward increases, and the number of patients in the waiting queue decreases. The reason is that different types of beds are in short supply for admitting all patients requiring hospitalization. When $N = 326$ and 366, the number of patients in the waiting queue decreases from day 13 to 14. The reason is that there is a sufficient supply of buffer beds to allow elective patients to be admitted.

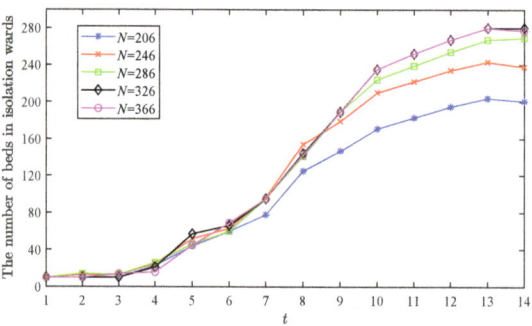

Figure 6. The number of beds in isolation wards in case 1.

Table 5. Comparison of optimal decision schemes in case 1.

Decision Variable	N	t = 1	t = 2	t = 3	t = 4	t = 5	t = 6	t = 7	t = 8	t = 9	t = 10	t = 11	t = 12	t = 13	t = 14
$n_{1,t}$	206	0	0	13	21	16	18	47	22	24	12	12	9	0	0
	246	3	0	12	27	11	33	58	25	31	12	12	9	0	0
	286	4	0	13	20	14	35	46	48	35	15	15	13	2	0
	326	0	0	11	36	9	29	49	45	46	17	15	13	0	0
	366	0	4	2	29	24	26	48	46	46	17	15	13	0	0
$n_{2,t}$	206	3	41	36	13	16	5	15	32	16	0	9	0	0	0
	246	27	57	36	20	5	5	12	34	19	1	10	0	0	1
	286	56	51	53	12	11	7	0	22	19	29	2	3	0	2
	326	58	50	61	45	11	0	0	13	19	22	17	3	0	0
	366	75	34	48	78	27	0	0	8	16	22	17	11	0	1
$n_{3,t}$	206	0	0	0	0	0	0	0	0	0	0	0	0	3	0
	246	0	0	0	0	0	0	0	0	0	0	0	0	5	0
	286	0	1	0	0	0	0	0	0	0	0	0	0	3	0
	326	0	0	0	0	0	0	0	0	0	0	0	0	0	5
	366	0	0	0	0	0	0	0	0	0	0	0	0	3	7
$n_{4,t}$	206	0	0	0	0	0	0	0	0	0	0	0	0	0	0
	246	0	0	0	0	0	0	0	0	0	0	0	0	1	0
	286	0	0	0	0	0	0	0	0	0	0	0	0	0	0
	326	0	0	0	0	0	0	0	0	0	0	0	0	2	0
	366	0	0	0	0	0	0	1	0	0	0	0	0	1	0
x_t	206	13	37	34	28	53	27	12	6	12	11	9	0	1	1
	246	34	54	34	27	25	22	12	6	12	11	10	0	3	4
	286	60	51	50	25	28	20	8	8	20	28	15	6	9	11
	326	61	50	55	54	30	19	1	9	25	34	27	20	27	33
	366	61	50	55	76	43	18	1	9	31	34	27	33	33	39

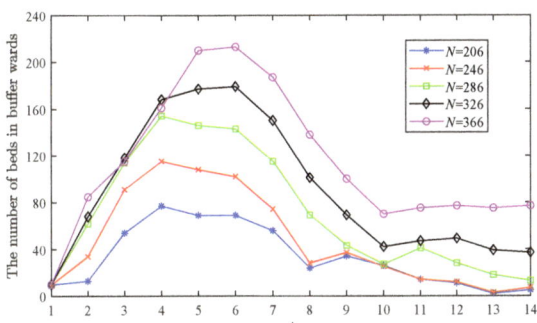

Figure 7. The number of beds in buffer wards in case 1.

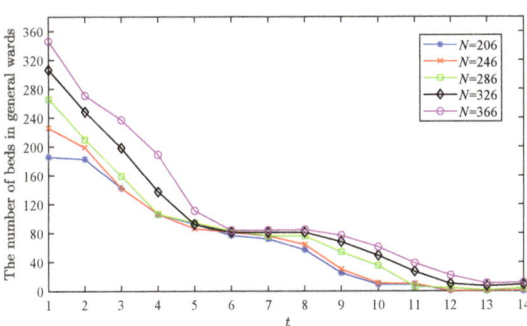

Figure 8. The number of beds in general wards in case 1.

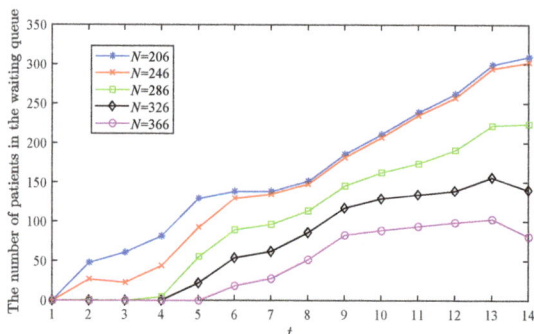

Figure 9. The number of patients in the waiting queue in case 1.

6.3.2. Impact of the Arrival Rate of COVID-19 Patients

We now consider the impact of the arrival rate of COVID-19 patients by varying $\lambda_{1,1,t}$ from 0.5 to 1.5 times the base case's value with a difference of 0.25. Table 6 shows the execution time of the BBO-DBPA algorithm in seconds and the total operating cost depending on the arrival rate of COVID-19 patients.

Table 6. The execution time and optimization results in case 2.

Multiple of Base Case's $\lambda_{1,1,t}$	0.5	0.75	1	1.25	1.5
The execution time	982	970	980	985	963
The total operating cost	8125	17982	26142	49188	79268

We investigate the impact of the arrival rate of COVID-19 patients on the optimal dynamic policy in Table 7. We can see that the trend of each decision variable is roughly the same as the base case when we change the arrival rate of COVID-19 patients. Moreover, the larger the arrival rate of COVID-19 patients, the larger the number of buffer beds retrofitted to isolation beds, and the smaller the number of elective patients admitted. It suggests that hospitals should admit fewer elective patients, thus freeing up beds to admit more new arriving COVID-19 patients to reduce the total operating cost.

Table 7. Comparison of optimal decision schemes in case 2.

Decision Variable	Multiple of Base Case's $\lambda_{1,1,t}$	t = 1	t = 2	t = 3	t = 4	t = 5	t = 6	t = 7	t = 8	t = 9	t = 10	t = 11	t = 12	t = 13	t = 14
$n_{1,t}$	0.5	4	0	0	8	10	22	27	25	27	14	9	0	0	0
	0.75	4	0	2	7	15	36	36	36	35	17	13	5	0	0
	1	4	0	3	16	19	45	45	48	38	17	13	10	0	0
	1.25	4	0	8	15	20	60	69	20	29	10	13	12	0	0
	1.5	4	0	2	22	25	58	64	20	25	11	14	12	0	0
$n_{2,t}$	0.5	57	51	54	47	3	0	0	0	9	21	7	1	0	4
	0.75	58	54	57	34	7	0	0	3	9	20	11	5	0	4
	1	58	54	61	32	6	1	0	18	18	7	6	4	0	0
	1.25	57	59	57	19	8	5	7	26	7	0	11	5	0	0
	1.5	58	53	62	24	9	0	5	25	7	2	11	5	0	0
$n_{3,t}$	0.5	0	0	0	0	0	0	0	0	0	0	0	2	2	9
	0.75	0	0	0	0	0	0	0	0	0	0	0	0	0	4
	1	0	0	0	0	0	0	0	0	0	0	0	0	0	0
	1.25	0	0	0	0	0	0	0	0	0	0	0	0	2	1
	1.5	0	0	0	0	0	0	0	0	0	0	0	0	5	0
$n_{4,t}$	0.5	0	0	0	0	0	0	0	0	0	0	0	0	1	0
	0.75	0	0	0	0	0	0	0	0	0	0	0	0	1	0
	1	0	0	0	0	0	0	0	0	0	0	0	0	0	0
	1.25	0	0	0	0	0	0	0	0	0	0	0	0	0	0
	1.5	0	0	0	0	0	0	0	0	0	0	0	0	0	0
x_t	0.5	60	49	55	45	43	26	13	26	37	37	40	32	36	38
	0.75	62	50	55	30	28	16	7	17	32	39	33	25	29	30
	1	62	50	49	19	19	10	9	11	16	17	12	6	6	5
	1.25	62	49	36	12	3	0	13	6	13	12	12	2	6	7
	1.5	62	50	38	10	2	0	13	6	13	12	12	2	6	5

Figures 10–13 show the number of beds in each type of ward and the number of patients in the waiting queue under different arrival rates of COVID-19 patients, respectively. In Figures 10–13, the blue, red, green, black, and mauve lines represent the corresponding indicator values when the number of COVID-19 patients ($\lambda_{1,1,t}$) is 0.5, 0.75, 1, 1.25, and 1.5 multiples of the value of $\lambda_{1,1,t}$ in the base case, respectively. As the arrival rate of COVID-19 patients increases, the number of beds in isolation wards increases, the number of beds in buffer wards increases, the number of beds in general wards remains roughly the same, and the number of patients in the waiting queue increases. The reason is that different types of beds are in short supply for receiving all patients requiring hospitalization.

The number of the three types of beds is almost the same from day 1 to 4. The reason is that the isolation beds are in adequate supply due to the small number of arriving COVID-19 patients, and the buffer beds are in short supply because of the large number of non-COVID-19 patients. Thus, the empty beds in the general wards are mainly retrofitted to buffer beds to serve non-COVID-19 patients. When the arrival rate of COVID-19 patients is at 1.25 and 1.5 times the base case, the number of beds in all three different types is almost the same from day 10 to day 14. The reason is that hospital beds are almost already occupied by many COVID-19 patients, so there are no beds available to retrofit into isolation beds.

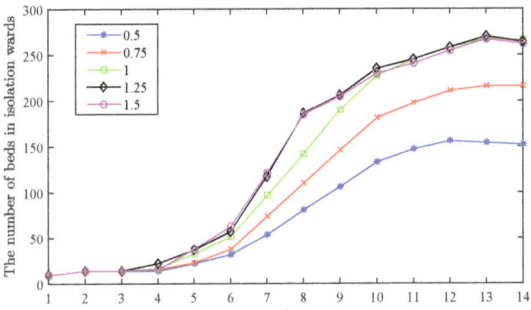

Figure 10. The number of beds in isolation wards in case 2.

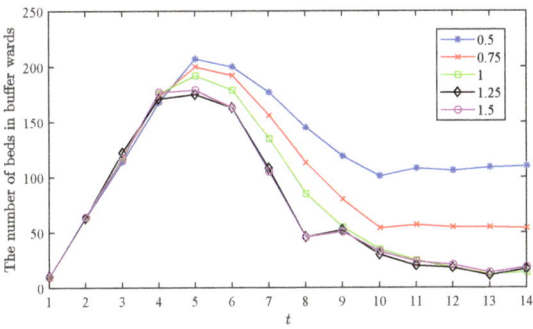

Figure 11. The number of beds in buffer wards in case 2.

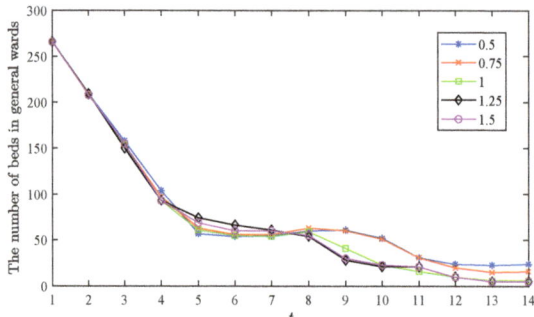

Figure 12. The number of beds in general wards in case 2.

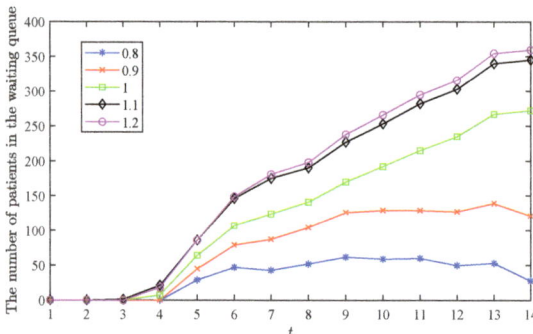

Figure 13. The number of patients in the waiting queue in case 2.

6.3.3. Impact of the Arrival Rate of Elective Patients

We now consider the impact of the arrival rate of elective patients by varying $\lambda_{3,2,t}$ from 0.8 to 1.2 times the base case's value with a difference of 0.1. Table 8 shows the execution time of the BBO-DBPA algorithm in seconds and the total operating cost depending on the arrival rate of elective patients.

Table 8. The execution time and optimization results in case 3.

Multiple of Base Case's $\lambda_{3,2,t}$	0.8	0.9	1	1.1	1.2
The execution time	972	980	965	975	973
The total operating cost	20,937	21,602	22,605	23,611	24,833

Furthermore, we investigate the impact of the arrival rate of elective patients on the optimal dynamic policy in Table 9. We can see that the trend of each decision variable is roughly the same as the base case when we change the arrival rate of elective patients. Moreover, the larger the arrival rate of elective patients, the larger the number of general beds retrofitted to buffer beds, and the larger the number of elective patients admitted. That is because the bigger the arrival rate of elective patients, the higher the demand for buffer beds.

Figures 14–17 show the number of beds in each type of ward and the number of patients in the waiting queue under different arrival rates of elective patients, respectively. In Figures 14–17, the blue, red, green, black, and mauve lines show the corresponding indicator values when the number of elective patients ($\lambda_{3,2,t}$) is 0.8, 0.9, 1, 1.1, and 1.2 multiples of the value of $\lambda_{3,2,t}$ in the base case, respectively. As the arrival rate of elective patients increases, the number of beds in isolation wards remains roughly the same, the number of beds in buffer wards increases, the number of beds in general wards decreases, and the number of patients in the waiting queue increases. This is because the bed demand for

COVID-19 patients has been met, and empty isolation beds are retrofitted to buffer beds to receive arriving elective patients.

Table 9. Comparison of optimal decision schemes in case 3.

Decision Variable	Multiple of Base Case's $\lambda_{3,2,t}$	$t=1$	$t=2$	$t=3$	$t=4$	$t=5$	$t=6$	$t=7$	$t=8$	$t=9$	$t=10$	$t=11$	$t=12$	$t=13$	$t=14$
$n_{1,t}$	0.8	1	0	8	24	14	40	44	48	31	16	12	13	0	0
	0.9	2	0	12	22	15	34	46	48	31	17	13	13	0	0
	1	3	0	13	23	16	31	46	48	36	13	15	13	1	0
	1.1	5	0	14	25	12	29	46	48	39	12	15	13	0	0
	1.2	6	0	15	27	11	26	46	48	44	9	15	13	1	0
$n_{2,t}$	0.8	44	40	46	25	8	15	4	22	16	26	16	2	0	0
	0.9	49	47	52	17	13	4	2	22	17	29	7	6	0	2
	1	54	52	55	15	13	2	1	21	19	28	1	3	0	3
	1.1	62	58	46	18	9	3	0	22	21	19	5	1	0	3
	1.2	67	62	46	19	8	3	0	20	23	8	8	1	0	2
$n_{3,t}$	0.8	0	0	0	0	0	0	0	0	0	0	0	0	0	0
	0.9	0	0	0	0	0	0	0	0	0	0	0	0	1	1
	1	0	0	1	0	0	0	0	0	0	0	0	0	0	0
	1.1	0	0	0	0	0	0	0	0	0	0	0	0	0	0
	1.2	0	0	0	0	0	0	0	0	0	0	0	0	0	0
$n_{4,t}$	0.8	0	0	0	0	0	0	0	0	0	0	0	0	2	0
	0.9	0	0	0	0	0	0	0	0	0	0	0	0	5	0
	1	0	0	0	0	0	0	0	0	0	0	0	0	3	0
	1.1	0	0	0	0	0	0	0	0	0	0	0	0	3	0
	1.2	0	0	0	0	0	0	0	0	0	0	0	0	2	0
x_t	0.8	48	41	44	27	17	6	1	0	10	20	20	10	17	16
	0.9	53	47	49	27	23	11	4	4	14	22	21	9	14	18
	1	59	52	52	25	30	18	5	7	21	28	14	9	9	13
	1.1	66	56	45	32	37	27	9	8	24	30	12	8	9	12
	1.2	70	60	44	34	44	38	8	13	28	28	16	5	8	10

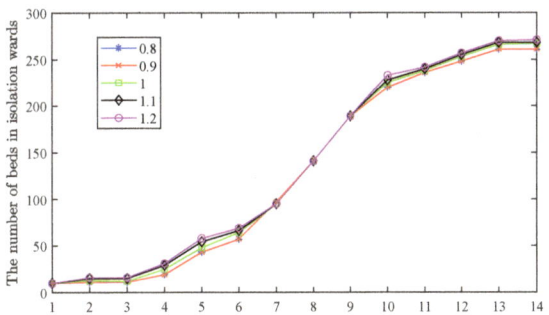

Figure 14. The number of beds in isolation wards in case 3.

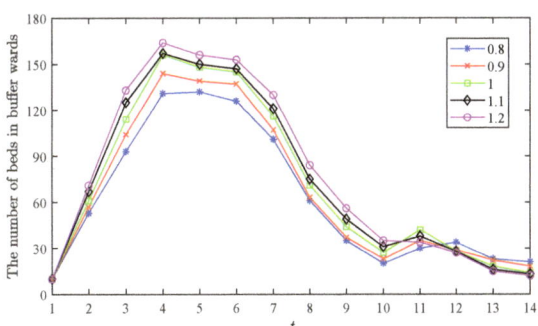

Figure 15. The number of beds in buffer wards in case 3.

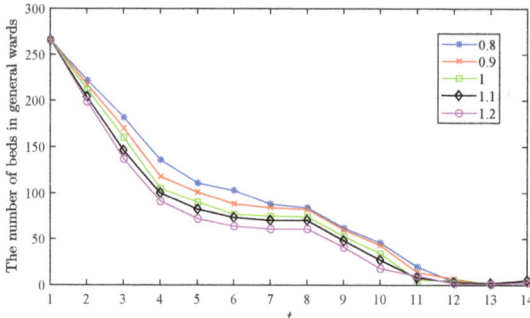

Figure 16. The number of beds in general wards in case 3.

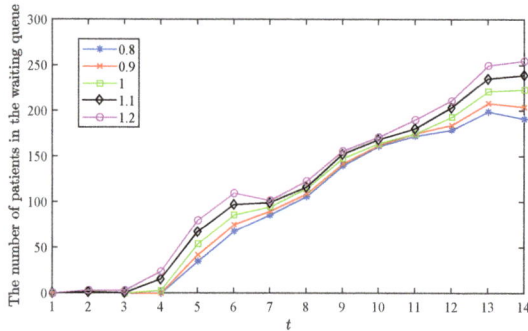

Figure 17. The number of patients in the waiting queue in case 3.

6.3.4. Performance Evaluation with Benchmark Policies

We explore the performance evaluation of the optimal dynamic policy by comparing it with some benchmark policies. Inspired by the different hospital operational management, we propose the following three benchmark policies from the perspective of bed retrofit policy and patient admission control policy: (1) only adopting bed retrofit policy (dynamic bed allocation), (2) only adopting patient admission control policy, and (3) neither adopting bed retrofit policy nor patient admission control policy. For simplicity, we denote the three benchmark policies above as BR policy, AC policy, and nBR–nAC policy, respectively. We define the optimal dynamic policy proposed in this paper (i.e., simultaneously adopting bed retrofit policy and patient admission control policy) as BR–AC policy.

These benchmark policies have data settings that are consistent with the base case to guarantee fairness. Obviously, some parameters are not available under a specific policy. Our objective is to measure the total operating cost in four different dynamic policies.

Figure 18 shows the total operating cost under the four different policies. We can see that the BR–AC policy and BR policy are always better than the AC policy and the nBR–nAC policy. The reason is that the surge of COVID-19 patients and those requiring observation leads to an elevated demand for isolation beds and buffer beds. Thus adopting the bed retrofit policy can significantly reduce the total rejection cost for COVID-19 patients and the total waiting cost for elective patients, thereby significantly reducing the total operating cost of the hospital.

It also shows that the BR–AC policy always performs better than the BR policy. The reason is that based on using the bed retrofit policy and adopting the patient admission control policy can delay some treatment of elective patients and reserve some empty beds for emergency and COVID-19 patients who arrive in the future through the bed retrofit policy. Intuitively, the difference in the total operating cost between the AC policy and the nBR–nAC policy is slight as the total number of beds increases.

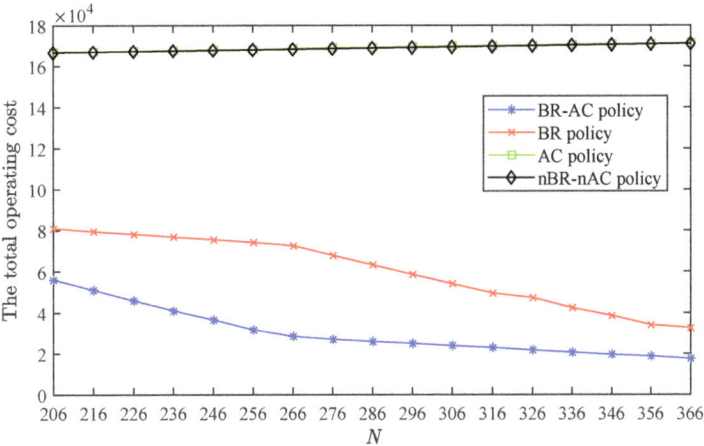

Figure 18. The total operating cost under four different policies.

We also find that the total operating cost under the AC policy and the nBR–nAC policy increase as N increases. In contrast, the total operating cost under the BR–AC policy and BR policy decreases as N increases. That is because our experimental setup is to add beds to the general wards. Thus the more general beds there are, the higher the empty cost the hospital has, thereby increasing the total operating cost. However, the BR–AC and BR policies can significantly reduce the total rejection cost for COVID-19 patients and the total waiting cost for elective patients. Moreover, the more general beds there are, the lower the hospital's total operating cost.

7. Conclusions and Future Research

We introduce a new problem of dynamic bed allocation and patient admission control for hospitals with three different types of wards and three kinds of patients during pandemics. In addition to isolation wards for COVID-19 patients and general wards for non-COVID-19 patients, we consider buffer wards for at-risk-of-COVID-19 patients to prevent nosocomial virus transmission further. To solve this problem, we formulate a MIP model to minimize the total operating cost of the hospital. By using the proposed BBO-DBPA algorithm, we find the approximate optimal solution. Through the analysis of numerical experiments, we discuss how the dynamic bed policy and patient admission control can effectively reduce the total operating cost of hospitals during the pandemic. In addition, we evaluate the performance of the optimal policy by comparing it with some benchmark policies. We conclude that when the admission control policy is used together with the dynamic bed policy, the total operating cost of the hospital is significantly reduced. Although our work is motivated by healthcare operations management under pandemics, our method and insights can also be applied to other service operations requiring screening and being assigned to different designated departments.

In future research, the proposed method could be extended to consider resource extension by adding additional medical staff and critical equipment or providing new suitable beds for hospitals and resource exchange among different hospitals. We can further study hospital resource allocation and patient admission control optimization by using the data-driven response to COVID-19. Note that intelligent medical care with the application of AI technology is an important direction for healthcare operations. Our future study will discuss the dynamic allocation of medical resources in hospitals with buffer wards based on machine learning technology.

Author Contributions: F.Y.: Conceptualization, Supervision, Methodology, Formal analysis, Writing—review & editing, Validation, Funding acquisition. C.W.: Methodology, Data curation, Investigation, Formal analysis, Software, Writing—original draft. Q.-L.L.: Investigation, Supervision, Writing—review & editing, Funding acquisition. All authors have read and agreed to the published version of the manuscript.

Funding: This work is sponsored by the National Natural Science Foundation of China under Grants 72202010, 71932002, 71671158, and the China Postdoctoral Science Foundation (2022M710275).

Data Availability Statement: The data of Appendix A1, A2, and A3 included in the current study has been uploaded to the database of Zenodo (https://doi.org/10.5281/zenodo.7107022).

Conflicts of Interest: The authors declare no conflict of interest.

Abbreviations

The following abbreviations are used in this manuscript:

COVID-19	Corona Virus Disease 2019
MIP	mixed-integer programming
BBO	biogeography-based optimization
BBO-DBPA	biogeography-based optimization for dynamic bed and patient admission

References

1. Yang, F.; Jiang, Y.; Tang, Z. Optimal admission control under premature discharge decisions for operational effectiveness. *Int. Trans. Oper. Res.* **2023**, *30*, 99–125. [CrossRef]
2. Huh, K.; Shin, H.S.; Peck, K.R. Emergent strategies for the next phase of COVID-19. *Infect. Chemother.* **2020**, *52*, 105. [CrossRef]
3. Shaheen, S.; Awwad, O.; Shokry, K.; Abdel-Hamid, M.; El-Etriby, A.; Hasan-Ali, H.; Shawky, I.; Magdy, A.; Nasr, G.; Kabil, H.; et al. Rapid guide to the management of cardiac patients during the COVID-19 pandemic in Egypt: "A position statement of the Egyptian Society of Cardiology". *Egypt. Heart J.* **2020**, *72*, 1–9.
4. Wee, L.E.; Conceicao, E.P.; Sim, X.Y.; Aung, M.K.; Tan, K.Y.; Wong, H.M.; Wijaya, L.; Tan, B.H.; Ling, M.L.; Venkatachalam, I. Minimizing intra-hospital transmission of COVID-19: The role of social distancing. *J. Hosp. Infect.* **2020**, *105*, 113–115. [CrossRef]
5. Asperges, E.; Novati, S.; Muzzi, A.; Biscarini, S.; Sciarra, M.; Lupi, M.; Sambo, M.; Gallazzi, I.; Peverini, M.; Lago, P.; et al. Rapid response to COVID-19 outbreak in Northern Italy: How to convert a classic infectious disease ward into a COVID-19 response centre. *J. Hosp. Infect.* **2020**, *105*, 477–479. [CrossRef]
6. Wee, L.E.I.; Sim, X.Y.J.; Conceicao, E.P.; Aung, M.K.; Tan, K.Y.; Ko, K.K.K.; Wong, H.M.; Wijaya, L.; Tan, B.H.; Venkatachalam, I.; et al. Containing COVID-19 outside the isolation ward: The impact of an infection control bundle on environmental contamination and transmission in a cohorted general ward. *Am. J. Infect. Control* **2020**, *48*, 1056–1061. [CrossRef] [PubMed]
7. He, H.; Jiarui, F.; Minghuan, G.; Ling, Y.; Shaohua, C.; Zhongxiang, C.; Xuan, S.; Yujia, C.; Hesheng, W.; Zongkui, M.; et al. Establishment and practice of "dual-triage and double-buffering" model in the management of COVID-19 in large comprehensive hospitals. *Chin. Hosp. Manag.* **2020**, *40*, 53–55. (In Chinese)
8. Wen, X.; Li, Y. Anesthesia procedure of emergency operation for patients with suspected or confirmed COVID-19. *Surg. Infect.* **2020**, *21*, 299. [CrossRef]
9. Heins, J.; Schoenfelder, J.; Heider, S.; Heller, A.R.; Brunner, J.O. A scalable forecasting framework to predict COVID-19 hospital bed occupancy. *INFORMS J. Appl. Anal.* **2022**, *52*, 508–523. [CrossRef]
10. Liu, M.; Cheng, S.Z.; Xu, K.W.; Yang, Y.; Zhu, Q.T.; Zhang, H.; Yang, D.Y.; Cheng, S.Y.; Xiao, H.; Wang, J.W.; et al. Use of personal protective equipment against coronavirus disease 2019 by healthcare professionals in Wuhan, China: Cross sectional study. *BMJ* **2020**, *369*, m2195. [CrossRef]
11. Hu, X.Y.; Yang, Q.X.; Xiao, C.Q.; Quan, L.L.; Chen, D.Y. Establishment and operation of buffer quarantine area in designated hospital during the pandemic of COVID-19. *Basic Clin. Med.* **2020**, *40*, 746. (In Chinese)
12. Hu, X.; Ma, X.; Hu, Y. Exploration and practice of setting up buffer wards in general hospitals in non-epidemic areas. *Chin. Hosp.* **2021**, *25*, 91–93.
13. Liu, R.; Xu, J.; Liu, Y. Dynamic patient admission control with time-varying and uncertain demands in Covid-19 pandemic. *IEEE Trans. Autom. Sci. Eng.* **2021**, *19*, 620–631. [CrossRef]
14. Pishnamazzadeh, M.; Sepehri, M.M.; Panahi, A.; Moodi, P. Reallocation of unoccupied beds among requesting wards. *J. Ambient. Intell. Humaniz. Comput.* **2021**, *12*, 1449–1469. [CrossRef]
15. Lei, X.; Na, L.; Xin, Y.; Fan, M. A mixed integer programming model for bed planning considering stochastic length of stay. In Proceedings of the 2014 IEEE International Conference on Automation Science and Engineering (CASE), New Taipei, Taiwan, 18–22 August 2014; pp. 1069–1074. [CrossRef]
16. Taramasco, C.; Olivares, R.; Munoz, R.; Soto, R.; Villar, M.; de Albuquerque, V.H. The patient bed assignment problem solved by autonomous bat algorithm. *Appl. Soft Comput.* **2012**, *81*, 105484. [CrossRef]

17. Bachouch, R.B.; Guinet, A.; Hajri-Gabouj, S. An integer linear model for hospital bed planning. *Int. J. Prod. Econ.* **2012**, *140*, 833–843. [CrossRef]
18. Wang, X.; Gong, X.; Geng, N.; Jiang, Z.; Zhou, L. Metamodel-based simulation optimization for bed allocation. *Int. J. Prod. Res.* **2020**, *58*, 6315–6335. [CrossRef]
19. Luo, L.; Li, J.; Xu, X.; Shen, W.; Xiao, L. A data-driven hybrid three-stage framework for hospital bed allocation: A case study in a large tertiary hospital in China. *Comput. Math. Methods Med.* **2019**, *2019*, 7370231. [CrossRef]
20. Zhou, L.; Geng, N.; Jiang, Z.; Wang, X. Multi-objective capacity allocation of hospital wards combining revenue and equity. *Omega* **2018**, *81*, 220–233. [CrossRef]
21. Sitepu, S.; Mawengkang, H.; Husein, I. Optimization model for capacity management and bed scheduling for hospital. *IOP Conf. Ser. Mater. Sci. Eng.* **2018**, *300*, 012016. [CrossRef]
22. Ma, X.; Zhao, X.; Guo, P. Cope with the COVID-19 pandemic: Dynamic bed allocation and patient subsidization in a public healthcare system. *Int. J. Prod. Econ.* **2022**, *243*, 108320. [CrossRef] [PubMed]
23. Demeester, P.; De Causmaecker, P.; Vanden Berghe, G. Applying a local search algorithm to automatically assign patients to beds. In Proceedings of the 22nd Conference on Quantitative Methods for Decision Making (ORBEL 22), Brussels, Belgium, 1–18 January 2008.
24. Demeester, P.; Souffriau, W.; De Causmaecker, P.; Berghe, G.V. A hybrid tabu search algorithm for automatically assigning patients to beds. *Artif. Intell. Med.* **2010**, *48*, 61–70. [CrossRef]
25. Bilgin, B.; Demeester, P.; Misir, M. One hyper-heuristic approach to two timetabling problems in health care. *J. Heuristics* **2012**, *18*, 401–434. [CrossRef]
26. Range, T.M.; Lusby, R.M.; Larsen, J. A column generation approach for solving the patient admission scheduling problem. *Eur. J. Oper. Res.* **2014**, *235*, 252–264. [CrossRef]
27. Hammouri, A.I.; Alrifai, B. Investigating biogeography based optimization for patient admission scheduling problems. *J. Theor. Appl. Inf. Technol.* **2014**, *70*, 413–421.
28. Hammouri, A.I. A modified biogeography-based optimization algorithm with guided bed selection mechanism for patient admission scheduling problems. *J. King Saud Univ.-Comput. Inf. Sci.* **2022**, *34*, 871–879. [CrossRef]
29. Turhan, A.M.; Bilgen, B. Mixed integer programming based heuristics for the patient admission scheduling problem. *Comput. Oper. Res.* **2017**, *80*, 38–49. [CrossRef]
30. Bastos, L.S.; Marchesi, J.F.; Hamacher, S.; Fleck, J.L. A mixed integer programming approach to the patient admission scheduling problem. *Eur. J. Oper. Res.* **2019**, *273*, 831–840. [CrossRef]
31. Ceschia, S.; Schaerf, A. Modeling and solving the dynamic patient admission scheduling problem under uncertainty. *Artif. Intell. Med.* **2012**, *56*, 199–205. [CrossRef]
32. Bolaji, A.L.; Bamigbola, A.F.; Shola, P.B. Late acceptance hill climbing algorithm for solving patient admission scheduling problem. *Knowl.-Based Syst.* **2018**, *145*, 197–206. [CrossRef]
33. Zhu, Y.H.; Toffolo, T.A.; Vancroonenburg, W.; Berghe, G.V. Compatibility of short and long term objectives for dynamic patient admission scheduling. *Comput. Oper. Res.* **2019**, *104*, 98–112. [CrossRef]
34. Heydar, M.; O'Reilly, M.M.; Trainer, E.; Fackrell, M.; Taylor, P.G.; Tirdad, A. A stochastic model for the patient-bed assignment problem with random arrivals and departures. *Ann. Oper. Res.* **2022**, *315*, 813–845. [CrossRef]
35. Engl, T.; Harper, P.; Crosby, T.; Gartner, D.; Arruda, E.F.; Foley, K.; Williamson, I. Modelling lung cancer diagnostic pathways using discrete event simulation. *J. Simul.* **2021**, *2021*, 1–11. [CrossRef]
36. van den Broek d'Obrenan, A.; Ridder, A.; Roubos, D.; Stougie, L. Minimizing bed occupancy variance by scheduling patients under uncertainty. *Eur. J. Oper. Res.* **2020**, *286*, 336–349. [CrossRef]
37. Simon D. Biogeography-based optimization. *IEEE Trans. Evol. Comput.* **2008**, *12*, 702–713. [CrossRef]
38. Pollock, A.M.; Lancaster, J. Asymptomatic transmission of COVID-19. *BMJ* **2020**, *371*, m4851. [CrossRef]
39. Lauer, S.A.; Grantz, K.H.; Bi, Q.; Jones, F.K.; Zheng, Q.; Meredith, H.R.; Azman, A.S.; Reich, N.G.; Lessler, J. The incubation period of coronavirus disease 2019 (COVID-19) from publicly reported confirmed cases: Estimation and application. *Ann. Intern. Med.* **2020**, *172*, 577–582. [CrossRef]
40. Guan, W.J.; Ni, Z.Y.; Hu, Y.; Liang, W.H.; Ou, C.Q.; He, J.X.; Liu, L.; Shan, H.; Lei, C.L.; Hui, D.S. Clinical characteristics of coronavirus disease 2019 in China. *N. Engl. J. Med.* **2020**, *382*, 1708–1720. [CrossRef]
41. Zhao, S.; Musa, S.S.; Lin, Q.; Ran, J.; Yang, G.; Wang, W.; Lou, Y.; Yang, L.; Gao, D.; He, D.; et al. Estimating the unreported number of novel coronavirus (2019-nCoV) cases in China in the first half of January 2020: A data-driven modelling analysis of the early outbreak. *J. Clin. Med.* **2020**, *9*, 388. [CrossRef]

Disclaimer/Publisher's Note: The statements, opinions and data contained in all publications are solely those of the individual author(s) and contributor(s) and not of MDPI and/or the editor(s). MDPI and/or the editor(s) disclaim responsibility for any injury to people or property resulting from any ideas, methods, instructions or products referred to in the content.

Article

Defects Classification of Hydro Generators in Indonesia by Phase-Resolved Partial Discharge

Chun-Yao Lee [1,*], Nando Purba [2] and Guang-Lin Zhuo [1]

1. Department of Electrical Engineering, Chung Yuan Christian University, Taoyuan 320314, Taiwan
2. Indonesia Asahan Aluminum Co., Ltd., Pintu Pohan Merant, Toba 22384, Indonesia
* Correspondence: cyl@cycu.edu.tw; Tel.: +886-3-2654827

Abstract: This paper proposed a phase-resolved partial discharge (PRPD) shape method to classify types of defect generator units by using offline partial discharge (PD) measurement instruments. In this paper, the experimental measurement was applied to two generators in the Inalum hydropower plant, located in North Sumatera, Indonesia. The recorded PRPD using the instrument MPD600 can illustrate the PRPD patterns of generator defects. The proposed PRPD shape method is used to mark auxiliary lines on the PRPD patterns. Moreover, four types of defects refer to the IEC 60034-27 standard, which are microvoid (S1), delamination tape layer (S2), slot defect (S3), and internal delamination (S4) and are used to classify the defect types of the generators. The results show that the proposed method performs well to classify types of defect generator units.

Keywords: partial discharge (PD); phase-resolved PD (PRPD); rotating machine; stator coil

MSC: 35Q68

1. Introduction

Partial discharge (PD) phenomena are produced from the concentration of the local electrical stresses in electrical insulation [1–3]. PD activity may deploy to failure resulting in serious damage. Eventually, it would undermine the essential elements of the power network [4]. Therefore, it is compulsory to check, identify, and monitor the PD activity of the main rotating machine, motors, or generators [5,6]. Detection, measurement, and interpretation of PD are great challenges due to the large variety and complexity of PD signals [7–9]. However, PD measurements are still a widely accepted method for insulation diagnosis, and they are specified for the type, routine, and on-site tests for the highest voltage (HV) assets [10,11].

Generally, PD can be developed at locations where the dielectric properties of insulating materials are inhomogeneous. The local electric field strength may be enhanced in such locations [12]. This may lead to a local partial breakdown regarding local electrical overstressing. This partial breakdown does not result in the total breakdown of the insulation system [13]. Although the stator winding insulation system in HV machines normally has some PD activity, it is inherently resistant to PD regarding the inorganic mica components [14]. The significance of PD in these machines generally can be said as a symptom of insulation deficiencies, such as manufacturing problems or in-service deterioration, that finally become a direct cause of failure [15]. In conclusion, PD occurrences in machines may directly damage the insulation, hence influencing the aging process, which depends on the machine processes [16]. The failure time may not correlate with the PD levels, but we are significantly looking at other factors, e.g., site operating temperature, condition of the wedging, level of contamination, etc. [17].

The developments of digital technology, both for the equipment and software, have created innovative solutions for improving the sensitivity, significance, and reproducibility of power systems. For example, Li et al. developed an adaptive virtual synchronous

generator (VSG) controller. This controller can implement optimal control policies in a no-expert or model-free manner [18]. Zhang et al. proposed an event-triggered decentralized hybrid control scheme for the economic cost of an integrated energy system (IES) composed by a cluster of energy hubs (EHs) [19]. Gopinath et al. demonstrated a hybrid method for predicting the insulation state of stator windings using an artificial neural network (ANN) and an optimization algorithm [20]. Nair et al. successfully found slot discharges at low frequencies, which, in practice, can significantly reduce the size and cost of test sources [21]. The developments are, by far, exceeding the capabilities of old analog systems to make it easier both for analyzing and interpreting insulation conditions in rotating machines [22].

PD measurement from stator coil windings can be conducted in two ways [23]—(1) online measurement [24]: the rotating machine is normally operated and connected to the power system; and (2) offline measurement [25]: the stator winding is separated from the power system by giving a power supply to energize the winding during the standstill of the machine.

Indonesia Asahan Aluminum Co. Ltd, hereinafter called Inalum, is an aluminum company in Indonesia, which has two hydropower stations that use water flow from the Asahan River to produce electricity for the Inalum Smelting Plant. One of the power stations is called Siguragura Power (SGP) with a capacity of 4×71.5 MW with a voltage of 11 kV, and another one is called Tangga Power (TNP) with a capacity of 4×79.2 MW with a voltage of 11 kV; this together is called the Inalum Power Plant (IPP), as shown in Figure 1 [26]. The routine maintenance of the main machines in the IPP has been properly conducted to keep power without any stoppage to fulfill the load demand at the smelting plant, i.e., maintenance of the water turbine, generator, and equipment.

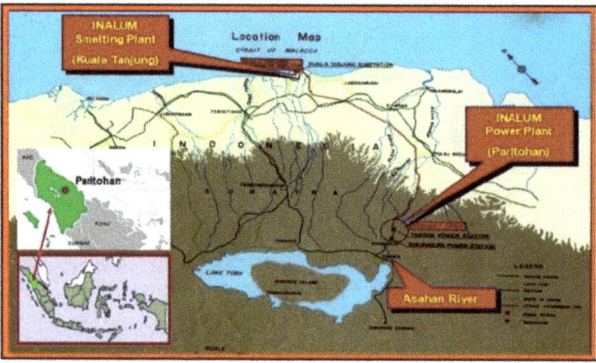

Figure 1. Location of Inalum Hydropower Plant, Paritohan, North Sumatera, Indonesia.

PD measurement at the generator intends to assess the stator coil insulation system condition [27]. This PD measurement is applied for the first time to Inalum's generator since its operation in 1983, 37 years ago, to assess the stator coil of generator TNP units 2 and 3. Furthermore, the intention of this paper was to compare the PD result of two rotating machines with similar ratings and designs [28].

The paper is organized as follows: PD measurement for rotating machines is discussed in Section 2. PD measurement connection is presented in Section 3. Case studies of partial discharge measurement are discussed in Section 4. Discussion is provided in Section 5, and the conclusions are given in Section 6.

2. Partial Discharge Measurement for Rotating Machines

In relation to the operating lifetime, the rotating HV machines continuously and periodically face thermal, electrical, ambient, and mechanical stress. Conseil International des Grands Reseaux Electriques (CIGRE), also called the International Council on Large Electric System, conducted an interesting and important statistic by observing hydro generators. CIGRE observed 1199 units of generators, then recorded and analyzed

69 incidents, and found that 56% of the failed machines are related to insulation damage. The top 3 root causes leading to insulation damage are aging (31%), contamination of winding (25%), and internal PD (22%). The others are shown in Table 1 [29].

Table 1. Root cause of insulation damage.

Root Cause of Insulation Damage	Percentage of Failures (%)
Aging	31
Contamination of winding	25
Internal PD	22
Loosing of bars	10
Thermal cycling of overloading	7
Defective corona protection	3
Overvoltage	2

Some machines have been designed to be able to withstand an appreciable level of discharge without significantly affecting the insulation properties based on the mica–epoxy insulation system. For instance, the internal discharge in small volumes and some other PD activities are even strongly detrimental to the insulation system. Moreover, the PD in HV can be used to detect the insulation aging and evaluate the insulation condition [30].

A specific level of PD is allowed to occur in the stator insulation of a large HV rotating machine. Admittedly, degradation of stator insulation always increases PD activity, particularly in phase winding. It means that PD events represent certain symptoms or even causes of winding insulation defects, depending on their location of occurrence on the winding [31].

PD measurement can identify stator coils that have insulation problems and evaluate the condition of stator coil insulation systems. The rotating machines that do not have specific acceptable PD levels are unusual among high-voltage equipment [32] because the mica-based insulation can tolerate the large magnitudes and huge difference in acceptable magnitude to different types of PD sources in the stator insulation. PD measurement has been used for many years as a powerful tool to detect and interpret the signs of locally confined insulation defects.

The factors that affect the insulation such as corona can be described based on the research of hydro generator damage samplings. At least, the data give a hint that the original design of the winding has changed, e.g., by aging. Hence, the main challenge in PD measurement is to classify the PD events to diagnose a damaged one. A sensitive and selective PD measurement is suitable to discover a potential defect in stator insulation before failure. Therefore, periodical PD measurement is expected to provide warning for appropriate decisions and actions to minimize the possibility of risk failure in service. Many methods are available to detect the PD activity for motors and generators. This paper used MPD600 and its acquisition unit as the tool to measure, collect, and analyze the PD data from the generators.

PD measurement detects most, but not all, of the common manufacturing and deterioration problems in the form-wound stator windings, including the following [33]:

(1) Overheating or deterioration of thermal cycling in the long term;
(2) Poor impregnation of the epoxy inside;
(3) Improper coating of the semiconductive;
(4) Insufficient spacing between coils in the end-winding area;
(5) Looseness of coils in the slot;
(6) Contamination of winding by dust, dirty oil, moisture, etc.;
(7) Cycling problems of the load;
(8) Improper electrical connections.

Normally, a PD pattern is viewed as a PD distribution map, in which the specific PD quantity is correlated in a scatter plot, in obtaining information on the PD activity and its sources. Usually, the PD distribution is in two dimensions for visualization. A PD pattern consists of three items, ϕ, q, and n. The pattern is recommended to identify the causes of PD in the stator winding insulation, where ϕ is the phase of occurrence, q is the PD magnitude, and n is the frequency of PD occurrence. The frequency of PD occurrence normally is put in the scatter plot within each phase-magnitude window, and it should be displayed by a suitable color type whose scale can be visualized on the right side of the plot. The PD measurement shows the three-item ϕ-q-n pattern as the output of the phase-resolved partial discharge (PRPD) pattern, which sometimes is called the fingerprint ϕ-q-n diagram. In addition, PD characteristics can be displayed in bipolar patterns to show the characteristic of PD (symmetrical or asymmetrical) by displaying the PD events during interval time recording versus discharge magnitude [34].

2.1. Definitions

The PD activity in the generator usually occurs in the stator coils. The stator coils have many parts protecting the core winding. This paper did not include every type of fault, e.g., mechanical faults such as broken strands. The assembly of a stator coil is simplified with the aim to show the PD detected location found in the stator coil, as shown in Figure 2. The simplified signs marked as S1 are microvoids, S2 is the delamination of tape layers, S3 is the slot discharge-semiconductive paint abrasion, and S4 is the delamination of winding from the main insulation of the conductor. The purpose of signs S1, S2, S3, and S4 is to make the recognition and interpretation of PRPD patterns easier [35].

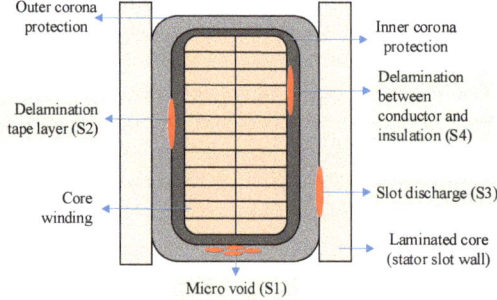

Figure 2. Stator coil part and typical PD faults.

Table 2 refers to the nature of PD in rotating machines and displays some basic ideas regarding the risk associated with some major PD sources. The risk assessment is stated based on experience with modern resin-impregnated mica tape-based HV insulation systems and may vary depending on the insulation material, surface conditions, location of the PD source, etc. [36].

PD parameters, such as apparent charge, pulse repetition rate, current discharge, etc., should be recorded at each voltage as stated and defined in the standard and the PRPD diagram; the so-called fingerprints ought to be recorded as well. Limitations for the meaning of apparent charge levels are not defined in any standard. Evaluation for the rotating machines is a more complex procedure based on several results, such as the number of measured PD magnitudes, PRPD pattern, Q_{Peak}, etc. The condition of the background environment is important for evaluation.

The PD pulse repetition rate, n (kPDs/s), is the ratio between the total number of PD recorded in the interval time selected and the duration of this certain time interval, t [16]. Q_{IEC}, which is expressed in pC or nC, is an apparent charge, which is measured according to the IEC standard, sometimes called Q of an individual PD. An apparent charge is not equal to the amount of charge locally involved at the site of discharge and cannot be directly measured [23].

Table 2. Basic risk assessment of PD fault.

PD Source	Risk	Remarks
Microvoid (S1)	Low	Does not indicate aging factors, whereas normal circumstances do not lead to remarkable aging.
Delamination tape layer (S2)	High	Internal delamination or tape layer commonly results from overheating and extreme mechanical forces, which can lead to separation of large areas of these layers.
Slot discharge (S3)	High	Generated by poor, missing, contact between field-grading layer and stator slot wall.
Delamination between conductors and insulation (S4)	High	Commonly results from overheating and extreme mechanical forces, which can lead to separation of large areas of these layers.

The number of charges can be measured as in (1) for testing and measuring the void of the test object.

$$Q = \Delta V_1 \times C_F = \int_{t_0}^{t_m} i(t)dt \tag{1}$$

where Q is the apparent charge, ΔV_1 is the instantaneous applied voltage to the test object, C_F is the capacitance inside the void of the test object, t_0 is the starting time, t_m is the completion time, and m is the number of the final pulse during t.

Q_{Peak} is the PD magnitude of the largest absolute discharge of any PD event seen during the evaluation interval. Q_{Avg} is the average Q_{IEC} value during the evaluation interval. I_{Dis} is the average discharge current over the evaluation interval. The statistical computation of MPD600 shows the I_{Dis} value, which refers to the IEC standard [6], by adopting the formula as shown in (2).

$$I_{Dis} = \frac{Q_1 + Q_2 + \ldots + Q_m}{t_m - t_0} = \sum_{j=1}^{m} \frac{Q_j}{t_m - t_0} \tag{2}$$

where I_{Dis} is the average discharge current; and Q_1, Q_2, until Q_m are the apparent charges, transferred in PD pulse 1 through m [4].

P_{Dis} is the average discharge power, which is discharge current times instantaneous AC voltage over the evaluation interval. The statistical PRPD pattern result of MPD600 shows the values of P_{Dis} and D as calculated from the formulas shown in (3) and (4), respectively.

$$P_{Dis} = \frac{1}{t}(Q_1 V_1 + Q_2 V_2 + \ldots + Q_i V_i) = (1/t)\sum_{i=1}^{m} Q_i V \tag{3}$$

$$D = 1/t(Q_1^2 + Q_2^2 + \ldots + Q_m^2) \tag{4}$$

where P_{Dis} is the discharge power, t is the time period, Q_i is the magnitude of the i-th pulse in terms of the charge transfer at the system terminals, and V_i is the instantaneous value of the applied test voltage in volts at which the i-th pulse happens. D is the quadratic rate over the evaluation interval of the sum of the individual discharge magnitudes [5]. The quadratic rate is expressed as coulombs square per second.

2.2. PRPD Pattern of Microvoids (S1)

Microvoid discharge refers to the internal discharges that occur within the insulation ground wall, inside small voids. Internal activity always occurs on HV machines, for example, measured at 13.8 kV generators under normal operating conditions [6]. During offline measurement, it is normal that the activity appears at the lowest voltage, except in the presence of severe problems such as slot discharge activity or severe damage of the stress-grading paint. Microvoid activity is characterized by symmetry in the maximum amplitude and in the number of discharge pulses when the activity occurring in both voltage half-cycles is compared. Figure 3 shows a typical PRPD pattern of the microvoid activity. In addition, this microvoid pattern shows the symmetry of the positive discharges, occurring during the negative cycle of the voltage, and the negative discharges, occurring during the positive cycle of the voltage, which has long been recognized as a characteristic of microvoid discharges [28].

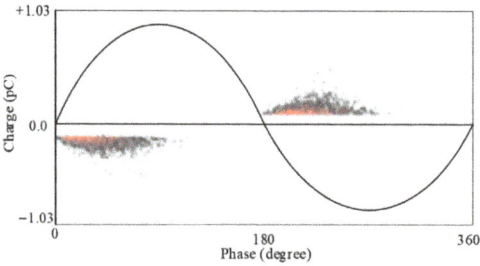

Figure 3. PRPD pattern of microvoid measured on stator bar (S1).

2.3. PRPD Pattern of Delamination Tape Layer (S2)

Delamination discharge is the discharge that occurs between conductors and an insulation layer generated within air or gas filled in the longitudinal direction, which is embedded between the main insulation and field-grading material [6].

This phenomenon is often created by overheating or extreme mechanical forces that lead to the separation of large areas between two layers. Although a distinctive asymmetry was recorded for this defect, it disappeared after a short exposure time to HV as shown in Figure 4.

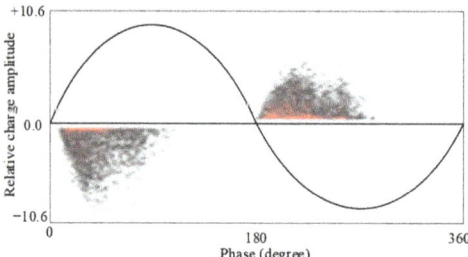

Figure 4. PRPD pattern of delamination tape layers (S2).

The asymmetrical PRPD pattern, followed by a sickle or bow shape as shown in Figure 5, is an important attribute for the PRPD analysis of delamination discharges. In many cases, the sickle shapes stick out of bigger symmetrical inner microvoids [6].

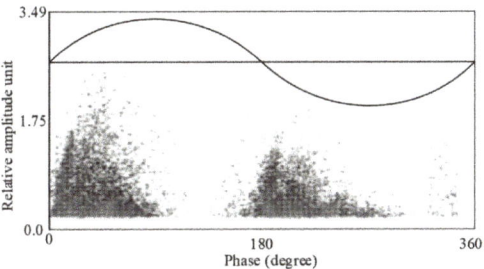

Figure 5. Another PRPD pattern of delamination tape layers (S2).

2.4. PRPD Pattern of Slot Defect (S3)

In the presence of slot discharge, the PRPD pattern is completely different from what is seen in the internal PD. A typical PRPD pattern that resulted from slot discharges exists in the air gap between the magnetic core and the side of stator bars [28] as shown in Figure 6. The occurrence of slot discharge activity obviously increases the risk of in-service failure.

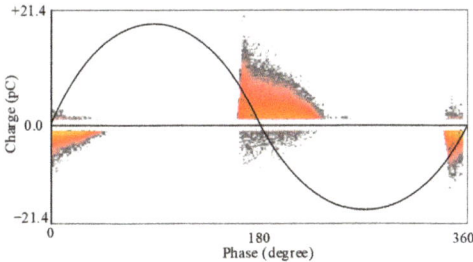

Figure 6. PRPD pattern of slot discharge (S3).

This activity manifested a PRPD pattern stated as slot discharge at the slot area of the stator coil. It can break the insulation gap of the stator. In comparison with the internal PD, the PRPD pattern results from an asymmetrical shape with a magnitude of charges at the negative cycle that is larger than the positive cycle, combined with a triangular shape [6,28]. Moreover, another feature of this PRPD pattern is typical of slot discharge marked with a steep edge in front of a triangular pattern.

2.5. PRPD Pattern of Internal Delamination Discharge (S4)

Internal delamination is generated within air or gas filled in a longitudinal direction that is embedded within the main insulation. This activity often results from overheating of the main insulation or extreme mechanical force that leads to the separation of large areas between insulation layers. The delamination tape layer pattern is an asymmetric pattern with a higher PD reading in the negative half-wave in the AC voltage as shown in Figure 7. The delamination reduces thermal conductivity and accelerates aging [23,28].

Large voids potentially develop over a large surface resulting in discharges of relatively high energy, which may significantly attack the insulation. Particularly, delamination reduces the thermal conductivity of the insulation, which might lead to accelerated aging or even a thermal runaway. Thus, delamination needs deep attention when PD activity is being assessed [6].

Delamination is located between copper strands and the ground-wall insulation found on the generator bars with a resin-rich mica–epoxy insulation system. This delamination is associated with the resin decomposition area that was caused by the PD activity in this delamination [36]. The appearance of the decomposed resin can be figured as a white powder. Specifically, the resin was found totally decomposed at the edges.

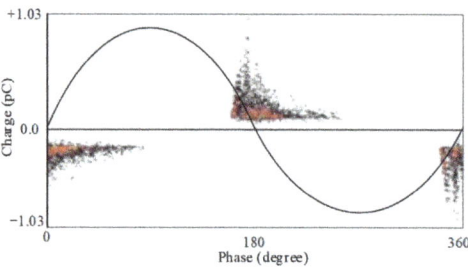

Figure 7. PRPD pattern at internal delamination discharges (S4).

3. Partial Discharge Measurement Connection

The PD measurement in this paper was conducted in offline condition. Firstly, both generators were completely shut down and separated from the system before measurement (see Figure 8a). After the generators were completely shut down, the HV controller and its HV-source 12 kV transformer were set up and connected to a compensating reactor that needed the test source to deliver the impedance part of the current (see Figure 8b,c). The test voltage was gradually stepped up by this HV controller. Then the output of the HV controller was connected to all three HV phase terminals R, S, and T of the generator as the test object was synchronously performed, and the channel had a digital band-pass filter [35] (see Figure 8d).

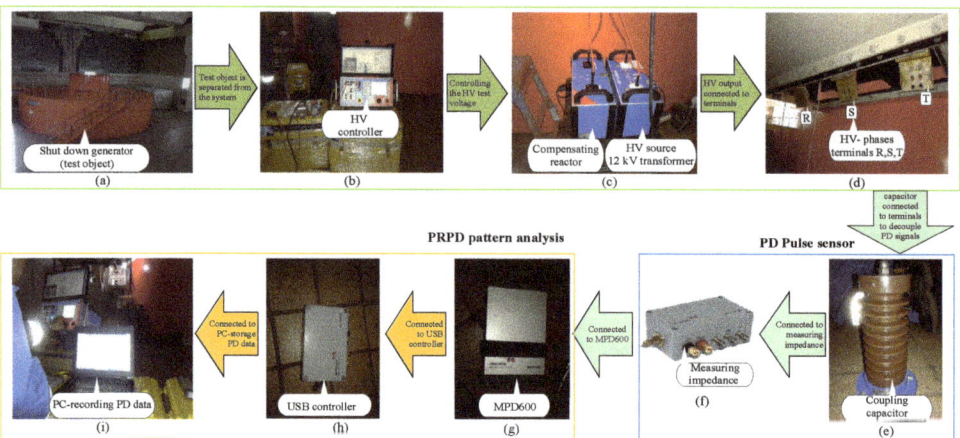

Figure 8. PD measurement instrument and equipment connection to the generator as test object. (**a**) Test object. (**b**) HV controller. (**c**) Compensating reactor and transformer. (**d**) Three phases' terminals. (**e**) Coupling capacitor. (**f**) Measuring impedance. (**g**) MPD600. (**h**) USB controller. (**i**) Recording data.

The measurement used a coupling capacitor as the sensor. Coupling capacitor MCC124 was used as the mounted sensor within the generator's terminals R, S, and T to decouple the PD signal and connected to measuring impedance (see Figure 8e). The sensor was easily integrated into the old machine as a test object after being separated from the power system. The MPD600 PD acquisition unit completely encapsulated components without any control element. The impedance was measured as the input was connected to MPD600 (see Figure 8f). Then MPD600 was connected to a USB controller. The USB controller and all connected MPD600 units were restarted, and the software continued to perform measurements (see Figure 8g).

The collected data were transmitted to a server via cable providers. A PC received the recording PD data from the acquisition unit MPD600 by using a USB controller (see Figure 8h). PD data were displayed, recorded, and analyzed through a PRPD streamer that had been stored at the PC for every stage of the test voltages (see Figure 8i). The PD measurement equipment connection can be seen as shown in Figure 8.

The principal difference between the various PD measuring systems is the bandwidth. The PD pulses arriving at the terminals have a frequency spectrum characterized by the transmission function of the machine winding. Following IEC 60270, PD measurement systems are defined as a wide band if their bandwidth exceeds 100 kHz [6].

The range of the bandwidth for the PD record is from 100 kHz to 400 kHz, which is the PD measurement instrument specification of MPD600. This setting follows the IEC standard for PD setting measurement [23].

The test circuit instrument requires calibration using the CAL542D charge calibrator by 10 nC by a calibration factor before performing measurement [5,6]. The aim of the calibration is to compare various influences of the test circuit, e.g., power supply connection, stray capacitance, coupling capacitance, and test object capacitance, by injecting a better value-defined reference at the terminal after the test circuit is completely connected [23].

The lower cutoff frequency should be in the range of dozens of kilohertz following the IEC standards [23]. It should be noted that resonance phenomena that are in the frequency range of the PD measuring device may occur and, therefore, may also influence the PD results depending on the winding design and measurement arrangement used.

4. Case Studies of Partial Discharge Measurement

The PD measurement uses the frequency integration at 250 kHz ± 300 kHz from 100 kHz to 400 kHz referring to the specification of MPD600 to follow the IEC standards [23,35]. The testing voltage for the PD measurement is carried out by gradually injecting the voltage to the test objects, initially from 20%, 40%, 60%, 80%, to 100% of the phase-to-phase voltage 6.35 kV, which is obtained by dividing 11 kV by $\sqrt{3}$ and hereinafter called the U_n [5,23]. The voltage of the test procedure gradually stepped up from 1.27 kV to 6.35 kV including the following stages: 1.27 kV–2.54 kV–3.81 kV–5.08 kV–6.35 kV–5.08 kV –3.81 kV–2.54 kV–1.27 kV, as shown in Figure 9.

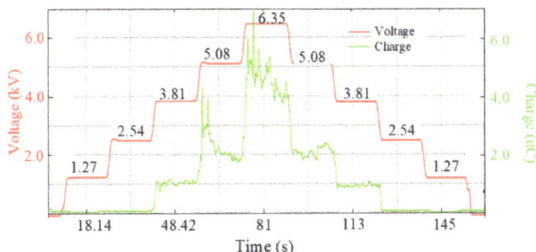

Figure 9. Gradual step-up test voltage for offline PD measurement on rotating machines.

Offline PD measurement was conducted with the system presented above using MPD600 on hydropower generator units 2 and 3 with a capacity of 79.2 MW with a voltage of 11 kV as test objects located in TNP, IPP, North Sumatera, Indonesia. There are four units of generators at TNP as shown in the single-line diagram of TNP in Figure 10 [26].

This paper focused on units 2 and 3 for PD data measurement. The purpose was to assess and compare the stator coil insulation condition by PRPD analysis of the PD level in the stator coil [27]. The main objective of the purpose of the PD measurement is to interpret the result. The PD measurement is a powerful tool for detecting and diagnosing the locally confined insulation defects in rotating machines [35]. The minimum magnitude of the PD quantities that can be measured in a particular test is, in general, limited by disturbances. These can effectively be eliminated by suitable techniques by choosing the appropriate coupling capacitor sensor; additional limits are obtained by the internal noise levels of the measuring instruments and systems, physical dimensions and layout of the test circuit, and values of the test circuit parameters.

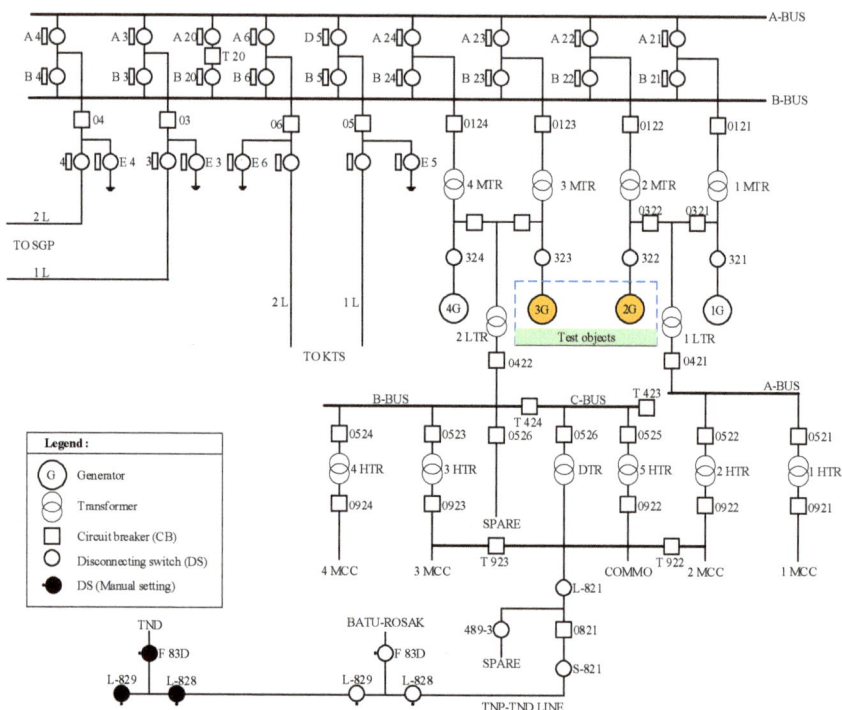

Figure 10. Single-line diagram of TNP, Inalum Power Plant, Indonesia.

Another consideration and limit for the measurement of a minimum PD quantity are set by the capacitance ratio of C_t/C_C and the optimal values for the input impedance of the coupling device and its matching to the measuring instruments used. C_t is the capacitance of the test objects, and C_C is the capacitance of the coupling capacitor. The highest sensitivity would be realized if C_C is greater than C_t; this condition is generally inconvenient to satisfy due to the additional loading of the HV supply. Thus, the nominal value of C_C is limited for the actual tests, but acceptable sensitivity is usually achieved with C_C being about 1 nF or higher [23]. The coupling capacitor as a sensor in this offline PD measurement uses the coupling-capacitor-type MCC124, 24 kV, with the capacitance 1.1 nF and Z_m C542: 30 µF, 0.5 A, with the frequency bandwidth of PD measurement of MPD600 100–400 kHz following the IEC standards. Sometimes, the PD measurement uses a coupling capacitor with a capacitance of 80 pF with reference to the IEEE 1434 standard.

The test objects are connected to the offline PD measurement equipment. The test voltage is increased until reaching the maximum test voltage of 6.35 kV. The PRPD pattern, partial discharge inception voltage (PDIV), partial discharge extinction voltage (PDEV), and the largest repeated occurrences of PD magnitude referred to as Q_{Peak} are the basic results to interpret from any offline PD measurement on the stator, recorded during the interval time of measurement [6]. The values of the PDIV and PDEV are influenced by many constraints, including the rate where the voltage gradually increased as well as the history of the voltage applied in the winding or other components thereof. In most cases of the PD measurement, the PDIV is larger than the PDEV, which is related to the following factors: statistical time lags of the availability of the initial electron, oxidation for the consumption of oxygen, and residual voltage [5,23]. Both the PDIV and PDEV may define the limit of permissible background noise.

The PD detector obtains several important parameters from the PD measurement, such as the PDIV, PDEV, and PD magnitude in pC. The advantages of the PD measurement are given as follows [4]:

(1) Getting the series prediction and an indication of the insulation degradation in advance prior to failure;
(2) Avoiding unexpected in-service failures of the equipment, furthermore, can extend uptime between outages;
(3) Avoiding service that is not important and repairing old equipment by maximizing the operating hours;
(4) Finding a problem and repairing it before it has a chance to fail the equipment;
(5) Finding a problem with new equipment that is still under warranty;
(6) Evaluating the quality of maintenance and repairing whether to rewind it before and after testing;
(7) Comparing the results of similar equipment to decide on maintenance on those with higher levels of PD;
(8) Identifying the root cause of the failure mechanism in the equipment to determine the action prior to an outage;
(9) Improving the overall reliability of the equipment.

4.1. PD Measurement Test Procedures

The PD measurement for generator units 2 and 3 was conducted on 27 January 2016 and that for unit 3 on 28 January 2016. The balance power generation unit is properly regulated during the measurement to fulfill load demand at the smelting plant. These procedures are briefly described as shown in Figure 11 and applied to both generator units 2 and 3 as test objects for the PD measurement. The generators are shut down and separated from the power system network. The HV source test equipment should be well-prepared after the generators are completely stopped. The step procedures of the PD measurement for generator units 2 and 3 are briefly described as follows [35]:

Step (1) Preparing the HV source test equipment (see Figure 11a);
Step (2) Connecting the HV power output to the stator winding (see Figure 11b);
Step (3) Connecting the HV return to the ground (see Figure 11c);
Step (4) Connecting the PD sensor and coupling capacitor to stator winding (see Figure 11d);
Step (5) Connect the output from the PD sensor to the measurement unit (see Figure 11e);
Step (6) Connecting the PD measurement unit to the USB controller using fiber optic cable (see Figure 11e);
Step (7) Connecting the USB controller to the PC for measurement (see Figure 11f);
Step (8) Selecting the test voltage 20% Un (see Figure 11g);
Step (9) Operating the HV output button, making sure to observe safety rules (see Figure 11g);
Step (10) Recording the test voltage and PD stream as the PRPD output (see Figure 11h);
Step (11) Discharging the test object using the ground device after finishing the test (see Figure 11i);
Step (12) Following steps (8) to (12) for the test voltage 40%, 60%, 80%, and 100% Un.

The complete offline PD measurement procedures can be seen as shown in Figure 12. The first step is to completely shut down the generator and prepare the circuit of the PD equipment, and the last step is to record and analyze the PD data and then compare them with the ideal kind of PD defect provided by the standards IEC 60034-27 and IEC 60270.

Figure 11. Test procedures for offline PD measurement on generator units 2 and 3 Inalum hydro generators at TNP. (**a**) HV source test equipment. (**b**) Connecting HV output to stator winding. (**c**) Connecting HV return to the ground. (**d**) Connecting PD sensor capacitor to the stator winding. (**e**) Connecting output from PD sensor to PD measurement unit and PD measurement unit to USB controller. (**f**) Connecting USB controller to PC. (**g**) Selecting test voltage–HV output level. (**h**) Recording test voltage and PD stream. (**i**) Discharging test object using grounding device.

4.2. PD Test Result of Phase R + S + T- Unit 2

The PD stream has been recorded from stator coil unit 2 and analyzed by the PRPD pattern method. PD activities recorded in the range of bandwidth frequency from 100 to 400 kHz refer to the specification of the PD measurement instrument, MPD600 [23]. PRPD pattern results are recorded during the interval time for every stage of the test voltage. The maximum scale setting discharge on MPD600 during the test is set to 8 nC to capture the appropriate PRPD pattern.

(1) PRPD pattern result of 20%, and 40% U_n: The initial testing voltage was applied by injecting 20% U_n, 1.27 kV, to the stator coil with interval duration time. The value of the voltage is 1.27 kV, which gradually increased during a specific interval time. This pattern is recorded without knowing the kind of PD fault during this setup voltage. After recording the PD stream, the test voltage is increased to 40% U_n, 2.54 kV. The PRPD patterns in these two stages, 20% and 40% U_n, are still flat and small as shown in Figure 13a,b, respectively.

(2) PRPD pattern result of 60%, 80%, and 100% U_n: The next step is voltages are set up to 60%, 80%, and 100% U_n. The higher voltage obtains the higher PD magnitude as well. The PRPD pattern is shaped like a bowl and is asymmetric. The clearest pattern and largest PD magnitude are found in 100% U_n. The recorded PRPD pattern has a triangular shape and is asymmetric since the positive charge magnitude is higher than the negative charge on 60%, 80%, and 100% U_n as shown in Figure 13c–e, respectively. Hence, the PD fault from this PRPD pattern can be categorized as slot discharge (S3) as in the IEC standards [6,7,23]. The highest PD magnitude of the PRPD pattern result is during 100% U_n.

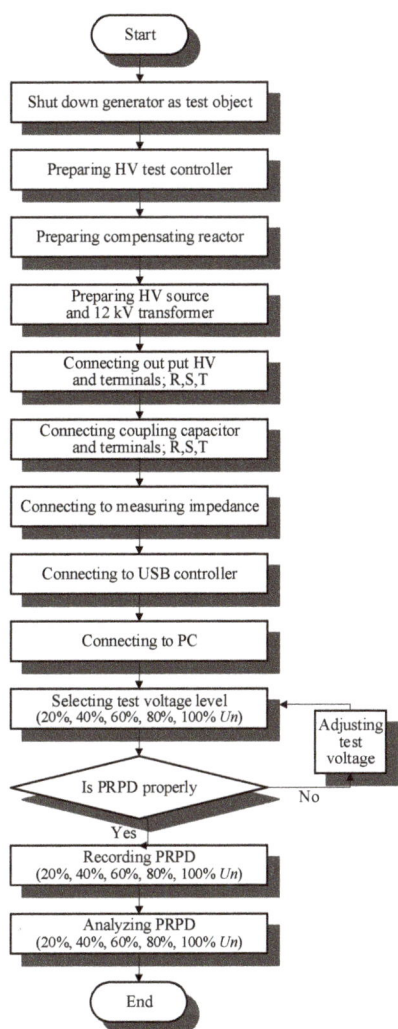

Figure 12. Flow chart of offline PD measurement.

The PD magnitude is set with a threshold of 50 PD/s pulse repetition and 3.5 nC with the PD magnitude maximum found at Q_{Peak} of 8098 pC and relatively can be categorized as a low PD magnitude, as shown in Figure 13f, for a service aged generator [26].

Data resulting from the measurement of all the levels of test voltage were collected for further analysis. The fingerprint data, PRPD pattern, were collected during the interval time testing. The output of the PD detector MPD600 is displayed in the PRPD pattern graph. The data result of the discharge magnitude of Q_{Peak} and Q_{Avg}, n, I_{Dis}, P_{Dis}, and D is higher when the voltage is set up higher. The maximum value of each variable resulted when the test voltage is 100% Un. The value for each level of voltage test can be seen as shown in Table 3.

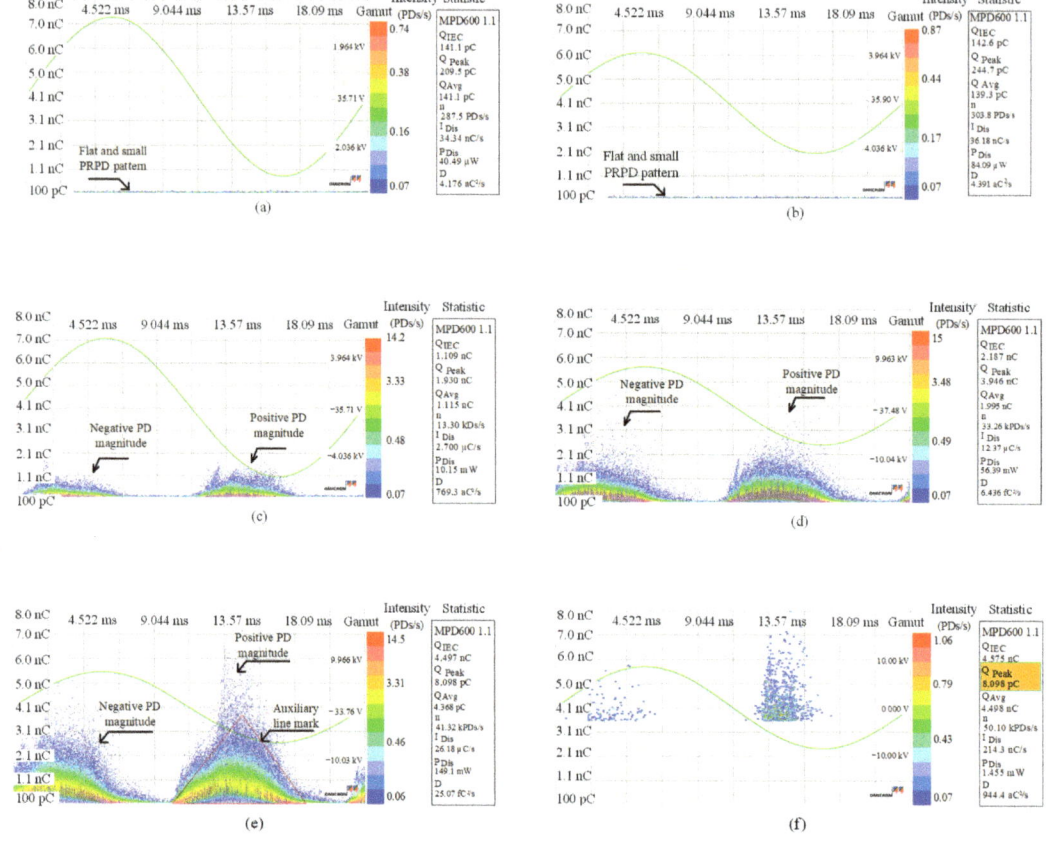

Figure 13. PD test result on generator unit 2, (**a**) PRPD pattern at 20% U_n, (**b**) PRPD pattern at 40% U_n, (**c**) PRPD pattern at 60% U_n, (**d**) PRPD pattern at 80% U_n, (**e**) PRPD pattern at 100% U_n, and (**f**) PD threshold 50 PD/s pulse repetition.

Table 3. PRPD parameter result on unit 2.

U_n (%)	Q_{Peak} (pC)	Q_{Avg} (pC)	n (kPDs/s)	I_{Dis} (nC/s)	P_{Dis} (μW)	D (aC²/s)
20	209.5	141.1	0.3	34.3	40.5	4.2
40	244.7	139.3	0.3	36.2	84.1	4.4
60	1930.0	1115.0	13.3	2,700.0	10,150.0	769.3
80	3946.0	1995.0	33.3	12,370.0	56,390.0	6436.0
100	8098.0	4368.0	41.3	26,180.0	149,100.0	25,070.0

The common representation of the PD events versus discharge value can display the analysis and interpretation of the PD fault from unit 2. The display is in bipolar shape from both negative and positive discharges [34]. It is easy to differentiate the slot discharge and internal PD from the phase-resolved representation, and over the last decade, it has replaced other types of representation such as bipolar or unipolar shape [7]. The level of discharge patterns at low voltage, 20% and 40% U_n, is lower compared with that at 60%, 80%, and 100% U_n. The bipolar shape patterns from 20% and 40% U_n are not clear since the total amounts of PD events are 4131 and 4483 PDs as shown in Figure 14a,b in the maximum event scale of approximately 5000 PDs.

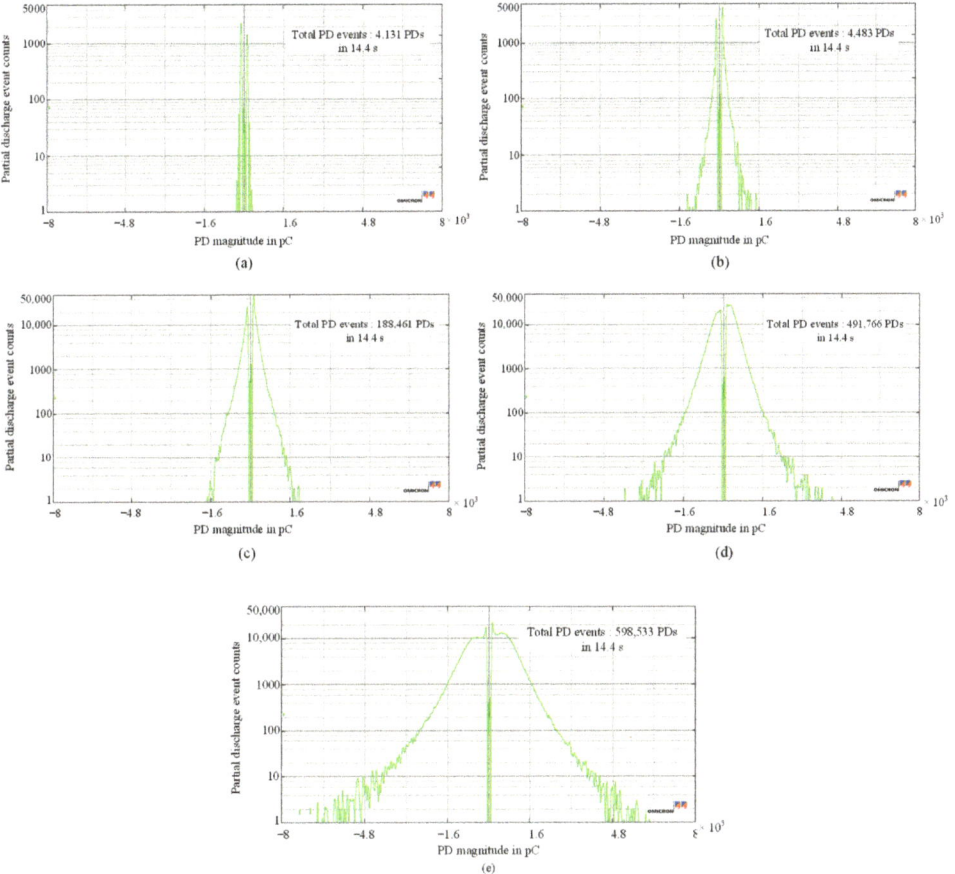

Figure 14. Bipolar pattern of PD events on generator unit 2, (**a**) 20% U_n, (**b**) 40% U_n, (**c**) 60% U_n, (**d**) 80 % U_n, and (**e**) 100% U_n.

The time duration for recording is 14.4 s. The bipolar shapes for higher voltage 60%, 80%, and 100% U_n are more rounded with the total amount of PD events larger than that of 20% and 40% U_n, i.e., 188,461 PDs, 491,766 PDs, and 598,533 PDs within the same duration recording time of 14.4 s with the maximum events scale approximately 50,000 events as shown in Figure 14c–e, respectively. The bipolar patterns have triangular shapes and similar asymmetric patterns. The PD events in the positive cycle are larger than those in the negative cycle. The bipolar pattern is in asymmetric shape, which shows as the slot discharge referring to the IEC pattern [23,34].

The PD fault on stator coil unit 2 as slot discharge can be indicated from the frequency spectrum of PD pulses as shown in Figure 15. The frequency spectrum is viewed for a wider bandwidth up to 32 MHz to compare with the slot discharge spectrum in the IEC standard as shown in Figure 16. PD activities are recorded in the range of bandwidth frequency from 100 to 400 kHz to refer to the specification of the PD measurement instrument MPD600 [23]. Slot discharge was detected along the frequency test during the measurement. It happened along the frequency bandwidth, even though the trend is not similar for all the percentages of U_n as shown in Figure 17.

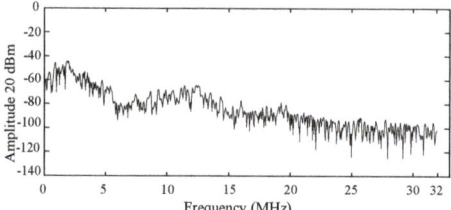

Figure 15. Frequency spectrum pattern of slot discharge pulses on unit 2.

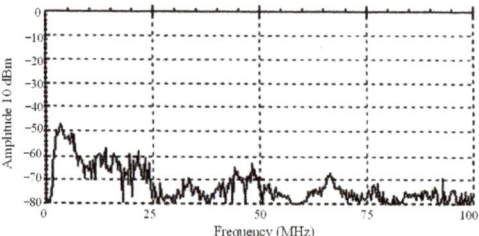

Figure 16. Frequency spectrum of slot discharge in IEC standards.

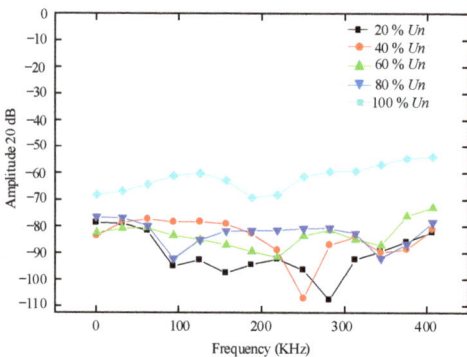

Figure 17. Frequency spectrum of slot discharge MPD600 on unit 2.

Through the PRPD pattern, PD bipolar characteristic, and PD spectrum frequency analysis, the PD defect on generator unit 2 was analyzed and interpreted as slot discharge (S3). Slot discharge in high machines develops when the conductive slot portion coating is damaged due to the stator bar–coil movement in the slot or the slot exit area, e.g., by loss of wedging pressure due to settlement, erosion of the material, abrasion, chemical attack, or manufacturing deficiencies [5,23]. The high-energy discharge develops when serious mechanical damage or void occurs [4,16]. It can result in additional damage to the main insulation and eventually cause an insulation fault. The level of risk of insulation damage is high since the stator coil has slot discharge (S3).

The initial threshold of 500 pC set to determine the PDIV of unit 2 obtains a voltage of 3.846 kV. This value is 60.57% Un, and the PDEV is obtained at 2.524 kV. The highest PDIV and PDEV occur when the threshold is at 2500 pC, since the PDIV is 5.189 kV, which is about 81.72% Un. The PDIV and PDEV are recorded with various thresholds rather than recording the PRPD patterns during the PD measurement, as shown in Table 4 [5,16]. The recording can be figured out in the graph since the PDIV is larger than the PDEV, as shown in Figure 18.

Table 4. PDIV and PDEV with various thresholds on unit 2.

PD Threshold (pC)	PDIV (kV)	PDEV (kV)
500	3.846 (60.57%)	2.524
1000	3.857 (60.74%)	2.528
1500	4.926 (77.57%)	3.831
2000	5.185 (81.65%)	4.046
2500	5.189 (81.72%)	5.155

Note: PD threshold 3000 pC result is PDIV < PDEV (not typical), Un base is 6.35 kV.

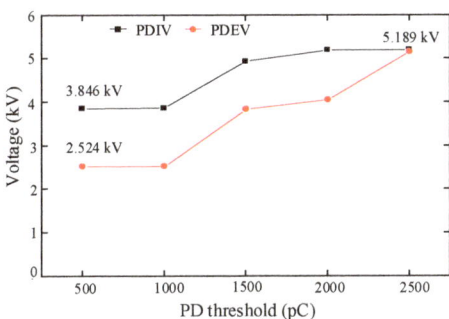

Figure 18. PDIV and PDEV with various thresholds on unit 2.

4.3. PD Test Result of Phase R + S + T- Unit 3

The PD stream that has been recorded from stator coil unit 3 is analyzed by the PRPD pattern method in the same way as that carried out in unit 2. PD activities recorded in the range of bandwidth frequency from 100 to 400 kHz refer to the specification of the PD measurement instrument MPD600 [23]. PRPD pattern results were recorded during the interval time for every stage of the test voltage. The maximum discharge setting on MPD600 during the test is set to 14 nC to capture the appropriate PRPD pattern since the unit 3 charge magnitude is higher than the unit.

(1) PRPD pattern result of 20% and 40% *Un*: The initial testing voltage was applied by injecting 20% Un, 1.27 kV, to the stator coil with interval duration time. The value of the voltage is 1.27 kV, which gradually increased during a specific interval time. This pattern is recorded without knowing the kind of PD fault during this setup voltage. The PD magnitude during this voltage stage is small. After recording the PD stream, the test voltage is increased to 40% Un, 2.54 kV. The PRPD pattern and magnitudes of 40% Un are still small but larger than those of 20% Un. During this stage, there are not enough PRPD pattern results to recognize the kind of PD defect. However, the result is still higher than unit 2 since the maximum scale of the discharge was set to 14 nC compared with 8 nC for unit 2. The PRPD patterns and magnitudes of 20% and 40% Un are recorded as the output of MPD600 for further analysis as shown in Figure 19a,b, respectively.

(2) PRPD pattern result of 60%, 80%, and 100% *Un*: The next step is the voltages are increased to 60%, 80%, and 100% Un, with the maximum scale of discharge set to 14 nC. The higher voltage obtains the higher PD magnitude. The pattern is shaped like a bowl and asymmetric since the negative charge magnitude is higher than the positive charge. The PRPD patterns and magnitudes for 60%, 80%, and 100% Un are larger than those for 20% and 40%. PRPD pattern results can be recognized for the kind of PD defect. The patterns have triangular shapes, are asymmetric, and have sickle shapes before having a bowl shape, as shown in Figure 19c–e, respectively. Referring to the PRPD pattern result, the PD defect can be indicated as delamination

(S2) and slot discharge (S3), which also refers to the IEC standards and experiences of PD measurements [7,23].

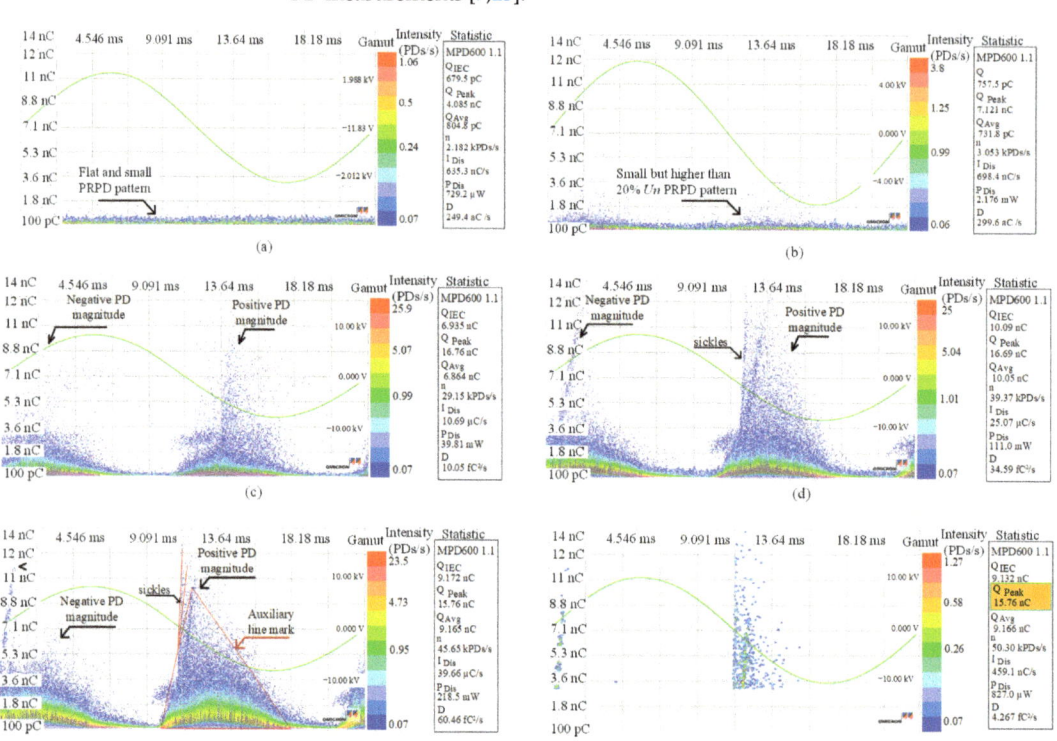

Figure 19. PD test result on generator unit 3, (**a**) PRPD pattern at 20% U_n, (**b**) PRPD pattern at 40% U_n, (**c**) PRPD pattern at 60% U_n, (**d**) PRPD pattern at 80% U_n, (**e**) PRPD pattern at 100% U_n, and (**f**) PD threshold 50 PD/s pulse repetition.

The PD magnitude with a threshold at 50 PD/s pulse repetition is 7.65 nC with the PD magnitude maximum Q_{Peak} of 15,760 pC detected as shown in Figure 19f and relatively can be categorized as the medium PD magnitude for the 33-year operation of the generator.

Similar with the treatment in unit 2, the data resulting from the measurement of all the levels of test voltage were collected for further analysis. The PD stream data were collected in PC software. This PD stream is the PRPD pattern, and the value is displayed on the statistics of the MPD600 result, on the right side of the PRPD pattern. The fingerprint data, PRPD pattern, are collected during the sine-wave cycle. The output of the PD detector MPD600 is displayed in the PRPD pattern graph. Similar with unit 2, the data result of the discharge magnitude of Q_{Peak} and Q_{Avg}, n, I_{Dis}, P_{Dis}, and D is higher when the voltage is set up higher. The maximum value of each variable resulted when the test voltage is 100% U_n. The value for each level of test voltage is shown in Table 5.

The analysis and interpretation of the PD fault from unit 3 can be displayed by the common representation of the PD events versus discharge [34]. The display pattern from MPD600 is bipolar. The level of slot discharge is low at 20% and 40% U_n. The bipolar patterns have triangular shapes with the total amount of PD events being 25,168 PDs and 29,583 PDs, during the duration interval of 14.4 s with maximum event scales of approximately 5000 and 10,000 events as shown in Figure 20a,b, respectively. Anyhow, the asymmetrical shape is not clear during this stage. However, the bipolar patterns for 60%, 80%, and 100% U_n have a more rounded and triangular shape asymmetrically. The total amount of PD events in the negative cycle is larger than that in the positive cycle, i.e.,

418,894 PDs, 563,461 PDs, and 698,192 PDs during the interval time of 14.4 s as shown in Figure 20c–e with a maximum PD event scale of approximately 50,000 events, respectively. The bipolar pattern of PD events has an asymmetrical shape since the negative cycle is larger than the positive cycle, and the triangular shape can be indicated as the PD defect on the slot area also has delamination at the tape layer and is referred to as the IEC standard pattern [23,34].

Table 5. PRPD parameter result on unit 3.

U_n (%)	Q_{Peak} (pC)	Q_{Avg} (pC)	n (kPDs/s)	I_{Dis} (nC/s)	P_{Dis} (µW)	D (aC^2/s)
20	4085	804.8	2.2	635.3	729.2	249.4
40	7121	731.8	3.1	698.4	2176.0	299.6
60	16,760	6864.0	29.2	10,690.0	39,810.0	10,050.0
80	16,690	10,050.0	39.4	25,070.0	111,000.0	34,590.0
100	15,760	9165.0	45.7	39,660.0	218,500.0	60,460.0

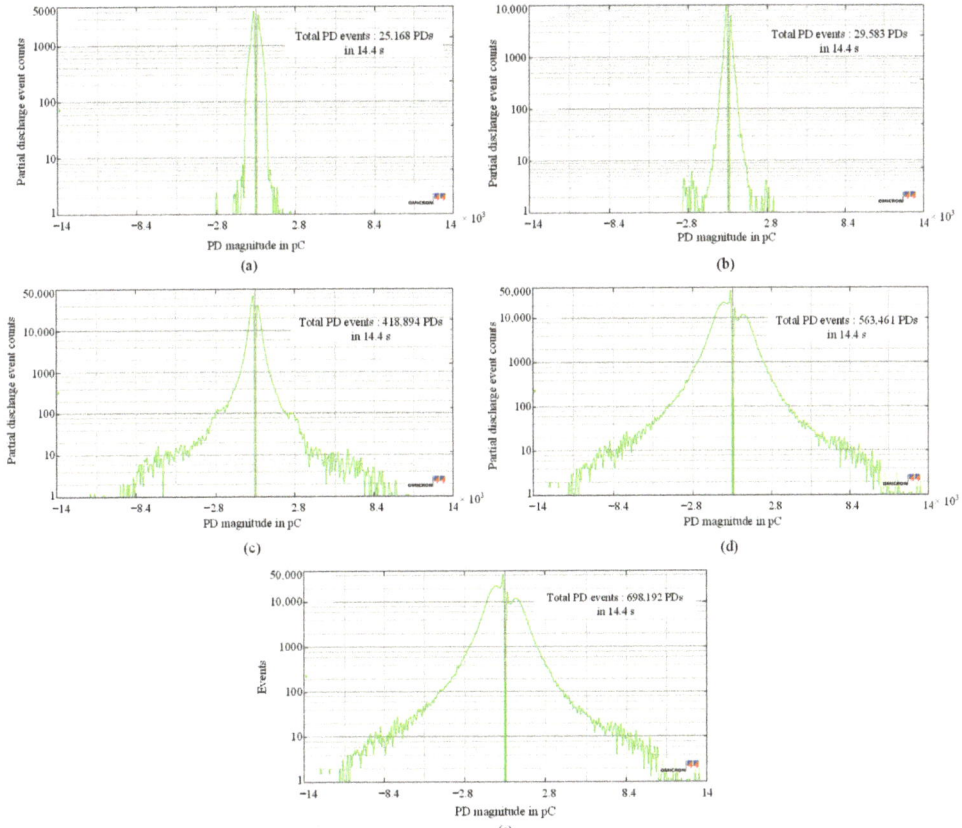

Figure 20. Bipolar pattern of PD events on generator unit 3, (**a**) 20% U_n, (**b**) 40% U_n, (**c**) 60% U_n, (**d**) 80 % U_n, and (**e**) 100% U_n, respectively.

Delamination discharge can be explained through PRPD, and the bipolar pattern as above refers to the experiences of such PD measurements [7,23]. The frequency spectrum can be viewed for a wider bandwidth up to 32 MHz from PD pulses to compare with the standard since the pattern is like the slot discharge pattern in the IEC standards, as shown in Figure 21. The recorded frequency spectrum refers to the bandwidth of MPD600 in the range of 100–400 kHz. The slot discharge happened even though the magnitude is randomly not similar, but it could be seen along the frequency setting, as shown in Figure 22. The PD pulse was recorded higher than the spectrum in unit 2. It cannot be distinguished whether the pulse is slot discharge or delamination through this spectrum, but the pulse has been detected along the frequency test. The other important parameters that needed to be recorded during the PD measurement are the PDIV and PDEV. The initial threshold, 500 pC, is set to determine the PDIV of unit 3 and obtain the voltage of 1.262 kV. This value is 19.87% Un, and the PDEV is obtained at 1.216 kV. The highest PDIV and PDEV occur when the threshold is at 11,500 pC and the PDIV is 5.731 kV, which is about 90.25% Un. The PDIV and PDEV are recorded with various thresholds rather than recording the PRPD patterns during the PD measurement, as shown in Table 6 [5,16]. The recording data are figured out in the graph since the PDIV is larger than the PDEV as shown in Figure 23.

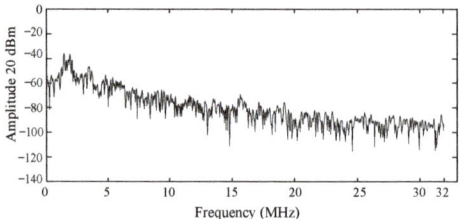

Figure 21. Frequency spectrum pattern of slot discharge pulses on unit 3.

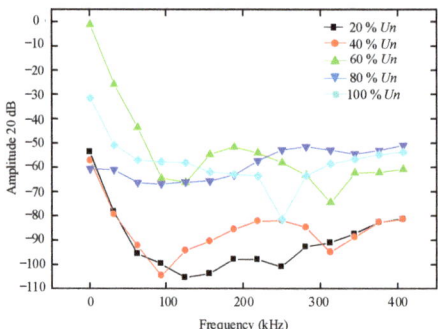

Figure 22. Frequency spectrum of slot discharge MPD600 on unit 3.

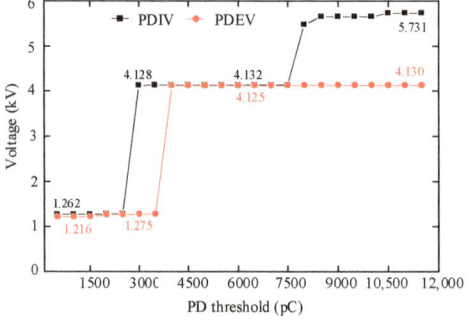

Figure 23. PDIV and PDEV with various thresholds on unit 3.

Table 6. PDIV and PDEV with various thresholds on unit 3.

PD Threshold (pC)	PDIV (kV)	PDEV (kV)
500	1.262 (19.87%)	1.216
1000	1.262 (19.87%)	1.216
1500	1.262 (19.87%)	1.216
2000	1.275 (20.08%)	1.263
2500	1.275 (20.08%)	1.263
3000	4.128 (65.01%)	1.275
3500	4.132 (65.07%)	1.275
4000	4.132 (65.07%)	4.124
4500	4.132 (65.07%)	4.124
5000	4.132 (65.07%)	4.124
5500	4.132 (65.07%)	4.125
6000	4.132 (65.07%)	4.125
6500	4.133 (65.08%)	4.125
7000	4.133 (65.08%)	4.125
7500	4.133 (65.08%)	4.130
8000	5.481 (86.32%)	4.130
8500	5.657 (89.08%)	4.130
9000	5.657 (89.08%)	4.130
9500	5.657 (89.08%)	4.130
10,000	5.657 (89.08%)	4.130
10,500	5.731 (90.25%)	4.130
11,000	5.731 (90.25%)	4.130
11,500	5.731 (90.25%)	4.130

Note: PD threshold 12,000 pC result is PDIV < PDEV (not typical), U_n = 6.35 kV

4.4. PD Defect Measurement Found

Based on the PRPD pattern, PD bipolar characteristic, and PD spectrum frequency analysis, the PD defect on generator unit 3 was analyzed and interpreted as the combination of thermal aging or delamination (S2) and slot discharge (semicon paint abrasion, S3). The internal delamination within the main insulation can be caused by imperfect curing of the insulation system during manufacturing or by mechanical and thermal overstressing during operation. The level of risk of insulation damage for both S2 and S3 is high based on the PRPD pattern results [6,23].

Delamination, which is located at the interface of the copper conductor and the main insulation, mostly results from excessive thermal cycling and is harmful, and the delamination can cause the turn or strand of the insulation's conductor to be severely broken. Therefore, this delamination phenomenon must be paid attention to and should be firstly maintained to avoid more severe damage.

The PD data results show that the values of Q_{Peak} and Q_{Avg} in unit 3 are not rapidly increasing similar with those in unit 2. Data show that in 100% U_n, Q_{Peak} and Q_{Avg} are lower than those in 80% and 60%. This condition is probably caused by contamination occurring on unit 3; hence, at that stage voltage, the PD is decreased. Since PD is a symptom affected by many parameters, such as contamination, manufacturing issues, and incorrect design, there are thermal and mechanical stresses in operation. By considering this phenomenon, generator unit 3 should be put in priority to check the stator coil condition in the maintenance plan schedule.

4.5. Actual Experimental Inspection Found

The intention of this research was to compare the PD fault result from two generators with similar rates and designs by using the same testing methods, equipment, and characteristics as well, and it was found that there are different PD faults on generator units 2 and unit 3 of the Inalum hydro generator. Therefore, the maintenance plan should be stipulated for unit 3 as the priority while keeping the monitoring of the PD activity by periodically measuring, for instance, every six months [30].

Slot discharges in HV machines develop when the conductive portion coating is damaged when there is bar or coil movement in the slot exit area, e.g., by loss of wedging pressure due to settlement, erosion of material, abrasion, chemical attack, or manufacturing deficiencies. These are the root causes of producing slot discharge [6]. The fault typically appears during the operation of the machine and is caused by electromechanical forces, resulting in arcing, which can be measured as slot discharge [35].

A typical delamination tape layer develops when there is a separation of large areas between two insulation layers in a longitudinal direction. It often results from overheating, extreme mechanical force, or imperfect curing of the insulation system. Delamination is dangerous since the turn or strand insulation of the conductors can be severely damaged [6].

Based on inspection experience as evidence, slot discharges in generator stator coil units 2 and 3 at TNP were found, as shown in Figures 24 and 25. Maintenance treatment is carried out for the stator coil as countermeasures after conducting the inspection, such as

(1) Checking the wedges of the stator coil for each stator slot as shown in Figures 24a and 25a, overheating areas for units 2 and 3, respectively;
(2) Marking the loosened wedges for every slot so that they can be replaced by appropriate new wedges as shown in Figure 24b, wedge at slot no. 86, and Figure 25b for units 2 and 3, respectively.
(3) Inspecting and marking the loosened wedges for every slot number of the stator coil, as shown in Figure 24c, wedge at slot no. 126, and Figure 25c, wedge at slot no. 47 for units 2 and 3, respectively.

Loose and wounded wedges were found during the routine maintenance work on 27 January 2016. In the inspection procedure, pressure meters were used to obtain the pressure magnitude to realize the status of wedges, as shown in Figures 24a and 25a for units 2 and 3, respectively. In the measurement, loose and wounded wedges were found at slot nos. 126 and 86, as shown in Figures 24b and 25b for units 2 and 3, respectively. Meanwhile, other loose and wounded wedges were inspected at slot nos. 126 and 47 as shown in Figures 24c and 25c for units 2 and 3, respectively. The locations of the wedges are almost similar with the locations of the conductor partial discharge nearby.

Some countermeasures need to be applied to the stator coil after collecting data such as

(1) Tightening the loosened wedges by adding the pieces of wedges;
(2) Replacing broken wedges with new ones, with the same dimension as well;
(3) Cleaning the slot area of the stator coil by smoothly scrubbing it;
(4) Re-taping the stator coil bar for the slightly broken stator bar;
(5) Replacing the broken stator coil with a new one since there is a spare in the warehouse;
(6) Renew all the total stator coils with new ones by conducting a precise inspection or major overhaul of the whole parts of the generator machine including turbine parts.

The last part of this countermeasure was not included in this paper, since the intention is to compare the PD magnitude of two rotating machines with a similar rating and design only.

(a)

(b)

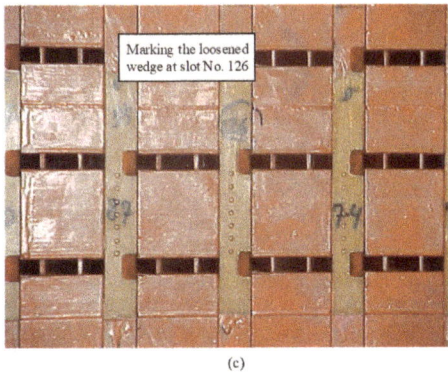

(c)

Figure 24. Visual checking on stator slot of generator unit 2. (**a**) Engineer checking the wedge by gauge pressure. (**b**) Loosening of the wedge in slot no. 86. (**c**) Loosening of the wedge in slot no. 126.

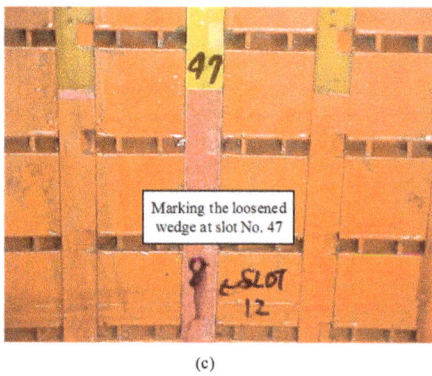

Figure 25. Visual checking on stator slot of generator unit 3. (**a**) Engineer checked and found marking such as overheating. (**b**) Marking the loosened wedge. (**c**) Loosening of the wedge in slot no. 47.

5. Discussion

The PD measurement methods can bring a new point of view and contribution to other similar rotating machines. The stator coil with the greatest activity should be subjected to further inspections instead of the other. To summarize, the advantages of applying PRPD pattern analysis can be listed for several types of discharge in the rotating machine as follows:

(1) Knowing the stator coil condition: The PD measurement can be stated as the preliminary checking of the condition of the stator coil without pulling out the rotor of

the generator. The interpretation of PRPD analysis is necessary to indicate the stator coil condition prior to being inspected. The results of the PRPD pattern analysis in this research found that the defect on the stator coil on unit 2 is slot discharge (S3) with a high-risk level; unit 3 has delamination (S2) and slot discharge (S3) with a high-risk level.
(2) Early detection for stator coil treatment: The PD measurement of units 2 and 3 shows the result condition of the stator coil insulation system. The result contributes to early detection for the future planning of the stator coil treatment by finding out whether to re-tape it or replace it with a new stator coil.
(3) Priority maintenance plan of the generator: The PD fault interpreted by the results of the PRPD analysis can explain which unit of the generator has more PD activity. Then, the stator with the highest PD magnitude should be subjected to further inspection. Based on the result of this research, generator unit 3 should be planned to be inspected first rather than generator unit 2 since the former has a higher peak Q_{Peak}. The PD measurement is suggested to be periodically conducted to see the trend of PD activity on the stator coil.

6. Conclusions

PD measurement that has been conducted in hydropower generators was presented in this paper. The intention is to compare the PD magnitude and pattern from two rotating machines that have similar ratings and designs. The measurement result shows that the two generators have different PD fault on the stator coil.

The measurement results show that the stator coil defect of unit 2 is slot discharge (S3), and unit 3 has delamination (S2) and slot discharge (S3). Based on the PRPD analysis, the PD fault of the generator unit on generator unit 2 is a slot defect caused by stator coil–bar movement in the slot area, but unit 3 has not only a slot defect but also delamination at the tape layer, which is caused by mechanical overstressing during operation. Moreover, due to the higher peak Q_{Peak} of unit 3, inspections should be scheduled first. Finally, after a maintenance inspection, the stator coils of TNP generator units 2 and 3 were found to have loose and damaged wedges. The location of the wedge is almost the same as the location of the partial discharge from nearby conductors.

The benefit of the PRPD analysis on the offline PD measurements was shown in this thesis. It certainly can provide more clear information and reference to other similar rotating machines about PD activity. For future work, some studies are of great interest: for instance, the new identification method of delamination and slot discharge could be verified for the insulation condition of the stator coil for other rotating machines.

Author Contributions: Methodology, C.-Y.L. and N.P.; visualization, C.-Y.L., N.P. and G.-L.Z.; software, C.-Y.L.; data curation, N.P.; writing—original draft preparation, N.P.; writing—review and editing, C.-Y.L. and G.-L.Z. All authors have read and agreed to the published version of the manuscript.

Funding: This research received no external funding.

Institutional Review Board Statement: Not applicable.

Informed Consent Statement: Not applicable.

Data Availability Statement: Not applicable.

Acknowledgments: The authors are grateful to all engineers of Inalum Co. Ltd. and Omicron Co. Ltd. who were involved in the PD measurements and provided the PD data. The authors also would like to thank the top management of Inalum Co. Ltd. that provided the authors with encouragement and financial support during the study and completion of this research.

Conflicts of Interest: The authors declare no conflict of interest.

References

1. Koltunowicz, W.; Badicu, L.-V.; Broniecki, U.; Belkov, A. Increased operation reliability of HV apparatus through PD monitoring. *IEEE Trans. Dielectr. Electr. Insul.* **2016**, *23*, 1347–1354. [CrossRef]
2. Cavallini, A.; Montanari, G.; Puletti, F.; Contin, A. A new methodology for the identification of PD in electrical apparatus: Properties and applications. *IEEE Trans. Dielectr. Electr. Insul* **2005**, *12*, 203–215. [CrossRef]
3. Seo, I.-J.; Khan, U.A.; Hwang, J.-S.; Lee, J.-G.; Koo, J.-Y. Identification of Insulation Defects Based on Chaotic Analysis of Partial Discharge in HVDC Superconducting Cable. *IEEE Trans. Appl. Supercond.* **2015**, *25*, 5402005. [CrossRef]
4. Omicron Energy Monitoring Solution Brochure. *Partial Discharge Monitoring of High Voltage Assets*; Omicron: Asotin, WA, USA, 2015.
5. IEEE Std. 1434-2000 (R2005); IEEE Guide to the Measurement of Partial Discharges in Rotating Machinery. IEEE: New York, NY, USA, 2005.
6. IEC60034-27; Rotating Electrical Machines - PD Measurements of Rotating Machinery. IEC Std.: Worcester, MA, USA, 2006.
7. Hudon, C.; Belec, M. Partial discharge signal interpretation for generator diagnostics. *IEEE Trans. Dielectr. Electr. Insul.* **2005**, *12*, 297–319. [CrossRef]
8. Baug, A.; Choudhury, N.R.; Ghosh, R.; Dalai, S.; Chatterjee, B. Identification of single and multiple partial discharge sources by optical method using mathematical morphology aided sparse representation classifier. *IEEE Trans. Dielectr. Electr. Insul.* **2017**, *24*, 3703–3712. [CrossRef]
9. Lee, S.B.; Naeini, A.; Jayaram, S.; Stone, G.C.; Šašić, M. Surge Test-Based Identification of Stator Insulation Component With Partial Discharge Activity for Low Voltage AC Motors. *IEEE Trans. Ind. Appl.* **2020**, *56*, 2541–2549. [CrossRef]
10. Johnson, J.S.; Warren, M. Detection of Slot Discharges in HV Stator Windings During Operation. *Trans. AIEE* **2009**, *70*, 1998–2000.
11. Renforth, L.A.; Giussani, R.; Dodd, L.; Mendiola, M. On-line partial discharge insulation condition monitoring of complete high voltage (HV) networks. *IEEE Trans. Ind. Appl.* **2019**, *55*, 1021–1029. [CrossRef]
12. Mondal, M.; Kumbhar, G.B.; Kulkarni, S.V. Localization of Partial Discharges inside a Transformer Winding Using a Ladder Network Constructed from Terminal Measurements. *IEEE Trans. Power Deliv.* **2018**, *33*, 1035–1043. [CrossRef]
13. Petr Mraz, I. Aspect of Partial Discharge Activity Evaluation. Ph.D. Dissertation, Pilsen University, Pilsen, Czech Republic, 2014.
14. Lwin, K.-S.; Park, N.-J.; Kim, H.-D.; Ju, Y.-H.; Park, D.-H. Off-line PD Diagnosis for Stator Winding of Rotating Machines using a UWB Sensor. *J. Electr. Eng. Technol.* **2008**, *3*, 263–269. [CrossRef]
15. Stone, G.C.; Sasic, M.; Dunn, D.; Culbert, I. Recent Problems Experienced with Motor and Generator Windings. In Proceedings of the Petroleum and Chemical Industry Conference, Industry Applications Society 56th Annual, Anaheim, CA, USA, 14–16 September 2009.
16. Wang, X. Partial Discharge Analysis of Stator Insulation at Arbitrary Voltage Waveform Stimulus. Ph.D. Dissertation, KTH Electrical Engineering, Stockholm, Sweden, 2015.
17. Altenburger, R.; Heitz, C.; Timmer, J. Analysis of phase-resolved partial discharge patterns of voids based on a stochastic process approach. *J. Phys. D Appl. Phys.* **2002**, *35*, 1149. [CrossRef]
18. Li, Y.; Gao, W.; Huang, S.; Wang, R.; Yan, W.; Gevorgian, V.; Gao, D.W. Data-driven Optimal Control Strategy for Virtual Synchronous Generator via Deep Reinforcement Learning Approach. *J. Mod. Power Syst. Clean Energy* **2021**, *9*, 919–929. [CrossRef]
19. Zhang, N.; Sun, Q.; Yang, L.; Li, Y. Event-Triggered Distributed Hybrid Control Scheme for the Integrated Energy System. *IEEE Trans. Ind. Informat.* **2022**, *18*, 835–846. [CrossRef]
20. Gopinath, S.; Sathiyasekar, K.; Padmanaban, S.; Chokkalingam, B. Insulation Condition Assessment of High Voltage Rotating Machines Using Hybrid Techniques. *IET Gener. Transm. Distrib.* **2019**, *13*, 171–180. [CrossRef]
21. Nair, R.P.; Sumangala, B.V.; Rao, N.B. Identification of slot discharges in rotating machine insulation system using variable frequency PD measurement. *IET High Volt.* **2018**, *3*, 179–186. [CrossRef]
22. CIGRE Technical Brochure 258, Application of On-Line Partial Discharge Tests to Rotating Machines. 2015. Available online: https://e-cigre.org/publication/258-application-of-on-line-partial-discharge-tests-to-rotating-machines (accessed on 1 September 2022).
23. IEC 60270; High–Voltage Test Techniques–Partial Discharge Measurements. 3rd ed. IEC Std.: Worcester, MA, USA, 2000.
24. Parent, G.; Rossi, M.; Duchesne, S.; Dular, P. Determination of Partial Discharge Inception Voltage and Location of Partial Discharges by Means of Paschen's Theory and FEM. *IEEE Trans. Magn.* **2019**, *55*, 7023504. [CrossRef]
25. Stone, G.C.; Sedding, H.G.; Chan, C. Experience with online partial-discharge measurement in high-voltage inverter-fed motors. *IEEE Trans. Ind. Appl.* **2018**, *54*, 866–872. [CrossRef]
26. Nippon Koei Co., Ltd. *Project Completion Report, Vol. III Main Text (3)*; PT. Indonesia Asahan Aluminium: Jakarta Selatan, Indonesia, 1984.
27. Nelson, J.K. *Assessment of Partial Discharge and Electromagnetic Interference On-Line Testing of Turbine-Driven Generator Stator Winding Insulation Systems*; EPRI: Palo Alto, CA, USA, 2003; p. 1007742.
28. Rotating Electrical Machines–Part 27-2: On-Line Partial Discharge Measurements on the Stator Winding Insulation of Rotating Electrical Machines, IEC/TS60034-27-2:2012-03. Available online: https://webstore.iec.ch/publication/131 (accessed on 1 September 2022).
29. Edin, H. Partial Discharges Studied With Variable Frequency of the Applied Voltage. Ph.D. Dissertation, KTH Royal Institute of Technology, Stockholm, Sweden, 2001.

30. Kurtz, M.; Lyles, J.F.; Stone, G.C. Application of partial discharge testing to hydro generator maintenance. *IEEE Trans. Power Appar. Syst.* **1984**, *PAS-103*, 2148–2157. [CrossRef]
31. Stone, G.C.; Goodeve, T.E.; Sedding, H.G.; McDermid, W. Unusual PD Pulse Phase Distributions in Operating Rotating Machines. *IEEE Trans Dielectr. Electr. Insul* **1995**, *2*, 567–577. [CrossRef]
32. Yue, B.; Chen, X.; Cheng, Y.; Song, J.; Xie, H. Diagnosis of stator winding insulation of large generator based on partial discharge measurement. *IEEE Trans. Energy Convers.* **2006**, *21*, 387–395. [CrossRef]
33. Stone, G.C.; Warren, V. Objective Methods to Interpret Partial-Discharge Data on Rotating-Machine Stator Windings. *IEEE Trans. Ind. Appl.* **2006**, *42*, 195–200. [CrossRef]
34. Yazici, B. Statistical Pattern Analysis of Partial Discharge Measurements for Quality Assessment of Insulation Systems in High-Voltage Electrical Machinery. *IEEE Trans. Ind. Appl.* **2004**, *40*, 1579–1594. [CrossRef]
35. MPD600 User Manual, Omicron Service Centers, www.omicronusa.net, a Publication of Omicron Electronics GmbH. 2013. Available online: http://www.ucaiug.org/Meetings/CIGRE_2014/USB%20Promo%20Content/OMICRON/Presentations/OMICRON-magazine-volume4-issue2-ENU.pdf (accessed on 1 September 2022).
36. Sumereder, C.; Weiers, T. Significance of Defects Inside In-Service Aged Winding Insulations. *IEEE Trans. Energy Convers.* **2008**, *23*, 9–14. [CrossRef]

Article

Filter-GAN: Imbalanced Malicious Traffic Classification Based on Generative Adversarial Networks with Filter

Xin Cao [1], Qin Luo [1,*] and Peng Wu [2]

[1] School of Computer Science, Southwest Petroleum University, Chengdu 610100, China
[2] School of Information and Engineering, Sichuan Tourism University, Chengdu 610100, China
* Correspondence: dorothy_lq@163.com

Abstract: In recent years, with the rapid development of Internet services in all walks of life, a large number of malicious acts such as network attacks, data leakage, and information theft have become major challenges for network security. Due to the difficulty of malicious traffic collection and labeling, the distribution of various samples in the existing dataset is seriously imbalanced, resulting in low accuracy of malicious traffic classification based on machine learning and deep learning, and poor model generalization ability. In this paper, a feature image representation method and Adversarial Generative Network with Filter (Filter-GAN) are proposed to solve these problems. First, the feature image representation method divides the original session traffic into three parts. The Markov matrix is extracted from each part to form a three-channel feature image. This method can transform the original session traffic format into a uniform-length matrix and fully characterize the network traffic. Then, Filter-GAN uses the feature images to generate few attack samples. Compared with general methods, Filter-GAN can generate more efficient samples. Experiments were conducted on public datasets. The results show that the feature image representation method can effectively characterize the original session traffic. When the number of samples is sufficient, the classification accuracy can reach 99%. Compared with unbalanced datasets, Filter-GAN has significantly improved the recognition accuracy of small-sample datasets, with a maximum improvement of 6%.

Keywords: malicious network traffic; GAN; imbalanced classification

MSC: 68M25

1. Introduction

The rapid development of information technology not only brings great convenience to network users but also brings many security threats. Network traffic is an important carrier for network information exchange and transmission. Many network attacks and threats also exist in network traffic, so malicious traffic classification is one of the research focuses of cyberspace security. Due to the wide application of application-layer encryption technology, traditional port matching [1], deep packet inspection (DPI) [2–4], and other technologies cannot accurately identify malicious traffic. Therefore, researchers try to classify malicious traffic using various machine learning algorithms such as SVM, decision tree, naive Bayes, etc. However, machine learning-based methods involve two problems. First, machine learning models always rely on the knowledge and experience of professional security personnel to extract and select traffic features. Second, machine learning models have low accuracy and poor generalization ability in multi-classification tasks. Compared with machine learning, deep learning is a more popular method. As an end-to-end learning method, it can automatically extract data features without human intervention. Although the deep learning network enhances the expressive power, the performance of this classification algorithm decreases in the case of an imbalanced class distribution of the dataset, especially for few samples.

Therefore, overcoming imbalanced class distribution is of great significance for the classification of malicious traffic. To solve the problem of poor generalization of the classification model and the feature representation in the case of a class imbalance dataset, a representation method based on the Markov transition matrix and Adversarial Generative Networks with Filters (Filter-GAN) is proposed in this paper.

The original input to the feature representation method is the traffic session. The method embeds the relevant features into the feature image through the feature image extraction algorithm. The feature images are then used to train a Generative Adversarial Network (GAN) model and data filter based on machine learning algorithms. Finally, the GAN model generates enough new samples to filter out more effective samples through the data filter. These more effective samples serve as a supplement to the original dataset to address the problem of sample imbalance.

Compared with traditional malicious traffic characterization methods and data enhancement methods, this method has a better feature representation effect and stronger data enhancement effect, which can make the classification model have a better generalization and higher classification accuracy. There are two main contributions of this paper:

- A new traffic feature representation method is proposed. The method embeds the header feature and payload feature of each data packet into a feature image, which realizes a unified representation method for traffic files. The method avoids information loss and redundancy during preprocessing because the traffic session file is not sliced or populated. Compared with the traditional grayscale image method, the feature image generated by this method is more friendly to the model.
- A generative adversarial network model with a sample filter is designed. The filter is trained and tested with real samples to screen the generated samples so that the generated samples that pass the screening are closer to the distribution of real samples.

The rest of the paper is organized as follows. The second part introduces the related work of malicious traffic classification. The third part elaborates the whole model framework and training process, including data preprocessing, feature image extraction, model structure, and algorithm. Section 4 describes the experimental details and result evaluation. Section 5 concludes and proposes future work.

2. Related Work

2.1. Classification of Malicious Traffic Based on Deep Learning

Deep learning has been widely used [5–10] in the field of traffic detection and classification. Wang et al. [11] combined deep learning with traffic analysis for the first time, pointing out the similarities between images and TCP traffic. Jia et al. [12] further studied the application of deep learning in traffic analysis, unifying the length of the data packets, so that the length of each data packet reaches 784 bytes. The flow vector is converted into a 28 × 28 byte matrix and fed into a convolutional neural network for malicious traffic classification. Wang et al. [13] converts the data packets of the same five-tuple into fixed-length byte vectors in sequence according to time and then forms feature vectors through data compression. The feature vector is classified using the convolutional neural network with the Gabor function to achieve the purpose of intrusion detection. The two methods inevitably fill or intercept bytes, resulting in loss of information.

Jiarui Man et al. [14] directly used 196 statistical features of malicious traffic to form images, and then used a residual network for intrusion detection. Although the use of a residual network has good advantages in multi-classification, this method does not consider that there is no spatial position information between statistical features. Simply converting a one-dimensional vector into a two-dimensional matrix causes redundancy of information. Huiwen Bai et al. [15] convert network traffic into text, in which the words in the text consist of every byte of the payload. We use the n-gram semantic neural network model to generate continuous domain vectors, and then use the gated recurrent unit (GRU) to obtain feature vectors for final classification. However, with the use of more encryption protocols, the packet payload is randomly encrypted and no longer has specific semantics. This makes semantic-based malicious traffic detection difficult. Marín [16] takes the network traffic byte stream directly as the input of the convolutional neural network and the recurrent neural network, and evaluates the feature representation effect at the packet and flow level. There are also many related works [17–20] that demonstrate the superiority of deep learning (DL) methods for malicious traffic analysis. We conclude that the DL method application technique consists of three steps: First, converting the data packet or pcap file into the standard input format of DL, then selecting a deep learning model according to the characteristics of the input data, and finally training the DL classifier to automatically extract and classify the characteristics of the traffic.

2.2. Common Methods for Dealing with Sample Imbalances

In the field of network traffic classification, the class imbalance problem can be expressed as an order of magnitude difference in the number of samples of traffic data in each application category, resulting in the classifier being overwhelmed by the majority class and ignoring the minority class. Misidentifying small categories is often costly. For example, in intrusion detection, the attack class is a small class relative to normal traffic, and misclassifying the attack class may cause network paralysis. There are generally three ways to deal with data imbalance: modify the objective cost function, change the sampling strategy, and generate artificial data as shown in Table 1. The method of modifying the loss function can alleviate the problem of quantity imbalance through different weighting processes according to different sample sizes. This approach gives higher scores to small classes and penalizes large classes for updating the parameters of the classification model.

Methods to address sample imbalance also include random undersampling (RUS) and random oversampling (ROS) strategies [21–23]. Undersampling increases the number of samples in the secondary class by discarding some sample data, thereby reducing the sample size in the main class. Oversampling increases the amount of data for samples with fewer classes by reusing data from classes with fewer classes. However, if the sample size of the minority class is very small, then discarding a large number of samples from the majority class will result in a loss of sample distribution information. While the oversampling method repeats samples leading to severe overfitting problems, which has been the main disadvantage of oversampling.

Table 1. A brief summary of methods for dealing with imbalanced datasets.

Author	Method	Reference
Wang	Random Over-sampling (ROS)	[21]
Vu	Random Under-sampling (RUS)	[22]
Cieslak	RUS + ROS	[23]
Chawla	Synthetic Minority Over-sampling Technique (SMOTE)	[24]
Chen	Adaptive Synthetic Sampling (ADASYN)	[25]
Nguyen	SVM-SMOTE	[26]
Last, F	Kmeans-SMOTE	[27]

As a method of oversampling, SMOTE (Adaptive Synthetic Sampling) [24] is also widely used in the literature to solve the class imbalance problem. However, it relies on interpolation for oversampling, resulting in poor representation of synthetic samples. SVM-SMOTE method [26] use support vector machine (SVM) classifiers to train the support vectors on the original training set. Based on the majority sample density of the nearest neighbors, interpolation or extrapolation techniques are used to combine each minority class support vector with its nearest neighbors to generate new samples. Chen et al. [25] proposed the ADASYN (Adaptive Synthetic Sampling) method for data generation based on the SMOTE method. However, the experimental results show that the distribution of the generated data is quite different from the real data. Last et al. [27] applied the Kmeans algorithm to the SMOTE method, taking inter- and intra-class relationships into account in the generated data.

The classic approach to generating artificial data is based on Generative Adversarial Networks (GAN), which are trained using a few samples as training data, rather than simply replicating it. Related research [28] shows that GANs can efficiently generate high-quality synthetic samples. Vu et al. [29] used the GAN model to generate data to supplement a small number of categories. The SVM, decision tree, and random forest models were trained on mixed data and achieved high classification accuracy. Wang et al. [30] generated multiple minority class data simultaneously through a conditional GAN model. The generated data are then supplemented by the minority class, which effectively improved the accuracy compared to the original dataset. Wang et al. [31] used a GAN model for data generation on an unbalanced encrypted traffic dataset in units of network flows. Although perceptrons have been widely used to solve class imbalance problems, instability problems such as vanishing gradients, mode collapse, etc. have always been shortcomings of multilayer perceptrons. Furthermore, they do not evaluate the data distribution of the generated samples versus the real samples. Therefore, in this paper, we propose to use filters trained on real samples to filter the generated samples, directly avoiding crashes and instability problems in the model. At the same time, the generated samples are evaluated using mathematical statistical methods.

3. The Proposed Method

This section discusses the framework for malicious traffic classification based on the Filter-GAN model, shown in Figure 1. It is divided into three stages: the data processing stage, data enhancement stage, and classification stage. In particular, the difference between the Filter-GAN model-based framework and the general method framework is the data processing stage and the data augmentation stage.

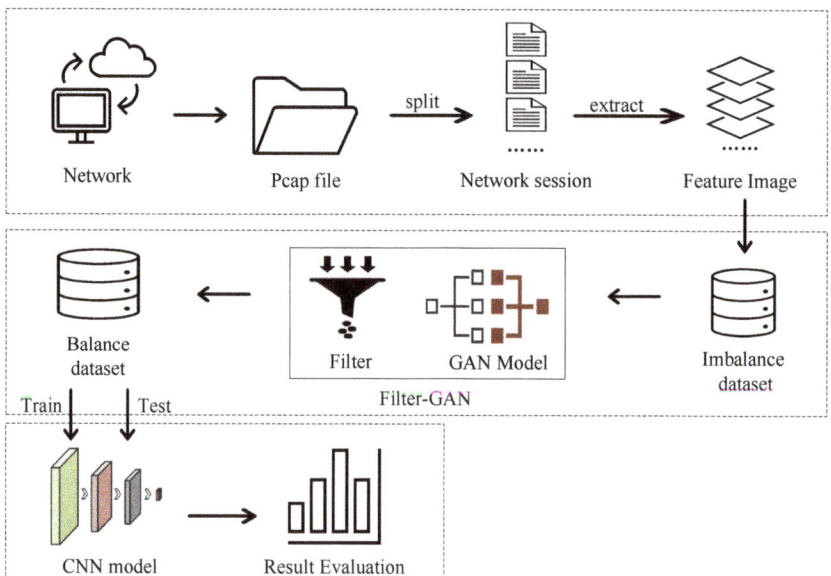

Figure 1. Architecture of Filter-GAN.

In the data processing stage, the original traffic file is divided into network session files according to the network quintuple. The network session file is used as the input of the feature image algorithm. The algorithm generates data matrices of uniform size without filling or intercepting valid fields. Then, these data matrices are converted into feature images to form feature image datasets.

The data augmentation stage is mainly used to generate data to supplement the minority class. Due to the imbalanced distribution of categories in the original traffic dataset, the feature image set still suffers from imbalanced problem. Therefore, firstly, through the adversarial generative network (GAN), enough new feature images are generated and sent to the filter to screen more effective samples as a supplement to the original feature image set to enhance the diversity of the original feature images. It is worth mentioning that here, the generator generates feature images instead of the original raw traffic files.

In the classification stage, a convolutional neural network model is used as the classification model. The training set and the test set are the mixed feature image dataset and the original feature image dataset, respectively. Finally, the classification effect is evaluated.

3.1. Feature Image Extraction Algorithm

Traffic sessions have statistical, timing, and payload-related features. To compress all the features into one image as much as possible and improve the representation ability of the feature image, the feature image extraction algorithm converts the header field, source payload, and destination payload into three matrices, which are compressed into three channels of a picture to form a complete feature image. The specific process is shown in Figure 2.

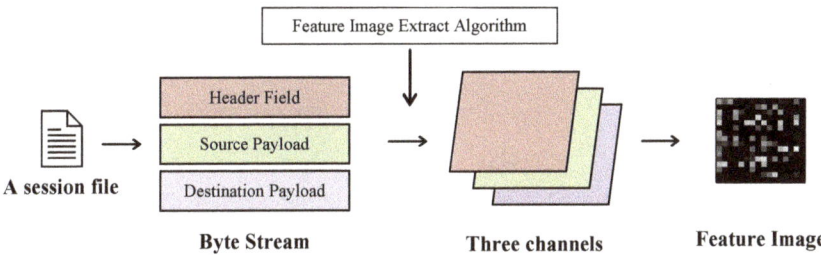

Figure 2. Feature image extraction.

There are data packets in two directions in a network session and the header fields of the information about the data packets themselves. The header field of each data packet needs to remove noise and useless information, such as data link layer information (mac address, frame type, etc.), and truncates the IP address. These data can usually be regarded as a bit stream, and each bit string has different state transition probabilities. This transmission process has the characteristics of a Markov chain. Therefore, the use of Markov models can effectively characterize the spatiotemporal features of session payloads.

We read the header field and payload of each data packet in the session file in binary mode, and then divide the payload into source payload and destination payload. Then , we take every four bits as a value. It can be expressed as:

$$bits = \{b_1, b_2, \ldots, b_{N \times 8}\}, b_i \in (0,1) \tag{1}$$

$$v = \{s_1, s_2, \ldots, s_{\frac{N \times 8}{4}}\}, s_i \in (0,1,2,\ldots,15) \tag{2}$$

where N is the byte length and the vector v is the encoded state vector. Consider v as a Markov chain, calculate the probability that two adjacent states s_{i+1} appear after s_i, denoted by $P(s_{i+1}|s_i)$:

$$P_{s_{i+1},s_i} = \frac{P(s_{i+1},s_i)}{p(s_i)} = \frac{P(s_{i+1},s_i)}{\sum_{j=0}^{i} P(s_i|s_j))} \tag{3}$$

where $s_i, s_{i+1} \in (0,1,2,\ldots,15)$. All can form a Markov probability transition matrix:

$$M = \begin{bmatrix} P_{0,0} & P_{0,1} & \cdots & P_{0,15} \\ P_{1,0} & P_{1,1} & \cdots & P_{1,15} \\ \vdots & \vdots & \ddots & \vdots \\ P_{15,0} & P_{15,1} & \cdots & P_{15,15} \end{bmatrix} \quad (4)$$

Figure 3 is the process of converting binary data into a Markov matrix. Each value of the Markov matrix of malicious traffic is the transmission probability of a fixed-length bit string, not the actual value of the bit string. They represent the distribution characteristics of network session fields. After converting the payload and the header fields into Markov matrices, they are used as three channels of the feature image, respectively. Each value in the matrix is used as a pixel point of the feature image to form a feature image as in feature image extraction Algorithm 1.

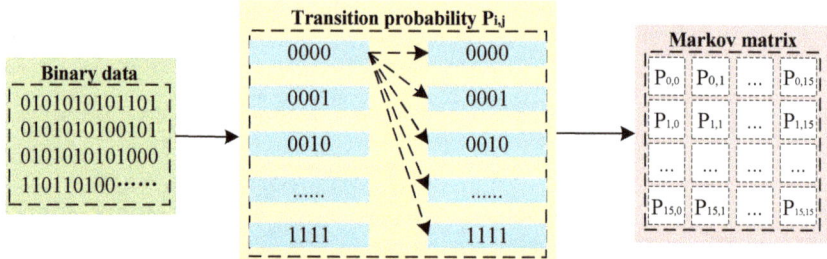

Figure 3. The process of converting binary data into Markov matrix.

Algorithm 1: Feature Image Extract

Input: Network traffic Session(Pcap)
Output: Feature Image
Data: SrcPayloadBits,DstPayloadBits,HeaderBits;
1 **for** *Packets* **do**
2   Extract header , source payload and destination payload
3   SrcPayloadBits = SrcPayloadBits + source payload
4   DstPayloadBits = DstPayloadBits + destination payload
5   HeaderBits = HeaderBits + header
6 **end**
7 $M_1, M_2, M_3 \leftarrow$ Convert Bits to Markov matrix // using the Markov algorithm
8 Encoding M1, M2, M3 matrices as Feature Images;

3.2. Filter-Gan Model Based on Gan with Machine Learning Filter

The structure of Filter-GAN is shown in Figure 4, including generator, discriminator, and sample filter. The first step is GAN network training. Random noise is sent to the generator to generate enough samples, then the generated samples and real samples are sent to the discriminator for backward propagation of the loss function so that the entire model can generate a generated sample that is closer to the real sample image. In the second step, the filter consisting of a machine learning model uses real data for training and testing. When the best classification effect is achieved, it is used to screen the samples generated in the first step. In step 3, the samples generated by the GAN model are fed into the filter to screen more effective samples.

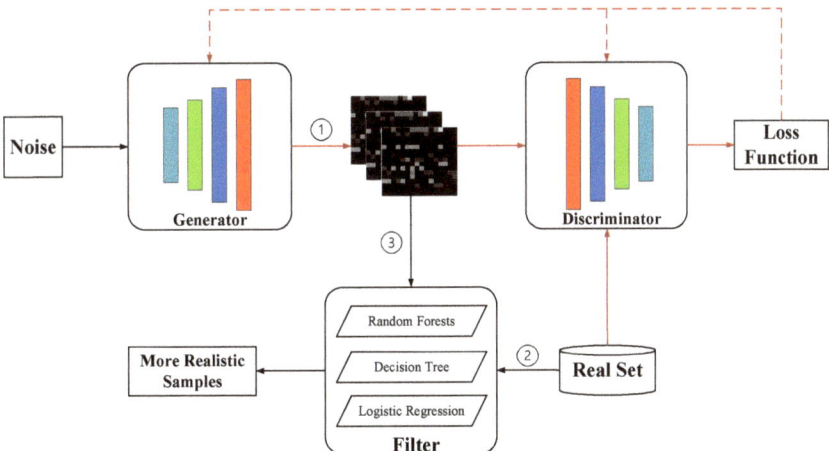

Figure 4. Architecture of Filter-GAN.

3.2.1. Gan Model and Loss Function

GAN [32] includes a generator (G) and a discriminator (D). The structure of the GAN network model constructed in this paper is shown in Tables 2 and 3. In the original imbalanced data, for the minority attack class, the real sample $\mathbf{x}$ is randomly selected as the input of D. $D(\mathbf{x})$ is the output of D, representing the probability that the data distribution of $\mathbf{x}$ belongs to the real data distribution $\mathbb{P}_r$. A noise vector $\mathbf{z}$ is randomly generated in the normal distribution $\mathbb{P}_z$ as the input to G. G generates synthetic samples $G(\mathbf{z})$. This generated sample is then used as the input of the discriminator, which is used to predict the probability $D(G(\mathbf{z}))$ of $G(\mathbf{z})$ in the generated data distribution $\mathbb{P}_g$.

Table 2. The detailed network structure of the discriminator. The input data dimension is (3, 16, 16).

Layer (Type)	Output
Input	(3, 16, 16)
Flatten	(768, 1)
Dense 1	(512, 1)
Dense 2	(256, 1)
Dense 3	(128, 1)
Dense 4	(64, 1)
Output	(1,)

Table 3. The detailed network structure of the generator, the input data is a random latent vector of length 100.

Layer (Type)	Output
Latent dim	(100, 1)
Dense 1	(128, 1)
Dense 2	(256, 1)
Dense 3	(512, 1)
Dense 4	(1024, 1)
Dense 5	(768, 1)
Reshape and output	(3, 16, 16)

The objective function of GAN is given as follows:

$$\min_G \max_D \mathbb{E}_{\mathbf{x}\sim\mathbb{P}_r(\mathbf{x})}[\log D(\mathbf{x})] + \mathbb{E}_{\mathbf{z}\sim\mathbb{P}_z(\mathbf{z})}[\log(1 - D(G(\mathbf{z})))] \tag{5}$$

The purpose of GAN is to maximize the discriminator D and minimize the generator G. $\mathbb{P}_r$ and $\mathbb{P}_z$ are the probability distributions of the real data and latent vectors, respectively. Accordingly, the loss functions of D and G are:

$$\mathcal{L}_D = -\mathbb{E}_{\mathbf{x}\sim\mathbb{P}_r(\mathbf{x})}[\log D(\mathbf{x})] + \mathbb{E}_{\mathbf{z}\sim\mathbb{P}_z(\mathbf{z})}[\log(1 - D(G(\mathbf{z})))] \tag{6}$$

$$\mathcal{L}_G = \mathbb{E}_{\mathbf{z}\sim\mathbb{P}_z(\mathbf{z})}[\log(1 - D(G(\mathbf{z})))] \tag{7}$$

3.2.2. Sample Filter Based on Machine Learning

GAN uses the maximum similarity to measure the loss of the entire model training. When the data are distributed in high dimensions, the similarity of the data is difficult to define, which can cause the generated samples to not be close to the real samples. However, since GAN models can generate infinite samples, we use decision trees, random forests, and logistic regression models to compose a sample filter to filter the generated samples. The screening process is shown in Figure 5.

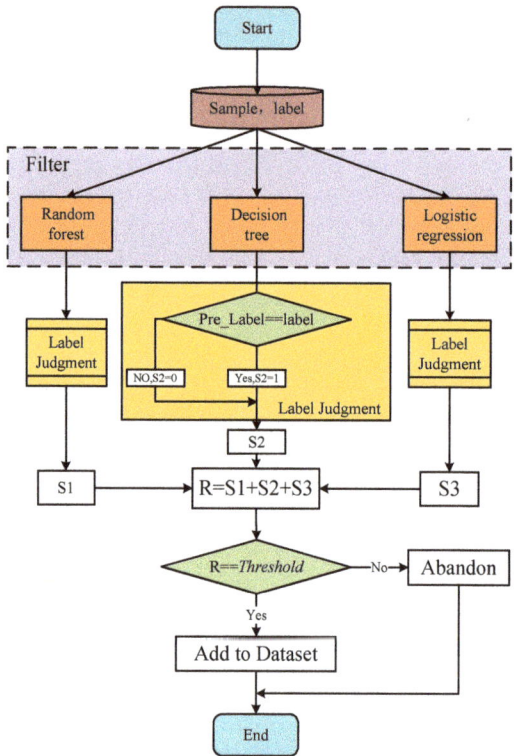

Figure 5. The process of filtering generated samples.

Each generated sample with a label is sent to three machine learning models to obtain predicted labels. The value is 1 if the predicted label is the same as the label of the generated sample, and 0 otherwise. Finally, we add the results of the three models to obtain R, $R \in (0, 1, 2, 3)$. For example, when a sample obtains $R = 2$ through the filter, meaning that the sample is judged to be of this class by the two machine learning models in the filter.

To limit the filtering granularity of the filter, a *Threshold* is set. If R is greater than or equal to the *Threshold*, the generated sample is added to the dataset, otherwise, it is discarded. Algorithm 2 is the training process of Filter-GAN.

Algorithm 2: Filter-GAN Training process.

Input: Real feature images set
Output: Discriminator D, Genarator G of GAN and Filter F

1 **for** *each feature image* **do**
   `// Traning GAN`
2   Feed the feature image into discriminator D to calculate loss
3   Randomly generate Gaussian noise z
4   Feed the z Genarator G to generate generated samples X_{fake}
5   Feed X_{fake} into discriminator D to Calculate loss
6   Compute the training error
7   Update weight and bias
   `// Training Filter`
8   Convert feature images to a one-dimensional feature data X_{data}
9   Feed X_{data} to Random Forests, Decision Trees, Logistic Regression model for training
10 **end**
11 Combining three machine learning models as a filter F

4. Experimental Evaluation

4.1. The Datasets and Evaluation Metrics

4.1.1. Malicious Traffic Dataset

The dataset in the experiments comes from the Malware Capture Facility project [33], which collects malicious traffic over a long period. The datasets released by this project contain malicious traffic generated by various malicious attack methods, such as ransomware, DDoS attacks, and Trojan horse attacks. Many of these malicious programs cannot generate enough network traffic during the attack or propagation process, resulting in an imbalanced number of malicious traffic samples.

Twelve types of malicious traffic were selected. The SplitCap.exe tool [34] was used to split the original traffic file PCAP into network sessions, which were converted to feature images using the feature image extraction algorithm.

In Table 4, it can be seen that there is an extreme imbalance between the samples. For example, MinerTrojan's samples only accounted for 1.23% of the entire dataset, and PUA only accounted for 0.69% of the entire dataset. Therefore, there was a distribution imbalance problem between the categories of this dataset, which can be used to verify the method and model proposed in this paper.

Table 4. Dataset distribution after segmentation and feature image transformation.

Class Name	Size	Session Number	Rate
CoinMiner(CM)	54 M	10,385	7.11%
WebCompanion(WebC)	227 M	6442	4.41%
Trickbot(Tbot)	33 M	30,052	20.58%
Sathurbot(Sbot)	244 M	11,453	7.84%
Ursnif	150M	10,558	7.23%
Artemis Trojan(AT)	773 M	16,719	11.45%
HPEMOTET(HPE)	70 M	13,737	9.41%
Wannacry Ransomware(WR)	6.8 M	10,829	7.41%
Necurse	20 M	2633	1.81%
Magic Hound(M-H)	20 M	30,431	20.84%
MinerTrojan(MinerT)	309 M	1795	1.23%
PUA	54 M	1008	0.69%
Total	1.91G	146,042	100%

4.1.2. Evaluation Metrics

To evaluate the performance of our method on imbalanced datasets from multiple perspectives, we used accuracy, precision, recall, and F1:

$$ACCURACY = \frac{TP + TN}{TP + TN + FP + FN} \tag{8}$$

$$PRECISION = \frac{TP}{TP + FP} \tag{9}$$

$$RECALL = \frac{TP}{TP + FN} \tag{10}$$

$$F1 = 2 \cdot \frac{Precision \cdot Recall}{Precision + Recall} \tag{11}$$

4.1.3. Experimental Platform And Configuration

The training and testing of the model have been carried out under the Windows 10 operating system. The deep learning model was implemented using the Python language based on the Torch framework. The parameters are listed in Table 5.

Table 5. Generator structure parameters.

Category	Version
GPU	Nvidia GPU(GeForce GTX 2080TI)
Operating System	Windows 10, 64 bit
Deep Learining Platform	Torch
DeepLearning Backend	Torch-gpu
Cuda version	11.6
CuDNN version	7.1.4

4.2. Experimental Results and Analysis

The experiment was carried out from two aspects, the first is to prove whether the feature extraction algorithm can effectively characterize malicious traffic. The second is to prove the data generation model and data filter proposed in this paper, which can effectively supplement the samples with an unbalanced number of samples.

4.2.1. Feature Image Representation Ability Experiment

To verify that the feature extraction algorithm proposed in this paper can effectively characterize malicious network traffic, the feature image sets obtained after data processing are respectively sent to the machine learning model and the neural network model for multi-classification experiments. Machine learning models include random forest (rf), decision trees (dt), and logistic regression (lr) models.

In the machine learning model, each pixel of the three-dimensional feature image (dimension (3, 16, 16)) is regarded as a feature, converted into a one-dimensional vector with a feature number of 768, and normalized as a machine input to the learning model. The neural network model includes the residual convolutional neural network (res, ResNet), which directly uses the three-dimensional feature image as the input of the model. The training parameters are shown in Table 6.

The results of Precision, Recall, and F1 for each category in the classification results are shown in Figure 6. the classification effects of various categories are the ResNet model, Random Forest, Decision Tree, and Logistic Regression. The ResNet model performs significantly better than the machine learning model, because the feature images generated by the feature image extraction algorithm are essentially three-channel images. Each pixel on the image is the transition probability of a fixed-length bit string in the traffic field, which represents the feature distribution of the field. In the field of image classification, ResNet has a very large advantage, so the results of the ResNet model are better than the classification results of the machine learning model. At the same time, it also shows that the feature image extraction algorithm proposed can effectively extract malicious traffic session features when there are enough samples in the dataset.

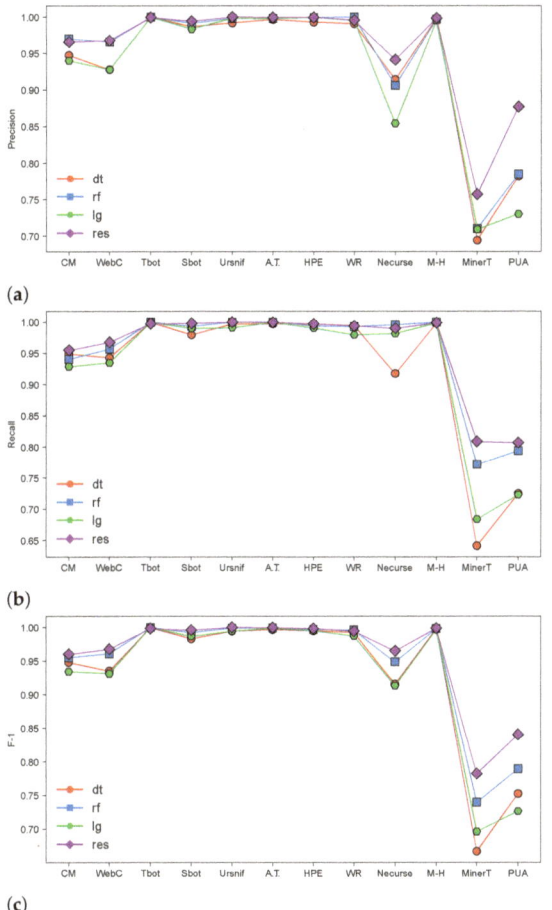

Figure 6. Experimental results of random forest (rf), decision trees (dt), logistic regression (lr), and residual networks (res). (**a**) Precision. (**b**) Recall. (**c**) F1.

In an addition, Figure 6 shows the detection accuracy of each category using the ResNet model, which shows results above 0.95 for most classes, except Necurse, MinerTrojan, and PUA. In particular, the number of samples in these three categories accounts for less than 2% of the total number of samples, and the number of training samples is less than 1000, which is very small as the amount of pre-training data for deep learning models. Therefore, the reason for the low classification accuracy of these three categories is largely due to the insufficient number of samples, resulting in the imbalance of sample classes.

Table 6. The training parameters in ResNet model.

Training Parameters	Optimizer	Learning Rate	Loss Function	Epochs	Mini_Batch
Value	SGD	0.001	crossentropy	100	128

To solve this problem, in the following experiments, according to the distribution of the sample size of the original dataset, Filter-GAN was used to perform data enhancement for the categories with less than 10,000 samples.

4.2.2. Data Generation and Dataset Balancing

The network session was transformed into feature images through feature extraction algorithms to form feature image datasets. The number of various feature images in the feature image set also inherits this shortcoming due to the unbalanced number of web sessions per class. According to the results of the above experiments, it can be seen that the imbalance in the amount of data between samples leads to poor classification results.

Therefore, for categories with less than 10,000 feature images in the dataset, including WebCompanion, Necurse, MinerTrojan, and PUA, the Filter-GAN model was used for data augmentation. These feature image datasets were trained as input to the GAN model in Filter-GAN. The featured image was then converted into a 1D vector (one feature per pixel) and fed to the filter for training. Finally, the trained GAN model was used for sample generation, and the generated samples were screened by the filter. The samples generated by screening were closer to the data distribution of the real samples.

Samples that can pass the filter were selected and those that did not pass were discarded directly. Because a GAN model can use random noise as input, it can keep generating samples until enough valid samples are generated. Figure 7 shows the comparison of the amount of data before and after the four small sample balances in the dataset so that the entire dataset achieves class balance.

To highlight the effect of the filter, we use the following statistical methods to compare the effectiveness of generated samples and real data. Considering the real data samples $\mathbf{A} = \{\mathbf{a}_i\}_{i=1}^{M} \sim \mathbb{P}_r$, and the generated data samples $\mathbf{B} = \{\mathbf{b}_j\}_{j=1}^{N} \sim \mathbb{P}_g$, where $\mathbf{a}_i, \mathbf{b}_j \in \mathbb{R}^D$. The average of the real and generated data samples is computed as $\mu_A = \frac{1}{M} \sum_{i=1}^{M} \mathbf{a}_i$ and $\mu_B = \frac{1}{N} \sum_{j=1}^{N} \mathbf{b}_j$, respectively.

1. Euclidean distance: Euclidean distance (ED) is used to evaluate the distance of two samples in Euclidean space. As shown in Equation (12), the lower ED indicates that the real sample and the generated sample are more similar.

$$ED(\mathbf{A}, \mathbf{B}) = \|\mu_\mathbf{A} - \mu_\mathbf{B}\|^2 = \sum_{d=1}^{D} (\mu_{\mathbf{A},d} - \mu_{\mathbf{B},d})^2 \qquad (12)$$

2. Correlation Coefficient: The Pearson correlation coefficient ($CC \in [-1, 1]$) assesses the correlation between two samples, as shown in Equation (13). The higher the correlation between the two samples, the closer the CC is to 1.

$$CC(\mathbf{A}, \mathbf{B}) = \frac{D \sum_d \mu_{\mathbf{A},d} \mu_{\mathbf{B},d} - \sum_d \mu_{\mathbf{A},d} \mu_{\mathbf{B},d}}{c_1 \times c_2}$$
$$c_1 = \sqrt{D \sum_d \mu_{\mathbf{A},d}^2 - (\sum_d \mu_{\mathbf{A},d})^2} \qquad (13)$$
$$c_2 = \sqrt{D \sum_d \mu_{\mathbf{B},d}^2 - (\sum_d \mu_{\mathbf{B},d})^2}$$

3. Fréchet distance: The Fréchet distance (FD) is given by Equation (14). Evaluating the distance of two samples in metric space is a robust measure relative to Euclidean distance. A lower FD indicates that the two samples are more similar.

$$FD(\mathbf{A}, \mathbf{B}) = \|\mu_\mathbf{A} - \mu_\mathbf{B}\|^2 + Tr(\Sigma'_{AB})$$
$$\Sigma'_{AB} = \Sigma_A + \Sigma_B - 2\sqrt{\Sigma_A \Sigma_B}$$
$$\Sigma_A = \frac{1}{M-1} \sum_{i=1}^{M} (\mathbf{a}_i - \mu_\mathbf{A})(\mathbf{a}_i - \mu_\mathbf{A})^T \quad (14)$$
$$\Sigma_B = \frac{1}{N-1} \sum_{i=1}^{N} (\mathbf{b}_i - \mu_\mathbf{B})(\mathbf{b}_i - \mu_\mathbf{B})^T$$

In order to evaluate the effect of the filter, we set different *thresholds*, including 1, 2, and 3, to generate sample screening. For example, a threshold of 2 indicates that the generated samples pass both machine learning models in the filter. The generated samples of each class are screened, and the similarity estimates are calculated with the real samples, including ED, CC, and FD. The results are shown in Table 7.

For the result of each class of samples and each threhold, the result that generated samples pass the three machine learning models in the filter is the best; that is, the ED and FD are the smallest, and the CC value is the largest. This shows that the filter built by machine learning is able to filter out generated samples that are more similar to the real samples. In other words, compared with the general GAN model, the samples that Filter-GAN generate are closer to the real samples.

Table 7. Statistical evaluation of data augmentation methods.

Class	Filter Threshold	ED	CC	FD
PUA	1	1.4233	0.7396	0.2764
	2	1.5597	0.74910	0.2380
	3	**0.7429**	**0.8763**	**0.1475**
WebCompanion	1	3.3419	0.2437	0.7057
	2	1.4356	0.6712	0.34327
	3	**0.7512**	**0.8776**	**0.2236**
Necure	1	1.8990	0.5266	0.3572
	2	1.1253	0.7132	0.2105
	3	**1.0797**	**0.7808**	**0.1730**
MinerTrojan	1	1.0582	0.7802	0.1510
	2	0.8240	0.8421	0.1332
	3	**0.6757**	**0.8895**	**0.1061**

Note: Bold represents best values.

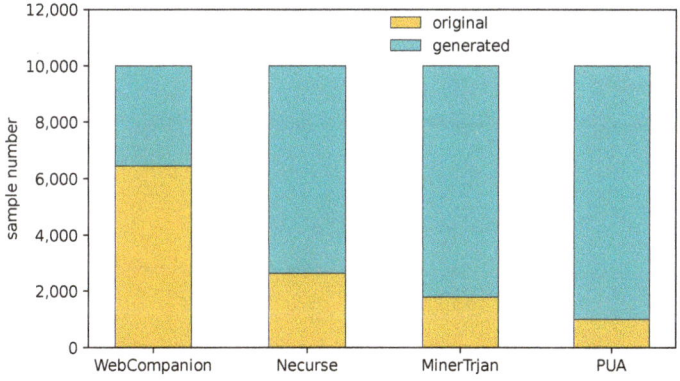

Figure 7. Data distribution after balancing subclasses.

4.2.3. Experimental Results on Balanced Datasets

To compare the filtering effect of Filter on the generated samples. Experiments are carried out on imbalanced datasets and balanced datasets with different filter thresholds. As can be seen in Section 3.2.2, when the threshold = 1 is set, the sample passes only one machine learning model in the filter. As can be seen from Table 8, when only the imbalance feature image set is used as the training set for classification, the accuracy of the small sample categories such as Necurse, MinerTrojan, and PUA is very low.

Table 8. Comparative experimental results based on balanced and unbalanced datasets.

Traffic Class Name	Imbalance Dataset			Threshold = 1			Threshold = 2			Threshold = 3		
	Pre	Rec	F1	Pre	Rec	F1	Pre	Rec	F1	Pre	Rec	F1
CoinMiner	0.9656	0.955	0.9603	0.9671	0.9523	0.9596	0.9654	0.9574	0.9614	0.9753	0.9599	0.9675
WebCompanion	0.9676	0.9676	0.9676	0.9627	0.962	0.9623	0.9697	0.9711	0.9704	0.9607	0.9699	0.9653
Trickbot1	0.9995	0.9974	0.9984	0.9968	0.9967	0.9967	0.9975	0.9988	0.9981	0.9983	0.997	0.9976
Sathurbot	0.9944	0.9979	0.9961	0.9916	0.9947	0.9931	0.9948	0.9965	0.9956	0.9907	0.996	0.9933
Ursnif	1.0	1.0	1.0	0.9977	0.9986	0.9981	0.9995	0.999	0.9992	0.9995	0.9981	0.9988
Artemis Trojan	0.9994	0.9997	0.9995	0.9982	0.9994	0.9988	0.9997	0.9994	0.9995	0.9994	1.0	0.9997
HPEMOTET	0.9993	0.9971	0.9982	0.9982	0.9994	0.9988	0.9971	0.9971	0.9971	0.9993	0.9946	0.9969
Wannacry-R	0.9956	0.9937	0.9946	0.9977	0.9926	0.9951	0.9937	0.9914	0.9925	0.9981	0.9963	0.9972
Necurse	0.9412	0.99	0.965	0.9452	0.9848	0.9646	0.955	0.9903	0.9723	0.9303	0.9848	0.9568
Magic Hound	0.9984	0.9992	0.9988	0.9987	0.9998	0.9992	0.9987	0.9992	0.9989	0.9984	0.9995	0.9989
MinerTrojan	0.757	0.8087	0.782	0.7303	0.767	0.7482	0.7872	0.7521	0.7692	**0.8187**	0.821	0.8198
PUA	0.8767	0.8067	0.8402	0.8497	0.8283	0.8389	0.8394	0.8592	0.8492	0.8535	0.8622	0.8578
Avarage	0.9578	0.9594	0.9584	0.9528	0.9563	0.9545	0.9581	0.9593	0.9586	0.9602	0.9649	0.9625

Note: Bold represents best values.

When using a balanced dataset with the filter, $Threshold = 1$. We use generated feature image samples as a complement to the few-shot class training set. Compared with using only the imbalanced dataset, the classification accuracy of this case is not significantly improved, which is large because the data distribution of the samples generated by the GAN network is not close to the real samples. That is to say, the sample size of these four types of samples used to train the GAN network model is too small so that the GAN network model cannot fully learn the data distribution of the small sample category so that the generated samples of effective data distribution cannot be accurately generated. Therefore, it is necessary to use filters to screen the generated samples.

When the $Threshold = 2$ or 3, the generated samples as supplementary four-type small samples pass the classification of at least one machine learning model in the filter. The results show that the classification results of MinerTrojan, WebCompanion, and Necurse are improved. The F-1 indicators all rose above 0.97. Necurse's Precision and F-1 metrics improved by 1%. In particular, the MinerTrojan category achieved an accuracy of 0.8187, an improvement of 6%. This shows that through the filtering of the filter, the data distribution of the generated samples is closer to the real samples, which effectively solves the problem of class imbalance in the real dataset. Filter-GAN considers the diversity and accuracy of the generated samples, making the classification effect of the samples more significant.

4.2.4. Comparative Experiment

We implement the commonly used methods for dealing with data imbalance as a comparative experiment for Filter-GAN. The first method is *the Random Oversampling (ROS)* [22], which aims to improve the sampling rate of small classes. ROS generates some copies of the secondary class examples. The method is simple to implement and requires little computation. The second way is the *synthetic minority over-sampling technique (SMOTE)* [24]. The SMOTE method generates samples by evaluating the feature space of the sample and its k-nearest neighbors, where k is determined by the number of minority samples. Specifically, first let the d_i vector be different from the feature vector of the minority sample x_i, that is, the k nearest neighbors, let $d'_i = d_i \times r$ where $r \in [0,1]$. Then, the new sample $x'_i = x_i + d'_i$. Further, some derivatives of SMOTE are also implemented, such as SVM-SMOTE [26], ADASYN [25].

Table 9 shows the results of the comparison experiments. The table shows the overall accuracy for the classification task and the classification accuracy for the four minority classes. The overall accuracy of our method is higher than other methods. Secondly, the accuracy rates of CM, WebC, MinerT, and PUA are also higher than other research methods. Therefore, the Filter-GAN method outperforms other compared methods, which shows that our method has advantages in malicious traffic characterization and data augmentation.

Table 9. The result of comparative experiment.

Method	Overall Accuracy	CM	WebC	Necurse	MinerT	PUA
ROS	0.9867	0.9623	0.9599	0.9392	0.7058	0.8462
RUS	0.9691	0.8907	0.8586	0.8734	0.7808	0.7972
SMOTE	0.9841	0.9578	0.9465	0.9392	0.7519	0.7168
SVM-SMOTE	0.9856	0.951	0.9502	0.9516	0.7365	0.8112
ADASYN	0.987	0.9639	0.9647	0.9417	0.7038	0.8112
GAN without Filter	0.9852	0.9603	0.9627	0.9452	0.7303	0.8497
Filter-GAN	0.9907	0.9753	0.9607	0.9303	0.8187	0.8535

5. Conclusions

The class imbalance of malicious traffic datasets leads to the low classification accuracy of deep learning and weak generalization ability. It is solved by two aspects in this paper: on the one hand, the features of the network session are mapped to the feature image, which makes the low-rank feature space of the image represent the diversity of the original traffic session. This method can generate images of uniform size and realize the uniform expression of features in different sessions. On the other hand, to balance the original traffic session dataset, the Filter-GAN model continuously generates new feature images through the GAN model and uses filter to filter the generated samples, so that the generated samples are closer to the distribution of real data. Experimental results show that the feature image representation method can effectively classify malicious traffic families. When there are enough class samples, the detection accuracy of the samples can reach 99%. In the case of unbalanced samples of malicious traffic families, after using the Filter-GAN model to enhance the small sample data, the detection and classification accuracy is also significantly improved up to 6%.

Author Contributions: Conceptualization, X.C. and Q.L.; methodology, X.C.; software, P.W.; resources, X.C.; data curation, X.C.; writing—original draft preparation, X.C.; writing—review and editing, X.C.; visualization, P.W.; supervision, Q.L.; project administration, P.W.; funding acquisition, Q.L. All authors have read and agreed to the published version of the manuscript.

Funding: This research was funded by the National Natural Science Foundation of China under Grant 61902328 and Key R&D projects of Sichuan Science and technology plan (2022YFG0323).

Data Availability Statement: The data presented in this study are available on request from the corresponding author. The data are not publicly available due to lab privacy.

Acknowledgments: The authors wish to thank the editor and the anonymous reviewers for their valuable suggestions on improving this paper.

Conflicts of Interest: The authors declare no conflict of interest.

References

1. Cotton, M.; Eggert, L.; Touch, D.J.D.; Westerlund, M.; Cheshire, S. Internet Assigned Numbers Authority (IANA) Procedures for the Management of the Service Name and Transport Protocol Port Number Registry. RFC 6335, 2011. Available online: https://www.rfc-editor.org/info/rfc6335 (accessed on 24 October 2020).
2. Khalife, J.; Hajjar, A.; Diaz-Verdejo, J. A multilevel taxonomy and requirements for an optimal traffic-classification model. *Int. J. Netw. Manag.* **2014**, *24*, 101–120. [CrossRef]
3. Park, B.C.; Won, Y.J.; Kim, M.S.; Hong, J.W. Towards automated application signature generation for traffic identification. In Proceedings of the NOMS 2008—2008 IEEE Network Operations and Management Symposium, Bahia, Brazil, 7–11 April 2008; pp. 160–167.
4. Sherry, J.; Lan, C.; Popa, R.A.; Ratnasamy, S. Blindbox: Deep packet inspection over encrypted traffic. In Proceedings of the 2015 ACM Conference on Special Interest Group on Data Communication, London, UK, 17–21 August 2015; pp. 213–226.
5. Zhang, K.; Wang, Z.; Chen, G.; Zhang, L.; Yang, Y.; Yao, C.; Wang, J.; Yao, J. Training effective deep reinforcement learning agents for real-time life-cycle production optimization. *J. Pet. Sci. Eng.* **2022**, *208*, 109766. [CrossRef]
6. Yin, F.; Xue, X.; Zhang, C.; Zhang, K.; Han, J.; Liu, B.; Wang, J.; Yao, J. Multifidelity genetic transfer: An efficient framework for production optimization. *SPE J.* **2021**, *26*, 1614–1635. [CrossRef]
7. Zhang, K.; Zhang, J.; Ma, X.; Yao, C.; Zhang, L.; Yang, Y.; Wang, J.; Yao, J.; Zhao, H. History matching of naturally fractured reservoirs using a deep sparse autoencoder. *SPE J.* **2021**, *26*, 1700–1721. [CrossRef]
8. Ma, X.; Zhang, K.; Zhang, L.; Yao, C.; Yao, J.; Wang, H.; Jian, W.; Yan, Y. Data-driven niching differential evolution with adaptive parameters control for history matching and uncertainty quantification. *SPE J.* **2021**, *26*, 993–1010. [CrossRef]
9. Xu, X.; Wang, C.; Zhou, P. GVRP considered oil-gas recovery in refined oil distribution: From an environmental perspective. *Int. J. Prod. Econ.* **2021**, *235*, 108078. [CrossRef]
10. Xu, X.; Hao, J.; Zheng, Y. Multi-objective artificial bee colony algorithm for multi-stage resource leveling problem in sharing logistics network. *Comput. Ind. Eng.* **2020**, *142*, 106338. [CrossRef]
11. Wang, Z. The applications of deep learning on traffic identification. *BlackHat USA* **2015**, *24*, 1–10.
12. Jia, W.; Liu, Y.; Liu, Y.; Wang, J. Detection Mechanism Against DDoS Attacks based on Convolutional Neural Network in SINET. In Proceedings of the 2020 IEEE 4th Information Technology, Networking, Electronic and Automation Control Conference (ITNEC), Chongqing, China, 12–14 June 2020; Volume 1, pp. 1144–1148.
13. Wang, Y.; Jiang, Y.; Lan, J. Fcnn: An efficient intrusion detection method based on raw network traffic. *Secur. Commun. Netw.* **2021**, *2021*, 5533269. [CrossRef]
14. Man, J.; Sun, G. A residual learning-based network intrusion detection system. *Secur. Commun. Netw.* **2021**, *2021*, 5593435. [CrossRef]
15. Bai, H.; Liu, G.; Liu, W.; Quan, Y.; Huang, S. N-gram, semantic-based neural network for mobile malware network traffic detection. *Secur. Commun. Netw.* **2021**, *2021*, 5599556. [CrossRef]
16. Marín, G.; Caasas, P.; Capdehourat, G. Deepmal-deep learning models for malware traffic detection and classification. In *Data Science–Analytics and Applications*; Springer: Berlin/Heidelberg, Germany, 2021; pp. 105–112.
17. Hwang, R.H.; Peng, M.C.; Huang, C.W.; Lin, P.C.; Nguyen, V.L. An unsupervised deep learning model for early network traffic anomaly detection. *IEEE Access* **2020**, *8*, 30387–30399. [CrossRef]
18. Wang, W.; Zhu, M.; Wang, J.; Zeng, X.; Yang, Z. End-to-end encrypted traffic classification with one-dimensional convolution neural networks. In Proceedings of the 2017 IEEE International Conference on Intelligence and Security Informatics (ISI), Beijing, China, 22–24 July 2017; pp. 43–48.
19. Zhang, W.; Wang, J.; Chen, S.; Qi, H.; Li, K. A framework for resource-aware online traffic classification using cnn. In Proceedings of the 14th International Conference on Future Internet Technologies, Phuket, Thailand, 7–9 August 2019; pp. 1–6.
20. Lotfollahi, M.; Jafari Siavoshani, M.; Shirali Hossein Zade, R.; Saberian, M. Deep packet: A novel approach for encrypted traffic classification using deep learning. *Soft Comput.* **2020**, *24*, 1999–2012. [CrossRef]
21. Wang, P.; Chen, X. SAE-based encrypted traffic identification method. *Comput. Eng.* **2018**, *44*, 140–147.
22. Vu, L.; Van Tra, D.; Nguyen, Q.U. Learning from imbalanced data for encrypted traffic identification problem. In Proceedings of the Seventh Symposium on Information and Communication Technology, Ho Chi Minh, Vietnam, 8–9 December 2016; pp. 147–152.
23. Cieslak, D.A.; Chawla, N.V.; Striegel, A. Combating imbalance in network intrusion datasets. In Proceedings of the GrC, Citeseer, Atlanta, GA, USA, 10–12 May 2006; pp. 732–737.
24. Chawla, N.V.; Bowyer, K.W.; Hall, L.O.; Kegelmeyer, W.P. SMOTE: Synthetic minority over-sampling technique. *J. Artif. Intell. Res.* **2002**, *16*, 321–357. [CrossRef]
25. Chen, Z.; Zhou, L.; Yu, W. ADASYN- Random Forest Based Intrusion Detection Model. In Proceedings of the 2021 4th International Conference on Signal Processing and Machine Learning, Beijing, China, 18–20 August 2021; pp. 152–159.
26. Nguyen, H.M.; Cooper, E.W.; Kamei, K. Borderline over-sampling for imbalanced data classification. In Proceedings of the Proceedings: Fifth International Workshop on Computational Intelligence & Applications, IEEE SMC Hiroshima Chapter, Hiroshima City, Japan, 10–12 November 2009; Volume 2009, pp. 24–29.
27. Last, F.; Douzas, G.; Bacao, F. Oversampling for imbalanced learning based on k-means and smote. *arXiv* **2017**, arXiv:1711.00837.
28. Hu, W.; Tan, Y. Generating adversarial malware examples for black-box attacks based on GAN. *arXiv* **2017**, arXiv:1702.05983.

29. Vu, L.; Bui, C.T.; Nguyen, Q.U. A deep learning based method for handling imbalanced problem in network traffic classification. In Proceedings of the Eighth International Symposium on Information and Communication Technology, Nha Trang, Vietnam, 7–8 December 2017; pp. 333–339.
30. Wang, P.; Li, S.; Ye, F.; Wang, Z.; Zhang, M. PacketCGAN: Exploratory study of class imbalance for encrypted traffic classification using CGAN. In Proceedings of the ICC 2020—2020 IEEE International Conference on Communications (ICC), Dublin, Ireland, 7–11 June 2020; pp. 1–7.
31. Wang, Z.; Wang, P.; Zhou, X.; Li, S.; Zhang, M. FLOWGAN: Unbalanced network encrypted traffic identification method based on GAN. In Proceedings of the 2019 IEEE Intl Conf on Parallel & Distributed Processing with Applications, Big Data & Cloud Computing, Sustainable Computing & Communications, Social Computing & Networking (ISPA/BDCloud/SocialCom/SustainCom), Xiamen, China, 16–18 December 2019; pp. 975–983.
32. Goodfellow, I.; Pouget-Abadie, J.; Mirza, M.; Xu, B.; Warde-Farley, D.; Ozair, S.; Courville, A.; Bengio, Y. Generative adversarial nets. *Commun. ACM* **2014**, *27*, 139–144.
33. The CTU Dataset from Malware Capture Facility Project. Available online: https://www.stratosphereips.org/datasets-malware (accessed on 15 March 2021).
34. SplitCap.exe Tool. Available online: https://www.netresec.com/?page=SplitCap (accessed on 24 October 2020).

Article

Dynamic Model Selection Based on Demand Pattern Classification in Retail Sales Forecasting

Erjiang E [1,*], Ming Yu [2], Xin Tian [3,4,*] and Ye Tao [5]

1 School of Management, Guangxi Minzu University, Nanning 530006, China
2 Department of Industrial Engineering, Tsinghua University, Beijing 100084, China
3 School of Economics and Management, University of Chinese Academy of Sciences, Beijing 100190, China
4 Research Center on Fictitious Economy and Data Science, Chinese Academy of Sciences, Beijing 100190, China
5 Beijing Haolinju CVS Co., Ltd., Beijing 100190, China
* Correspondence: eej22@gxmzu.edu.cn (E.E.); tianx@ucas.ac.cn (X.T.)

Abstract: Many forecasting techniques have been applied to sales forecasts in the retail industry. However, no one prediction model is applicable to all cases. For demand forecasting of the same item, the different results of prediction models often confuse retailers. For large retail companies with a wide variety of products, it is difficult to find a suitable prediction model for each item. This study aims to propose a dynamic model selection approach that combines individual selection and combination forecasts based on both the demand patterns and the out-of-sample performance for each item. Firstly, based on both metrics of the squared coefficient of variation (CV^2) and the average inter-demand interval (ADI), we divide the demand patterns of items into four types: smooth, intermittent, erratic, and lumpy. Secondly, we select nine classical forecasting methods in the M-Competitions to build a pool of models. Thirdly, we design two dynamic weighting strategies to determine the final prediction, namely DWS-A and DWS-B. Finally, we verify the effectiveness of this approach by using two large datasets from an offline retailer and an online retailer in China. The empirical results show that these two strategies can effectively improve the accuracy of demand forecasting. The DWS-A method is suitable for items with the demand patterns of intermittent and lumpy, while the DWS-B method is suitable for items with the demand patterns of smooth and erratic.

Keywords: sales forecasting; demand pattern; dynamic weighting; model selection; retail

MSC: 62P30

1. Introduction

Retailers are under enormous pressure to grow their sales, profit, and market share [1]. Sales forecasts play a crucial role in the operation of the retail industry. Reliable sales forecasts can significantly enhance the effectiveness of business strategy quality, reduce operating expenses, and improve customer satisfaction. However, sales forecasting is not an easy task due to a variety of factors affecting demand and supply. For example, numerous factors, including weather, promotions, and pricing, have an impact on product sales [2]. Thus, for those retailers who supply a wide range of stock-keeping units (SKUs), accurately predicting the sales of each product will be a complex task.

Currently, many forecasting techniques have been applied to sales forecasts in the retail industry. Simple moving averages and sophisticated machine learning algorithms are among the techniques used. The amount of data and computing complexity required for these models varies greatly. Many academics have attempted to assess and contrast the effectiveness of various forecasting techniques, such as M-Competitions. However, some scholars have found that some models perform well in a specific scene but perform poorly in another scene [3,4]. No single prediction model is ever universally applicable in all cases [5]. Moreover, for demand forecasting of the same item, the different results of prediction models often confuse retailers. In practice, a key issue is how managers choose the right predictive model for each product in a variety of forecasting techniques. The sales volume and data length of each product widely vary. For example, Haolingju, a large chain of convenience stores in Beijing, stocks more than 5000 different items in its distribution center and has more than 800 stores. The best-selling products can sell tens of thousands a day, such as Nongfu Spring Mineral Water. In addition, managers need to remove low-volume products from the shelves and launch new products to meet consumer demand. Some products are sold for a short period of time or have high volatility and skewness. New product forecasts are ranked by forecasters as one of the most complex forecasting tasks they encounter, as little or no historical data are available for reference [6,7].

This study proposes a dynamic model selection approach that combines individual selection and combination forecasts based on both the demand patterns and the out-of-sample performance for each item. Firstly, we selected nine classical forecasting methods in the M-Competitions to build a model pool. The M-Competitions aim to learn how to improve prediction accuracy and how to apply this learning to promote prediction theory and practice [8]. Secondly, based on both indicators of the squared coefficient of variation (CV^2) and the average inter-demand interval (ADI), we divided the demand patterns of items into four types: smooth, intermittent, erratic, and lumpy. For instance, the smooth pattern is characterized by low CV^2 and short ADI, while the intermittent pattern is characterized by low CV^2 and long ADI. The erratic pattern is characterized by high CV^2 and short ADI, while the lumpy pattern is characterized by high CV^2 and long ADI. Thirdly, we designed two dynamic weighting strategies to determine the final prediction, namely DWS-A and DWS-B. Finally, we demonstrated the effectiveness of this approach by using two large datasets from a large offline retailer (Haolinju) and a large online retailer (JD) in China. We implemented multi-round rolling forecast with different horizons. The results show that the proposed dynamic weighting strategies outperformed the benchmark and winner prediction models in M-Competitions, including Naïve, Comb S-H-D, and simple combination of univariate models (SCUM). Further, we investigated the optimal weighting strategy for each demand pattern. The analysis results suggest that the DWS-A method is applicable to the items of intermittent and lumpy patterns, and the DWS-B method is applicable to the items of smooth and erratic patterns.

The rest of the paper is organized as follows. Section 2 presents a literature review of the forecasting methods and model selection. Section 3 describes the methodology of sales forecasting. Section 4 presents the results of a sales forecasting system for two real-world problems. Lastly, Section 5 provides a summary of the results and concludes the study.

2. Literature Review

2.1. Demand Forecasting Method in Retailing

Over the past few decades, many researchers have proposed a new prediction or revised existing models based on application requirements. Traditional quantitative prediction methods include times series, econometric models, and machine learning. At present, scholars increasingly pay attention to the integration of mixed and combined models of two or more models.

2.1.1. Individual Methods

(a) Time series method. Some prediction methods, such as Naïve, seasonal Naïve, and moving averages, are very simple and effective [9]. These methods are often used as a benchmark for new demand forecasting methods. However, the performance of the Naïve model will drop in the long-term predictions or predicting the series of structural mutations. Exponential smoothing is a simple and practical point prediction method in which predictions are constructed from exponentially weighted averages of past observations. Simple exponential smoothing is suitable for forecasts without significant trends or seasonal patterns. In contrast, double exponential smoothing models, such as Brown's DES and Holt's DES, were developed to deal with time series of linear trends [10,11]. Holt–Winter's model was developed to handle time series with trends or seasonal patterns [11,12], whereas the ARMA model, proposed by Box and Jenkins in 1976 [13], is one of the most widely used to predict various time series. For instance, Ali et al. [14] found that simple time series techniques perform very well for periods without promotions.

(b) Econometric model. An econometric model is a useful tool for economic forecasting and causality analysis. As a typical example of econometric models, the traditional regression method can be used to analyze the causal relationship between product sales and the factors affecting it [15]. For example, Divakar et al. [16] proposed a sales forecasting model by using a dynamic regression model to capture the effects of such variables as past sales, trend, temperature, significant holidays, etc.

(c) Machine learning method. The artificial neural network (ANN) models are widely used in retail sales forecasts. Kong and Martin [17] found that the backpropagation neural network (BPN) is a useful tool to generate sales forecasts and outperform statistical methods. Meanwhile, Lee et al. [18] used the BPN method to establish a convenience store sales forecasting model. Furthermore, Chen and Ou [19] proposed a model that integrates grey correlation analysis and a multi-layer functional link network to predict the actual sales data in the retail industry.

2.1.2. Hybrid Methods

No general predictive model is applicable to different types of problems. Some researchers argued that hybrid models integrate two or more models with different capabilities, which are more accurate than a single specific model with limited capabilities [2]. Aburto and Weber [20] proposed a hybrid system of combing ARIMA and neural networks to predict the daily demand of a Chilean supermarket. They showed an increase in predictive accuracy and proposed a replenishment system that reduces sales failures and inventory levels compared with previous solutions. Meanwhile, Arunraj and Ahrens [2] developed seasonal autoregressive combined moving averages using external variable models to predict the daily sales of banana in a retail store in Germany. Furthermore, Liu et al. [21] combined time series and hidden Markov models to improve the reliability of the prediction. Rubio and Alba [22] proposed a hybrid model combing ARIMA and support vector machine to predict Colombian shares. Wang et al. [23] proposed an error compensation mechanism to address the user's ability to correct the model in practice and designed a hybrid LSTM-ARMA model for demand forecasting.

2.1.3. Combination Methods

Combining forecast refers to the averaging forecasts of component methods to reduce forecast error [24]. Makridakis and Hibon [25] proposed a combination method in the M3 competition, namely, Comb S-H-D. This method is a simple arithmetic mean of single exponential smoothing (SES), Holt exponential smoothing, and exponential smoothing with the damped trend. This combination method is more accurate than the above three methods. Makridakis, Spiliotis, and Assimakopoulos [8] found that of the 17 most accurate methods of the M4 competition, 12 are 'combinations' of statistical methods. Meanwhile, Aye et al. [26] found that the combined forecasting models perform better in forecasting aggregate retail sales than the single models and are not affected by the business cycle and time horizon.

2.2. Model Selection

The existing literature indicates that the performance of forecasting models largely depends on the choice of error measures, the model used for comparison, the forecasting horizon, and the type of data. Zhang [27] argued that no single prediction model is applicable to all cases. For instance, Aburto and Weber [20] found that neural networks are superior to ARIMA models, and the proposed additive hybrid approach yields the best results. Lee, Chen, Chen, Chen, and Liu [18] found that logistic regression performed better than BPNN and moving average, and Kuo [28] found that the fuzzy neural network has better performance than conventional statistical methods. Thus, which forecasting techniques should be chosen when retailers face complex environments in production operations and management?

Since no single model always outperforms other candidate models in all cases, it is necessary to find a model selection method for any given SKU or item. Recently, some scholars have paid more attention to the topic of forecasting model selection. Table 1 shows typical papers that have investigated forecasting model selection and presents the contribution of our study to the literature. The strategies for selecting the best prediction model according to the historical performance of candidate models can be classified into three types: individual selection, aggregate selection, and combination forecasts. Individual selection refers to finding the most suitable prediction model for each SKU or item. Instead, aggregate selection refers to when a single forecasting model is used for all SKUs or items [29]. Combined forecasts combine a set of forecasting models by building a weight coefficient vector. Individual model selection is more effective than most aggregation model selection methods, but the former has the disadvantage of higher complexity and computational costs [30]. In the individual selection procedure, information criteria (such as Akaike information), time series features, in-sample performance, and out-of-sample performance are usually used as model selection criteria. For instance, Villegas et al. [31] proposed a model selection method that combines information criteria and in-sample performance using a support vector machine. Taghiyeh, Lengacher, and Handfield [30] developed an approach that combines both in-sample and out-of-sample performance. Ulrich, Jahnke, Langrock, Pesch, and Senge [4] considered model selection as a classification problem and proposed a model selection framework via classification based on the labeled training data. Combining different models is another effective way to improve the performance of prediction [27]. However, Claeskens, Magnus, Vasnev, and Wang [3] showed that simple weighting schemes, such as arithmetic mean, usually produce equally good or better predictions than more complex weighting schemes.

Table 1. Review of published literature for forecasting model selection.

Article	Model Selection Strategy	Model Selection Criteria	Candidate Model
Fildes [29]	Aggregate selection	Out-of-sample performance	Filter model; Robust Trend Estimation
Taghiyeh, Lengacher, and Handfield [30]	Individual selection	In-sample performance. Out-of-sample performance	Naïve; Exponential Smoothing Models; ARIMA; Theta
Villegas, Pedregal, and Trapero [31]	Individual selection	Information criteria. In-sample performance	White Noise; Moving Average; Simple Exponential Smoothing; Mean; Median
Ulrich, Jahnke, Langrock, Pesch, and Senge [4]	Individual selection	Feature-based	Linear Regression; Generalized Additive Models; Quantile Regression; ARIMAX
Our study	Individual selection. Combination forecasts	Feature-based. Out-of-sample performance	Benchmark and winning models in M-Competitions

The contribution of our study is to determine the corresponding model selection strategies that combine individual selection and combination forecasts based on both the demand patterns and the out-of-sample performance for each item. Further, we selected the benchmark and winning models in M-Competitions as the candidate models.

3. Methodology

In this section, we designed an automatic forecasting system to address model selection of sales forecasting in the retail industry. Figure 1 shows the flowchart of the system framework, which was designed to include four steps: data input and pre-processing, construction of model pool and forecasting, classification of demand pattern and model selection, and final prediction output and database update.

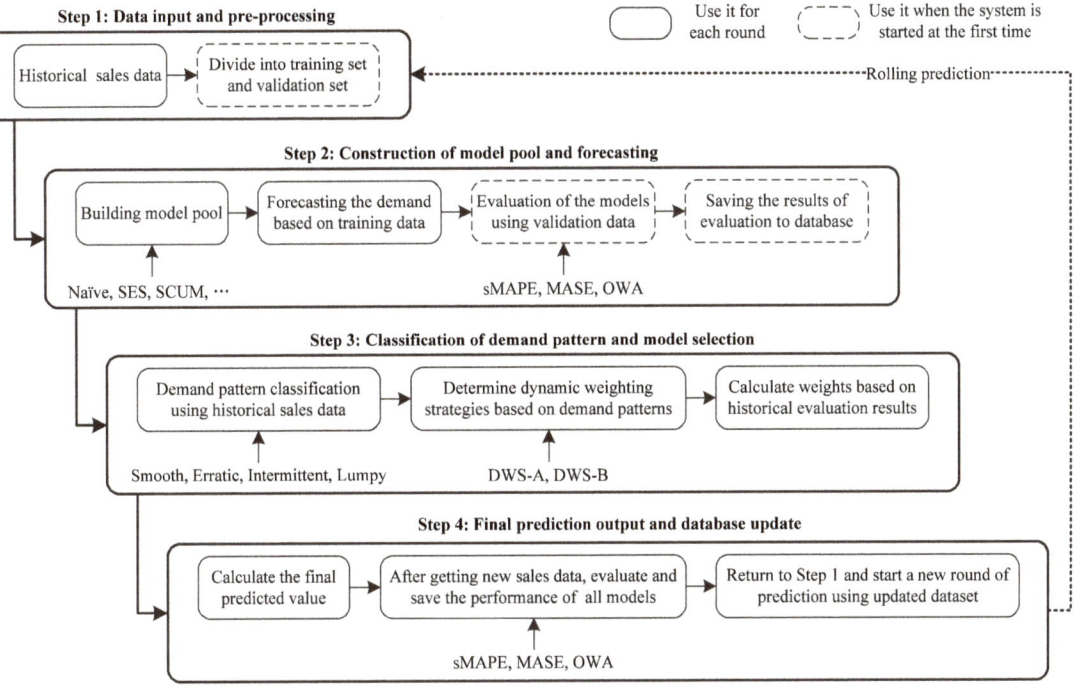

Figure 1. The system framework flowchart.

3.1. Design of Forecasting Model Pool

According to Figure 1, we know that the sales characteristics of different items vary greatly. Moreover, the sales characteristics of each item will also change over time. Therefore, no single forecasting method can maintain the advantage in the demand forecasting of all items. In this study, the idea of dynamic optimization is introduced into the task of forecasting. Firstly, a model pool composed of multiple prediction methods was constructed. Secondly, a vector of dynamic weight coefficients was determined based on the performance of the prediction methods in practice. Finally, the prediction of each item was determined according to the corresponding demand pattern and weight vector of the item.

Based on M-Competitions, this study selected the nine most popular forecasting models to build a pool of models for predicting sales of retail products.

Sub-Model 1: Naïve. The value of the last sales is simply used for all forecasts.

Sub-Model 2: Seasonal Naïve. Considering the sales characteristics of retail products, the model uses daily sales for the previous week as the forecast for the same day of the week.

Sub-Model 3: Single exponential smoothing (SES). The SES model weights the sum of the predicted and actual values of historical sales through the smoothing coefficient.

Sub-Model 4: Holt's linear exponential smoothing. The Holt model considers the linear trend of the sequence on the basis of the SES model [11].

Sub-Model 5: Dampened trend exponential smoothing. The damped model considers the damping trend on the basis of the Holt model [32].

Sub-Model 6: Comb S-H-D. The 'Comb S-H-D' method is the simple arithmetic average of Models 3, 4, and 5. The Comb S-H-D model is more accurate than the three individual methods in M3 competition [25].

Sub-Model 7: Theta. The theta model decomposes the time series into two or more curves, which are combined by theta coefficients [33].

Sub-Model 8: 4Theta. The 4Theta model takes into account the nonlinear pattern of trend and the strength of adjustment trend on the basis of the theta model, and introduces a multiplication term into the model [34].

Sub-Model 9: Simple combination of univariate model. The SCUM model combines four methods: exponential smoothing, complex exponential smoothing, ARIMA, and dynamic optimization theta, and takes the median of the predicted values of the four models as the final predicted value [35]. The SCUM model outperformed most models and improved by 5.6% compared with the benchmark model in M4 competition [8].

3.2. Demand Pattern Classification

For retail stores, the sales characteristics of different items vary greatly. The coefficient of variation is an effective index to measure the volatility of an item's demand, which is defined by the ratio of the standard deviation to the mean demand. The squared coefficient of variation (CV^2) of the demand sizes is given by:

$$CV^2 = \frac{\sigma^2}{\mu^2} \quad (1)$$

The demand for some products may be zero in some time periods. The average inter-demand interval (ADI) is another important indicator to describe the demand characteristics of items. The ADI is calculated as follows:

$$ADI = \frac{Z}{I} \quad (2)$$

where Z is the number of zero demand, and I is the number of intervals. For example, the daily demand of an item is [3,0,2,0,0,3,0,1,0,4], and then the average inter-demand interval is 5/4.

Based on the series' average inter-demand interval and the squared coefficient of variation of the demand sizes, Syntetos et al. [36] proposes a rule to classify demand patterns into four categories: smooth ($CV^2 < 0.49$ and $ADI < 1.32$), intermittent ($CV^2 < 0.49$ and $ADI \geq 1.32$), erratic ($CV^2 \geq 0.49$ and $ADI < 1.32$), and lumpy ($CV^2 \geq 0.49$ and $ADI \geq 1.32$).

Figure 2 shows an example of four items selling on JD, a large B2C online retailer in China. According to CV^2 and ADI, these four items represent the sales characteristics of the four demand patterns, respectively. The smooth pattern is characterized by relatively stable demand volatility and a short average inter-demand interval. The lumpy pattern is characterized by high demand volatility and a long average inter-demand interval. Obviously, the demand prediction of the lumpy pattern will be more difficult than that of the smooth pattern.

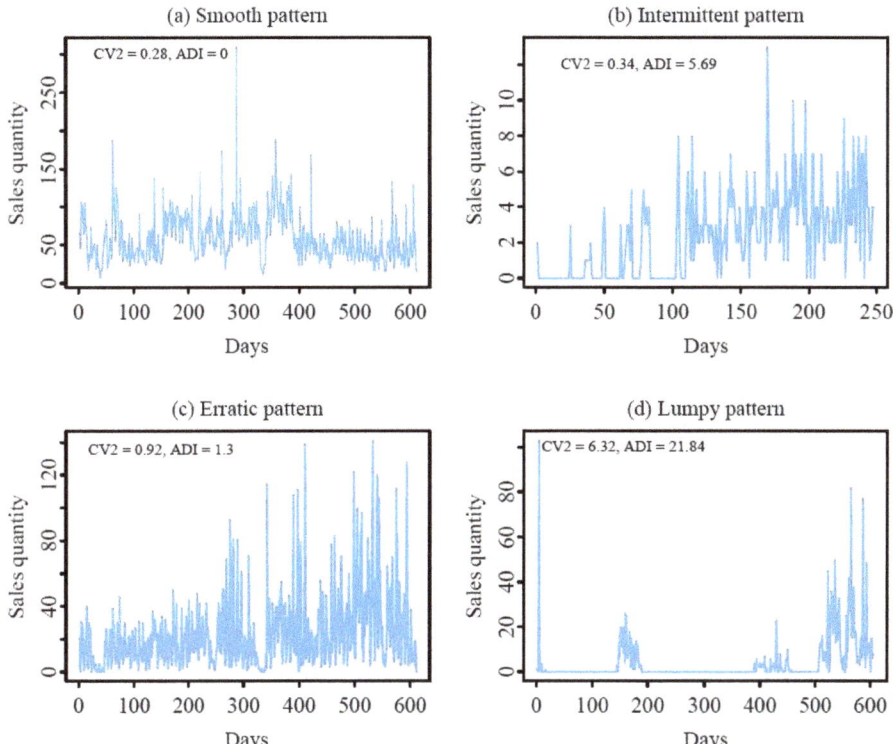

Figure 2. Typical sales characteristics of retail products of the four demand patterns.

3.3. Design of Dynamic Weighting Strategy

Suppose that the model pool M has m sub-models. The sub-model i predicts the demand $\hat{y}_{i,T+1}$ at $T+1$ based on the historical observations $y = \{y_1, \ldots, y_T\}$.

$$\hat{y}_{i,T+1} = f_i(y|y_1, \ldots, y_T), \ i \in M \tag{3}$$

Let $\mathbf{w} = [w_1, \ldots, w_m]$ present a weight vector. The objective of the ensemble model is to determine the weight coefficient of each sub-model (w_i) and to obtain the final prediction value by weighted summation of the output of the sub-model.

$$\hat{Y}_{T+1} = \sum_{i=1}^{m} w_{i,T+1} \hat{y}_{i,T+1}, w_{i,T+1} = [0,1], \sum w_{i,T+1} = 1 \tag{4}$$

The weight coefficient will change with the performance of the model in multi-round rolling prediction. $e_{i,t}$ denotes the error metric of model i at t, such as the root mean square error or symmetric mean absolute percentage error, and $E_{i,k}$ represents the performance of model i over a period of time:

$$E_{i,k} = \frac{1}{k} \sum_{t=T+1}^{T+k} e_{i,t}, t = \{T+1, T+2, \ldots, T+k\} \tag{5}$$

Based on the performance of the sub-models in reality, this study proposes two dynamic weighting strategies.

Dynamic weighting strategy A (DWS-A): The final predictions of DWS-A are the forecasts of that model, which outperforms other models on historical data. The weight coefficient of sub-model i under the DWS-A is as follows:

$$w_{i,k}^A = \begin{cases} 1, if\ E_{i,k} = \min\{E_k\}, \\ 0,\ otherwise. \end{cases} \quad (6)$$

where $E_k = \{E_{1,k}, \ldots, E_{i,k}, \ldots, E_{m,k}\}$ is the set of error metrics of all sub-models.

Dynamic weighting strategy B (DWS-B): The final predictions of DWS-A utilize all the sub-models, which are weighted according to their performance on historical data. The weight coefficient of sub-model i under the DWS-B is given by the formula:

$$w_{i,k}^B = \frac{\max\{E_k\} - E_{i,k}}{\sum_{i=1}^m (\max\{E_k\} - E_{i,k})} \quad (7)$$

In the real world, the value of error metrics will change dynamically as the models roll forward. Thus, the weight coefficients ($w_{i,k}^A$ and $w_{i,k}^B$) will also change with k. The final predictions of DWS-A and DWS-B at $T + k + 1$ are given by the formula:

$$\hat{Y}_{T+k+1}^j = \sum_{i=1}^m w_{i,k}^j \hat{y}_{i,T+k+1}, j \in \{A, B\} \quad (8)$$

3.4. Model Evaluation

Cross-validation is a primary method of measuring the predictive performance of a model. In this study, symmetric mean absolute percentage error (sMAPE), mean absolute scaled error (MASE), and overall weighted average (OWA) were used to evaluate the performance of the forecasting methods [8,25,37]. The sMAPE is defined as:

$$\text{sMAPE} = \frac{1}{h} \sum_{t=1}^h \frac{2|y_t - \hat{y}_t|}{|y_t| + |\hat{y}_t|}. \quad (9)$$

where y_t is the real sales at point t, $\hat{y}_t$ is the forecasting sales, and h is the forecasting horizon. Items with intermittent demand and lumpy demand are very common in retailing. The problem of large error can be avoided by using symmetric MAPE when the actual values, y_t, are close to zero.

The MASE is defined as:

$$\text{MASE} = \frac{1}{h} \frac{\sum_{t=1}^h |y_t - \hat{y}_t|}{\frac{1}{n-r}\sum_{t=r+1}^n |y_t - y_{t-r}|} \quad (10)$$

where r is the frequency of the data and n is the number of historical observations. The MASE is a scale-free error metric. It never yields undefined or infinite values and therefore is a good choice for intermittent demand and lumpy demand.

The OWA is computed by averaging the relative MASE and the relative sMAPE for all samples. The OWA is defined as:

$$\text{OWA}_i = \frac{1}{2}\left(\frac{\sum_1^s \text{sMAPE}_i}{\sum_1^s \text{sMAPE}_1} + \frac{\sum_1^s \text{MASE}_i}{\sum_1^s \text{MASE}_1}\right), i \in M \quad (11)$$

where OWA_i is the OWA of method i, s is the number of series, and sMAPE_1 and MASE_1 are the performance measures of Naïve. The OWA is an effective metric to compare the performance difference between proposed models and the benchmark model. If the OWA of the proposed model is lower than 1, it means that the proposed model outperformed the benchmark model, and vice versa.

4. Empirical Analysis

4.1. Empirical Data

We demonstrate the applicability of the sales forecasting methods using two real-world problems. The first dataset was taken from Haolinju, a large chain of a convenience store in Beijing, China. Haolinju has more than 800 stores and typically stocks more than 5000 different items in its distribution center. Haolinju's sales data ranges from 9 July 2016 to 8 July 2018 and contains 5383 items of different categories and various time horizons. The second dataset was taken from JD, also known as Jingdong, a large B2C online retailer in China. JD's sales data ranges from 1 January 2016 to 31 December 2017 and contains 1000 items of different categories and various time horizons. It should be noted that JD's data in June and November are excluded due to promotional activities. Since some forecasting methods require historical data for training, we removed items with sales records less than 40 days. Then, there were 4027 items in Haolinju's data and 936 items in JD's data that met the requirements.

According to the indicators of CV^2 and ADI, those items in both retailers were divided into four demand patterns: smooth, intermittent, erratic, and lumpy. Table 2 shows the detailed descriptive statistics of CV^2 and ADI on those four demand patterns. There were 1336 (33.2%) items in Haolinju's data and 34 (3.6%) items in JD's data that met the smooth demand pattern. The CV^2 of nonzero demand of Haolinju and JD was 0.223 and 0.376, respectively, and the ADI of both retailers was 0.096 and 0.607, respectively. There were 1211 (30.1%) items in Haolinju's data and 700 (74.8%) items in JD's data that met the lumpy demand pattern. The CV^2 of nonzero demand of Haolinju and JD was 1.586 and 3.408, respectively, and the ADI of Haolinju and JD was 7.096 and 3.862, respectively. In the lumpy pattern, the sales volatility of Haolinju was less than JD, but the former had a longer demand interval.

Table 2. Characteristics of the sales of the offline retailer (Haolinju) and the online retailer (JD).

Characteristics	Haolinju	JD
Total items		
No. of series	4027	936
Mean obs./series	535.0	209.4
Smooth pattern		
No. of series	1336 (33.2%)	34 (3.6%)
% Zero values	0.3 (2.2)	2.1 (4.5)
Average of nonzero demand	471.4 (1155.5)	49.8 (50.9)
CV^2 of nonzero demand	0.223 (0.128)	0.376 (0.084)
ADI	0.096 (0.302)	0.607 (0.554)
Intermittent pattern		
No. of series	713 (17.7%)	40 (4.3%)
% Zero values	56.8 (25.5)	12.4 (14.9)
Average of nonzero demand	38.7 (172.7)	45.6 (121.6)
CV^2 of nonzero demand	0.315 (0.109)	0.403 (0.059)
ADI	6.949 (17.059)	3.739 (3.986)
Erratic pattern		
No. of series	767 (19.0%)	162 (17.3%)
% Zero values	1.1 (3.4)	2.9 (4.7)
Average of nonzero demand	295.4 (667.4)	91.7 (171.1)
CV^2 of nonzero demand	2.340 (4.124)	2.641 (6.377)
ADI	0.290 (0.476)	0.781 (0.518)
Lumpy pattern		
No. of series	1211 (30.1%)	700 (74.8%)
% Zero values	45.8 (23.5)	21.9 (18.4)
Average of nonzero demand	34.0 (189.5)	42.3 (102.1)
CV^2 of nonzero demand	1.586 (3.023)	3.408 (7.795)
ADI	7.096 (36.012)	3.862 (6.421)

ADI: average demand interval; CV: the coefficient of variation. Means (standard deviation) are presented in the table.

4.2. Empirical Results

Based on the two datasets drawn from an offline retailer and an online retailer, we examined the performance of two dynamic weighting strategies by comparing with benchmark models such as Naïve, Comb S-H-D, and SCUM. We implemented multi-round rolling forecast with different horizons. The last 10 days of each series were used to test the performance of the models. We conducted the experiment with ten rounds and one horizon for short-term forecasting, and the experiment with four rounds and seven horizons for long-term forecasting. For example, suppose 1 item has 40 days of sales data, and we set the forecasting horizon equal to 1. Before starting the forecasting system, we used the sales data from day 1 to day 29 to train the sub-models and forecast the demand on day 30. In round 1, based on the performance of each sub-model on day 30, the sales data of the first 30 days were used to predict the demand on day 31. In round 10, the sales data of the first 39 days were used to forecast the demand on day 40. In this study, we measured the performance of the proposed methods with Windows 10, Intel(R) Core(TM) i7-8550U CPU @ 1.80 GHz, 8.00 GB RAM. The forecasting process was performed by using R Studio Version 4.0.5. The performances of two dynamic weighting strategies in four demand patterns were analyzed, respectively.

4.2.1. Smooth Pattern

The forecast accuracy comparisons for different methods with different forecasting horizons in the smooth pattern are shown in Table 3. The Comb S-H-D outperformed the other eight methods in the model pool for Haolinju's data when the horizon was equal to one. In the remaining three datasets, the SCUM outperformed the other eight sub-models. Surprisingly, the DWS-B outperformed all sub-models on all datasets, and the DWS-A performed better than all sub-models for Haolinju's data and JD's data when the horizon was equal to seven. For instance, for Haolinju's data when the horizon was equal to seven, the sMAPE of Naïve was 22.114%, that of Comb S-H-D was 18.749%, that of SCUM was 18.947%, while for DWS-A and DWS-B they were 17.588% and 17.387%, respectively. We also calculated the improvement in OWA of the Comb S-H-D, the SCUM, and the two proposed dynamic weighting strategies over the Naïve. According to OWA, for Haolinju's data when the horizon was equal to seven, the DWS-B was 18.4% more accurate than the Naïve and 5.23% more than the SCUM. In general, the forecast results in the smooth pattern indicate that the proposed DWS-B performed better than the DWS-A method and the other three benchmark models.

4.2.2. Intermittent Pattern

The pattern of intermittent demand is characterized by a long average inter-demand interval and a low coefficient of variation. The results of Table 4 show that the Naïve model provided more accuracy than all other sub-models for Haolinju's data and JD's data when the horizon was equal to one. This means that forecasting intermittent demand is not an easy task. However, the DWS-A outperformed all sub-models for Haolinju's data and JD's data. For instance, for Haolinju's data when the horizon was equal to seven, the sMAPE of Naïve was 82.682%, that of Comb S-H-D was 124.918%, that of SCUM was 126.654%, while for DWS-A it was 75.052%. According to OWA for Haolinju's data when the horizon was equal to seven, the DWS-A was 11.1% more accurate than the Naïve and 7% more than the best sub-model, sNaïve.

Table 3. The performance of the five methods for rolling forecast testing in the smooth pattern.

Model	sMAPE	MASE	OWA	% Improvement of Method over the Naïve
Haolinju: Horizon = 1 (Obs. = 1336 × 1 × 10) [a]				
Naïve	19.948 (1.991)	0.801 (0.152)	1.000 (0.000)	-
Comb S-H-D	17.366 (1.812)	0.707 (0.126)	0.883 (0.076)	11.7%
SCUM	17.714 (1.966)	0.696 (0.128)	0.885 (0.070)	11.5%
DWS-A	18.594 (1.961)	0.763 (0.135)	0.942 (0.069)	5.8%
DWS-B	17.387 (1.972)	0.701 (0.133)	0.873 (0.071)	12.7%
Haolinju: Horizon = 7 (Obs. = 1336 × 7 × 4) [b]				
Naïve	22.114 (0.967)	0.926 (0.054)	1.000 (0.000)	-
Comb S-H-D	18.749 (0.135)	0.811 (0.009)	0.863 (0.043)	13.7%
SCUM	18.947 (0.216)	0.796 (0.008)	0.861 (0.043)	13.9%
DWS-A	17.588 (0.158)	0.768 (0.020)	0.813 (0.036)	18.7%
DWS-B	17.797 (0.334)	0.764 (0.010)	0.816 (0.038)	18.4%
JD: Horizon = 1 (Obs. = 34 × 1 × 10) [b]				
Naïve	49.071 (8.709)	0.975 (0.161)	1.000 (0.000)	-
Comb S-H-D	42.648 (9.694)	0.876 (0.158)	0.897 (0.129)	10.3%
SCUM	41.644 (9.287)	0.845 (0.144))	0.871 (0.119)	12.9%
DWS-A	45.632 (6.064)	0.933 (0.234)	0.975 (0.140)	2.5%
DWS-B	40.476 (8.104)	0.819 (0.160)	0.858 (0.118)	14.2%
JD: Horizon = 7 (Obs. = 34 × 7 × 4) [b]				
Naïve	52.739 (3.593)	1.075 (0.121)	1.000 (0.000)	-
Comb S-H-D	41.531 (0.594)	0.903 (0.027)	0.841 (0.055)	25.9%
SCUM	40.942 (0.657)	0.877 (0.024)	0.821 (0.050)	27.9%
DWS-A	38.658 (1.515)	0.838 (0.009)	0.789 (0.033)	31.1%
DWS-B	38.707 (0.387)	0.823 (0.004)	0.782 (0.782)	31.8%

[a] The Comb S-H-D outperformed the other sub-models in this dataset. [b] The SCUM outperformed the other sub-models in these datasets.

Table 4. The performance of the five methods for rolling forecast testing in the intermittent pattern.

Model	sMAPE	MASE	OWA	% Improvement of Method over the Naïve
Haolinju: Horizon = 1 (Obs. = 713 × 1 × 10) [a]				
Naïve	78.516 (3.403)	1.401 (0.142)	1.000 (0.000)	-
Comb S-H-D	123.704 (2.298)	1.257 (0.088)	1.241 (0.068)	−24.1%
SCUM	125.214 (2.144)	1.249 (0.091)	1.248 (0.066)	−24.8%
DWS-A	79.247 (3.445)	1.349 (0.097)	0.989 (0.035)	1.1%
DWS-B	111.481 (13.306)	1.254 (0.090)	1.164 (0.127)	−16.4%
Haolinju: Horizon = 7 (Obs. = 713 × 7 × 4) [b]				
Naïve	82.682 (3.055)	1.532 (0.127)	1.000 (0.000)	-
Comb S-H-D	124.918 (0.553)	1.315 (0.017)	1.175 (0.061)	−17.5%
SCUM	126.654 (0.344)	1.302 (0.016)	1.181 (0.063)	−18.1%
DWS-A	75.052 (1.303)	1.361 (0.071)	0.889 (0.029)	11.1%
DWS-B	120.953 (1.360)	1.295 (0.029)	1.146 (0.061)	−14.6%
JD: Horizon = 1 (Obs. = 40 × 1 × 10) [a]				
Naïve	49.867 (7.385)	1.094 (0.139)	1.000 (0.000)	-
Comb S-H-D	52.398 (9.005)	1.057 (0.167)	1.025 (0.193)	−2.5%
SCUM	55.184 (8.113)	1.037 (0.162)	1.046 (0.171)	−4.6%
DWS-A	47.535 (7.858)	1.050 (0.157)	0.960 (0.106)	4.0%
DWS-B	48.858 (7.067)	0.994 (0.160)	0.949 (0.118)	5.1%
JD: Horizon = 7 (Obs. = 40 × 7 × 4) [c]				
Naïve	56.265 (5.720)	1.251 (0.044)	1.000 (0.000)	-
Comb S-H-D	55.036 (1.417)	1.157 (0.037)	0.955 (0.083)	4.5%
SCUM	57.666 (0.224)	1.135 (0.038)	0.974 (0.077)	2.6%
DWS-A	47.379 (0.724)	1.058 (0.051)	0.857 (0.074)	14.3%
DWS-B	52.147 (1.313)	1.062 (0.020)	0.903 (0.084)	9.7%

[a] The Naïve outperformed the other sub-models in these datasets. [b] The sNaïve outperformed the other sub-models in this dataset (OWA = 0.956). [c] The 4Theta outperformed the other sub-models in this dataset (OWA = 0.940).

4.2.3. Erratic Pattern

The pattern of erratic demand is characterized by a short average inter-demand interval and a high coefficient of variation. The results of Table 5 show that the DWS-B outperformed all sub-models for Haolinju's data and JD's data. For example, for Haolinju's data when the horizon was equal to one, the sMAPE of Naïve was 32.220%, that of Comb S-

H-D was 31.539%, that of SCUM was 29.752%, while for DWS-B it was 28.731%. According to OWA for Haolinju's data, when the horizon was equal to one, the DWS-B was 8.5% more accurate than the Naïve and 4.29% than the best sub-model, SCUM.

Table 5. The performance of the five methods for rolling forecast testing in the erratic pattern.

Model	sMAPE	MASE	OWA	% Improvement of Method over the Naïve
Haolinju: Horizon = 1 (Obs. = 767 × 1 × 10) [a]				
Naïve	32.220 (2.656)	0.978 (0.686)	1.000 (0.000)	-
Comb S-H-D	31.539 (1.565)	0.975 (0.670)	1.007 (0.127)	−0.7%
SCUM	29.752 (1.562)	0.934 (0.667)	0.956 (0.119)	4.4%
DWS-A	30.604 (2.485)	0.976 (0.713)	0.958 (0.116)	4.2%
DWS-B	28.731 (1.563)	0.945 (0.720)	0.915 (0.089)	8.5%
Haolinju: Horizon = 7 (Obs. = 767 × 7 × 4) [a]				
Naïve	36.492 (1.616)	1.259 (0.293)	1.000 (0.000)	-
Comb S-H-D	35.613 (0.853)	1.332 (0.253)	1.025 (0.049)	−2.5%
SCUM	33.380 (0.660)	1.248 (0.208)	0.969 (0.093)	3.1%
DWS-A	30.258 (1.428)	1.058 (0.258)	0.841 (0.069)	15.9%
DWS-B	31.030 (0.656)	1.140 (0.326)	0.886 (0.048)	11.4%
JD: Horizon = 1 (Obs. = 162 × 1 × 10) [b]				
Naïve	59.324 (8.485)	1.451 (0.597)	1.000 (0.000)	-
Comb S-H-D	63.360 (11.363)	1.407 (0.523)	1.046 (0.191)	−4.6%
SCUM	61.548 (10.980)	1.343 (0.511)	1.003 (0.171)	−0.3%
DWS-A	56.958 (6.653)	1.328 (0.482)	0.956 (0.093)	4.4%
DWS-B	56.821 (8.354)	1.298 (0.496)	0.942 (0.097)	5.8%
JD: Horizon = 7 (Obs. = 162 × 7 × 4) [a]				
Naïve	63.030 (3.753)	1.431 (1.115)	1.000 (0.000)	-
Comb S-H-D	62.366 (1.894)	1.472 (0.070)	1.022 (0.027)	−2.2%
SCUM	60.903 (1.585)	1.409 (0.090)	0.983 (0.024)	1.7%
DWS-A	52.883 (2.642)	1.303 (0.889)	0.889 (0.020)	11.1%
DWS-B	54.516 (1.838)	1.294 (0.898)	0.898 (0.012)	10.2%

[a] The SCUM outperformed the other sub-models in these datasets. [b] The Naïve outperformed the other sub-models in this dataset.

4.2.4. Lumpy Pattern

The pattern of lumpy demand, which is characterized by a long average inter-demand interval and a high coefficient of variation, is a common phenomenon in online and offline retail. The results of Table 6 show that the DWS-A provided more accuracy than all sub-models for Haolinju's data and JD's data. For example, for JD's data when the horizon was equal to seven, the MASE of Naïve was 75.817%, that of Comb S-H-D was 74.057%, that of SCUM was 74.092%, while for DWS-A it was 64.560%. According to OWA for JD's data, when the horizon was equal to seven, the DWS-A was 14.7% more accurate than the Naïve and 8.38% than the best sub-model, SCUM.

Table 6. The performance of the five methods for rolling forecast testing in the lumpy pattern.

Model	sMAPE	MASE	OWA	% Improvement of Method over the Naïve
Haolinju: Horizon = 1 (Obs. = 1211 × 1 × 10) [a]				
Naïve	80.997 (3.429)	1.176 (0.158)	1.000 (0.000)	-
Comb S-H-D	108.250 (1.737)	1.072 (0.102)	1.127 (0.061)	−12.7%
SCUM	110.246 (1.581)	1.059 (0.103)	1.134 (0.062)	−13.4%
DWS-A	81.301 (3.306)	1.143 (0.141)	0.983 (0.014)	1.7%
DWS-B	98.551 (9.256)	1.078 (0.123)	1.065 (0.073)	−6.5%
Haolinju: Horizon = 1 (Obs. = 1211 × 7 × 4) [a]				
Naïve	86.245 (0.944)	1.361 (0.112)	1.000 (0.000)	-
Comb S-H-D	110.943 (0.141)	1.207 (0.035)	1.078 (0.031)	−7.8%
SCUM	113.245 (0.468)	1.187 (0.034)	1.084 (0.031)	−8.4%
DWS-A	76.947 (0.515)	1.218 (0.026)	0.884 (0.033)	11.6%
DWS-B	106.015 (0.426)	1.178 (0.027)	1.038 (0.028)	−3.8%
JD: Horizon = 1 (Obs. = 700 × 1 × 10) [b]				
Naïve	70.315 (4.558)	1.487 (0.368)	1.000 (0.000)	-
Comb S-H-D	72.850 (8.011)	1.384 (0.386)	0.987 (0.083)	1.3%
SCUM	73.208 (7.767)	1.352 (0.383)	0.980 (0.079)	2.0%
DWS-A	68.414 (4.737)	1.401 (0.348)	0.969 (0.042)	3.1%
DWS-B	68.991 (6.494)	1.316 (0.376)	0.941 (0.055)	5.9%
JD: Horizon = 7 (Obs. = 700 × 7 × 4) [b]				
Naïve	75.817 (1.651)	1.549 (0.041)	1.000 (0.000)	-
Comb S-H-D	74.057 (0.600)	1.414 (0.079)	0.945 (0.031)	5.5%
SCUM	74.092 (0.707)	1.370 (0.075)	0.931 (0.030)	6.9%
DWS-A	64.56 (0.387)	1.341 (0.097)	0.853 (0.033)	14.7%
DWS-B	69.691 (0.719)	1.319 (0.085)	0.880 (0.029)	12.0%

[a] The Naïve outperformed the other sub-models in these datasets. [b] The SCUM outperformed the other sub-models in these datasets.

4.3. Optimal Dynamic Weighting Strategy for Each Demand Pattern

Based on the empirical analysis results, as shown in Figure 3, we can determine an optimal dynamic weighting strategy for each demand pattern. For items in the smooth or erratic pattern, it is recommended to use the DWS-B method to output the final predicted value. For items in the intermittent or lumpy pattern, it is recommended to use the DWS-A method to output the final predicted value. This means that for such items with intermittent or lumpy patterns, retailers only need to consider the output of the optimal sub-model as the final predictions.

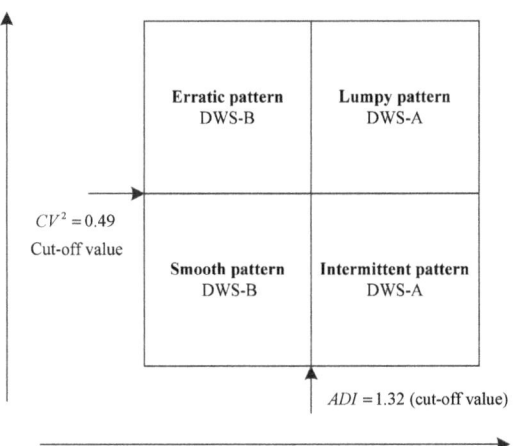

Figure 3. Optimal dynamic weighting strategies in the four demand patterns.

5. Conclusions

In this paper, we proposed dynamic model selection based on demand pattern classification as a new approach in the retailing forecasting area. This approach offers a framework to address the challenge of model selection with complex demand patterns in retail practice. Based on a series' average inter-demand interval and the squared coefficient of variation of the demand sizes, we divided the demand patterns of all items of retailers into four types: smooth, intermittent, erratic, and lumpy. Some studies have proposed specific prediction methods for certain demand patterns, such as Syntetos-Boylan Approximation and Croston methods for intermittent demand [38]. However, the demand pattern of items may change over time. Moreover, any single model for demand forecasting cannot be the most accurate in all periods of an item. It is necessary to monitor and update the demand pattern and switch appropriate forecasting methods. We first built a pool of models, including nine classical methods, in the M-Competitions. Then, we proposed two dynamic weighting strategies based on the historical performance of all candidate models, namely DWS-A and DWS-B. The DWS-A method only selects the best prediction model in the past as the final model. The DWS-B method sets different weights according to the historical performance of candidate models. The weights of both strategies change dynamically over time. This framework can provide automatic model selection for retail demand forecasting. Further, this approach has better interpretability and may be more acceptable to decision makers.

We verified the effectiveness of this approach by using two large datasets from an offline retailer and an online retailer in China. We implemented multi-round rolling forecast with different demand patterns and horizons to verify the generalization ability of this approach. The pattern of smooth demand, which is characterized by low volatility and short intervals, is easier to predict. For this pattern, the DWS-B delivered more accuracy at various forecast horizons. Additionally, the DWS-B in the pattern of erratic demand outperformed all models in the pool. This means that the combination forecast is more suitable for items with a short ADI. The demand patterns of intermittent and lumpy, which are characterized by a high proportion of zero values, are not easier to predict. However, the DWS-A still outperformed all models in the pool. This means that individual selection is more suitable for items with a long ADI. In general, the proposed dynamic weighting strategies dominated the benchmark and winning prediction models in M-Competitions, including Naïve, Comb S-H-D, and SCUM. We suggest that the DWS-A method is applicable to the items of intermittent and lumpy patterns, and the DWS-B method is applicable to the items of smooth and erratic patterns.

We did not consider additional prediction methods in the pool of models, such as deep learning methods, as several models take extra time in the calculation and have higher complexity, and their performance is not necessarily as good as statistical models [8]. However, the model pool and empirical results of this study are sufficient to prove the effectiveness of the proposed model selection approach. In future studies, additional models and factors that affect consumer demand should be included in this forecasting system to improve the forecast accuracy.

Author Contributions: Conceptualization, E.E. and M.Y.; methodology, E.E. and X.T.; validation, E.E. and Y.T.; formal analysis, X.T.; data curation, Y.T.; writing—original draft preparation, E.E.; writing—review and editing, M.Y., X.T., and Y.T. All authors have read and agreed to the published version of the manuscript.

Funding: This research was funded by the National Natural Science Foundation of China (72172145, 71932002), the Beijing Natural Science Foundation (9212020), and the Fundamental Research Funds for the Central Universities.

Institutional Review Board Statement: Not applicable.

Informed Consent Statement: Not applicable.

Data Availability Statement: Not applicable.

Conflicts of Interest: The authors declare no conflict of interest.

References

1. Simchi-Levi, D.; Wu, M.X. Powering retailers' digitization through analytics and automation. *Int. J. Prod. Res.* **2018**, *56*, 809–816. [CrossRef]
2. Arunraj, N.S.; Ahrens, D. A hybrid seasonal autoregressive integrated moving average and quantile regression for daily food sales forecasting. *Int. J. Prod. Econ.* **2015**, *170*, 321–335. [CrossRef]
3. Claeskens, G.; Magnus, J.R.; Vasnev, A.L.; Wang, W. The forecast combination puzzle: A simple theoretical explanation. *Int. J. Forecast.* **2016**, *32*, 754–762. [CrossRef]
4. Ulrich, M.; Jahnke, H.; Langrock, R.; Pesch, R.; Senge, R. Classification-based model selection in retail demand forecasting. *Int. J. Forecast.* **2022**, *38*, 209–223. [CrossRef]
5. Makridakis, S.; Andersen, A.; Carbone, R.; Fildes, R.; Hibon, M.; Lewandowski, R.; Newton, J.; Parzen, E.; Winkler, R. The accuracy of extrapolation (time series) methods: Results of a forecasting competition. *J. Forecast.* **1982**, *1*, 111–153. [CrossRef]
6. Ching-Chin, C.; Ieng, A.I.K.; Ling-Ling, W.; Ling-Chieh, K. Designing a decision-support system for new product sales forecasting. *Expert Syst. Appl.* **2010**, *37*, 1654–1665. [CrossRef]
7. Neelamegham, R.; Chintagunta, P.K. Modeling and Forecasting the Sales of Technology Products. *Qme-Quant. Mark. Econ.* **2004**, *2*, 195–232. [CrossRef]
8. Makridakis, S.; Spiliotis, E.; Assimakopoulos, V. The M4 Competition: Results, findings, conclusion and way forward. *Int. J. Forecast.* **2018**, *34*, 802–808. [CrossRef]
9. Hyndman, R.J.; Athanasopoulos, G. *Forecasting: Principles and Practice*; OTexts: Melbourne, Australia, 2018.
10. Brown, R.G. *Smoothing, Forecasting and Prediction of Discrete Time Series*; Courier Corporation: Chelmsford, MA, USA, 2004.
11. Holt, C.C. Forecasting seasonals and trends by exponentially weighted moving averages. *Int. J. Forecast.* **2004**, *20*, 5–10. [CrossRef]
12. Winters, P.R. Forecasting sales by exponentially weighted moving averages. *Manag. Sci.* **1960**, *6*, 324–342. [CrossRef]
13. Box, G.E.; Jenkins, G.M.; Reinsel, G.C.; Ljung, G.M. *Time Series Analysis: Forecasting and Control*; John Wiley & Sons: Hoboken, NJ, USA, 2015.
14. Ali, Ö.G.; Sayın, S.; van Woensel, T.; Fransoo, J. SKU demand forecasting in the presence of promotions. *Expert Syst. Appl.* **2009**, *36*, 12340–12348. [CrossRef]
15. Peng, B.; Song, H.; Crouch, G.I. A meta-analysis of international tourism demand forecasting and implications for practice. *Tour. Manag.* **2014**, *45*, 181–193. [CrossRef]
16. Divakar, S.; Ratchford, B.T.; Shankar, V. Practice Prize Article—CHAN4CAST: A Multichannel, Multiregion Sales Forecasting Model and Decision Support System for Consumer Packaged Goods. *Mark. Sci.* **2005**, *24*, 334–350. [CrossRef]
17. Kong, J.; Martin, G. A backpropagation neural network for sales forecasting. In *Proceedings of Proceedings of ICNN'95-International Conference on Neural Networks, Perth, Australia, 27 November 1995*; pp. 1007–1011.
18. Lee, W.-I.; Chen, C.-W.; Chen, K.-H.; Chen, T.-H.; Liu, C.-C. Comparative study on the forecast of fresh food sales using logistic regression, moving average and BPNN methods. *J. Mar. Sci. Technol.* **2012**, *20*, 142–152. [CrossRef]
19. Chen, F.; Ou, T. Gray relation analysis and multilayer functional link network sales forecasting model for perishable food in convenience store. *Expert Syst. Appl.* **2009**, *36*, 7054–7063. [CrossRef]
20. Aburto, L.; Weber, R. Improved supply chain management based on hybrid demand forecasts. *Appl. Soft Comput.* **2007**, *7*, 136–144. [CrossRef]
21. Liu, J.; Liu, C.; Zhang, L.; Xu, Y. Research on sales information prediction system of e-commerce enterprises based on time series model. *Inf. Syst. E-Bus. Manag.* **2019**, *18*, 1–14. [CrossRef]
22. Rubio, L.; Alba, K. Forecasting Selected Colombian Shares Using a Hybrid ARIMA-SVR Model. *Mathematics* **2022**, *10*, 2181. [CrossRef]
23. Wang, C.-C.; Chang, H.-T.; Chien, C.-H. Hybrid LSTM-ARMA Demand-Forecasting Model Based on Error Compensation for Integrated Circuit Tray Manufacturing. *Mathematics* **2022**, *10*, 2158. [CrossRef]
24. Armstrong, J.S. Combining forecasts. In *Principles of forecasting*; Springer: Berlin/Heidelberg, Germany, 2001; pp. 417–439.
25. Makridakis, S.; Hibon, M. The M3-Competition: Results, conclusions and implications. *Int. J. Forecast.* **2000**, *16*, 451–476. [CrossRef]
26. Aye, G.C.; Balcilar, M.; Gupta, R.; Majumdar, A. Forecasting aggregate retail sales: The case of South Africa. *Int. J. Prod. Econ.* **2015**, *160*, 66–79. [CrossRef]
27. Zhang, G.P. Time series forecasting using a hybrid ARIMA and neural network model. *Neurocomputing* **2003**, *50*, 159–175. [CrossRef]
28. Kuo, R. A sales forecasting system based on fuzzy neural network with initial weights generated by genetic algorithm. *Eur. J. Oper. Res.* **2001**, *129*, 496–517. [CrossRef]
29. Fildes, R. Evaluation of Aggregate and Individual Forecast Method Selection Rules. *Manag. Sci.* **1989**, *35*, 1056–1065. [CrossRef]
30. Taghiyeh, S.; Lengacher, D.C.; Handfield, R.B. Forecasting model selection using intermediate classification: Application to MonarchFx corporation. *Expert Syst. Appl.* **2020**, *151*, 113371. [CrossRef]
31. Villegas, M.A.; Pedregal, D.J.; Trapero, J.R. A support vector machine for model selection in demand forecasting applications. *Comput. Ind. Eng.* **2018**, *121*, 1–7. [CrossRef]
32. Gardner, E.S.; Mckenzie, E. Forecasting Trends in Time Series. *Manag. Sci.* **1985**, *31*, 1237–1246. [CrossRef]

33. Assimakopoulos, V.; Nikolopoulos, K. The theta model: A decomposition approach to forecasting. *Int. J. Forecast.* **2000**, *16*, 521–530. [CrossRef]
34. Spiliotis, E.; Assimakopoulos, V. 4Theta: Generalizing the Theta Method for Automatic Forecasting. Available online: https://github.com/M4Competition/M4-methods (accessed on 1 July 2022).
35. Petropoulos, F.; Svetunkov, I. A simple combination of univariate models. *Int. J. Forecast.* **2020**, *36*, 110–115. [CrossRef]
36. Syntetos, A.A.; Boylan, J.E.; Croston, J.D. On the categorization of demand patterns. *J. Oper. Res. Soc.* **2005**, *56*, 495–503. [CrossRef]
37. Hyndman, R.J.; Koehler, A.B. Another look at measures of forecast accuracy. *Int. J. Forecast.* **2006**, *22*, 679–688. [CrossRef]
38. Tian, X.; Wang, H. Forecasting intermittent demand for inventory management by retailers: A new approach. *J. Retail. Consum. Serv.* **2021**, *62*, 102662. [CrossRef]

Article

Tourist Arrival Forecasting Using Multiscale Mode Learning Model

Kaijian He [1,†], Don Wu [2,3,†] and Yingchao Zou [1,*,†]

1. College of Tourism, Hunan Normal University, Changsha 410081, China
2. School of Tourism Management, Macao Institute of Tourism Studies, Macao, China
3. Department of Marketing, City University of Hong Kong, Hong Kong, China
* Correspondence: evangeline1203@hunnu.edu.cn; Tel.: +86-18511075982
† These authors contributed equally to this work.

Abstract: The forecasting of tourist arrival depends on the accurate modeling of prevalent data patterns found in tourist arrival, especially for daily tourist arrival, where tourist arrival changes are more complex and highly nonlinear. In this paper, a new multiscale mode learning-based tourist arrival forecasting model is proposed to exploit different multiscale data features in tourist arrival movement. Two popular Mode Decomposition models (MD) and the Convolutional Neural Network (CNN) model are introduced to model the multiscale data features in the tourist arrival data The data patterns at different scales are extracted using these two different MD models which dynamically decompose tourist arrival into the distinctive intrinsic mode function (IMF) data components. The convolutional neural network uses the deep network to further model the multiscale data structure of tourist arrivals, with the reduced dimensionality of key multiscale data features and finer modeling of nonlinearity in tourist arrival. Our empirical results using daily tourist arrival data show that the MD-CNN tourist arrival forecasting model significantly improves the forecasting reliability and accuracy.

Keywords: tourist arrival forecast; variational mode decomposition; empirical mode decomposition; multiscale analysis; deep learning model; convolutional neural network model; seasonal ARIMA; ARIMA

MSC: 42C99; 62M10; 91B84; 68T05

1. Introduction

As one of the cornerstones of the rapidly developing service economy, the tourism industry is intertwined with the development of different sectors of the economy. It is subject to the influences of a very complicated and diversified range of factors for different purposes over a different time horizon [1,2]. For example, key tourist motivations may include pleasure, business visiting, relatives, conferences, study, and others [3]. The long-term influencing factors may include macroeconomic policy adjustments. The short-term influencing factors may include weather, diseases, exchange rate changes, natural hazards, major recreation, sports events, changes in essential inputs, and trade barriers [4–12]. As these factors come and go over time, their joint influence on the tourist arrival determination process has resulted in an unstable and nonstationary tourist arrival changing process. It represents significant factors for the sustained development of the tourism industry, from tourism planning to budgeting. Various issues concerning different aspects of tourist arrival have attracted significant attention from academics, practitioners, and investors.

The tourism demand forecasting research has profound implications for both public and private parts of the economy [1]. The private or industrial sectors rely on accurate tourist demand forecasting for their efficient operations, i.e., they need accurate tourist forecasts to plan, set appropriate prices, recruit enough staff, and allocate sufficient resources to meet the tourism demand for products and services in the holiday season and under rapidly changing market circumstances. The public sectors, such as local governments, rely on accurate tourist demand forecasting for public policy formulation, transportation development, the promotion and development of specific tools, tourism industry, and related industrial development in the supply chain [13,14]. Developing a more accurate and reliable tourist arrival forecasting model is, therefore, very important for the efficient operation of the tourism industry and academic research [1,15].

The forecasting of tourist arrival and tourist demand has been a main research topic in the literature over the years [16,17]. Song and Li [16] presented a comprehensive survey on the early development of tourism demand forecasting. The mainstream tourism demand forecasting models are classified as either qualitative models, such as judgmental methods, or quantitative models, such as econometrics models, time series models, or other emerging models such as Artificial Intelligence (AI) models [14,16]. The structural econometrics model has been used to investigate the impacts of different influencing factors on tourist arrival. For example, Nguyen and Valadkhani [5] studied the sensitivity of the exchange rate to tourist arrival. The main problem with this approach is that the influencing factors of tourist arrivals are very complicated and diversified. It is difficult to identify these influencing factors exactly with high accuracy, not to mention the modeling of the relationship between these influencing factors and tourist arrival. In the meantime, another popular approach is the time series approach, which extracts patterns from the analysis of the historical observation and current value of tourist arrival, and ultimately tries to infer the future changes [18]. Mainstream time series models such as the Autoregressive Integrated Moving Average (ARIMA) model, Seasonal ARIMA, Generalized Autoregressive Conditional Heteroskedasticity (GARCH) model, Exponential Smoothing (ETS), Naive, etc. have been developed to capture some of the most widely acknowledged data patterns in the tourist demand forecasting literature such as autocorrelation, volatility clustering, and seasonality [16,19]. Aside from these approaches, the tourism demand forecasting literature has paid increasing attention to the potential of Artificial Intelligence and Machine Learning models to capture and model the nonlinear data features in tourist arrivals with an assumption-free and data-driven approach [20]; typical models include Neural Networks and Support Vector Regression [21]. For example, Cang [22] found that the neural network and support vector regression-based combination model achieves the best forecasting accuracy compared to the individual models. However, the neural network is known to suffer from the overfitting problem, especially when it is applied to a small sample size, such as low-frequency data. In recent years, Deep Learning, as one of the latest developments in the field, has brought much hope and been widely applied in the economics and finance field [23,24]. It has become more and more popular in the tourism research literature [13,25–27]. For example, Law et al. [25] proposed a bagging-based multivariate simple deep learning model to forecast the monthly tourist arrival. It is constructed based on individual models such as stacked autoencoder and the kernel-based extreme learning machine. It refers to a collection of rapidly developing models in the Artificial Intelligence field, such as Convolutional Neural Network (CNN) and Long Short-Term Memory (LSTM) [28–32]. Song et al. [17] provided an updated comprehensive review on the latest developments in tourism demand forecasting. It is interesting to see how the focus of the tourism demand forecasting models has gradually shifted from the mostly econometric and time series approach to the more recent artificial intelligence and data analysis model.

Until now, no consensus on the optimal tourist arrival forecasting model has been reached in the literature after years of development [20,33,34]. The rich set of data features in the tourist arrival data at higher frequency and larger sample size would lead to exponential increasing level of model risk and lower level of generalization in forecasting, which has brought new challenges as well as opportunities for better tourist arrival modeling and forecasting [14]. When modeling and analysis are performed at a much shorter time scale, such as at the daily or intraday frequency, many different data characteristics such as seasonality, autocorrelation, multiscale, etc. may prevail, with the disruptions of transient or extreme factors [6,10]. Among the newly emerging data characteristics, the multiscale data feature is one of the most important and promising data features. The multiscale data feature is widely found in natural and economic systems, such as energy markets and exchange markets. Motivations for tourist travel decisions and tourist destination supply also vary with different time horizon focuses and budget scales, which results in the multiscale characteristics in the tourist arrival changes. However, in the tourist arrival forecasting and tourism management literature, the modeling of multiscale data features has only received limited attention.

To model the multiscale data characteristics, there have been two interesting developments in the recent literature. Firstly, multiscale data decomposition models such as Empirical Mode Decomposition (EMD) and Variational Mode Decomposition (VMD) have received increasing attention in tourism demand forecasting [35–38]. For example, Xing et al. [37] proposed an adaptive multiscale ensemble model that combines VMD with the ARIMA, SARIMA, and LSSVR models; it models data features such as trend and seasonality to produce tourist arrival forecasts with improved accuracy. Xie et al. [38] combined Complete Ensemble EMD with Adaptive Noise (CEEMDAN) with Elman's neural network model to enhance the predictive accuracy of tourist arrival forecasts. Between EMD and VMD models, EMD has been known to suffer from the inherent mode mixing issue, which poses difficulty to its estimation accuracy. As its name implies, the mode mixing problem refers to the fact that the supposedly unique intrinsic modes may share common characteristics and demonstrate similar data patterns, making them indistinguishable from each other [39]. The root cost is the biased estimation such that the decomposed components do not center around unique frequency. The reduction of the mode mixing problem may come at the cost of added noise to the intrinsic modes, while VMD takes a completely different approach. VMD is a more recent development that takes the alternative optimization-based approach to address the data decomposition and mode-mixing problem [40]. It can achieve more accurate decomposition than the EMD model. These studies provide initial evidence that multiscale models contribute to the construction of a more-accurate forecasting model. With the accelerating development of different multiscale models in the literature, the choice among rapidly emerging different multiscale models have attracted increasing attention. Secondly, multiscale data features have also been incorporated in the deep learning models, particularly in the form of filters in the Convolutional Neural Network model. CNN uses the filters to extract the hierarchical information across different scales [41,42]. It serves as a promising intelligence model to further extract multiscale and hierarchical information from the data with mixed features.

The general research question of this study is the construction of a new tourist arrival forecasting model that better takes advantage of multiscale data features and produces accurate forecasts, given the development of different multiscale models such as EMD and VMD models. In this paper, we propose a new MD-CNN tourist arrival forecasting model that aims to take advantage of the multiscale data characteristics with the multiscale mode learning approach. The proposed model takes a two-step approach. It firstly reveals the complex heterogeneous factor structure using the MD model, including EMD and VMD models, and identifies the optimal scale for the transient factor. It uses CNN models with different parameters to further extract the multiscale data features and forecast tourist arrivals with an artificial intelligence approach. Through empirical studies using the latest tourist arrival data, we find that the extraction of multiscale factors and their incorporation in the modeling would lead to a significant performance improvement.

Work in this paper contributes to the relevant literature by proposing a new mode-learning-based forecasting model to capture better the multiscale data features in tourist arrival changes. Early work in the risk forecasting area has demonstrated the potential contribution of multiscale deep-learning-based models to risk forecasting accuracy improvement [43–45]. Theoretically, we propose a multiscale structure of influencing factors for tourist arrival changes. Some factors such as macroeconomic factors and infrastructure structures generate impacts on the decision to travel on a long-term scale while some other factors such as tsunamis and pandemics are more short-term focused. Empirically, we found that the current different Mode Decomposition (MD) models and CNN model all provide different perspectives on multiscale modeling, the combination of which would lead to better modeling and forecasting accuracy. We found that signal processing techniques such as the Mode Decomposition (MD) model can be used to uncover the underlying dynamic structure while deep learning models such as CNN can extract multiscale data features further and produce optimized forecasts based on these data features. We show empirical evidence that the incorporation of multiscale factors lead to a positive performance improvement in forecasting accuracy.

The rest of the paper proceeds as follows. In Section 2, we explain and illustrate the algorithmic details of different models involved in this paper, such as the MD models (i.e., EMD and VMD models), the CNN model, and the proposed MD-CNN model. Results from empirical studies applying these models to tourist arrival data are reported in Section 3. Section 4 presents some summarizing remarks.

2. Methodology

2.1. Mode Decomposition (MD) Model

Since the original proposition of the EMD model in geophysical research in 1998, MD models have developed further and attracted significant attention in different disciplines, such as vibration engineering, biomedicine, computer science, and economics and finance [35,46,47]. Typical mode decomposition models include Ensemble EMD (EEMD), Complete Ensemble EMD (CEEMD) and CEEMDAN, and VMD [35,39,40,48–50]. EMD extracts several Intrinsic Mode Functions (IMFs) at several different characterizing scales from the original tourist arrival data. In the literature, EMD is usually perceived to be a better choice than wavelet analysis as it represents better the physical characteristics of the nonstationary or nonlinear signal. The classical EMD decomposition theory assumes the white noise assumptions. It assumes that each decomposed IMF can fully represent the underlying data characteristics at different scales [35]. However, the real-world time series often do not exactly conform to the white noise definition. With practical data, EMD decomposition may fail to extract the unique frequency-scale components. During the decomposition process, the extracted IMFs need to satisfy two assumptions, usually as the stopping criteria. The difference between zero-crossing and extrema of an ideal IMF is less than one when the defined envelopes are symmetric. The EMD model involves several steps, collectively known as the sitting process, which are as follows [35]:

(1) Find all local maximum and minimum points of $y_{m,t}$.
(2) Use two separate cubic spline curves to connect all local maximum and minimum points for constructing the upper envelope and the lower envelope, respectively.
(3) Calculate the local mean curve of the upper and lower envelopes.
(4) Calculate the difference between the local mean curve and the data.
(5) Repeat the previous steps until the difference satisfies the assumption of IMFs.
(6) Calculate the residual. Use the residual to replace the original signal as a new y_t. Repeat the previous steps until no more IMFs can be identified or the stopping criteria are satisfied.
(7) Eventually, the original tourist arrival data after m repetitions can be expressed as the sum of IMF components and a residual component, as in Equation (1):

$$y_{m,t} = \sum_{j=1}^{J} c_{m,j,t} + r_{m,t}. \qquad (1)$$

where $y_{m,t}$ is the tourist arrival data at time t after m repetitions, $c_{m,j,t}$ is the j_{th} IMF components at time t, and $r_{m,t}$ is the residual at time t.

There have been different extensions to the original EMD in the literature, such as EEMD, CEEMD, and CEEMDAN [39,48–50]. If the empirical data satisfy the model assumptions of particular MD models such as CEEMDAN, it can become the preferred choice among different EMD extensions and can be combined with CNN model. To reduce the model risk when no single model may fit the data perfectly, the MD-CNN approach can be used. It is possible to replace EMD with CEEMDAN in MD-CNN model. MD-CNN is proposed as a general model that could be easily extended by including a wide range of EMD extensions such as EEMD, CEEMD, or CEEMDAN. Overall, CEEMDAN still adopts the iterative decomposition approach. In the meantime, Variational Mode Decomposition (VMD) is a new MD model proposed in recent years [40]. Compared with the classic Empirical Mode Decomposition (EMD), it takes an alternative nonrecursive, nonlinear optimization approach to solve for the modes decomposed from the tourist arrival data. Different from the recursive one-by-one mode decomposition process in the EMD model, the VMD model produces the decomposed modes simultaneously. As for the well-known mode mixing problem in the EMD model, VMD leaves it to the theoretical judgment, which sets the number of modes. If the assumption of the number of modes is correct, VMD is expected to produce unique modes. Naturally, there is a significant model risk if the number of modes set is biased. To solve for the modes from the tourist arrival data, the VMD model formulates the following constrained optimization equations in Equation (2) [40].

$$Min_{\mu,\omega} = \sum_k ||\partial_t[(\vartheta(t) + \frac{j}{\pi t}) * \mu_k(t)]e^{-j\omega_k t}||_2^2$$
$$s.t. \sum_k \mu_k = f \quad (2)$$

where μ_k is the k_{th} mode (subsignals), ω is the k_{th} center frequency, ϑ is the Dirac distribution, and $*$ is the convolution operator.

The augmented Lagrange function is constructed as in Equation (3) [40].

$$Ł(\mu_k, \omega_k, \lambda) = \alpha \sum_k ||\partial_t[(\vartheta(t) + \frac{j}{\pi t}) * \mu_k(t)]e^{-j\omega_k t}||_2^2 + ||f(t) - \sum_k \mu_k(t)||_2^2 + <\lambda(t), f(t) - \sum_k \mu_k(t)> \quad (3)$$

where λ is the Lagrange multiplier.

The optimal modes $\hat{\mu}$ and $\hat{\omega}$ are calculated as in Equation (4) [40].

$$\hat{\mu}_k^{n+1}(\omega) = \frac{(\hat{f}(\omega) - \sum_{u \neq k} \hat{\mu}_i(\omega) + \frac{\lambda(\omega)}{2})}{1 + 2\alpha(\omega - \omega_k)^2}$$
$$\hat{\omega}_k^{n+1} = \frac{\int_0^\infty \omega |\hat{\mu}_k(\omega)|^2 d\omega}{\int_0^\infty |\hat{\mu}_k(\omega)|^2 d\omega} \quad (4)$$

2.2. Convolutional Neural Network Model

The classic neural network model mimics the human brain structure to process the complex mixture of data features in the nonlinear tourist arrival data [51]. The training process to determine the network structure and parameters may become computationally infeasible due to the high dimensional search space for parameters. The new-generation neural network, known as the deep learning model, moves one step further to incorporate the specific data features in the network structure, which results in a significantly reduced number of estimated parameters [52]. As is demonstrated in the empirical and theoretical research, a deep learning network enjoys better functional approximation and improved generalization in the face of the overfitting situation. CNN is one popular deep learning model that mimics human visual processing by emphasizing the major space-invariant data features in terms of abstraction and ignoring the trivial [53]. It recognizes feature abstraction by the depth of layers at different scales. Motivated by the activation of certain groups of neurons by the particular information feedback in the human visual processing system, filters in the CNN model are used to perform linear convolutional transformation on the original tourist arrival data. The same filters are used by neurons at the same layer while filters across different layers can be different to represent different data features. The feature maps are introduced to contain the transformed tourist arrival data using the filters. When the data are processed through different convolutional layers in the CNN model, different targeted data features are continuously produced and a series of feature maps are produced to represent the continuous processing of information. By convolution and pooling operations, the feature maps at deeper layers contain more abstract data features.

In the CNN model, there are two main groups of layers, i.e., feature extraction and nonlinearity learning. The feature extraction layer attempts to extract the key features across different scales in a hierarchical manner and reduce the dimensionality of the input feature as much as possible while the nonlinearity learning layer attempts to model the nonlinear relationship between tourist arrivals and the extracted features [41]. In the network training process, the weights of the neurons are continuously adjusted to reduce the training errors as much as possible. In the model forecasting process, these layers work together to produce forecasts as accurately as possible [54].

In the CNN model, the main feature extraction layers include the convolutional layers and pooling layer. The convolutional layers use filter functions to perform the convolutional operation and produce feature maps that contain the identified key feature data from the original tourist arrival data. With input data X, the feature map at the next layer is calculated as in Equation (5) [55]:

$$X_{l+1} = f(W_{l+1} \otimes dX_l + b_{l+1}) \quad (5)$$

where $X_l + 1$ is the feature map at layer $l + 1$, W is the weight matrix, b is the bias matrix, and f is the activation function for nonlinear transformation of the output data. Typical activation functions may include Rectified Linear Unit (ReLU), Sigmoid, Tanh, among others [55].

The pooling layer attempts to reduce the dimensionality and signify the importance of the extracted feature. It is calculated as in Equation (6) [55]:

$$d(X) = T_{r \in R}(X_{i \times T + r}) \quad (6)$$

where T is the maximization or mean operation.

There are also several ancillary layers that are added to tackle the overfitting issue and improve the generalization of the network [41,56]. Typical ancillary layers include dropout layers, fully connected layers, batch normalization layers, etc.

2.3. MD-CNN Forecasting Model

As suggested in numerous empirical studies, there are far too many factors that jointly affect the movement of tourist arrivals. This would result in significant fluctuations in tourist arrival changes with complex and heterogeneous properties. Theoretically, we assume that J influencing factors for tourist arrival y are defined with unique time scale characteristics at time t as in Equation (7):

$$y_t = \sum_{j=1}^{J} c_{j,t} \quad (7)$$

where y_t is tourist arrival at time t and $c_{j,t}$ is the j_{th} intrinsic modes at time t.

Since the true generating process and multiscale structure are unknown, the multiscale structure for tourist arrival represented by the decomposed data components is determined using m different criteria and algorithm. For example, EMD relies on the stationarity of the decomposed data component to identify the multiscale structure while VMD relies on theoretical guidance to identify multiscale structure. There are estimation biases in both approaches, as in Equation (8):

$$y_t = \sum_{j=1}^{J} \sum_{m=1}^{M} \hat{c}_{j,t,m} + \epsilon_{m,t} \tag{8}$$

where y_t is the tourist arrival data at t and $\hat{c}_{j,t,m}$ is the j_{th} intrinsic modes at time t using the m mode decomposition model.

The future movement of tourist arrival changes are defined as the function of its estimated J influencing factors over time, using M algorithms under different assumptions and criteria, as in Equation (9)

$$\hat{y}_{t+1} = f(C) \tag{9}$$

where $C = \hat{c}_{j,t,m}, j \in 1, \ldots, J, t \in 1, \ldots, T, m \in 1, \ldots, M$, $\hat{y}_{t+1}$ is the tourist arrival forecast at time $t + 1$.

In this paper, we take VMD and EMD as two MD models and CNN as the final estimation model, and propose a new MD-CNN forecasting model. The general structure of the MD-CNN tourist arrival forecasting model is illustrated in Figure 1.

As illustrated in Figure 1, given MD models $m, m \in \{EMD, VMD\}$, the tourist arrival data y_t are decomposed into a series of IMFs accordingly, as in Equation (10).

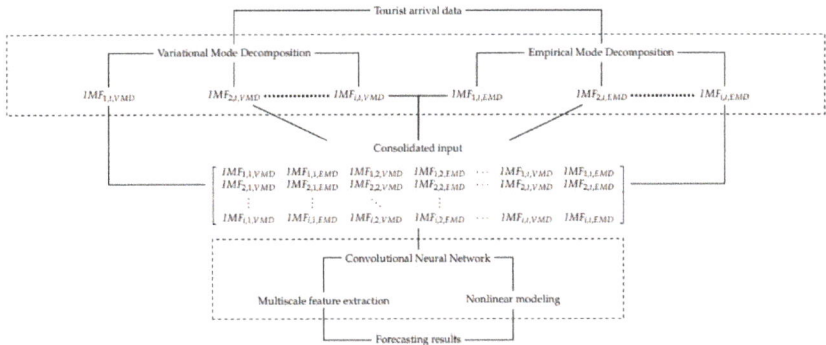

Figure 1. Flowchart for the MD-CNN model.

$$y_{m,t} = \sum_{j=1}^{J} c_{j,t,m} + r_{m,t}, \tag{10}$$

where $y_{m,t}$ is the tourist arrival data using the m mode decomposition model at time t, $c_{j,t,m}$ is the j_{th} intrinsic mode component, and $r_{m,t}$ is the residual component at time t.

IMFs matrices calculated with different MD models $IMF_{j,t,m}, m = \{EMD, VMD\}$ are combined together to construct the consolidated IMFs matrix as $M_{j,t}$. For example, if EMD and VMD—two major decomposition models in the literature—are used, the consolidated IMF matrix is constructed as in Equation (11):

$$\hat{M}_{i,t} = \begin{bmatrix} IMF_{1,1,VMD} & IMF_{1,1,EMD} & IMF_{1,2,VMD} & IMF_{1,2,EMD} & \cdots & IMF_{1,t,VMD} & IMF_{1,t,EMD} \\ IMF_{2,1,VMD} & IMF_{2,1,EMD} & IMF_{2,2,VMD} & IMF_{2,2,EMD} & \cdots & IMF_{2,t,VMD} & IMF_{2,t,EMD} \\ \vdots & \vdots & \ddots & \vdots & & \vdots & \vdots \\ IMF_{j,1,VMD} & IMF_{j,1,EMD} & IMF_{j,2,VMD} & IMF_{j,2,EMD} & \cdots & IMF_{j,t,VMD} & IMF_{j,t,EMD} \end{bmatrix} \tag{11}$$

$IMF_{j,t,m}$ is the t_{th} intrinsic modes at scale j using multiscale models m.

The Convolutional Neural Network model is used to model the nonlinear map function f between the higher dimensional matrix $\hat{M}_{j,t}$ and the tourist arrival data $\hat{y}_{t+1}$, as in Equation (12).

$$\hat{y}_{t+1} = f(\hat{M}_{j,t}) \qquad (12)$$

$\hat{y}_{t+1}$ is the tourist arrival data at time $t + 1$, $f(\hat{M}_{j,t})$ is the nonlinear function using CNN.

3. Empirical Results

Data Description and Descriptive Statistics

In our empirical study, Macao is selected as the subject of the empirical analysis to evaluate the forecasting accuracy of different models because it is one of the most active tourist attractions in the world. It receives an active inflow of tourists from around the world and represents an interesting case both for city tourism and international tourism. The dataset for tourist arrival is extensive to reflect the dynamics in the tourism industry so that the modeling accuracy and the generalizations of the MD-CNN model can be evaluated comprehensively in this paper. More importantly, the Macao Government Tourism Office (MGTO) provides data at a daily level while most tourist destinations provide data at a monthly or lower frequency, from the annual statistical report. Therefore, we use the daily tourist arrival data in Macao from five major countries or regions to estimate the model parameters and evaluate the forecasting accuracy of different models. These countries include China, Hong Kong (HK), Indonesia, Philippines, and Singapore. The dataset spans from 1 January 2017 to 13 February 2020 and is preprocessed to remove the anomalies and outliers. The dataset is obtained from the Statistics and Census Service (DSEC), Government of Macao SAR, China. Following the data analysis and machine learning literature, the dataset is divided into three parts with a 49%–21%–30% ratio, which corresponds to the training–validation–test sub-dataset.

The basic descriptive statistics for tourist arrival are reported in Table 1.

Table 1. Descriptive statistics and statistical tests for tourist arrivals from different countries or regions.

Statistics	$Mean_{\times 10^4}$	$Standard\ Deviation_{\times 10^4}$	Skewness	Kurtosis	p_{JB}	p_{BDS}
China	6.6678	1.7571	1.4807	7.5316	0.001	0
HK	1.7382	4.7507	1.6218	7.7804	0.001	0
Indonesia	0.0508	0.0290	2.1270	9.0066	0.001	0
Philippines	0.0862	0.0333	1.7717	8.8315	0.001	0
Singapore	0.0374	0.0150	0.6695	3.2716	0.001	0

Table 1 shows that tourist arrivals from different countries or regions have a significant level of kurtosis, mostly bigger than 7, except for Singapore. This indicates the prevalence of nonuniform extreme events and significant fluctuations in tourist arrival. Skewness values have positive signs at a non-negligible scale, bigger than 1. Standard deviations also reach the level of significance. The distributions of tourist arrival from different countries or regions do not conform to the normal distribution, indicated by a p-value less than 0.05 for both the Jarque–Bera (JB) test of normality and the BDS test of nonlinear independence. There may exist nonlinear dynamics such as multiscale data features in the tourist arrival changes.

Then, we forecast the MSEs of tourist arrival forecasts in different countries or regions over the time period covered by the validation dataset. The MD-CNN model network structure is Conv1(1,1)-Pool(2,2)-Conv2(1,1)-Pool(2,2)-FC(1) for all countries and regions. Results are reported in Table 2.

Table 2. Performance of MD-CNN model with different parameters using the model tuning dataset.

Models	$MSE_{China, \times 10^8}$	$MSE_{HK, \times 10^7}$	$MSE_{Indonesia, \times 10^4}$	$MSE_{Philippines, \times 10^4}$	$MSE_{Singapore, \times 10^3}$
$MD-CNN_{(1,1)}$	1.6773	1.1280	2.3589	7.8064	9.6990
$MD-CNN_{(1,2)}$	1.7660	1.1260	2.7853	10.5543	8.3517
$MD-CNN_{(2,1)}$	1.7654	1.1214	2.2340	8.2777	8.6854
$MD-CNN_{(2,2)}$	1.7365	1.2332	2.3452	9.2343	8.4691

$CNN_{(k,p)}$ refers to the CNN model with parameter k for the filter size and p for the pooling size. The number of filters is set to 11.

As reported in Table 2, the forecasting accuracy using MD-CNN with different hyperparameters varies. There is no optimal set of hyperparameters for MD-CNN models in all countries or regions. In this paper, we follow the principle of MSE minimization to select the hyperparameters for MD-CNN models with minimal MSE in different countries or regions, respectively. In the end, we chose $MD-CNN_{(1,1)}$ in China and Philippines, $MD-CNN_{(2,1)}$ for tourist arrivals from HK and Indonesia, and $MD-CNN_{(1,2)}$ for tourist arrivals from Singapore, since the parameters are optimized for the tourist arrival of particular countries and regions. This implies that the factors for tourist arrivals from different countries or regions have unique data characteristics and need to be captured within different parameters.

With the optimized parameters, tourist arrivals in different countries or regions are calculated in Table 3; we report the out-of-sample performance comparison using the test data. The model comparison has been conducted between four models, with three benchmark models, i.e., the Random Walk (RW), ARIMA, Seasonal ARIMA models, and our MD-CNN model.

Table 3. Model performance using out-of-sample dataset.

Models	$MSE_{China, \times 10^8}$	$MSE_{HK, \times 10^7}$	$MSE_{Indonesia, \times 10^4}$	$MSE_{Philippines, \times 10^4}$	$MSE_{Singapore, \times 10^3}$
RW	5.7607	4.4349	8.3045	3.1473	21.5561
ARIMA	2.0019	2.0368	5.4306	1.7129	9.8781
Seasonal ARIMA	1.8434	2.2151	5.8317	1.9324	5.5029
MD-CNN	1.5185	1.6382	2.8709	1.2432	5.0741

In Table 3, it is clear that the MD-CNN model produces the most accurate forecasts with the smallest MSEs, compared with the performance of the benchmarks RW, ARIMA, and Seasonal ARIMA models.

The superior forecasting performance of the proposed multiscale deep-learning-based model indicates the effectiveness of the incorporation of multiscale data features during the modeling and forecasting process. More specifically, the better performance of the MD-CNN model is attributed to the modeling of multiscale data features during the forecasting process, beyond the linear autocorrelation and seasonal data features captured by the ARIMA and Seasonal ARIMA models. Meanwhile, the better performance of the MD-CNN model compared with the RW model confirms that it is important to consider specific data features such as multiscale and autocorrelation data features in the modeling and forecasting process [36–38].

4. Conclusions

In this paper, a new multiscale mode-learning-based (MD-CNN) forecasting model is proposed to predict tourist arrival changes. MD-CNN uses different MD algorithms to model the transient factors. The CNN model is used to aggregate different factors and forecast tourist arrival changes. A comprehensive performance evaluation was conducted using tourist arrival data, which provides empirical evidence for the superior tourist arrival forecasting accuracy of the MD-CNN model.

The success of the introduction of the convolutional neural network model implies that more advanced artificial intelligence models such as deep learning models can contribute to better modeling of tourist arrival change. These models can be designed to target and model specific data features such as multiscale hierarchical structure. Secondly, the results in this paper suggest that the empirical analysis results and the forecasting performance are sensitive to the choice of different multiscale models. The significant model risk may result from the lack of theoretical foundation for the choice of particular multiscale models. Thirdly, the proposed MD-CNN model is constructed as a general multiscale-based forecasting methodology that is flexible enough to be extended to address different modeling issues when it is presented with different tourist destinations data, beyond the Macao tourist arrival data and EMD and VMD models used in this paper.

Author Contributions: Conceptualization, K.H. and Y.Z.; methodology, Y.Z.; writing—original draft preparation, K.H.; writing—review and editing, D.W.; funding acquisition, K.H. All authors have read and agreed to the published version of the manuscript.

Funding: This research was funded by the National Natural Science Foundation of China, grant number 71671013; Hunan Provincial Natural Science Foundation of China, grant number 2022JJ30401; the Humanities and Social Sciences Youth foundation of Ministry of Education of China, grant number 16YJC790026; and partially sponsored by a scholarship from the Macao Foundation.

Institutional Review Board Statement: Not applicable.

Informed Consent Statement: Not applicable.

Data Availability Statement: Publicly available datasets were analyzed in this study. These data can be found here: Available online: https://www.dsec.gov.mo/ (accessed on 20 June 2021).

Conflicts of Interest: The authors declare no conflict of interest.

References

1. Dharmaratne, G.S. Forecasting tourist arrivals in Barbados. *Ann. Tour. Res.* **1995**, *22*, 804–818. [CrossRef]
2. Hadavandi, E.; Ghanbari, A.; Shahanaghi, K.; Abbasian-Naghneh, S. Tourist arrival forecasting by evolutionary fuzzy systems. *Tour. Manag.* **2011**, *32*, 1196–1203. [CrossRef]
3. Yang, Y.; Chen, M.H.; Su, C.H.J.; Lin, Y.X. Asymmetric effects of tourist arrivals on the hospitality industry. *Int. J. Hosp. Manag.* **2020**, *84*, 102323. [CrossRef]
4. Deng, T.; Gan, C.; Du, H.; Hu, Y.; Wang, D. Do high speed rail configurations matter to tourist arrivals? Empirical evidence from China's prefecture-level cities. *Res. Transp. Econom.* **2020**, *90*, 100952. [CrossRef]
5. Nguyen, J.; Valadkhani, A. Dynamic responses of tourist arrivals in Australia to currency fluctuations. *J. Hosp. Tour. Manag.* **2020**, *45*, 71–78. [CrossRef]
6. Huang, L.; Yin, X.; Yang, Y.; Luo, M.; Huang, S.S. Blessing in disguise: The impact of the Wenchuan earthquake on inbound tourist arrivals in Sichuan, China. *J. Hosp. Tour. Manag.* **2020**, *42*, 58–66. [CrossRef]
7. Demir, E.; Simonyan, S.; Chen, M.H.; Marco Lau, C.K. Asymmetric effects of geopolitical risks on Turkey's tourist arrivals. *J. Hosp. Tour. Manag.* **2020**, *45*, 23–26. [CrossRef]
8. Tiwari, A.K.; Das, D.; Dutta, A. Geopolitical risk, economic policy uncertainty and tourist arrivals: Evidence from a developing country. *Tour. Manag.* **2019**, *75*, 323–327. [CrossRef]
9. Fourie, J.; Santana-Gallego, M. The impact of mega-sport events on tourist arrivals. *Tour. Manag.* **2011**, *32*, 1364–1370. [CrossRef]
10. Mao, C.K.; Ding, C.G.; Lee, H.Y. Post-SARS tourist arrival recovery patterns: An analysis based on a catastrophe theory. *Tour. Manag.* **2010**, *31*, 855–861. [CrossRef]
11. Su, Y.W.; Lin, H.L. Analysis of international tourist arrivals worldwide: The role of world heritage sites. *Tour. Manag.* **2014**, *40*, 46–58. [CrossRef]
12. Yang, C.H.; Lin, H.L.; Han, C.C. Analysis of international tourist arrivals in China: The role of World Heritage Sites. *Tour. Manag.* **2010**, *31*, 827–837. [CrossRef] [PubMed]
13. Bi, J.-W.; Li, H.; Fan, Z.-P. Tourism demand forecasting with time series imaging: A deep learning model. *Ann. Tour. Res.* **2021**, *90*, 103255. [CrossRef]
14. Song, H.; Wen, L.; Liu, C. Density tourism demand forecasting revisited. *Ann. Tour. Res.* **2019**, *75*, 379–392. [CrossRef]
15. Gounopoulos, D.; Petmezas, D.; Santamaria, D. Forecasting Tourist Arrivals in Greece and the Impact of Macroeconomic Shocks from the Countries of Tourists? Origin. *Ann. Tour. Res.* **2012**, *39*, 641–666. [CrossRef]
16. Song, H.; Li, G. Tourism demand modelling and forecasting—A review of recent research. *Tour. Manag.* **2008**, *29*, 203–220. [CrossRef]

17. Song, H.; Qiu, R.T.; Park, J. A review of research on tourism demand forecasting: Launching the Annals of Tourism Research Curated Collection on tourism demand forecasting. *Ann. Tour. Res.* **2019**, *75*, 338–362. [CrossRef]
18. Yang, X.; Pan, B.; Evans, J.A.; Lv, B. Forecasting Chinese tourist volume with search engine data. *Tour. Manag.* **2015**, *46*, 386–397. [CrossRef]
19. Vergori, A.S. Patterns of seasonality and tourism demand forecasting. *Tour. Econ.* **2017**, *23*, 1011–1027. [CrossRef]
20. Hassani, H.; Silva, E.S.; Antonakakis, N.; Filis, G.; Gupta, R. Forecasting accuracy evaluation of tourist arrivals. *Ann. Tour. Res.* **2017**, *63*, 112–127. [CrossRef]
21. Li, S.; Chen, T.; Wang, L.; Ming, C. Effective tourist volume forecasting supported by PCA and improved BPNN using Baidu index. *Tour. Manag.* **2018**, *68*, 116–126. [CrossRef]
22. Cang, S. A Comparative Analysis of Three Types of Tourism Demand Forecasting Models: Individual, Linear Combination and Non-linear Combination. *Int. J. Tour. Res.* **2014**, *16*, 596–607. [CrossRef]
23. Long, W.; Lu, Z.; Cui, L. Deep learning-based feature engineering for stock price movement prediction. *Knowl. Based Syst.* **2019**, *164*, 163–173. [CrossRef]
24. Lahmiri, S.; Bekiros, S. Cryptocurrency forecasting with deep learning chaotic neural networks. *Chaos Solitons Fractals* **2019**, *118*, 35–40. [CrossRef]
25. Law, R.; Li, G.; Fong, D.K.C.; Han, X. Tourism demand forecasting: A deep learning approach. *Ann. Tour. Res.* **2019**, *75*, 410–423. [CrossRef]
26. Kulshrestha, A.; Krishnaswamy, V.; Sharma, M. Bayesian BILSTM approach for tourism demand forecasting. *Ann. Tour. Res.* **2020**, *83*, 102925. [CrossRef]
27. Bi, J.W.; Liu, Y.; Li, H. Daily tourism volume forecasting for tourist attractions. *Ann. Tour. Res.* **2020**, *83*, 102923.
28. Chen, J.; Zhu, X.; Zhong, M. Nonlinear effects of financial factors on fluctuations in nonferrous metals prices: A Markov-switching VAR analysis. *Resour. Policy* **2018**, *61*, 489–500. [CrossRef]
29. Tzirakis, P.; Trigeorgis, G.; Nicolaou, M.A.; Schuller, B.W.; Zafeiriou, S. End-to-End Multimodal Emotion Recognition Using Deep Neural Networks. *IEEE J. Sel. Top. Signal Process.* **2017**, *11*, 1301–1309. [CrossRef]
30. McCann, M.T.; Jin, K.H.; Unser, M. Convolutional Neural Networks for Inverse Problems in Imaging A review. *IEEE Signal Process. Mag.* **2017**, *34*, 85–95. [CrossRef]
31. Rawat, W.; Wang, Z. Deep Convolutional Neural Networks for Image Classification: A Comprehensive Review. *Neural Comput.* **2017**, *29*, 2352–2449. [CrossRef]
32. Lago, J.; Ridder, F.D.; Schutter, B.D. Forecasting spot electricity prices: Deep learning approaches and empirical comparison of traditional algorithms. *Appl. Energy* **2018**, *221*, 386–405; Erratum in *Appl. Energy* **2018**, *229*, 1286. [CrossRef]
33. Peng, B.; Song, H.; Crouch, G.I. A meta-analysis of international tourism demand forecasting and implications for practice. *Tour. Manag.* **2014**, *45*, 181–193. [CrossRef]
34. Coshall, J.T.; Charlesworth, R. A management orientated approach to combination forecasting of tourism demand. *Tour. Manag.* **2011**, *32*, 759–769. [CrossRef]
35. Huang, N.E.; Shen, Z.; Long, S.R.; Wu, M.C.; Shih, H.H.; Zheng, Q.; Yen, N.C.; Tung, C.C.; Liu, H.H. The empirical mode decomposition and the Hilbert spectrum for nonlinear and non-stationary time series analysis. *Proc. R. Soc. Lond. Ser. A Math. Phys. Eng. Sci.* **1998**, *454*, 903–995. [CrossRef]
36. Zhang, C.; Jiang, F.; Wang, S.; Sun, S. A new decomposition ensemble approach for tourism demand forecasting: Evidence from major source countries in Asia-Pacific region. *Int. J. Tour. Res.* **2021**, *23*, 832–845. [CrossRef]
37. Xing, G.; Sun, S.; Bi, D.; Guo, J.E.; Wang, S. Seasonal and trend forecasting of tourist arrivals: An adaptive multiscale ensemble learning approach. *Int. J. Tour. Res.* **2022**, *24*, 425–442. [CrossRef]
38. Xie, G.; Qian, Y.; Wang, S. A decomposition-ensemble approach for tourism forecasting. *Ann. Tour. Res.* **2020**, *81*, 102891. [CrossRef]
39. Wu, Z.; Huang, N.E. Empirical mode decomposition: A noise-assisted data analysis method. *Adv. Adapt. Data Anal.* **2009**, *1*, 1–41. [CrossRef]
40. Dragomiretskiy, K.; Zosso, D. Variational Mode Decomposition. *IEEE Trans. Signal Process.* **2014**, *62*, 531–544. [CrossRef]
41. Lecun, Y.; Bottou, L.; Bengio, Y.; Haffner, P. Gradient-based learning applied to document recognition. *Proc. IEEE* **1998**, *86*, 2278–2324. [CrossRef]
42. van Noord, N.; Postma, E. Learning scale-variant and scale-invariant features for deep image classification. *Pattern Recognit.* **2017**, *61*, 583–592. [CrossRef]
43. Zou, Y.; Yu, L.; Tso, G.K.; He, K. Risk forecasting in the crude oil market: A multiscale Convolutional Neural Network approach. *Phys. A: Stat. Mech. Appl.* **2020**, *541*, 123360. [CrossRef]
44. He, K.; Tso, G.K.; Zou, Y.; Liu, J. Crude oil risk forecasting: New evidence from multiscale analysis approach. *Energy Econ.* **2018**, *76*, 574–583. [CrossRef]
45. He, K.; Zou, Y. Crude oil risk forecasting using mode decomposition based model. *Procedia Comput. Sci.* **2022**, *199*, 309–314. [CrossRef]
46. Wang, J.; Wang, J. Forecasting stochastic neural network based on financial empirical mode decomposition. *Neural Netw.* **2017**, *90*, 8–20. [CrossRef]

47. Qiu, X.; Ren, Y.; Suganthan, P.N.; Amaratunga, G.A. Empirical Mode Decomposition based ensemble deep learning for load demand time series forecasting. *Appl. Soft Comput.* **2017**, *54*, 246–255. [CrossRef]
48. Torres, M.E.; Colominas, M.A.; Schlotthauer, G.; Flandrin, P. A complete ensemble empirical mode decomposition with adaptive noise. In Proceedings of the 2011 IEEE International Conference on Acoustics, Speech and Signal Processing (ICASSP), Prague, Czech Republic, 22–27 May 2011, pp. 4144–4147. [CrossRef]
49. Yeh, J.R.; Shieh, J.S.; Huang, N.E. Complementary ensemble empirical mode decomposition: A novel noise enhanced data analysis method. *Adv. Adapt. Data Anal.* **2010**, *2*, 135–156. [CrossRef]
50. Liu, T.; Luo, Z.; Huang, J.; Yan, S. A Comparative Study of Four Kinds of Adaptive Decomposition Algorithms and Their Applications. *Sensors* **2018**, *18*, 2120. [CrossRef]
51. Schmidhuber, J. Deep learning in neural networks: An overview. *Neural Netw.* **2015**, *61*, 85–117. [CrossRef]
52. Hinton, G.E.; Salakhutdinov, R.R. Reducing the dimensionality of data with neural networks. *Science* **2006**, *313*, 504. [CrossRef] [PubMed]
53. Hinton, G.E.; Osindero, S.; Teh, Y.W. A Fast Learning Algorithm for Deep Belief Nets. *Neural Comput.* **2014**, *18*, 1527–1554. [CrossRef] [PubMed]
54. Liu, C.; Hou, W.; Liu, D. Foreign Exchange Rates Forecasting with Convolutional Neural Network. *Neural Process. Lett.* **2017**, *46*, 1095–1119. [CrossRef]
55. Zhao, Z.; Zhang, Y.; Deng, Y.; Zhang, X. ECG authentication system design incorporating a convolutional neural network and generalized S-Transformation. *Comput. Biol. Med.* **2018**, *102*, 168–179. [CrossRef] [PubMed]
56. Lee, W.Y.; Park, S.M.; Sim, K.B. Optimal hyperparameter tuning of convolutional neural networks based on the parameter-setting-free harmony search algorithm. *Optik* **2018**, *172*, 359–367. [CrossRef]

Article

Research on Hybrid Multi-Attribute Three-Way Group Decision Making Based on Improved VIKOR Model

Jiekun Song *, Zeguo He *, Lina Jiang, Zhicheng Liu and Xueli Leng

School of Economics and Management, China University of Petroleum, Qingdao 266580, China
* Correspondence: songjiekun@upc.edu.cn (J.S.); z21080318@s.upc.edu.cn (Z.H.)

Abstract: In the era of internet connection and IOT, data-driven decision-making has become a new trend of decision-making and shows the characteristics of multi-granularity. Because three-way decision-making considers the uncertainty of decision-making for complex problems and the cost sensitivity of classification, it is becoming an important branch of modern decision-making. In practice, decision-making problems usually have the characteristics of hybrid multi-attributes, which can be expressed in the forms of real numbers, interval numbers, fuzzy numbers, intuitionistic fuzzy numbers and interval-valued intuitionistic fuzzy numbers (IVIFNs). Since other forms can be regarded as special forms of IVIFNs, transforming all forms into IVIFNs can minimize information distortion and effectively set expert weights and attribute weights. We propose a hybrid multi-attribute three-way group decision-making method and give detailed steps. Firstly, we transform all attribute values of each expert into IVIFNs. Secondly, we determine expert weights based on interval-valued intuitionistic fuzzy entropy and cross-entropy and use interval-valued intuitionistic fuzzy weighted average operator to obtain a group comprehensive evaluation matrix. Thirdly, we determine the weights of each attribute based on interval-valued intuitionistic fuzzy entropy and use the VIKOR method improved by grey correlation analysis to determine the conditional probability. Fourthly, based on the risk loss matrix expressed by IVIFNs, we use the optimization method to determine the decision threshold and give the classification rules of the three-way decisions. Finally, an example verifies the feasibility of the hybrid multi-attribute three-way group decision-making method, which provides a systematic and standard solution for this kind of decision-making problem.

Keywords: hybrid multi-attribute; three-way group decision making; VIKOR model; grey correlation analysis; interval-valued intuitionistic fuzzy numbers

MSC: 90B50; 03E72

1. Introduction

With the rapid popularization of the internet and the internet of things, the generation and collection speed of various decision-making data in economic production and life is rapidly increasing. Due to the limitations of data collection technology and expert judgment [1,2], the decision-making data show the characteristics of incompleteness, uncertainty, incongruity, fuzziness and hesitation [3,4]. For this kind of decision-making problem with complex decision data and uncertain evaluation information, the traditional optimization mechanism model based on function relationship becomes more difficult in decision analysis and problem-solving. In fact, there is a large amount of effective decision information hidden in the decision data. Based on the existing decision data, we use scientific data processing technology to objectively analyze and evaluate them and transform them into effective decision indicators and knowledge, which can provide reliable and reasonable suggestions and decision support for decision-makers. This data-driven decision-making has become a new trend in modern decision-making [5–7].

Multi-attribute decision making (MADM) is the most common decision-making problem in practice. Objects are evaluated and sorted according to the comprehensive performance of multi-attribute. In order to reflect the uncertainty of human cognition, Zadeh proposed fuzzy set theory [8], linguistic variable [9–11] and possibility measure and introduced them into the MADM problem [12]. Nowadays, fuzzy set theory has been developed and produced in many forms. Because the fuzzy set only has a membership index of fuzzy objects, it is difficult to describe people's subjective understanding of fuzzy concepts completely. Atanassov proposed intuitive fuzzy sets by adding a non-membership degree and hesitation degree to the relationship between objects and sets [13], which can more truly reflect the subject's understanding of the fuzzy nature of objective things when expressing uncertain information [14]. Since the membership degree and non-membership degree may also be uncertain, Atanassov and Gargov further extended them into the form of interval numbers and proposed the interval-valued intuitive fuzzy set (IVIFS) [15]. Intuitionistic fuzzy sets and interval-valued intuitionistic fuzzy sets have been introduced into many traditional decision models to solve MADM problems, such as the combination with AHP (Analytic Hierarchy Process) [16,17], TOPSIS (Technique for Order Preference by Similarity to an Ideal Solution) [18,19], VIKOR (VlseKriterijumska Optimizacija I Kompromisno Resenje) [20], ELECTRE (Elimination et Choice Translating Reality) [21,22], PROMETHEE (preference ranking organization methods for enrichment evaluations) [23], etc.

We can sort and select different schemes by MADM. However, in practice, we often encounter the following situation: we plan to select the top 10 of the 15 suppliers as the access suppliers, but after a comprehensive evaluation, the evaluation results of the ninth to 11th suppliers may be slightly different. There are certain risks in accepting or rejecting these three suppliers, and further field visits may be required. This means that the 15 suppliers can be divided into three types, i.e., accepted, rejected and to be further determined. The three-way decision theory can make exactly three kinds of decisions in this situation. The three-way decision is a new theory proposed by Yao on the basis of the rough set theory. A rough set applies the lower and upper approximations of equivalence relation to divide the universe of objects into three pair-wise disjoint regions, i.e., positive region, negative region and boundary region [24]. In a classical rough set, the positive region and the associated positive rules are the focus of attention, as these rules produce consistent acceptance and rejection decisions. However, the decisions are made without any tolerance of uncertainty, which is too strict for dealing with incomplete and noisy data and is insensitive to the cost of classification errors. In order to overcome these deficiencies, Yao et al. introduced the Bayesian minimum risk decision theory and proposed the decision-theoretic rough set models [25], which can allow a tolerance of inaccuracy in lower and upper approximations and define three regions including probabilistic positive, boundary, and negative regions. However, there is difficulty in interpreting rules in the decision-theoretic rough set models. For example, an object in the probabilistic positive region does not certainly belong to the decision class, but with a high probability (i.e., the probability value is above a certain threshold) [26], so a rule from the probabilistic positive region may be uncertain and nondeterministic. In order to better interpret the rules qualitatively, Yao et al. introduced the notion of three-way decision rules [27]. Positive, negative, and boundary rules are constructed from the corresponding regions, and they represent the results of a three-way decision of acceptance, rejection, or abstaining. In addition, the decisions of acceptance and rejection are made with certain levels of tolerance for errors, which reflects the cost sensitivity of decision-makers to incorrect classification decisions. Obviously, the semantics of three-way decisions are consistent with the thinking of human beings in dealing with complex decision-making problems. At present, three-way decision has been widely used in the field of MADM and produced good results [28–31]. In reality, the various indicators of evaluation objects have different expression forms. Some indicators can be expressed in exact real numbers, some can be expressed in uncertain interval numbers, some can be expressed as the fuzzy values of qualitative linguistic variables, and some can be expressed in the forms of fuzzy numbers, intuitive fuzzy numbers, IVIFNs, etc. Therefore, it is of great significance to discuss the three-way decisions under a hybrid multi-attribute environment, especially in the case of attributes represented by intuitionistic fuzzy numbers or IVIFNs with more fuzzy information.

The representative studies on the three-way decisions under intuitionistic fuzzy or interval-valued intuitionistic fuzzy multi-attribute environments are shown in Table 1.

Table 1. The representative three-way decision methods under intuitionistic fuzzy or interval-valued intuitionistic fuzzy multi-attribute environment.

Method	Basic Principle	Characteristics
Jia and Liu [32]	• The conditional probability is calculated by TOPSIS.	• It is easy to understand the geometric position proximity to the ideal points, but it does not take into account the inherent characteristics of the data, such as the similarity with the ideal points.
Liu et al. [33]	• The conditional probability is calculated based on the grey correlation degree between each scheme and the ideal scheme. • The losses are determined based on the preference coefficient and the distance from the ideal point, and then the threshold is determined by the Bayesian deduction formula.	• It reflects the similarity with the ideal scheme represented by a positive ideal point and reflects the inherent characteristics of data. • The loss function has certain objectivity, but the risk-taking level needs to be determined according to the personal preference coefficient.
Gao et al. [34]	• The conditional probability is calculated by VIKOR. • The attribute weights are calculated according to the method of maximizing the deviation.	• From the whole perspective of all attributes, the group utility and individual regret relative to the ideal point can be considered, and the factors are more comprehensive.
Xue et al. [35]	• The comprehensive evaluation value of each scheme is obtained by intuitionistic fuzzy additive operation between each attribute value and the attribute weight. Combining the hesitation degree and threshold pair, the threshold of each scheme is obtained, and then the classification of each scheme is given.	• The calculation is simple, but the attribute weight is not fully used when calculating the conditional probability value with an intuitive fuzzy logic operation.
Xue et al. [36,37]	• Based on the intuitionistic fuzzy possibility measure, the threshold pair and three decision classifications are determined, and then the selected schemes are further ranked based on the decision risk.	• The classification based on probabilistic positive region, negative region and boundary region has clear meaning, but the attribute weight is not considered, and the schemes in negative and boundary regions cannot be further sorted.
Liu et al. [38]	• Three-way decision rules are formed based on the intuitive fuzzy similarity, risk costs and closeness degree between schemes, combined with the ordering method of an intuitive fuzzy number.	• The classification based on similarity is easy to understand, but attribute weights are not considered.
Ye et al. [39]	• The interval-valued intuitionistic fuzzy weighted averaging operation is used to aggregate the group opinions on the losses, and the score and accuracy of the expected loss are used to determine the classification of each scheme. • The weights of experts are determined by grey correlation analysis.	• The classification of each scheme is determined based on the expected loss after the aggregation of the loss of each expert, which fails to reflect the attribute value of the scheme.
Liu et al. [40,41]	• Based on the optimization model and Karush–Kuhn–Tucker condition, a new method to determine the threshold is proposed.	• It provides an idea for determining the threshold pair of risk losses expressed by intuitionistic fuzzy numbers and IVIFNs.

The main methods for determining conditional probability in three-way decisions include TOPSIS [32], grey correlation analysis [33] and VIKOR [34]. Two methods are used to determine the decision thresholds: one is to use the optimization method to determine the thresholds based on the subjective risk loss matrix [40,41]; the second is to determine the losses based on the preference coefficient and the distance from the ideal points and then use the formula derived from Bayesian decision to determine the thresholds [33]. In addition, some scholars put forward the method of weight determination based on deviation [34], and some scholars put forward the method of grey correlation analysis to determine the weights of experts in group decision-making [39].

The above literature provides a good foundation for this study. However, the existing studies still have the following contents that may be deepened. Firstly, there is a lack of discussion on the hybrid multi-attribute three-way decision, even the study on the interval-valued intuitionistic fuzzy three-way decision is relatively lacking. Secondly, there are few discussions about expert weight and attribute weight in the interval-valued intuitionistic fuzzy three-way group decisions. In fact, the interval-valued intuitionistic fuzzy group decision matrix contains a lot of information. It is of great significance to make effective use of the information and give the scientific weights of experts and attributes for decision results. Thirdly, the determination method of conditional probability in the three-way decision can be further improved. For example, the advantages of VIKOR, TOPSIS and grey correlation analysis can be fully integrated to form a grey correlation improved VIKOR model, which can give the conditional probability more objectively. In order to make up for the above deficiencies, we will discuss the hybrid multi-attribute three-way group decision-making method. The attribute values of different forms are unified into IVIFNs with the least information distortion. Based on the IVIFNs group decision matrix, the expert weight and attribute weight are determined. Then the conditional probability is determined by using the improved VIKOR model based on grey correlation, and the three-way decision rules can be formed by comparing with the threshold pair based on optimization.

The rest of this paper is organized as follows. Section 2 proposes research preliminaries, including interval-valued intuitionistic fuzzy sets and three-way decisions. Section 3 proposes a hybrid multi-attribute three-way group decision method based on an improved VIKOR model. Section 4 provides an illustrative example to verify the validity of the method. Section 5 summarizes the conclusions of this study.

2. Preliminaries

2.1. Interval-Valued Intuitionistic Fuzzy Sets

Definition 1 [15]. *Let X be a non-empty set and an IVIFS $\widetilde{A}$ in X is expressed as follows:*

$$\widetilde{A} = \{\langle x, \widetilde{\mu}_{\widetilde{A}}(x), \widetilde{v}_{\widetilde{A}}(x)\rangle | x \in X\} = \{\langle x, [\mu^L_{\widetilde{A}}(x), \mu^R_{\widetilde{A}}(x)], [v^L_{\widetilde{A}}(x), v^R_{\widetilde{A}}(x)]\rangle | x \in X\} \quad (1)$$

where, $\mu^L_{\widetilde{A}}(x)$ and $\mu^R_{\widetilde{A}}(x)$, respectively, represent the upper and lower boundaries of the membership degree $\widetilde{\mu}_{\widetilde{A}}(x)$ of the element x in X belonging to $\widetilde{A}$; $v^L_{\widetilde{A}}(x)$ and $v^R_{\widetilde{A}}(x)$, respectively, represent the upper and lower boundaries of the non-membership degree $\widetilde{v}_{\widetilde{A}}(x)$ of the element x that belong to $\widetilde{A}$. For each $x \subset X$, it satisfies the conditions: $0 \leq \mu^L_{\widetilde{A}}(x) \leq \mu^R_{\widetilde{A}}(x) \leq 1, 0 \leq v^L_{\widetilde{A}}(x) \leq v^R_{\widetilde{A}}(x) \leq 1$, $0 \leq \mu^R_{\widetilde{A}}(x) + v^R_{\widetilde{A}}(x) \leq 1, \forall x \in X$.

Definition 2 [15]. *For an IVIFS $\widetilde{A}$, the hesitation degree of element x in $\widetilde{A}$ is:*

$$\pi_{\widetilde{A}}(x) = 1 - \widetilde{\mu}_{\widetilde{A}}(x) - \widetilde{v}_{\widetilde{A}}(x) = [\pi^L_{\widetilde{A}}(x), \pi^R_{\widetilde{A}}(x)] = [1 - \mu^R_{\widetilde{A}}(x) - v^R_{\widetilde{A}}(x), 1 - \mu^L_{\widetilde{A}}(x) - v^L_{\widetilde{A}}(x)] \quad (2)$$

Definition 3 [42]. *For an IVIFS $\widetilde{A}$, the fuzzy degree $\Delta_{\widetilde{A}}(x)$ of element x belonging to $\widetilde{A}$ is given as follows:*

$$\Delta_{\widetilde{A}}(x) = \sqrt{\frac{\left(\Delta^L_{\widetilde{A}}(x)\right)^2 + \left(\Delta^R_{\widetilde{A}}(x)\right)^2}{2}} \quad (3)$$

where:

$$\Delta^L_{\widetilde{A}}(x) = \left|\mu^L_{\widetilde{A}}(x) - v^L_{\widetilde{A}}(x)\right|, \Delta^R_{\widetilde{A}}(x) = \left|\mu^R_{\widetilde{A}}(x) - v^R_{\widetilde{A}}(x)\right| \quad (4)$$

Definition 4 [15]. *The complement of an IVIFS $\tilde{A}$ is given as follows:*

$$\tilde{A}^C = \{\langle x, \tilde{v}_{\tilde{A}}(x), \tilde{\mu}_{\tilde{A}}(x)\rangle | x \in X\} \tag{5}$$

Definition 5 [15]. *Given three IVIFNs $\tilde{\alpha} = ([a, b], [c, d])$, $\tilde{\alpha}_1 = ([a_1, b_1], [c_1, d_1])$ and $\tilde{\alpha}_2 = ([a_2, b_2], [c_2, d_2])$, their basic operations are summarized as follow:*
(1) $\tilde{\alpha}_1 + \tilde{\alpha}_2 = ([a_1 + a_2 - a_1 a_2, b_1 + b_2 - b_1 b_2], [c_1 c_2, d_1 d_2])$;
(2) $\tilde{\alpha}_1 \otimes \tilde{\alpha}_2 = ([a_1 a_2, b_1 b_2], [c_1 + c_2 - c_1 c_2, d_1 + d_2 - d_1 d_2])$;
(3) $\lambda \tilde{\alpha} = \left(\left[1 - (1-a)^\lambda, 1 - (1-b)^\lambda\right], [c^\lambda, d^\lambda]\right), \lambda \geq 0$;
(4) $\tilde{\alpha}^\lambda = \left([a^\lambda, b^\lambda], \left[1 - (1-c)^\lambda, 1 - (1-d)^\lambda\right]\right), \lambda \geq 0$.

Definition 6 [42]. *Let IVIFSs(X) be the set of all IVIFSs in X, a real-valued function E: IVIFS(X) [0, 1] is called an entropy measure for IVIFSs if it satisfies the following axiomatic requirements:*

(1) $E(\tilde{A}) = 0$, if and only if $\tilde{A}$ is an exact set, namely.
$\tilde{A} = \{\langle x, [1, 1], [0, 0]\rangle$ or $\langle x, [0, 0], [1, 1]\rangle | x \in X\}$;
(2) $E(\tilde{A}) = 1$, if and only if $\tilde{A} = \{\langle x, [0, 0], [0, 0]\rangle | x \in X\}$;
(3) $E(\tilde{A}) = E(\tilde{A}^C)$;
(4) For a constant a in (0, 1), let Δ_a^L, Δ_a^R, π_a^L and π_a^R be the sets of all IvIFSs $\{\langle x, \tilde{\mu}_{\tilde{A}}(x), \tilde{v}_{\tilde{A}}(x)\rangle\}$ in X with $\Delta_{\tilde{A}}^L(x) = a$, $\Delta_{\tilde{A}}^R(x) = a$, $\pi_{\tilde{A}}^L(x) = a$, $\pi_{\tilde{A}}^R(x) = a$, respectively. $E(\tilde{A})$ is strictly monotone decreasing with respect to $\Delta_{\tilde{A}}^L(x)$ on Δ_a^L and $\Delta_{\tilde{A}}^R(x)$ on Δ_a^R respectively and is strictly monotone increasing with respect to $\pi_{\tilde{A}}^L(x)$ on π_a^L and $\pi_{\tilde{A}}^R(x)$ on π_a^R, respectively.

Definition 7. *In [43], for an IVIFS $\tilde{A}$ in X, X = $\{x_1, x_2, \ldots, x_n\}$, the authors define the following entropy function:*

$$E(\tilde{A}) = \frac{1}{n}\sum_{i=1}^{n} \frac{2 - 2(\Delta_{\tilde{A}}(x_i))^3 + \left(\pi_{\tilde{A}}^L(x_i)\right)^3 + \left(\pi_{\tilde{A}}^R(x_i)\right)^3}{4} \tag{6}$$

It is not difficult to prove that the above entropy function satisfies the axiomatic condition of interval-valued intuitionistic fuzzy entropy in Definition 6.

Definition 8 [44]. *Given two IVIFSs $\widetilde{A}$ and $\widetilde{B}$ in X, X = $\{x_1, x_2, \ldots, x_n\}$, the cross entropy of them is defined as follows:*

$$D(\widetilde{A}, \widetilde{B}) = \sum_{i=1}^{n}\left[d_{\widetilde{A}}(x_i)\ln\frac{d_{\widetilde{A}}(x_i)}{\frac{1}{2}(d_{\widetilde{A}}(x_i) + d_{\widetilde{B}}(x_i))} + (1 - d_{\widetilde{A}}(x_i))\ln\frac{1 - d_{\widetilde{A}}(x_i)}{\frac{1}{2}(2 - d_{\widetilde{A}}(x_i) - d_{\widetilde{B}}(x_i))}\right] \tag{7}$$

where:

$$d_{\widetilde{A}}(x_i) = \frac{1}{2}\left[\frac{\mu_{\widetilde{A}}^L(x_i) + \mu_{\widetilde{A}}^R(x_i)}{2} + 1 - \frac{v_{\widetilde{A}}^L(x_i) + v_{\widetilde{A}}^R(x_i)}{2}\right] = \frac{\mu_{\widetilde{A}}^L(x_i) + \mu_{\widetilde{A}}^R(x_i) + 2 - v_{\widetilde{A}}^L(x_i) - v_{\widetilde{A}}^R(x_i)}{4} \tag{8}$$

$$d_{\widetilde{B}}(x_i) = \frac{1}{2}\left[\frac{\mu_{\widetilde{B}}^L(x_i) + \mu_{\widetilde{B}}^R(x_i)}{2} + 1 - \frac{v_{\widetilde{B}}^L(x_i) + v_{\widetilde{B}}^R(x_i)}{2}\right] = \frac{\mu_{\widetilde{B}}^L(x_i) + \mu_{\widetilde{B}}^R(x_i) + 2 - v_{\widetilde{B}}^L(x_i) - v_{\widetilde{B}}^R(x_i)}{4} \tag{9}$$

Obviously, $0 \leq D(\widetilde{A}, \widetilde{B}) \leq n\ln 2$, and $D(\widetilde{A}, \widetilde{B}) = 0$, if and only if $\tilde{\mu}_{\widetilde{A}}(x) = \tilde{\mu}_{\widetilde{B}}(x)$, $\tilde{v}_{\widetilde{A}}(x) = \tilde{v}_{\widetilde{B}}(x)$. The cross entropy can also be called the relative entropy or divergence measure, which indicates the discrimination degree of IVIFS $\widetilde{A}$ from $\widetilde{B}$. Since the cross entropy formula does not satisfy the symmetry, we rewrite it as follows:

$$D^*\left(\widetilde{A}, \widetilde{B}\right) = D\left(\widetilde{A}, \widetilde{B}\right) + D\left(\widetilde{B}, \widetilde{A}\right) \tag{10}$$

It is not difficult to prove that the following relationships hold: $D^*\left(\widetilde{A}, \widetilde{B}\right) = D^*\left(\widetilde{A}^C, \widetilde{B}^C\right)$, $D^*\left(\widetilde{A}, \widetilde{B}\right) = D^*\left(\widetilde{B}, \widetilde{A}\right)$ and $0 \leq D^*\left(\widetilde{A}, \widetilde{B}\right) \leq 2n \ln 2$.

Definition 9 [15]. Let $\tilde{\alpha}_j = \left([a_j, b_j], [c_j, d_j]\right)$ ($j = 1, 2, \cdots, n$) be a set of IVIFNs, interval-valued intuitionistic fuzzy weighted averaging operator is as follows:

$$IvIFWA_\omega(\tilde{\alpha}_1, \tilde{\alpha}_2, \cdots, \tilde{\alpha}_n) = \left(\left[1 - \prod_{j=1}^n (1-a_j)^{\omega_j}, 1 - \prod_{j=1}^n (1-b_j)^{\omega_j}\right], \left[\prod_{j=1}^n c_j^{\omega_j}, \prod_{j=1}^n d_j^{\omega_j}\right]\right) \tag{11}$$

where $\omega = (\omega_1, \omega_2, \cdots, \omega_n)^T$ is the weighting vector of the IVIFNs $\tilde{\alpha}_j$ ($j = 1, 2, \cdots, n$).

Definition 10 [45]. Given two IVIFNs $\tilde{\alpha}_1 = ([a_1, b_1], [c_1, d_1])$ and $\tilde{\alpha}_2 = ([a_2, b_2], [c_2, d_2])$, the distance of them is as follows:

$$d(\tilde{\alpha}_1, \tilde{\alpha}_2) = \frac{1}{6}(|a_1 - a_2| + |b_1 - b_2| + |c_1 - c_2| + |d_1 - d_2| + |e_1 - e_2| + |f_1 - f_2|) \tag{12}$$

where $\pi_{\tilde{\alpha}_1} = [e_1, f_1]$ and $\pi_{\tilde{\alpha}_2} = [e_2, f_2]$ are the hesitation degree of $\tilde{\alpha}_1$ and $\tilde{\alpha}_2$, respectively.

2.2. Three-Way Decision

Assuming U is a finite nonempty set, R is an equivalence relation defined on U, and $apr_{(\alpha,\beta)} = (U, R)$ is a probabilistic rough approximation space, then for $X \subseteq U$, let $0 \leq \beta \leq \alpha \leq 1$, the upper and lower (α, β)- approximation sets of $apr_{(\alpha,\beta)}$ can be expressed as [25]:

$$\begin{cases} \underline{apr}_{(\alpha,\beta)}(X) = \{x \in U | \Pr(X|[x]) \geq \alpha\} \\ \overline{apr}_{(\alpha,\beta)}(X) = \{x \in U | \Pr(X|[x]) > \beta\} \end{cases} \tag{13}$$

where $[x]$ is the equivalence class of X with respect to R.

In the above formula, $\Pr(X|[x]) = |[x] \cap X|/|[x]|$ represents the conditional probability of classification, and $|\cdot|$ represents the cardinality of elements in the set. (α, β)-upper and lower approximation sets divide the domain into three parts, i.e., positive domain $POS_{(\alpha,\beta)}(X)$, negative domain $NEG_{(\alpha,\beta)}(X)$ and boundary domain $BND_{(\alpha,\beta)}(X)$ [27]:

(a) $POS_{(\alpha,\beta)}(X) = \{x \in U | \Pr(X|[x]) \geq \alpha\}$;
(b) $BND_{(\alpha,\beta)}(X) = \{x \in U | \beta < \Pr(X|[x]) < \alpha\}$;
(c) $NEG_{(\alpha,\beta)}(X) = \{x \in U | \Pr(X|[x]) \leq \beta\}$.

The thresholds α and β are often given artificially in advance, and so are too subjective and difficult to obtain. Decision rough set introduces Bayesian theory into probability rough set and uses loss function to construct the division strategy of three-way decision with the minimum overall risk, which promotes the development of rough set theory. The decision rough set describes three-way decision processes through the state set $\Omega = \{X, \neg X\}$ and the action set $A = \{a_P, a_B, a_N\}$. The state set $\Omega = \{X, \neg X\}$ represents two states of events, that is, belonging to concept X and not belonging to concept X. The action set $A = \{a_P, a_B, a_N\}$ indicates that three action strategies of acceptance, delay and rejection can be adopted for different states. Considering that different actions will cause different losses, we record that $\lambda_{PP}, \lambda_{BP}$ and λ_{NP}, respectively, represent the losses of actions a_P, a_B and a_N when $x \in X$, and $\lambda_{PN}, \lambda_{BN}$ and λ_{NN}, respectively, represent the losses of actions

a_P, a_B and a_N when $x \notin X$. Therefore, the expected losses of actions a_P, a_B and a_N can be expressed as:

$$\begin{cases} L(a_P|[x]) = \lambda_{PP}\Pr(X|[x]) + \lambda_{PN}\Pr(\neg X|[x]) \\ L(a_B|[x]) = \lambda_{BP}\Pr(X|[x]) + \lambda_{BN}\Pr(\neg X|[x]) \\ L(a_N|[x]) = \lambda_{NP}\Pr(X|[x]) + \lambda_{NN}\Pr(\neg X|[x]) \end{cases} \quad (14)$$

According to Bayesian decision criteria, we select the action set with the minimum expected loss as the best action scheme, and obtain the following three decision criteria [27]:

(**P**): Both $L(a_P|[x]) \leq L(a_B|[x])$ and $L(a_P|[x]) \leq L(a_N|[x])$ are satisfied, then x ∈ POS(X);

(**B**): Both $L(a_B|[x]) \leq L(a_P|[x])$ and $L(a_B|[x]) \leq L(a_N|[x])$ are satisfied, then x ∈ BND(X);

(**N**): Both $L(a_N|[x]) \leq L(a_P|[x])$ and $L(a_N|[x]) \leq L(a_B|[x])$ are satisfied, then x ∈ NEG(X).

Because $\Pr(X|[x]) + \Pr(\neg X|[x]) = 1$, the above rules (**P**)~(**N**) are only related to the conditional probability $\Pr(X|[x])$ and the loss function $\lambda_{\bullet\bullet}$ (• = P, B, N). Generally, the loss of accepting the right thing is not greater than that of delaying to accept it, and both of them are less than the loss of rejecting the right thing. The loss of rejecting the wrong thing is not greater than that of delaying rejecting it, and both of them are less than the loss of accepting the wrong thing. Therefore, these loss parameters satisfy the following relationships: $0 \leq \lambda_{PP} \leq \lambda_{BP} < \lambda_{NP}$, $0 \leq \lambda_{NN} \leq \lambda_{BN} < \lambda_{PN}$, and the decision rules (**P**)~(**N**) can be rewritten as [27]:

(**P1**): If $\Pr(X|[x]) \geq \alpha$, $x \in POS(X)$;
(**B1**): If $\beta < \Pr(X|[x]) < \alpha$, $x \in BND(X)$;
(**N1**): If $\Pr(X|[x]) \leq \beta$, $x \in NEG(X)$.
where:

$$\begin{cases} \alpha = \frac{\lambda_{PN} - \lambda_{BN}}{(\lambda_{PN} - \lambda_{BN}) + (\lambda_{BP} - \lambda_{PP})} \\ \beta = \frac{\lambda_{BN} - \lambda_{NN}}{(\lambda_{BN} - \lambda_{NN}) + (\lambda_{NP} - \lambda_{PP})} \end{cases} \quad (15)$$

3. Hybrid Multi-Attribute Three-Way Group Decision Based on Improved VIKOR Model

Several experts evaluate multiple programs based on multiple indicators. Quantitative indicators may be expressed as exact real numbers, or as interval numbers with minimum and maximum boundaries. Qualitative indicators may be expressed by proper linguistic expressions (values of some linguistic variables), fuzzy numbers, intuitionistic fuzzy numbers or IVIFNs. In accordance with the actual situation, all experts adopt the same expression for the same indicator of each scheme. For this hybrid multi-attribute group decision-making problem, scholars have proposed two different methods. One is to directly construct a hybrid multi-attribute decision matrix and apply TOPSIS, prospect theory, or other methods to make decisions [46,47]. Another is to transform different forms of attributes into the same form and construct a decision model based on a single form of attributes [48–51]. IVIFNs are more flexible and practical in dealing with fuzziness and uncertainty, and other forms of expression can be regarded as special forms of IVIFNs. Therefore, transforming hybrid multi-attribute values into IVIFNs can minimize information distortion. Moreover, after being transformed to the same form, we can effectively calculate the expert weight and attribute weight. Therefore, we choose the latter method for the hybrid multi-attribute group decision-making. The overall decision-making steps are shown in Figure 1.

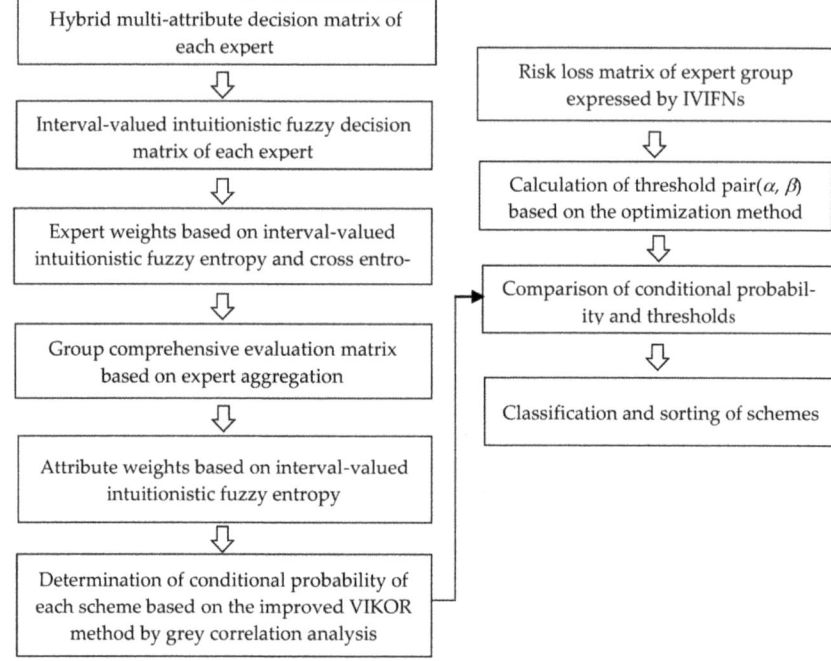

Figure 1. The steps of hybrid multi-attribute three-way group decision making.

3.1. IVIFN Conversion of Different Forms of Attributes

Let scheme set $G = \{G_1, G_2, \ldots, G_n\}$, attribute set $A = \{A_1, A_2, \ldots, A_m\}$ and decision maker set $D = \{D_1, D_2, \ldots, D_l\}$. The decision maker D_k applies real numbers, interval numbers, values of linguistic variables, intuitionistic fuzzy numbers and IVIFNs to give evaluation value $r_{ij}^{(k)}$ for the attribute A_j ($j = 1, 2, \ldots, m$) of the scheme G_i ($I = 1, 2, \ldots, n$), thus forming a hybrid multi-attribute decision-making matrix: $R^{(k)} = [r_{ij}^{(k)}]_{n \times m}$. Where, $r_{ij}^{(k)} = x_{ij}^{(k)}$ is expressed by an exact real number, $r_{ij}^{(k)} = [x_{ij}^{L(k)}, x_{ij}^{R(k)}]$ by an interval number, $r_{ij}^{(k)} = s_{ij}^{(k)}$ by a linguistic variable value, $r_{ij}^{(k)} = (\mu_{ij}^{(k)}, v_{ij}^{(k)})$ by an intuitionistic fuzzy number, and $r_{ij}^{(k)} = \left(\tilde{\mu}_{ij}^{(k)}, \tilde{v}_{ij}^{(k)}\right) = \left(\left[\mu_{ij}^{L(k)}, \mu_{ij}^{R(k)}\right], \left[v_{ij}^{L(k)}, v_{ij}^{R(k)}\right]\right)$ by an IVIFN.

For the intuitionistic fuzzy number $(u_{ij}^{(k)}, v_{ij}^{(k)})$, we can transform it to an IVIFN as follows:

$$\tilde{r}_{ij}^{(k)} = \left(\left[\mu_{ij}^{(k)}, \mu_{ij}^{(k)}\right], \left[v_{ij}^{(k)}, v_{ij}^{(k)}\right]\right) \tag{16}$$

For a real number $x_{ij}^{(k)}$, we first use the linear proportion, vector normalization, extreme value transformation, or other methods to make dimensionless processing. For example, the calculation formula of the linear proportion method is as follows:

$$y_{ij}^{(k)} = \begin{cases} \dfrac{x_{ij}^{(k)}}{\max\limits_{h=1,2,\cdots,n} x_{hj}^{(k)}}, & j \in J_1 \\[2ex] \dfrac{\max\limits_{h=1,2,\cdots,n} x_{hj}^{(k)} - x_{ij}^{(k)}}{\max\limits_{g=1,2,\cdots,n}\left(\max\limits_{h=1,2,\cdots,n} x_{hj}^{(k)} - x_{gj}^{(k)}\right)}, & j \in J_2 \end{cases} \tag{17}$$

where J_1 is an indicator of benefit type that the larger the better, and J_2 is an indicator of cost type that the smaller the better. Then we transform $y_{ij}^{(k)}$ into an intuitionistic fuzzy number $r_{ij}^{(k)} = (y_{ij}^{(k)}, 1 - y_{ij}^{(k)})$, and transform $r_{ij}^{(k)}$ into an IVIFN $\widetilde{r}_{ij}^{(k)} = \left(\left[y_{ij}^{(k)}, y_{ij}^{(k)}\right], \left[1 - y_{ij}^{(k)}, 1 - y_{ij}^{(k)}\right]\right)$.

For an interval number $[x_{ij}^{L(k)}, x_{ij}^{R(k)}]$, we first carry out dimensionless processing. For example, the calculation formula of the linear proportion method is as follows:

$$y_{ij}^{L(k)} = \begin{cases} \dfrac{x_{ij}^{L(k)}}{\max\limits_{h=1,2,\cdots,n} x_{hj}^{R(k)}}, & j \in J_1 \\[2ex] \dfrac{\max\limits_{h=1,2,\cdots,n} x_{hj}^{R(k)} - x_{ij}^{R(k)}}{\max\limits_{g=1,2,\cdots,n}\left(\max\limits_{h=1,2,\cdots,n} x_{hj}^{R(k)} - x_{gj}^{L(k)}\right)}, & j \in J_2 \end{cases} \quad (18)$$

$$y_{ij}^{R(k)} = \begin{cases} \dfrac{x_{ij}^{R(k)}}{\max\limits_{h=1,2,\cdots,n} x_{hj}^{R(k)}}, & j \in J_1 \\[2ex] \dfrac{\max\limits_{h=1,2,\cdots,n} x_{hj}^{R(k)} - x_{ij}^{L(k)}}{\max\limits_{g=1,2,\cdots,n}\left(\max\limits_{h=1,2,\cdots,n} x_{hj}^{R(k)} - x_{gj}^{L(k)}\right)}, & j \in J_2 \end{cases} \quad (19)$$

Then we transform $[y_{ij}^{L(k)}, 1 - y_{ij}^{R(k)}]$ into an IVIFN $\widetilde{r}_{ij}^{(k)} = ([y_{ij}^{L(k)}, y_{ij}^{L(k)}], [1 - y_{ij}^{R(k)}, 1 - y_{ij}^{R(k)}])$.

Let a linguistic evaluation set $S^q = \left\{S_i^q \middle| i \in \left\{-\frac{q-1}{2}, \cdots, -1, 0, 1, \cdots, \frac{q-1}{2}\right\}\right\}$, here q is an odd positive number, the IVIFN corresponding to the q linguistic evaluation granularity can be expressed as [52]:

$$\begin{aligned}\widetilde{\mu}^q &= \left(\widetilde{\mu}^q_{-\frac{q-1}{2}}, \widetilde{\mu}^q_{-\frac{q-1}{2}+1}, \cdots, \widetilde{\mu}^q_0, \cdots, \widetilde{\mu}^q_{\frac{q-1}{2}-1}, \widetilde{\mu}^q_{\frac{q-1}{2}}\right) \\ &= \left(\left(\widetilde{\mu}^q_0\right)^{\frac{q+1}{2}}, \left(\widetilde{\mu}^q_0\right)^{\frac{q+1}{2}-1}, \cdots, \widetilde{\mu}^q_0, \cdots, \left(\widetilde{\mu}^q_0\right)^{1/(\frac{q+1}{2}-1)}, \left(\widetilde{\mu}^q_0\right)^{1/(\frac{q+1}{2})}\right)\end{aligned} \quad (20)$$

$$\begin{aligned}\widetilde{v}^q &= \left(\widetilde{v}^q_{-\frac{q-1}{2}}, \widetilde{v}^q_{-\frac{q-1}{2}+1}, \cdots, \widetilde{v}^q_0, \cdots, \widetilde{v}^q_{\frac{q-1}{2}-1}, \widetilde{v}^q_{\frac{q-1}{2}}\right) \\ &= \left(1 - \left(1 - \widetilde{v}^q_0\right)^{\frac{q+1}{2}}, 1 - \left(1 - \widetilde{v}^q_0\right)^{\frac{q+1}{2}-1}, \cdots, \widetilde{v}^q_0, \cdots, 1 - \left(1 - \widetilde{v}^q_0\right)^{1/(\frac{q+1}{2}-1)}, 1 - \left(1 - \widetilde{v}^q_0\right)^{1/(\frac{q+1}{2})}\right)\end{aligned} \quad (21)$$

where $\widetilde{\mu}^q_0 = \widetilde{v}^q_0 = \left[0.5 - \frac{1}{2q}, 0.5\right]$. Then, for a linguistic variable value $s_{ij}^{(k)}$, we determine the linguistic evaluation value of the corresponding level in the q granularity, and then express it with the corresponding IVIFN.

In this way, we can transform the hybrid multi-attribute decision-making matrix $R^{(k)}$ into an interval-valued intuitionistic fuzzy decision matrix $\widetilde{R}^k = \left[\widetilde{r}_{ij}^{(k)}\right]_{n \times m}, k = 1, 2, \ldots, l$, where $\widetilde{r}_{ij}^{(k)} = \left(\widetilde{\mu}_{ij}^{(k)}, \widetilde{v}_{ij}^{(k)}\right) = \left(\left[\mu_{ij}^{L(k)}, \mu_{ij}^{R(k)}\right], \left[v_{ij}^{L(k)}, v_{ij}^{R(k)}\right]\right)$.

3.2. Determination of Expert Weight Based on Entropy and Cross Entropy

In multi-attribute group decision-making, the smaller the difference between the evaluation value of a decision-maker and other decision-makers, the greater weight should be given to this decision-maker. At the same time, the higher the effectiveness of information in a decision-maker's evaluation matrix, that is, the smaller the redundancy, the greater the weight of this decision-maker. In evaluating the redundancy and difference of information, we introduce entropy and cross-entropy to measure them, respectively, and then build a model to determine the weights of experts.

For the evaluation matrix of a single decision maker, we use entropy $E^{(k)}$ to express the redundancy of evaluation information, and the formula is as follows:

$$E^{(k)} = \frac{1}{m} \sum_{j=1}^{m} E_j^{(k)} \quad (22)$$

where $E_j^{(k)}$ represents the entropy of the jth indicator obtained from the decision matrix of the kth expert. According to Definition 7, its expression is as follows:

$$E_j^{(k)} = \frac{1}{n} \sum_{i=1}^{n} \frac{2 - 2\left(\Delta_{\tilde{A}}\left(\tilde{r}_{ij}^{(k)}\right)\right)^3 + \left(\pi_{\tilde{A}}^L\left(\tilde{r}_{ij}^{(k)}\right)\right)^3 + \left(\pi_{\tilde{A}}^R\left(\tilde{r}_{ij}^{(k)}\right)\right)^3}{4}, \quad (23)$$
$$j = 1, 2, \cdots, m$$

Based on the entropy of each expert, we can calculate the expert weight as follows:

$$w_1^{(k)} = \frac{1 - E^{(k)}}{\sum_{h=1}^{l}\left[1 - E^{(h)}\right]}, \quad k = 1, 2, \cdots, l \quad (24)$$

To reflect the difference between a single decision-making matrix and the other decision-making matrices, we define the cross entropy as follows:

$$D^{(k)} = \frac{1}{(l-1)mn} \sum_{t=1, t \neq k}^{l} D^*\left(r^{(k)}, r^{(t)}\right) \quad (25)$$

According to Definition 8, the formula of $D^*\left(r^{(k)}, r^{(t)}\right)$ is as follows:

$$D^*\left(r^{(k)}, r^{(t)}\right)$$
$$= \sum_{i=1}^{n} \sum_{j=1}^{m} [d\left(\tilde{r}_{ij}^{(k)}\right) \ln \frac{d\left(\tilde{r}_{ij}^{(k)}\right)}{\frac{1}{2}\left(d\left(\tilde{r}_{ij}^{(k)}\right) + d\left(\tilde{r}_{ij}^{(t)}\right)\right)}$$
$$+ \left(1 - d\left(\tilde{r}_{ij}^{(k)}\right)\right) \ln \frac{1 - d\left(\tilde{r}_{ij}^{(k)}\right)}{\frac{1}{2}\left(2 - d\left(\tilde{r}_{ij}^{(k)}\right) - d\left(\tilde{r}_{ij}^{(t)}\right)\right)} \quad (26)$$
$$+ d\left(\tilde{r}_{ij}^{(t)}\right) \ln \frac{d\left(\tilde{r}_{ij}^{(t)}\right)}{\frac{1}{2}\left(d\left(\tilde{r}_{ij}^{(k)}\right) + d\left(\tilde{r}_{ij}^{(t)}\right)\right)}$$
$$+ \left(1 - d\left(\tilde{r}_{ij}^{(t)}\right)\right) \ln \frac{1 - d\left(\tilde{r}_{ij}^{(t)}\right)}{\frac{1}{2}\left(2 - d\left(\tilde{r}_{ij}^{(k)}\right) - d\left(\tilde{r}_{ij}^{(t)}\right)\right)}]$$

Because $0 \leq D^*\left(r^{(k)}, r^{(t)}\right) \leq 2mn \ln 2$, $0 \leq D^{(k)} \leq 2 \ln 2$. Then, based on the cross-entropy, we can calculate the expert weight as follows:

$$w_2^{(k)} = \frac{2 \ln 2 - D^{(k)}}{\sum_{h=1}^{l}\left[2 \ln 2 - D^{(h)}\right]}, \quad k = 1, 2, \cdots, l \quad (27)$$

By aggregating $w_1^{(k)}$ and $w_2^{(k)}$ with weight coefficients γ and $(1-\gamma)$, respectively, we can calculate the final expert weight as follows:

$$w_k = \gamma w_1^{(k)} + (1-\gamma) w_2^{(k)} \quad (28)$$

3.3. Determination of Group Comprehensive Evaluation Matrix

Combined with all the experts' weights, we apply the interval-valued intuitionistic fuzzy weighted averaging operator to calculate the group comprehensive evaluation matrix $X = [\tilde{x}_{ij}]_{n \times m}$, where:

$$\tilde{x}_{ij} = \left(\left[\mu_{ij}^L, \mu_{ij}^R\right], \left[v_{ij}^L, v_{ij}^R\right]\right) = IIFWA_w\left(\tilde{r}_{ij}^{(1)}, \tilde{r}_{ij}^{(2)}, \cdots, \tilde{r}_{ij}^{(l)}\right)$$
$$= \left(\left[1 - \prod_{k=1}^{l}\left(1 - \mu_{ij}^{L(k)}\right)^{w_k}, 1 - \prod_{k=1}^{l}\left(1 - \mu_{ij}^{R(k)}\right)^{w_k}\right], \left[\prod_{k=1}^{l}\left(v_{ij}^{L(k)}\right)^{w_k}, \prod_{k=1}^{l}\left(v_{ij}^{R(k)}\right)^{w_k}\right]\right) \quad (29)$$

3.4. Determination of Attribute Weight Based on Entropy

Based on the group comprehensive evaluation matrix, we apply the entropy value method to determine the weight of each attribute:

$$\omega_j = \frac{1 - E_j}{\sum_{h=1}^{m}(1 - E_h)}, \quad j = 1, 2, \cdots, m \quad (30)$$

where:

$$E_j = \frac{1}{n}\sum_{i=1}^{n}\frac{2 - 2(\Delta_{\tilde{A}}(\tilde{x}_{ij}))^3 + \left(\pi_{\tilde{A}}^L(\tilde{x}_{ij})\right)^3 + \left(\pi_{\tilde{A}}^R(\tilde{x}_{ij})\right)^3}{4}, \quad j = 1, 2, \cdots, m \quad (31)$$

3.5. Determination of Conditional Probability

The determination of conditional probability is the key to a three-way decision. The VIKOR method originates from TOPSIS and can take group utility and individual regret into account. Grey correlation analysis can make full use of sample information to reflect the internal law of sample data. We use the VIKOR method improved by grey correlation analysis to determine the conditional probability, and the concrete steps are as follows:

Step 1: According to the evaluation matrix X, the positive and negative ideal solutions are as follows:

$$\tilde{x}^+ = (\tilde{x}_1^+, \tilde{x}_2^+, \cdots, \tilde{x}_m^+), \tilde{x}^- = (\tilde{x}_1^-, \tilde{x}_2^-, \cdots, \tilde{x}_m^-) \quad (32)$$

where:

$$\begin{cases} \tilde{x}_j^+ = \left(\left[\max_i \mu_{ij}^L, \max_i \mu_{ij}^R\right], \left[\min_i v_{ij}^L, \min_i v_{ij}^R\right]\right) \\ \tilde{x}_j^- = \left(\left[\min_i \mu_{ij}^L, \min_i \mu_{ij}^R\right], \left[\max_i v_{ij}^L, \max_i v_{ij}^R\right]\right) \end{cases} \quad (33)$$

Step 2: Calculate the group utility value S_i and the individual regret value R_i of the ith scheme:

$$S_i = \sum_{j=1}^{m}\frac{\omega_j d\left(\tilde{x}_j^+, \tilde{x}_{ij}\right)}{d\left(\tilde{x}_j^+, \tilde{x}_j^-\right)}, \quad R_i = \max_{j=1,2,\cdots,m}\frac{\omega_j d\left(\tilde{x}_j^+, \tilde{x}_{ij}\right)}{d\left(\tilde{x}_j^+, \tilde{x}_j^-\right)}, \quad i = 1, 2, \ldots, n \quad (34)$$

where $d(x, y)$ represents the distance between two IVIFNs x and y, which can be calculated according to Definition 10. The smaller the value of S_i, the higher the group utility. The smaller the value of R_i, the smaller the individual regret.

Step 3: Determine the best and the worst group utility values as follows:

$$S^+ = \min_{i=1,2,\cdots,n} S_i, \quad S^- = \max_{i=1,2,\cdots,n} S_i \quad (35)$$

The best and the worst individual regret values are:

$$R^+ = \min_{i=1,2,\cdots,n} R_i, \quad R^- = \max_{i=1,2,\cdots,n} S_i \quad (36)$$

Step 4: Calculate the grey correlation degree between the ith scheme and the positive and negative ideal solutions as follows:

$$\varepsilon_i^+ = \frac{1}{m}\sum_{j=1}^{m}\varepsilon_{ij}^+, \quad \varepsilon_i^- = \frac{1}{m}\sum_{j=1}^{m}\varepsilon_{ij}^-, \quad i = 1, 2, \cdots, n \quad (37)$$

where:

$$\varepsilon_{ij}^+ = \frac{\min\limits_{g=1,2,\cdots,m}\min\limits_{nh=1,2,\cdots,m}\omega_h d\left(\tilde{x}_h^+,\tilde{x}_{gh}\right) + \rho \max\limits_{g=1,2,\cdots,m}\max\limits_{nh=1,2,\cdots,m}\omega_h d\left(\tilde{x}_h^+,\tilde{x}_{gh}\right)}{w_j d\left(\tilde{x}_j^+,\tilde{x}_{ij}\right) + \rho \max\limits_{g=1,2,\cdots,m}\max\limits_{nh=1,2,\cdots,m}\omega_h d\left(\tilde{x}_h^+,\tilde{x}_{gh}\right)} \tag{38}$$

$$\varepsilon_{ij}^- = \frac{\min\limits_{g=1,2,\cdots,m}\min\limits_{nh=1,2,\cdots,m}\omega_h d\left(\tilde{x}_h^-,\tilde{x}_{gh}\right) + \rho \max\limits_{g=1,2,\cdots,m}\max\limits_{nh=1,2,\cdots,m}\omega_h d\left(\tilde{x}_h^-,\tilde{x}_{gh}\right)}{w_j d\left(\tilde{x}_j^-,\tilde{x}_{ij}\right) + \rho \max\limits_{g=1,2,\cdots,m}\max\limits_{nh=1,2,\cdots,m}\omega_h d\left(\tilde{x}_h^-,\tilde{x}_{gh}\right)} \tag{39}$$

In the above formula, $\rho \in [0,1]$ is the distinguishing coefficient. The smaller the value of ρ, the greater the distinguishing ability. Generally, ρ is taken as 0.5.

Step 5: Calculate the group utility value and individual regret value of the ith scheme based on grey correlation analysis as follows:

$$\zeta_i = \frac{\varepsilon_i^-}{\varepsilon_i^+}, \; \xi_i = \max_j \frac{\varepsilon_{ij}^-}{\varepsilon_{ij}^+}, \; i = 1,2,\cdots,n \tag{40}$$

Both the group utility value and the individual regret value are indicators that the smaller the better. Then the best and the worst group utility values are, respectively:

$$\zeta^+ = \min_{i=1,2,\cdots,n}\zeta_i, \; \zeta^- = \max_{i=1,2,\cdots,n}\zeta_i \tag{41}$$

The best and the worst individual regret values are:

$$\xi^+ = \min_{i=1,2,\cdots,n}\xi_i, \; \xi^- = \max_{i=1,2,\cdots,n}\xi_i \tag{42}$$

Step 6: Determine the benefit ratio of the ith scheme based on the VIKOR-grey correlation analysis method as follows:

$$Q_i = \sigma\left(\frac{S_i\zeta_i - S^+\zeta^+}{S^-\zeta^- - S^+\zeta^+}\right) + (1-\sigma)\left(\frac{R_i\xi_i - R^+\xi^+}{R^-\xi^- - R^+\xi^+}\right), \; i = 1,2,\cdots,n \tag{43}$$

where σ represents the compromise coefficient between group utility and individual regret, $0 \leq \sigma \leq 1$. If $\sigma > 0.5$, it represents the principle of conformity.

Step 7: The smaller the benefit ratio of the ith scheme, the greater the probability that it belongs to the acceptable state Z. The conditional probability can be calculated as follows:

$$\Pr(Z|[G_i]) = 1 - Q_i \tag{44}$$

3.6. Determination of Decision Thresholds

The threshold pair (α, β) is another key parameter of a three-way decision, which is determined by the loss function. In practice, it is difficult for decision-makers to give the exact value of risk loss of each action under different states. They prefer to use uncertain expressions, such as interval number, fuzzy number, linguistic variable value, intuitionistic fuzzy number and IVIFN. According to the linear or nonlinear ordering rules of various uncertain forms, scholars proposed the corresponding determination methods of the threshold pair [40,41,53,54]. Considering the deficiency of large information distortion in linear ordering, Liu et al. proposed a generalized scalable and nonlinear sorting method to determine the threshold pair for the risk loss matrix represented by IVIFNs from the perspective of optimization [41].

The expert group expresses the risk loss values of three actions a_P (acceptance), a_B (delay) and a_N (rejection) under two states Z (acceptable) and Z^C (unacceptable) as IVIFNs, as shown in Table 2.

Table 2. Risk loss matrix.

	Z	Z^C
a_P	$([\mu_{PZ}^L, \mu_{PZ}^R], [v_{PZ}^L, v_{PZ}^R])$	$([\mu_{PZ^C}^L, \mu_{PZ^C}^R], [v_{PZ^C}^L, v_{PZ^C}^R])$
a_B	$([\mu_{BZ}^L, \mu_{BZ}^R], [v_{BZ}^L, v_{BZ}^R])$	$([\mu_{BZ^C}^L, \mu_{BZ^C}^R], [v_{BZ^C}^L, v_{BZ^C}^R])$
a_N	$([\mu_{NZ}^L, \mu_{NZ}^R], [v_{NZ}^L, v_{NZ}^R])$	$([\mu_{NZ^C}^L, \mu_{NZ^C}^R], [v_{NZ^C}^L, v_{NZ^C}^R])$

Then the optimization model for solving α and β is as follows [41]:

$$\alpha = \min g$$

$$s.t. \begin{cases} \frac{2-(v_{PZ}^L)^g(v_{PZ^C}^L)^h - (v_{PZ}^R)^g(v_{PZ^C}^R)^h}{2+(1-\mu_{PZ}^L)^g(1-\mu_{PZ^C}^L)^h + (1-\mu_{PZ}^R)^g(1-\mu_{PZ^C}^R)^h - (v_{PZ}^L)^g(v_{PZ^C}^L)^h - (v_{PZ}^R)^g(v_{PZ^C}^R)^h} \leq \\ \frac{2-(v_{BZ}^L)^g(v_{BZ^C}^L)^h - (v_{BZ}^R)^g(v_{BZ^C}^R)^h}{2+(1-\mu_{BZ}^L)^g(1-\mu_{BZ^C}^L)^h + (1-\mu_{BZ}^R)^g(1-\mu_{BZ^C}^R)^h - (v_{BZ}^L)^g(v_{BZ^C}^L)^h - (v_{BZ}^R)^g(v_{BZ^C}^R)^h} \\ \frac{2-(v_{PZ}^L)^g(v_{PZ^C}^L)^h - (v_{PZ}^R)^g(v_{PZ^C}^R)^h}{2+(1-\mu_{PZ}^L)^g(1-\mu_{PZ^C}^L)^h + (1-\mu_{PZ}^R)^g(1-\mu_{PZ^C}^R)^h - (v_{PZ}^L)^g(v_{PZ^C}^L)^h - (v_{PZ}^R)^g(v_{PZ^C}^R)^h} \leq \\ \frac{2-(v_{NZ}^L)^g(v_{NZ^C}^L)^h - (v_{NZ}^R)^g(v_{NZ^C}^R)^h}{2+(1-\mu_{NZ}^L)^g(1-\mu_{NZ^C}^L)^h + (1-\mu_{NZ}^R)^g(1-\mu_{NZ^C}^R)^h - (v_{NZ}^L)^g(v_{NZ^C}^L)^h - (v_{NZ}^R)^g(v_{NZ^C}^R)^h} \\ g+h=1, \; g,h \geq 0 \end{cases} \quad (45)$$

$$\beta = \max g$$

$$s.t. \begin{cases} \frac{2-(v_{NZ}^L)^g(v_{NZ^C}^L)^h - (v_{NZ}^R)^g(v_{NZ^C}^R)^h}{2+(1-\mu_{NZ}^L)^g(1-\mu_{NZ^C}^L)^h + (1-\mu_{NZ}^R)^g(1-\mu_{NZ^C}^R)^h - (v_{NZ}^L)^g(v_{NZ^C}^L)^h - (v_{NZ}^R)^g(v_{NZ^C}^R)^h} \leq \\ \frac{2-(v_{PZ}^L)^g(v_{PZ^C}^L)^h - (v_{PZ}^R)^g(v_{PZ^C}^R)^h}{2+(1-\mu_{PZ}^L)^g(1-\mu_{PZ^C}^L)^h + (1-\mu_{PZ}^R)^g(1-\mu_{PZ^C}^R)^h - (v_{PZ}^L)^g(v_{PZ^C}^L)^h - (v_{PZ}^R)^g(v_{PZ^C}^R)^h} \\ \frac{2-(v_{NZ}^L)^g(v_{NZ^C}^L)^h - (v_{NZ}^R)^g(v_{NZ^C}^R)^h}{2+(1-\mu_{NZ}^L)^g(1-\mu_{NZ^C}^L)^h + (1-\mu_{NZ}^R)^g(1-\mu_{NZ^C}^R)^h - (v_{NZ}^L)^g(v_{NZ^C}^L)^h - (v_{NZ}^R)^g(v_{NZ^C}^R)^h} \leq \\ \frac{2-(v_{BZ}^L)^g(v_{R7C}^L)^h - (v_{BZ}^R)^g(v_{R7C}^R)^h}{2+(1-\mu_{BZ}^L)^g(1-\mu_{BZ^C}^L)^h + (1-\mu_{BZ}^R)^g(1-\mu_{BZ^C}^R)^h - (v_{BZ}^L)^g(v_{BZ^C}^L)^h - (v_{BZ}^R)^g(v_{BZ^C}^R)^h} \\ g+h=1, \; g,h \geq 0 \end{cases} \quad (46)$$

3.7. Classification and Sorting of Schemes

According to the value of the threshold (α, β), we can classify schemes:

(1) If the conditional probability of the ith scheme $\Pr(Z|[G_i]) \geq \alpha$, the scheme G_i can be accepted;
(2) If $\Pr(Z|[G_i]) \leq \beta$, the scheme G_i shall be rejected;
(3) If $\beta < \Pr(Z|[G_i]) < \alpha$, the scheme G_i can be used as a candidate scheme and needs further evaluation.

In addition, the larger the value of $\Pr(Z|[G_i])$, the greater the possibility of selecting the scheme G_i. If $\alpha = \beta$, the three-way decision model degenerates into a two-way decision-making model. If $\Pr(Z|[G_i]) \geq \alpha$, we accept the scheme G_i; Otherwise, we reject the scheme G_i.

4. An Illustrative Example

We use the latent dirichlet allocation topic model to mine customers' demand factors for mobile phone performance, and extract six features, namely appearance (A_1), fast response (A_2), endurance (A_3), screen definition (A_4), running fluency (A_5) and battery heating (A_6). We organize four experts D_1, D_2, D_3 and D_4 from China Mobile Communications, China United Network Communications and China Telecommunications in the field of mobile communication performance evaluation to evaluate the above characteristics of the five mobile phone brands $G_1 \sim G_5$. In order to verify the feasibility of the method proposed in this paper, after discussion with experts, the forms of different indicators are set as follows:

(1) A1 is evaluated in the form of percentage real number. The prettier the mobile phone, the larger the value of A1.
(2) A2 is evaluated in the form of percentage interval number. For example, if an expert thinks that a mobile phone responds well to various functional requirements, according to the percentage system, it can be regarded as more than 80, but less than 85, then he can give an evaluation value of [80, 85].
(3) A3 and A6 are evaluated in the form of seven granularity values of linguistic evaluation variables {very poor, poor, relatively poor, average, relatively good, good, very good}. For example, if an expert thinks the battery life of a mobile phone is very good, he can assign A3 to it as "very good".
(4) A4 is evaluated in the form of an intuitive fuzzy number. For example, an expert thinks that the membership degree of a clear screen display of a mobile phone is 0.8 and that of unclear is 0.1, or he organizes 10 people to vote on whether the screen display of a mobile phone is "clear", with eight supporting, one opposing and one neutral. In this case, he can value A4 as an intuitive fuzzy number [0.8, 0.1].
(5) A5 is evaluated in the form of IVIFN. For example, an expert thinks that the membership degree of the smooth operation of a mobile phone is [0.6, 0.7] and that of unsmooth operation is [0.1, 0.2], he can value A5 as an IVIFN ([0.6, 0.7], [0.1, 0.2]). Or, an expert organizes 10 people to vote on whether the operation of a mobile phone is smooth or not, six of them think it is definitely smooth, and one thinks it is smooth, but hesitate; one thinks it is definitely not smooth, one thinks it is not smooth but hesitates; one is not sure whether it is smooth and chose to abstain. In this case, he can also value A5 as an IVIFN ([0.6, 0.7], [0.1, 0.2]).

The evaluation matrices of the four experts are shown in Tables 3–6, respectively. We will select the brands that can be agented, rejected and pending from the five mobile brands.

Table 3. The evaluation matrix of expert D_1.

Brand	A_1	A_2	A_3	A_4	A_5	A_6
G_1	82	(90, 95)	poor	[0.8, 0.15]	([0.6, 0.7], [0.2, 0.25])	average
G_2	90	(70, 73)	good	[0.45, 0.5]	([0.3, 0.34], [0.5, 0.5])	very good
G_3	96	(80, 85)	relatively poor	[0.9, 0.05]	([0.8, 0.85], [0.05, 0.1])	relatively poor
G_4	75	(92, 96)	relatively good	[0.6, 0.2]	([0.5, 0.6], [0.2, 0.4])	very good
G_5	87	(80, 88)	average	[0.8, 0.05]	([0.6, 0.75], [0.1, 0.18])	relatively good

Table 4. The evaluation matrix of expert D_2.

Brand	A_1	A_2	A_3	A_4	A_5	A_6
G_1	90	(88, 98)	relatively poor	(0.7, 0.24)	([0.8, 0.82], [0.1, 0.12])	relatively poor
G_2	88	(70, 75)	good	(0.3, 0.62)	([0.4, 0.6], [0.32, 0.35])	good
G_3	94	(83, 90)	poor	(0.88, 0.1)	(0.9, 0.05)	relatively poor
G_4	82	(77, 86)	good	(0.8, 0.1)	([0.4, 0.6], [0.3, 0.35])	relatively good
G_5	83	(75, 85)	relatively good	(0.75, 0.15)	([0.65, 0.72], [0.1, 0.15])	relatively good

Table 5. The evaluation matrix of expert D_3.

Brand	A_1	A_2	A_3	A_4	A_5	A_6
G_1	84	(92, 94)	relatively poor	(0.9, 0.1)	([0.63, 0.73], [0.12, 0.14])	relatively poor
G_2	90	(86, 91)	average	(0.5, 0.35)	([0.7, 0.75], [0.15, 0.19])	average
G_3	92	(88, 94)	relatively poor	(0.75, 0.14)	([0.5, 0.65], [0.12, 0.14])	relatively good
G_4	87	82	relatively good	(0.65, 0.24)	([0.82, 0.82], [0.15, 0.15])	good
G_5	91	(79, 85)	good	(0.88, 0.05)	([0.69, 0.74], [0.22, 0.26])	average

Table 6. The evaluation matrix of expert D_4.

Brand	A_1	A_2	A_3	A_4	A_5	A_6
G_1	82	(88, 90)	poor	(0.73, 0.15)	([0.82, 0.9], [0.08, 0.1])	relatively good
G_2	88	(84, 90)	relatively good	(0.55, 0.42)	([0.63, 0.7], [0.13, 0.18])	very good
G_3	87	90	relatively poor	(0.73, 0.27)	([0.5, 0.55], [0.3, 0.38])	average
G_4	94	(92, 96)	relatively good	(0.78, 0.18)	([0.71, 0.77], [0.15, 0.23])	relatively good
G_5	91	(86, 89)	average	(0.86, 0.1)	([0.6, 0.66], [0.2, 0.24])	relatively poor

We transform all the elements in the above four evaluation matrices into IVIFNs. The results are shown in Tables 7–10.

Table 7. The transformed evaluation matrix of expert D_1.

Brand	A_1	A_2	A_3
G_1	([0.9574, 0.9574], [0.0426, 0.0426])	([0.9375, 0.9375], [0.0104, 0.0104])	([0.0787, 0.125], [0.8231, 0.875])
G_2	([0.9362, 0.9362], [0.0638, 0.0638])	([0.7292, 0.7292], [0.2396, 0.2396])	([0.754, 0.7937], [0.1751, 0.2063])
G_3	([1, 1], [0, 0])	([0.8542, 0.8542], [0.1146, 0.1146])	([0.1837, 0.25], [0.6848, 0.75])
G_4	([0.8723, 0.8723], [0.1277, 0.1277])	([0.9583, 0.9583], [0, 0])	([0.6547, 0.7071], [0.2507, 0.2929])
G_5	([0.883, 0.883], [0.117, 0.117])	([0.8333, 0.8333], [0.0833, 0.0833])	([0.4286, 0.5], [0.4286, 0.5])
Brand	A_4	A_5	A_6
G_1	([0.8, 0.8], [0.15, 0.15])	([0.6, 0.7], [0.2, 0.25])	([0.4286, 0.5], [0.4286, 0.5])
G_2	([0.45, 0.45], [0.5, 0.5])	([0.3, 0.34], [0.5, 0.5])	([0.8091, 0.8409], [0.1344, 0.1591])
G_3	([0.9, 0.9], [0.05, 0.05])	([0.8, 0.85], [0.05, 0.1])	([0.1837, 0.25], [0.6848, 0.75])
G_4	([0.6, 0.6], [0.2, 0.2])	([0.5, 0.6], [0.2, 0.4])	([0.8091, 0.8409], [0.1344, 0.1591])
G_5	([0.8, 0.8], [0.05, 0.05])	([0.6, 0.75], [0.1, 0.18])	([0.6547, 0.7071], [0.2507, 0.2929])

Table 8. The transformed evaluation matrix of expert D_2.

Brand	A_1	A_2	A_3
G_1	([0.8542, 0.8542], [0.1458, 0.1458])	([0.898, 0.898], [0, 0])	([0.1837, 0.25], [0.6848, 0.75])
G_2	([0.9375, 0.9375], [0.0625, 0.0625])	([0.7143, 0.7143], [0.2347, 0.2347])	([0.754, 0.7937], [0.1751, 0.2063])
G_3	([1, 1], [0, 0])	([0.898, 0.898], [0.0816, 0.0816])	([0.0787, 0.125], [0.8231, 0.875])
G_4	([0.7813, 0.7813], [0.2188, 0.2188])	([0.7857, 0.7857], [0.1224, 0.1224])	([0.754, 0.7937], [0.1751, 0.2063])
G_5	([0.8854, 0.8854], [0.1146, 0.1146])	([0.7245, 0.7245], [0.1633, 0.1633])	([0.6547, 0.7071], [0.2507, 0.2929])
Brand	A_4	A_5	A_6
G_1	([0.7, 0.7], [0.24, 0.24])	([0.8, 0.82], [0.1, 0.12])	([0.1837, 0.25], [0.6848, 0.75])
G_2	([0.3, 0.3], [0.62, 0.62])	([0.4, 0.6], [0.32, 0.35])	([0.754, 0.7937], [0.1751, 0.2063])
G_3	([0.88, 0.88], [0.1, 0.1])	([0.9, 0.9], [0.05, 0.05])	([0.1837, 0.25], [0.6848, 0.75])
G_4	([0.8, 0.8], [0.1, 0.1])	([0.4, 0.6], [0.3, 0.35])	([0.6547, 0.7071], [0.2507, 0.2929])
G_5	([0.75, 0.75], [0.15, 0.15])	([0.65, 0.72], [0.1, 0.15])	([0.6547, 0.7071], [0.2507, 0.2929])

Table 9. The transformed evaluation matrix of expert D_3.

Brand	A_1	A_2	A_3
G_1	([0.913, 0.913], [0.087, 0.087])	([0.9684, 0.9684], [0.0105, 0.0105])	([0.1837, 0.25], [0.6848, 0.75])
G_2	([0.9783, 0.9783], [0.0217, 0.0217])	([0.9053, 0.9053], [0.0421, 0.0421])	([0.4286, 0.5], [0.4286, 0.5])
G_3	([1, 1], [0, 0])	([0.9474, 0.9474], [0, 0])	([0.1837, 0.25], [0.6848, 0.75])
G_4	([0.9457, 0.9457], [0.0543, 0.0543])	([0.8632, 0.8632], [0.1368, 0.1368])	([0.6547, 0.7071], [0.2507, 0.2929])
G_5	([0.9565, 0.9565], [0.0435, 0.0435])	([0.8316, 0.8316], [0.1053, 0.1053])	([0.754, 0.7937], [0.1751, 0.2063])
Brand	A_4	A_5	A_6
G_1	([0.9, 0.9], [0.1, 0.1])	([0.63, 0.73], [0.12, 0.14])	([0.1837, 0.25], [0.6848, 0.75])
G_2	([0.5, 0.5], [0.35, 0.35])	([0.7, 0.75], [0.15, 0.19])	([0.4286, 0.5], [0.4286, 0.5])
G_3	([0.75, 0.75], [0.14, 0.14])	([0.5, 0.65], [0.12, 0.14])	([0.6547, 0.7071], [0.2507, 0.2929])
G_4	([0.65, 0.65], [0.24, 0.24])	([0.82, 0.82], [0.15, 0.15])	([0.754, 0.7937], [0.1751, 0.2063])
G_5	([0.88, 0.88], [0.05, 0.05])	([0.69, 0.74], [0.22, 0.26])	([0.4286, 0.5], [0.4286, 0.5])

Table 10. The transformed evaluation matrix of expert D_4.

Brand	A_1	A_2	A_3
G_1	([0.8723, 0.8723], [0.1277, 0.1277])	([0.9167, 0.9167], [0.0625, 0.0625])	([0.0787, 0.125], [0.8231, 0.875])
G_2	([0.9362, 0.9362], [0.0638, 0.0638])	([0.875, 0.875], [0.0625, 0.0625])	([0.6547, 0.7071], [0.2507, 0.2929])
G_3	([0.9255, 0.9255], [0.0745, 0.0745])	([0.9375, 0.9375], [0.0625, 0.0625])	([0.1837, 0.25], [0.6848, 0.75])
G_4	([1, 1], [0, 0])	([0.9583, 0.9583], [0, 0])	([0.6547, 0.7071], [0.2507, 0.2929])
G_5	([0.9681, 0.9681], [0.0319, 0.0319])	([0.8958, 0.8958], [0.0729, 0.0729])	([0.4286, 0.5], [0.4286, 0.5])
Brand	A_4	A_5	A_6
G_1	([0.73, 0.73], [0.15, 0.15])	([0.82, 0.9], [0.08, 0.1])	([0.6547, 0.7071], [0.2507, 0.2929])
G_2	([0.55, 0.55], [0.42, 0.42])	([0.63, 0.7], [0.13, 0.18])	([0.8091, 0.8409], [0.1344, 0.1591])
G_3	([0.73, 0.73], [0.27, 0.27])	([0.5, 0.55], [0.3, 0.38])	([0.4286, 0.5], [0.4286, 0.5])
G_4	([0.78, 0.78], [0.18, 0.18])	([0.71, 0.77], [0.15, 0.23])	([0.6547, 0.7071], [0.2507, 0.2929])
G_5	([0.86, 0.86], [0.1, 0.1])	([0.6, 0.66], [0.2, 0.24])	([0.1837, 0.25], [0.6848, 0.75])

According to Formulas (22)–(23), we calculate that the values of entropy $E^{(1)}$, $E^{(2)}$, $E^{(3)}$ and $E^{(4)}$ are 0.341134, 0.360570, 0.331364 and 0.336861, respectively. Then, according to (24), the four experts' weights $w_1^{(1)}$, $w_1^{(2)}$, $w_1^{(3)}$ and $w_1^{(4)}$ are 0.250513, 0.243123, 0.254227 and 0.252137, respectively. According to (25)–(26), the values of cross entropy $D^{(1)}$, $D^{(2)}$, $D^{(3)}$ and $D^{(4)}$ are 0.03027, 0.033022, 0.035811 and 0.037154, respectively, and according to (27), the expert' weights $w_2^{(1)}$, $w_2^{(2)}$, $w_2^{(3)}$ and $w_2^{(4)}$ are 0.222170, 0.242347, 0.262814 and 0.272669, respectively. Taking the weight coefficient γ as 0.5 and substituting it with (28), the final expert weights w_1, w_2, w_3 and w_4 are 0.236341, 0.242735, 0.258521 and 0.262403, respectively. Combined with expert weights, we apply the formula (29) to calculate the group comprehensive evaluation matrix, as shown in Table 11.

Table 11. The group comprehensive evaluation matrix.

Brand	A_1	A_2	A_3
G_1	([0.9079, 0.9079], [0.0921, 0.0921])	([0.9364, 0.9364], [0, 0])	([0.1329, 0.1901], [0.7506, 0.8099])
G_2	([0.9519, 0.9519], [0.0481, 0.0481])	([0.8293, 0.8293], [0.1069, 0.1069])	([0.6657, 0.7157], [0.2425, 0.2843])
G_3	([1, 1], [0, 0])	([0.9177, 0.9177], [0, 0])	([0.1594, 0.2214], [0.7161, 0.7786])
G_4	([1, 1], [0, 0])	([0.9157, 0.9157], [0, 0])	([0.682, 0.731], [0.2298, 0.269])
G_5	([0.9359, 0.9359], [0.0641, 0.0641])	([0.8331, 0.8331], [0.1006, 0.1006])	([0.5933, 0.6507], [0.2985, 0.3493])
Brand	A_4	A_5	A_6
G_1	([0.8004, 0.8004], [0.1514, 0.1514])	([0.7313, 0.8067], [0.1165, 0.1416])	([0.4013, 0.4675], [0.4709, 0.5325])
G_2	([0.4602, 0.4602], [0.4589, 0.4589])	([0.5418, 0.6303], [0.2308, 0.2731])	([0.7305, 0.7722], [0.1934, 0.2278])
G_3	([0.8281, 0.8281], [0.1202, 0.1202])	([0.7276, 0.7742], [0.1003, 0.1309])	([0.4049, 0.4712], [0.467, 0.5288])
G_4	([0.7208, 0.7208], [0.1724, 0.1724])	([0.6521, 0.7186], [0.19, 0.2599])	([0.725, 0.7684], [0.1972, 0.2316])
G_5	([0.8315, 0.8315], [0.0783, 0.0783])	([0.6375, 0.7186], [0.1471, 0.2042])	([0.5071, 0.5696], [0.3749, 0.4304])

According to (31), we calculate that the entropy values of six attributes are 0.105597, 0.187031, 0.439343, 0.378227, 0.423710 and 0.469141, respectively. Then, according to (30), the six attributes' weights are 0.223771, 0.203397, 0.140271, 0.155562, 0.144183 and 0.132816, respectively. According to (32)–(33), we obtain the positive and negative ideal solutions are:

$$\tilde{x}^+ = (([1, 1], [0, 0]), ([0.9364, 0.9364], [0, 0]), ([0.682, 0.731], [0.2298, 0.269]), ([0.8315, 0.8315], [0.0783, 0.0783]), ([0.7313, 0.8067], [0.1003, 0.1309]), ([0.7305, 0.7722], [0.1934, 0.2278]))$$

$$\tilde{x}^- = (([0.9079, 0.9079], [0.0921, 0.0921]), ([0.8293, 0.8293], [0.1069, 0.1069]), ([0.1329, 0.1901], [0.7506, 0.8099]), ([0.4602, 0.4602], [0.4589, 0.4589]), ([0.1329, 0.1901], [0.7506, 0.8099]), ([0.4602, 0.4602], [0.4589, 0.4589]), ([0.5418, 0.6303], [0.2308, 0.2731]), ([0.4013, 0.4675], [0.4709, 0.5325]))$$

According to (34)–(44), We calculate the group utility value S_i, the individual regret value R_i, the group utility value ζ_i of grey correlation analysis, the individual regret value ξ_i of grey correlation analysis, the benefit ratio Q_i and the conditional probability $\Pr(G_i)$ of each mobile phone brand in turn. The results are shown in Table 12.

Table 12. The conditional probability value of each scheme based on improved VIKOR model.

Brand	S_i	R_i	ζ_i	ξ_i	Q_i	$\Pr(G_i)$
G_1	0.537312	0.223771	1.111560	3	0.917785	0.082215
G_2	0.624022	0.203397	1.060860	2.549017	0.84188	0.158121
G_3	0.330910	0.132834	0.924580	2.581907	0.387610	0.612390
G_4	0.172601	0.086148	0.622639	1.027416	0	1
G_5	0.534577	0.196129	0.913147	1.499537	0.501100	0.498900

The four experts jointly give the risk loss matrix represented by IVIFNs, as shown in Table 13.

Table 13. Risk loss matrix results.

Action	Z	Z^C
a_P	([0.015, 0.100], [0.805, 0.836])	([0.865, 0.900], [0.000, 0.066])
a_B	([0.555, 0.650], [0.300, 0.320])	([0.250, 0.355], [0.452, 0.536])
a_N	([0.951, 0.982], [0.007, 0.018])	([0.024, 0.085], [0.818, 0.840])

We substitute the data in the above table into the nonlinear programming models (45) and (46) and obtain that $\alpha = 0.608646$ and $\beta = 0.122339$. It can be seen that the conditional probabilities of G_3 and G_4 are greater than α, indicating that the two mobile phone brands can be chosen as an agent. If the conditional probability of G_1 is less than β, this mobile phone brand shall be excluded. The conditional probabilities of G_2 and G_5 are between α and β, so they need to be further investigated

In order to reflect the difference between the improved VIKOR model and other conditional probability models, we calculated the conditional probability results and the three classification results under TOPSIS, grey correlation analysis and traditional VIKOR models. The results are shown in Table 14.

Table 14. The results under TOPSIS, grey correlation analysis and VIKOR models.

Brand	TOPSIS		Grey Correlation Analysis		VIKOR	
	Relative Proximity to the Weighted Negative Ideal Point	Classification	Grey Correlation Degree	Classification	Conditional Probability	Classification
G_1	0.482436	delay	0.738883	accept	0.096041	reject
G_2	0.178874	delay	0.752781	accept	0.074021	reject
G_3	0.821297	accept	0.794445	accept	0.655037	accept
G_4	0.891682	accept	0.897226	accept	1	accept
G_5	0.253693	delay	0.773943	accept	0.199499	delay

It can be seen that the conditional probability results of grey correlation analysis are too close to effectively distinguish the differences between brands. TOPSIS results of different brands are different to some extent, but brands G_1, G_2 and G_3 are all pending, which indicates that the distinction is not obvious enough. Of course, this is related to the risk loss matrix given by decision-makers. However, considering only the proximity to positive and negative ideal points, it is difficult to reflect the intrinsic characteristics of data. Nor does it capture decision-makers' attitudes to utility and regret. The results of the VIKOR method are similar to those of improved VIKOR, but there are differences in brand G_1, which is greatly related to the addition of grey correlation analysis results reflecting the inherent characteristics of data. In general, the improved VIKOR model can not only reflect the proximity to the ideal points, but also reflect the inherent characteristics of data and decision-makers' trade-offs on utility and regret, and the results of it are relatively objective.

5. Conclusions

For the hybrid multi-attribute decision-making problem, we propose a three-way group decision-making method based on the improved VIKOR model. Based on the transformed interval-valued intuitionistic fuzzy decision matrix, we apply entropy and cross-entropy to determine the expert weights and obtain the group comprehensive evaluation matrix. Then, we use entropy to obtain attribute weights. By using the improved VIKOR method by grey correlation analysis, we determine conditional probability. By comparing the conditional probability with the decision threshold pair based on optimization, we obtain the classification rules of the three-way decision. The example analysis shows that the method has good three-way classification and can provide support for actual management decision-making. This study has the following features and benefits: First, it considers the hybrid multi-attribute environment, especially the interval-valued intuitionistic fuzzy environment containing more fuzzy information, which is closer to the actual decision-making and has better universality. Second, considering the group decision-making environment, the hybrid multi-attribute evaluation matrix is given by each expert, which is more consistent with reality. Moreover, the proposed expert weight determination method can not only reflect the differences among experts' opinions, but also reflect the uncertainty degree of each expert's evaluation opinion, and the obtained weights are more reasonable and objective. Different from scholars' studies, this paper mainly has three aspects of innovation. First, from the perspective of research, it expands the research of hybrid multi-attribute decision-making and three-way group decision-making. Second, it deepens the research on expert weights and attribute weights in interval-valued intuitionistic fuzzy group decision making and improves the objectivity of weights. Thirdly, an improved VIKOR model based on grey correlation analysis is proposed to determine the conditional probability, which improves the scientificity of the conditional probability.

There are some shortcomings in this study. First, in the determination of expert weights and attribute weights, only one form of interval-valued intuitionistic fuzzy entropy is considered. In fact, there are many forms of interval-valued intuitionistic fuzzy entropy that meet the axiom conditions. How do they affect the weight results and final results, and whether there will be contradictory conclusions? These are not tested. Second, for the risk loss matrix represented by IVIFNs, we use the threshold determination method based on the optimization model, but there is another interactive threshold determination method, that is, to determine the losses based on the preference coefficient and the distance from the ideal points, and then calculate the thresholds. How much is the difference between the results of these two methods? In addition, is it more advantageous to combine the two, that is, to first determine the threshold loss matrix in an interactive way and then determine the thresholds by an optimization method? These aspects are also not explored. Third, we adopt the method of conditional probability determination of the improved VIKOR model. In fact, the prospect theory based on an ordinary utility curve is being gradually introduced to determine conditional probability. Limited by the fact that the prospect theory based on the IVIFN decision matrix is not perfect, we have not conducted research on this aspect. Based on the shortcomings of the method, further research can be conducted in the following aspects. First, we can analyze the influence of other forms of interval-valued intuitionistic fuzzy entropy on expert weights, attribute weights, and the final results. Second, based on the risk loss matrix expressed by IVIFNs, we can discuss the impact of other threshold determination methods on the decision results. Third, we can further improve the prospect theory based on the IVIFN decision matrix and introduce it into the determination of the conditional probability of a three-way decision.

Author Contributions: Conceptualization, J.S.; methodology, J.S.; writing—original draft preparation, Z.H.; investigation, L.J.; writing—review and editing, Z.L.; supervision, X.L.; project administration, Z.L. and L.J. All authors have read and agreed to the published version of the manuscript.

Funding: This research was funded by National Natural Science Foundation of China. (NO.71871222).

Institutional Review Board Statement: Not applicable.

Informed Consent Statement: Not applicable.

Data Availability Statement: Not applicable.

Acknowledgments: We greatly appreciate the associate editor and the anonymous reviewers for their insightful comments and constructive suggestions, which have greatly helped us to improve the manuscript and guide us forward to the future research.

Conflicts of Interest: The authors declare no conflict of interest.

References

1. Dong, Y.C.; Hong, W.C.; Xu, Y.; Yu, S. Selecting the individual numerical scale and prioritization method in the analytic hierarchy process: A 2-tuple fuzzy linguistic approach. *IEEE Trans. Fuzzy Syst.* **2011**, *19*, 13–25. [CrossRef]
2. Zhang, Y.Y.; Li, T.R.; Luo, C.; Zhang, J.B.; Chen, H.M. Incremental updating of rough approximations in interval-valued information systems under attribute generalization. *Inf. Sci.* **2016**, *373*, 461–475. [CrossRef]
3. Doumpos, M.; Zopounidis, C. *Multicriteria Decision Aid Classification Methods*; Kluwer Academic Publishers: Dordrecht, The Netherlands, 2002.
4. Li, X.L.; Jusup, M.; Wang, Z.; Li, H.J.; Shi, L.; Podobnik, B.; Stanley, H.E.; Havlin, S.; Boccaletti, S. Punishment diminishes the benefits of network reciprocity in sicial dilemma experiments. *Proc. Natl. Acad. Sci. USA* **2017**, *115*, 30–35. [CrossRef] [PubMed]
5. Grechuk, B.; Zabarankin, M. Direct data-based decision making under uncertainty. *Eur. J. Oper. Res.* **2018**, *267*, 200–211. [CrossRef]
6. Fu, C.; Xu, C.; Xue, M.; Liu, W.Y.; Yang, S.L. Data-driven decision making based on evidential reasoning approach and machine learning algorithms. *Appl. Soft Comput.* **2021**, *11*, 107622. [CrossRef]
7. Ullah, A.M.M.S.; Noor-E-Alam, M. Big data driven graphical information based fuzzy multi criteria decision making. *Appl. Soft Comput.* **2018**, *63*, 23–38. [CrossRef]
8. Zadeh, L.A. Fuzzy sets. *Inf. Control* **1965**, *8*, 338–353. [CrossRef]
9. Zadeh, L.A. The concept of a linguistic variable and its applications to approximate reasoning Part I. *Inf. Sci.* **1975**, *8*, 199–249. [CrossRef]
10. Zadeh, L.A. The concept of a linguistic variable and its applications to approximate reasoning Part II. *Inf. Sci.* **1975**, *8*, 301–357. [CrossRef]
11. Zadeh, L.A. The concept of a linguistic variable and its applications to approximate reasoning Part III. *Inf. Sci.* **1975**, *9*, 43–80. [CrossRef]
12. Zadeh, L.A. Fuzzy sets as a basis for a theory of possibility. *Fuzzy Sets Syst.* **1978**, *1*, 3–28. [CrossRef]
13. Atanassov, K.T. Intuitionistic fuzzy sets. *Fuzzy Sets Syst.* **1986**, *20*, 87–96. [CrossRef]
14. Liu, H.W.; Wang, G.J. Multi-criteria decision-making methods based on Intuitionistic fuzzy sets. *Eur. J. Oper. Res.* **2007**, *179*, 220–233. [CrossRef]
15. Atanassov, K.; Gargov, G. Interval valued intuitionistic fuzzy sets. *Fuzzy Sets Syst.* **1989**, *31*, 343–349. [CrossRef]
16. Tavana, M.; Zareinejad, M.; Caprio, D.D.; Kaviani, M.A. An integrated intuitionistic fuzzy AHP and SWOT method for outsourcing reverse logistics. *Appl. Soft Comput.* **2016**, *40*, 544–557. [CrossRef]
17. Wu, J.; Huang, H.-B.; Cao, Q.-W. Research on AHP with interval-valued intuitionistic fuzzy sets and its application in multi-criteria decision making problems. *Appl. Math. Model.* **2013**, *37*, 9898–9906. [CrossRef]
18. Boran, F.E.; Genç, S.; Kurt, M.; Akay, D. A multi-criteria intuitionistic fuzzy group decision making for supplier selection with TOPSIS method. *Expert Syst. Appl.* **2009**, *36*, 11363–11368. [CrossRef]
19. Gupta, P.; Mehlawat, M.K.; Grover, N.; Pedrycz, W. Multi-attribute group decision making based on extended TOPSIS method under interval-valued intuitionistic fuzzy environment. *Appl. Soft Comput.* **2018**, *69*, 554–567. [CrossRef]
20. Zeng, S.; Chen, S.-M.; Kuo, L.-W. Multiattribute decision making based on novel score function of intuitionistic fuzzy values and modified VIKOR method. *Inf. Sci.* **2019**, *488*, 76–92. [CrossRef]
21. Erdebilli, B. The intuitionistic fuzzy ELECTRE model. *Int. J. Manag. Sci. Eng. Manag.* **2018**, *13*, 139–145.
22. Devi, K.; Yadav, S.P. A multicriteria intuitionistic fuzzy group decision making for plant location selection with ELECTRE method. *Int. J. Adv. Manuf. Technol.* **2013**, *66*, 1219–1229. [CrossRef]
23. Chen, T.-Y. IVIF-PROMETHEE outranking methods for multiple criteria decision analysis based on interval-valued intuitionistic fuzzy sets. *Fuzzy Optim. Decis. Mak.* **2015**, *14*, 173–198. [CrossRef]
24. Pawlak, Z. Rough set. *Int. J. Comput. Inf. Sci.* **1982**, *11*, 341–356. [CrossRef]
25. Yao, Y.Y. Probabilistic approaches to rough sets. *Expert Syst.* **2003**, *20*, 287–297. [CrossRef]
26. Ziarko, W. Probabilistic approach to rough sets. *Int. J. Approx. Reason.* **2008**, *49*, 272–284. [CrossRef]
27. Yao, Y.Y. Three-way decisions with probabilistic rough sets. *Inf. Sci.* **2010**, *180*, 341–353. [CrossRef]
28. Liang, D.C.; Pedrycz, W.; Liu, D.; Hu, P. Three-way decisions based on decision-theoretic rough sets under linguistic assessment with the aid of group decision making. *Appl. Soft Comput.* **2015**, *29*, 256–269. [CrossRef]
29. Pang, J.; Guan, X.; Liang, J.; Wang, B.; Song, P. Multi-attribute group decision-making method based on multi-granulation weights and three-way decisions. *Int. J. Approx. Reason.* **2020**, *117*, 122–147. [CrossRef]
30. Wang, W.; Zhan, J.; Zhang, C. Three-way decisions based multi-attribute decision making with probabilistic dominance relations. *Inf. Sci.* **2021**, *559*, 75–96. [CrossRef]
31. Wang, J.; Ma, X.; Xu, Z.; Pedrycz, W.; Zhan, J. A three-way decision method with prospect theory to multi-attribute decision-making and its applications under hesitant fuzzy environments. *Appl. Soft Comput.* **2022**, *126*, 109283. [CrossRef]

32. Jia, F.; Liu, P. Multi-attribute three-way decisions based on ideal solutions under interval-valued intuitionistic fuzzy environment. *Int. J. Approx. Reason.* **2021**, *138*, 12–37. [CrossRef]
33. Liu, P.; Wang, Y.; Jia, F.; Fujita, H. A multiple attribute decision making three-way model for intuitionistic fuzzy numbers. *Int. J. Approx. Reason.* **2020**, *119*, 177–203. [CrossRef]
34. Gao, Y.; Huang, Y.C.; Cheng, G.B.; Duan, L. Multi- target threat assessment method based on VIKOR and three-way decisions under intuitionistic fuzzy information. *Acta Electron. Sin.* **2021**, *49*, 542–549.
35. Xue, Z.A.; Zhu, T.L.; Xue, T.Y.; Liu, J.; Wang, N. Model of three-way decision theory based on intuitionistic fuzzy sets. *Comput. Sci.* **2016**, *43*, 283–288.
36. Xue, Z.A.; Xin, X.W.; Yuan, Y.L.; Xue, T.Y. Research on the three-way decisions model based on intuitionistic fuzzy possibility measures. *J. Nanjing Univ. Nat. Sci.* **2016**, *52*, 1065–1074.
37. Xue, Z.A.; Xin, X.W.; Yuan, Y.L.; Lv, M.J. Study on three-way decisions based on intuitionistic fuzzy probability distribution. *Comput. Sci.* **2018**, *45*, 135–139.
38. Liu, J.B.; Zhang, L.B.; Zhou, X.Z.; Huang, B.; Li, H.X. Three-way decision model under intuitionistic fuzzy information system environment. *J. Chin. Comput. Syst.* **2018**, *39*, 1281–1285.
39. Ye, D.; Liu, D.; Hu, P. Three-way decisions with interval-valued intuitionistic fuzzy decision-theoretic rough sets in group decision-making. *Symmetry* **2018**, *10*, 281. [CrossRef]
40. Liu, J.B.; Li, H.X.; Zhou, X.Z.; Huang, B.; Wang, T.X. An optimization-based formulation for three-way decisions. *Inf. Sci.* **2019**, *495*, 185–214. [CrossRef]
41. Liu, J.B.; Ju, H.R.; Li, H.X.; Huang, B.; Bu, X.Z. Three-way group decisions with interval-valued intuitionistic fuzzy information based on optimization method. *J. Shanxi Univ. Nat. Sci. Ed.* **2020**, *43*, 817–827.
42. Zhao, N.; Xu, Z.S. Entropy measures for interval-valued intuitionistic fuzzy information from a comparative perspective and their application to decision making. *Informatica* **2015**, *27*, 203–229. [CrossRef]
43. Yang, S.K.; Tian, Z.J.; Lv, Y.J. Fuzzy entropy based on the new fuzziness of interval-valued intuitionistic fuzzy set and its application. *J. Guangxi Univ. Nat. Sci. Ed.* **2018**, *43*, 2478–2489.
44. Zhang, Q.S.; Jiang, S.Y.; Jia, B.G.; Luo, S.H. Some information measures for interval- valued intuitionistic fuzzy sets. *Inf. Sci.* **2010**, *180*, 5130–5145. [CrossRef]
45. Xu, Z.S. A method based on distance measure for interval-valued intuitionistic fuzzy group decision making. *Inf. Sci.* **2010**, *180*, 181–190. [CrossRef]
46. Yu, X.; Xu, Z.; Chen, Q. A method based on preference degrees for handling hybrid multiple attribute decision making problems. *Expert Syst. Appl.* **2011**, *38*, 3147–3154. [CrossRef]
47. Mi, W.J.; Dai, Y.W. Risk mixed multi-criteria fuzzy group decision-making approach based on prospect theory. *Control Decis.* **2017**, *32*, 1279–1285.
48. Bao, T.T.; Xie, X.L.; Meng, P.P. Intuitionistic fuzzy hybrid multi- criteria decision making based on prospect theory and evidential reasoning. *Syst. Eng. Theory Pract.* **2017**, *37*, 460–468.
49. Luo, C.K.; Chen, Y.X.; Gu, T.Y.; Xiang, H.C. Method for hybrid multi-attribute decision making based on prospect theory and evidential reasoning. *J. Natl. Univ. Def. Technol.* **2019**, *41*, 49–55.
50. Song, J.K.; Zhao, Z.H.; Zhang, Y.M.; Chen, R. Study on the evaluation of enterprise competitive intelligence system under the background of big data. *J. Intell.* **2020**, *39*, 186 192.
51. Song, J.; Zhang, Y.; Zhao, Z.; Chen, R. Research on the evaluation model for wireless sensor network performance based on mixed multiattribute decision-making. *J. Sens.* **2021**, *2021*, 8885009. [CrossRef]
52. Qi, X.W.; Liang, C.Y.; Huang, Y.Q.; Ding, Y. Multi-attribute group decision making method based on hybrid evaluation matrix. *Syst. Eng. Theory Practice* **2013**, *33*, 473–481.
53. Liang, D.C.; Liu, D. Deriving three-way decisions from intuitionistic fuzzy decision-theoretic rough sets. *Inf. Sci.* **2015**, *300*, 28–48. [CrossRef]
54. Liang, D.C.; Liu, D. Systematic studies on three-way decisions with interval-valued decision-theoretic rough sets. *Inf. Sci.* **2014**, *276*, 186–203. [CrossRef]

Article

A Two-Stage Model with an Improved Clustering Algorithm for a Distribution Center Location Problem under Uncertainty

Jun Wu [1], Xin Liu [1], Yuanyuan Li [1], Liping Yang [1], Wenyan Yuan [2] and Yile Ba [1,*]

[1] School of Economics and Management, Beijing University of Chemical Technology, Beijing 100029, China; wujun@mail.buct.edu.cn (J.W.); 2020200839@buct.edu.cn (X.L.); lyyletter@126.com (Y.L.); lipingphd@163.com (L.Y.)
[2] School of Mathematics and Physics, Beijing University of Chemical Technology, Beijing 100029, China; yuanwy@mail.buct.edu.cn
* Correspondence: bayile@163.com

Abstract: Distribution centers are quite important for logistics. In order to save costs, reduce energy consumption and deal with increasingly uncertain demand, it is necessary for distribution centers to select the location strategically. In this paper, a two-stage model based on an improved clustering algorithm and the center-of-gravity method is proposed to deal with the multi-facility location problem arising from a real-world case. First, a distance function used in clustering is redefined to include both the spatial indicator and the socio-economic indicator. Then, an improved clustering algorithm is used to determine the optimal number of distribution centers needed and the coverage of each center. Third, the center-of-gravity method is used to determine the final location of each center. Finally, the improved method is compared with the traditional clustering method by testing data from 12 cities in Inner Mongolia Autonomous Region in China. The comparison result proves the proposed method's effectiveness.

Keywords: multi-facility location problem; clustering algorithm; center-of-gravity method

MSC: 68T20

1. Introduction

Selecting a proper site for a distribution center can effectively save costs, increase profits, improve customer satisfaction and reduce circulation time. Therefore, the location problem has been one of the most important decisions in logistics system planning [1]. Among these, the selection of distribution center sites has become one of the most popular research interests in logistics management. Readers interested in this field could refer to some recent research [2–7].

As the logistics in real-world become increasingly complicated due to factors that significantly increase the uncertainty in logistics planning, such as economy development, the prevalence of online retailing, increasing natural disasters, etc. It is necessary to introduce more indicators to deal with the uncertainty during the site selection process. This research includes demand uncertainty in the model described in a proper mathematical function, which takes both the spatial condition and the economic condition into consideration when selecting the proper locations for distribution centers. Hopefully, this research could provide a planning strategy for the selection of distribution center sites.

In this paper, all data is extracted from a real case of 12 cities in Inner Mongolia Autonomous Region, China. The author proposes a two-stage model based on an improved clustering algorithm and the center-of-gravity method to solve the location problem of distribution centers and provides a strategy for the logistics transportation in this case. The improved model proposed in this paper is compared with the traditional clustering method

by testing data from 12 cities and is proved to be effective. The main work of this paper is as follows:

1. Proposes a modified distance function takes both spatial indicators and socio-economic indicators into consideration, which makes the model match the real case better.
2. Divides demand points into different regions using an improved clustering algorithm first, then uses the center-of-gravity method to modify the clustering center to select the location of the distribution center in each region.
3. Compares the new model with the traditional clustering method using the data from a real case. The results indicate that the method proposed in this paper has a better performance.

The remainder of this paper is organized as follows. Section 2 reviews the literature on location problems. Section 3 presents the methodology of a two-stage model, including the improved clustering algorithm and the center-of-gravity method. Section 4 describes the obtained results using the proposed model. Section 5 compares the results between proposed model and different clustering algorithms. Section 6 concludes the research.

2. Literature Review

The location problem (LP) is a classical problem. The original problem can be traced back to the Fermat problem. The first industrial application of the Fermat problem was proposed by Alfred Weber in 1909 and called the Weber problem [8]. The purpose of the Weber problem is to find the location of a warehouse to minimize the total distance among all customers. Ever since Weber's seminal work, LP has been booming in both the academical world and the industrial world. In previous researches, LP is well classified on the basis of model assumptions, constraints and objectives functions [9].

Based on the number of facilities involved, the location problem could also be classified into two categories, the single-facility location problem (SFLP) or the multi-facility location problem (MFLP). The SFLP is to determine the location of a single facility using the criteria of distance and cost. The common methods include the Weiszfeld method [10] and the center-of-gravity method [11]. However, one single facility might not be able to meet the increased service demand for its capacity is limited. This is where it becomes a multi-facility location problem, which is the problem to be studied in this paper.

The MFLP is commonly seen in humanitarian relief [12,13], emergency response [14], health care facility locations [15,16] and other fields. The objective function and criteria for facility location are considered from different perspectives in many studies, such as total cost, total transportation time and satisfaction [17]. Because MFLP covers a wide range and need to consider many factors, it can be divided into different problems, for example, it could be divided as the deterministic problem if the information in the problem is determined, and the probabilistic and stochastic problem if not. The former mainly focuses on coverage maximization [18,19] and resource minimization [20]. The latter had been largely discussed in earlier researches on the uncertainties of location problems, such as uncertain demand [21,22] and disruption risk [23]. Probabilistic and stochastic location problems can be divided into stochastic programming problems [24] and robust optimization problems [25]. For the detailed classification of MFLPs, interested readers can refer to Wang et al. [26].

There are two commonly methodologies used in MFLP researches: exact methods and heuristic algorithms [27]. In early researches, the scale of the location problem is usually small. Branch-and-bound [28] and cutting plane [29] are quite popular. However, with the expansion of the problem scales and the increase of the constraints, it becomes difficult to obtain the accurate solution. Finding a proper solution of a large-scale problem in a reasonable time has become the mainstream of LP researches, among which, the heuristic algorithm has been proposed for this purpose. Commonly used heuristic algorithms include genetic algorithm [30], particle swarm optimization [31], tabu search [32], cuckoo search [33] and Lagrangian relaxation [34]. However, the most distinctive disadvantage of heuristic algorithms is the computationally burdensome to find the best solution.

How to deal with the computational burden has then become many researchers' interests. One widely adopted perspective is the clustering-based algorithms. By defining the location problem as a kind of clustering problem, the researcher would divide customers or demand points into different clusters, each of which is supplied by one facility. Then there would be only one SFLP in each cluster needs to be solved. Thus, by decomposing the multi-facility location problem (MFLP) into multiple single-facility location problems (SFLP), the researcher could simplify the complexity of calculation [35]. Among those researchers, Esnaf and Kucukdeniz [36] proposed a hybrid method using the fuzzy clustering algorithm to divide the whole region into certain number of areas, each supplied by one very facility, then they used the center-of-gravity method to select the location point of each facility. Kuecuekdeniz et al. [37] proposed a method which integrates fuzzy c-means and convex programming for solving a capacitated MFLP, where fuzzy c-means is used to convert an MFLP to an SFLP. Gupta et al. [38] used fuzzy c-means and particle swarm optimization to optimize the locations of public service centers. Researches mentioned above proved that the clustering-based algorithms are applicable in practice [39]. Nonetheless, few researchers have dedicated to improving the distance function in clustering.

In this paper, an MFLP of distribution centers arising from a real-world case is studied with clustering-based algorithms. The author uses the clustering algorithm to decompose the MFLP into multiple SFLPs and then uses the center-of-gravity method to select the locations of distribution centers by solving each SFLP. The work differs clearly from the previous literature. In this paper, both spatial and socio-economic indicators are well embedded in the clustering method. An improved distance function is proposed to explain the clustering results affected by the two types of indicators. Furthermore, the effectiveness of the proposed method is proved by a comparison on different methods.

3. Methodology

The proposed two-stage model (2SM) aims to compute the optimal number and locations of distribution centers with minimal total transportation cost. The structure of the model is composed of two sequential stages.

1. Determine the optimal number of distribution centers by improved clustering for an MFLP.

In this stage, the author proposes an improved K-Medoids clustering algorithm to classify the demand points and determine the optimal clustering strategy. The improved clustering algorithm can be summarized as follows:
- Redefine the distance function by introducing three socio-economic indicators.
- Select the initial clustering center based on the density to improve the algorithm's efficiency.
- Use the elbow method to determine the optimal number of clusters.

2. Determine the optimal distribution center location by the center-of-gravity method for each SFLP.

After clustering, the location of each cluster distribution center is solved as a SFLP by employing the center-of-gravity method, which optimizes transportation cost. The framework of the model is given in Figure 1.

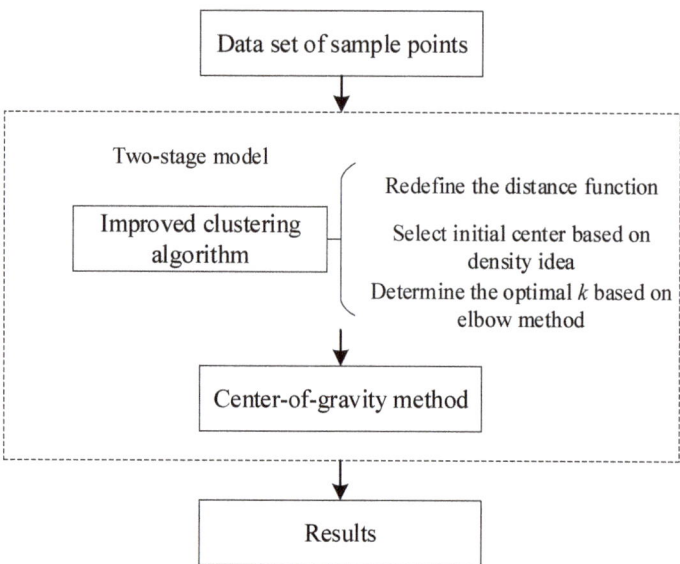

Figure 1. Framework of the proposed model.

3.1. Improved Clustering Algorithm

The clustering algorithm [40] is a kind of unsupervised machine learning method. Its main idea is to divide the objects into different clusters to maximize the object similarity in each cluster and minimize the object similarity between any two clusters. To deal with noise data and outliers effectively, the author employs the K-Medoids clustering algorithm and modifies it to fit the work. The K-Medoids clustering algorithm [41,42] is an adjustment of the classical K-Means clustering algorithm. The pseudocodes for the K-Medoids are shown in Algorithm 1.

Algorithm 1 K-Medoids Clustering Algorithm

Input: Data points $\{x_i\}_{i=1}^{N}$, number of clusters K
Choose different x_i as initial clustering center c_k for $k = 1$ to K
Set $C_k \leftarrow \{c_k\}$ for $k = 1$ to K
for $i = 1$ to K **do**
$C_p \leftarrow C_p \cup \{x_i\}$, where p = $\mathrm{argmin}_{p \in I_1^k} d(x_i, c_p)$
end
while allocation result of any x_i changed **do**
for $k = 1$ to K

$$c_k \leftarrow \mathrm{argmin}_{x_i \in C_k} \sum_{x_t \in C_k} d(x_t, x_i)$$

end
for $i = 1$ to N **do**
    if $x_i \in C_{k'}$ and $d(x_i, c_k) < d(x_i, c_{k'})$ **then**
    $C_k \leftarrow C_k \cup \{x_i\}$ and $C_{k'} \leftarrow C_{k'} \setminus \{x_i\}$
    end
end
end
Output: Clustering results $\{C_k\}_{k=1}^{K}$

Different from the K-Means, in the iterative process, the K-Medoids selects the data point closest to the data's mean in the cluster as the new clustering center instead of choosing the average of all data points.

In the clustering algorithms, there are three factors affect the performance of clustering directly: distance measurement, algorithm efficiency and number of clusters. In consideration of the factors, an improved clustering method is proposed to meet the real-world situation.

3.1.1. Redefine the Distance Function

Euclidean distance is a common distance function in clustering algorithm that measures the distance between two points in m-dimensional space. The two-dimensional distance function considering the longitude and the latitude is as follows:

$$D_{ij} = \sqrt{(x_i - x_j)^2 - (y_i - y_j)^2} \qquad (1)$$

where D_{ij} measures the distance between point i and point j; x_i and x_j are the longitudes of point i and point j, respectively; and y_i and y_j are the latitudes of point i and point j, respectively.

Euclidean distance is simple and effective when dealing with homogeneous indicators. But when the indicators are different, it misses some practical interpretability. To cope with this setback, the author redefines the distance function considering both spatial indicators and socio-economic indicators. The spatial indicators represent the actual distance between two points. The socio-economic indicators reflect the logistics-level score of each point. The detailed computing process is as follows.

(1) Compute the logistics-level score.

The logistics-level score proposed in this research mainly considers three dimensions: economy development, traffic congestion and total logistics demand, which is represented respectively by the per capita disposable income of urban residents, the population density and the permanent urban population, as shown in Table 1. Note that there is no available data on population density. Instead, the ratio of permanent urban residents to urban built-up area is used as in Equation (2).

$$population\ density = \frac{permanent\ urban\ population}{urban\ built\ up\ area} \qquad (2)$$

Table 1. The indicator composition of the logistics-level score.

Dimension	Indicator
Economy development	per capita disposable income of urban residents
Traffic congestion	population density
Total logistics demand	permanent urban population

As the actual data of the corresponding indicators is obtained, the author computes each city's logistics-level score using the entropy weight method, which is used to determine the weight coefficient of each indicator by computing the information entropy. To a certain extent, the entropy weight method can avoid subjective judgment when determining weight coefficients [43]. The smaller the information entropy value of one indicator is, the larger the weight coefficient assigned to it becomes [44]. The logistics-level score is computed as Equations (3)–(8):

First, the data are normalized by Equations (3) and (4):

$$Y_{ij} = \frac{X_{ij} - \min_i(X_{ij})}{\max_i(X_{ij}) - \min_i(X_{ij})} \qquad (3)$$

$$Y_{ij} = \frac{\max_i(X_{ij}) - X_{ij}}{\max_i(X_{ij}) - \min_i(X_{ij})} \quad (4)$$

Equation (3) is the normalized formula of the utility indicator, and Equation (4) is the normalized formula of the cost indicator. X_{ij} is the jth ($j = 1, 2 \ldots, m$) indicator of city i ($i = 1, 2 \ldots, n$). Y_{ij} is the indicator data after normalization. Since the greater the population density is, the greater the traffic congestion becomes, population density should be considered as the cost indicator. The other two indicators are utility indicators.

Then, the information entropy is computed by Equations (5) and (6):

$$P_{ij} = Y_{ij} / \sum_{i=1}^{n} Y_{ij} \quad (5)$$

$$E_j = -\frac{1}{\ln n} \sum_{i=1}^{n} P_{ij} \ln P_{ij} \quad (6)$$

where P_{ij} is the weight of city i in the jth indicator and E_j is the information entropy of the jth indicator.

After that, the weights of the indicators are computed by Equation (7):

$$W_j = (1 - E_j) / \left(n - \sum_{j=1}^{m} E_j\right) \quad (7)$$

where W_j is weight of the jth indicator.

Finally, the logistics-level score of each city is computed by Equation (8):

$$Z_i = \sum_{j=1}^{m} Y_{ij} W_j \quad (8)$$

where Z_i is the logistics-level score of city i.

(2) Define the distance between two points:

$$D(X_i, X_j) = \frac{D_{ij}^2}{(Z_i Z_j)^u} \quad (9)$$

In Equation (9), $D(X_i, X_j)$ measures the distance between any two cities, which is affected by two distance indicators: spatial and socio-economic. D_{ij}^2 is the spatial distance between any two cities, which represents the spatial indicators. The greater the spatial distance is, the greater the distance between the two cities becomes. $Z_i Z_j$ is the logistics score distance between any two cities, which represents the socio-economic indicators. Z_i and Z_j are the logistics-level scores of city i and city j, respectively. The greater the logistics score distance is, the closer the connection between the two cities at the logistics level lies, and the smaller the distance between the two cities in the clustering process becomes. u represents the degree of influence of the logistics-level score in the distance function between any two cities. The larger u is, the greater the influence of the logistics-level score becomes. When u is 0, the distance function is equivalent to the Euclidean distance.

3.1.2. Select the Initial Clustering Center

To reduce the time complexity of the clustering algorithm effectively and avoid the interference of noise data, the author introduces the idea of density into the clustering algorithm to determine the initial clustering center in this research. The steps of selecting the initial clustering center are as follows.

First, the domain radius r_a of the demand points X_i is computed by Equation (10):

$$r_a = \frac{1}{2} max\{\|X_i - X_k\|\} \quad (10)$$

The domain radius r_a measures the maximum distance between X_i and other demand points.

Then, the density factor D_i of X_i is computed by Equation (11):

$$D_i = \sum_{j=1}^{n} exp\left[-\frac{\|X_i - X_j\|^2}{(2r_a)^2}\right] \tag{11}$$

A larger D_i means that more demand points surround X_i, i.e., X_i has a closer relationship with other points. The point with a greater density factor is more likely to be a clustering center. The exponential function could make sure that the point surrounded by more demand has a greater density factor.

After figuring out the density factors of all demand points, the factors are arranged in the descend order. Then, the demand points are selected corresponding to the top k density factors as the initial clustering center.

3.1.3. Determine the Optimal k

The clustering algorithm aims to divide the similar sample points into the same cluster and effectively distinguish the dissimilar sample points. In this process, k will significantly affect the final clustering performance. To obtain the optimal clustering results, it is necessary to determine the optimal selection of k before clustering. In this research, the elbow method is used to obtain the optimal k by computing the sum of the squares of error (SSE) between the sample points and their respective clustering centers. The equation for computing SSE is Equation (12):

$$SSE = \sum_{i=1}^{k} \sum_{x \in C_i} (x - P_i)^2 \tag{12}$$

where C_i represents the ith cluster, P_i is the clustering center of C_i and x is the point belonging to the C_i.

The core idea of the elbow method lies in the following: With the increase in cluster number k, sample division will be more refined, and the aggregation degree of each cluster will be gradually improved; thus, SSE will gradually become smaller. In addition, when k is less than the optimal cluster number, SSE decreases greatly because the increase of k will greatly increase the degree of aggregation of each cluster. However, when k reaches the optimal cluster number, the return of aggregation degree obtained by increasing k decreases rapidly. This means decrease of SSE will tend to be gentler as k continues to increase.

3.1.4. The Flowchart of Clustering Algorithm

Based on the improvements discussed above, the clustering algorithm flow is as follows:

Step 1: Obtain the data of each city required by the model, normalize the data for each indicator to eliminate the dimensional influence.

Step 2: Compute the density factor of each city and arrange each city in the order of density factor from large to small.

Step 3: Take the top k points in Step 2 as clustering centers and take the remaining $n - k$ points as sample points for clustering. Corresponding clustering results are obtained.

Step 4: Compute the sum of distances between each point in the cluster and the remaining points in the same cluster, redetermine the center of each cluster according to the principle of the minimum sum of distances. On this basis, obtain the results by clustering again.

Step 5: Repeat Step 4 until clustering result obtained becomes stable. Take this result as the result under k.

Step 6: Change the value of k ($k \leq \sqrt{n}$) and repeat Steps 3–5 to obtain clustering results under different k.

Step 7: Use the elbow method to obtain the optimal k and the optimal clustering scheme.
Step 8: Output the optimal clustering results.
Figure 2 shows the flow chart of the clustering algorithm.

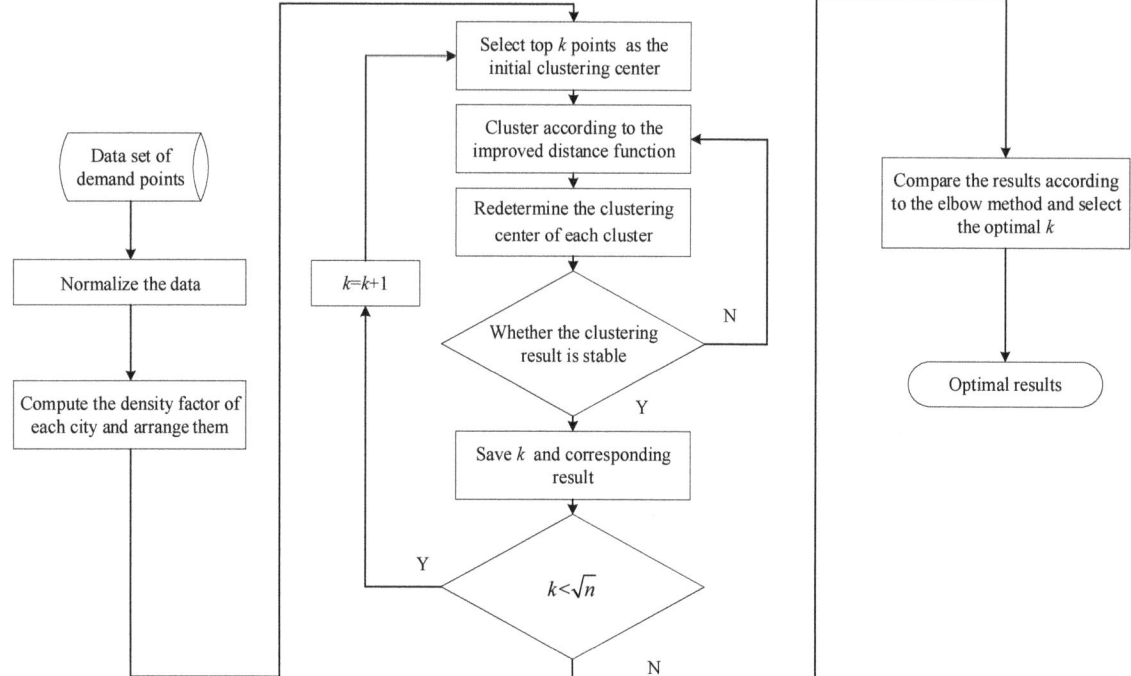

Figure 2. The flow chart of the clustering algorithm.

3.2. The Center-of-Gravity Method

The center-of-gravity method is used to obtain the optimal distribution center location within each cluster after clustering. The point is to minimize the transportation cost between any demand point and the distribution center.

In the logistics distribution system, the coordinate of each logistics demand point is defined as $i(x_i, y_i)(i = 1, 2, \ldots, n)$ according to geographical location, and the coordinate of distribution center P is set as (x_0, y_0). Equation (13) shows the objective function:

$$H = \sum_{i=1}^{n} h_i w_i d_i \tag{13}$$

where H is total transportation cost, h_i is demand of goods at point i, w_i is transportation cost from distribution center to point i and d_i is distance of distribution center to point i.

Here h_i is defined as follows:

$$h_i = \sum_{s \in S} p_{is} a_{is} u_i = u_i \sum_{s \in S} p_{is} a_{is} \tag{14}$$

where S is the set of scenarios, p_{is} is the probability of scenario s occurring at point i, a_{is} is the demand coefficient when scenario s occurs at point i, $a_{is} = 1$ denotes a stable demand case and u_i is per capita disposable income of urban residents at point i.

In the first stage of this method, the gravity centers of each cluster are computed by the following formulas:

$$x_0 = \frac{\sum_{i=1}^{n} h_i w_i x_i / d_i}{\sum_{i=1}^{n} h_i w_i / d_i} \quad (15)$$

$$y_0 = \frac{\sum_{i=1}^{n} h_i w_i y_i / d_i}{\sum_{i=1}^{n} h_i w_i / d_i} \quad (16)$$

$$d_i = \sqrt{(x_0 - x_i)^2 + (y_0 - y_i)^2} \quad (17)$$

$P(x_0, y_0)$ is the extreme point, which is a necessary condition for the optimal solution. If it is not optimal, the iterative method is introduced to find the optimal solution. The solution formulas are as follows:

$$x_0^{(q+1)} = \frac{\sum_{i=1}^{n} h_i w_i x_i / d_i^{(q+1)}}{\sum_{i=1}^{n} h_i w_i / d_i^{(q+1)}} \quad (18)$$

$$y_0^{(q+1)} = \frac{\sum_{i=1}^{n} h_i w_i y_i / d_i^{(q+1)}}{\sum_{i=1}^{n} h_i w_i / d_i^{(q+1)}} \quad (19)$$

$$d_i^{(q+1)} = \sqrt{\left(x_0^{(q+1)} - x_i\right)^2 + \left(y_0^{(q+1)} - y_i\right)^2} \quad (20)$$

This computing process ends when the difference between the last two coordinates of distribution center is lower than a specific minimal value.

3.3. Evaluation Function

In this paper, the evaluation function's object is evaluating the sum of the transportation costs from each distribution center to its responsible demand points. To describe the function accurately, assumptions should be made and given as follows. The capacity of each distribution center can always meet all the demands of the points covered by it. Each demand point is supplied by only one distribution center. Omit the rental, maintenance and other costs related to transporting vehicles during the transportation process. Transportation costs include only freight rates and transportation distance, with the exclusion of labor costs incurred from loading and unloading. Based on the assumptions above, the evaluation function can be calculated as follows:

$$F = \sum_{i=1}^{k} \sum_{j \in N_i} m_{ij} w_{ij} J \quad (21)$$

where i indicates the distribution center, j indicates the demand point, N_i is the set of all requirement points covered by i distribution center, m_{ij} is the transportation distance from the distribution center i to the demand point j, w_{ij} is the total weight of goods transported from distribution center i to the demand point j, and J is the unit rate from distribution center i to the demand point j.

4. Case Study

In this section, taking Inner Mongolia Autonomous Region as an example, the author analyzes the locations of distribution centers in 12 cities to provide a better solution for its logistics transportation. The algorithm is implemented in Python version 3.8.

4.1. Data Collection and Processing

There are six indicators involved: the longitude, the latitude, the per capita disposable income of urban residents, the permanent urban population, the urban built-up area and the population density.

The longitude and the latitude are obtained from Baidu Maps. The per capita disposable income of urban residents, the permanent population and the urban built-up area of each city in 2019 are downloaded from the official website of the Inner Mongolia Bureau of Statistics. The population density of each city is computed by Equation (2). Table 2 shows the initial data used in this case.

Table 2. The initial data.

City Name	Longitude	Latitude	PCDIUR [1]	PUP [2]	Population Density	Z
Hohhot	111.7555	40.8484	49397	265.5	0.8019	0.7287
Baotou	109.8465	40.6629	50427	232.48	0.9408	0.6293
Hulun Buir	119.7814	49.1724	35482	116.41	0.5209	0.4503
Xing'an	122.0406	46.0893	30408	75.13	0.6744	0.2171
Tongliao	122.2505	43.6580	34127	143.03	0.8690	0.2561
Chifeng	118.8938	42.2608	34101	211.42	0.8636	0.3397
Xilin Gol	116.0486	43.9390	40778	80.2	0.4478	0.5496
Ulanqab	113.1314	41.0003	33042	100.29	0.4569	0.4218
Ordos	109.7886	39.6136	49768	165.04	0.5958	0.7352
Bayannur	107.3950	40.7494	32634	91.77	0.6942	0.2676
Wuhai	106.8010	39.6629	45010	52.9	0.8491	0.3668
Alxa	105.7354	38.8583	42983	21.06	0.3637	0.5696

[1] PCDIUR: Per capita disposable income of urban residents. [2] PUP: Permanent urban population.

In order to eliminate the influence of data dimension on the results, all indicators are normalized in advance.

4.2. The Location Problem's Solution

According to the methodology proposed in Section 3, the location problem is solved as follows.

Compute the domain radius r_a and the density factor D_i of each city using the latitude and the longitude. Sort the density factor in the descend order, as shown in Table 3.

Table 3. Domain radius r_a and density factor D_i for each city.

City Name	Domain Radius	Density Factor	Ranking
Hohhot	0.503365	4.328515	1
Baotou	0.468513	4.25465	2
Bayannur	0.520765	4.245805	3
Ordos	0.577318	4.18387	4
Wuhai	0.614253	4.003441	5
Ulanqab	0.43221	3.649514	6
Alxa	0.64415	2.272527	7
Tongliao	0.511665	2.100625	8
Xing'an	0.543144	1.842189	9
Chifeng	0.421892	1.756682	10
Xilin Gol	0.34472	1.590949	11
Hulun Buir	0.64415	1.275099	12

Select the top k cities in Table 3 as the initial centers for clustering. Use the elbow method to evaluate the clustering results with different k.

Since it contains 12 demand points in total, the value range of k lies in [2, 4] according to the principle of $k \leq \sqrt{n}$. Figure 3 shows the sum of the squares of error (SSE) when k takes the values in [2, 6]. The optimal value is $k = 3$.

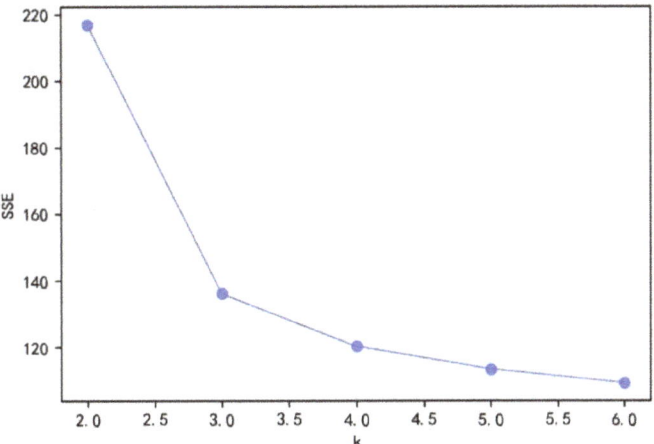

Figure 3. The *SSE* when k lies in [2, 6].

After selecting the optimal k, clustering results are obtained according to the improved clustering algorithm, which is shown in Table 4.

Table 4. The clustering results for the optimal k.

Regions	Central City	Covered Cities
Region 1	Xing'an	Tongliao, Chifeng, Hulun Buir
Region 2	Hohhot	Ulanqab, Baotou, Ordos, Xilin Gol
Region 3	Wuhai	Bayannur, Alxa

The result is modified by the center-of-gravity method. In this process, the permanent urban population is taken to represent the demand of each city. The modified results are shown in Table 5 and Figure 4. C0, C1, C2 and Center are in different colors in Figure 4.

Table 5. The location results for the 2SM.

Clustering	City Name	Longitude	Latitude	Demand
C0	Xing'an	122.0406	46.08926	75.13
	Tongliao	122.2505	43.65798	143.03
	Chifeng	118.8938	42.26083	211.42
	Hulun Buir	121.8592	50.18671	116.41
	Center 0	121.2842	44.08581	
C1	Hohhot	111.7555	40.84842	265.5
	Ulanqab	112.2595	42.44243	100.29
	Baotou	110.3877	42.15471	232.48
	Ordos	109.7886	39.61359	165.04
	Xilin Gol	114.1209	44.03614	80.2
	Center 1	111.4345	41.1818	
C2	Wuhai	106.801	39.6629	52.9
	Bayannur	107.8949	41.73579	91.77
	Alxa	101.339	41.36085	21.06
	Center 2	107.849	41.68704	

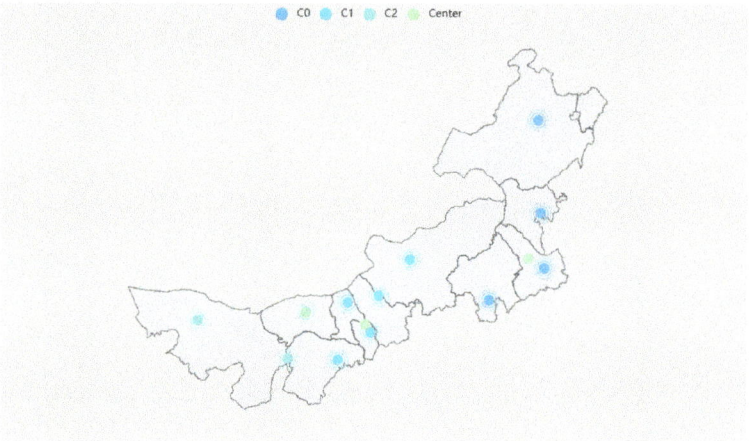

Figure 4. The location results for the 2SM.

A distribution center cannot be set up outside the city because of its infrastructure requirements. So, the distribution center is sited in a city closest to the location results for the 2SM. The results are shown in Table 6.

Table 6. The final location results for the 2SM.

Regions	Central City	Covered Cities
Region 1	Tongliao	Chifeng, Hulun Buir, Xing'an
Region 2	Hohhot	Ulanqab, Baotou, Ordos, Xilin Gol
Region 3	Bayannur	Alxa, Wuhai

5. Evaluation

To evaluate the effectiveness of the two-stage model (2SM), the author makes a comparison on the results of it with three models' based on the traditional K-means algorithm. For each model, k is set as 3. Details are shown in the following.

Model 1: Geographic clustering model (GCM). This model considers only the geographical indicator. It takes the linear distance between cities as the similarity measurement. The distance between cities is computed based on the longitude and the latitude of each city. The location results are obtained by K-means clustering. The results are shown in Table 7 and Figure 5. C0, C1, C2 and Center are in different colors in Figure 5.

Table 7. The location results for the GCM.

Clustering	City Name	Longitude	Latitude	Demand
C0	Hulun Buir	121.8592	50.18671	116.41
	Center 0	121.8592	50.18671	
C1	Hohhot	111.7555	40.84842	265.5
	Baotou	110.3877	42.15471	232.48
	Ulanqab	112.2595	42.44243	100.29
	Ordos	109.7886	39.61359	165.04
	Bayannur	107.8949	41.73579	91.77
	Wuhai	106.801	39.6629	52.9
	Alxa	101.339	41.36085	21.06
	Center 1	108.6037	41.11695	
C2	Xing'an	122.0406	46.08926	75.13
	Tongliao	122.2505	43.65798	143.03
	Chifeng	118.8938	42.26083	211.42
	Xilin Gol	114.1209	44.03614	80.2
	Center 2	119.3265	44.01106	

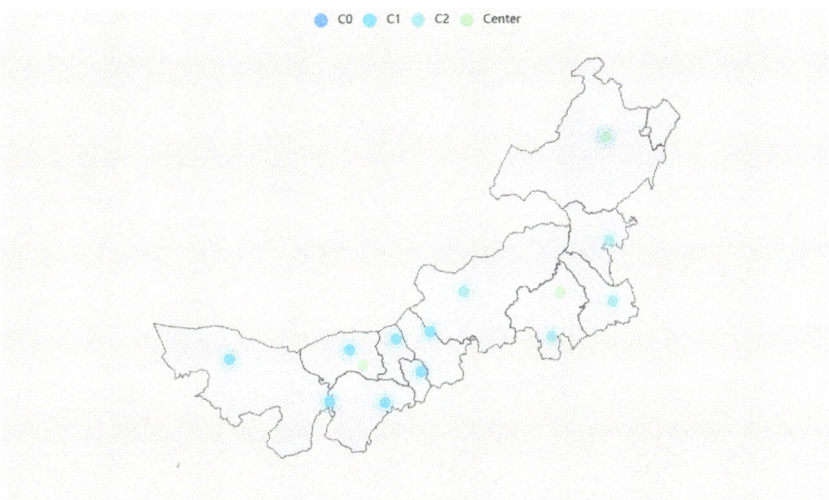

Figure 5. The location results for the GCM.

Model 2: Five-indicator clustering model (5ICM). This model contains five normalized indicators used in this paper: the longitude, the latitude, the per capita disposable income of urban residents, the permanent urban population and the population density. Euclidean distance is used to compute the distance between cities, the results are obtained by K-means clustering as shown in Table 8 and Figure 6. C0, C1, C2 and Center are in different colors in Figure 6.

Table 8. The location results for the 5ICM.

Clustering	City Name	Longitude	Latitude	Demand
	Hulun Buir	121.8592	50.18671	116.41
	Xing'an	122.0406	46.08926	75.13
C0	Tongliao	122.2505	43.65798	143.03
	Chifeng	118.8938	42.26083	211.42
	Center 0	121.261	45.5487	
	Xilin Gol	114.1209	44.03614	80.2
	Ulanqab	112.2595	42.44243	100.29
C1	Bayannur	107.8949	41.73579	91.77
	Alxa	101.339	41.36085	21.06
	Center 1	108.9036	42.3938	
	Hohhot	111.7555	40.84842	265.5
	Baotou	110.3877	42.15471	232.48
C2	Ordos	109.7886	39.61359	165.04
	Wuhai	106.801	39.6629	52.9
	Center 2	109.6832	40.5699	

Model 3: Improved five-indicator clustering model (I5ICM). Based on the result of Model 2, this model incorporates the center-of-gravity method to obtain lower transportation costs. The results are shown in Table 9 and Figure 7. C0, C1, C2 and Center are in different colors in Figure 7.

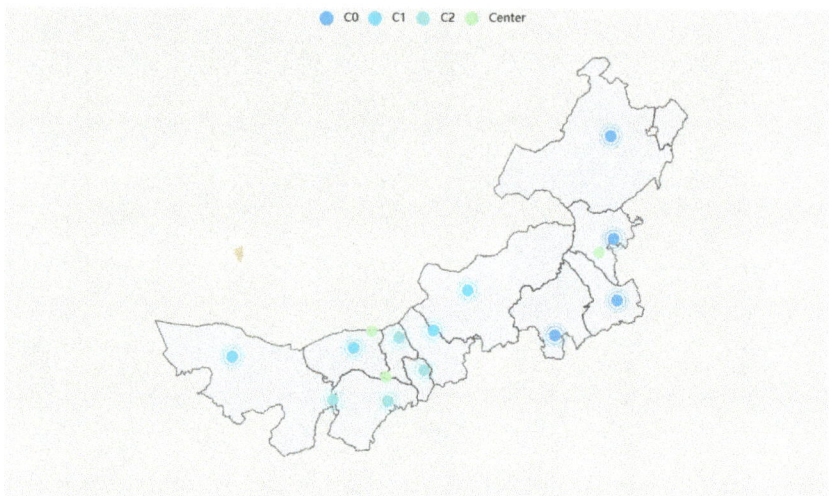

Figure 6. The location results for the 5ICM.

Table 9. The location results for the I5ICM.

Clustering	City Name	Longitude	Latitude	Demand
C0	Hulun Buir	121.8592	50.18671	116.41
	Xing'an	122.0406	46.08926	75.13
	Tongliao	122.2505	43.65798	143.03
	Chifeng	118.8938	42.26083	211.42
	Center 0	121.2842	44.08581	
C1	Xilin Gol	114.1209	44.03614	80.2
	Ulanqab	112.2595	42.44243	100.29
	Bayannur	107.8949	41.73579	91.77
	Alxa	101.339	41.36085	21.06
	Center 1	112.2504	42.44865	
C2	Hohhot	111.7555	40.84842	265.5
	Baotou	110.3877	42.15471	232.48
	Ordos	109.7886	39.61359	165.04
	Wuhai	106.801	39.6629	52.9
	Center 2	110.9376	41.0485	

The total transportation costs of the four models are shown in Table 10.

Table 10. The transportation costs of the four models.

	GCM	5ICM	I5ICM	2SM
Transportation cost	3864.2391	4100.9813	3539.9559	3220.9834

As shown in Table 10, the 2SM proposed in this research has the lowest total transportation cost. Furthermore, compared with the three traditional models, the following conclusions can be drawn:

1. Compared with the result of the geographic clustering model (GCM), clustering with five indicators (5ICM) has an increase in cost, this indicates that if the distance function or algorithm is not adjusted, the result will be worse than the original method.
2. Using the center-of-gravity method to modify the clustering with five indicators (I5ICM) significantly reduces the cost.

3. If the distance function is modified reasonably and the algorithm is improved into the two-stage model (2SM) proposed in this study, the cost will be further reduced.

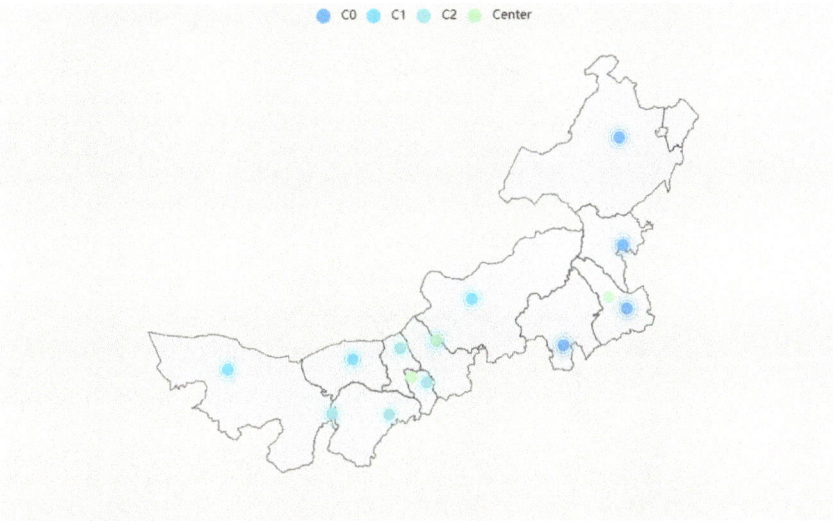

Figure 7. The location results for the I5ICM.

6. Results and Conclusions

In this research, a two-stage location selection model based on an improved clustering algorithm and the center-of-gravity method is proposed for an MFLP arising from a real-world problem. This methodology is proved to be effective and contributing to future logistics system planning strategy researches. The following conclusions are drawn as follows.

First, the more indicators introduced into LP, the more realistic the research becomes. In this paper, three socio-economic indicators, namely, economy development, traffic congestion degree and total logistics demand, are introduced in defining a distance function used in clustering, each of which could affect the decision on the site of a distribution center. Different from most of the existing researches, which only used spatial indicators, this research introduces three socio-economic indicators to evaluate a city's potential to accommodate a distribution center, described as the logistics-level score. This method provides a more comprehensive perspective for decision-makers to choose proper sites for distribution.

Second, an improved clustering algorithm is used to divide demand points into different regions. The improved algorithm redefines the traditional distance function, which could not reflect the distance result caused by the socio-economic indicators. The improved distance function takes both the positive effect of the three socio-economic indicators and the passive effect caused by the spatial indicators into consideration, and proved to be more effective than GCM, 5ICM and I5ICM in the case study.

Third, based on the methodology discussed above, this research divides 12 cities in Inner Mongolia into 3 regions and selects 1 city for each region as the regional distribution center. This is consistent with the government's current logistics center planning strategy. Such consistency indicates that this methodology could be used as an optional reference for local governments' logistics planning.

The limitation of this paper may lie in the selection of the clustering indicators. Although three socio-economic indicators are introduced in the 2SM, it is still impossible to describe the complexity of the logistics in real world. This means more socio-economic indicators or even more kinds of indicators should be introduced into LP researches. Besides, during the SFLP process, the author takes only the total transportation cost as the final objective and omits some other influential decision making factors. In subsequent research, other objectives/constraints such as carbon emission reduction and sustainable development can be added to the existing research.

Author Contributions: Conceptualization, J.W. and Y.B.; methodology, J.W., X.L. and Y.L.; software, X.L.; validation, J.W., X.L., Y.L. and W.Y.; formal analysis, J.W. and Y.B.; investigation, J.W. and Y.B.; resources, Y.B.; data curation, X.L. and Y.L.; writing—original draft preparation, J.W., X.L. and L.Y.; writing—review and editing, J.W., X.L. and Y.L.; visualization, X.L. and L.Y.; supervision, J.W., W.Y. and Y.B.; project administration, J.W. and Y.B.; funding acquisition, J.W. and Y.B. All authors have read and agreed to the published version of the manuscript.

Funding: This research received no external funding.

Institutional Review Board Statement: Not applicable.

Informed Consent Statement: Not applicable.

Data Availability Statement: Not applicable.

Conflicts of Interest: The authors declare no conflict of interest.

References

1. Ozmen, M.; Aydogan, E.K. Robust multi-criteria decision making methodology for real life logistics center location problem. *Artif. Intell. Rev.* **2020**, *53*, 725–751. [CrossRef]
2. Zhuge, D.; Yu, S.; Zhen, L.; Wang, W. Multi-period distribution center location and scale decision in supply chain network. *Comput. Ind. Eng.* **2016**, *101*, 216–226. [CrossRef]
3. He, Y.; Wang, X.; Lin, Y.; Zhou, F.; Zhou, L. Sustainable decision making for joint distribution center location choice. *Transp. Res. Part D Transp. Environ.* **2017**, *55*, 202–216. [CrossRef]
4. Zhang, H.; Beltran-Royo, C.; Wang, B.; Zhang, Z. Two-phase semi-lagrangian relaxation for solving the uncapacitated distribution centers location problem for B2C E-commerce. *Comput. Optim. Appl.* **2019**, *72*, 827–848. [CrossRef]
5. Zhou, Y.; Xie, R.; Zhang, T.; Holguin-Veras, J. Joint distribution center location problem for restaurant industry based on improved k-means algorithm with penalty. *IEEE Access* **2020**, *8*, 37746–37755. [CrossRef]
6. Zhang, S.; Chen, N.; She, N.; Li, K. Location optimization of a competitive distribution center for urban cold chain logistics in terms of low-carbon emissions. *Comput. Ind. Eng.* **2021**, *154*, 107120. [CrossRef]
7. Pérez-Mesa, J.C.; Serrano-Arcos, M.M.; Jiménez-Guerrero, J.F.; Sánchez-Fernández, R. Addressing the location problem of a perishables redistribution center in the middle of Europe. *Foods* **2021**, *10*, 1091. [CrossRef]
8. Fearon, D. *Alfred Weber: Theory of the Location of Industries, 1909*; Center for Spatially Integrated Social Science: CA, USA, 2006.
9. Afsharian, M. The p-efficient problem in location analytics: Definitions, formulations, applications, and future research directions. *Healthc. Anal.* **2022**, *2*, 100014. [CrossRef]
10. Chen, R. Optimal location of a single facility with circular demand areas. *Comput. Math. Appl.* **2001**, *41*, 1049–1061. [CrossRef]
11. Zeferino, E.F.S.; Mpofu, K.; Makinde, O.A.; Ramatsetse, B.I.; Daniyan, I.A. FR/CoG multi-attribute-based comparison methods for selection of the location of a research institute. *J. Facil. Manag.* **2020**, *18*, 20–35. [CrossRef]
12. Trivedi, A.; Singh, A. Facility location in humanitarian relief: A review. *Int. J. Emerg. Manag.* **2018**, *14*, 213–232. [CrossRef]
13. Alizadeh, R.; Nishi, T. Hybrid set covering and dynamic modular covering location problem: Application to an emergency humanitarian logistics problem. *Appl. Sci.* **2020**, *10*, 7110. [CrossRef]
14. Liu, Y.; Yuan, Y.; Shen, J.; Gao, W. Emergency response facility location in transportation networks: A literature review. *J. Traffic Transp. Eng. (Engl. Ed.)* **2021**, *8*, 153–169. [CrossRef]
15. Ahmadi-Javid, A.; Seyedi, P.; Syam, S.S. A survey of healthcare facility location. *Comput. Oper. Res.* **2017**, *79*, 223–263. [CrossRef]
16. De Vries, H.; Van de Klundert, J.; Wagelmans, A.P. The roadside healthcare facility location problem a managerial network design challenge. *Prod. Oper. Manag.* **2020**, *29*, 1165–1187. [CrossRef]
17. Nasiri, M.M.; Mahmoodian, V.; Rahbari, A.; Farahmand, S. A modified genetic algorithm for the capacitated competitive facility location problem with the partial demand satisfaction. *Comput. Ind. Eng.* **2018**, *124*, 435–448. [CrossRef]
18. Farahani, R.Z.; Asgari, N.; Heidari, N.; Hosseininia, M.; Goh, M. Covering problems in facility location: A review. *Comput. Ind. Eng.* **2012**, *62*, 368–407. [CrossRef]
19. Alizadeh, R.; Nishi, T.; Bagherinejad, J.; Bashiri, M. Multi-period maximal covering location problem with capacitated facilities and modules for natural disaster relief services. *Appl. Sci.* **2021**, *11*, 397. [CrossRef]
20. Sarker, B.R.; Wu, B.; Paudel, K.P. Optimal location for renewable gas production and distribution facilities: Resource planning and management. *BioEnergy Res.* **2022**, *15*, 650–666. [CrossRef]
21. Cheng, C.; Adulyasak, Y.; Rousseau, L.M. Robust facility location under demand uncertainty and facility disruptions. *Omega* **2021**, *103*, 102429. [CrossRef]

22. Zhu, T.; Boyles, S.D.; Unnikrishnan, A. Two-stage robust facility location problem with drones. *Transp. Res. Part C Emerg. Technol.* **2022**, *137*, 103563. [CrossRef]
23. Cui, T.; Ouyang, Y.; Shen, Z.J.M. Reliable facility location design under the risk of disruptions. *Oper. Res.* **2010**, *58 Pt 1*, 998–1011. [CrossRef]
24. Shang, X.; Yang, K.; Wang, W.; Wang, W.; Zhang, H.; Celic, S. Stochastic hierarchical multimodal hub location problem for cargo delivery systems: Formulation and algorithm. *IEEE Access* **2020**, *8*, 55076–55090. [CrossRef]
25. Snyder, L.V.; Daskin, M.S. Reliability models for facility location: The expected failure cost case. *Transp. Sci.* **2005**, *39*, 400–416. [CrossRef]
26. Wang, W.; Wu, S.; Wang, S.; Zhen, L.; Qu, X. Emergency facility location problems in logistics: Status and perspectives. *Transp. Res. Part E Logist. Transp. Rev.* **2021**, *154*, 102465. [CrossRef]
27. Gargouri, M.A.; Hamani, N.; Mrabti, N.; Kermad, L. Optimization of the collaborative hub location problem with metaheuristics. *Mathematics* **2021**, *9*, 2759. [CrossRef]
28. Akyuz, M.H.; Oncan, T.; Altınel, I.K. Branch and bound algorithms for solving the multi-commodity capacitated multi-facility Weber problem. *Ann. Oper. Res.* **2019**, *279*, 1–42. [CrossRef]
29. Yang, Z.; Chen, H.; Chu, F.; Wang, N. An effective hybrid approach to the two-stage capacitated facility location problem. *Eur. J. Oper. Res.* **2019**, *275*, 467–480. [CrossRef]
30. Silva, A.; Aloise, D.; Coelho, L.C.; Rocha, C. Heuristics for the dynamic facility location problem with modular capacities. *Eur. J. Oper. Res.* **2021**, *290*, 435–452. [CrossRef]
31. Ozgun-Kibiroglu, C.; Serarslan, M.N.; Topcu, Y.I. Particle swarm optimization for uncapacitated multiple allocation hub location problem under congestion. *Expert Syst. Appl.* **2019**, *119*, 1–19. [CrossRef]
32. Ramshani, M.; Ostrowski, J.; Zhang, K.; Li, X. Two level uncapacitated facility location problem with disruptions. *Comput. Ind. Eng.* **2019**, *137*, 106089. [CrossRef]
33. Li, J.; Xiao, D.D.; Lei, H.; Zhang, T.; Tian, T. Using cuckoo search algorithm with q-learning and genetic operation to solve the problem of logistics distribution center location. *Mathematics* **2020**, *8*, 149. [CrossRef]
34. Rostami, M.; Bagherpour, M. A lagrangian relaxation algorithm for facility location of resource-constrained decentralized multi-project scheduling problems. *Oper. Res.* **2020**, *20*, 857–897. [CrossRef]
35. Iyigun, C.; Ben-Israel, A. A generalized Weiszfeld method for the multi-facility location problem. *Oper. Res. Lett.* **2020**, *38*, 207–214. [CrossRef]
36. Esnaf, S.; Kuçukdeniz, T. A fuzzy clustering-based hybrid method for a multi-facility location problem. *J. Intell. Manuf.* **2009**, *20*, 259–265. [CrossRef]
37. Kuçukdeniz, T.; Baray, A.; Ecerkale, K.; Esnaf, S. Integrated use of fuzzy c-means and convex programming for capacitated multi-facility location problem. *Expert Syst. Appl.* **2012**, *39*, 4306–4314. [CrossRef]
38. Gupta, R.; Muttoo, S.K.; Pal, S.K. Fuzzy c-means clustering and particle swarm optimization based scheme for common service center location allocation. *Appl. Intell.* **2017**, *47*, 624–643. [CrossRef]
39. Gao, X.; Park, C.; Chen, X.; Xie, E.; Huang, G.; Zhang, D. Globally optimal facility locations for continuous-space facility location problems. *Appl. Sci.* **2021**, *11*, 7321. [CrossRef]
40. Pérez-Suárez, A.; Martínez-Trinidad, J.F.; Carrasco-Ochoa, J.A. A review of conceptual clustering algorithms. *Artif. Intell. Rev.* **2019**, *52*, 1267–1296. [CrossRef]
41. Ushakov, A.V.; Vasilyev, I. Near-optimal large-scale k-medoids clustering. *Inf. Sci.* **2021**, *545*, 344–362. [CrossRef]
42. Wang, T.; Li, Q.; Bucci, D.J.; Liang, Y.; Chen, B.; Varshney, P.K. K-medoids clustering of data sequences with composite distributions. *IEEE Trans. Signal Process.* **2019**, *67*, 2093–2106. [CrossRef]
43. Bai, H.; Feng, F.; Wang, J.; Wu, T. A combination prediction model of long-term ionospheric foF2 based on entropy weight method. *Entropy* **2020**, *22*, 442. [CrossRef] [PubMed]
44. Lin, H.; Du, L.; Liu, Y. Soft decision cooperative spectrum sensing with entropy weight method for cognitive radio sensor networks. *IEEE Access* **2020**, *8*, 109000–109008. [CrossRef]

Article

Mining Plan Optimization of Multi-Metal Underground Mine Based on Adaptive Hybrid Mutation PSO Algorithm

Yifei Zhao, Jianhong Chen, Shan Yang * and Yi Chen

School of Resource and Safety Engineering, Central South University, Changsha 410083, China; zhaoyifei@csu.edu.cn (Y.Z.); jhchen@csu.edu.cn (J.C.); dlx8529@csu.edu.cn (Y.C.)
* Correspondence: yangshan@csu.edu.cn

Abstract: Mine extraction planning has a far-reaching impact on the production management and overall economic efficiency of the mining enterprise. The traditional method of preparing underground mine production planning is complicated and tedious, and reaching the optimum calculation results is difficult. Firstly, the theory and method of multi-objective optimization are used to establish a multi-objective planning model with the objective of the best economic efficiency, grade, and ore quantity, taking into account the constraints of ore grade fluctuation, ore output from the mine, production capacity of mining enterprises, and mineral resources utilization. Second, an improved particle swarm algorithm is applied to solve the model, a nonlinear dynamic decreasing weight strategy is proposed for the inertia weights, the variation probability of each generation of particles is dynamically adjusted by the aggregation degree, and this variation probability is used to perform a mixed Gaussian and Cauchy mutation for the global optimal position and an adaptive wavelet variation for the worst individual optimal position. This improved strategy can greatly increase the diversity of the population, improve the global convergence speed of the algorithm, and avoid the premature convergence of the solution. Finally, taking a large polymetallic underground mine in China as a case, the example calculation proves that the algorithm solution result is 10.98% higher than the mine plan index in terms of ore volume and 41.88% higher in terms of economic efficiency, the algorithm solution speed is 29.25% higher, and the model and optimization algorithm meet the requirements of a mining industry extraction production plan, which can effectively optimize the mine's extraction plan and provide a basis for mine operation decisions.

Keywords: multi-objective optimization; mining plan; metal mines; adaptive; hybrid mutation

MSC: 90C29

1. Introduction

The preparation of the extraction plan, as a basic link in the production operation of a mining enterprise, is one of the most critical tasks in the production decision of a mine, and the rationality of the plan preparation directly affects the efficiency of the subsequent production links and the overall economic efficiency of the mining enterprise [1–3]. The traditional manual preparation method is not only time-consuming and intensive but also has poor accuracy and is difficult to modify. The reason for this is mainly the complex underground mine conditions during the preparation of the plan, which requires comprehensive consideration of the spatial and temporal constraints between the production processes and the mines and their continuity. Therefore, how to develop the underground mine production plan quickly and accurately has been an urgent problem to be solved.

With the continuous advancement of computer technology and operations research theory, many researchers have started to try to use the powerful simulation computing power of computers to simulate the mine production process, so as to continuously optimize the mine extraction plan [4,5]. Several researchers recognize that integer programming can solve discrete production scheduling decision problems in the mining industry [6,7]. Many studies on mine production planning related to integer programming theory were subsequently carried out [3,8–12]. Dimitrakopoulos and Ramazan [13] developed an optimization framework for stochastic mine production scheduling considering mine uncertainties based on an ore body model and an integer planning approach. Weintraub et al. [14] developed a large, aggregated integer planning model (MIP) based on cluster analysis for mine planning at CODELCO, a national copper mine in Chile, through which data information of all CODELCO mines can be obtained to optimize the mine extraction planning. Newman et al. [15] developed a mixed integer planning model for underground mining operations in Kiruna mine, Sweden. This optimization model identifies an operationally feasible recovery sequence that minimizes deviations from the planned production quantities. Terblanche and Bley [16] used a mixed integer planning approach to construct a theoretical model applicable to the optimization of extraction production plans for open pit and underground mines but did not verify the feasibility of the model. Nehring et al. [17] proposed an improved modified model formulation for the classical model of long-term mine planning, assigning different human resources and equipment to each mining area. In the classical model, only one binary variable is assigned to each activity in each mining area, whereas the improved model assigns one binary variable to all activities under a more stringent assumption.

Although there are more existing studies on mathematical planning methods, most of these models achieve the solution of mine production planning with a single economic indicator; however, since mine extraction production planning is a complex system of engineering, it is difficult to highlight the production plan preparation and optimization effect by considering only a single economic indicator [18]. In order to overcome these difficulties, researchers have used a variety of computational intelligence methods to solve multi-objective prediction and optimization problems, and heuristic algorithms are effective methods to improve the solution speed and avoid involving local optimal solutions, while having unique advantages for multi-objective optimization problems (MOP). Little and Topal [19] investigated the methodology of whole life of mine (LOM) production planning generated using a simulated annealing technique and stochastic simulation representation of the ore body with the objective of maximizing the net present value (NPV) of the mine. Hou et al. [20] addressed the production planning for the next three years of the mine using an artificial bee colony optimization algorithm. Otto and Bonnaire [21] developed a "Greedy randomized adaptive search" program to help solve models for copper mining development and improve the speed of solution. O'Sullivan and Newman [22] proposed an optimization heuristic algorithm to set a complex set of constraints based on an optimization algorithm in a mining operation model for an underground lead–zinc mine in Ireland. Wang et al. [23] proposed a multi-objective optimization model formulation by taking the grade of mined and processed ore as the main constraint, maximizing mining returns and efficient use of natural resources as the objective function, and used a genetic algorithm to find the optimal solution to the multi-objective optimization problem. Nesbitt et al. [24] considered the uncertainty faced in the economic value of minerals faced by mines with long operating cycles. For a hard rock mine, the method of creating a stochastic integer program helps the mine to customize a mining schedule with a high degree of feasibility.

However, the use of traditional heuristic algorithms in the preparation of mining industry extraction production plans leads to slow solution speed and reduced global convergence performance, which brings many difficulties to the preparation and optimization effect of the actual production operation plan in real time and has a profound impact on the production management and economic efficiency of the enterprise. Therefore, in order to solve these problems, which are due to the complexity of multi-metal mine production planning, and since it is difficult to achieve the optimal results by traditional methods, this paper takes the best economic efficiency, grade, and ore volume as the goal and integrates constraints such as ore grade fluctuation, ore output of mining sites, mine production capacity, and mineral resource utilization. A production planning model is established, and the model is optimally solved by an improved particle swarm optimization (PSO) algorithm with nonlinear inertia weights and adaptive mutation probability (NAMPSO) in the context of an engineering example to improve the model's solving speed and increase the global convergence performance of the algorithm, thereby verifying the feasibility of the model solution method.

2. Balanced Mining Plan Model

2.1. Model Analysis

There are many factors that need to be considered comprehensively in the preparation of an underground mine extraction plan, and by analyzing the current situation faced by underground mining and the existing mining technology conditions [25–30], the main factors that need to be considered in the process of extraction plan preparation are shown in Figure 1.

(1) Economic efficiency: when mining in the market economy, the first factor to consider is the economic factors, that is, to ensure that the mining enterprise can obtain a better economic benefit.
(2) The planned quantity of mining: for mining enterprises to carry out normal operations, mining plans must be able to ensure the mine's subsequent production of ore demand.
(3) Planned metal quantity: for mines with metal quantity as the production target, the quantity of ore mined should be guaranteed to meet the requirements of metal quantity for production and processing.
(4) Ore loss and dilution ratios: in the process of balanced mining in underground metal mines, ore loss and dilution ratios must be controlled in order to ensure the maximization of the comprehensive benefits of the enterprise and the maximization of resource recovery and utilization.
(5) Ore quality and grade: due to the variability of mineral resources endowment, there are differences in quality and grade of ore per mining site; therefore, the development of the extraction plan needs to take full account of such differences and achieve the requirements of the extracted ore in terms of quality and grade through reasonable planning.
(6) Ore reserves: to achieve balanced mining, the development of the extraction plan must take into account the limits of the ore reserve of each mineral deposit and mine excavation.
(7) Operating capability: mining enterprises need to have a full understanding of the existing production technology conditions of the mine, production equipment, and the ability and quality of operators when formulating the extraction plan.
(8) Production continuity requirements: once the mine is established, it must ensure that production activities can be carried out continuously and steadily; therefore, the mine's mining plan must consider the ore reserves of the mineral deposit, cutting, retrieval, and preparation for mining to ensure that the mine production activities can be carried out continuously and steadily.
(9) Mine transportation and hoisting capacity: Most of the waste rock and all the ore produced by underground metal mines rely on haulage and hoisting equipment to transport and hoist. The production capacity of the mine must be matched with the transport and hoisting capacity of the mine.
(10) Mine processing plant capacity: in order to avoid the long-term backlog of mined ore, resulting in increased mining production costs or affecting underground mining operations, the total output of ore during the planning period is generally required to be on par with the processing capacity of the plant.

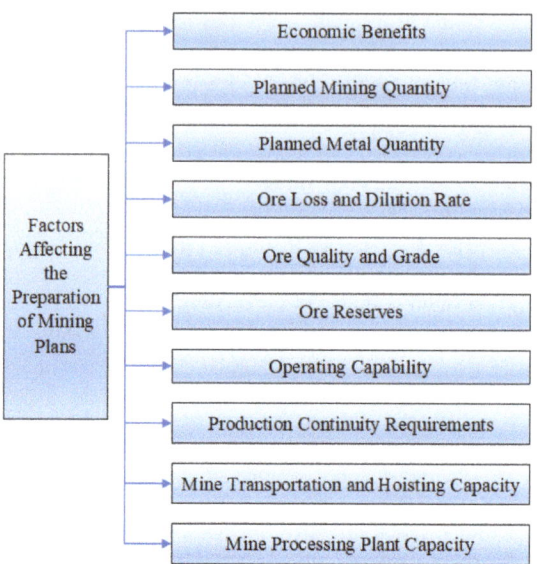

Figure 1. Factors affecting the preparation of the mining plan.

In principle, each underground metal mine plan should consider all the factors in Figure 1, but in practice some factors can be combined and simplified according to the actual situation of the specific mine. For example, only one of the planned mining quantities and planned metal quantity are required, and only the smaller of the mine transport and hoisting capacity and mine processing plant capacity should be considered. At the same time, it is possible to add other influencing factors.

The process of preparing an extraction plan based on balanced mining is essentially a process of seeking an extraction solution that meets the requirements of various stakeholders in the process of comprehensive coordination of various constraints. Therefore, with the help of the objective optimization method in operations research theory, the complex extraction planning can be transformed into an MOP problem model by converting various restrictions into constraints and the final objective into an objective function, thus turning the complex programming process into a mathematical optimization problem.

2.2. Model Building

2.2.1. Model Assumptions

This modeling is carried out based on the following three basic assumptions:

(1) The mining method assumed for the model is room-and-pillar mining. The mine development system has been completed before the preparation of the mining plan, and the mining plan constructed in this paper mainly includes the output of each mineral deposit and the mining cut of each block during the planning period.
(2) The ore reserves, the grade of each metallic element in the ore, and the content of contaminants in each mineral deposit (including the mined room, the mined pillar, the mined and cut room, the mined and cut pillar, and the complete block that has not yet been mined) have all been proven.
(3) The planned mineral deposits should be capable of simultaneous mining operations.

2.2.2. Model Parameters Definition

This model parameters are defined at the end of the paper.

2.2.3. Objective Functions

Equation (1) indicates the maximization of corporate revenue: from the perspective of corporate profitability, one of the purposes of mining enterprises conducting extractive operations is to obtain economic benefits, so the maximization of corporate revenue is one of the main objectives of the preparation of the extraction plan.

$$\max Q = \sum_{h=1}^{H}\sum_{b=1}^{B} x_b u e_{bh} s_h p_h + \sum_{h=1}^{H}\sum_{r=1}^{R} y_r e_{rh} s_h p_h + \sum_{h=1}^{H}\sum_{k=1}^{K} z_k e_{kh} s_h p_h \qquad (1)$$

$$\min E_h = |\sigma_h - \sigma_h^*| = \left| \frac{\sum_{b=1}^{B} x_b u e_{bh} + \sum_{r=1}^{R} y_r e_{rh} + \sum_{k=1}^{K} z_k e_{kh}}{\sum_{b=1}^{B} x_i u + \sum_{r=1}^{R} y_r + \sum_{k=1}^{K} z_k} - \sigma_h^* \right| \qquad (2)$$

$$\max A = \sum_{b=1}^{B} x_i u + \sum_{r=1}^{R} y_r + \sum_{k=1}^{K} z_k \qquad (3)$$

Equation (2) indicates the grade optimization: from the perspective of mineral processing, due to the variability of mineral resource endowment, the development of the extraction plan needs to take full account of such differences to achieve the minimum fluctuations in the average grade of the extracted ore.

Equation (3) indicates the ore production maximization: the more ore extracted during the planning period, the higher the production efficiency and the better the mining operation.

2.2.4. Constraints

After establishing the target of the extraction plan, it is necessary to transform each restriction into the constraint of the target function. Combined with the actual underground mining, the constraints are mainly the following six kinds.

$$\sum_{b=1}^{B} x_b u e_{bh} s_h + \sum_{r=1}^{R} y_r e_{rh} s_h + \sum_{k=1}^{K} z_k e_{kh} s_h > S_h \qquad (4)$$

$$\begin{cases} x_b \leq X_b \\ y_r \leq Y_r \\ z_k \leq Z_k \end{cases} \qquad (5)$$

$$\begin{cases} \sum_{b=1}^{B} x_b \leq D_1 \\ \sum_{r=1}^{R} y_r \leq D_2 \\ \sum_{k=1}^{K} z_k \leq D_3 \end{cases} \qquad (6)$$

$$\sum_{b=1}^{B} U x_b \geq (\sum_{r=1}^{R} y_r + \sum_{k=1}^{K} z_k) \times \eta \qquad (7)$$

$$\sum_{b=1}^{B} x_i u + \sum_{r=1}^{R} y_r + \sum_{k=1}^{K} z_k \leq A_1 \qquad (8)$$

$$\begin{cases} x_b \geq 0 \\ y_r \geq 0 \\ z_k \geq 0 \end{cases} \qquad (9)$$

Equation (4) indicates the metal quantity constraint: the actual quantity of metal produced cannot be lower than the minimum amount of metal required during the planning period.

Equation (5) indicates the ore reserve constraint: the ore reserves of each mine room and pillar, as well as the ore reserves of the mining preparation works, are limited and cannot be exceeded.

Equation (6) indicates the production capacity constraints: the development of extraction plans needs to consider the existing technical conditions of the mine's production and production equipment, etc., and cannot exceed the maximum production capacity.

Equation (7) indicates the production continuity constraints: once the mine is fully operational, it must ensure that production activities can be carried out continuously and steadily; therefore, the mine's mining plan must be prepared to consider mining preparation blocks. Back mining blocks in the ore reserves can be articulated reasonably as the general requirements of the planned period for mining preparation blocks, and the ore reserves are not less than the planned period for back mining of ore to ensure that the mine production activities can be carried out continuously and steadily.

Equation (8) indicates the mine hoisting capacity constraint: the mining capacity cannot exceed the maximum hoisting capacity of equipment during the planning period.

Equation (9) represents the variable non-negative constraint: recovery of ore quantity in all mine rooms and pillar and mining preparation block quantity are non-negative quantities that are greater than or equal to zero.

2.3. Optimized Solution

The optimal solution $(\overline{x_b}, \overline{y_r}, \overline{z_k})$ to the objective is the optimal operation plan for the planning period. However, due to the large number of decision variables, it is difficult to find the optimal solution by manual calculation. In order to solve the above MOP problem, this paper does not use the traditional single-objective processing methods, such as weight coefficient summation or objective constraint, but finds a set of feasible solutions based on the Pareto optimal solution set in order to provide more decision options for the decision maker. Therefore, it is necessary to find an appropriate algorithm and then solve the problem with the powerful computing facilities. In this paper, an improved particle swarm algorithm is adopted to solve the above MOP problem [31].

3. Materials and Methods

3.1. Basic Particle Swarm Optimization Algorithm

The particle swarm algorithm was proposed by Kennedy, an American psychologist, and Dr. Eberhart, an electrical engineer, in 1995 [32]. This algorithm is used to guide the updating of the velocity and position of the next generation of particles by the individual optimal position and the global optimal position of the particles in the population, so that the particles always move toward the individual optimal position and the global optimal position and finally converge to the global optimal position [33,34].

In the M-dimensional search space, there exists a population x_{ij} consisting of N particles, where $i \in \{1, \ldots, N\}, j \in \{1, 2, \cdots, M\}$; the velocity and position components of the i particle at the t iteration in the j dimension are $v_{ij}(t)$ and $x_{ij}(t)$, respectively; $P_{best,ij}(t)$ denotes the optimal position component of the particle; $g_{best,j}(t)$ denotes the optimal position component of the population; w is the inertia weight coefficient; c_1, c_2 is the learning factor; r_1, r_2 is a random number obeying uniform distribution within $(0, 1)$ [35].

The velocity and position update of the basic particle swarm algorithm are as indicated by Equations (10) and (11) [36].

$$v_{ij}(t+1) = wv_{ij}(t) + c_1 r_1 (P_{best,ij}(t) - x_{ij}(t)) + c_2 r_2 (G_{best,j}(t) - x_{ij}(t)) \quad (10)$$

$$x_{ij}(t+1) = x_{ij}(t) + v_{ij}(t+1) \quad (11)$$

3.2. Optimization Strategies

3.2.1. Nonlinear Dynamic Decreasing Inertia Weighting Strategy

The inertia weight w is one of the important parameters affecting the performance of PSO algorithm. The larger the inertia weight is, the faster the particle swarm moves, the ability to search the local space is reduced, and the ability to detect the global space is enhanced; the smaller the inertia weight is, the lower the speed of the particle moves, the ability to search the local space is enhanced, and the ability to detect the global space is reduced. Therefore, appropriate improvement of inertia weights can improve the performance of the PSO algorithm. For this reason, Shi [37] proposed a linear decreasing particle swarm optimization (LDPSO) algorithm, with the following linear decreasing inertia weight strategy:

$$w = (w_{\max} - w_{\min}) \times \left(\frac{t_{\max} - t}{t_{\max}}\right) + w_{\min} \qquad (12)$$

where t_{max} denotes the maximum number of iterations; t denotes the current number of iterations; w_{max} and w_{min} denote the set maximum inertia weights and minimum inertia weights, respectively. Through several experimental analyses, the authors found that as the number of iterations increases, when $w_{max} = 0.9, w_{min} = 0.4$, the search performance of the algorithm is greatly improved [38,39].

In this paper, based on the LDPSO algorithm and inspired by the ideas in the literature [39–42], we propose a nonlinear dynamic decreasing weight strategy particle swarm optimization (NDIWPSO) algorithm in which the inertia weights are set as nonlinear exponential functions, as shown in Equation (13):

$$w = (w_{\max} - w_{\min}) \times \left(1 - \frac{1}{1 + \exp((-kt) \div t_{\max})}\right) + w_{\min} \qquad (13)$$

where k is the control factor. Compared with LDPSO, when w is close to w_{max}, the value of w increases, and NDIWPSO is dominated by the first term of Equation (10) during most of the iterations. Then, the ability of the particle to expand the search space is enhanced, and it is more advantageous in searching the global space, while the contraction ability of the particle to the location of the optimal value decreases, and the ability to search the local space is then weakened; when w is close to w_{min}, the value of w decreases and NDIWPSO is dominated by the last two terms of Equation (10) during most of the iterations, and then the particle is more advantageous in searching for the optimal value in the local interval, and the ability to search the global space is weakened. So, the nonlinear exponential function, Equation (13), can coordinate the algorithm to achieve better between the ability of local search and global search.

3.2.2. Dynamic Learning Factor Strategy

In addition to the inertia weights ω, the learning factors C_1, C_2 also need to be improved to make them more suitable for system optimization search.

$$c_1 = 1 - \ln 2\left(\frac{t}{t_{\max}}\right) \qquad (14)$$

$$c_2 = 1 + \ln 2\left(\frac{t}{t_{\max}}\right) \qquad (15)$$

Equations (14) and (15) are the improvement of the learning factor [42]; as the iterative process proceeds, c_1 decreases while c_2 increases, and in the early iterative process, the particles are mainly influenced by the individual information, which is beneficial to increase the population diversity. In the later iterative process, the particles are mainly influenced by the population information, which is beneficial to the particles to rapidly approach the global extremes and obtain the optimal solution.

3.2.3. Adaptive Variation Probability and Global Optimal Hybrid Mutation Strategy

In order to increase the diversity of the population, a variation strategy is applied to it based on the previous optimization, which leads the particles to jump out of the local optimal value points and search in a more global space. The specific implementation is as follows.

If f_{avg}^t, f_{max^t}, f_{min^t} represent the mean, maximum and minimum values of particle fitness in the t generation, respectively, then Equation (16) for the aggregation degree δ of particles in the t generation is as follows.

$$\delta = \frac{1}{N}\sum_{i=1}^{N}\left|\frac{f(x_i^t) - f_{avg}^t}{f_{max^t} - f_{min^t}}\right| \tag{16}$$

When the deviation of the fitness of individual particles from the overall average fitness is larger, the diversity of particles is better, and vice versa, the diversity of particles is worse. Therefore, when δ is larger, the diversity of particles is better, and when δ is smaller, the diversity of particles is worse. Therefore, the aggregation degree δ can be used to dynamically adjust the probability of variation of particles in each generation, and let the probability of variation in the t generation be p_m^t, as shown in Equation (17). α is used to regulate how fast the variance probability changes and is a constant that takes values in the range [2,4].

$$p_m^t = \delta e^{-\alpha(1+\frac{t}{t_{max}})} \tag{17}$$

In this paper, a mutation on the optimal position of the particle is used, and if $rand \in [0, p_m^t]$, a mixture of Gaussian (Equation (18)) and Cauchy (Equation (19)) distributions is used to vary the optimal position of the particle. pg denotes a random one of the global optimal and global suboptimal positions; g_{best} denotes the global optimal position; $randn$ is a random number of Gaussian distribution; $Cauchy$ is a random number of Cauchy distribution.

$$g_{best} = pg \times (1 + 0.5 \times randn) \tag{18}$$

$$Cauchy = \tan(\pi \times (rand - 0.5)) \tag{19}$$

$$g_{best} = pg \times (1 + 0.5 \times Cauchy) \tag{20}$$

The pseudo-code for the global optimal hybrid mutation strategy is **Mut1** (Algorithm 1).

Algorithm 1: Mut1.

begin
    Evaluate the best position g_{best}
    and the second best position p_{sec}
    if rand < 0.5
        $pg = g_{best}$
    else
        $pg = p_{sec}$
    end
    if rand < p_m^t
        $g_{best} = (1 + 0.5 \times randn)$;
    end
    if rand < p_m^t
        $Cauchy = \tan(\pi(randn - 0.5))$;
        $g_{best} = pg \times (1 + 0.5 \times Cauchy)$;
    end
end

3.2.4. Worst Personal-Best Position Adaptive Wavelet Mutation Strategy

In the above hybrid variation strategy, the global optimal and suboptimal extremes are utilized for variation, while the worse individual extremes are not utilized. In fact, in the population, the worse individual extremes have limited guiding effect on the particles; thus, variation on the worse individual extremes is beneficial to accelerate the convergence of the population.

The worst individual optimal adaptive wavelet variation strategy [43] (**Mut2**):

The worst individual extreme value particle m is selected, and the search boundary of the selected particle in the j dimension is $P_{best,mj} \in [x_{min}, x_{max}]$. $P_{best,mj}$ is varied according to Equation (21), and in this paper, adaptive wavelet variation is used to improve the worst individual extreme value to speed up the evolution of the population. δ is the wavelet function value, $\psi(x)$ is the wavelet function, and Morlet wavelet is chosen as the wavelet base in Equations (22)–(24). a is the scale parameter, and more than 99% of the energy of the wavelet function is contained in $(-2.5, 2.5)$, so the range of values of φ in the formula is the pseudo-random number of $(-2.5a, 2.5a)$ [44]. The wavelet amplitude decreases continuously with the increase of parameter $\psi(x)$. In order to adjust the wavelet amplitude $\psi(x)$ adaptively, the adaptive parameter a is proposed in this paper, and its expression is Equation (25). k and a_0 are positive constants, and this paper sets $k = 10, a_0 = 5$.

$$P_{best,mj} = \begin{cases} P_{best,mj} + \sigma\left(x_{max} - P_{best,mj}\right), \text{if } \sigma > 0 \\ P_{best,mj} + \sigma\left(P_{best,mj} - x_{min}\right), \text{if } \sigma \leq 0 \end{cases} \quad (21)$$

$$\sigma = \frac{1}{\sqrt{a}} \psi\left(\frac{\varphi}{a}\right) \quad (22)$$

$$\psi(x) = e^{-\frac{x^2}{2}} \cos(5x) \quad (23)$$

$$\sigma = \frac{1}{\sqrt{a}} e^{-\frac{(\frac{\varphi}{a})^2}{2}} \cos\left(5\left(\frac{\varphi}{a}\right)\right), \varphi \in [-2.5a, 2.5a] \quad (24)$$

$$a = kt + a_0 \quad (25)$$

3.3. Algorithm Steps

Step 1. (Initialization): set the current number of iterations $t = 1$, the maximum number of iterations t_{max}, the population size N, the dimensionality of the search space M, and the initial position and velocity of each particle generated randomly.

Step 2. (Optimal update): the velocity and current position of each particle are updated according to Equations (10), (11) and (13)–(15), and the value of the fitness function $f(x_i)$ is calculated for each particle.

Step 3. (Individual Optimal Update): for each particle x_i, if the current fitness function value $f(x_i)$ is better than the individual historical optimal position $f(g_{best})$, update the individual optimal g_{best}.

Step 4. (Global Optimal Update): for each particle x_i, if the current fitness function value $f(x_i)$ is better than the global optimal position $f(g_{best})$, the global optimal g_{best} is updated.

Step 5. Calculate the aggregation degree δ and the variation probability p_m^t of the particle population according to Equation (16); if $rand \in [0, p_m^t]$, mutate according to the mutation strategies Mut1 and Mut2 in Sections 3.2.3 and 3.2.4.

Step 6. Calculate the particle fitness and update p_{best} and g_{best}.

Step 7. $t = t + 1$ and return to step 2 until t reaches the set maximum number of iterations and stop.

Step 8. The optimal result is output, and the algorithm is finished.

3.4. Construction of the Fitness Evaluation Function

For the MOP problem model of the extraction plan, this paper uses the evaluation function method to construct the fitness function. Specifically, we set an arbitrary best value Q^* and A^* for the objective functions $Q(x_i, y_j, z_k)$ and $A(x_i, y_j, z_k)$ respectively, and construct the fitness evaluation function $F(x_i, y_j, z_k)$ of the extraction plan by calculating the difference between each objective function and it and pursuing the minimum of the sum. Equation (26). A^* is the planned quantity of ore to be produced, Q^* is the planned economic efficiency of the enterprise during the plan period.

$$F(x_i, y_j, z_k) = \sqrt{(\frac{Q-Q^*}{Q^*})^2} + \sqrt{(\frac{A-A^*}{A^*})^2} + \sqrt{(\frac{\sigma_t - \sigma_t^*}{\sigma_t^*})^2} \tag{26}$$

4. Engineering Applications and Results Analysis

4.1. Mine Engineering Overview and Basic Data

In order to verify the effectiveness of the NAMPSO algorithm for industrial mining planning of multi-metal mines, the actual mining production data of a large underground metal mine rich in gold (Au), antimony (Sb), and tungsten (WO$_3$) in Hunan Province, China, are taken as an example, and the numerical model of the mine is shown in Figure 2. In this paper, the annual production task index of this mine and the actual situation of the mine are combined, and the balanced mining extraction plan model established in Section 2 and the NAMPSO algorithm for solving multi-objective optimization problems proposed in Section 3 are applied to optimize the extraction plan of this mine for each quarter and obtain the annual optimal mining plan.

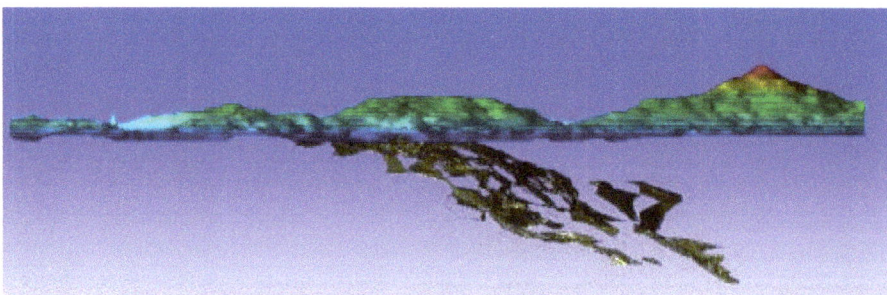

Figure 2. Digital model of underground multi-metal mine.

The production target of the mining company for this mine in the current year is shown in Table 1.

Table 1. Production task indicators.

Total Ore Production	80,000 t	Excavation footage	480 m
Mining Quantity	78,000 t	Excavation ore quantity	2000 t

Metal	Au	Sb	WO$_3$
Comprehensive Ore Grade	3.75 g/t	0.188%	0.125%
Metal Quantity	300 kg	150 t	100 t
Mineral Processing Recovery Rate (%)	89.7	97.0	70.0

Among them, after the completion of the mining tasks of the previous year, the ore reserves of the mine's preparation rooms (13) and preparation pillars (8), as well as the part of the works of the excavated blocks (9) that need to be completed in this year, are shown in Table 2.

Table 2. Parameters of the mine rooms, mine pillars, and excavated blocks.

Name	Number		Mining Quantity/Extraction Footage	Grade(e_1, e_2, e_3)		
				Au (g/t)	Sb (%)	WO$_3$ (%)
Mined pillar	1314-1	b_1	1089 t	7.1	0.21	0.17
	1102-1II	b_2	2543 t	10.93	0.25	0.08
	⋮	⋮	⋮	⋮	⋮	⋮
	708-1	b_8	12,312 t	6.16	0.11	0.14
Mined room	508-1	r_1	25,854 t	6.97	0.23	0.16
	2516-1	r_2	2709 t	6.71	0.23	0.11
	⋮	⋮	⋮	⋮	⋮	⋮
	12,514-1	r_{13}	5180 t	5.62	0.13	0.65
Excavated block	12,520	k_1	80.1 m	4.52	0.16	0.16
	12,520-1	k_2	56.3 m	4.37	0.21	0.23
	⋮	⋮	⋮	⋮	⋮	⋮
	5016	k_9	94.7 m	3.25	0.00	0.00

4.2. Balanced Mining Model Parameters

According to the balanced mining extraction plan model constructed in Section 2.2 of this paper, the parameters involved in the mathematical model of the extraction plan are organized as follows, considering the actual situation of the mine and referring to the production experience of the mine in previous years:

(1) Excavated blocks $B = 9$, Mine pillars $K = 8$, Mine rooms $R = 13$.
(2) Production ore quantity factor for block mining preparation works $u = 4.2$ t/m, Quantity of ore contained in 1 m of mining preparation $U = 166.7$ t/m.
(3) Quantity factor of prepared mining blocks/ during the plan period $\eta = 1$.
(4) Maximum mining capacity: $D_1 = 25{,}000$ t, $D_2 = 25{,}000$ t, $D_3 = 180$ m.
(5) Metal types $H = 3$, Average quarterly ore output $A = 20{,}000$ t, Maximum underground hoisting capacity quarterly $A_1 = 35{,}000$ t.
(6) Gold concentrate contains gold price (metal price) $p_1 = 235{,}000$ Yuan/kg, antimony concentrate contains antimony price (metal price) $p_2 = 29{,}700$ Yuan/t (antimony concentrate valuation coefficient is 0.6), tungsten concentrate contains tungsten price $p_3 = 150{,}000$ Yuan/t. The quarterly revenue required by the enterprise can be calculated according to the quarterly metal quantity task as $Q^* = 22{,}488{,}750$.

4.3. Algorithm Parameter Setting

For the above engineering example data and the constructed model, the algorithm is applied on the MATLAB platform to solve the plan model optimally. There are 30 parameters of decision variables in this metal mine mining planning model, so the dimension of each particle in the algorithm $M = 30$; the population size of particles $N = 150$, the number of iterations $T = t_{\max} = 3000$; the learning factor c_1, c_2 varies with the number of iterations t; the ore loss rate of the mining site is considered to be 5%.

4.4. Engineering Example Simulation

Based on the equilibrium mining model and the data in Tables 1 and 2, the PSO algorithm and the NAMPSO algorithm were applied to find the optimal extraction plan for each quarter of a year, and the iterative convergence process of the model solution was calculated to obtain four quarters, as shown in Figure 3. From the fitness function curves, we can see that the fitness function values of the two algorithms are close to the improved algorithm slightly better, but the convergence speed of the improved PSO algorithm is significantly faster in the first two quarters (PSO converges around the 1550th, 450th, 1400th, and 120th generations, and NAMPSO converges around the 1100th, 250th, 1200th, and 80th generations), the convergence speed is improved by about 29.25%, and the specific results of the balanced extraction plan are shown in Tables 3–5.

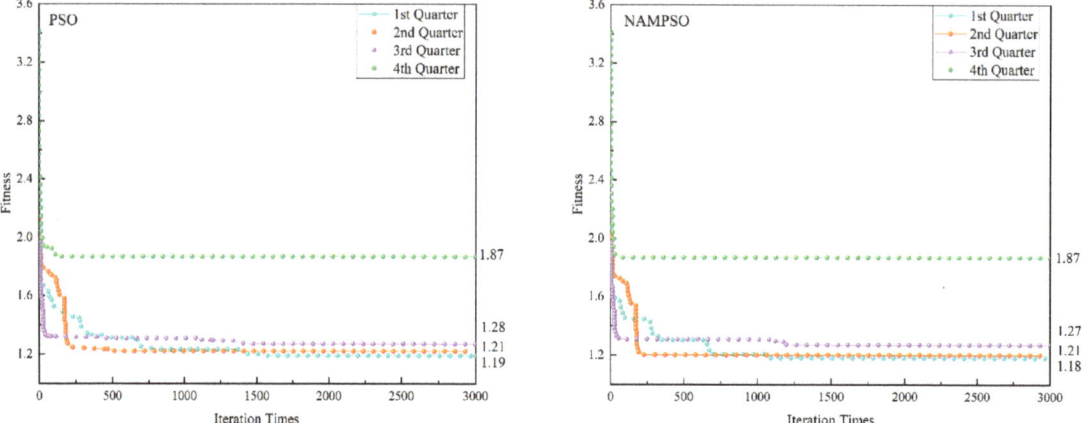

Figure 3. Convergence curve of the optimal adaptation degree of the mining plan.

Table 3. Quarterly and annual mining plan.

Name		Mining Quantity				
		Q1	Q2	Q3	Q4	Full Year
Mine pillar	1314-1	201.6	47.8	492.8	196.3	938.4
	1102-1II	74.7	166.0	43.0	443.6	727.3
	⋮	⋮	⋮	⋮	⋮	⋮
	708-1	1151.0	3697.0	3903.4	3439.0	12,190.4
Mine room	508-1	2247.4	1808.9	850.7	11,899.8	16,806.8
	2516-1	430.7	362.8	819.7	733.0	2346.2
	⋮	⋮	⋮	⋮	⋮	⋮
	12,514-1	1261.2	1397.7	1652.5	676.0	4987.5
Total		22,297.1	21,082.3	20,751.3	22,305.4	86,436.1

Table 4. Quarterly and annual excavation plan.

Name		Excavation Footage (m)				
		Q1	Q2	Q3	Q4	Full Year
Excavated block	12,520	23.6	5.0	7.6	9.9	46.1
	12,520-1	18.5	17.9	5.0	10.6	51.9
	⋮	⋮	⋮	⋮	⋮	⋮
	5016	15.4	36.9	30.9	4.3	87.5
Total (m)		174.3	179.4	134.3	72.1	560.1
By-product ore quantity (t)		731.9	753.7	564.0	302.7	2352.3

From the convergence curve in Figure 3, it can be seen that when the NAMPSO algorithm is used to solve the extraction plan, the value of the objective function fluctuates between 3.2 and 1.2 when the number of iterations is between 0 and 500, indicating that the algorithm converges to the global optimal solution slowly at the early stage of iterative computation when the number of particles within the population is high under a certain initial population size and at the late stage of iterative computation, i.e., after 500 iterations, the algorithm starts to converge smoothly and rapidly to the global optimal solution of the objective function. It can also be seen that the NAMPSO algorithm, when solving the production planning model with complex constraints, performs nonlinear dynamic optimization of the inertia weights of the algorithm and introduces an adaptive variational probability strategy to make the particles outside the feasible domain enter the feasible domain quickly, which leads to a slow convergence computation at the early stage of the algorithm search, while the computation speed of the algorithm is faster at the later stage, and it is easy to jump out of the local optimal solution problem.

Table 5. Extraction plan optimization results by quarter and year.

Time	Economic Benefits	Total Ore Quantity (t)	Au		Sb		WO$_3$	
			Quantity (kg)	Grade (g/t)	Quantity (t)	Grade (%)	Quantity (t)	Grade (%)
Q1	30,498,831.0	23,028.9	108.3	5.244	43.5	0.195	25.0	0.155
Q2	30,168,711.6	21,836.0	107.4	5.482	39.8	0.188	25.0	0.164
Q3	30,382,181.5	21,315.3	108.4	5.668	38.9	0.188	25.1	0.168
Q4	36,643,023.2	22,608.1	134.3	6.623	44.6	0.204	25.0	0.158
Full Year	127,692,747.3	88,788.3	458.4	5.755	166.8	0.194	100.1	0.161

4.5. Analysis of Results

Combined with the enterprise's target requirements for the mine's extraction production, a comparative analysis of the extraction plans given in this paper for each quarter shows that:

(1) As shown in Figure 4, in terms of mining quantity, the actual mining quantity of each quarter and year in the balanced mining plan is slightly higher than the planned mining quantity, which can meet the annual mining quantity target specified by the enterprise. At the same time, the proportion of mining quantity in each quarter is 26%, 25%, 24%, and 25%, respectively, which meets the requirement of balanced mining.

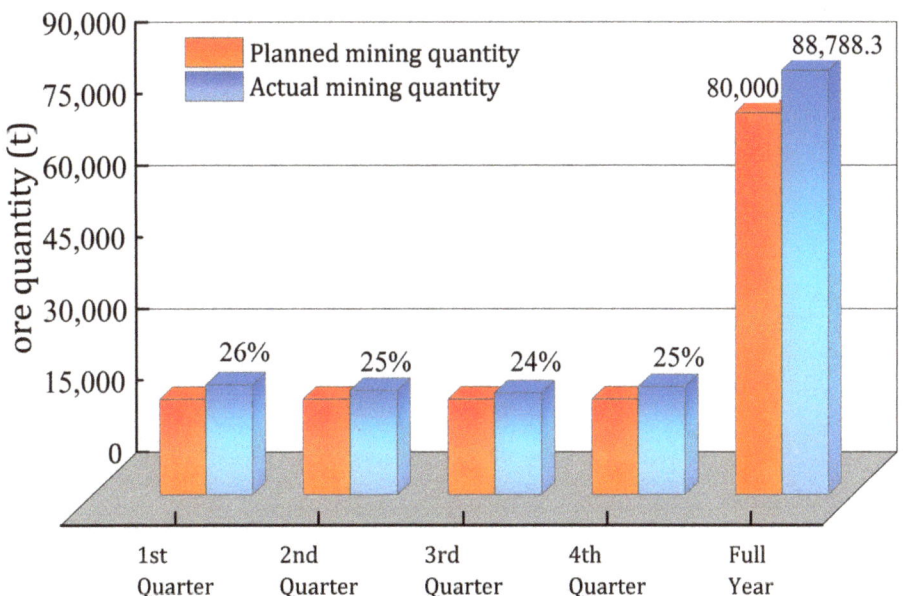

Figure 4. Convergence curve of the optimal adaptation degree of the mining plan.

(2) As shown in Figure 5, in terms of the production of gold, antimony, and tungsten, the actual production for each quarter and year in the extraction plan given in this paper is slightly higher or equal to the planned production, which fully meets the annual metal production target set by the enterprise. The percentages of gold production in each quarter are 24%, 23%, 24%, and 29%, respectively; the percentages of antimony production in each quarter are 26%, 24%, 23%, and 27%, respectively; and the percentages of tungsten production in each quarter are 25%, 25%, 25%, and 25%, respectively. From the absolute uniform distribution of tungsten production in each quarter, it can be seen that the algorithm takes the achievement of tungsten production as one of the key conditions when searching for the optimal mining plan, which fully meets the metal content constraint requirement of the model, and because the grade of tungsten is relatively the lowest among the three metals in the ore of each mining site, the value of tungsten is relatively the lowest among the three metals, and the recovery rate of tungsten beneficiation is also the lowest.

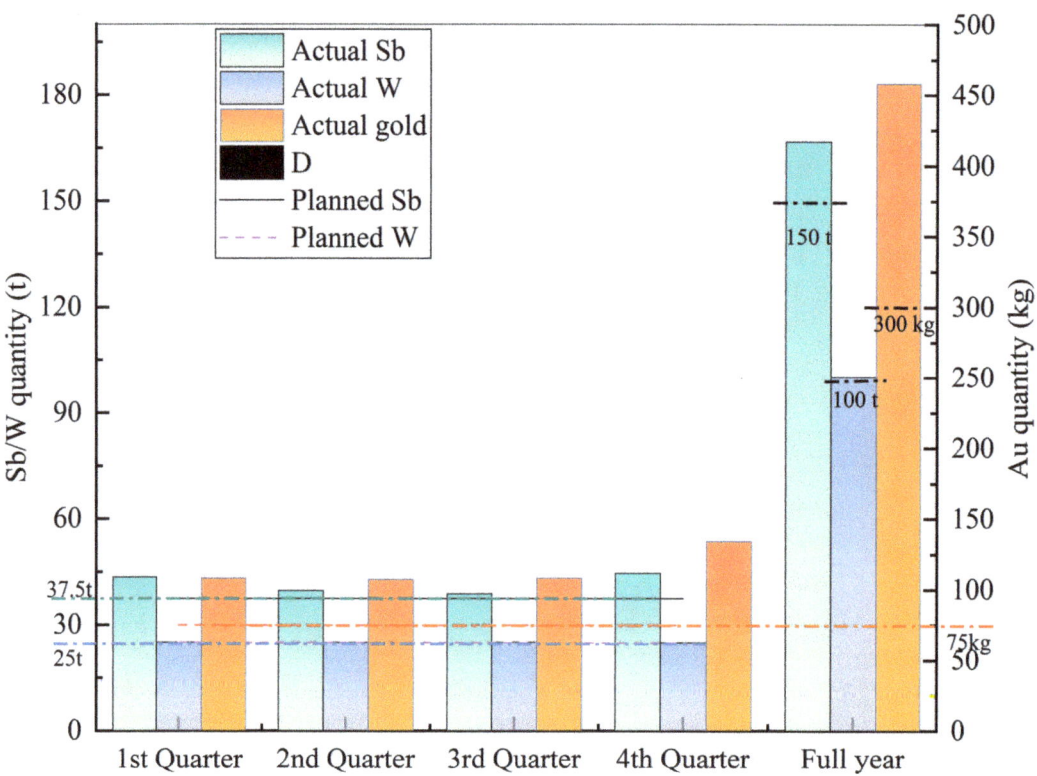

Figure 5. Comparison of actual and planned production of metal quantities.

(3) As shown in Figure 6, the average grade of gold and tungsten is higher than the planned ore grade, the average grade of gold and tungsten in the ore mined in each quarter is basically balanced, and the average grade of antimony in the ore mined in each quarter is basically the same as the planned grade. Therefore, the mining plan searched by the method of this paper achieves the balance of the ore grade, and the ore grade fluctuation is small.

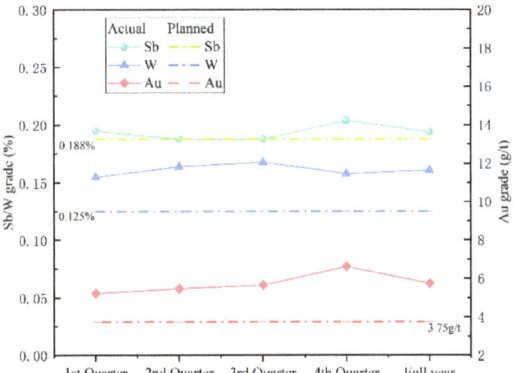

Figure 6. Comparison of actual grade and planned grade of ore mined.

(4) As shown in Figure 7, in terms of economic benefits, the annual economic benefits of the extraction plan given in this paper increased by 41.88% compared to the planned economic benefits. The actual production of each quarter and year is slightly higher than the planned production, and the production of each metal also meets the requirements, so the economic benefits of each quarter and year are necessarily higher than the planned economic benefits, and the actual benefits of each quarter account for 24%, 23%, 24%, and 29%, respectively, and in general, the economic benefits of each quarter are balanced and stable, which can well fulfill the benefit targets given by the company.

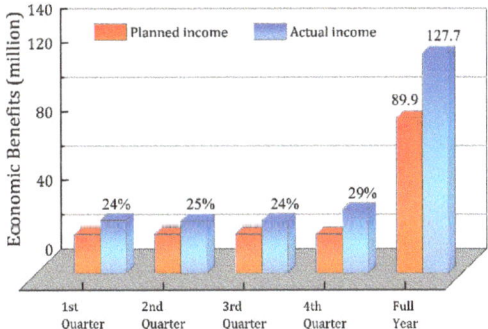

Figure 7. Comparison of actual and planned economic benefits.

(5) As shown in Figure 8, in terms of mining balance, in order to seek the quarterly quantity of ore production that satisfies each constraint, the quantity of ore mined from each mineral deposit (including the mine room and pillar) varies each quarter, which reflects the equilibrium process of ore matching. Through four quarters of mining, the ore reserves of each mining field are basically depleted, and in actual production the ore reserves of the mining field can be considered as the end of mining when they are below a certain value. After one year of mining, most of the 21 recovery mining fields involved in the plan can be considered as completed. In order to ensure that mine production can be carried out continuously, it is necessary to adhere to the principle of balanced mining and excavation with excavation first. In this paper, the mining plan is formulated mainly through the balance between the recovery quantity and mining preparation quantity to ensure the continuity of production, as shown in Figure 9. This paper contains nine mining preparation fields, each of which has a different footage of excavation in each quarter, and the reason for this is that the

quantity of ore production from each mining preparation project also must meet the production constraints. After four quarters of mining preparation work, the nine mining preparation fields are basically finished and can be used as back mining fields for the next year, which can ensure the continuous progress of production work in the next year.

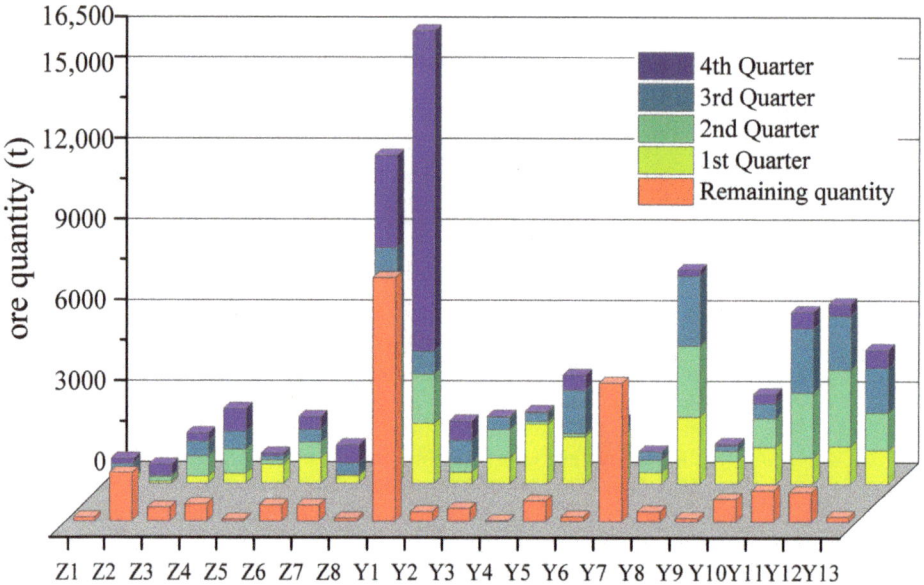

Figure 8. Distribution of ore production and remaining ore in each mining field by quarter.

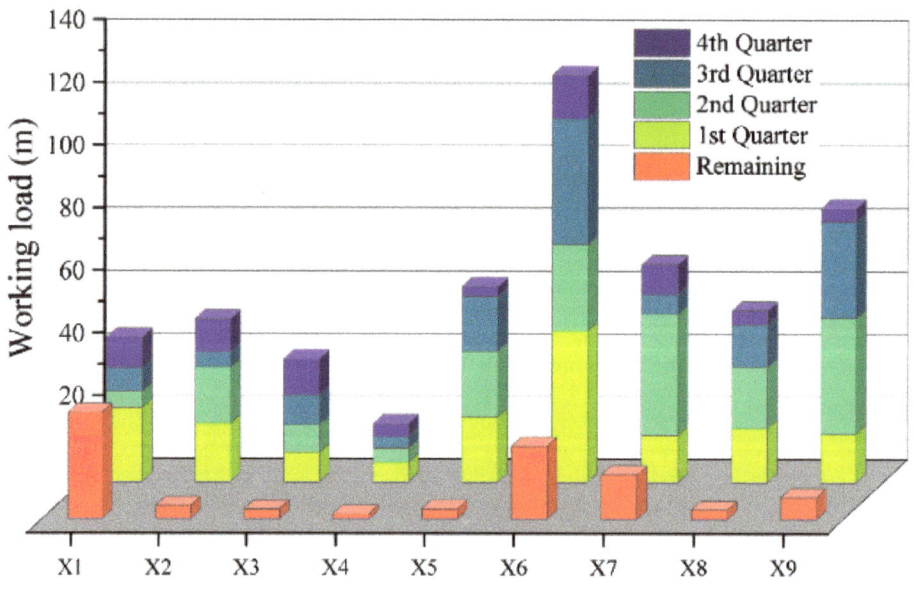

Figure 9. Distribution of excavation works and remaining works in each mining field by quarter.

5. Conclusions

Aiming at the multi-objective optimization problem faced by underground multi-metal mine extraction plans, this paper proposes an improved particle swarm optimization algorithm, which makes the global relative optimal solution converge smoothly and quickly by nonlinear dynamic optimization of inertia weights of a particle swarm algorithm, while introducing an adaptive mutation probability strategy, mixed mutation strategy for relatively optimal individuals, and adaptive wavelet mutation strategy for the poorer optimal individuals to achieve the solution of the balanced mining plan. The optimal extraction plan searched was compared and analyzed with the production target proposed by the enterprise in five aspects: economic efficiency, ore production, metal quantity, ore grade, and extraction balance. The results prove that the balanced mining plan model constructed by using this paper and the quarterly and annual mining plans obtained by using the NAMPSO algorithm not only fully meet the production task requirements, but also the algorithm solution results are 10.98% higher than the mine plan index in terms of ore quantity, 41.88% higher in terms of economic efficiency, and 29.25% higher in terms of algorithm solution speed, which can well achieve the balanced production of the mine. Thus, the practicality and feasibility of the model and algorithm are highlighted.

The optimization of the engineering examples in this paper focuses on optimization with deterministic information and has limitations that can provide a reference for decision makers. Future research will focus on optimization under uncertainty, seeking quantitative methods for the uncertain information in the complex system of a mine. At the same time, the optimization algorithm solution can be adapted in the future not only in the mine quarry but in the whole mine system, as it is included in the optimization model, while updating the optimization algorithm to achieve the optimization of the mine system from a single link to the whole, thus helping the mining enterprises to obtain greater economic benefits and improve the efficient use of limited mineral resources.

Author Contributions: Conceptualization, methodology, formal analysis, and writing—review and editing, Y.Z.; software, investigation, and visualization, Y.C.; writing—original draft preparation and validation, Y.Z. and Y.C.; resources and data curation, S.Y.; supervision, project administration, and funding acquisition, J.C. All authors have read and agreed to the published version of the manuscript.

Funding: This research was funded by the National Natural Science Foundation Project of China, grant no. 72088101, no. 5140430, and no. 551374242, and the Graduated Students' Research and Innovation Fund Project of Central South University, grant no. 2021zzts0283.

Data Availability Statement: Not applicable.

Acknowledgments: The authors would like to express thanks to the National Natural Science Foundation and Innovation Fund Project of Central South University.

Conflicts of Interest: The authors declare no conflict of interest.

Abbreviations

Model parameters definition

Indices	Definition
B	number of mining preparation blocks within the orebody model
R	number of mining rooms within the orebody model
K	number of mine pillar rooms within the orebody model
H	number of metal types
b	set of preparation blocks, $b \in \{1, \ldots, B\}$
r	set of mine rooms, $r \in \{1, \ldots, R\}$
k	set of mine pillars, $k \in \{1, \ldots, K\}$
h	set of metal types, $h \in \{1, \ldots, H\}$

Parameters

X_b	Mining preparation work for block b, meter
Y_r	Ore reserves in the mine room r, ton
Z_k	Ore reserves in the mine pillar k, ton
D_1	Maximum block mining preparation capacity, meter/a plan period
D_2	Maximum mine room recovery capacity, ton/a plan period
D_3	Maximum mine pillar recovery capacity, ton/a plan period
η	Quantity factor of prepared mining blocks during the plan period, 1~2
A	Ore production during the plan period, ton
A_1	Maximum hoisting capacity of underground hoisting equipment, ton
Q	Enterprise revenue during the plan period, yuan
p_h	The price of the h ore produced during the plan period, yuan/ton
U	Quantity of ore contained in 1 meter of mining preparation, ton/meter
u	Production ore quantity factor for block mining preparation works, ton/meter
s_h	mineral processing recovery rate of h metal, %
S_h	Minimum requirements for h metal production during the plan period, ton
σ_h	The average grade of h metal in the production ore
σ_h^*	The grade required by the enterprise for h metal in the ore
$e_{bh}\ e_{rh}\ e_{kh}$	The average grade of h metal in the mining preparation blocks b, mine room r mine pillar k, %

Variables

x_b	Mining preparation work for block b in the mining plan, meter/a period
y_r	Recovery of ore quantity in mine room r of the mining plan, ton/a period
z_k	Recovery of ore quantity in mine pillar k of the mining plan, ton/a period

References

1. Zhu, M.; Sun, J.; Liu, W.; Zhang, A.; Zhou, H.; Ai, L.; Peng, J.; Jia, Y.; Wang, L. Mining Plan Optimization Based on Linear Programming in Shirengou Iron Mine. In *Proceedings of the Manufacturing Systems Engineering*; Yang, G., Ed.; Trans Tech Publications Ltd.: Durnten-Zurich, Switzerland, 2012; Volume 429, p. 206.
2. Musingwini, C. Presidential Address: Optimization in Underground Mine Planning-Developments and Opportunities. *J. S. Afr. Inst. Min. Metall.* **2016**, *116*, 809–820. [CrossRef]
3. Kumral, M.; Sari, Y.A. Underground Mine Planning for Stope-Based Methods. In *Proceedings of the 2nd International Conference on Earth Science, Mineral, and Energy*; Prasetya, J.D., Cahyadi, T.A., Muangthai, I., Widodo, L.E., Ardian, A., Syafrizal, S., Rahim, R., Eds.; American Institute of Physics: Melville, NY, USA, 2020; Volume 2245, p. 030014.
4. Sundar, D.K.; Acharya, D. Blast Schedule Planning and Shiftwise Production Scheduling of an Opencast Iron Ore Mine. *Comput. Ind. Eng.* **1995**, *28*, 927–935. [CrossRef]
5. Chanda, E. An Application of Integer Programming and Simulation to Production Planning for a Stratiform Ore Body. *Min. Sci. Technol.* **1990**, *11*, 165–172. [CrossRef]
6. Carlyle, W.M.; Eaves, B.C. Underground Planning at Stillwater Mining Company. *Interfaces* **2001**, *31*, 50–60. [CrossRef]
7. Dagdelen, K.; Topal, E.; Kuchta, M. *Linear Programming Model Applied to Scheduling of Iron Ore Production at the Kiruna Mine, Sweden*; Mine Planning and Equipment Selection 2000; Routledge: London, UK, 2018.
8. Nehring, M.; Topal, E.; Knights, P. Dynamic Short Term Production Scheduling and Machine Allocation in Underground Mining Using Mathematical Programming. *Min. Technol.* **2010**, *119*, 212–220. [CrossRef]
9. Leite, A.; Dimitrakopoulos, R. Stochastic Optimisation Model for Open Pit Mine Planning: Application and Risk Analysis at Copper Deposit. *Min. Technol.* **2013**, *116*, 109–118. [CrossRef]
10. Nehring, M.; Topal, E. Production Schedule Optimisation in Underground Hard Rock Mining Using Mixed Integer Programming. *Australas. Inst. Min. Metall.* **2007**, *7*, 169–175. [CrossRef]
11. Guo, Q.; Zhang, Z.; Li, Z.; Liu, K.; Liu, H. Mining Method Optimization Based on Fuzzy Comprehensive Evaluation. In *Proceedings of the Sustainable Development of Natural Resources*; Pts 1–3; Trans Tech Publications Ltd.: Stafa-Zurich, Switzerland, 2013; Volume 616–618, pp. 365–369.
12. Huang, S.; Li, G.; Ben-Awuah, E.; Afum, B.O.; Hu, N. A Robust Mixed Integer Linear Programming Framework for Underground Cut-and-Fill Mining Production Scheduling. *Int. J. Min. Reclam. Environ.* **2020**, *34*, 397–414. [CrossRef]
13. Dimitrakopoulos, R.; Ramazan, S. Stochastic Integer Programming for Optimising Long Term Production Schedules of Open Pit Mines: Methods, Application and Value of Stochastic Solutions. *Min. Technol.* **2013**, *117*, 155–160. [CrossRef]
14. Weintraub, A.; Pereira, M.; Schultz, X. A Priori and A Posteriori Aggregation Procedures to Reduce Model Size in MIP Mine Planning Models. *Electron. Notes Discret. Math.* **2009**, *30*, 297–302. [CrossRef]

15. Newman, A.M.; Kuchta, M. Using Aggregation to Optimize Long-Term Production Planning at an Underground Mine. *Eur. J. Oper. Res.* **2007**, *176*, 1205–1218. [CrossRef]
16. Terblanche, S.E.; Bley, A. An Improved Formulation of the Underground Mine Scheduling Optimisation Problem When Considering Selective Mining. *ORiON* **2015**, *31*, 1–16. [CrossRef]
17. Nehring, M.; Topal, E.; Little, J. A New Mathematical Programming Model for Production Schedule Optimization in Underground Mining Operations. *J. S. Afr. Inst. Min. Metall.* **2010**, *110*, 437–446. [CrossRef]
18. Chowdu, A.; Nesbitt, P.; Brickey, A.; Newman, A.M. Operations Research in Underground Mine Planning: A Review. *INFORMS J. Appl. Anal.* **2022**, *52*, 109–132. [CrossRef]
19. Little, J.; Topal, E. Strategies to Assist in Obtaining an Optimal Solution for an Underground Mine Planning Problem Using Mixed Integer Programming. *Int. J. Min. Miner. Eng.* **2011**, *3*, 152–172. [CrossRef]
20. Hou, J.; Li, G.; Wang, H.; Hu, N. Genetic Algorithm to Simultaneously Optimise Stope Sequencing and Equipment Dispatching in Underground Short-Term Mine Planning under Time Uncertainty. *Int. J. Min. Reclam. Environ.* **2019**, *34*, 307–325. [CrossRef]
21. Otto, E.; Bonnaire, X. A New Strategy Based on GRASP to Solve a Macro Mine Planning. In Proceedings of the International Symposium on Foundations of Intelligent Systems, Prague, Czech Republic, 14–17 September 2009.
22. O'Sullivan, D.; Newman, A. Extraction and Backfill Scheduling in a Complex Underground Mine. *Oper. Res.* **2015**, *5722*, 483–492. [CrossRef]
23. Wang, X.; Gu, X.; Liu, Z.; Wang, Q.; Xu, X.; Zheng, M. Production Process Optimization of Metal Mines Considering Economic Benefit and Resource Efficiency Using an NSGA-II Model. *Processes* **2018**, *6*, 228. [CrossRef]
24. Nesbitt, P.; Blake, L.R.; Lamas, P.; Goycoolea, M.; Brickey, A. Underground Mine Scheduling Under Uncertainty. *Eur. J. Oper. Res.* **2021**, *294*, 340–352. [CrossRef]
25. Nwaila, G.T.; Zhang, S.E.; Tolmay, L.C.K.; Frimmel, H.E. Algorithmic Optimization of an Underground Witwatersrand-Type Gold Mine Plan. *Nat. Resour. Res.* **2021**, *30*, 1175–1197. [CrossRef]
26. Campeau, L.-P.; Gamache, M. Short-Term Planning Optimization Model for Underground Mines. *Comput. Oper. Res.* **2020**, *115*, 104642. [CrossRef]
27. Campeau, L.-P.; Gamache, M.; Martinelli, R. Integrated Optimisation of Short- and Medium-Term Planning in Underground Mines. *Int. J. Min. Reclam. Environ.* **2022**, *36*, 235–253. [CrossRef]
28. Zhang, Z.; Liu, Z.; Bo, L.; Yue, Y.; Wang, Y. Economic Optimal Allocation of Mine Water Based on Two-Stage Adaptive Genetic Algorithm and Particle Swarm Optimization. *Sensors* **2022**, *22*, 883. [CrossRef]
29. Gu, Q.; Liu, Y.; Chen, L.; Xiong, N. An Improved Competitive Particle Swarm Optimization for Many-Objective Optimization Problems. *Expert Syst. Appl.* **2022**, *189*, 116118. [CrossRef]
30. Gu, Q.; Zhang, X.; Chen, L.; Xiong, N. An Improved Bagging Ensemble Surrogate-Assisted Evolutionary Algorithm for Expensive Many-Objective Optimization. *Appl. Intell.* **2022**, *52*, 5949–5965. [CrossRef]
31. Nhleko, A.S.; Musingwini, C. Optimisation of Three-Dimensional Stope Layouts Using a Dual Interchange Algorithm for Improved Value Creation. *Minerals* **2022**, *12*, 501. [CrossRef]
32. Kennedy, J.; Eberhart, R. Particle Swarm Optimization. In Proceedings of the Icnn95-International Conference on Neural Networks, Perth, WA, Australia, 27 November 1995.
33. Li, Z.; Zhu, T. Research on Global-Local Optimal Information Ratio Particle Swarm Optimization for Vehicle Scheduling Problem. In Proceedings of the International Conference on Intelligent Human-Machine Systems & Cybernetics, Hangzhou, China, 23 November 2015.
34. Yunkai, L.; Yingjie, T.; Zhiyun, O.; Lingyan, W.; Tingwu, X.; Peiling, Y.; Huanxun, Z. Analysis of Soil Erosion Characteristics in Small Watersheds with Particle Swarm Optimization, Support Vector Machine, and Artificial Neuronal Networks. *Environ. Earth Sci.* **2009**, *60*, 92–96. [CrossRef]
35. Dejun, A.E.; Lipengcheng, B.; Pengzhiwei, C.; Oujiaxiang, D. Research of Voltage Caused by Distributed Generation and Optimal Allocation of Distributed Generation. In Proceedings of the 2014 International Conference on Power System Technology (POWERCON), Chengdu, China, 20 October 2014.
36. Ren, Y.; Liu, S. Modified Particle Swarm Optimization Algorithm for Engineering Structural Optimization Problem. In Proceedings of the International Conference on Computational Intelligence & Security, Hong Kong, China, 15 December 2017.
37. Shi, Y. A Modified Particle Swarm Optimizer. In Proceedings of the IEEE ICEC Conference, Anchorage, AK, USA, 4 May 1998.
38. Yong, F.; Teng, G.F.; Wang, A.X.; Yao, Y.M. Chaotic Inertia Weight in Particle Swarm Optimization. In Proceedings of the International Conference on Innovative Computing, Kumamoto, Japan, 5–7 September 2007.
39. Firs, R.; Malik, A.; Rahman, T.A.; Zaiton, S.; Hashim, M.; Ngah, R.; Malik, R.F. New Particle Swarm Optimizer with Sigmoid Increasing Inertia Weight. *Int. J. Comput. Sci. Secur.* **2007**, *1*, 35–44.
40. Chen, G.; Huang, X.; Jia, J.; Min, Z. Natural Exponential Inertia Weight Strategy in Particle Swarm Optimization. In Proceedings of the World Congress on Intelligent Control & Automation, Dalian, China, 21 June 2006.
41. Chatterjee, A.; Siarry, P. Nonlinear Inertia Weight Variation for Dynamic Adaptation in Particle Swarm Optimization. *Comput. Oper. Res.* **2006**, *33*, 859–871. [CrossRef]

42. Li, H.; Gao, Y. *Particle Swarm Optimization Algorithm with Exponent Decreasing Inertia Weight and Stochastic Mutation*; IEEE: Manchester, UK, 2009.
43. Ling, S.H.; Iu, H.C.; Chan, K.Y.; Lam, H.K.; Leung, F. Hybrid Particle Swarm Optimization with Wavelet Mutation and Its Industrial Applications. *IEEE Trans. Syst. Man Cybern.* **2008**, *38*, 743. [CrossRef]
44. Zhai, J.C.; Zhao, Z.; Zhang, P. An Improved Teaching-Learning Based Optimization Algorithm. *Comput. Technol. Dev.* **2019**, *29*, 37–41. [CrossRef]

Article

SEPSI: A Secure and Efficient Privacy-Preserving Set Intersection with Identity Authentication in IoT

Bai Liu [1,*], Xiangyi Zhang [1], Runhua Shi [1], Mingwu Zhang [1,*] and Guoxing Zhang [2]

1. The School of Computer Science, Hubei University of Technology, Wuhan 430068, China; xiangyizhang@foxmail.com (X.Z.); hfsrh@sina.com (R.S.)
2. School of Management, Lanzhou University, Lanzhou 730000, China; guoxingzh@lzu.edu.cn
* Correspondence: liubai@hbut.edu.cn (B.L.); csmwzhang@gmail.com (M.Z.)

Abstract: The rapid development of the Internet of Things (IoT), big data and artificial intelligence (AI) technology has brought extensive IoT services to entities. However, most IoT services carry the risk of leaking privacy. Privacy-preserving set intersection in IoT is used for a wide range of basic services, and its privacy protection issues have received widespread attention. The traditional candidate protocols to solve the privacy-preserving set intersection are classical encryption protocols based on computational difficulty. With the emergence of quantum computing, some advanced quantum algorithms may undermine the security and reliability of traditional protocols. Therefore, it is important to design more secure privacy-preserving set intersection protocols. In addition, identity information is also very important compared to data security. To this end, we propose a quantum privacy-preserving set intersection protocol for IoT scenarios, which has higher security and linear communication efficiency. This protocol can protect identity anonymity while protecting private data.

Keywords: private set intersection; quantum authentication; oblivious quantum key distribution; Internet of Things

MSC: 81P94

1. Introduction

In the Internet of Things (IoT), many devices are connected to exchange data through the internet [1,2]. The core components of IoT are smart devices, the internet and connectivity, where IoT devices collect information about personal behavior. In recent years, the development of IoT has brought about many practical scenarios, such as the Internet of Medical Things (IoMT) [3], smart cities [4], and smart homes [5]. IoT services bring great convenience to human life.

As a basic service, privacy-preserving set intersection (PSI) in IoT is widely used in various practical environments. For example, in IoMT, hospitals cannot share electronic medical records while protecting patient privacy. Patients with similar symptoms also cannot exchange and share medical information. Therefore, there exists the phenomenon of information islands in IoMT. In this regard, personal health information (PHI) can be securely shared through profile matching [6] based on PSI. In a cloud environment, Abadi et al. [7] proposed an efficient delegated privacy set intersection scheme on outsourced private datasets. In addition, private graph intersection operation also plays an important role in social networks. Zuo et al. [8] proposed an efficient and privacy-preserving verifiable graph intersection scheme using cryptographic accumulators in social networks.

Because of its importance and wide applicability, many privacy-preserving set intersection (PSI) protocols have been proposed. In 2004, Friedman et al. [9] proposed the first PSI protocol, where a set can be used with homomorphic encryption to ensure secure computation. In 2019, Le et al. [10] proposed a PSI protocol based on secret sharing, which removes the trusted third party of the protocol [11]. Kolesnikov et al. [12] proposed a new PSI protocol, which improved the communication efficiency of the protocol [13] by 2.9–3.3 times. In 2020, Chase et al. [14] proposed a novel lightweight multi-point oblivious pseudorandom function protocol based on oblivious OT extension and utilized it to construct a PSI scheme. In 2021, Badrina Rayanan et al. [15] proposed an updated privacy set intersection protocol, which allows two parties that have constantly updated sets to calculate their privacy set intersections.

However, most existing PSI protocols are based on difficulty assumptions, which are vulnerable to attacks by quantum technology. As a consequence, classical PSI protocols may not have long-term security and the design of quantum-resistant PSI protocols becomes a research hot spot. In addition, quantum cryptography [16,17] has emerged, which can guarantee information-theoretic security.

In this article, we propose a general system model of privacy-preserving set intersection in IoT, which is aided with edge computation (ED). Then, we present a quantum protocol for a private-preserving set intersection with identity authentication. A novel quantum PSI in IoT is designed with the help of obvious quantum key distribution, quantum authentication and count Bloom filter.

Our contributions, in this paper, are summarized as follows:

- We propose a general system model aided with ED of PSI, which is suitable for IoT applications.
- we present a novel quantum updatable PSI protocol in IoT, which can be roughly divided into three phases: key generation, encryption and decryption.
- We analyze security and communication efficiency of the protocol. The protocol has efficient communication efficiency, i.e., linear communication complexity $O(\tau)(\tau \ll N)$ qubits, where N is the size of the universal set. The proposed protocol has higher security. The protocol also provides identity authentication to protect identity information and to maintain the integrity of the transmitted information.

The remainder of this article is organized as follows. In Section 2, we introduce the related works of a privacy-preserving set intersection in a quantum setting. Then, we describe our system model, security model and design goals in Section 3. In Section 4, we present our quantum PSI protocol, followed by security analysis and performance evaluation in Section 5. Then, we have some discussions in Section 6. Finally, we draw our conclusions in Section 7.

2. Related Works

2.1. Quantum PSI Protocol

In 2015, Shi et al. [18] first proposed a cheat-sensitive quantum PSI protocol using phase-encoded private query. Then, Cheng et al. [19] presented a new quantum PSI protocol, which is cryptanalysis and an improvement of the protocol [18]. Cheng's protocol shows that the protocol [18] is not as efficient as claimed because the communication complexity should be $O(nlogN)$ instead of $O(n)$. Later, Maitra [20] presented a fair quantum PSI protocol based on a set membership decision protocol [21]. However, these protocols need complicated oracle operators and multi-particle entangled states. Subsequently, in order to enhance the realizability, Kumar [22] introduced a feasible quantum private set intersection protocol with single photons using the flexible oblivious quantum key distribution (OQKD) [23]. Based on the quantum PSI protocol [22], Debnath et al. [24] presented an efficient quantum PSI protocol, which reduced communication complexity. However, a multi feasible OQKD protocol [25] was broken by the protocol [26] using the man-in-the-middle attack. Therefore, the security of protocols [22,24] may not be guaranteed.

2.2. Oblivious Quantum Key Distribution

In 2011, Jakobi et al. [27] proposed a practical oblivious quantum key distribution (OQKD) protocol, which guaranteed better efficiency and feasibility of a private quantum query. The oblivious key can be distributed between two parties by using SARG04 QKD [28], where the sender knows the whole key while the receiver only knows a single or a few bits of the key. The main process of OQKD can be briefly described as follows:

The sender, i.e., Alice, generates a long quantum sequence including states $|\uparrow\rangle, |\downarrow\rangle$, $|\leftarrow\rangle, |\rightarrow\rangle$, where two quantum states carry a bit of classical information, e.g., $\{|\downarrow\rangle, |\uparrow\rangle\}$ represent the bit 0 and $\{|\leftarrow\rangle, |\rightarrow\rangle\}$ denote the bit 1. Then, Alice sends the quantum sequence to the receiver. After receiving it, the receiver, i.e., Bob, measures each qubit randomly in $\leftrightarrow$ basis or $\updownarrow$ basis.

Then, Bob announces that he successfully measured the positions of the qubits and discards the missed or undetected qubits. For each qubit that Bob successfully measured, Alice announces a pair of verification qubits to verify the correctness of Bob's measured results. Due to the uncertainty of measurements in quantum mechanics, Bob only obtains partial values that match a pair of qubits published by Alice. In other words, Bob can only obtain partially correct values of the key. In order to reduce Bob's information on the raw key, two parties cut the raw key into multiple substrings of length N and added these strings bitwise to obtain the final key with length N.

Then, Gao et al. [23] proposed a variant OQKD protocol in which a variable angle θ was introduced in the protocol [27]. That is, they use four generalized states $\{|0\rangle, |1\rangle, |0'\rangle, |1'\rangle\}$, where $|0'\rangle = cos\theta|0\rangle + sin\theta|1\rangle$ and $|1'\rangle = cos\theta|0\rangle - sin\theta|1\rangle$.

Later, Xiao et al. [29] integrated an identity authentication mechanism into the OQDK protocol [27] to present a new OQKD protocol that can implement mutual identity authentication to resist malicious adversary attacks. First, two parties register with a trusted third party (Certificate Authority, CA) to obtain their respective identity information, i.e., Alice's identity string ID_C and Bob's identity string ID_S. Then, Alice sends the qubits used as the original key (QOK) along with the qubits for authentication (QA) to CA. All qubits need to be forwarded by the CA to Bob, where QA are modified by the CA based on the identity strings of both parties. Both parties can authenticate with QA to obtain a key K that can be used for subsequent anonymous authentication. Another difference with the OQDK protocol [27] is that instead of directly disclosing the quantum bit pairs used to verify Bob's measurement results, Alice encrypts them with the key K and sends them to Bob. The system model is shown in Figure 1.

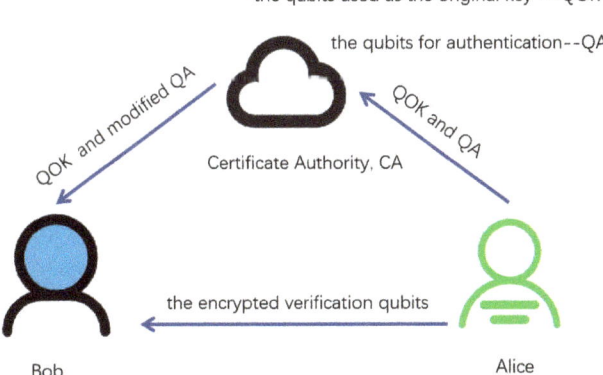

Figure 1. System model of the OQKD protocol [29].

2.3. Quantum Authentication

Quantum message authentication is an important research direction in quantum cryptography and is divided into two parts: authentication of classical information [30] and authentication of quantum information [31]. Curty et al. [30] proposed the first protocol for classical information by quantum entangled states. Subsequently, Xi et al. [32] proposed a quantum authentication scheme that required only single photons. This protocol assumes that two parties pre-share a classical key and a pair of quantum operators. Then, the sender converts a classical message into quantum bits and transmits these qubits to the receiver through the quantum channel. Finally, the receiver verifies the authenticity of the qubits.

The main process of the protocol [32] is as follows:

Suppose that Alice has a classical set $\{m_1, m_2, ... m_n\}$, where $m_i \in \{0,1\}$ and $i \in \{1, 2, ..., n\}$. Two parties, Alice and Bob, share a secret key $\{s_1, s_2, ... s_{n+1}\}$ in advance, where $s_i \in \{0,1\}$ and $i \in \{1, 2, ..., n+1\}$. Then, two parties also pre-share two publicly quantum unitary operations, U_0 and U_1, which should satisfy the following conditions:

1. $U_0|v\rangle\langle v|U_0^+ + U_1|v\rangle\langle v|U_1^+ \neq 0$.
2. There is no a unitary operation U_e to make $\langle v|U_i^+ U_e U_i|v\rangle = 0$, where $i \in \{0,1\}$.
3. $\langle v|U_0^+ U_1|v\rangle \neq 0$.

where $|v\rangle$ is an arbitrary qubit.

Two parties select two pairs of arbitrary quantum states, i.e., $|\varphi_0\rangle, |\varphi_1\rangle$, and $|\psi_0\rangle, |\psi_1\rangle$, where $\langle\varphi_0|\varphi_1\rangle = 0$ and $\langle\psi_0|\psi_1\rangle = 0$. As shown in Tables 1 and 2, Alice generates a pair of quantum states $\{|a_i\rangle|t_i\rangle\}$, where the first qubit represents the quantization of m_i and the second qubit implies the relevant label of m_i. Alice transforms classical information $\{m_1, m_2, ... m_n\}$ to obtain a quantum sequence $\{|a_1\rangle, |t_1\rangle, |a_2\rangle, |t_2\rangle, ... |a_n\rangle, |t_n\rangle\}$ by the method in Tables 1 and 2, then sends the quantum sequence to Bob.

After receiving the quantum sequence, Bob selects suitable measurement bases by the method in Table 3, then measures the quantum sequence $\{|a_1\rangle, |t_1\rangle, |a_2\rangle, |t_2\rangle, ... |a_n\rangle, |t_n\rangle\}$. If each quantum pair satisfies the equation $|t_i\rangle_m = U_{s_{i+1}}|a_i\rangle_m$, where $|t_i\rangle_m$ and $|a_i\rangle_m$ are measurement results of $|t_i\rangle$ and $|a_i\rangle$, respectively, the quantum sequence passes the verification of Bob.

Table 1. The value of $|a_i\rangle$.

s_i/m_i [1]	0	1
0	$\|a_i\rangle = \|\varphi_0\rangle$	$\|a_i\rangle = \|\varphi_1\rangle$
1	$\|a_i\rangle = \|\psi_0\rangle$	$\|a_i\rangle = \psi_1\rangle$

[1] The row represents the value of m_i, while the column represents the value of s_i.

Table 2. The value of $|t_i\rangle$.

s_{i+1}	$\|t_i\rangle$
0	$U_0\|a_i\rangle$
1	$U_1\|a_i\rangle$

Table 3. Measurement basis of $|t_i\rangle$.

s_{i+1}/s_i [1]	0	1
0	$\{U_0\|\varphi_0\rangle, U_0\|\varphi_1\rangle\}$	$\{U_1\|\varphi_0\rangle, U_1\|\varphi_1\rangle\}$
1	$\{U_0\|\psi_0\rangle, U_0\|\psi_1\rangle\}$	$\{U_1\|\psi_0\rangle, U_1\|\psi_1\rangle\}$

[1] The row represents the value of s_i, while the column represents the value of s_{i+1}.

2.4. Count Bloom Filter

A Bloom filter is an efficient data structure that is mainly used to determine or find whether an element exists in a set. The Bloom filter was first proposed by B.H. Bloom in 1970 [33]. Since Bloom filters do not support delete operations, it cannot be adapted to dynamic data environments. A counting Bloom filter that can support a delete operation is proposed in the protocol in [34].

Figure 2 shows the composition of a counting Bloom filter. It mainly consists of two tools: an array of size m and k different collision-resistant hash functions $\{H_1, ..., H_k\}$, where $H_i : \{0,1\}^* \longrightarrow \{1, ..., m\}$ for $i \in \{1, 2, ..., k\}$. Suppose Alice has a private set $S = \{s_1, s_2, ..., s_n\}$. She wants to map all elements of S into the m-size array CBF_s by k hash functions. Initially, Alice obtains an empty array CBF_s, where all elements are set to 0. For each element x of S, Alice uses hash functions $\{H_1, ..., H_k\}$ to obtain positions $\{H_1(x)th, ..., H_k(x)th\}$ in CBF_s, and adds 1 to the values in these positions.

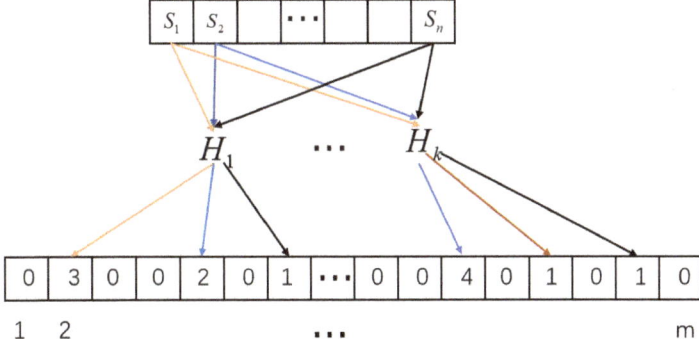

Figure 2. Counting bloom filter.

In general, if someone wants to insert an element into CBF_s, he can use hash functions to map the element to the corresponding positions in CBF_s and add one to the values in these positions. In addition, if someone wants to query whether an element x belongs to S, he only needs to map the element x to the corresponding positions in CBF_s by hash functions. Then, he determines whether the values in all these positions are non-zero. If there exists a position where the value is 0, then it means that the element x cannot belong to S. If Alice wants to delete an element x of S to CBF_s, she only needs to map the element x to the corresponding positions in CBF_s and reduces the value of all positions by one unit (value = value $-$ 1). Please note that x must belong to S. However, if the values in all positions are non-zero, it is possible that x is not in S. That is, the count Bloom filter has false positives.

3. Models and Design Goal

3.1. System Model

In this section, we will illustrate our design of the privacy-preserving set intersection from a system perspective. Our system model consists of five groups of entities: (1) IoT devices; (2) devices for an edge device; (3) a server provider; (4) a client and (5) a certificate authority, as shown in Figure 3.

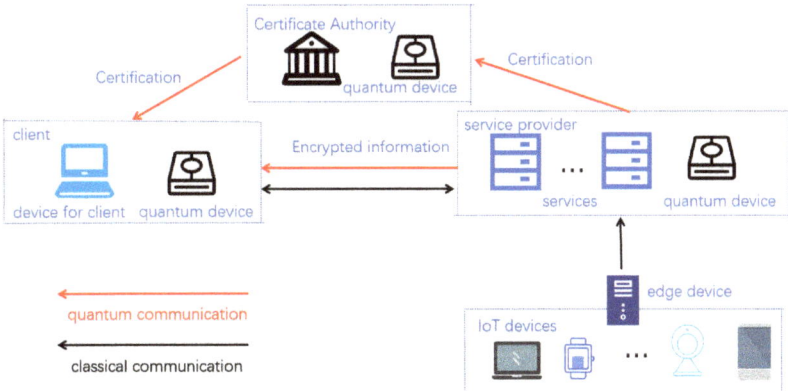

Figure 3. System model aided with ED of PSI in IoT scenarios.

IoT Devices: IoT devices equipped with sensing and communication capabilities are deployed in areas of interest. IoT devices generate real-time data and periodically report data to the edge device. Communication between IoT devices and edge devices is classic communication.

Edge Devices (ED): In order to improve efficient communication, an edge device is deployed at the network edge, which receives the data reported from IoT devices. After receiving data, it locally processes, aggregates, and forwards data to a service provider.

Service Provider (SP): An SP might consist of servers equipped with quantum devices. The SP directly provides the IoT services to the end client. Specifically, we take the IoMT scenario as an example to describe the privacy-preserving set intersection. In hospitals, various IoT devices monitor patients' physical health, such as physiological parameters and living habits. After IoT devices report data to an ED, ED first processes data locally. Then, the ED forwards processing results to SP through wireless communication. When physicians belonging to other hospitals want to obtain data on patients with similar diseases, SP will respond to the client according to this protocol.

Client: A client may be an end device that is equipped with quantum devices. She receives anonymous encrypted data from SP and calculates the privacy intersection of their sets.

Certificate Authority (CA): A CA is a trusted third party that generates identity information for clients and servers. CA is also equipped with quantum devices that can forward quantum states to the client. CA is only used in the basic building block of the protocol: oblivious key distribution scheme [29], which is introduced in Section 2.2.

In this paper, the quantum devices required above only need to support single-photon preparation, measurement, and simple single-bit operations. That is, the quantum device we describe is not a full-fledged quantum computer including quantum random memory but has some basic devices [35–38] and single-bit circuits that can support single-photon operations.

3.2. Security Model

We consider honest-but-curious parties, where adversaries may attempt to learn more information from a given protocol execution but are not able to deviate from the protocol.

Definition 1. *Privacy-preserving set intersection (PSI) protocol—there are two communicating parties, i.e., a client with a private set C and an SP with a private set S. After executing a PSI protocol, the client outputs the intersection of their respective private sets, i.e., $C \cap S$, but the SP obtains nothing. Furthermore, a PSI protocol should meet the following privacy requirements:*

(1) SP Privacy: The client learns no information about the SP's private set except the intersection $C \cap S$.

(2) Client Privacy: SP cannot obtain any private information about the client's private set.

Traditionally, PSI uses a static setting where computation is performed only once on both parties' input sets. We also consider that parties can periodically calculate the intersection of their private updatable sets.

In addition, we also consider external adversary attacks and authentication analysis to enhance security. That is, the protocol should also meet the following security requirement:

(3) Authentication: If the tag passes authentication, the client will continue to execute the protocol, otherwise, terminate.

Due to the focus on privacy-preserving of two parties, i.e., a client and an SP, during the interaction, we do not consider the honesty of IoT devices and EDs. That is, they faithfully report data and are not subject to attack.

3.3. Design Goal

The design goals are as follows.

- The proposed protocol can not only protect the private data of both parties but also protect the identity information of both parties. The protocol needs to ensure correctness without losing the ability to protect privacy. In order to enhance privacy protection, the protocol is required to protect the identity information of both parties. In addition, the protocol may be subject to external attacks with quantum devices, so it needs to have a certain resistance to external attacks.
- The proposed protocol should have efficient communication efficiency. This protocol only needs the linear communication complexity of $O(\tau)$ qubits.

4. Proposed Protocol

In this protocol, assume that a client has a private set $C = \{c_1, c_2, ..., c_v\}$ and an SP has a private set $S = \{s_1, s_2, ..., s_w\}$, where $w > v$. All elements of sets C and S lie in Z_N, where $Z_N = \{0, 1, 2, .., N-1\}$.

Furthermore, SP and the client have the same count Bloom filter parameters, i.e., hash functions $\{h_1, h_2, ..., h_\lambda\}$ and the length τ of the count Bloom filter [34,39].

The protocol consists of three main parts, including key generation phase, encryption phase and decryption phase. Next, we will describe these phases. In addition, specific notations used in the following text are illustrated in Table 4.

Table 4. Definitions of notations.

Notations	Definitions
C	The client's private set
S	The SP's private set
$\{h_1, h_2, ..., h_\lambda\}$	The hash functions
τ	The length of the count Bloom filter
k_B	The raw key distributed by the SP
K	The message authentication key from the protocol [29]
k_b	The intermediate key after checking the SP's honesty
k_b^*, k^*	The final key distributed by the SP
CBF	The SP's count Bloom filter
BF	The variant of CBF
KBF	Encryption result of the array BF by the key k^*
$\|a_i\rangle, \|t_i\rangle$	The ith element of the encryption result of the array KBF by the key K
CBF_C	The client's count Bloom filter
$\{p_1, , p_2 ..., p_m\}$	The positions index of non-zero items of CBF_C

4.1. Key Generation

In this section, two parties, i.e., a client and an SP, will be distributed a special asymmetric key. SP knows every bit of the key, while the client only knows partial bits of the key, where each bit that the client knows is associated with a unique element of her private set. For instance, assume that position indexes of the key bits start from 0 to $N-1$. Suppose that Alice has a set $X = \{x_1, x_2..., x_n\}$, where $x_i \in \{0, 1, , ...N-1\}$ and $n < N$. Then, Alice only knows the x_1th, x_2th, ...and x_nth bits of the key.

Step 1: The client and SP invoke Xiao's Oblivious Quantum Key Distribution (OQKD) protocol [29] to share a random secret $(\tau + q)$-bit key k_B. SP knows the whole key k_B, and the client only knows $m + q$ bits of key k_B (note that m is the number of non-zero items in the client's array CBF_C during decryption phase, τ is the size of SP's array BF in encryption phase and q is a security parameter).

Furthermore, as for reference [29], we can also obtain the $\tau + 1$ bits message authentication key K, which only are known by the SP and client.

Step 2: Then, the client randomly chooses q bits of the key to check whether SP is honest. That is, she requests SP to announce the values of these checked bits. If these values published by SP do not entirely match those that she has deciphered, it would indicate that SP is dishonest or there is an outside eavesdropper. If the client discovered a dishonest SP or any outside eavesdropping, she would terminate this protocol, otherwise, continue to the next step.

Step 3: SP and the client discard q checked bits of the raw key k_B and further obtain the intermediate key k_b of length τ. Similarly, the client only knows m bits of key k_b, while SP still knows all bits. Actually, the client knows not only m-bit values: $k_b(j_1), k_b(j_2), ..., k_b(j_m)$ but also their respective position indexes: $\{j_1, j_2, ..., j_m\}$, where $k_b(j_i)$ denotes the j_i th bit of k_b. In addition, SP does not know the bits which the client knows.

Step 4: The client generates a random permutation π of an τ-element sequence by position index set $\{j_1, j_2, ..., j_m\}$ and non-zero items' position index set $\{p_1, p_2, ..., p_m\}$ of the count Bloom filter CBF_C, which must meet the following condition

$$\{k_b(j_1), \ldots, k_b(j_m)\} = \{k_b^*(p_1), , \ldots, k_b^*(p_m)\} \quad (1)$$

where k_b^* is a new sequence after applying the permutation π to τ-element sequence k_b, i.e., $k_b^* = \pi(k_b)$. Then the client announces the permutation π to SP.

Step 5: SP obtains the final key $k_b^* = \pi(k_b)$ from key k_b by permutation π. Obviously, the client only knows partial bits: $k_b^*(p_1), k_b^*(p_2), \ldots, k_b^*(p_m)$, where $k_b^*(p_i)$ denotes the p_ith bit of k_b^* for $i = \{1, 2, ..., m\}$. However, SP does not know any secret information about position index set $\{p_1, p_2, ..., p_m\}$ without $\{j_1, j_2, ..., j_m\}$.

Here, we give a simple example to illustrate how to generate an oblivious key between the client and SP, as shown in Figure 4. The client and SP share the length $\tau = 14$ of the count Bloom filter. The client has position indexes, $\{p_1 = 4, p_2 = 7, p_3 = 8, p_4 = 14\}$, of non-zero items in the count Bloom filter, and thus finally, she only knows $k_b^*(4), k_b^*(7), k_b^*(8)$ and $k_b^*(14)$, while SP knows all bits of k_b^*. The elements of Figure 4 with blue background are the checked qubits, such as $k_B(11)$ and $k_B(15)$. The elements with black slashes are the checked qubits that have been discarded, such as $k_b(15)$ and $k_b(16)$.

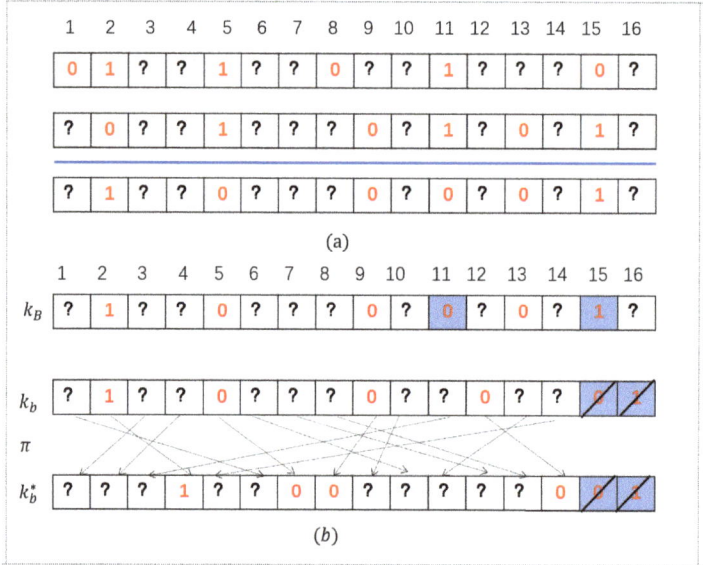

Figure 4. Illustration of generating the key. (**a**) How to reduce the client's information in the key. (**b**) How to obtain the final key k_b^* from the raw key k_B.

4.2. Encryption

Suppose that SP has a private set $S = \{s_1, s_2, ..., s_w\}$, where every element lies in Z_N. She employs λ independent collision resistant hash functions $\{h_1, h_2, ..., h_\lambda\}$.

Step 6: In this step, SP utilizes Algorithm 1 to generate an array of τ elements. First, SP maps the private set $S = \{s_1, s_2, ..., s_w\}$ to the counting Bloom filter $CBF = \{CBF_1, CBF_2, ..., CBF_\tau\}$ through hash functions $\{h_1, h_2, ..., h_\lambda\}$. Then, SP selects an array $BF = \{BF_1, BF_2, ..., BF_\tau\}$, where all elements initialize to 0. All elements of corresponding positions in BF are set to 1, according to non-zero items in CBF. SP has position indexes $\{q_1, q_2, ..., q_l\}$ of non-zero items in the array BF. The construction process is shown in Figure 5.

Furthermore, SP's database is constantly changing in the actual environment. Therefore, SP synchronously modifies the local counting Bloom filter through Algorithms 2 and 3.

Algorithm 1 Generating an array of τ elements

Require: $\{s_1, s_2, ..., s_w\}$.
Ensure: $BF \in \{0,1\}^\tau$.
1: **for** $i = 1$ to τ **do**
2:     $CBF[i] = 0$
3:     $BF[i] = 0$
4: **end for**
5: // All τ elements in CBF and BF are set to 0 initially.
6: **for** $i = 1$ to w **do**
7:     **for** $j = 1$ to λ **do**
8:        $CBF[h_j(s_i)] = CBF[h_j(s_i)] + 1$;
9:     **end for**
10: **end for**
11: // That is, for each element s_i of the private set S, the $h_1(s_i)th, h_2(s_i)th, ...,$ and $h_\lambda s_i th$ the elements of CBF all plus 1.
12: **for** $i = 1$ to τ **do**
13:     **if** CBF[i] > 0 **then**
14:        BF[i] = 1;
15:     **end if**
16: **end for**
17: // That is, for each element s_i of the private set S, the $h_1(s_i)th, h_2(s_i)th, ...,$ and $h_\lambda(s_i)th$ the elements of BF all set 1.

Algorithm 2 Adding an element to count Bloom filter

Require: x.
Ensure: BF and CBF, where $CBF = CBF \cup x$.
1: Execute Algorithm 1 to generate CBF and BF
2: **for** $i = 1$ to λ **do**
3:     $CBF[h_i(x)] = CBF[h_i(x)] + 1$;
4:     **if** BF[i] = 0 **then**
5:        BF[i] = 1;
6:     **end if**
7: **end for**

Algorithm 3 Deleting an existing element from count Bloom filter

Require: x;
Ensure: BF and CBF, where $CBF = CBF - x$;
1: Execute Algorithm 1 to generate CBF and BF
2: **for** $i = 1$ to k **do**
3:   CBF[i] = CBF[i]-1;
4:   **if** CBF[i] = 0 **then**
5:     BF[i] = 0 ;
6:   **end if**
7: **end for**
8: //Please note that it must guarantee that the element indeed belongs to the set associated with count Bloom filter before deleting it.

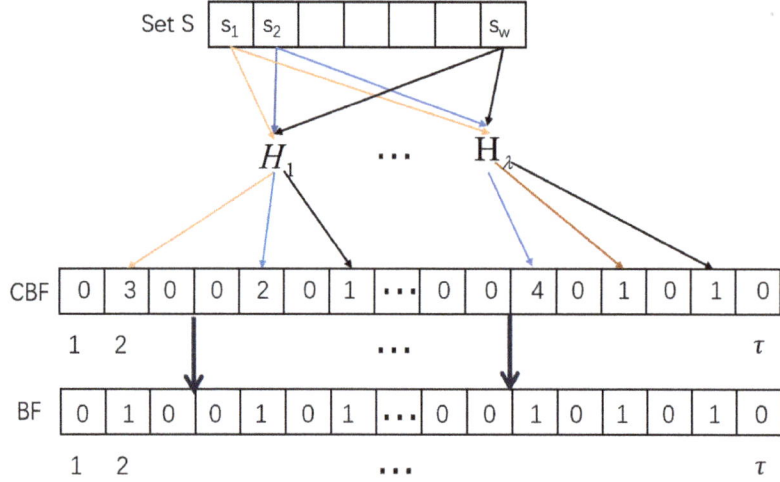

Figure 5. The process of transforming data.

Step 7: After obtaining the array BF, SP encrypts it with the key k^* ($k^* = k_b^*$) to obtain

$$KBF = k^* \oplus BF \\ = \{k_1^* \oplus BF[1], k_2^* \oplus BF[2], ..., \{k_n^* \oplus BF[\tau]\} \\ = \{KBF_1, ...KBF_\tau\}. \qquad (2)$$

Then, as for reference [32], the client and SP publicly select two unitary quantum operations U_0, U_1, which should satisfy the conditions of Section 2.3.

According to the key K and operations U_0, U_1, SP transforms $KBF\}$ into τ pairs of qubits $\{|a_1\rangle, |t_1\rangle, |a_2\rangle, |t_2\rangle, ..., |a_\tau\rangle, |t_\tau\rangle\}$, where each item KBF_j is associated with a pair of qubits $|a_j\rangle, |t_j\rangle$. First qubit $|a_j\rangle$ is the quantization of KBF_j and the second $|t_j\rangle$ is the tag of KBF_j. Finally, SP sends this quantum sequence to the client.

4.3. Decryption

Suppose that a client has a private set $C = \{c_1, c_2, ..., c_v\}$, where every element lies in Z_N. He also employs λ independent collision resistant hash functions $\{h_1, h_2, ..., h_\lambda\}$.

Step 8: The client also generates a count Bloom filter CBF_C of τ size and can obtain position indexes of non-zero items in CBF_C, i.e., $\{p_1, p_2, ..., p_m\}$.

Furthermore, the client's database is also constantly changing in actual environments. Therefore, the client synchronously modifies the local counting Bloom filter through

Algorithms 2 and 3. However, different from SP, the client does not need to generate the array BF_C that is similar to BF.

Step 9: After receiving the quantum sequence from SP, the client verifies each pair of qubits. As previously introduced in Section 2.3, if the client finds that equation $|t_i\rangle_m = U_{K_{i+1}}|a_i\rangle_m$ holds, where $i \in \{1, 2, ..., \tau\}$, the verification will succeed, otherwise, it will fail. $|t_i\rangle_m$ and $|a_i\rangle_m$ are measurement results of $|t_i\rangle$ and $|a_i\rangle$, respectively. If the client discovered a dishonest SP or any outside eavesdropping, she would terminate this protocol, otherwise, continue to the next step. After successful authentication, the client obtains a correct encrypted array $KBF = \{KBF_1, ..., KBF_\tau\}$. Then the client decrypts KBF to obtain decrypted values of partial position indexes $\{p_1, p_2, ..., p_m\}$ in KBF by k^*, where the client only knows m bits of k^*. Furthermore, the decryption of array KBF is also reflected in Algorithm 4.

Finally, the client continues to execute Algorithm 4 to obtain the desired private set intersection $C \cap S$.

Algorithm 4 Obtaining the set intersection

Require: $C = \{c_1, c_2, ..., c_v\}, KBF, \{p_1, p_2, ..., p_m\}, k^*$;
Ensure: $\chi \in \{0, 1..., N-1\}^\tau$, where $\chi = C \cap S$;
1: **for** $i = 1$ to τ **do**
2:     PBF[i] = 0;
3:     χ[i] = 0;
4: **end for**
5: **for** $i = p_1$ to p_m **do**
6:     PBF[i] = KBF[i] $\oplus k^*$[i];
7: **end for**
8: //Initialization and setting values;
9: z = 0;
10: **for** $i = 1$ to v **do**
11:     **for** $j = 1$ to λ **do**
12:        **if** $PBF[h_j(c[i])] = 0$ **then**
13:           Break;
14:        **end if**
15:     **end for**
16:     χ[++z] = c[i];
17: **end for**
18: //Testing membership tests

5. Security Analysis and Performance Evaluation

In this section, we mainly analyze the security and performance evaluation of this protocol. In the above definition 1, PSI protocol satisfies the following three security properties:

1. Correctness: After executing the protocol, the client should obtain the correct set intersection ($C \cap S$).

2. SP Privacy: The client learns no information about SP's set except $C \cap S$.

3. Client Privacy: SP cannot obtain any private information about the client's set.

Next, we specifically analyze three properties of this protocol.

5.1. Correctness

As we know, the client has a private set $C = \{c_1, c_2, ..., c_v\}$ and SP has a private set $S = \{s_1, s_2, ..., s_w\}$, where $w > v$. All elements of sets, i.e., C and S, lie in Z_N, where $Z_N = \{0, 1, 2, .., N-1\}$.

Furthermore, SP and the client have same count Bloom filter parameters: hash functions $\{h_1, h_2, ..., h_\lambda\}$ and the size τ of the count Bloom filter. Then, SP has position indexes

$\{q_1, q_2, ..., q_l\}$ of non-zero items in BF. The client also has position indexes $\{p_1, p_2, ..., p_m\}$ of non-zero items in the count Bloom filter CBF_C. Then, we will obtain

$$i \in S \cap C \iff i \in S \land i \in C$$
$$\implies BF[j] \neq 0 \land CBF_C[j] \neq 0$$
$$\land j \in \{h_1(i), h_2(i), ..., h_\lambda(i)\}$$
$$\text{(by hash functions } \{h_1, h_2, ..., h_\lambda\})$$
$$\implies BF[j] \neq 0 \land j \in \{p_1, p_2, ..., p_m\}$$
$$\implies BF[j] \land j \in \{q_1, q_2, ..., q_l\} \land j \in \{p_1, ..., p_m\}$$
$$\implies BF[j] \land j \in \{q_1, q_2, ..., q_l\} \cap \{p_1, p_2, ..., p_m\}$$
$$\implies KBF[j] \land j \in \{q_1, q_2, ..., q_l\} \cap \{p_1, p_2, ..., p_m\}$$
$$\text{(by Equations (2))}$$
$$\implies PBF[j] \land j \in \{q_1, q_2, ..., q_l\} \cap \{p_1, p_2, ..., p_m\}$$
$$\text{(by step 1} \sim \text{7 of Algorithm 4)}$$
$$\implies i \in \chi \iff i \in S \cap C$$
$$\text{(by step 10} \sim \text{17 Algorithm 4)}$$

Therefore, the set of all parameters i satisfying condition $i \in \chi$ is equal to the intersection of their respective private sets, i.e., $C \cap S$. Thus, the proposed protocol is correct.

Furthermore, we give an example to clearly illustrate correctness of the protocol from Figure 6. In this example, the client has a private set $C = \{25, 34, 56, 36, 57\}$ and SP has a private set $S = \{20, 34, 56, 38, 50\}$, where all elements of sets C and S lie in Z_{60}.

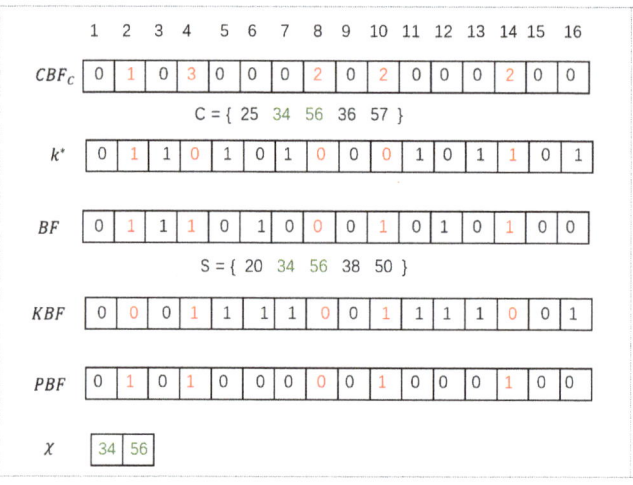

Figure 6. An example of privately computing $C \cap S$.

Two parties have the same count Bloom filter parameters: hash functions h_1, h_2 and the length of the count Bloom filter $\tau = 16$. First, SP and the client successfully construct their own count Bloom filters, i.e., CBF and CBF_C. In addition, SP extends count Bloom filter CBF to obtain an array BF. Then, SP has position indexes $\{2, 3, 4, 6, 10, 12, 14\}$ of non-zero items in BF. The client also has position indexes $\{2, 3, 4, 6, 10, 14\}$ of non-zero items in the count Bloom filter CBF_C.

In addition, the quantum sequence $\{a_1, t_1, a_2, t_2 ..., a_\tau, t_\tau\}$ has no influence on the correctness of the protocol. Therefore, we do not consider the quantum sequence in the following example.

After the key generation phase, SP secretly obtains the final key k^* ($k^* = k_b^*$), where the client obtains values of position indexes of red digits in the key k^*. Obviously, $CBF_C[h_1(i)] \neq 0$ and $CBF_C[h_2(i)] \neq 0$ if $i \in C$. If $i \in S$, $BF[h_1(i)] \neq 0$ and $BF[h_2(i)] \neq 0$, because $CBF[h_1(i)] \neq 0$ and $CBF[h_2(i)] \neq 0$. Therefore, $\{CBF_C[h_1, h_2(i)] \cap BF[h_1, h_2(i)]\} \neq 0$, if $i \in C \cap S$. Please look at those positions in BF, where the number color is red and the number is 1. After encryption and decryption, these positions are still representations of set intersection in the array PBF, i.e., $j \in red \wedge PBF[red] = 1$, if $i \in C \cap S$ and $j \in \{h_1(i), h_2(i)\}$. Furthermore, KBF is an encrypted array of BF by the key k^*, where SP knows all elements. This array PBF is an array that partially decrypts KBF with the key k^*, where the client only knows part of the elements. In our example, $j \in \{2, 4, 10, 14\}$, if $i \in C \cap S$. Then, the client uses the array PBF to obtain the set intersection χ, i.e., $\{34, 56\}$, by Algorithm 4.

5.2. Security

The protocol consists of three main parts, i.e., key generation phase, encryption phase and decryption phase. The security analysis of the protocol will be orderly presented.

5.2.1. SP privacy

During key generation, the security of Step 1 is guaranteed by Xiao et al.'s OQKD protocol [29]. By the analysis of reference [29], a dishonest client will not receive more bits than expected, i.e., $m + q$-bit, even with more efficient measures, such as the optimal unambiguous state discrimination (USD) measurement.

During the encryption phase, SP firstly maps a private set $S = \{s_1, s_2, ..., s_w\}$ to an array $CBF = \{CBF_1, CBF_2, ..., CBF_\tau\}$ through hash functions $\{h_1, h_2, ..., h_\lambda\}$ that the client also knows. Then, SP changes $CBF = \{CBF_1, CBF_2, ..., CBF_\tau\}$ to obtain an array $BF = \{BF_1, BF_2, ..., BF_\tau\}$. That is, if a dishonest client obtains BF, she may obtain SP's private set $S = \{s_1, s_2, ..., s_w\}$. However, SP encrypts BF by the key k^*, where SP knows all the bits of the key, while the client only knows the partial bits. The security of BF has information-theoretic security because SP uses one-time pad encryption. During the decryption phase, the client can just decrypt the encrypted array KBF to obtain partial values of BF by k^*, where she only knows m-bit of the key. That is to say, the client cannot have more information about SP's private set S.

In a word, the protocol can protect the privacy information of SP.

5.2.2. Client Privacy

Specifically, if a dishonest SP wants to eavesdrop on the client's private key during the key generation phase, the probability that his dishonesty will be detected by his client is at least $1 - \frac{1}{2^q}$, where q is a secure parameter.

The security in Step 1 of key generation is guaranteed by Xiao et al.'s OQKD protocol [29]. Based on reference [29], a dishonest SP will introduce bit errors. That is, if SP obtains a message on the conclusiveness of the client's bits, he will lose information on the bit values that the client has recorded. Actually, it is impossible for SP to have both correct bit value and conclusiveness message of the client's measurement, i.e., position index of the correct basis. Therefore, SP cannot simultaneously obtain a bit value $k_b(j)$ that is a correct result deciphered by the client and its corresponding index j.

In Step 2 of key generation, the client randomly compares q bits of the key with corresponding bits announced by SP to decide whether SP is dishonest. SP cannot know which bits will be taken as the checked bits before the client declares them.

Moreover, for each checked bit, if SP does not honestly execute the protocol, he will receive an error probability of $\frac{1}{2}$ in the honesty test. Therefore, for a dishonest SP, the successful probability of completely passing the honest test is less than $\frac{1}{2^q}$.

Finally, in Step 4 of key generation, the client declares the permutation π to SP, which is defined by two sets $\{j_1, j_2, ..., j_m\}$ and $\{p_1, p_2, ..., p_m\}$. Next, the condition probability $P(\{j_1, j_2, ..., j_m\}, \{p_1, p_2, ..., p_m\} | \pi)$ will be analyzed. Although the permutation π is randomly selected by the client, it still must satisfy Equation (1). That is, the client announces a random permutation π with m fixed points, where fixed points are private, but the permutations are public. Accordingly, the number of permutations satisfies the condition $m!(\tau - m)!$.

For simplicity, suppose that JM denotes two arrays $\{j_1, j_2, ..., j_m\}$ and $\{p_1, p_2, ...p_m\}$. $p(|)$ and $I(;)$ denote the conditional probability and mutual information, respectively. Then, we deduce following results:

$$P(\pi) = \frac{1}{\tau!} \tag{3}$$

$$P(\pi \mid JM) = \frac{1}{m!(\tau - m)!} \tag{4}$$

$$P(JM) = \frac{1}{C_\tau^m \cdot C_\tau^m} \tag{5}$$

$$\begin{aligned} I(\pi; JM) &= \log \frac{P(\pi \mid JM)}{P(\pi)} \\ &= \log \frac{\frac{1}{t!(\tau-m)!}}{\frac{1}{\tau!}} = \log \frac{\tau!}{t!(\tau - m)!} \end{aligned} \tag{6}$$

$$\begin{aligned} I(JM) &= -\log P(JM) = -\log \frac{1}{C_\tau^m \cdot C_\tau^m} \\ &= 2\log C_\tau^m = 2\log \frac{\tau!}{t!(\tau - m)!} \end{aligned} \tag{7}$$

$$\begin{aligned} I(JM \mid \pi) &= I(JM) - I(\pi; JM) \\ &= 2\log \frac{\tau!}{t!(\tau - m)!} - \log \frac{\tau!}{t!(\tau - m)!} \\ &= \log \frac{\tau!}{t!(\tau - m)!} \end{aligned} \tag{8}$$

$$I(JM \mid \pi) = -\log P(JM \mid \pi) \tag{9}$$

$$P(JM \mid \pi) = \frac{1}{\frac{\tau!}{m!(\tau-m)!}} = \frac{1}{C_\tau^m} \tag{10}$$

The probability of successfully guessing values of two arrays $\{j_1, j_2, ..., j_m\}$ and $\{p_1, p_2, ..., p_m\}$ through the public permutation π is negligible, i.e., $\frac{1}{C_\tau^m}$.

As we know that $p(M) = \frac{1}{C_\tau^m}$, so $p(JM|\pi) = p(M)$. In other words, the probability of successfully guessing these sets $\{j_1, j_2, ..., j_m\}$ and $\{p_1, p_2, ...p_m\}$ with the public permutation π is equal to the probability of directly guessing values of set $\{p_1, p_2, ...p_m\}$ without π. In addition, the set $\{j_1, j_2, ..., j_m\}$ is the client's private message. Therefore, it is difficult for the SP to obtain the private set $\{p_1, p_2, ...p_m\}$ even if the client declares the permutation π.

In a word, the honest test (i.e., q checked bits) ensures the honesty of SP during the key generation phase. The probability of successfully guessing the private sets by the public permutation π is negligible, i.e., $\frac{1}{C_\tau^m}$.

Furthermore, the client does not send any information during encryption and decryption phases, so private information is not leaked. Therefore, the protocol can protect the client's private information.

5.3. External Security Analysis and Anonymity Analysis

In this protocol, we not only consider the three basic properties above but also consider external adversary security analysis and anonymity analysis.

5.3.1. External Security Analysis

During the key generation phase, the external security of Step 1 is guaranteed by Xiao et al.'s OQKD protocol [29]. Their protocol is resistant to external attacks, such as impersonation and man-in-the-middle attacks, through quantum bits for authentication (QA). Thus, our protocol can resist external attacks in the key generation phase.

Furthermore, they also use quantum bits to generate a key K, which is shared by SP and the client.

In the Step 7 of the encryption phase, even if a malicious adversary impersonates the client, she cannot obtain SP's private set $S = \{s_1, s_2, ..., s_w\}$ by the encrypted quantum sequence $\{|a_1\rangle, |t_1\rangle, |a_2\rangle, |t_2\rangle, ..., |a_\tau\rangle, |t_\tau\rangle\}$. First, the quantum sequence is obtained by encrypting the array KBF with the key K. The adversary cannot obtain values of K, which is only known by the client and SP. Secondly, the adversary also cannot know the values of the array KBF, where the security is information-theoretic security. Therefore, even if the adversary pretends to be the client to obtain the quantum sequence $\{|a_1\rangle, |t_1\rangle, |a_2\rangle, |t_2\rangle, ..., |a_\tau\rangle, |t_\tau\rangle\}$, he cannot obtain SP's private information.

Furthermore, a malicious adversary may apply man-in-the-middle attack in Step 7 of encryption and Step 9 of decryption phases. She first intercepts the quantum sequence sent by SP and then sends fake information to the client so that the client decrypts fake information. However, the client verifies the correctness of the transmitted information. Once any bit is wrong, the client will think there is an external adversary or SP is dishonest. The adversary cannot obtain values of the key K, so fake information cannot pass verification. Therefore, in the encryption and decryption phases, our protocol can resist impersonation and man-in-the-middle attacks.

In a word, the protocol can resist external attacks, such as impersonation and man-in-the-middle attacks.

5.3.2. Anonymity Analysis

In the key generation phase, the anonymity analysis of Step 1 is guaranteed by Xiao et al.'s OQKD protocol [29]. They send quantum sequences through CA.

During the encryption phase, SP only sends quantum sequences $\{a_1, t_1, a_2, t_2, ..., a_\tau, t_\tau\}$ to clients that SP already knows in step 1 of the key generation phase. However, in decryption phase, the client cannot directly determine whether the quantum sequence $\{a_1, t_1, a_2, t_2, ..., a_\tau, t_\tau\}$ is sent from the actual SP, even if quantum information indeed comes from SP. Because the client cannot determine the source of the quantum sequence. Therefore, the protocol provides an authentication function. That is, if the quantum sequence $\{a_1, t_1, a_2, t_2, ..., a_\tau, t_\tau\}$ passes authentication, the sequence is indeed sent by SP. After the quantum sequence $\{a_1, t_1, a_2, t_2, ..., a_\tau, t_\tau\}$ are authenticated, the client can obtain the actual encrypted array KBF from SP.

Therefore, the protocol can guarantee the anonymity of the communicating parties.

5.4. Performance

In the key generation of the protocol, it uses single photons as quantum resources. There are no complicated quantum operators except projective measurements of single photons and simple single-bit operators. In encryption and decryption, the protocol only uses simple single-bit operators and projective measurements of single photons; thus, it is easy to implement this protocol in a real-life setting.

Next, we will consider the role of protocol in updatable databases. In encryption and decryption, counting Bloom filters are employed to reduce communication overhead and accommodate dynamic databases. Counting Bloom filters are employed to handle the updated data from Algorithms 2 and 3. With the increase in data, we only need to change corresponding values in the count Bloom filter according to updatable values, instead of creating a completely new Bloom filter at each modification. At the same time, the size τ of the count Bloom filter will not be changed when updating the database on a small scale.

Instead, the protocol only increases the size of the counting Bloom filter to reduce the false rate after that data increases to a certain threshold.

With the size τ of the count Bloom filter remaining the same, if the client needs more key bits due to the increase in data, the client only needs to request insufficient key bits from SP, not all bits of the key. For example, the client and SP had the key k_1^* of the τ length, where the client only knew k-bit values of the key, while SP knew all bits of the key. Now, the client has the size $l(l > k)$ of position indexes of non-zero items in the count Bloom filter. Then, the client only needs to obtain a new key k_2^* of the $p(p <= \tau)$ length from SP, where the client only knows $(k - l)$-bit. Later, the client combines the key k_1^* and k_2^* to form a new key k_3^* of τ length after applying the permutation pl, where the client knows l-bit of k_3^*. The effect of pl is similar to the effect of π. Then, the client announces the permutation pl to SP. In this way, we can reduce the communication overhead of keys and the cost of preparing them. Of course, we consider the semi-honest model, where the client should not deceive SP. Thus, the protocol can significantly reduce computation and storage overhead.

From Table 5, we can see a comparative summary of existing quantum private set intersection (QPSI) protocols. The communication complexity of our protocol is $O(\tau)$-qubit. The transmitted qubits of the OQKD protocol [29] in key generation are $\kappa(\tau + q) + z$ qubits, where z is the number of the qubits for authentication, κ is a security parameter and $\kappa \approx \log\sqrt{(\tau + q)}$. Then, in the encryption phase, SP only transmits 2τ-qubit to the client. Therefore, the communication complexity (qubit) of our protocol depends on the communication complexity (qubit) of OQKD protocol, i.e., $O(\tau)$, because $\tau \gg q$ in $O(\kappa(\tau + q) + z)$. The client needs a single-photon measurements of the $\kappa(\tau + q) + z$-qubit in the key generation phase. CA only needs to change the quantum state of the z-bit in the key generation. Therefore, the computation complexity of the key is $O(\tau)$. SP needs to generate 2τ-qubit while performing quantum transformations on them in the encryption phase. The client needs single-photon measurements of 2τ-qubit in the decryption phase. Therefore, the computation complexity of transmitted messages is $O(\tau)$. The computation complexity of this protocol is $O(\tau)$.

Table 5. Comparison summary.

Protocol	Ours	[24]	[22]	[18]	[19]	[20]
Quantum resource	single photons	single photons	single photons	multi-particle entangled states	multi-particle entangled states	multi-particle entangled states
Complicated oracle operators	no	no	no	yes	yes	yes
Dimension of the Hilbert Space	2	2	2	N	N	N
Quantum measurements	single-photon measurements	single-photon measurements	single-photon measurements	projective measurements	projective measurements	projective measurements
Intersection cardinality revealed to SP	no	no	no	no	no	yes
Communication complexity (qubit)	$O(\tau)$	$O(\varsigma)$	$O(N)$	$O(v \log N)$	$O(v \log N)$	$O(v+l)\log N$
Computation complexity (qubit)	$O(\tau)$	$O(\varsigma)$	$O(N)$	$O(v)$	$O(v)$	$O(N+l)$
Round complexity in the set intersection	1	1	1	2	3	4
Resistant to external attacks	yes	no	no	no	no	no

Similarly, we analyze that the communication complexity of the protocol [24] should be $O(\varsigma)$-qubit ($N \gg \varsigma \gg q$), because the OQKD protocol [23] that they cite needs to transmit $\omega(\varsigma + q)$-qubit, where a security parameter is $\omega \approx \log\sqrt{(\varsigma + q)}$. The communication complexity of the protocol [22] should be $O(N)$-qubit ($N \gg \varsigma \gg q$) because the OQKD protocol [23] that they cite needs to transmit $\omega(N + q)$-qubit, where a security parameter is $\omega \approx \log\sqrt{(N + q)}$.

In addition, our protocol only needs single photons, which are easier to achieve in a real-life setting. We also have a linear communication performance $O(\tau)$, where $\tau \approx \varsigma \ll N$ and $\tau < v$ in large-scale data. We need only one round of communication during the data transfer phase, i.e., $\{|a_1\rangle, |t_1\rangle, |a_2\rangle, |t_2\rangle, ..., |a_\tau\rangle, |t_\tau\rangle\}$.

6. Discussion

PSI have a wide range of application environments in IoT. In this paper, a novel quantum PSI in IoT is designed with the help of OQKD, quantum authentication and count Bloom filter. We describe the correctness and security of this protocol by formal expressions. Of course, there is also some security analysis software for reference, such as AVISPA and SCYTHER. In this paper, we extend the OQKD method to PSI. In Table 6, we describe some differences between this paper and the underlying protocol.

Table 6. Comparison with the OQKD protocol [29].

Protocol	Research Themes	SP (Server) Honesty Test	The Data Process	Matching Method between Keys and Data
Ours	private query	no	no	a shift value
[29]	PSI	yes	count Bloom filter	a permutation

Below we present some limitations of the protocol and the direction of future work. Limited by the current development of quantum technology, we are not able to conduct experiments and perform practical validation of the protocols in the IoT. Although the development of quantum facilities is still immature, there already exist some programming environments capable of simulating a small number of quantum bits, e.g., HiQ quantum cloud platform, IBM quantum cloud platform. The OQKD of key generation is similar to that of quantum key distribution (QKD). As far as we know, the key rate of QKD is 14.5 b/s under experimental conditions of 75 MHz clock rate and time bin encoding [40], which is the most advanced development [41]. Quantum devices are also subject to this protocol. We hope to perform experimental validation of the protocol in the future. The OQKD protocol [29] is the first protocol that combines OQKD methods with quantum authentication, but to our knowledge, its efficiency is not optimal. In the future, we can improve the efficiency of the overall protocol with other existing OQKD protocols [42–44]. The quantum authentication method used in the overall protocol requires relatively more conditions. In the future, we will improve the authentication method with better quantum authentication protocols. In addition, we hope to combine this protocol with existing classical methods so that the protocol can contribute to the development of research in other directions [7,45]. At the same time, we would like to promote a new idea: the most likely faster implementation of OQKD or QKD as a basic building block for other research topics. We hope to combine QKD and OQKD with other technologies to create a whole new security system.

7. Conclusions

In this paper, we proposed a generic system model aided with ED for PSI in IoT. Then, we presented a quantum PSI protocol in IoT. Our proposed quantum PSI protocol obtained higher security and only needed the communication complexity of $O(\tau)$ qubits. The proposed protocol can not only protect the private data of two parties but also protect identity information of two parties. The proposed protocol had an authentication function to prevent malicious adversary attacks and maintain information integrity.

Author Contributions: Conceptualization: B.L. and X.Z.; methodology, B.L. and X.Z.; validation: B.L., X.Z. and M.Z.; formal analysis: B.L. and M.Z.; investigation: B.L. and X.Z.; resources: M.Z.; data curation: B.L. and X.Z.; writing—original draft preparation: B.L. and X.Z.; writing—review and editing: B.L., X.Z. and R.S.; visualization: B.L. and X.Z.; supervision: M.Z. and G.Z.; project administration: B.L. and M.Z.; funding acquisition: B.L. and M.Z. All authors have read and agreed to the published version of the manuscript.

Funding: This work was supported by the National Natural Science Foundation of China (62002105, 62072134, U2001205, 61902116) and The Key Research and Development Program of Hubei (2021BEA163).

Institutional Review Board Statement: Not applicable.

Informed Consent Statement: Not applicable.

Data Availability Statement: Not applicable.

Conflicts of Interest: The authors declare no conflict of interest.

References

1. Yang, Y.; Wu, L.; Yin, G.; Li, L.; Zhao, H. A survey on security and privacy issues in Internet-of-Things. *IEEE Internet Things J.* **2017**, *4*, 1250–1258. [CrossRef]
2. Xu, X.; He, Y. Blockchain application in modern logistics information sharing: A review and case study analysis. In *Production Planning & Control*; Taylor & Franics: Abingdon, UK, 2022; pp. 1–15.
3. Qadri, Y.A.; Nauman, A.; Zikria, Y.B.; Vasilakos, A.V.; Kim, S.W. The future of healthcare Internet of Things: A survey of emerging technologies. *IEEE Commun. Surv. Tutorials* **2020**, *22*, 1121–1167. [CrossRef]
4. Zhang, K.; Ni, J.; Yang, K.; Liang, X.; Ren, J.; Shen, X.S. Security and privacy in smart city applications: Challenges and solutions. *IEEE Commun. Mag.* **2017**, *55*, 122–129. [CrossRef]
5. Chakravorty, A.; Wlodarczyk, T.; Rong, C. Privacy preserving data analytics for smart homes. In Proceedings of the 2013 IEEE Security and Privacy Workshops, San Francisco, CA, USA, 23–24 May 2013; IEEE: Piscataway, NJ, USA, 2013; pp. 23–27.
6. Qian, Y.; Shen, J.; Vijayakumar, P.; Sharma, P.K. Profile matching for IoMT: A verifiable private set intersection scheme. *IEEE J. Biomed. Health Inform.* **2021**, *25*, 3794–3803. [CrossRef] [PubMed]
7. Abadi, A.; Terzis, S.; Metere, R.; Dong, C. Efficient delegated private set intersection on outsourced private datasets. *IEEE Trans. Dependable Secur. Comput.* **2017**, *16*, 608–624. [CrossRef]
8. Zuo, X.; Li, L.; Luo, S.; Peng, H.; Yang, Y.; Gong, L. Privacy-Preserving Verifiable Graph Intersection Scheme With Cryptographic Accumulators in Social Networks. *IEEE Internet Things J.* **2020**, *8*, 4590–4603. [CrossRef]
9. Freedman, M.J.; Nissim, K.; Pinkas, B. Efficient private matching and set intersection. In Proceedings of the International Conference on the Theory and Applications of Cryptographic Techniques, Interlaken, Switzerland, 2–6 May 2004; Springer: Cham, Switzerland, 2004; pp. 1–19.
10. Le, P.H.; Ranellucci, S.; Gordon, S.D. Two-party private set intersection with an untrusted third party. In Proceedings of the 2019 ACM SIGSAC Conference on Computer and Communications Security, London, UK, 11–15 November 2019; pp. 2403–2420.
11. Hazay, C.; Nissim, K. Efficient set operations in the presence of malicious adversaries. In Proceedings of the International Workshop on Public Key Cryptography, Xi'an, China, 30 May–3 June 2016; Springer: Berlin/Heidelberg, Germany, 2010; pp. 312–331.
12. Kolesnikov, V.; Kumaresan, R.; Rosulek, M.; Trieu, N. Efficient batched oblivious PRF with applications to private set intersection. In Proceedings of the 2016 ACM SIGSAC Conference on Computer and Communications Security, Vienna, Austria, 24–28 October 2016; pp. 818–829.
13. Pinkas, B.; Schneider, T.; Segev, G.; Zohner, M. Phasing: Private set intersection using permutation-based hashing. In Proceedings of the 24th USENIX Security Symposium (USENIX Security 15), Washington, DC, USA, 12–14 August 2015; pp. 515–530.
14. Chase, M.; Miao, P. Private set intersection in the internet setting from lightweight oblivious PRF. In Proceedings of the Annual International Cryptology Conference, Santa Barbara, CA, USA, 18–22 August 2020; Springer: Berlin/Heidelberg, Germany, 2020; pp. 34–63.
15. Badrinarayanan, S.; Miao, P.; Xie, T. Updatable Private Set Intersection. *Cryptol. ePrint Arch.* **2021**. Available online: https://eprint.iacr.org/2021/1349 (accessed on 15 March 2022).
16. Cho, K.; Miyano, T. Chaotic cryptography using augmented Lorenz equations aided by quantum key distribution. *IEEE Trans. Circuits Syst. I: Regul. Pap.* **2014**, *62*, 478–487. [CrossRef]
17. Shi, R.H. Anonymous Quantum Sealed-bid Auction. *IEEE Trans. Circuits Syst. II Express Briefs* **2021**, *69*, 414–418. [CrossRef]
18. Shi, R.H.; Mu, Y.; Zhong, H.; Cui, J.; Zhang, S. An efficient quantum scheme for Private Set Intersection. *Quantum Inf. Process.* **2016**, *15*, 363–371. [CrossRef]

19. Cheng, X.; Guo, R.; Chen, Y. Cryptanalysis and improvement of a quantum private set intersection protocol. *Quantum Inf. Process.* **2017**, *16*, 37. [CrossRef]
20. Maitra, A. Quantum secure two party computation for set intersection with rational players. *Quantum Inf. Process.* **2018**, *17*, 197. [CrossRef]
21. Shi, R.H.; Mu, Y.; Zhong, H.; Zhang, S. Quantum oblivious set-member decision protocol. *Phys. Rev. A* **2015**, *92*, 022309. [CrossRef]
22. Debnath, S.K.; Dey, K.; Kundu, N.; Choudhury, T. Feasible private set intersection in quantum domain. *Quantum Inf. Process.* **2021**, *20*, 41. [CrossRef]
23. Gao, F.; Liu, B.; Wen, Q.Y.; Chen, H. Flexible quantum private queries based on quantum key distribution. *Opt. Express* **2012**, *20*, 17411–17420. [CrossRef]
24. Debnath, S.K.; Srivastava, V.; Mohanty, T.; Kundu, N.; Sakurai, K. Quantum Secure Privacy Preserving Technique to Obtain the Intersection of Two Datasets for Contact Tracing. *IACR Cryptol. ePrint Arch.* **2021**, *2021*, 618. [CrossRef]
25. Ye, T.; Li, H.K.; Hu, J.L. Multi-User Quantum Private Query Protocol. *Int. J. Theor. Phys.* **2020**, *59*, 2867–2874. [CrossRef]
26. Zhu, D.; Wang, L.; Zhu, H. Cryptanalysis of Multi-User Quantum Private Query Protocol. *Int. J. Theor. Phys.* **2021**, *60*, 284–292. [CrossRef]
27. Jakobi, M.; Simon, C.; Gisin, N.; Bancal, J.D.; Branciard, C.; Walenta, N.; Zbinden, H. Practical private database queries based on a quantum-key-distribution protocol. *Phys. Rev. A* **2011**, *83*, 22301. [CrossRef]
28. Bennett, C.H. Quantum cryptography: Public key distribution and coin tossing. In Proceedings of the IEEE International Conference on Computers, Bangalore, India, 9–12 December 1984.
29. Xiao, M.; Lei, S. Quantum private query with authentication. *Quantum Inf. Process.* **2021**, *20*, 166. [CrossRef]
30. Curty, M.; Santos, D. Quantum authentication of classical messages. *Phys. Rev. A* **2012**, *64*, 168. [CrossRef]
31. Curty, M.; Santos, D.J.; Pérez, E.; García-Fernández, P. Qubit authentication. *Phys. Rev. A* **2002**, *66*, 022301. [CrossRef]
32. Xin, X.; Li, F. Quantum Authentication of Classical Messages without Entangled State as Authentication Key. *Int. J. Multimed. Ubiquitous Eng.* **2015**, *10*, 199–206. [CrossRef]
33. Bloom, B.H. Space/time trade-offs in hash coding with allowable errors. *Commun. ACM* **1970**, *13*, 422–426.
34. Fan, L. Summary Cache: A Scalable Wide-area Web Cache Sharing Protocol. *ACM SIGCOMM Comput. Commun. Rev.* **1998**, *28*, 254–265. [CrossRef]
35. Xu, F.; Ma, X.; Zhang, Q.; Lo, H.K.; Pan, J.W. Secure quantum key distribution with realistic devices. *Rev. Mod. Phys.* **2020**, *92*, 025002. [CrossRef]
36. Liu, H.; Wang, W.; Wei, K.; Fang, X.T.; Li, L.; Liu, N.L.; Liang, H.; Zhang, S.J.; Zhang, W.; Li, H.; et al. Experimental demonstration of high-rate measurement-device-independent quantum key distribution over asymmetric channels. *Phys. Rev. Lett.* **2019**, *122*, 160501. [CrossRef]
37. Gisin, N.; Ribordy, G.; Tittel, W.; Zbinden, H. Quantum cryptography. *Rev. Mod. Phys.* **2002**, *74*, 145. [CrossRef]
38. Liu, B.; Xia, S.; Xiao, D.; Huang, W.; Xu, B.; Li, Y. Decoy-state method for quantum-key-distribution-based quantum private query. *Sci. China Phys. Mech. Astron.* **2022**, *65*, 240312. [CrossRef]
39. Liu, B.; Ruan, O.; Shi, R.; Zhang, M. Quantum private set intersection cardinality based on bloom filter. *Sci. Rep.* **2021**, *11*, 17332. [CrossRef]
40. Goldreich, O. Secure multi-party computation. *Manuscript. Prelim. Version* **1998**, *78*, 110.
41. Shor, P.W. Polynomial-Time Algorithms for Prime Factorization and Discrete Logarithms on a Quantum Computer. *SIAM Rev.* **1999**, *41*, 303–332. [CrossRef]
42. Gao, F.; Qin, S.; Huang, W.; Wen, Q. Quantum private query: A new kind of practical quantum cryptographic protocol. *Sci. China Physics Mech. Astron.* **2019**, *62*, 70301. [CrossRef]
43. Wei, C.Y.; Cai, X.Q.; Wang, T.Y.; Qin, S.J.; Gao, F.; Wen, Q.Y. Error tolerance bound in QKD-based quantum private query. *IEEE J. Sel. Areas Commun.* **2020**, *38*, 517–527. [CrossRef]
44. Wei, C.Y.; Cai, X.Q.; Liu, B.; Wang, T.Y.; Gao, F. A generic construction of quantum-oblivious-key-transfer-based private query with ideal database security and zero failure. *IEEE Trans. Comput.* **2017**, *67*, 2–8. [CrossRef]
45. Xu, X.; Wei, Z.; Ji, Q.; Wang, C.; Gao, G. Global renewable energy development: Influencing factors, trend predictions and countermeasures. *Resour. Policy* **2019**, *63*, 101470. [CrossRef]

Article

Markovian Demands on Two Commodity Inventory System with Queue-Dependent Services and an Optional Retrial Facility

K. Jeganathan [1], M. Abdul Reiyas [2], S. Selvakumar [1], N. Anbazhagan [3], S. Amutha [4], Gyanendra Prasad Joshi [5,*], Duckjoong Jeon [6] and Changho Seo [6,*]

- [1] Ramanujan Institute for Advanced Study in Mathematics University of Madras, Chepauk, Chennai 600005, India; kjeganathan@unom.ac.in (K.J.); illoduselvakumar@gmail.com (S.S.)
- [2] Department of Food Business Management, College of Food and Dairy Technology, The Tamil Nadu Veterinary and Animal Sciences University (TANUVAS), Chennai 600051, India; mabdulreiyas74@gmail.com
- [3] Department of Mathematics, Alagappa University, Karaikudi 630003, India; anbazhagann@alagappauniversity.ac.in
- [4] Ramanujan Centre for Higher Mathematics, Alagappa University, Karaikudi 630003, India; amuthas@alagappauniversity.ac.in
- [5] Department of Computer Science and Engineering, Sejong University, Seoul 05006, Korea
- [6] Department of Convergence Science, Kongju National University, Gongju 32588, Korea; jooniii@tta.or.kr
- * Correspondence: joshi@sejong.ac.kr (G.P.J.); chseo@kongju.ac.kr (C.S.)

Abstract: The use of a Markovian inventory system is a critical part of inventory management. The purpose of this study is to examine the demand for two commodities in a Markovian inventory system, one of which is designated as a major item (Commodity-I) and the other as a complimentary item (Commodity-II). Demand arrives according to a Poisson process, and service time is exponential at a queue-dependent rate. We investigate a strategy of (s, Q) type control for commodity-I with a random lead time but instantaneous replenishment for commodity-II. If the waiting hall reaches its maximum capacity of N, any arriving primary client may enter an infinite capacity orbit with a specified ratio. For orbiting consumers, the classical retrial policy is used. In a steady-state setting, the joint probability distributions for commodities and the number of demands in the queue and the orbit, are derived. From this, we derive a waiting time analysis and a variety of system performance metrics in the steady-state. Additionally, the physical properties of various performance measures are evaluated using various numerical assumptions associated with diverse stochastic behaviours.

Keywords: classical retrial policy; queue dependent service rate; waiting time analysis; infinite orbit

MSC: 60K20; 60K25

1. Introduction

The function or usage of one product may be dependent on another product in general. The first product is the major commodity and the second one is the complimentary of the first product, such as mobile phone with memory card, bike with helmet, printer with ink cartridge, computer with software, torch with battery, etc. From the production point of view, both commodities are correlated with each other. According to the demand of both commodities, a firm will sell them abundantly to the targeted population who are economically benefited with the purchase.

Elaborately if the cost of one product increases, the customer demand for the corresponding complimentary product decreases. So the customers' interest towards the product will be changed. Furthermore, it will spoil the existing quantity of the product and hence, the company may encounter lose in their sales. In order to maintain the goodwill of business, the company should sell their product along with its complimentary product. Furthermore any company must plan to introduce a new product as a compliment of another product that will gain customers interests towards the new product with positive feedback. It can be applied in any industry right from software to dairy products. These impacts make us analyze the economic strategy of multi inventory system which sells both products with an affordable cost.

In reality, many servers can adjust the speed of service according to customer satisfaction which impacts brand reputation. In a queuing system, some authors considered queue length-dependent service times (see Abolnikov [1], Dshalalow [2], Fakinos [3], Harris [4] and Ivnitskiy et al. [5]). Furthermore, if an arriving customer finds the waiting room full, the customer decides to reattempt to get the entry with certain proportion. Under such real conditions, the proposed model deals with two commodity perishable inventory system that is the novelty of this paper. The next section elaborates the Review Literature of this model. System description is presented in Section 3. Under stability conditions, the mathematical and waiting time of the model is studied in Sections 4 and 5, respectively. System characteristics and numerical analysis are presented in Sections 6 and 7, respectively. Conclusion of the deal is presented in the final section.

Related Works

The relevant features of the present study are discussed in various modeling of queuing inventory system. Before making procurement of some products in an inventory system, a customer should need some demonstration about the product. It will take some positive time for a server showing its demonstration. In that duration, any arriving customer may wait for his/her turn. An inventory system with arbitrary service time was first studied by Sigman and Simchi-levi [6]. Schwarz et al. [7] first developed an inventory queuing system for which lead time, service time and the time between each arrival into the system are all considered to be independent exponential distributions. This was discussed by Berman et al. [8]. Recently, regarding service facilities one can refer [9].

Gebhard [10] considered a M/M/1 queuing system with two rate of service policy. Sangeetha and Sivakumar [11] studied a perishable inventory system for MAP arrival and Phase type service distribution environment and found an optimal policies of service rates in order to minimize the expected total cost. Under the steady state approximation, the probability of empty state and mean queue length are also obtained. Furthermore Doo Il Choi et al. [12] individually studied the queue dependent service time with finite capacity and infinite capacity queue. In these models, one rate of service is fixed up to a certain level in the queue and another rate of service is provided after finding the queue size beyond that level. Jeganathan et al. [13] considered an inventory queuing system which provides k independent phases of services with each service rate depending upon two discrete states of queue length.

Keerthana et al. [14] considered the postponed and renewal demands on their inventory system in which they follow arbitrary demand distribution for the inter-arrival times. The economical advantages of an inventory system are analyzed with three kinds of retrial mode by Krishnamoorthy and Jose [15]. Amirthakodi and Sivakumar [16] investigated the feedback mechanism on their inventory system with an orbital search policy. Dhanya Shajin and Krishnamoorthy [17] explored the advanced reservation, cancellation, overbooking with an impatient customers. Furthermore, more queries regarding inventory and production inventory discussion, can be referred through [18–21].

Paul Manuel et al. [22] studied a perishable finite capacity retrial inventory system with service facilities. The inter-retrial time and life time of a stored item for each model discussed here are exponentially distributed. Furthermore, Paul Manuel et al. [23] counted a constant rate of retrial from infinite space orbit is dealt with a finite queuing perishable inventory. Kathiresan et al. [24] considered an inventory system with finite capacity waiting hall. In this model,any arriving customer can also use a finite capacity orbit whenever there is no vacant in waiting hall and there is a vacant in the orbit with constant rate of retrial. Most of the times, the nature of the retrial policy is dependent on the size of the customers in the orbit which is discussed as a classical retrial policy (CRP). Artaljeo et al. [25] and Ushakumari [26] both elaborately discussed CRP in an inventory system.

The merits of multi item service facilities are pointed out in some publications. The optimum ordering policy of multi-item inventory system under some different constraints of total cost function was studied by Veinott and Wagner [27] and Wagner et al. [28]. Alscher and Schneider [29] determined a multi-item inventory control model undertaking with varying costs of multi items. Kalpakam and Arivarignan [30] considered a joint (s,S) reordering policy of a multi-item inventory. In this model, S denotes the aggregate of maximum stock level of each commodity and whenever the aggregate stock level reaches to s, the quantity of each commodity are ordered up to its maximum stock level and the replenishment time of any joint new order is zero. Anbazhagan and Arivarignan [31–33] analyzed the different ordering policies of two commodities inventory system under the assumption of various random conditions. Sivakumar et al. [34] studied two commodity inventory queuing system where any one of two item is replaceable when a demanded item is not available. Instead of a finite waiting hall, Sivakumar [35] studied the same with retrial demand.

Yadavalli et al. [36] studied a two commodity coordinated inventory system in which demand of each commodity is sold with another commodity under a distinct Bernoulli schedule and arrival pattern of a customer is poisson. Furthermore, Yadavalli et al. [36] thoroughly investigated two perishable commodity inventory system with three types of customers where the demand of one commodity is always bulk. Anbazhagan et al. [37] introduced the gift item for a customer whenever the quantity of the demand of the main product is beyond certain level. Under a base stock ordering policy, a two commodity inventory system with a finite capacity waiting hall was analyzed by Gomathi et al. [38]. Anbazhagan and Jeganathan [39] independently studied the ordering policies of primary product and gift item, but compliment item may also be sold when a customer do not make any demand of primary product.

2. System Description

A single server two commodity inventory system with a limited queue of size N and an optional retrial facility of indefinite size is considered in this model, in which one commodity is designated as a significant item and the other as a complimentary item is taken into consideration. When a customer first enters the system, they purchase a large item and depart with a complementary item after the service is completed. The interval between the arrival times of any two customers is exponentially distributed with rate λ between them. The single server delivers queue-dependent service at a rate of $x\mu$, where x denotes the number of consumers currently waiting in line at the time of the request. If there is no available space in the queue, any new customers who join in an endless retrial orbit with a rate of $q\lambda$. After some exponential time has passed, the customer can be reintroduced into the system to satisfy his or her demand, with the rate of reintroduction being $u\lambda_r$, where u represents the number of orbital clients present at the time.

For each commodity, a continuous review ordering policy is considered: (s, Q) and $(0, S_2)$ (instantaneous) are the ordering policies for the major item and complimentary item, respectively; further, anytime the level of stock for a major item falls below s, the system immediately places an order for quantity Q of the major item, and the time it takes for the ordered quantity of major item to arrive is exponential with rate β, as shown in the following diagram. However, whenever the stock of the complimentary item reaches zero, the order for quantity S_2 is placed immediately. The deteriorating times of both items are random and exponential in nature, with intensities of γ_1 and γ_2 for the major item and γ_2 for the complimentary item, respectively.

3. Analysis of the Model

Let $X_1(t), X_2(t), X_3(t), W(t)$ described number of demands in the orbit, current inventory level of first commodity (CIL1), current inventory level of second commodity (CIL2), number of demands in the waiting hall (queue), respectively. Assumption developed on the birth death process make a stochastic process $Y(t) = \{(X_1(t), X_2(t), X_3, W(t)), t \geq 0\}$ and it is also said to be a continuous-time stochastic process (CTSP) having the state space E such that $E = \{(\wp_1, \wp_2, \wp_3, \wp_4) : \wp_1 = 0, 1, \cdots; \wp_2 = 0, 1, \cdots, S_1; \wp_3 = 1, \cdots, S_2; \wp_4 = 0, 1, \cdots, N\}$.

3.1. Construction of Infinitesimal Generator Matrix

Indicating to the discrete state space and continuous time Markov chain, the transition matrix of $Y(t)$ having the structure as follows:

$$B = \begin{pmatrix} \mathbb{B}_{00} & \mathbb{B}_{01} & 0 & 0 & 0 & \cdots \\ \mathbb{B}_{10} & \mathbb{B}_{11} & \mathbb{B}_{01} & 0 & 0 & \cdots \\ 0 & \mathbb{B}_{20} & \mathbb{B}_{21} & \mathbb{B}_{01} & 0 & \cdots \\ \vdots & \vdots & \ddots & \ddots & \ddots & \ddots \end{pmatrix},$$

where

$$\mathbb{B}_{01} = \begin{cases} q\lambda & \wp'_1 = \wp_1, & \wp_1 \in \{0, 1, 2, \cdots\} \\ & \wp'_2 = \wp_2, & \wp_2 \in \{0, 1, 2, \cdots S_1\} \\ & \wp'_3 = \wp_3, & \wp_3 \in \{1, 2, \cdots S_2\} \\ & \wp'_4 = \wp_4, & \wp_4 = N \\ 0, & \text{otherwise.} \end{cases},$$

$$\mathbb{B}_{\wp_1 0} = \begin{cases} \wp_1 \lambda_r, & \wp'_1 = \wp_1 - 1, & \wp_1 \in \{1, 2, \cdots\} \\ & \wp'_2 = \wp_2, & \wp_2 \in \{0, 1, 2, \cdots, S_1\} \\ & \wp'_3 = \wp_3, & \wp_3 \in \{1, 2, \cdots, S_2\} \\ & \wp'_4 = \wp_4, & \wp_4 \in \{0, 1, 2, \cdots, N-1\} \\ 0, & \text{otherwise.} \end{cases}$$

and

$$
\mathbb{B}_{\wp_1,\wp_1'} = \begin{cases}
\beta & \begin{aligned}\wp_1' &= \wp_1, \\ \wp_2' &= \wp_2 + Q, \\ \wp_3' &= \wp_3, \\ \wp_4' &= \wp_4,\end{aligned} & \begin{aligned}\wp_1 &\in \{0,1,2,\ldots\} \\ \wp_2 &\in \{0,1,2,\ldots,s\} \\ \wp_3 &\in \{1,2,\ldots,S_2\} \\ \wp_4 &\in \{0,1,\ldots,N\}\end{aligned} \\[1em]
\lambda & \begin{aligned}\wp_1' &= \wp_1, \\ \wp_2' &= \wp_2, \\ \wp_3' &= \wp_3, \\ \wp_4' &= \wp_4,\end{aligned} & \begin{aligned}\wp_1 &\in \{0,1,2,\ldots\} \\ \wp_2 &\in \{0,1,2,\ldots,S_1\} \\ \wp_3 &\in \{1,2,\ldots,S_2\} \\ \wp_4 &\in \{0,1,\ldots,N-1\}\end{aligned} \\[1em]
\wp_2 \gamma_1 & \begin{aligned}\wp_1' &= \wp_1, \\ \wp_2' &= \wp_2 - 1, \\ \wp_3' &= \wp_3, \\ \wp_4' &= \wp_4,\end{aligned} & \begin{aligned}\wp &\in \{0,1,2,\ldots\} \\ \wp_2 &\in \{1,2,\ldots,S_1\} \\ \wp_3 &\in \{1,2,\ldots,S_2\} \\ \wp_4 &\in \{0,1,\ldots,N\}\end{aligned} \\[1em]
\wp_3 \gamma_2 & \begin{aligned}\wp_1' &= \wp_1, \\ \wp_2' &= \wp_2, \\ \wp_3' &= S_2, \\ \wp_3' &= \wp_3 - 1, \\ \wp_4' &= \wp_4,\end{aligned} & \begin{aligned}\wp_1 &\in \{0,1,2,\ldots\} \\ \wp_2 &\in \{0,1,2,\ldots,S_1-1\} \\ \wp_3 &= 1 \\ \wp_3 &\in \{2,3,\ldots,S_2\} \\ \wp_4 &\in \{0,1,\ldots,N\}\end{aligned} \\[1em]
\wp_4 \mu & \begin{aligned}\wp_1' &= \wp_1, \\ \wp_2' &= \wp_2 - 1, \\ \wp_3' &= S_2, \\ \wp_3' &= \wp_3 - 1, \\ \wp_4' &= \wp_4 - 1,\end{aligned} & \begin{aligned}\wp_1 &\in \{0,1,2,\ldots\} \\ \wp_2 &\in \{1,2,\ldots,S_1\} \\ \wp_3 &= 1 \\ \wp_3 &\in \{2,3,\ldots,S_2\} \\ \wp_4 &\in \{1,2,\ldots,N\}\end{aligned} \\[1em]
\begin{aligned}-[H(s-\wp_2)\beta + \wp_2\gamma_1 \\ + \wp_3\gamma_2 + v_2\delta_{0\wp_2}\wp_4\mu \\ \delta_{N\wp_4}q\lambda + \delta_{N\wp_4}\wp_1\lambda_r]\end{aligned} & \begin{aligned}\wp_1' &= \wp_1, \\ \wp_2' &= \wp_2, \\ \wp_3' &= \wp_3, \\ \wp_4' &= \wp_4,\end{aligned} & \begin{aligned}\wp_1 &\in \{0,1,2,\ldots\} \\ \wp_2 &\in \{0,1,2,\ldots,S_1\} \\ \wp_3 &\in \{1,2,\ldots,S_2\} \\ \wp_4 &\in \{0,1,\ldots,N\}\end{aligned} \\[1em]
0, & \text{otherwise.}
\end{cases}
$$

The infinitesimal generator matrix, B, is to be obtained by the transitions as follows:

1. $(\wp_1, \wp_2, \wp_3, N) \xrightarrow{q\lambda} (\wp_1 + 1, \wp_2, \wp_3, N)$ $\wp_1 = 0,1,2,\cdots$; $\wp_2 = 0,1,2,\cdots S_1$; $\wp_3 = 1,2,\cdots S_2$.

2. $(\wp_1, \wp_2, \wp_3, \wp_4) \xrightarrow{\wp_1\lambda_r} (\wp_1 - 1, \wp_2, \wp_3, \wp_4 + 1)$ $\wp_1 = 0,1,2,\cdots$; $\wp_2 = 0,1,2,\cdots S_1$; $\wp_3 = 1,2,\cdots S_2$; $\wp_4 = 0,1,2,\cdots N-1$.

3. $(\wp_1, \wp_2, \wp_3, \wp_4) \xrightarrow{\beta} (\wp_1, \wp_2 + Q, \wp_3, \wp_4)$ $\wp_1 = 0,1,2,\cdots$; $\wp_2 = 0,1,2,\cdots s$; $\wp_3 = 1,2,\cdots S_2$; $\wp_4 = 0,1,2,\cdots N$.

4. $(\wp_1, \wp_2, \wp_3, \wp_4) \xrightarrow{\lambda} (\wp_1, \wp_2, \wp_3, \wp_4 + 1)$ $\wp_1 = 0,1,2,\cdots$; $\wp_2 = 0,1,2,\cdots S_1$; $\wp_3 = 1,2,\cdots S_2$; $\wp_4 = 0,1,2,\cdots N-1$.

5. $(\wp_1, \wp_2, \wp_3, \wp_4) \xrightarrow{\wp_2\gamma_1} (\wp_1, \wp_2 - 1, \wp_3, \wp_4)$ $\wp_1 = 0,1,2,\cdots$; $\wp_2 = 1,2,\cdots S_1$; $\wp_3 = 1,2,\cdots S_2$; $\wp_4 = 0,1,2,\cdots N$.

6. $(\wp_1, \wp_2, \wp_3, \wp_4) \xrightarrow{\wp_3\gamma_1} (\wp_1, \wp_2, \wp_3 - 1, \wp_4)$ $\wp_1 = 0,1,2,\cdots$; $\wp_2 = 0,1,2,\cdots S_1$; $\wp_3 = 1,2,\cdots S_2$; $\wp_4 = 0,1,2,\cdots N$.

7. $(\wp_1, \wp_2, \wp_3, \wp_4) \xrightarrow{\wp_4\mu} (\wp_1, \wp_2 - 1, \wp_3 - 1, \wp_4 - 1)$ $\wp_1 = 0,1,2,\cdots$; $\wp_2 = 1,2,\cdots S_1$; $\wp_3 = 1,2,\cdots S_2$; $\wp_4 = 1,2,\cdots N$.

3.2. Matrix Geometric Approximation

Steady State Analysis

Consider the point at which this truncation procedure stops for the matrix-geometric approximation to be K. In order to identify the steady state of the considered system using Neut's Rao truncation approach, we make the assumptions that $B_{i0} = B_{K0}$ and $B_{i1} = B_{K1}$ for all $i \geq K$. In addition, the updated generator matrix for the truncated system with the following structure is created.

$$\hat{\mathbb{B}} = \begin{pmatrix} \mathbb{B}_{00} & \mathbb{B}_{01} & 0 & 0 & 0 & \cdots & 0 & 0 & 0 & 0 & 0 & \cdots \\ \mathbb{B}_{10} & \mathbb{B}_{11} & \mathbb{B}_{01} & 0 & 0 & \cdots & 0 & 0 & 0 & 0 & 0 & \cdots \\ 0 & \mathbb{B}_{20} & \mathbb{B}_{21} & \mathbb{B}_{01} & 0 & \cdots & 0 & 0 & 0 & 0 & 0 & \cdots \\ \vdots & \vdots & \vdots & \vdots & \vdots & \ddots & \vdots & \vdots & \vdots & \vdots & \vdots & \ddots \\ 0 & 0 & 0 & 0 & 0 & \cdots & \mathbb{B}_{K0} & \mathbb{B}_{K1} & \mathbb{B}_{01} & 0 & 0 & \cdots \\ 0 & 0 & 0 & 0 & 0 & \cdots & 0 & \mathbb{B}_{K0} & \mathbb{B}_{K1} & \mathbb{B}_{01} & 0 & \cdots \\ \vdots & \vdots & \vdots & \vdots & \vdots & \ddots & \vdots & \vdots & \vdots & \vdots & \vdots & \ddots \end{pmatrix},$$

Theorem 1. *The steady-state probability vector, χ, where*

$$\chi = (\chi^{(0)}, \chi^{(1)}, \cdots, \chi^{(S_1)}),$$
$$\chi^{(\wp_2)} = \chi^{(\wp_2,0)}, \chi^{(\wp_2,1)}, \cdots, \chi^{(\wp_2,S_2)} \wp_2 = 0,1,\cdots,S_1$$
$$\chi^{(\wp_2,\wp_3)} = \chi^{(\wp_2,\wp_3,0)}, \chi^{(\wp_2,\wp_3,1)}, \cdots, \chi^{(\wp_2,\wp_3,N)} \wp_2 = 0,1,\cdots,S_1 \text{ and } \wp_3 = 0,1,\cdots,S_2$$

that corresponds to the generator matrix is denoted by $\mathbb{B}_K$ where $\mathbb{B}_K = \mathbb{B}_{K0} + \mathbb{B}_{K1} + \mathbb{B}_{01}$ is given by

$$\chi^{(i)} = \chi^{(Q)} e_i, \quad i = 0, 1, \ldots, S_1.$$

where

$$e_i = \begin{cases} (-1)^{Q-i} F_Q E_{Q-1}^{-1} F_{Q-1} \cdots F_{i+1} E_i^{-1}, & i = 0, 1, \cdots, Q-1 \\ I, & i = Q \\ (-1)^{2Q-i+1} \sum_{j=0}^{S_1-i} [(F_Q E_{Q-1}^{-1} F_{Q-1} \cdots F_{s+1-j} E_{s-j}^{-1}) \times \\ \quad G E_{S_1-j}^{-1} (F_{S_1-j} E_{S_1-j-1}^{-1} F_{S_1-j-1} \cdots F_{i+1} E_i^{-1})], & i = Q+1, Q+2, \cdots, S_1 \end{cases}$$

and $\chi^{(Q)}$ is obtained by solving

$$\chi^{(Q)}[(-1)^Q \sum_{j=0}^{s-1} [(F_Q E_{Q-1}^{-1} F_{Q-1} \cdots F_{s+1-j} E_{s-j}^{-1}) G E_{S_1-j}^{-1} (F_{S_1-j} E_{S_1-j-1}^{-1} F_{S_1-j-1} \cdots F_{i+1} E_i^{-1})]$$
$$F_{Q+1} + E_Q + (-1)^Q F_Q E_{Q-1}^{-1} F_{Q-1} \cdots F_1 E_0^{-1} G] = 0$$

and $\sum_{j=1}^{S_1} \chi^{(i)} \mathbf{e} = 1$.

Proof. We have

$$\chi \mathbb{B}_K = 0 \text{ and } \chi \mathbf{e} = 1 \tag{1}$$

where

$$[\mathbb{B}_K]_{ij} = \begin{cases} E_i & j = i, & i = 0,1,2,\cdots,S_1; \\ F_i & j = i-1, & i = 1,2,\cdots,S_1; \\ G & j = i+Q, & i = 0,1,2,\cdots,s; \\ 0 & \text{otherwise} \end{cases}$$

The first equation of the above framework yields the following set of equations:

$$\chi^{(i+1)} F_{i+1} + \chi^{(i)} E_i = 0, i = 0, 1, \cdots, Q-1$$
$$\chi^{(i+1)} F_{i+1} + \chi^{(i)} E_i + \chi^{(i-Q)} G = 0, i = Q, Q+1, \cdots, S_1 - 1$$
$$\chi^{(i)} E_i + \chi^{(i-Q)} G = 0, i = S_1$$

Solving the system of equations, we will get the stated result. □

Theorem 2. *The stability condition of the system at the truncation point K is given by*

$$r_1 q \lambda < r_2 K \lambda_r$$

where $r_1 = \sum_{\wp_2=0}^{S_1} \sum_{\wp_3=1}^{S_2} \chi^{(\wp_2,\wp_3,N)}$ *and* $r_2 = \sum_{\wp_2=0}^{S_1} \sum_{\wp_3=1}^{S_2} \sum_{\wp_4=1}^{N} \chi^{(\wp_2,\wp_3,\wp_3)}$.

Proof. From the well known result of Neuts on the positive recurrence of $\mathbb{B}_K$ we have

$$\chi^{(K)} \mathbb{B}_{01} \mathbf{e} < \chi^{(K)} \mathbb{B}_{K0} \mathbf{e}$$

and by exploiting the structure of the matrices $\mathbb{B}_{01}$ and $\mathbb{B}_{K0}$, we get, for $\wp_2 = 0, 1, 2, \cdots, S_1$, $\wp_3 = 1, 2, \cdots, S_2$ and $\wp_4 = 0, 1, 2, \cdots, N$.

$$\chi^{(\wp_2,\wp_3,\wp_4)} \mathbb{B}_{01} \mathbf{e} < \chi^{(\wp_2,\wp_3,\wp_4)} \mathbb{B}_{K0} \mathbf{e}.$$

First, $[\chi^{(0)}, \chi^{(1)}, \cdots, \chi^{(S_1)}] \mathbb{B}_{01} \mathbf{e} < [\chi^{(0)}, \chi^{(1)}, \cdots, \chi^{(S_1)}] \mathbb{B}_{K0} \mathbf{e}$
Due to the structure of B_0, L.H.S becomes

$$\chi^{(\wp_2)} B_0 = \chi^{(\wp_2,\wp_3,N)} q \lambda.$$

On the other hand, due to structure of B_1 R.H.S becomes

$$\chi^{(\wp_2)} B_1 = [\chi^{(\wp_2,\wp_3,1)}, \chi^{(\wp_2,\wp_3,2)}, \cdots, \chi^{(\wp_2,\wp_3,N)}] K \lambda_r$$

Therefore, the last inequality becomes

$$\sum_{\wp_2=0}^{S_1} \sum_{\wp_3=1}^{S_2} \chi^{(\wp_2,\wp_3,N)} q \lambda < \sum_{\wp_2=0}^{S_1} \sum_{\wp_3=1}^{S_2} \sum_{\wp_4=1}^{N} \chi^{(\wp_2,\wp_3,\wp_4)} K \lambda_r$$

Hence,

$$r_1 q \lambda < r_2 K \lambda_r$$

where $r_1 = \sum_{\wp_2=0}^{S_1} \sum_{\wp_3=1}^{S_2} \chi^{(\wp_2,\wp_3,N)}$ and $r_2 = \sum_{\wp_2=0}^{S_1} \sum_{\wp_3=1}^{S_2} \sum_{\wp_4=1}^{N} \chi^{(\wp_2,\wp_3,\wp_4)}$ as desired. □

Remark 1. *Using* $r_1 q \lambda < r_2 K \lambda_r$, *we get,*

$$\frac{r_1 q \lambda}{r_2 K \lambda_r} < 1$$

If $\frac{r_1}{r_2 K} = m(say)$, *then*

$$\frac{\lambda}{\lambda_r} < \frac{1}{m}.$$

3.3. Limiting Probability Distribution

It can be seen from the structure of the rate matrix B and from the Theorem 3, that the Markov process $\{X_1(t), X_2(t), X_3(t), W(t), t \geq 0\}$ with the state space E is regular. Henceforth, the limiting probability distribution

$$Y^{(\wp_1,\wp_2,\wp_3,\wp_4)} = \lim_{t \to \infty} Pr[X_1(t) = \wp_1, X_2(t) = \wp_2, X_3(t) = \wp_3, W(t) = \wp_4 | X_1(0), X_2(0), X_3(0), W(0)],$$

exists and is independent of the initial state.

Let $Y = \left(Y^{(0)}, Y^{(1)}, \ldots, \right)$ satisfies

$$YB = 0, \quad Ye = 1.$$

We can partition the vector $Y^{(\wp_1)}$, as

$$Y^{(\wp_1)} = \left(Y^{(\wp_1,0)}, Y^{(\wp_1,1)}, \ldots, Y^{(\wp_1,S_1)}\right), \wp_1 \geq 0$$

and

$$Y^{(\wp_1,\wp_2)} = \left(Y^{(\wp_1,\wp_2,1)}, Y^{(\wp_1,\wp_2,2)}, \ldots, Y^{(\wp_1,\wp_2,S_2)}\right), \wp_1 \geq 0, 0 \leq \wp_2 \leq S_1$$

$$Y^{(\wp_1,\wp_2,\wp_3)} = \left(Y^{(\wp_1,\wp_2,\wp_3,0)}, Y^{(\wp_1,\wp_2,\wp_3,1)}, \ldots, Y^{(\wp_1,\wp_2,\wp_3,N)}\right), \wp_1 \geq 0, 0 \leq \wp_2 \leq S_1, 0 \leq \wp_3 \leq N$$

Theorem 3. *Utilizing the vector $Y = (Y^{(0)}, Y^{(1)}, \ldots,)$ and the specific structure of B, R can be determined by*

$$R^2 \mathbb{B}_{K0} + R \mathbb{B}_{K1} + \mathbb{B}_{01} = 0$$

where R is the minimal non-negative of the matrix quadratic equation.

Proof. Assume

$$R = \begin{pmatrix} D_{00} & D_{01} & \cdots & D_{0S_1} \\ D_{10} & D_{11} & \cdots & D_{1S_1} \\ D_{20} & D_{21} & \cdots & D_{2S_1} \\ \vdots & \vdots & \ddots & \vdots \\ D_{S_10} & D_{S_11} & \cdots & D_{S_1S_1} \end{pmatrix}$$

where

$$D_{ij} = \begin{pmatrix} R_{11} & R_{12} & \cdots & R_{1S_2} \\ R_{21} & R_{22} & \cdots & R_{2S_2} \\ R_{31} & R_{32} & \cdots & R_{3S_2} \\ \vdots & \vdots & \ddots & \vdots \\ R_{S_21} & R_{S_22} & \cdots & R_{S_2S_2} \end{pmatrix}, i,j \in 1, 2, \cdots, S_2$$

Since the block matrix $\mathbb{B}_{01}$ has $(S_1+1)(S_2)$ number of nonzero rows, the assumed R matrix also has the same number of nonzero rows. Now, due to the specified structure of $\mathbb{B}_{01}$, the structure of the block matrix R_{mn} is of the form

$$R_{mn} = \begin{pmatrix} 0 & 0 & 0 & 0 & 0 & \cdots & 0 \\ 0 & 0 & 0 & 0 & 0 & \cdots & 0 \\ 0 & 0 & 0 & 0 & 0 & \cdots & 0 \\ \vdots & \vdots & \vdots & \vdots & \vdots & \ddots & \vdots \\ l^0_{mn} & l^1_{mn} & l^2_{mn} & l^3_{mn} & l^4_{mn} & \cdots & l^N_{mn} \end{pmatrix}, m, n \in 1, 2, \cdots, S_2$$

is also square matrix of dimension $N+1$.

Now, exploiting the coefficient matrices $\mathbb{B}_{K0}, \mathbb{B}_{K1}, \mathbb{B}_{01}$ with R^2 and R equating with 0, we obtain a system of $(N+1)$-dimensional vector as follows:

For $i = 0, 1, \cdots, S_1, j = 0, m = 1, 2, \cdots, S_2, n = 1, 2, \cdots, S_2 - 1$, $C_h^{(j)}$ be the diagonal elements of the corresponding matrix E_j where $j = 0, 1, 2, \cdots, S_1$ and $h = 1, 2, \cdots, S_2(N+1)$.

$(l_{mn}^0 C_{(n-1)(N+1)+1}^{(j)} + l_{m(n+1)}^0 (n+1)\gamma_2 + l_{mn}^0 (j+1)\gamma_1 + l_{m(n+1)}^1 1\mu, l_{mn}^0 \lambda + l_{mn}^1 C_{(n-1)(N+1)+2}^{(j)} + l_{m(n+1)}^1 (n+1)\gamma_2 + l_{mn}^1 (j+1)\gamma_1 + l_{m(n+1)}^2 2\mu, \cdots, l_{mn}^{N-2} \lambda + l_{mn}^{N-1} C_{(n-1)(N+1)+N}^{(j)} + l_{m(n+1)}^{N-1} (n+1)\gamma_2 + l_{mn}^{N-1}(j+1)\gamma_1 + l_{m(n+1)}^N N\mu, l_{mn}^{N-1}\lambda + l_{mn}^N C_{n(N+1)}^{(j)} + l_{m(n+1)}^N (n+1)\gamma_2 + l_{mn}^N (j+1)\gamma_1 + \delta_{i0}q\lambda) = 0$

For $j = 0, m = 1, 2, \cdots, S_2, n = S_2$

$(l_{mn}^0 C_{(n-1)(N+1)+1} + l_{m1}^0 1\gamma_2 + l_{mn}^0 (j+1)\gamma_1 + l_{m1}^1 1\mu, l_{mn}^0 \lambda + l_{mn}^1 C_{(n-1)(N+1)+2} + l_{m1}^1 1\gamma_2 + l_{mn}^1 (j+1)\gamma_1 + l_{m1}^2 2\mu, \cdots, l_{mn}^{N-2}\lambda + l_{mn}^{N-1} C_{(n-1)(N+1)+N} + l_{m1}^{N-1} 1\gamma_2 + l_{mn}^{N-1}(j+1)\gamma_1 + l_{m1}^N N\mu, l_{mn}^{N-1}\lambda + l_{mn}^N C_{n(N+1)} + l_{m1}^N 1\gamma_2 + l_{mn}^N (j+1)\gamma_1 + \delta_{i0}q\lambda) = 0$

For $j = 1, 2, \cdots, S_1 - 1, m = 1, 2, \cdots, S_2, n = 1, 2, \cdots, S_2 - 1$

$(l_{mn}^0 C_{(n-1)(N+1)+1}^{(j)} + l_{m(n+1)}^0 (n+1)\gamma_2 + l_{mn}^0 (j+1)\gamma_1 + l_{m(n+1)}^1 1\mu + H(s-j)l_{mn}^0 \beta$

$\sum_{d=1}^{S_2} l_{md}^0 l_{dn}^0 N\lambda_r + l_{mn}^0 \lambda + l_{mn}^1 C_{(n-1)(N+1)+2}^{(j)} + l_{m(n+1)}^1 (n+1)\gamma_2 + l_{mn}^1 (j+1)\gamma_1 + l_{m(n+1)}^2 2\mu +$

$H(s-j)l_{mn}^1 \beta, \cdots, \sum_{d=1}^{S_2} l_{md}^{N-2} l_{dn}^{N-2} N\lambda_r + l_{mn}^{N-2}\lambda + l_{mn}^{N-1} C_{(n-1)(N+1)+N}^{(j)} + l_{m(n+1)}^{N-1} (n+1)\gamma_2 + l_{mn}^{N-1}(j+1)\gamma_1 + l_{m(n+1)}^N N\mu +$

$H(s-j)l_{mn}^{N-1}\beta, \sum_{d=1}^{S_2} l_{md}^{N-1} l_{dn}^{N-1} N\lambda_r + l_{mn}^{N-1}\lambda + l_{mn}^N C_{n(N+1)}^{(j)} + l_{m(n+1)}^N (n+1)\gamma_2 + l_{mn}^N (j+1)\gamma_1$

$+ \delta_{ij}q\lambda + H(s-j)l_{mn}^N \beta) = 0$

For $j = 1, 2, \cdots, S_1 - 1, m = 1, 2, \cdots, S_2, n = S_2$

$(l_{mn}^0 C_{(n-1)(N+1)+1} + l_{m1}^0 1\gamma_2 + l_{mn}^0 (j+1)\gamma_1 + l_{m1}^1 1\mu + H(s-j)l_{mn}^0 \beta, \sum_{d=1}^{S_2} l_{md}^0 l_{dn}^0 N\lambda_r + l_{mn}^0 \lambda +$

$l_{mn}^1 C_{(n-1)(N+1)+2}^{(j)} + l_{m1}^1 1\gamma_2 + l_{mn}^1 (j+1)\gamma_1 + l_{m1}^2 2\mu + H(s-j)l_{mn}^1 \beta, \cdots, \sum_{d=1}^{S_2} l_{md}^{N-2} l_{dn}^{N-2} N\lambda_r +$

$l_{mn}^{N-2}\lambda + l_{mn}^{N-1} C_{(n-1)(N+1)+N} + l_{m1}^{N-1} 1\gamma_2 + l_{mn}^{N-1}(j+1)\gamma_1 + l_{m1}^N N\mu +$

$H(s-j)l_{mn}^{N-1}\beta, \sum_{d=1}^{S_2} l_{md}^{N-1} l_{dn}^{N-1}$

$N\lambda_r + l_{mn}^{N-1}\lambda + l_{mn}^N C_{n(N+1)} + l_{m1}^N 1\gamma_2 + l_{mn}^N (j+1)\gamma_1 + \delta_{ij}q\lambda + H(s-j)l_{mn}^N \beta) = 0$

For $j = S_1, m = 1, 2, \cdots, S_2, n = 1, 2, \cdots, S_2 - 1$

$(l_{mn}^0 C_{(n-1)(N+1)+1}^{(j)} + l_{m(n+1)}^0 (n+1)\gamma_2 + H(s-j)l_{mn}^0 \beta, \sum_{d=1}^{S_2} l_{md}^0 l_{dn}^0 N\lambda_r +$

$l_{mn}^0 \lambda + l_{mn}^1 C_{(n-1)(N+1)+2}^{(j)} + l_{m(n+1)}^1 (n+1)\gamma_2 + H(s-j)l_{mn}^1 \beta, \cdots, \sum_{d=1}^{S_2} l_{md}^{N-2} l_{dn}^{N-2} N\lambda_r + l_{mn}^{N-2}\lambda +$

$l_{mn}^{N-1} C_{(n-1)(N+1)+N}^{(j)} +$

$l_{m(n+1)}^{N-1} (n+1)\gamma_2 + H(s-j)l_{mn}^{N-1}\beta, \sum_{d=1}^{S_2} l_{md}^{N-1} l_{dn}^{N-1} N\lambda_r + l_{mn}^{N-1}\lambda + l_{mn}^N C_{n(N+1)}^{(j)} + l_{m(n+1)}^N (n+$

$1)\gamma_2 + \delta_{ij}q\lambda + H(s-j)l_{mn}^N \beta) = 0$

For $j = S_1, m = 1, 2, \cdots, S_2, n = S_2$

$$(l_{mn}^0 C_{(n-1)(N+1)+1} + l_{m1}^0 1\gamma_2 + H(s-j)l_{mn}^0 \beta, \sum_{d=1}^{S_2} l_{md}^0 l_{dn}^0 N\lambda_r + l_{mn}^0 \lambda + l_{mn}^1 C_{(n-1)(N+1)+2}^{(j)} +$$

$$l_{m1}^1 1\gamma_2 + H(s-j)l_{mn}^1 \beta, \cdots, \sum_{d=1}^{S_2} l_{md}^{N-2} l_{dn}^{N-2} N\lambda_r + l_{mn}^{N-2}\lambda + l_{mn}^{N-1} C_{(n-1)(N+1)+N} + l_{m1}^{N-1} 1\gamma_2 +$$

$$H(s-j)l_{mn}^{N-1}\beta, \sum_{d=1}^{S_2} l_{md}^{N-1} l_{dn}^{N-1} N\lambda_r + l_{mn}^{N-1}\lambda + l_{mn}^{N} C_{n(N+1)} + l_{m1}^{N} 1\gamma_2 + \delta_{ij} q\lambda + H(s-j)l_{mn}^{N}\beta) = 0$$

Equating the $(N+1)$-dimensional vector to zero vector we obtain a set of equations, after solving such equations, one can obtain the elements of R matrix. □

Theorem 4. *Due to the specific structure of B the vector Y can be determined by*

$$Y^{(i+K-1)} = Y^{(K-1)} R^i; i \geq 0 \qquad (2)$$

where R is the solution of

$$R^2 \mathbb{B}_{K0} + R\mathbb{B}_{K1} + \mathbb{B}_{01} = 0 \qquad (3)$$

and the vector $Y^{(i)}, i \geq 0$

$$Y^{(i)} = \begin{cases} \sigma X^{(0)} \prod_{j=i+1}^{K} \mathbb{B}_{j0}(-\mathbb{B}_{j-1}), 0 \leq i \leq K-1 \\ \sigma X^{(0)} R^{(i-K)}, i \geq K \end{cases} \qquad (4)$$

where

$$\sigma = [1 + X^{(0)} \sum_{i=0}^{K-1} \prod_{j=i+1}^{K} \mathbb{B}_{j0}(-\mathbb{B}_{j-1})\mathbf{e}]^{-1}. \qquad (5)$$

Proof. The sub vector $(Y^{(0)}, Y^{(1)}, \ldots, Y^{(K-1)})$ and the block partitioned matrix of B satisfies the following set of equations

$$\begin{aligned} Y^{(0)}\mathbb{B}_{00} + Y^{(1)}\mathbb{B}_{10} &= 0 \\ Y^{(i-1)}\mathbb{B}_{01} + Y^{(i)}\mathbb{B}_{i1} + Y^{(i+1)}\mathbb{B}_{(i+1)0} &= 0; 1 \leq i \leq K-1 \\ Y^{(K-2)}\mathbb{B}_{01} + Y^{(K-1)}(\mathbb{B}_{(K-1)1} + R\mathbb{B}_2) &= 0; \end{aligned} \qquad (6)$$

using Equation (6), we get,

$$Y^{(i)} = Y^{(i+1)} \mathbb{B}_{(i+1)0}(-B_i)^{-1}, 0 \leq i \leq K-1 \qquad (7)$$

where

$$B_i = \begin{cases} \mathbb{B}_{i0}, & i = 0 \\ (\mathbb{B}_{i1} - \mathbb{B}_{i0}(-B_{i-1})^{-1}\mathbb{B}_{01}), & 1 \leq i \leq K \end{cases}$$

Then

$$(Y^{(K)}, Y^{(K+1)}, Y^{(K+2)} \ldots) \begin{pmatrix} B_K & \mathbb{B}_{01} & 0 & 0 & 0 & \cdots \\ \mathbb{B}_{K0} & \mathbb{B}_{K1} & \mathbb{B}_{01} & 0 & 0 & \cdots \\ 0 & \mathbb{B}_{K0} & \mathbb{B}_{K1} & \mathbb{B}_{01} & 0 & \cdots \\ \vdots & \vdots & \vdots & \vdots & \vdots & \ddots \end{pmatrix} = 0 \qquad (8)$$

Assume,

$$\sigma = \sum_{i=K}^{\infty} Y^{(i)} \mathbf{e} \quad (9)$$

$$X^{(i)} = \sigma^{-1} Y^{(K+i)}, i \geq 0 \quad (10)$$

where X is also a 4-dimensional continuous time Markov chain such as Y. The similar partitions are also applicable to X. From (8) we get

$$Y^{(K)} B_N + Y^{(K+1)} \mathbb{B}_{K0} = 0$$
$$Y^{(K+i)} = Y^{(K+i-1)} R, i \geq 1$$

This can be written as

$$X^{(0)} B_N + X^{(1)} \mathbb{B}_{01} = 0$$
$$X^{(i)} = X^{(i-1)} R, i \geq 1$$

Since $\sum_{i=0}^{\infty} X^{(i)} \mathbf{e} = 1$, then

$$X^{(0)} (I - R)^{-1} \mathbf{e} = 1$$

Hence,

$$Y^{(i)} = \sigma X^{(0)} R^{(i-K)}, i \geq K \quad (11)$$

Again by (7) and (10),

$$Y^{(i)} = \sigma X^{(0)} \prod_{j=i+1}^{K} \mathbb{B}_{j0}(-B_{j-1}), 0 \leq i \leq K-1 \quad (12)$$

Therefore, combining (11) and (12), we get (4) and $X^{(0)}$ is the unique solution of the system

$$X^{(0)} (B_K + R \mathbb{B}_{K0}) = 0 \quad (13)$$
$$X^{(0)} (I - R)^{-1} \mathbf{e} = 1 \quad (14)$$

Since $\sum_{i=0}^{\infty} Y^{(i)} \mathbf{e} = 1$ and (13),

$$\sigma X^{(0)} \sum_{i=0}^{K-1} \prod_{j=i+1}^{K} \mathbb{B}_{j0}(-B_{j-1}) \mathbf{e} + \sigma X^{(0)} \sum_{K}^{\infty} R^{(i-K)} \mathbf{e} = 1$$

which gives (5). □

4. Waiting Time Analysis

The waiting time of a customer is defined as the time interval between the customer enters into the waiting hall and leaves the system after the service completion. Using the Laplace–Stieltjes transform (LST), we look at the waiting time of demand in the queue as well as the orbit independently for each node. Since the state space of the proposed model is infinite, the analytical work on finding the waiting time distribution is a difficult task to do so naturally. Thus, we restrict the orbit size to be finite say $L(L > K)$ to find the waiting time of a customer in the waiting hall and orbit. We denote W_p and W_o are continuous random variables to represent the waiting time distribution of a customer in the queue and orbit, respectively. The objective is to describe the probability that a customer has to wait, the distribution of the waiting time and nth order moments.

Waiting Time of a Demand in Queue

To enable waiting time distribution of W_p, we shall define some complementary variables. Suppose that the QIS is at state $(\wp_1, \wp_2, \wp_3, \wp_4), \wp_4 > 0$ at an arbitrary time t:

1. $W_p(\wp_1, \wp_2, \wp_3, \wp_4)$ is the time until chosen demand become satisfied.
2. LST of $W_p(\wp_1, \wp_2, \wp_3, \wp_4)$ is $^*W_p(\wp_1, \wp_2, \wp_3, \wp_4)(y)$, and we denote W_p by $^*W_p(y)$.
3. $^*W_p(y) = E\left[e^{yW_p}\right]$ LST of unconditional waiting time (UWT).
4. $^*W_p(\wp_1, \wp_2, \wp_3, \wp_4)(y) = E\left[e^{yW_p(\wp_1,\wp_2,\wp_3,\wp_4)}\right]$ LST of conditional waiting time (CWT).

Theorem 5. *The expected waiting time of a demand in the queue is defined by*

$$E[W_p] = \sum_{\wp_1=0}^{L} \sum_{\wp_2=0}^{S_1} \sum_{\wp_3=0}^{S_2} \sum_{\wp_4=0}^{N-1} \Upsilon^{(\wp_1,\wp_2,\wp_3,\wp_4)} E[W_p(\wp_1, \wp_2, \wp_3, \wp_4 + 1)] \qquad (15)$$

Proof. To obtain the CWT, we apply first step analysis as follows:
For $0 \leq \wp_1 \leq L, \wp_2 = 0, 1 \leq \wp_3 \leq S_2, 1 \leq \wp_4 \leq N$

$$\begin{aligned}
^*W_p(\wp_1, 0, \wp_3, \wp_4)(y) &= \frac{\bar{\delta}_{N\wp_4}\lambda}{a}\,^*W_p(\wp_1, 0, \wp_3, \wp_4 + 1)(y) + \\
&\quad \frac{\wp_3 \gamma_2}{a}\,^*W_p(\wp_1, 0, \wp_3 - 1, \wp_4)(y) + \frac{\beta}{a}\,^*W_p(\wp_1, Q, \wp_3, \wp_4)(y) + \\
&\quad \frac{\bar{\delta}_{N\wp_4}\wp_1 \lambda_r}{a}\,^*W_p(\wp_1 - 1, 0, \wp_3, \wp_4 + 1)(y) + \\
&\quad \frac{\bar{\delta}_{N\wp_4}\bar{\delta}_{L\wp_1} q\lambda}{a}\,^*W_p(\wp_1 + 1, 0, \wp_3, \wp_4)(y),
\end{aligned} \qquad (16)$$

where $a = (y + \bar{\delta}_{N\wp_4}\lambda + \wp_3 \gamma_2 + \beta + \bar{\delta}_{N\wp_4}\wp_1 \lambda_r + \bar{\delta}_{N\wp_4}\bar{\delta}_{L\wp_1} q\lambda)$.
For $0 \leq \wp_1 \leq L, 1 \leq \wp_2 \leq S_1, 1 \leq \wp_3 \leq S_2, 1 \leq \wp_4 \leq N$,

$$\begin{aligned}
^*W_p(\wp_1, \wp_2, \wp_3, \wp_4)(y) &= \frac{\bar{\delta}_{N\wp_4}\lambda}{b}\,^*W_p(\wp_1, \wp_2, \wp_3, \wp_4 + 1)(y) + \\
&\quad \frac{H(s - \wp_2)\beta}{b}\,^*W_p(\wp_1, \wp_2 + Q, \wp_3, \wp_4)(y) + \\
&\quad \frac{\wp_2 \gamma_1}{b}\,^*W_p(\wp_1, \wp_2 - 1, \wp_3, \wp_4)(y) + \frac{w\gamma_2}{b}\,^*W_p(\wp_1, \wp_2, \wp_3 - 1, \wp_4)(y) + \\
&\quad \frac{(\wp_4 - 1)\mu}{b}\,^*W_p(\wp_1, \wp_2 - 1, \wp_3 - 1, \wp_4 - 1)(y) + \\
&\quad \frac{\bar{\delta}_{N\wp_4}\wp_1 \lambda_r}{b}\,^*W_p(\wp_1 - 1, \wp_2, \wp_3, \wp_4 + 1)(y) + \frac{\bar{\delta}_{N\wp_1}\bar{\delta}_{L\wp_1} q\lambda}{b}\,^*W_p(\wp_1 + 1, \wp_2, \wp_3, \wp_4)(y) + \frac{\mu}{b}
\end{aligned} \qquad (17)$$

where, $b = (y + \bar{\delta}_{N\wp_4}\lambda + H(s - \wp_2)\beta + \wp_2 \gamma_1 + \wp_3 \gamma_2 + \wp_4 \mu + \bar{\delta}_{N\wp_4}\wp_1 \lambda_r + \bar{\delta}_{N\wp_4}\bar{\delta}_{L\wp_1} q\lambda)$.

Now, we differentiate the Equations (16) and (17) for $(n + 1)$ times and computing at $y = 0$, we have,
For $0 \leq \wp_1 \leq L, \wp_2 = 0, 1 \leq \wp_3 \leq S_2, 1 \leq \wp_4 \leq N$,

$$\begin{aligned}
E[W_p^{n+1}(\wp_1, 0, \wp_3, \wp_4)] &= \frac{\bar{\delta}_{N\wp_4}\lambda}{a} E[W_p^{n+1}(\wp_1, 0, \wp_3, \wp_4 + 1)] + \\
&\quad \frac{w\gamma_2}{b} E[W_p^{n+1}(\wp_1, \wp_2, \wp_3 - 1, \wp_4)] + \frac{\beta}{a} E[W_p^{n+1}(\wp_1, Q, \wp_3, \wp_4)] + \\
&\quad \frac{\bar{\delta}_{N\wp_4}\wp_1 \lambda_r}{a} E[W_p^{n+1}(\wp_1 - 1, 0, \wp_3, \wp_4 + 1)] + \\
&\quad \frac{\bar{\delta}_{N\wp_4}\bar{\delta}_{L\wp_1} q\lambda}{a} E[W_p^{n+1}(\wp_1 + 1, 0, \wp_3, \wp_4)] + (n + 1) E[W_p^{n+1}(\wp_1, \wp_2, \wp_3, \wp_4)],
\end{aligned} \qquad (18)$$

where $a = (y + \bar{\delta}_{N\wp_4}\lambda + \wp_3\gamma_2 + \beta + \bar{\delta}_{N\wp_4}\wp_1\lambda_r + \delta_{N\wp_4}\bar{\delta}_{L\wp_1}q\lambda)$.
For $0 \leq \wp_1 \leq L, 1 \leq \wp_2 \leq S_1, 1 \leq \wp_3 \leq S_2, 1 \leq \wp_4 \leq N$,

$$E[W_p^{n+1}(\wp_1, \wp_2, \wp_3, \wp_4)] = \frac{\bar{\delta}_{N\wp_4}\lambda}{b} E[W_p^{n+1}(\wp_1, \wp_2, \wp_3, \wp_4 + 1)] +$$
$$\frac{H(s-v)\beta}{b} E[W_p^{n+1}(u, v+Q, w, x)] + \frac{v\gamma_1}{b} E[W_p^{n+1}(\wp_1, \wp_2 - 1, \wp_3)] +$$
$$\frac{w\gamma_2}{b} E[W_p^{n+1}(\wp_1, \wp_2, \wp_3 - 1)] + \frac{(\wp_4 - 1)\mu}{b} E[W_p^{n+1}(\wp_1, \wp_2 - 1, \wp_3 - 1, \wp_4 - 1)] + \quad (19)$$
$$\frac{\bar{\delta}_{N\wp_4}\wp_1\lambda_r}{b} E[W_p^{n+1}(\wp_1 - 1, \wp_2, \wp_3, \wp_4 + 1)] +$$
$$\frac{\delta_{N\wp_4}\bar{\delta}_{L\wp_1}q\lambda}{b} E[W_p^{n+1}(\wp_1 + 1, \wp_2, \wp_3, \wp_4) + (n+1)E[W_p^{n+1}(\wp_1, \wp_2, \wp_3, \wp_4)]$$

where, $b = (y + \bar{\delta}_{N\wp_1}\lambda + H(s - \wp_2)\beta + \wp_2\gamma_1 + \wp_3\gamma_2 + \wp_4\mu + \bar{\delta}_{N\wp_4}\wp_1\lambda_r + \delta_{N\wp_4}\bar{\delta}_{L\wp_1}q\lambda)$.
The LST of UWT of a demand in the queue is given by

$$^*W_p(y) = 1 - \sum_{\wp_1=0}^{L} \sum_{\wp_2=0}^{S_1} \sum_{\wp_3=1}^{S_2} \sum_{\wp_4=0}^{N-1} \Upsilon^{(\wp_1, \wp_2, \wp_3, \wp_4)} + \quad (20)$$
$$\sum_{\wp_1=0}^{L} \sum_{\wp_2=0}^{S_1} \sum_{\wp_3=1}^{S_2} \sum_{\wp_4=0}^{N-1} \Upsilon^{(\wp_1, \wp_2, \wp_3, \wp_4)} {}^*W_p(\wp_1, \wp_2, \wp_3, \wp_4 + 1)(y)$$

The nth moments of UWT, using (20), is given by

$$E[W_p^n] = \delta_{0n} + (1 - \delta_{0n}) \sum_{\wp_1=0}^{L} \sum_{\wp_2=0}^{S_1} \sum_{\wp_3=1}^{S_2} \sum_{\wp_4=0}^{N-1} \Upsilon^{(\wp_1, \wp_2, \wp_3, \wp_4)} E[W_p^n(\wp_1, \wp_2, \wp_3, \wp_4 + 1)] \quad (21)$$

Using Equation (21) and substitute $n = 1$, we get the desired result as in (15). □

Corollary 1. *The expected waiting time of a orbital demand is defined by*

$$E[W_o] = \sum_{\wp_1=0}^{L-1} \sum_{\wp_2=0}^{S_1} \sum_{\wp_3=1}^{S_2} \sum_{\wp_4=0}^{N} \Upsilon^{(\wp_1, \wp_2, \wp_3, \wp_4)} E[W_o(\wp_1 + 1, \wp_2, \wp_3, \wp_4)] \quad (22)$$

5. System Characteristics

This section explores the necessary and sufficient system performance of the proposed model.

5.1. Mean Inventory Level for First Commodity

The mean inventory of the first commodity is defined as

$$\Delta_1 = \sum_{\wp_1=0}^{\infty} \sum_{\wp_2=1}^{S_1} \sum_{\wp_3=1}^{S_2} \sum_{\wp_4=0}^{N} \wp_2 \Upsilon^{(\wp_1, \wp_2, \wp_3, \wp_4)}$$

5.2. Mean Inventory Level for Second Commodity

The mean inventory of the second commodity is defined as

$$\Delta_2 = \sum_{\wp_1=0}^{\infty} \sum_{\wp_2=0}^{S_1} \sum_{\wp_3=1}^{S_2} \sum_{\wp_4=0}^{N} \wp_3 \Upsilon^{(\wp_1, \wp_2, \wp_3, \wp_4)}$$

5.3. Mean Reorder Rate for First Commodity

The mean reorder rate of first commodity is defined as

$$\Delta_3 = \sum_{\wp_1=0}^{\infty} \sum_{\wp_3=1}^{S_2} \sum_{\wp_4=1}^{N} \wp_4 \mu Y^{(\wp_1,s+1,\wp_3,\wp_4)} + \sum_{\wp_1=0}^{\infty} \sum_{\wp_3=1}^{S_2} \sum_{\wp_4=0}^{N} (s+1)\gamma_1 Y^{(\wp_1,s+1,\wp_3,\wp_4)}$$

5.4. Mean Reorder Rate for Second Commodity

The mean reorder rate of second commodity is defined as

$$\Delta_4 = \sum_{\wp_1=0}^{\infty} \sum_{\wp_2=1}^{S_1} \sum_{\wp_4=1}^{N} \wp_4 \mu Y^{(\wp_1,\wp_2,1,\wp_4)} + \sum_{\wp_1=0}^{\infty} \sum_{\wp_2=0}^{S_1} \sum_{\wp_4=0}^{N} \gamma_2 Y^{(\wp_1,\wp_2,1,\wp_4)}$$

5.5. Mean Perishable Rate for First Commodity

The mean perishable rate of first commodity is given by

$$\Delta_5 = \sum_{\wp_1=0}^{\infty} \sum_{\wp_2=1}^{S_1} \sum_{\wp_3=1}^{S_2} \sum_{\wp_4=0}^{N} \wp_2 \gamma_1 Y^{(\wp_1,\wp_2,\wp_3,\wp_4)}$$

5.6. Mean Perishable Rate for Second Commodity

The mean perishable rate of second commodity is given by

$$\Delta_6 = \sum_{\wp_1=0}^{\infty} \sum_{\wp_2=0}^{S_1} \sum_{\wp_3=1}^{S_2} \sum_{\wp_4=0}^{N} w \gamma_2 Y^{(\wp_1,\wp_2,\wp_3,\wp_4)}$$

5.7. Mean Number of Primary Customer Lost

The mean number of primary customer lost in the system is defined as

$$\Delta_{11} = \sum_{\wp_1=0}^{\infty} \sum_{\wp_2=0}^{S_1} \sum_{\wp_3=1}^{S_2} (1-q)\lambda Y^{(\wp_1,\wp_2,\wp_3,N)}$$

5.8. Overall Rate of Retrial

The expected overall rate of retrial of the orbit customer in the system is given by

$$\Delta_{12} = \sum_{\wp_1=1}^{\infty} \sum_{\wp_2=0}^{S_1} \sum_{\wp_3=1}^{S_2} \sum_{\wp_4=0}^{N} \wp_1 \lambda_r Y^{(\wp_1,\wp_2,\wp_3,\wp_4)}$$

5.9. Successful Rate of Retrial

The expected successful rate of retrial of the orbit customer in the system is given by

$$\Delta_{13} = \sum_{\wp_1=1}^{\infty} \sum_{\wp_2=0}^{S_1} \sum_{\wp_3=1}^{S_2} \sum_{\wp_4=0}^{N-1} \wp_1 \lambda_r Y^{(\wp_1,\wp_2,\wp_3,\wp_4)}$$

5.10. Fraction of Successful Rate of Retrial

The expected fraction of successful rate of retrial of the orbit customer in the system is given by

$$\Delta_{14} = \frac{\Delta_{13}}{\Delta_{12}}$$

6. Cost Analysis and Numerical Illustrations

The mean total cost (MTC) is given by

$$MTC = (C_{h1} * \Delta_1) + (C_{h2} * \Delta_2) + (C_{s1} * \Delta_3) + (C_{s2} * \Delta_4) + (C_{p1} * \Delta_5) + (C_{p2} * \Delta_6) + (C_{w1} * E[W_p]) + (C_{w2} * E[W_o]) + (C_b * \Delta_{11}).$$

To compute the MTC per unit time, the following costs are considered

C_{h1} = The holding cost of commodity-I per unit item per unit time t.
C_{h2} = The holding cost of commodity-II per unit item per unit time t.
C_{s1} = Set up cost of commodity-I per run.
C_{s2} = Set up cost of commodity-II per run.
C_{p1} = Perishable cost of commodity-I per unit item per unit time.
C_{p2} = Perishable cost of commodity-II per unit item per unit time.
C_{w1} = Waiting cost of a customer in the queue per unit time t.
C_{w2} = Waiting cost of a orbiting customer per unit time t.
C_b = Cost due to loss of customers per unit time.

Numerical Illustrations

Numerical analysis is an applied mathematics technique that allows staggeringly large amount of data to be processed and analyzed for trends, thereby aiding in forming conclusions. This is done nowadays in a computer environment, providing massive increases in speed and usefulness of calculations. This numerical work is carried out by fixing the parameters and cost values which are involved in the proposed mathematical model. Due to the nature of the proposed model, the determination of the parameter values assumed randomly under the satisfaction of the stability condition. The numerical value of stationary probability vector whose sum gives one. After such verification's (stability condition and normalising condition), we proceed the numerical works. To perform these numerical illustrations, we fix the parameter values as $C_{h1} = 0.001, C_{h2} = 0.01, s = 4, C_{s1} = 4.1, C_{s2} = 3.5, C_{p1} = 2, C_{p2} = 1.8, C_{w1} = 1.6, C_{w2} = 1.1, C_b = 3.6, N = 5, \lambda = 3.6, \beta = 0.93, \gamma_1 = 0.21, \gamma_2 = 0.2, \lambda_r = 4.46, q = 0.5, \mu = 25.5$. The proposed study is only valid if the assumed parameters must satisfy the stability condition and normalising condition.

Example 1. *From Table 1, for varying S_1, the economical capacity $S_1(S_1^*)$ is determined at each S_2 and is identified by the expected total cost which is column minimum with underline. Similarly, the economical capacity $S_2(S_2^*)$ is determined at each S_1 and is identified by the expected total cost which is row minimum and is given in bold form. When we increase the number of first commodity, the MTC holds the both decreasing and increasing properly. It shows that the MTC is not monotonic regarding the change in S_1. This will produce the minimum MTC at some S_1. Similarly, the same monotonic property holds for the second commodity. Therefore, we also obtain the minimum MTC for S_2. Since both S_1 and S_2 holds the minimum MTC, the proposed model produces the convex point at some (S_1, S_2) locally. Finally the local minimum expected total cost is determined at S_1^* and S_2^* where the row minimum and column minimum matches, so that the cost will be identified with both underlined and in bold script. Using Table 1, $S_1^* = 25, S_2^* = 7, MTC^* = 8.991429$.*

The graphical illustration of the optimum MTC is shown in Figure 1. If the values of S_1 increases, then the value of MTC have both increasing and increasing quality. It means that S_1 will give the optimum MTC. When we work on the S_2 with the similar manner as S_1, this also gives the minimum MTC. Finally, both S_1 and S_2 are increased together, we obtain the convex at some point of this proposed mathematical model. This convexity also helps us to determine the fixation of parameters and cost values of the model. Under the obtained convex result, we perform the further numerical work.

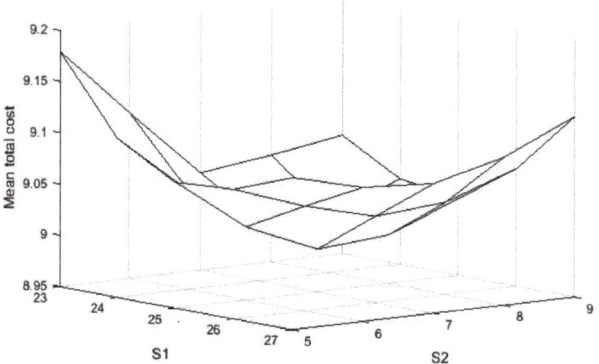

Figure 1. S_1 vs. S_2 on MTC.

Table 1. Mean total cost rate as a function of S_1 and S_2.

S_1/S_2	5	6	7	8	9
23	9.179124	9.105358	**9.072545**	9.076211	9.098163
24	9.111433	9.046548	**9.021119**	9.051946	9.080716
25	9.044719	9.008342	**8.991429**	9.033913	9.076386
26	9.054109	9.008624	**8.996934**	9.039765	9.094405
27	9.065483	9.032995	**9.024460**	9.064498	9.126085

Example 2. *From the exploration of Figures 2–6, the responses of $\Delta_3, \Delta_9, \Delta_{11}, \Delta_{13}$ and MTC under the subject of queue capacity and primary arrival rate are explained below.*

- When we increase λ, the number of arrival in the system as well as sales of first commodity are increased. So the number of customer and number of sold commodity are directly proportional to each other, the commodity-I reaches the reorder point as soon. Therefore, the mean reorder rate increases according to the increase of λ. Likewise, the queue size N also cause the increase of the mean reorder rate of the commodity-I. It is shown in Figure 2.
- As the increase of arrival rate, we observe that the number of customer in the waiting hall will increase from the Figure 3. The expansion of queue size N also cause the increase of number of customer in the waiting hall. Δ_9 monotonically increases as both N and λ increase.
- However, as we predicted, the customer lost rate will increase when λ increases due to the restriction of finite waiting hall size. Once the waiting hall starts overflow, the new arrivals at that moment either goes to an orbit or they considered as lost under the Bernoulli's schedule. It is shown in Figure 4. However, this can be controlled when we expand the queue size.
- As λ increases, the mean successful rate of retrial decrease. This is because the primary customer occupies the places in the waiting hall. When the orbit customer tries to enter into the waiting hall and finds that there will be very less seats available, the number of customer enters into the waiting hall will decrease. Similarly the same situation will happen when the queue size is expanded. This can be seen from Figure 5.
- According to occurrence of the arrival rate, the total cost of the system changed with the direct proportion. Since every customer requires an item, we should maintain the sufficient stock level according to the occurrence of customer in the waiting hall. So that the holding cost of the required items also increased accordingly. Thus the mean total cost value of the system increased as we increase both λ and N. It can be seen in Figure 6.

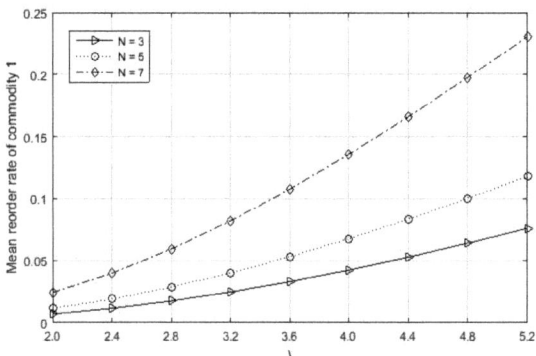

Figure 2. λ vs. N on Δ_3.

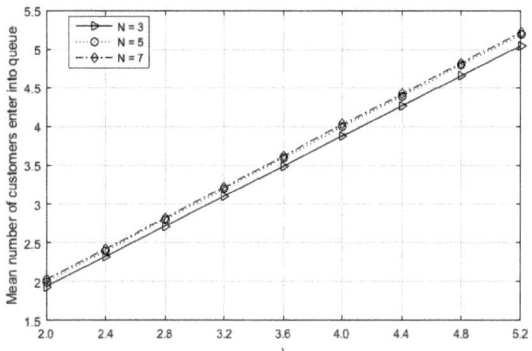

Figure 3. λ vs. N on Δ_9.

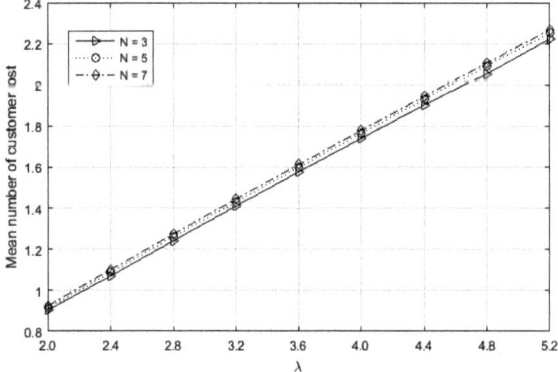

Figure 4. λ vs. N on Δ_{11}.

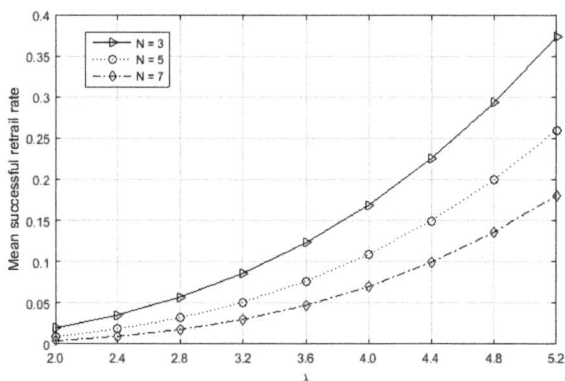

Figure 5. λ vs. N on Δ_{13}.

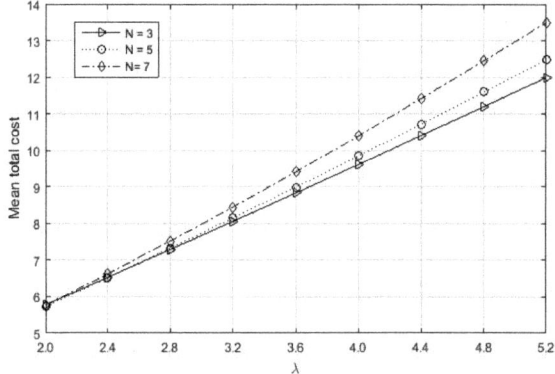

Figure 6. λ vs. N on MTC.

Example 3. *Table 2 shows the different characteristics of MTC and Δ_{11} with varying combinations Q, s, S_2 and q with set up cost dependent lead time for commodity 1.*

- *Basically the lead time of any receiving order depends upon the ordering quantity. Normally the lead time of an order decreases with increasing the order quantity. In addition, the set up cost per order may increase if the transportation cost increases with Q.*
- *But as β increases, MTC decreases due to high sensitive nature of lead time. β increases means that the average time of an ordered item to reach the system will be reduced. According to this fact the unnecessary delay of receiving the ordered items can be avoided. Relaxation of this delay time helps to reduce the MTC.*
- *As S_2 increases, MTC has both decreasing and increasing property under the given random environmental conditions. It possess the optimal MTC. As per the changes due to S_2, the C_{s2} will play the same role as S_2 on MTC.*
- *If we increase q, then the customer decides to leave the system without entering into the orbit. This leads to increase of mean customer lost. At the same time, it helps to reduce the mean total cost whenever it increases.*

Table 2. Mean total cost vs. Customer lost.

N	S_2	C_{s2}	$Q=18, s=2, q=0.5$ $\beta=1, C_{s1}=6$		$Q=18, s=2, q=0.75$ $\beta=1, C_{s1}=6$		$Q=16, s=4, q=0.5$ $\beta=0.75, C_{s1}=5.5$		$Q=16, s=4, q=0.75$ $\beta=0.75, C_{s1}=5.5$	
			MTC	Δ_{11}	MTC	Δ_{11}	MTC	Δ_{11}	MTC	Δ_{11}
2	2	3	8.7536	1.5519	7.5094	0.7532	9.0950	1.5882	8.0698	0.7743
	3	3.5	8.6646	1.5519	7.1303	0.7532	8.7645	1.5882	7.3157	0.7743
	4	4	8.7541	1.5519	7.0804	0.7532	8.7776	1.5882	7.1392	0.7743
4	2	3	10.3059	1.5886	9.9867	0.7724	12.5089	1.6150	13.0528	0.7870
	3	3.5	9.2156	1.5886	8.1644	0.7724	10.0960	1.6150	9.5449	0.7870
	4	4	9.1308	1.5886	7.8589	0.7724	9.7125	1.6150	8.7821	0.7870

Example 4. *From Table 3, Under the given cost structure and some parameters associated with service and any kind of arrivals, the comparisons of results of queue dependent with non-queue dependent service policies, the merits of the proposed model are studied and stated below:*

- *As μ increases, Δ_{11} and Δ_{14} increases. This is because the average service time per customer is reduced. So the overflowing of a customer in the waiting hall has been controlled by the server. Thus the attempt of an retrial customer to enter into the waiting hall becomes successful. In the mean time the customer lost is also controlled.*
- *At any given rate of primary arrival and retrial, the total cost curve is either decreased or convex under the given range of μ with non-queue dependent service time but it is lower at any given μ with queue dependent service time. Since the queue dependent service rate will reduce the average service time per customer, the optimal MTC of the proposed model is attained in the queue dependent service time cases only.*
- *As we expected $E[W_p], E[W_o], \Delta_{14}$ and MTC all increases as λ increases. The number of incoming arrival into the system generally increases the expected waiting time of a primary as well as retrial customer, MTC and customer lost when it increases.*
- *Further all these measures are much lower at queue dependent service time except Δ_{14}.*
- *As μ increases, MTC, $E[W_p]$ and $E[W_o]$ decreases and Δ_{11} and Δ_{14} decreases. This is due to the decreases of the mean service while increasing μ which reduces the number of customers in the waiting hall.*
- *We can notice that Δ_{14} decreases and others decrease on increasing the parameter vale of λ. Because the number of customers in the waiting hall increases if λ is increased.*
- *On comparing, the measures $E[W_p], E[W_o]$ and MTC under the parameter variation, Queue dependent service time is more effective than the non-queue dependent service time. For the others, non-queue dependent service time is effective.*

Table 3. Queue dependent service time Vs Non queue dependent service time.

λ	λ_r	μ	Queue Dependent Service Time					Non Queue Dependent Service Time				
			$E[W_p]$	$E[W_o]$	Δ_{14}	MTC	Δ_{11}	$E[W_p]$	$E[W_o]$	Δ_{14}	MTC	Δ_{11}
3.2	2.2	5	0.0325	0.0545	0.9283	7.7969	1.2069	0.0785	0.2167	0.8799	11.2858	0.7562
		10	0.0269	0.0431	0.9569	8.1573	1.2751	0.0349	0.0656	0.8950	8.9257	1.0759
		15	0.0256	0.0404	0.9689	8.6277	1.2930	0.0288	0.0497	0.9171	8.9840	1.1803
		20	0.0250	0.0393	0.9756	9.1269	1.3008	0.0268	0.0447	0.9326	9.3530	1.2259
	3.2	5	0.0224	0.0356	0.9273	7.6068	1.2671	0.0549	0.1433	0.8766	10.7980	0.7821
		10	0.0185	0.0280	0.9564	7.7515	1.3431	0.0241	0.0433	0.8925	8.4550	1.1201
		15	0.0176	0.0263	0.9685	7.9831	1.3634	0.0198	0.0326	0.9151	8.314	1.2347
		20	0.0172	0.0255	0.9753	8.2393	1.3722	0.0185	0.0292	0.9308	8.4485	1.2862
	4.2	5	0.0171	0.0263	0.9272	7.5383	1.3009	0.0422	0.1066	0.8749	10.5441	0.7975
		10	0.0141	0.0207	0.9564	7.6030	1.3823	0.0184	0.0323	0.8916	8.2765	1.1440
		15	0.0134	0.0194	0.9685	7.7398	1.4044	0.0151	0.0242	0.9144	8.0709	1.2644
		20	0.0131	0.0188	0.9752	7.8979	1.4140	0.0141	0.0217	0.9301	8.1125	1.3198

Table 3. Cont.

λ	λ_r	μ	Queue Dependent Service Time					Non Queue Dependent Service Time				
			$E[W_p]$	$E[W_o]$	Δ_{14}	MTC	Δ_{11}	$E[W_p]$	$E[W_o]$	Δ_{14}	MTC	Δ_{11}
3.6	2.2	5	0.0398	0.0716	0.9291	8.5298	1.3357	0.1020	0.3253	0.8859	12.8286	0.8124
		10	0.0324	0.0557	0.9572	9.0293	1.4180	0.0435	0.0889	0.8972	10.0259	1.1803
		15	0.0308	0.0521	0.9690	9.6480	1.4392	0.0351	0.0653	0.9181	10.0798	1.3060
		20	0.0301	0.0505	0.9756	10.2973	1.4484	0.0325	0.0581	0.9331	10.5559	1.3608
	3.2	5	0.0275	0.0467	0.9279	8.3045	1.4044	0.0718	0.2146	0.8828	12.2445	0.8386
		10	0.0224	0.0362	0.9566	8.5384	1.4962	0.0302	0.0586	0.8946	9.4455	1.2293
		15	0.0212	0.0338	0.9686	8.8598	1.5204	0.0243	0.0429	0.9159	9.2578	1.3674
		20	0.0207	0.0328	0.9753	9.2066	1.5308	0.0224	0.0380	0.9312	9.4438	1.4295
	4.2	5	0.0210	0.0345	0.9276	8.2237	1.4435	0.0554	0.1594	0.8810	11.9324	0.8546
		10	0.0170	0.0267	0.9565	8.3560	1.5418	0.0231	0.0437	0.8935	9.2145	1.2560
		15	0.0162	0.0249	0.9686	8.5547	1.5683	0.0185	0.0318	0.9150	8.9471	1.4011
		20	0.0158	0.0241	0.9752	8.7743	1.5796	0.0171	0.0281	0.9304	9.0161	1.4680

7. Conclusions

This paper analyses a single server two commodity inventory system with queue-dependent services for finite queue and an optional retrial facility. We applied a Neuts matrix geometric approach to resolve the infinitesimal generator matrix and further we derived a stability condition and the steady state probability vector of the system. Upon computing the necessary system characteristics of the system, we obtained the mean total cost of the considered model. This model explored the queue dependent and non-queue dependent service polices in a two commodity retrial inventory system. The minimal optimum mean total cost is obtained for the queue-dependent service policy. Indeed, this policy also helped to reduce the rate of customer lost and his/her expected waiting time. Apart from that the retrial customers successful retrial rate also increased as we expected. As for the consequences, the queue dependent service is more profitable when the major product attached with its complimentary. As a result of the numerical survey, maximum stock levels of both products are economically controlled. Furthermore, the fixed stocking capacities of inventory and the preference level of customer entering into the orbit, the system may control the size of queue with the ordering quantity which corresponds to lead time and set up cost. However, the comparison of queue dependent and non-queue dependent service polices will give a great impact on the inventory management. The readers can easily understand these different service polices which one is adoptable to bring out the profitable business. This model will be extended into a multi server service system in the future. In such an environment, one can analyse the impact of customer lost and their waiting time with the single server model. This analysis also helps to the business people to develop their business.

Author Contributions: Conceptualization, K.J.; data curation, K.J.; formal analysis, K.J., M.A.R. and S.A.; funding acquisition, G.P.J. and C.S.; investigation, N.A. and D.J.; methodology, M.A.R., S.S. and S.A.; project administration, G.P.J. and C.S.; software, M.A.R. and C.S.; supervision, C.S.; validation, G.P.J. and D.J.; visualization, S.S. and N.A.; writing—review and editing, G.P.J. All authors have read and agreed to the published version of the manuscript.

Funding: This work was supported by the Institute of Information and Communications Technology Planning and Evaluation (IITP) Grant by the Korean Government through MSIT (Development of User identity certification and management technology for self-sovereign identity applications.) under Grant 2021-0-00565.

Institutional Review Board Statement: Not applicable.

Informed Consent Statement: Not applicable.

Data Availability Statement: Not applicable.

Acknowledgments: Anbazhagan and Amutha would like to thank RUSA Phase 2.0 (F 24-51/2014-U), DST-FIST (SR/FIST/MS-I/2018/17), DST-PURSE 2nd Phase programme (SR/PURSE Phase 2/38), Govt. of India.

Conflicts of Interest: The authors declare no conflict of interest.

Notations

0	Null matrix of an appropriate order
e	A column vector of the each entries are one with an appropriate dimension
I	An identity matrix of an appropriate order
δ_{ij}	$\begin{cases} 1, & \text{if } j = i, \\ 0, & \text{otherwise} \end{cases}$
$H(z)$	$\begin{cases} 1, & \text{if } z \geq 0, \\ 0, & \text{otherwise} \end{cases}$
$\bar{\delta}_{ij}$	$1 - \delta_{ij}$

References

1. Abolnikov, L.; Dshalalow, J.H.; Dukhovny, A. On stochastic processes in a multilevel control bulk queueing system. *Stoch. Anal. Appl.* **1992**, *10*, 155–179. [CrossRef]
2. Dshalalow, J.H. Queueing systems with state-dependent parameters. In *Frontiers in Queueing: Models and Applications in Science and Engineering*; CRC Press: Boca Raton, FL, USA, 1995; pp. 61–116.
3. Fakinos, D. The G/G/1 (LCFS/P) queue with service depending on queue size. *Eur. J. Oper. Res.* **1992**, *59*, 303–307. [CrossRef]
4. Harris, C.M. Some results for bulk-arrival queue with state-dependent service times. *Manag. Sci.* **1970**, *16*, 313–326. [CrossRef]
5. Ivnitskiy, V.A. A stationary regime of a queueing system with parameters dependent on the queue length and with non-ordinary flow. *Eng. Cyb.* **1974**, *13*, 85–90.
6. Sigman, K.; Simchi-Lev, D. Light traffic heuristic for an M/G/1 queue with limited inventory. *Ann. Oper. Res.* **1992**, *40*, 371–380. [CrossRef]
7. Schwarz, M.; Sauer, C.; Daduna, H.; Kulik, R.; Szekli, R. M/M/1 queueing systems with inventory. *Queueing Syst.* **2006**, *54*, 55–78. [CrossRef]
8. Berman, O.; Kaplan, E.H.; Shimshak, D.G. Deterministic Approximations for Inventory Management at Service Facilities. *IIE Trans.* **1993**, *25*, 98–104. [CrossRef]
9. Jeganathan, K.; Reiyas, M.A.; Lakshmi, K.P.; Saravanan, S. Two server Markovian inventory systems with server interruptions: Heterogeneous vs. homogeneous servers. *Math. Comput. Simul.* **2019**, *155*, 177–200. [CrossRef]
10. Gebhard, R.F. A queueing process with bilevel hysteretic service-rate control. *Naval Res. Logist. Quart* **1967**, *14*, 55–68. [CrossRef]
11. Sangeetha, N.; Sivakumar, B. Optimal service rates of a perishable inventory system with service facility. *Int. J. Math. Oper. Res.* **2020**, *16*, 515–550. [CrossRef]
12. Choi, D.I.; Knessl, C.; Tier, C. A queueing system with queue length dependent service times, with applications to cell discarding in ATM networks *J. Appl. Math. Stoch. Anal.* **1999**, *12*, 35–62. [CrossRef]
13. Jeganathan, K.; Reiyas, M.A.; Padmasekaran, S.; Lakshmanan, K. An $M/E_k/1/N$ Queueing-Inventory System with Two Service Rates Based on Queue Lengths. *Int. J. Appl. Comput. Math.* **2017**, *3*, 357–386. [CrossRef]
14. Keerthana, M.; Sivakumar, B.; Manuel, P. An Inventory system with postponed and renewal demands. *Int. J. Syst. Sci. Oper. Logist.* **2021**, *9*, 180–198. [CrossRef]
15. Krishnamoorthy, A.; Jose, K.P. Comparison of inventory systems with service, positive lead-time, loss, and retrial of demands. *J. Appl. Math. Stoch. Anal.* **2007**, *2007*, 037848. [CrossRef]
16. Amirthakodi, M.; Sivakumar, B. An inventory system with service facility and feedback customers. *Int. J. Ind. Syst. Eng.* **2019**, *33*, 374–411.
17. Shajin, D.; Krishnamoorthy, A. On a queueing-inventory system with impatient customers, advanced reservation, cancellation, overbooking and common life time. *Oper. Res.* **2021**, *21*, 1229–1253. [CrossRef]
18. Anilkumar, M.P.; Jose, K.P. A Geo/Geo/1 inventory priority queue with self induced interruption. *Int. J. Appl. Comput. Math.* **2020**, *6*, 1–14. [CrossRef]
19. Jose, K.P.; Anilkumar, M.P. Stochastic Optimization of Local Purchase Quantities in a Geo/Geo/1 Production Inventory System. *Int. Conf. Distrib. Comput. Commun. Netw.* **2020**, *1337*, 206–220.
20. Jose, K.P.; Reshmi, P.S. A production inventory model with deteriorating items and retrial demands. *OPSEARCH* **2020**, *58*, 71–82. [CrossRef]
21. Reshmi, P.S.; Jose, K.P. A MAP/PH/1 Perishable Inventory System with Dependent Retrial Loss. *Int. J. Appl. Comput. Math.* **2020**, *6*, 1–11. [CrossRef]
22. Manuel, P.; Sivakumar, B.; Arivarignan, G. A perishable inventory system with service facilities, MAP arrivals and PH-service times. *J. Syst. Sci. Syst. Eng.* **2007**, *16*, 62–73. [CrossRef]
23. Manuel, P.; Sivakumar, B.; Arivarignan, G. A perishable inventory system with service facilities and retrial customers. *Comput. Ind. Eng.* **2008**, *54*, 484–501. [CrossRef]

24. Kathiresan, J.; Kokila, M.; Anbazhagan, N. Markovian Inventory System with Different Types of Service and Negative Customers. *Int. J. Pure Appl. Math.* **2018**, *120*, 7685–7699.
25. Artalejo, J.R.; Krishnamoorthy, A.; Lopez-Herrero, M.J. Numerical analysis of (s,S) inventory systems with repeated attempts. *Ann. Oper. Res.* **2006**, *141*, 67–83. [CrossRef]
26. Ushakumari, P.V. On (s,S) inventory system with random lead time and repeated demands. *J. Appl. Math. Stoch. Anal.* **2006**, *2006*, 081508. [CrossRef]
27. Veinott, F.V.; Wagner, H.M. Computing optimal (s, S) in inventory policies. *Manag. Sci.* **1965**, *11*, 525–552. [CrossRef]
28. Wagner, H.M.; Hagan, M.O.; Lundh, B. An empirical study of exactly and approximately optimal inventory policies. *Manag. Sci.* **1965**, *11*, 690–723. [CrossRef]
29. Alscher, T.; Schneider, H. Resolving a multi-item inventory problem with unknown costs. *Eng. Costs Prod. Econ.* **1982**, *6*, 9–15. [CrossRef]
30. Kalpakam, S.; Arivarignan, G. A coordinated multi commodity (s, S) inventory system. *Math. Comput. Model.* **1993**, *18*, 69–73. [CrossRef]
31. Anbazhagan, N.; Arivarignan, G. Analysis of two-commodity Markovian inventory system with lead time. *Korean J. Comput. Appl. Math.* **2001**, *8*, 427–438. [CrossRef]
32. Anbazhagan, N.; Arivarignan, G. Two-Commodity Inventory system with Individual and Joint Ordering Policies. *Int. J. Manag. Syst.* **2003**, *19*, 129–144.
33. Anbazhagan, N.; Arivarignan, G. Two-Commodity continuous review inventory system with coordinated reorder policy. *Int. J. Inf. Manag. Sci.* **2000**, *11*, 19–30.
34. Sivakumar, B.; Anbazhagan, N.; Arivarignan, G. A two-commodity perishable inventory system. *ORiON* **2005**, *21*, 157–172. [CrossRef]
35. Sivakumar, B. Two-commodity inventory system (TCIS) with retrial demand. *Eur. J. Oper. Res.* **2008**, *18*, 70–83. [CrossRef]
36. Yadavalli, V.S.S.; Adetunji, O.; Sivakumar, B.; Arivarignan, G. Two-commodity perishable inventory system with bulk demand for one commodity. *South Afr. J. Ind. Eng.* **2010**, *21*, 137–155. [CrossRef]
37. Anbazhagan, N.; Elango, C.; Kumaresan, V. Analysis of two-commodity inventory system with compliment for bulk demand. *Math. Model. Appl. Comput.* **2011**, *2*, 155–168.
38. Gomathi, D.; Jeganathan, K.; Anbazhagan, N. Two-Commodity Inventory System for Base-Stock Policy with Service Facility. *Glob. J. Sci. Front. Res. Math. Decis. Sci.* **2012**, *12*, 69–79.
39. Anbazhagan, N.; Jeganathan, K. Two-Commodity Markovian Inventory System with Compliment and Retrial Demand. *Br. J. Math. Comput. Sci.* **2013**, *3*, 115–134. [CrossRef]

Article

Equation for Egg Volume Calculation Based on Smart's Model

Yu-Kai Weng [1], Cheng-Han Li [1], Chia-Chun Lai [1] and Ching-Wei Cheng [2,*]

[1] Department of Bio-Industrial Mechatronics Engineering, National Chung Hsing University, Taichung 40227, Taiwan; ykweng@dragon.nchu.edu.tw (Y.-K.W.); cghan@smail.nchu.edu.tw (C.-H.L.); s39911050@gmail.com (C.-C.L.)

[2] Department of Computer Science and Information Engineering, National Taichung University of Science and Technology, Taichung 40401, Taiwan

* Correspondence: cwcheng@nutc.edu.tw; Tel.: +886-4-2219-5795

Abstract: In the egg industry, it is necessary to estimate the egg volume accurately when estimating egg quality or freshness in a non-destructive method. Egg volume and weight could obtain egg density and could be used to determine egg freshness. Therefore, the egg geometric must be obtained first to establish a volume equation with a geometric shape. This research proposes an innovative idea to derive the mathematical model and volume equation of egg shape, calculate its volume, and verify the accuracy of the mathematical equation proposed using the volume displacement method. Using the proposed equation, the minimum error between the calculated egg volume) and actual egg volume is 0.01%. The maximum volume error does not exceed 2%. The egg shape equation can accurately draw the outer contour curve of the egg by the half-length of the maximum long axis and maximum breadth of the short axis, and the distance from the center point of the egg to the maximum breadth (x_m).

Keywords: egg shape equation; displacement of volume method; egg volume

MSC: 14-11

1. Introduction

Egg geometry is often used in food research, agricultural engineering, biological sciences, mechanical engineering, architecture, and so on. This involves research on the classification and ecological morphology of poultry populations [1,2], predicting the weight relationship of chicks after egg hatching [3], and egg hatchability [4,5]. An egg can withstand external forces exerted during grading and transportation. Therefore, the mechanical properties of simulated eggshells are usually analyzed [6], and the best protection method is proposed. Eggshell shapes have also been used to design underwater installations, containers [7], and buildings [8]. Therefore, mathematical equations for egg shape, egg volume, and related parameters are required to perform related research and in applications.

Egg shape can be divided into oval, pyriform, circular, and elliptical forms [1,9]. The shape classification of eggs is mainly based on the ratio of the maximum breadth (B) to the maximum length (L) of the egg multiplied by 100, which is called the shape index (SI) [10,11]. The SI is used to judge whether the egg is approximately round or oval (i.e., degree of shape). Mathematically speaking, eggs are prolate spheroids [5], which approximate the volume of ellipsoids. Therefore, for egg volume calculation, the deformation equation with the volume of ellipsoids as the base is often used for calculation, as shown in Equation (1) [5,10].

$$V = k_v \frac{4}{3}\pi \left(\frac{L}{2}\right)\left(\frac{B}{2}\right)^2 \approx k_v LB^2. \qquad (1)$$

k_v is the compensating coefficient, B is the maximum width equatorial, and L is the maximum egg length. Eggs shape of various breeds is different, and the k_v value of the volume calculation Equation (1) will also change accordingly [12]. The commonly used $k_v = 0.5236$ is a standard ellipsoid. To increase the accuracy of the egg volume calculation, Narushin (1997) set $k_v = 0.496$ [13]. A follow-up study by Narushin (2005) proposed a more accurate correction equation for egg volume, $k_v = (0.6057 - 0.0018B)$, and the coefficient of determination reaching 0.958, as shown in Equation (2) [14]. It was subsequently proved that k_v is not a constant but a function of the linear parameters of the egg shape (that is, the maximum length L and maximum breadth B of the egg) [14–16]. Subsequently, Narushin (2021) again proposed that $k_v = 0.5136$ and Equation (2) can be more accurate and closer to the actual egg volume when calculations are performed [15].

$$V = \left(0.5202LB^2 - 0.4065\right). \tag{2}$$

In 1948, the German mathematician Fritz Hügelschäffer used two non-concentric circles to construct a deformed ellipse to form an egg-shaped curve [8,17]. Preston (1953) multiplied the basic ellipse equation by a cubic polynomial so that the deformed ellipse equation can describe a variety of egg shapes [18]. Smart (1969) found the tangent angle (taper angle) of the edge of the egg-shaped contour and introduced the short axis of the ellipse equation to describe the outer shape of the egg [19]. Narushin et al. (2020) applied Hügelschäffer's egg-shaped contour model to calculate the volume of an egg [20].

This study aims to derive a simplified equation that can quickly, directly, and accurately calculate the egg volume (V) based on the egg-shaped contour equation proposed by Smart (1969) and use the displacement of volume method to calculate volume. The egg volume calculated by the equation established in this paper is compared to the actual measured volume. This helps compare the theoretical equation and actual measurement error value as well as the accuracy of the theoretical equation. Further verifications were made by comparing the present results to the previously reported egg volume equations. The egg volume equation established in this study can be used as one of the reference methods for quick and accurate egg volume calculation. In addition, the egg-shaped contour equation was drawn and compared with the actual shooting shape, which further confirmed the reliability of the egg-shaped contour equation drawn in this research.

2. Materials and Methods

2.1. Egg Sample

The theoretical equation for egg volume proposed in this paper uses 47 eggs and measures the respective volume of each egg by the displacement of volume method. It is used to verify the difference between the egg volumes found using the theoretical equation and the actual experimental measurement.

2.2. Egg Dimension Parameter and Volume Measurement

For egg dimensions, a digital caliper is used to measure the maximum long (L) and maximum short (B) axes of eggs and the distance from the long axis half-length to the plane of the maximum breadth of eggs (x_m). The resolution of the digital caliper can reach 0.01 mm.

The actual volume of the egg is measured according to the volume displacement method, with the following practical guideline steps, as shown in Figure 1. Place the egg to be measured in a 500 mL graduated empty cylinder, and add water up to the 400 mL mark. Remove the egg from the measuring cylinder, reset the precision electronic balance (HG-2000, Shinko Denshi Co. Ltd., Tokyo, Japan) to zero, and then add the water in the measuring cylinder to 400 mL. As the density of water approaches 1 g/cm^3, the weight of the added water corresponds to the volume of the eggs. Removing the eggs from the graduated cylinder requires preventing the water in the graduated cylinder from overflowing. Therefore, let the water droplets adhering to the egg's surface remain in the measuring cylinder before removing the egg for higher precision. The water droplet adhering to the surface of the eggshell has a significant influence on the measurement of egg volume.

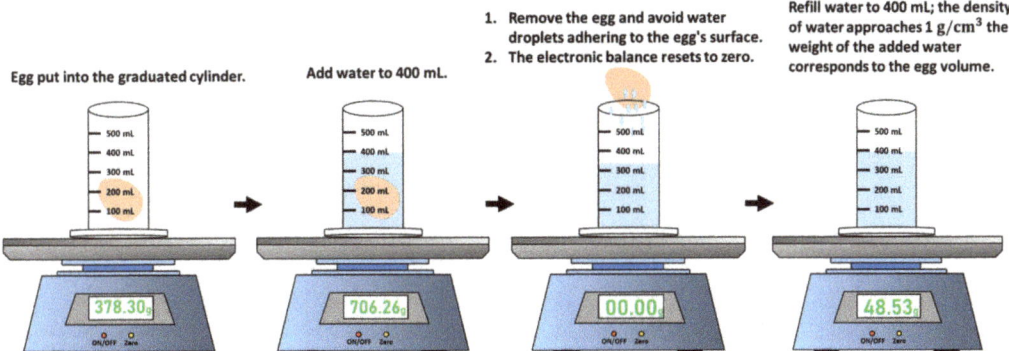

Figure 1. Flow chart of egg volume measurement.

2.3. Egg Volume Equation

Preston (1953) multiplied the basic ellipse equation by a polynomial to modify the ellipse shape to achieve a variety of egg shape equations for describing the geometric shapes of various bird eggs [18]. The follow-up work by Smart (1969) also used the ellipse equation as the basis to measure the tangent angle of the outer edge of the egg and introduced the ellipse equation to describe the shape of the egg [19], as follows:

$$\frac{x^2}{a^2} + \frac{y^2}{(b + x \tan \theta)^2} = 1. \tag{3}$$

Köller [21] multiplied the y^2 term by $t(x)$ based on the ellipse Equation:

$$\frac{x^2}{a^2} + \frac{y^2}{b^2} \cdot t(x) = 1, \tag{4}$$

where a and b are the long and short axes of the ellipse, respectively, as shown in Figure 2. $t(x) = 1 + kx$ is a simple function, which converts the ellipse into an egg-shaped curve. When the value of k is large, the y-axis of the ellipse is not symmetric. When the value of k is small, it will be closer to the standard ellipse shape, as shown in Figure 2b. $k = 0$ corresponds to the standard elliptic curve.

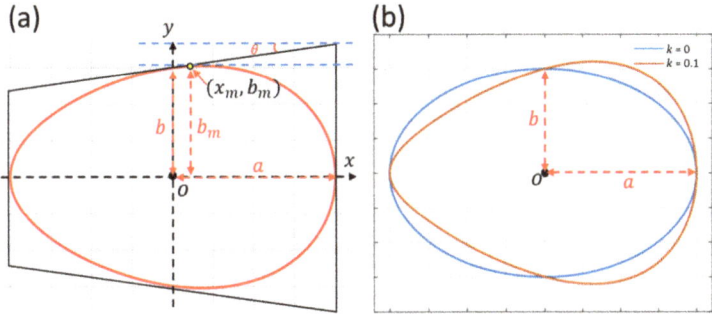

Figure 2. (**a**) Smart (1969) egg-shaped curve parameter location diagram. (**b**) Köller's egg-shaped curve diagram of the change of the function k value in Equation (4).

We have found that when $(b + x\tan\theta)^{-2}$ in Smart (1969) equation is converted by power series, $(1 + 2kx)$ can be obtained, and the conversion process is as follows:

Equation (5) can be obtained by expanding Equation (3) to power series as

$$\frac{x^2}{a^2} + \frac{y^2}{b^2}\left[\left(1 - 2\frac{\tan\theta}{b}x\right) + \frac{-2(-3)}{2!}\left(\frac{\tan\theta}{b}x\right)^2 + \cdots\right] = 1. \tag{5}$$

When $x = x_m$, Equation (6) can be obtained by neglecting the higher-order terms in Equation (5) as

$$\frac{x^2}{a^2} + \frac{y^2}{b^2}\left(1 - 2\frac{\tan\theta}{b}x\right) = 1 \tag{6}$$

and

$$\frac{x^2}{a^2} + \frac{y^2}{b^2}(1 + kx) = 1, \tag{7}$$

where $k = -\frac{2\tan\theta}{b}$.

From the above process, it can be seen that the egg-shaped contour equations of Köller (2000) and Smart (1969) are consistent. To calculate the egg volume, we use the Smart (1969) egg contour equation and find the egg volume from the equation by rotating the integral around the long axis. The process is as follows:

$$V = \int_{-a}^{a} \pi y^2 dx \tag{8}$$

$$= \int_{-a}^{a} \pi\left(1 - \frac{x^2}{a^2}\right)(b + x\tan\theta)^2 dx \tag{9}$$

$$= \frac{\pi}{a^2}\left[\frac{4}{3}a^3b^2 + \frac{4}{15}a^5\tan^2\theta\right]. \tag{10}$$

Finally, the egg volume equation is obtained:

$$V = \pi\left(\frac{4}{3}ab^2 + \frac{4}{15}a^3\tan^2\theta\right), \tag{11}$$

where a is the half-length of the long axis of the egg, b is the half-length of the short-axis breadth of point O in the center of the egg, and θ is the egg taper angle, as shown in Figure 2.

The short-axis breadth of the egg center point of the long axis ($2b$) and edge taper angle (θ) are not easy to measure. In this study, the half-length of the long axis of the egg (a), maximum breadth of the short axis of the egg (b_m), and distance from the long axis half-length to the plane of maximum breadth (x_m) are known conditions. The correct egg shape can be obtained by calculating the theoretical values b and $\tan\theta$ of the egg shape parameters.

Equation (12) can be obtained by sorting out Equation (6) as follows:

$$y^2 = \left(1 - \frac{x^2}{a^2}\right)\frac{b^2}{\left(1 - \frac{2}{b}\cdot x\cdot\tan\theta\right)}. \tag{12}$$

Equation (12) is differentiated such that:

$$y\frac{dy}{dx} = \frac{-x}{a^2}\frac{b^2}{\left(1 - \frac{2}{b}\cdot x\cdot\tan\theta\right)} + \frac{1}{b}\tan\theta\cdot\left(1 - \frac{x^2}{a^2}\right)\cdot\frac{b^2}{\left(1 - \frac{2}{b}\cdot x\cdot\tan\theta\right)^2}. \tag{13}$$

When $\frac{dy}{dx} = 0$ is the horizontal tangent of the maximum width of the egg, $x = x_m$, the result is as follows:

$$-x_m + \frac{a^2}{b}\tan\left(1-\left(\frac{x_m}{a}\right)^2\right)\cdot\frac{1}{1-\frac{x_m}{b}\cdot\tan\theta} = 0, \quad (14)$$

According to the actual measurements in Table 1, putting the x_m and egg length of half-length ($\frac{L}{2}$) average into $1 - \left(\frac{x_m}{a}\right)^2 = 0.99$ can be obtained. The short-axis breadth half-length (b) and egg maximum breadth half-length ($\frac{B}{2}$) are close, so we use the maximum breadth of half-length directly for calculation; alos obtaining $1 - \frac{x_m}{b}\cdot\tan\theta = 0.99$.

Table 1. Egg shape geometry parameters.

	Minimum Value	Maximum Value	Average	Standard Deviation	Coefficient of Variation (%)
Egg length (L) (mm)	54.11	63.01	58.75	2.31	3.93
Egg maximum breadth (B) (mm)	41.50	47.13	44.63	1.19	2.66
Weight (g)	52.05	74.40	65.54	5.17	7.88
Shape index	70.97	83.81	76.04	2.46	3.24
x_m (mm)	0.9	3.31	2.17	0.51	23.53
Taper angle (degree)	0.53	7.44	3.88	1.46	37.56
Actual egg volume (cm^2)	48.32	69.42	60.53	4.91	8.11

Therefore assume when, $1 - \left(\frac{x_m}{a}\right)^2 \cong 1$ and $1 - \frac{x_m}{b}\cdot\tan\theta \cong 1$, then:

$$x_m \cong \frac{a^2}{b}\tan\theta. \quad (15)$$

From Figure 2a, the following can be obtained:

$$\frac{b_m - b}{x_m} \cong \tan\theta. \quad (16)$$

From Equations (15) and (16), the short-axis breadth half-length (b) of point O in the egg can be obtained as follows (see Figure 2a):

$$b = \frac{a^2 b_m}{(x_m^2 + a^2)}. \quad (17)$$

By substituting Equations (15) and (17) into Equation (11), the final egg volume can be obtained as:

$$V = \pi a^3 \left(\frac{b_m}{x_m^2 + a^2}\right)^2 \cdot \left(\frac{4}{3}a^2 + \frac{4}{15}x_m^2\right), \quad (18)$$

where $b_m = \frac{B}{2}$ and $a = \frac{L}{2}$.

3. Results and Discussion

This paper uses 47 eggs to verify the egg volume equation (Equations (11) and (18)) established based on Smart's equation (Equation (3)). The actual measured parameter results of 47 eggs are shown in Table 1. The most significant variation of egg shape parameters is the actual volume of the egg and the coefficient of variation of x_m, which are 23.53% and 8.11%, respectively. Egg maximum breadth has the least variability.

The egg volume Equation (11) is introduced by Equations (15) and (17) to obtain the final egg theoretical volume Equation (18). The angle of taper (θ) of the egg and half the breadth of the center point (b) of the egg can be described by Equations (15)–(17). To confirm the accuracy of the calculated taper angle (θ) and the short-axis breadth (b) of the egg center point, we selected the egg SIs as large: 81.08, medium: 76.11, small: 70.97. The profile of actual eggs of different specifications was compared with the calculated curve profile, as shown in Figure 3 The volume percent errors of the three eggs were 0.32%, −0.58%, and 0.33%, respectively, within ±1%. MATLAB was used to draw the egg-shaped contour curve of Equation (3). b and $\tan\theta$ in Equation (3) were calculated using Equations (15)–(17). Actual pictures of the eggs were added. This helps to check whether the theoretical equation egg contour, taper angle (θ) and half of the short axis width of the egg center point (b) are consistent with the actual egg contour. The results are shown in Figure 3. The calculated egg taper angle (θ) and half of the short-axis width of the center point (b) are almost consistent with the actual egg contour.

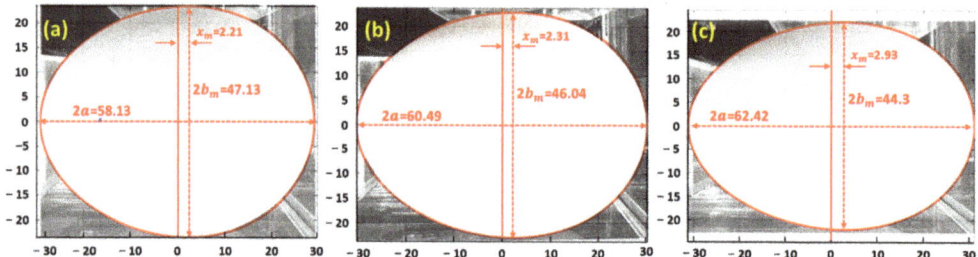

Figure 3. The actual egg shape and egg-shaped curve drawn by Equations (3) and (15)–(17). The SI (a) is 81.08; (b) 76.11; (c) 70.97.

The egg-shaped contour curve is converted into descriptions by a, b_m, and x_m from b and $\tan\theta$ in Equation (3). Therefore, the egg-shaped contour generated by the mathematical equation can approximate the real egg-shaped contour curve. However, according to the research and investigation in this study, there are still errors in the contour curves drawn by Equation (3) and Equations (15)–(17). In addition, because eggs are biological samples, they may be extruded deformed during production, resulting in an uneven shape.

For egg volume calculation, Equation (1) was used in the past. The k_v value was mainly set to 0.5236 for the elliptical volume equation. To make it more accurate, Narushin (2021) found that for $k_v = 0.5163$, calculation error variation can be reduced to a range of 0–3.7%, with an average of 1.1% [15]. Additionally, from the volume of the Hügelschäffer egg-shaped body and ellipsoids volume Equation (1) $k_v = 0.5236$, another Equation (2) for calculating the egg-shaped volume is obtained [15]. Equations (2) and (19) calculate the egg-shaped volume, with no significant difference between the two values obtained [15].

$$V = 0.5163 L B^2. \tag{19}$$

In this study, the actual volume of eggs was measured by the volume displacement method. The shape parameters of 47 eggs were substituted into the theoretical egg volume Equation (18), ellipse Equation (1), and egg volume Equations (2) and (19) proposed by Narushin (2021). Errors between the egg volume calculated by the four equations and the actual measured egg volume were compared. The root mean square (rms) error values obtained were 0.47, 0.96, 0.43, and 0.63, respectively. This indicates that our theoretical equation and that proposed by Narushin (2021) ($k_v = 0.5163$) can calculate relatively accurate egg volumes. With $k_v = 0.5236$ ellipse volume equation, the rms error of egg volume calculated is only 0.96. However, because eggs are not in a standard ellipse shape, the error between the egg volume calculated by the ellipse volume Equation (1) ($k_v = 0.5236$) and the actual measured volume will be more significant.

We use the actual measured volume of the egg and the calculated volume of the equation to express the percentage error, which is a standard used to measure the accuracy of the measurement results. It is calculated as the estimate minus the actual value divided by the actual value, multiplied by 100%. It is used to express the accuracy of the volume converted by its equation.

Figure 4a shows that from Narushin (2021) Equation (19), and theoretical calculation Equation (18) in this study, the calculated volume percentage errors are mainly distributed within ±2%. Therefore, from the volume obtained by the theoretical volume equation in this study and that measured by the volume of displacement method, the volume percentage errors of ±0.5%, ±1%, ±1.5%, and ±2% correspond to 22 eggs, 16 eggs, 7 eggs, and 2 eggs, respectively. Therefore, the standard deviation is 0.47%. The volume percentage errors calculated by Equation (19) of Narushin (2021) are ±0.5%, ±1%, ±1.5%, and 2%, corresponding to 22 eggs, 17 eggs, 7 eggs, and 1 egg, respectively. The standard deviation is 0.4%. For the theoretical volume equation (i.e., Equation (18)) in this study, the maximum volume error of the 47 eggs is 1.91%, minimum volume error is 0.01%. Narushin's equation (i.e., Equation (19)) maximum error is 1.59%, and the minimum volume error is 0.05%. The resulting data point distribution and volume calculation accuracy are roughly the same for our theoretical volume Equation (18) and Narushin's Equation (19). However, the maximum volume percentage error of Equation (18) proposed in this paper is 1.91%, which may be caused by the fact that Equation (5) is expanded by the power series method, and the higher-order terms of Equation (6) are omitted for the convenience of calculation. Another reason may be that $\tan\theta$ and b are approximate values obtained by converting Equations (15)–(17) after measuring a, b_m, and x_m, resulting in a slight error in using the theoretical volume Equation (18) in this study. The percentage of error in the volume calculation of the ellipse volume equation is mostly greater than 1.5%, the maximum volume error can reach 3%, and the standard deviation is 0.74%, while the egg volume calculated by Narushin's Equation (2) is mostly evenly distributed between 0 and 3%, as shown in Figure 4b. Figure 4a shows that the egg volume obtained by this theoretical Equation (18) and Narushin's (2021) Equation (19) is quite accurate. Therefore, both the theoretical equation and Equation (19) can accurately and quickly estimate the egg volume.

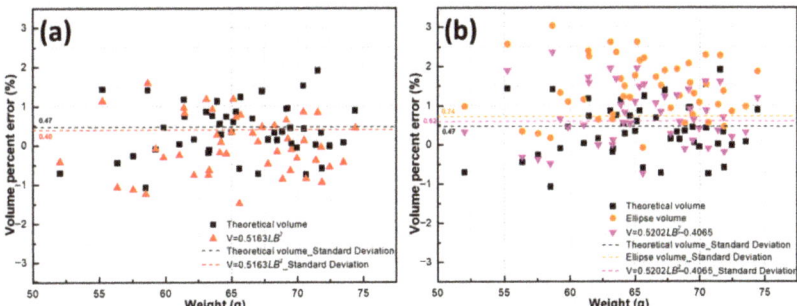

Figure 4. The volume percentage error corresponds to the actual weight of the egg. (**a**) theoretical volume Equations (18) and (19); (**b**) theoretical volume Equation (18), elliptical volume equation, Equation (2).

The theoretical egg volume Equation (18) established in this study is derived from Smart's egg-shaped curve Equation (3), with the parameters shown in Figure 2a including the taper angle (θ) and short-axis width (b) of the egg's geometric center point. The egg volume equation was verified using 47 eggs, and the egg volume could be accurately estimated when the SI of the egg ranged from 83.81 to 70.97. The research equation in this paper can be applied to analytical software such as the finite element method in the future to model eggshell or egg-shaped structures. Furthermore, it helps in improving the accuracy of the analysis in engineering or agriculture for analyzing parameters such as the mechanical strength of egg-shaped structures.

4. Conclusions

This study used the egg-shaped curve equation proposed by Smart (1969) [19] to extend the calculation equation of egg volume as:

$$V = \pi a^3 \left(\frac{b_m}{x_m^2 + a^2} \right)^2 \cdot \left(\frac{4}{3}a^2 + \frac{4}{15}x_m^2 \right). \tag{20}$$

The egg volume equation proposed in this study only requires the measurement of the half maximum length of the long axis (a), half maximum breadth of the short axis (b_m), and distance from the center of the egg to the maximum breadth of the short axis (x_m). Thus, it can quickly estimate the volume of the egg. It was verified that the egg volume with a SI of 70.97 to 83.81, the error range of the calculated theoretical volume and actual volume is within ±2%.

Another contribution of this study is that we do not need to measure the egg's outer taper angle (θ) and breadth (b) of the center point. Instead, it can be converted from x_m, b_m, and a using Equations (15)–(17) established in this work. By obtaining the length distance between θ and b, Smart's (1969) egg-shaped curve Equation (3) can be directly used to draw the egg-shaped curve that is almost the same as the actual egg shape. In addition, the equation proposed in this paper can be applied to the fields of agriculture or food to analyze and simulate the curve modeling of eggs, which will be of great help and can effectively improve the simulation accuracy.

Author Contributions: Y.-K.W., C.-H.L., C.-C.L. and C.-W.C. conceived and designed the experiments; Y.-K.W., C.-H.L., C.-C.L. and C.-W.C. performed the experiments; Y.-K.W., C.-H.L., C.-C.L. and C.-W.C. analyzed the data; Y.-K.W., C.-H.L., C.-C.L. and C.-W.C. wrote the paper; Y.-K.W., C.-H.L., C.-C.L. and C.-W.C. reviewed and edited the paper. All authors have read and agreed to the published version of the manuscript.

Funding: This research received no external funding.

Institutional Review Board Statement: Not applicable.

Informed Consent Statement: Not applicable.

Conflicts of Interest: The authors declare no conflict of interest.

References

1. Narushin, V.G.; Romanov, M.N.; Griffin, D.K. Egg and math: Introducing a universal formula for egg shape. *Ann. N. Y. Acad. Sci.* **2021**, *1505*, 169–177. [CrossRef] [PubMed]
2. Stoddard, M.C.; Yong, E.H.; Akkaynak, D.; Sheard, C.; Tobias, J.A.; Mahadevan, L. Avian egg shape: Form, function, and evolution. *Science* **2017**, *356*, 1249–1254. [CrossRef] [PubMed]
3. Narushin, V.G.; Romanov, M.N.; Bogatyr, V.P. Ap–animal production technology: Relationship between pre-incubation egg parameters and chick weight after hatching in layer breeds. *Biosyst. Eng.* **2002**, *83*, 373–381. [CrossRef]
4. Narushin, V.; Romanov, M. Physical characteristics of chicken eggs in relation to their hatchability and chick weight. In Proceedings of the ASAE Annual Meeting American Society of Agricultural and Biological Engineers, Chicago, IL, USA, 28–31 July 2002. [CrossRef]
5. Maclaury, D.W.; Insko, W.M.; Begin, J.J.; Johnson, T.H. Shape index versus hatchability of fertile eggs of Japanese quail (*Coturnix coturnix japonica*). *Poult. Sci.* **1973**, *52*, 558–562. [CrossRef]
6. Haiyan, S.; Fang, W.; Jianguo, Z.; Yinong, Z.; Shugang, Y. Finite element analysis of mechanical characteristics of dropped eggs based on fluid-solid coupling theory. *Shock. Vib.* **2017**, *2017*, 4512497. [CrossRef]
7. Zhang, J.; Wang, M.; Wang, W.; Tang, W. Buckling of egg-shaped shells subjected to external pressure. *Thin Walled Struct.* **2017**, *113*, 122–128. [CrossRef]
8. Petrovic, M.; Obradovic, M.; Mijailovic, R. Suitability analysis of Hügelschäffer's egg curve application in architectural structures' geometry. In Proceedings of the International Conference on Engineering Graphics and Design, ICEGD JASSY, Iași, Romania, 1 June 2011.
9. Nishiyama, Y. The mathematics of egg shape. *Int. J. Pure Appl. Math.* **2012**, *78*, 679–689.
10. Romanoff, A.L.; Romanoff, A.J. *The Avian Egg*; John Wiley & Sons: New York, NY, USA, 1949.
11. Brunson, C.C.; Godfrey, G.F. The relationship of egg shape, egg weight, specific gravity and 21-day incubation weight-loss to hatchability of broad-breasted bronze turkey eggs. *Poult. Sci.* **1953**, *32*, 846–849. [CrossRef]
12. Hoyt, D.F. Practical methods of estimating volume and fresh weight of bird eggs. *Auk* **1979**, *96*, 73–77. [CrossRef]
13. Narushin, V.G. The Avian Egg: Geometrical Description and Calculation of Parameters. *J. Agric. Eng. Res.* **1997**, *68*, 201–205. [CrossRef]
14. Narushin, V.G. Egg geometry calculation using the measurements of length and breadth. *Poult. Sci.* **2005**, *84*, 482–484. [CrossRef] [PubMed]
15. Narushin, V.G.; Romanov, M.N.; Griffin, D.K. Non-destructive measurement of chicken egg characteristics: Improved formulae for calculating egg volume and surface area. *Biosyst. Eng.* **2021**, *201*, 42–49. [CrossRef]

16. Narushin, V.G.; Lu, G.; Cugley, J.; Romanov, M.N.; Griffin, D.K. A 2-D imaging-assisted geometrical transformation method for non-destructive evaluation of the volume and surface area of avian eggs. *Food Control* **2020**, *112*, 107112. [CrossRef]
17. Petrovic, M.; Obradovic, M. The Complement of the Hügelschäffer's construction of the Egg Curve. In *BILTEN, Proceedings of 25th National and 2nd International Scientific Conference moNGeometrija, Beograd, Serbia, 24–27 June 2010*; Faculty of Architecture in Belgrade: Belgrade, Serbia; Serbian Society for Geometry and Graphics (SUGIG): Belgrade, Serbia, 2010; pp. 520–530.
18. Preston, F. The shapes of birds' eggs. *Auk* **1953**, *70*, 160–182. [CrossRef]
19. Smart, I.H. The method of transformed co-ordinates applied to the deformations produced by the walls of a tubular viscus on a contained body: The avian egg as a model system. *J. Anat.* **1969**, *104 (Pt 3)*, 507–518.
20. Narushin, V.G.; Romanov, M.N.; Lu, G.; Cugley, J.; Griffin, D.K. Digital imaging assisted geometry of chicken eggs using Hügelschäffer's model. *Biosyst. Eng.* **2020**, *197*, 45–55. [CrossRef]
21. Köller, J. Egg Curves and Ovals. 2000. Available online: http://www.mathematische-basteleien.de/eggcurves.htm (accessed on 13 April 2022).

Article

Reservoir Characterization and Productivity Forecast Based on Knowledge Interaction Neural Network

Yunqi Jiang [1], Huaqing Zhang [2], Kai Zhang [1,3,*], Jian Wang [2,*], Shiti Cui [4], Jianfa Han [4], Liming Zhang [1] and Jun Yao [1]

1. School of Petroleum Engineering, China University of Petroleum East China—Qingdao Campus, Qingdao 266580, China; jiangyunqi@s.upc.edu.cn (Y.J.); zhangliming@upc.edu.cn (L.Z.); rcogfr_upc@126.com (J.Y.)
2. College of Sciences, China University of Petroleum East China—Qingdao Campus, Qingdao 266580, China; zhh@upc.edu.cn
3. School of Science, Qingdao University of Technology, Qingdao 266580, China
4. Exploration and Development Research Institute of PetroChina Tarim Oilfield Company, Korla 841000, China; cuishiti-tlm@petrochina.com.cn (S.C.); hanjf-tlm@petrochina.com.cn (J.H.)
* Correspondence: zhangkai@upc.edu.cn (K.Z.); wangjiannl@upc.edu.cn (J.W.)

Abstract: The reservoir characterization aims to provide the analysis and quantification of the injection-production relationship, which is the fundamental work for production management. The connectivity between injectors and producers is dominated by geological properties, especially permeability. However, the permeability parameters are very heterogenous in oil reservoirs, and expensive to collect by well logging. The commercial simulators enable to get accurate simulation but require sufficient geological properties and consume excessive computation resources. In contrast, the data-driven models (physical models and machine learning models) are developed on the observed dynamic data, such as the rate and pressure data of the injectors and producers, constructing the connectivity relationship and forecasting the productivity by a series of nonlinear mappings or the control of specific physical principles. While, due to the "black box" feature of machine learning approaches, and the constraints and assumptions of physical models, the data-driven methods often face the challenges of poor interpretability and generalizability and the limited application scopes. To solve these issues, integrating the physical principle of the waterflooding process (material balance equation) with an artificial neural network (ANN), a knowledge interaction neural network (KINN) is proposed. KINN consists of three transparent modules with explicit physical significance, and different modules are joined together via the material balance equation and work cooperatively to approximate the waterflooding process. In addition, a gate function is proposed to distinguish the dominant flowing channels from weak connecting ones by their sparsity, and thus the inter-well connectivity can be indicated directly by the model parameters. Combining the strong nonlinear mapping ability with the guidance of physical knowledge, the interpretability of KINN is fully enhanced, and the prediction accuracy on the well productivity is improved. The effectiveness of KINN is proved by comparing its performance with the canonical ANN, on the inter-well connectivity analysis and productivity forecast tasks of three synthetic reservoir experiments. Meanwhile, the robustness of KINN is revealed by the sensitivity analysis on measurement noises and wells shut-in cases.

Keywords: reservoir characterization; productivity prediction; machine learning; knowledge interaction neural network; embedded model

MSC: 37M10

1. Introduction

In a waterflooding reservoir, the subsurface flow is invisible and influenced by the heterogenous geophysical properties, such as the porosity, compressibility, and especially permeability. As an important content of reservoir characterization, the inter-well connectivity analysis aims to quantify the contribution from an injection well to a production well, so as to reflect the relative permeability strength of the flowing channels. Based on the analysis of inter-well connectivity, the oil field enables the adjustment of the hydrodynamics, such as water shutoff, profile control, and well pattern optimization [1–5]. Commercial simulators can predict production and characterize reservoirs accurately. However, geological information is essential for the model development by simulators, which is difficult and expensive to obtain in practice. In addition, the simulation for complex reservoirs is pretty time-consuming, usually taking several hours or even days [6–8]. For most oil fields, the injection and production rates are often available, on which the simplified reservoir simulation models can be established.

Generally, characterization approaches for the inter-well connecting relationship can be classified into three categories:

(1) Statistical and signal processing methods. These methods are based on statistical analysis and signal processing techniques. Spearman rank correlations [9] were presented to measure the relationship between injectors and producers, while the authors also pointed out that this method was not completely robust and nor were the influence factors fully understood. Tian and Horne [10] proposed a modified Pearson's correlation coefficient method to capture the influence from injectors to producers, showing a more precise inter-well characterization ability than the Spearman rank correlation method. Wavelet analysis was adopted to infer the connecting relationships [11], revealing new insights into the inter-well connectivity analysis. Some novel signal processing approaches, like cross-correlation, spectral analysis, magnitude-squared coherence, and periodogram were also applied to infer the inter-well communication [12]. Although these methods have high computational efficiency by analyzing the correlation and mapping relationships between injection and production signals, they are not established on the physical laws of waterflooding. Therefore, the robustness of these methods is hard to be guaranteed, and these models are often combined together or served as complemental methods to reduce the uncertainty [9,11,12].

(2) Machine learning methods. These methods usually quantify inter-well connectivity through model parameters. Panda and Chopra [13] proposed a related approach, using artificial neural networks (ANNs) to estimate the interactions between injectors and producers, while the geological and geostatistical data were required to determine the model parameters. Artun [14] evaluated the inter-well connectivity via the products of weight matrices in ANNs, providing a new perception of the inter-well connectivity analysis. While Jensen [15] commented that Artun's ANNs model can't reflect the physical mechanism of the waterflooding process, so it was unclear for ANN's performance on the field disturbances (e.g., temporary shut-in or completion). Even though these machine learning (ML) methods are capable of inferring the inter-well connectivity via their strong nonlinear mapping abilities, they are considered as "black box" models, for their weakness in physical interpretation, limiting their practical applications.

(3) Physical models. These models are established on the physical process and derived from corresponding physical laws. Yousef et al. [16] used the capacitance resistance model (CRM or CRMIP) to reflect the connectivity and time lag between injector and producer pairs, which derived from the material balance equation and linear productivity model. Compared with the multiple linear regression (MLR) model [17], it considered the effects of compressibility and transmissibility. Based on the work of CRM, a series of models were introduced, such as the capacitance resistance model for the producer control volume (CRMP) [18] and the capacitance resistance model for a tank or field control volume (CRMT) [19] and. Different from CRMIP, CRMT and CRMP assign each drainage volume or each tank to a constant time delay, making the production signals react synchronously with the signals of all injectors. In addition, Sayarpour [20] proposed a CRM-blocks model, dividing the drainage volume into several blocks to calculate the flow rate. However, the complexity of the CRM-blocks model is inevitably increased, since it simulates the flowing process block by block, limiting its applications in complex cases. To infer the inter-well connectivity from multilayers, the multilayer CRM (ML-CRM) [21] was proposed, by modeling the injected fluids flowing across different layers with the help of production logging tools (PLT). Besides, Zhao et al. [22] presented an inter-well numerical simulation model (INSIM) to approximate the performance of waterflooding reservoirs. INSIM is derived from the mass material balance and front tracking equations, which consist of inter-well control units considering transmissibility and control pore volume. Moreover, considering more complex cases, such as the conversion from a producer to an injector, INSIM-FT [23] was designed; INSIM-FT-3D was proposed to simulate the flow in three dimensions with gravity [24]. Recently, INSIM-FPT [25] has been presented to reveal the inter-well connectivity via history matching data instead of the reservoir petrophysical properties. These physical models have clear physical assumptions and can be applied in other aspects, such as production optimization [26–29].

With the high computing efficiency, strong fitting ability, and excellent prediction accuracy, ML models have been widely utilized in the oil industry [28,30–36]. As an important kind of ML approach, ANNs enable to learn the complex mapping from the input variables to the desired output variables, by adjusting the weights of the internal synapses [37,38]. Nonetheless, the lack of trustworthiness is a big challenge for the further development of ANNs in real applications, since these models seldom consider physical knowledge and the model parameters do not have physical implications.

To improve the model reliability and generalizability, many researchers have tried to associate physical knowledge with ANNs in practical applications. A physics-guided neural network (PGNN) [39] was proposed to simulate the lake's temperature, using the results of physical models and leveraging physical rules to improve the scientific consistency of neural networks. In [40], physics-informed neural networks (PINN) were proposed, integrating the partial differential equation (PDE), boundary condition (BC), and initial condition (IC) into the objective function. PINN was improved in [41], which learned parameters and constitutive relationships in subsurface flow by minimizing the PDE (Darcy or Richards equation) residual. To reduce the sensitivity of initial parameters and too many iterations of primary PINN, a modified genetic algorithm is adopted in the model's optimization scheme, effectively resolving the linear elastic problems in the solid mechanics [42]. Moreover, a theory-guided neural network (TgNN) [43] was proposed to simulate the subsurface flow, which considered not only PDE, BC, and IC, but also expert knowledge and engineering controls. Csiszár et al. [44] combined continuous logic rules and multicriteria decision operators with networks, providing the semantic meaning for the values of the activation functions. In a social recommendation system, a Knowledge-aware Coupled Graph Neural Network (KCGN) is proposed, coupling the inter-dependent knowledge between items and users with the machine learning framework, which shows great performance on several real-world datasets [45]. On the one hand, most interpretable methods associate the physical knowledge with the objective function in the form of regularization terms, thus enforcing the neural networks to make predictions within certain physical constraints. However, penalty terms inevitably lead to the increase of hyperparameters, which are difficult to determine and negative to the model stability. On the other hand, the results of ML models are more consistent with the physical reality to a certain extent, yet they have a weak effect on strengthening the physical meaning of model parameters. Therefore, the "black box" can only be opened when ANNs have deeper physical interaction from the parameter level. Still, to the best of our knowledge, in terms of inter-well connectivity analysis problems, there are few studies focused on integrating the physical information with ANNs, not to mention assigning the knowledge to model parameters.

The goal of this study is to improve the accuracy and stableness of the inter-well connectivity characterization and enhance the prediction precision on well productivity, by combining the physical knowledge with machine learning techniques. The main contributions of this paper are outlined as follows.

(1) An innovative neural network is proposed to handle the reservoir characterization and productivity forecast problems, in which the material balance equation is embedded via three high transparent modules, thereby ensuring the physical sense of model parameters.

(2) A gate function is designed to evaluate the contributions from input signals to the output signals, which avoids the complex constraint optimization and guarantees the interpretability of function values.

(3) KINN reveals a successful paradigm to enhance the generalization capability and interpretability by integrating physical knowledge within the model architectures, which can be easily extended to a series of neural networks.

The rest of this paper is arranged as follows. In Section 2, we introduce the theoretical foundation (the material balance equation) of KINN. Then we provide the detailed workflow and explanation of model structures of KINN in Section 3. In Section 4, we reveal the effectiveness of KINN by comparing its performance with classical ANN on three reservoir simulation experiments and test the model's sensitivity to noisy data. Finally, we summarize this paper and get some conclusions in Section 5.

2. Methods

The material balance equation is the basic principle for a closed waterflooding reservoir, which describes the relationship between inflow, outflow, and the changes of flow among the water drainage volumes of the geological system. The inter-well connectivity analysis aims to generate a quantitative evaluation of the connecting strength for each injector-producer pair. During the waterflooding process, considering a single injector and single producer case, the material balance equation is:

$$C_t V_p \frac{d\overline{p}}{dt} = i(t) - q(t), \quad (1)$$

where C_t is the total compressibility; V_p represents the drainage pore volume; $\overline{p}$ is the average pressure of V_p; t represents the timestep; $i(t)$ and $q(t)$ are the vectors denote the injection rate and production rate, respectively. Equation (1) assumes that the total compressibility is a small constant, and no fluids flow into or out of the drainage volume. Assume that there is a case with M injectors and N producers, using superposition in space of M injectors and ignoring the response of the production signals before injection, the production rate for producer j is given by:

$$\sum_{k=1}^{M} C_{tkj} V_{pkj} \frac{d\overline{p}_{kj}}{dt} = \sum_{k=1}^{M} \lambda_{kj} i_k(t) - q_j(t), \quad (2)$$

where k is the injector index, $k = 1, 2, \ldots, M$; j is the producer index, $j = 1, 2, \ldots, N$; and λ_{kj} denotes the connectivity value between injector k and producer j.

3. Knowledge Interaction Neural Network (KINN)

As shown in Figure 1, KINN is a first-principle-based model with modularized architectures, where each module keeps a one-to-one correspondence with each item of the material balance equation. According to Equation (2), KINN is established on each producer, considering the flow from all injectors and the influence caused by the compressibility of the control volume. There are two input modules in KINN, named injection regulator module (IRM) and control volume module (CVM), respectively. IRM corresponds to the injection item in the material balance equation, using a gate function layer to quantitatively measure the contribution from each injector to the analyzed producer. CVM is used for approximating the fluid change rate in the control volume via a series of fully connected layers. Then, the model output of the analyzed producer is controlled by the output system, called the production monitor module (PMM). It aims to calculate the estimated production rate via the outputs of IRM and CVM according to the material balance equation. In brief, within the framework of the material balance equation, the three modules of KINN interact with physical knowledge corporately, then simulate the water flooding process and characterize inter-well connectivity through network parameters (gate functions).

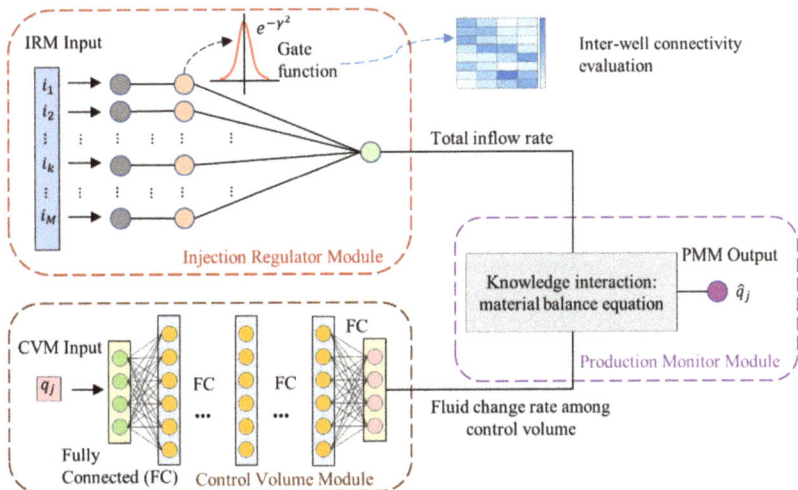

Figure 1. The architecture of KINN.

3.1. Injection Regulator Module (IRM)

The injection regulator module is an essential part of the input system in KINN, responsible for measuring the total flow from all injectors to the target producer (the first item on the right-hand side of Equation (2)) and inferring the inter-well connectivity by gate functions.

Let's assume that $I = [i_1, i_2, \ldots, i_k, \ldots, i_M]^T$ is the well water injection rate (WIR) data of M injectors, and $Q = [q_1, q_2, \ldots, q_j, \ldots, q_N]^T$ is the well liquid production rate (LPR) data of N producers, where i_k and q_j are vectors. As shown in Figure 1, the input data of IRM is I, followed by a gate function layer defined as:

$$g(\gamma_{kj}) = e^{-\gamma_{kj}^2}, \tag{3}$$

$$g(\gamma)_{M \times N} = \begin{pmatrix} g(\gamma_{11}) & \cdots & g(\gamma_{1N}) \\ \vdots & g(\gamma_{kj}) & \vdots \\ g(\gamma_{M1}) & \cdots & g(\gamma_{MN}) \end{pmatrix}, \tag{4}$$

where $g(\gamma)_{M \times N}$ denotes the inter-well connectivity matrix; $g(\gamma_{kj})$ is the connectivity value between injector k and producer j; and γ_{kj} denotes the independent variable of $g(\gamma_{kj})$.

The output of IRM is calculated by:

$$\Gamma_j = \sum_{k=1}^{M} g(\gamma_{kj}) \cdot i_k, \tag{5}$$

where · represents the product between one scalar and one vector and Γ_j denotes the comprehensive injection rate for producer j.

The multiplicity of the solution is a big challenge for inter-well connectivity analysis since it is a typical inverse problem. To reduce the multiplicity caused by the initialization of model parameters, Pearson correlation is employed in the initialization of $\gamma_{M\times N}$:

$$\rho(I,Q) = \frac{cov(I,Q)}{\sigma_I \cdot \sigma_Q}, \tag{6}$$

where $\rho(I,Q)$ and $cov(I,Q)$ are the correlation matrix and the covariance matrix between I and Q; σ_I, σ_Q are the standard deviations of I and Q. By calculating the reciprocal of each element in $\rho(I,Q)$, we can get $\gamma_{M\times N}$:

$$\gamma_{M\times N} = \begin{pmatrix} \gamma_{11} & \cdots & \gamma_{1N} \\ \vdots & \gamma_{kj} & \vdots \\ \gamma_{M1} & \cdots & \gamma_{MN} \end{pmatrix}, \tag{7}$$

where γ_{kj} is the reciprocal of the Pearson correlation coefficient between i_k and q_j.

For producer j, its initialized independent variable of the gate function, $\gamma_{M\times 1}$, is shown in Figure 2a, which is column j of $\gamma_{M\times N}$. During the initialization process, if the relationship between the signals of injector k and producer j is strong, their correlation coefficient would be big, and γ_{kj} would be close to 0, which means its gate value, $g(\gamma_{kj})$, would be large. In this way, each good pair would be assigned a fixed connectivity value according to the relation strength, which helps to decrease the multiplicity of the inter-well connectivity.

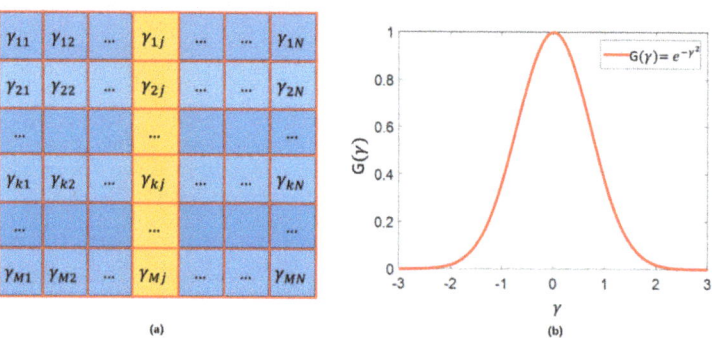

Figure 2. The curve of the gate function and its independent variables: (**a**) independent variables of the gate function; (**b**) curve of the gate function.

There are two major purposes for the presentation of the gate function.

(1) One purpose is that the negative connectivity value can be eliminated by the gate function, as its value is strictly constrained in (0, 1], as shown in Figure 2b. Therefore, the physical meaning of the gate function values can be guaranteed (the contribution from injector to producer). Moreover, γ_{kj} can be updated by normal unconstrained optimization methods, ensuring the fast convergence speed of KINN.

(2) The other purpose is that the proposed gate function has great significance for the stableness of KINN. As can be seen in Figure 2b, the gate function has a good sparsity, thereby only the strong connecting well pairs would be assigned to big connectivity values and the values of the weak or none connecting pairs would be maintained at a low level. In the machine learning field, it is common sense that the sparsity feature is helpful to support the model's robustness.

In IRM, for every producer, only $\gamma_{M\times 1}$ requires optimization, and the gate function layer can be used as inter-well connectivity indicators directly, once KINN has finished training.

3.2. Control Volume Module (CVM)

As shown in Figure 1, the control volume module is another part of the input system, aiming at computing the flow among the control volume, the left-hand side of Equation (2). In reservoir waterflood simulation, if the average reservoir pressure, $\bar{p}$, is a constant, the linear productivity model is often used to describe the relationship between production rate (q) and bottom hole pressure (p_{wf}). However, in an unstable flow case, q changes continuously, and the linear prediction model cannot represent the exact mapping relationship between q and p_{wf}. Figure 3 illustrates two inflow performance relationship (IPR) curves: one denotes the actual curve in the unstable flow case, and another represents the curve of the linear productivity model. Obviously, the linear model cannot provide a precise map between q and p_{wf} in the unstable flow case. To overcome this defect, some fully connected layers (some layers use nonlinear activation functions) are utilized in CVM to learn the nonlinear mapping relationships between q and p_{wf}. The motivation behind CVM is that the input variables can be mapped into a nonlinear space via the activation functions of nonlinear layers, thereby combining the connected weights to approximate the target output.

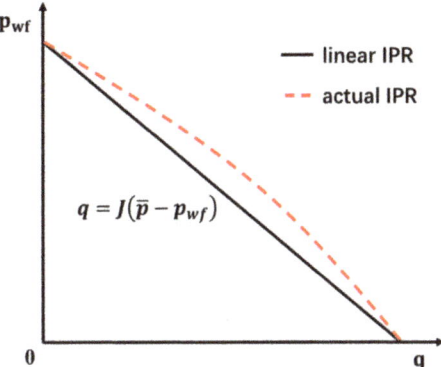

Figure 3. The inflow performance relationship (IPR) curves. The black line is the linear IPR prediction curve, and the red dashed line is the IPR curve of unstable flow.

Here, considering a single producer, we use:

$$q = \tilde{N}\left(\bar{p} - p_{wf}\right), \tag{8}$$

to represent the nonlinear relationship, where $\tilde{N}$ denotes a nonlinear mapping. In oil fields, $\bar{p}$ is usually unavailable, so we indicate the relationship between q and $\bar{p} - p_{wf}$ by:

$$\bar{p} - p_{wf} = N(q), \tag{9}$$

where N denotes another nonlinear mapping different from $\tilde{N}$. The differential form of Equation (9) with respect to the time step, t, is as follows:

$$\frac{d\bar{p}}{dt} - \frac{dp_{wf}}{dt} = \frac{dN(q)}{dt}. \tag{10}$$

Considering the case with constant BHP, Equation (10) can be simplified as:

$$\frac{d\bar{p}}{dt} = \frac{dN(q)}{dt}. \tag{11}$$

Multiply the left and right sides by $C_t V_p$ at the same time, and the change rate of the flow in the control volume is given by:

$$C_t V_p \frac{d\overline{p}}{dt} = C_t V_p \frac{dN(q)}{dt}. \tag{12}$$

For the analyzed producer j, considering M injectors, we utilize an amount of fully connected layers to approximate:

$$\sum_{k=1}^{M} C_{tkj} V_{pkj} \frac{d\overline{p}_{kj}}{dt} \sim Net(q_j), \tag{13}$$

where Net represents the connected layers in the network. In this paper, tansig function and Gaussian kernel function are employed as activation functions in CVM, respectively.

To sum up, several fully connected layers are used in CVM to approximate the sophisticated mapping from the LPR of the producer to the flow change rate among the control volume. Consequently, the robustness of KINN can be guaranteed even in the unstable flow case.

3.3. Production Monitor Module (PMM)

The production monitor module (PMM) is employed to calculate the liquid production rate of producer j, as shown in Figure 1. Based on the outputs generated by IRM and CVM, according to the material balance equation, the output of PMM can be given as:

$$\hat{q}_j = \Gamma_j - Net(q_j), \tag{14}$$

where $\hat{q}_j$ denotes the estimated production rate of producer j, the second item on the right-hand side of Equation (2). In this paper, the mean square error (MSE) function is used as the loss function:

$$MSE(q_j, \hat{q}_j) = \frac{1}{T} \sum_{t=1}^{T} (q_j(t) - \hat{q}_j(t))^2, \tag{15}$$

where t is the time step and T denotes the number of total time steps. Therefore, the difference between model output and target output can be monitored by PMM, and the waterflood simulation can be achieved by minimizing Equation (15).

As demonstrated in Figure 1, IRM and CVM are united with PMM under the control of the material balance equation, to approximate the influence caused by water injection and compressibility, respectively. Hence, KINN enables different modules to interact physical knowledge with each other during the learning process. Additionally, the transparency of KINN is significantly improved from the underlying parameter level, and both robustness and computation efficiency are successfully combined by integrating physical information within the ML framework.

3.4. Reservoir Characterization and Productivity Prediction

For producer j, considering the effect of all injection wells, KINN can be established on I and q_j, and each injector would obtain a gate function to evaluate its connectivity value with the producer j. The workflow of the KINN training procedure is shown in Figure 4, and the pseudocode is demonstrated in Algorithm 1. Firstly, $\gamma_{M \times N}$ must be initialized via Pearson correlation method with given I and Q, and the connecting weights in CVM also need an initialization. Afterward, guided by the material balance equation, IRM and CVM would cooperatively simulate the influence caused by water injection and compressibility in the waterflooding process. In the IRM part, the input comes from the water injection rate data of all injectors, and each vector would multiply a gate function, which is the inter-well connectivity indicator and has to be optimized during the training procedure. The output of IRM is the total inflow rate, the sum of all multiplied vectors. In the CVM part, a number of fully connected layers are utilized to realize the map from liquid production rate to the fluid change rate of the control volume, whose connecting weight matrices need optimization in the learning process. Afterward, both IRM and CVM would be combined by the material balance equation to calculate the model liquid production rate for producer j, and the loss between model output and target output can be measured by the loss function. It must be noted that the model loss comes from the outputs of both IRM and CVM, hence their physical knowledge would interact cooperatively with the model training process. During the optimization process, all the model parameters would be updated at the same time. When the stop criterion is satisfied, KINN would stop training, and the inter-well connectivity values can be inferred directly by gate functions.

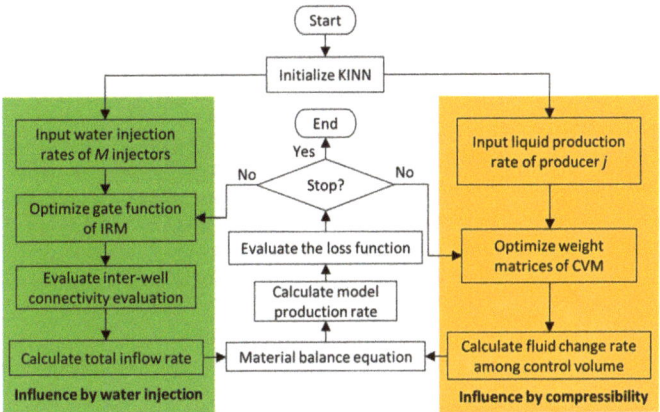

Figure 4. Flow diagram of KINN training.

Productivity forecast is the testing process of KINN, revealing its generalization performance. Unlike regular machine learning models, the liquid production rate is used as both input and output during the training procedure, as shown in Figure 1. When the training process is finished, all parameters of KINN are constants, then it can forecast the production rate $\hat{q}_j$ with given I, by solving the nonlinear equation:

$$\hat{q}_j - \Gamma_j + Net(\hat{q}_j) = 0. \qquad (16)$$

Algorithm 1: Knowledge Interaction Neural Network (KINN)

Input: I, WWIR for M injectors, and Q, WLPR for N producers
Output: $\hat{q}_j$

/*** **start KINN training** ***/
1 **Initialization** $\lambda_{M \times N}$: Compute $\gamma_{M \times N}$ using database I and Q by Equations (6) and (7), and initialize the parameters of ANN in CVM
2 **For** $j = 1$ to N **do**
3   **While** convergence tolerance is not met
    /*** **IRM calculation** ***/
4   Select the j_{th} column, $\gamma_{M \times 1}$, in $\gamma_{M \times N}$ as the independent variable of gate function;
5   Calculate the output of IRM, Γ_j, with $\gamma_{M \times 1}$ and I, using Equation (5)
    /*** **CVM calculation** ***/
6   Calculate the output of CVM, $Net(q_j)$, with q_j, using Equation (13)
    /*** **PMM calculation** ***/
7   Calculate the output of PMM, $\hat{q}_j$, using Equation (14)
    /*** **parameters update** ***/
8   Evaluate the loss function using Equation (15)
9   Update $\gamma_{M \times 1}$ and weight matrices of CVM via gradient descent algorithm
10   **End While**
11 **End For**
    /*** **end KINN training** ***/

4. Results

Three reservoir cases with various inter-well connecting conditions are studied in this section, including the streak reservoir case, the braided river reservoir case and Egg reservoir case, developed on ECLIPSE (Schlumberger Ltd., Houston, TX, USA). KINN has taken two activation functions (tansig function and Gaussian kernel function) in CVM, named KINN-tansig and KINN-Gaussian, respectively. To compare the performance of the proposed models and the classical neural network without the guidance of physical information, we demonstrate the results obtained by the single-hidden-layer feedforward neural network (SLFNN). The numbers of the input nodes and output nodes are equal to the numbers of injectors and producers. To keep the fairness of comparison, the number of hidden nodes, the activation function, the learning rate, the convergence error, and the optimization method are the same as those of KINN-tansig. The connectivity matrix of SLFNN is the normalized absolute value of the product between the input-hidden-layer weights and the hidden-output-layer weights. All three models use an Intel(R) Core (TM) i7-9700 CPU. The data are separated into two parts, where the former 80% are used in history matching and the latter 20% are utilized in productivity prediction. Table 1 shows the hyperparameters of KINN-tansig and KINN-Gaussian in three cases. To demonstrate the inter-well connectivity clearly and intuitively, the connectivity characterization results are visualized by heatmaps, where the deeper the block color, the stronger the injector-producer connectivity.

Table 1. The hyperparameters for KINN-tansig and KINN-Gaussian in three cases.

Hyperparameter	KINN-Tansig	KINN-Gaussian
Learning rate	0.05	0.05
Number of hidden layers in CVM	3	3
Number of neurons of each layer in CVM	[1, 10, 1]	[1, 10, 1]
Activation function in CVM	tansig function	Gaussian kernel function
Initialization range of weights in CVM	[0, 0.25]	[0, 0.25]
Initialization method of γ in IRM	Pearson Correlation	Pearson Correlation
Optimization algorithm	Gradient descent method	Gradient descent method
Convergence error (MSE)	10^{-6}	10^{-6}

4.1. The Streak Reservoir Case

This model is reconstructed from the work of [19], which consists of 31 × 31 single-layer grids in the X-Y plane, with 80, 80, and 12 ft in the X, Y, and Z axes, respectively. There are 5 injectors, named I1, I2, I3, I4, I5, and 4 producers, named P1, P2, P3, P4. As shown in Figure 5, the permeability of the matrix is 5 md, except for two high-permeability streaks. One streak is between I1 and P1 of 1000 md, and the other is 500 md between I3 and P4. The normal properties of the streak model are shown in Table 2. The simulated production lasts around 1800 days, and the timestep is 5 days. Because the permeability values of I1-P1 and I3-P4 are much higher than other well pairs, the fluids are less likely to flow into P2 and P3, thus their production rates are quite low. Here, only the history matching and production prediction results of P1 and P4 are given.

Table 2. Properties of the streak reservoir model.

Properties	Value
Model Size	31 × 31 × 1
Depth	2000 m
Initial pressure	2000 psi
Porosity	0.18
Initial water saturation	0.3
Density of oil	900 kg/m^3
Viscosity of oil	2.0 cp
Oil compressibility	5.0×10^{-6} bar^{-1}

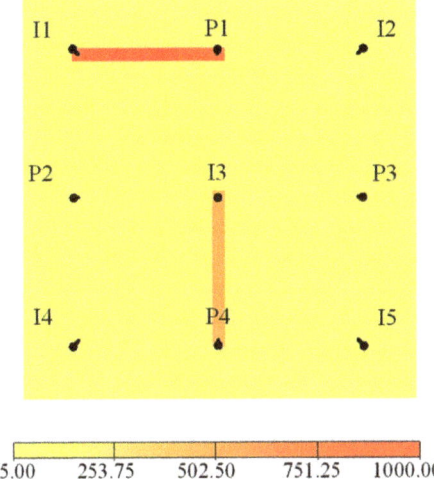

Figure 5. Permeability field of the streak reservoir case.

Figure 6a,b illustrate the history matching and productivity prediction results of P1 and P4, respectively. Obviously, the proposed two methods outperform SLFNN on both history matching and prediction periods. As shown in the figures, both KINN-tansig and KINN-Gaussian can obtain high fitness accuracy on P1 and P4 in the history matching period. And the two proposed models show different performances during the productivity prediction period. As illustrated in Figure 6a, there are three peaks in the prediction period of P1, which can be estimated accurately by KINN-tansig, while the forecast by KINN-Gaussian is lower than the actual values. Similar results can be found in Figure 6b, where KINN-tansig outperforms KINN-Gaussian in the prediction of P4. Figure 7 illustrates the training error (MSE) curves of KINN-tansig, KINN-Gaussian, and SLFNN, where both two proposed methods show smaller errors than SLFNN. Note that there are some fluctuations on the error curve of KINN-Gaussian, while the accuracy of KINN-Gaussian is equivalent to that of KINN-tansig when the training is finished. As shown in Table 3, KINN-tansig costs less computation time (0.3702 s) than KINN-Gaussian (2.3393 s) in this case, and the computation time of SLFNN (1.2737 s) is in the middle of the three methods. Both the history matching and prediction errors of KINN-tansig and KINN-Gaussian are around one order magnitude lower than those of SLFNN. Moreover, even though the history matching errors of KINN-tansig (0.0046) and KINN-Gaussian (0.0047) are very close to each other, the former outperforms the latter in the production prediction, with the errors of 0.0223 and 0.0256, respectively.

Table 3. The time consumption, training error (MSE) and testing error (MSE) of KINN-tansig, KINN-Gaussian and SLFNN in the streak reservoir case.

Methods	KINN-Tansig	KINN-Gaussian	SLFNN
Computation time (training and testing)	0.3702 s	2.3393 s	1.2737 s
Error of history matching (training error)	0.0046	0.0047	0.0976
Error of prediction (testing error)	0.0223	0.0256	0.1832

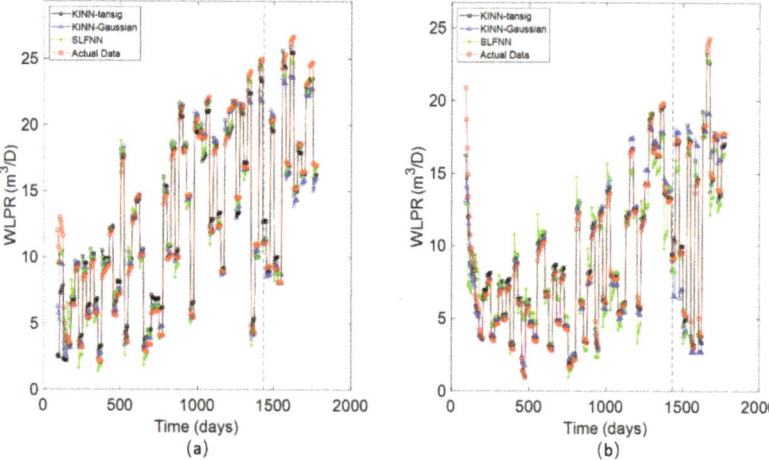

Figure 6. History matching results of the streak reservoir case by KINN-tansig, KINN-Gaussian and SLFNN. The black line with squares is the result obtained by KINN-tansig method; the blue line with triangles represents the result gotten by KINN-Gaussian method; the green line with stars is the results obtained by SLFNN; the red line with circles is the liquid production rate gotten by ECLIPSE; the grey vertical dashed line makes a separation of history matching period and the productivity forecast period: (**a**) P1; (**b**) P4.

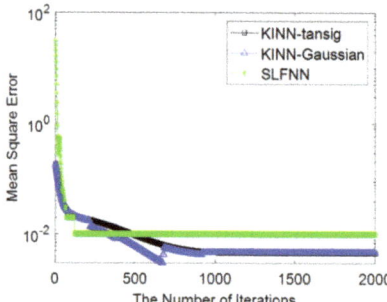

Figure 7. The training error (MSE) curves of KINN-tansig, KINN-Gaussian and SLFNN for the streak reservoir case. The black line with squares is the error curve of KINN-tansig; the blue line with triangles represents the error curve of KINN-Gaussian; and the green line with stars represent the error curve of SLFNN.

Figure 8 illustrates the inter-well connectivity analysis results produced by three models. Undoubtedly, I1-P1 and I3-P4 should be the top and the second highest connecting well pairs according to the permeability distribution in Figure 5, which are indicated truthfully by KINN-tansig and KINN-Gaussian. In detail, the permeability of the streak of I1-P1 is 1000 md, twice larger than the streak of I3-P4, so that their corresponding connectivity values should also reflect this difference. As shown in Figure 8a, the connectivity values of I1-P1 and I3-P4 obtained by KINN-tansig are 0.5974 and 0.2047, respectively. Similarly, as illustrated in Figure 8b, KINN-Gaussian assigns I1-P1 and I3-P4 with the values of 0.5138 and 0.2205, separately. However, as demonstrated in Figure 8c, the top two connectivity values are assigned to I4-P4 (1.000) and I1-P1 (0.9713), and the value of I3-P4 (0.7729) only ranks seventh, which means SLFNN mistakenly identifies the weak connecting well pairs as the strong connecting ones. In contrast, KINN-tansig and KINN-Gaussian successfully allocate the well pairs on the low permeability area with quite small connectivity values, showing great accordance with their actual geological properties.

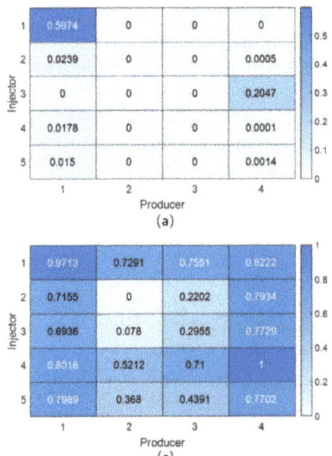

Figure 8. The heatmaps of the inter-well connectivity analysis by three models for the streak reservoir case: (**a**) KINN-tansig; (**b**) KINN-Gaussian; (**c**) SLFNN.

4.2. The Braided River Reservoir Case

To test the performance of KINN in other more complex cases, we have designed the braided river reservoir case, which is a classical fluvial deposition distributing in continental facies basin. There are 100 × 100 single-layer grids in the braided river reservoir model, where each grid is 80, 80 and 12 ft in the X, Y and Z axes, respectively. Except for the model size, the other properties of the braided river reservoir model are the same as shown in Table 4. As shown in Figure 9, the permeability distributions are significantly different between river channels and other areas, whose permeability values are set to be 1000 md and 50 md, respectively. The simulated production lasts around 1800 days and the time step is 1 day. In this case, there are also 5 injectors, named I1, I2, I3, I4 and I5, and 4 producers, called P1, P2, P3 and P4. I1 is located on the top left corner, connecting P1 through the river channel. P2, P3 and P4 are connected with I5 by three tributaries, respectively, where the tributary between I5 and P2 is widest. Besides, the tributaries of I5-P3 and I5-P4 are of similar width, while the distance of I5-P4 is longer than that of I5-P3.

Table 4. The time consumption, training error (MSE) and testing error (MSE) of KINN-tansig, KINN-Gaussian and SLFNN in the braided river reservoir case.

Methods	KINN-Tansig	KINN-Gaussian	SLFNN
Computation time (training and testing)	0.7417 s	3.4679 s	2.4602 s
Error of history matching (training error)	0.0052	0.0058	0.0104
Error of prediction (testing error)	0.0071	0.0065	0.0142

In the braided river reservoir case, even the production rates change significantly, the two proposed models are capable of matching the history of 4 producers with certain accuracy in general, as shown in Figure 10. In contrast, SLFNN shows a poorer performance than KINN-tansig and KINN-Gaussian, on both history matching and forecast tasks of all producers, where the green lines with stars often deviate from the actually observed curves (the red lines with circles). When it comes to the details, KINN-tansig and KINN-Gaussian show different performances on different producers. For instance, as can be seen in Figure 10a–d, the history matching results on P1 gotten by both two models are not as good as those on other producers, especially for KINN-tansig, whose estimated curve may be above or below the actual values. In the productivity prediction period, both KINN-tansig and KINN-Gaussian conduct results with significant fluctuations on P4, while they still show great performance on the other producers.

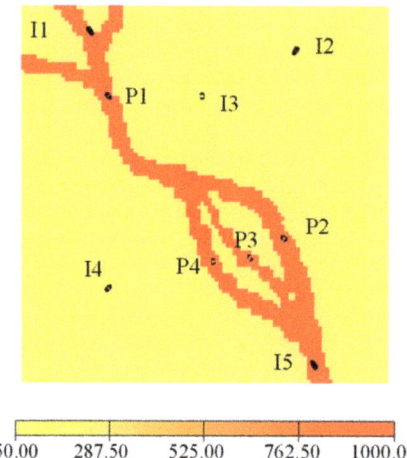

Figure 9. Permeability field of the braided river reservoir case.

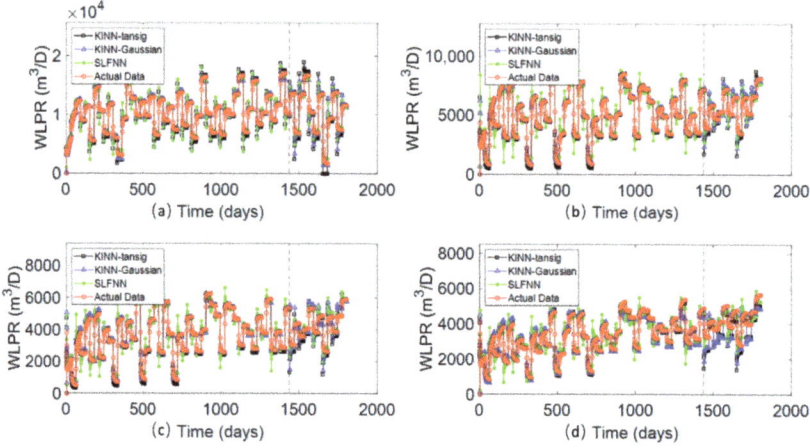

Figure 10. History matching results of the braided river reservoir case by KINN-tansig, KINN-Gaussian and SLFNN. The black line with squares is the result obtained by KINN-tansig method; the blue line with triangles represents the result gotten by the KINN-Gaussian method; the green line with stars is the results obtained by SLFNN; the red line with circles is the liquid production rate gotten by ECLIPSE; the grey vertical dashed line makes a separation of history matching period and the productivity forecast period: (**a**) P1; (**b**) P2; (**c**) P3; (**d**) P4.

As can be seen in Figure 11, KINN-tansig and KINN-Gaussian keep high computation efficiency in the braided river reservoir case, and their training errors converge to a neighborhood between 0.0050 and 0.0060, which is about a half of the error of SLFNN (0.0104). In addition, as shown in Table 4, it costs 0.7417 s for KINN-tansig and 3.4679 s for KINN-Gaussian to finish training and 2.4602 s for SLFNN. The proposed two approaches also have smaller training and testing errors than SLFNN in the braided river case.

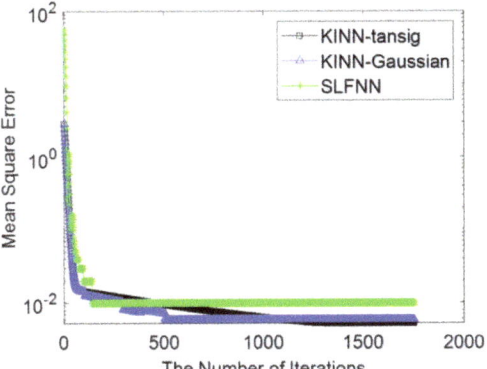

Figure 11. The training error (MSE) curves of KINN-tansig, KINN-Gaussian and SLFNN for the braided river reservoir case. The black line with squares is the error curve of KINN-tansig; the blue line with triangles represents the error curve of KINN-Gaussian; and the green line with stars represent the error curve of SLFNN.

According to the permeability distribution of the braided river reservoir case, the injector-producer pairs with high flow channels are I1-P1, I5-P2, I5-P3 and I5-P4, ranking by the strength of their connecting conditions. As shown in Figure 12, these strong connecting well pairs can be revealed directly through deep color grids in heatmaps. Figure 12a demonstrates that the inter-well connectivity can get a good reflection by KINN-tansig, as the top four connectivity values and the top four high connecting well pairs are one-to-one matched, where I1-P1 is biggest with 0.777, following I5-P2, I5-P3 and I5-P4, with 0.49, 0.4319 and 0.2963, respectively. Figure 12b shows that KINN-Gaussian generates similar characterization results with KINN-tansig, except that the value of I5-P3 (0.4696) is bigger than that of I5-P2 (0.4232). SLFNN enables to characterize three strong connecting well pairs, I5-P2, I1-P1 and I5-P4, with the values of 1, 0.8523 and 0.8409. Meanwhile, I5-P3 only obtains 0.3636, which is much lower than some actually weak connecting well pairs, such as I1-P3 (0.9205), I2-P1 (0.8295), I2-P4 (0.7841), I3-P1 (0.7841) and I3-P3 (0.875).

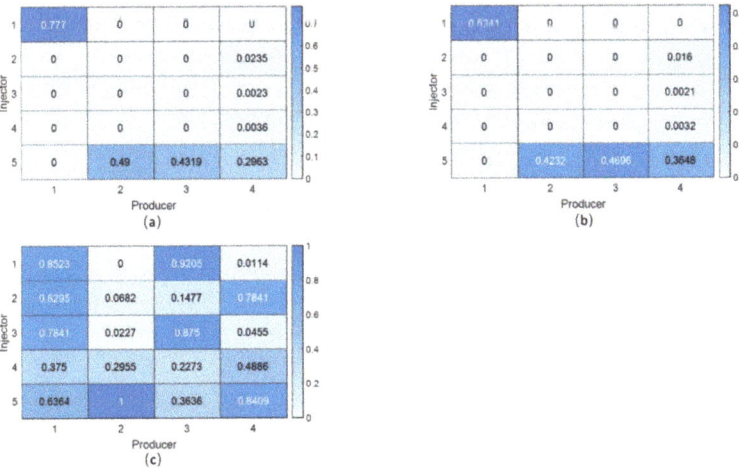

Figure 12. The heatmaps of the inter-well connectivity analysis by KINN-tansig and KINN-Gaussian for the streak reservoir case: (**a**) KINN-tansig; (**b**) KINN-Gaussian; (**c**) SLFNN.

4.3. Egg Reservoir Case

The initial Egg model can be seen in the work of [46], and some modifications are taken to make it more suitable for the inter-well connectivity analysis. This synthetic reservoir model consists of active 6910 grids, and the size of each grid in the X, Y, and Z directions is 8 m, 8 m, and 4 m, respectively. The important properties of Egg reservoir model are presented in Table 5. The simulated production lasts around 1200 days and the time step is 10 days. As shown in Figure 13a, the are 8 injectors and 4 producers in this case, and there are two faults in the Egg reservoir model, blocking the flow of underground fluid. In this way, the relationships between injectors and producers located on the different sides of the fault should be pretty weak. To understand the communications between injectors and producers in detail, the oil saturation distribution is demonstrated in Figure 13b.

Table 5. Properties of Egg reservoir model.

Properties	Value
Model Size	100 × 99 × 1
Depth	4000 m
Initial pressure	5765 psi
Porosity	0.2
Initial water saturation	0.1
Density of oil	900 kg/m^3
Viscosity of oil	2.0 cp
Oil compressibility	1.0×10^{-5} bar $^{-1}$

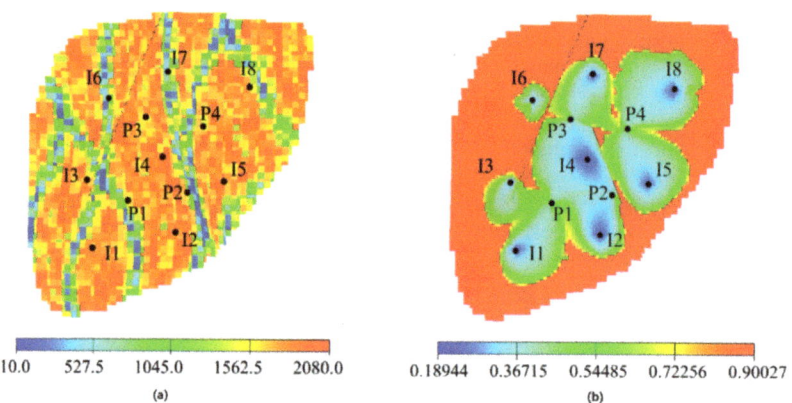

Figure 13. The permeability and oil saturation distribution of Egg reservoir case: (**a**) Permeability distribution; (**b**) oil saturation distribution.

As can be seen in Figure 14a–c, there are a certain number of points obtained by SLFNN (denoted by the green lines with stars) deviated from the actual ones (denoted by the red lines with circles), especially for the results on P4. Meanwhile, the proposed two methods (black lines with squares for KINN-tansig, and blue lines with triangles for KINN-Gaussian) show much better performance than SLFNN on the history matching and prediction for the LPR data of P1, P2 and P3. Besides, all three models show pretty good performance on P4, as shown in Figure 14d.

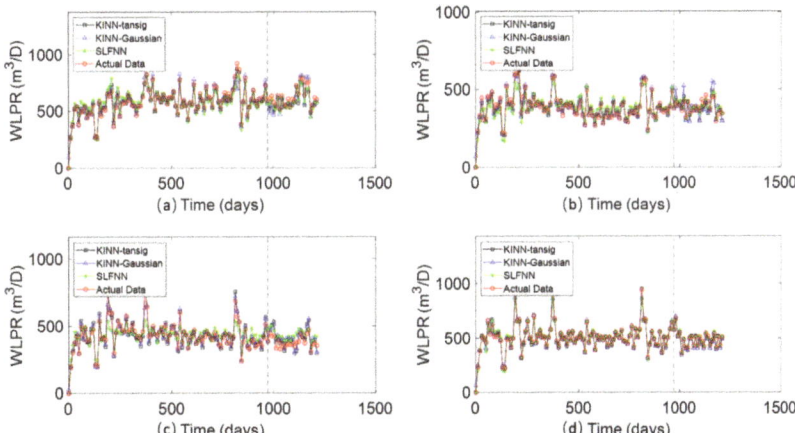

Figure 14. History matching results of the Egg reservoir case by KINN-tansig, KINN-Gaussian and SLFNN. The black line with squares is the result obtained by KINN-tansig method; the blue line with triangles represents the result gotten by KINN-Gaussian method; the green line with stars is the results obtained by SLFNN; the red line with circles is the liquid production rate gotten by ECLIPSE; the grey vertical dashed line makes a separation of history matching period and the productivity forecast period: (**a**) P1; (**b**) P2; (**c**) P3; (**d**) P4.

Figure 15 shows that KINN-tansig and KINN-Gaussian converge fast in the training process, where the MSE errors of both methods are reduced to less than 10^{-2} within 200 iterations. Meanwhile, the initial MSE for SLFNN is much bigger than that of KINN-tansig and KINN-Gaussian, and so is the converged error. As illustrated in Table 6, KINN-tansig, KINN-Gaussian, and SLFNN all demonstrate significant computation efficiency, taking 1.1282 s, 0.8539 s, and 0.3361 s, to finish training, respectively. As expected, both KINN-tansig and KINN-Gaussian are capable of producing more accurate results in history matching (0.0022 and 0.0035) and productivity prediction (0.0171 and 0.02263, respectively) than those obtained by SLFNN (0.0097 and 0.0426).

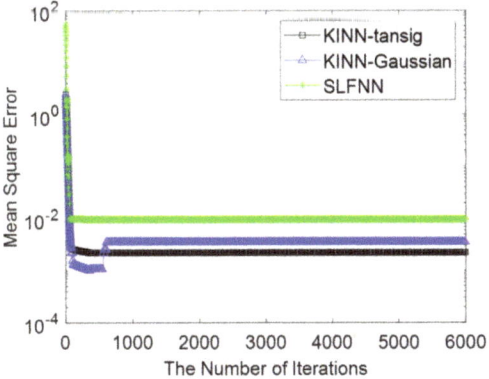

Figure 15. The training error (MSE) curves of KINN-tansig, KINN-Gaussian, and SLFNN for the Egg reservoir case. The black line with squares is the error curve of KINN-tansig; the blue line with triangles represents the error curve of KINN-Gaussian, and the green line with stars represents the error curve of SLFNN.

Table 6. The time consumption, training error (MSE), and testing error (MSE) of KINN-tansig, KINN-Gaussian, and SLFNN in the Egg reservoir case.

	KINN-Tansig	KINN-Gaussian	SLFNN
Computation time (training and testing)	0.1282 s	0.8539 s	0.3361 s
Error of history matching (training error)	0.0022	0.0035	0.0097
Error of prediction (testing error)	0.0171	0.0263	0.0426

Figure 16 reveals the inter-well connectivity characterization results obtained by three models. For P1, the production comes from the contribution of I1, I2, and I3. It is important to note that despite the fault between I3 and P1, the injected water of I3 still could reach P1 by getting round of the fault, as shown in Figure 13b. As shown in Figure 16a,b, I1-P1, I2-P1, and I3-P1 can be reflected correctly by the two proposed models, while I6-P1 is wrongly considered as a relatively high connecting well pair by both models. Moreover, the main contributors of P2 are I2 and I4; the main contributors of P3 are I4 and I7; and the flow of P4 comes from I5, I7, and I8. As shown in Figure 16a,b, all these strong connecting well pairs can be accurately revealed by the deeper color blocks of the heatmaps by the two models. However, SLFNN still struggles to characterize the relative connecting strength. For instance, the top four connectivity values obtained by SLFNN are assigned to I6-P4, I5-P2, I4-P1 and I6-P2, which are actually weak connecting well pairs.

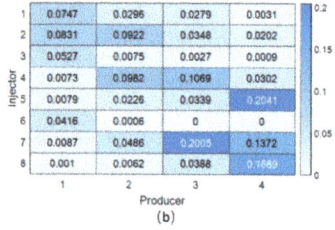

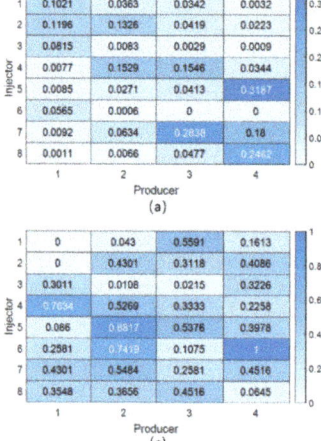

Figure 16. The heatmaps of the inter-well connectivity analysis by KINN-tansig and KINN-Gaussian for the Egg reservoir case: (a) KINN-tansig; (b) KINN-Gaussian; (c) SLFNN.

4.4. Sensitivity to Noise

The measurement noise and wells shut-in are unavoidable in real oilfield production, which are common challenges for all reservoir characterization methods. To evaluate the performance of KINN-tansig and KINN-Gaussian on these noisy data, we design the measurement noise case and wells shut-in cases for the braided river reservoir model. In the measurement noise case, all the injection data (5×1447 samples) and production data (4×1447 samples) are added with Gaussian noises, whose mean value is 1 and standard deviations range from 5%, 10%, 15%, 20%, 25% and 30%, respectively. In the wells shut-in case, 5 injectors and 4 producers are shut in from the time step 401 to 800.

Figure 17 shows the average absolute error of the connectivity values of KINN-tansig and KINN-Gaussian in the measurement noise case. As expected, the error of connectivity values grows slightly with the increase of measurement noise, where the two proposed models show great robustness. As can be seen in Figure 17, the average absolute errors of the connectivity values by the two models are less than 0.08, even though the noise reaches

30%. Figure 18 demonstrates the inter-well connecting relationship by KINN-tansig and KINN-Gaussian in the wells shut-in case against the basic case. KINN-Gaussian shows poor performance, since a part of connectivity values obtained by KINN-Gaussian are higher than 0 in the wells shut-in case, while they are very close to 0 in the basic case. This phenomenon means that the inter-well connectivity values of these weak connecting well pairs obtained by KINN-Gaussian are affected by wells shut-in. In detail, these weak connecting well pairs are likely to get bigger connectivity values in the wells shut-in case than those in the basic case. Nevertheless, KINN-tansig still demonstrates strong robustness in this case. As shown in Figure 18, the connectivity values obtained by KINN-tansig are close to the 45° line, which means that KINN-tansig can generate similar inter-well connectivity characterization results in wells shut-in case as in the basic case.

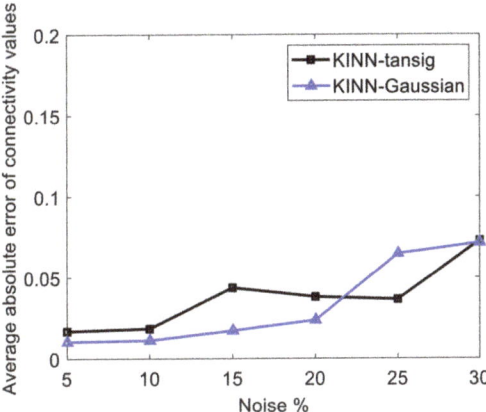

Figure 17. The average absolute error of connectivity values by KINN-tansig and KINN-Gaussian in the noise measurement case. The black line is the error curve of KINN-tansig and the blue line is the error curve of KINN-Gaussian.

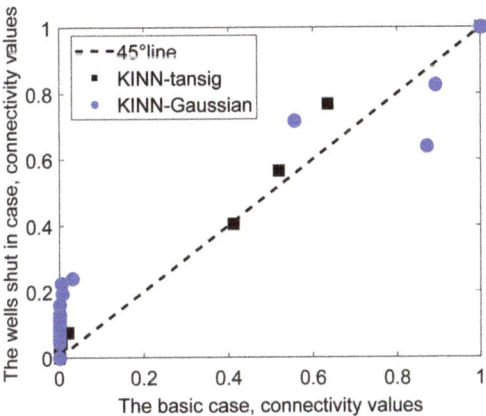

Figure 18. A cross plot of the connectivity values using KINN-tansig and KINN-Gaussian in the wells shut-in case against the basic case results. The black squares and blue circles represent the connectivity values of KINN-tansig and KINN-Gaussian, respectively, and the dashed is 45° line.

5. Discussion and Conclusions

The application of ANN in oil industry is limited by its unexplainability and poor generalizability. In this paper, we concentrate on associating the physical knowledge with neural networks to solve the reservoir characterization and production forecast problems.

Integrating the material balance equation with the machine learning techniques, the physical knowledge interaction neural networks have been proposed, combining both the merits of interpretability and robustness. Furthermore, the proposed gate functions have avoided the negative connectivity values without physical sense, and the computation efficiency has been fully improved by unconstraint optimization algorithm. In the end, the effectiveness of our models has been proved through several simulation experiments. Moreover, the performance of the proposed models on noisy data has been demonstrated. KINN illustrates a novel configuration to realize the cooperation and interaction between neural networks and physical knowledge. In the future, we would like to extend KINN to other areas, like production optimization, and try other machine learning optimization algorithms, like the fractional stochastic gradient descent method [47].

Author Contributions: Conceptualization, Y.J. and J.W.; methodology, K.Z.; software, Y.J.; validation, J.H. and S.C.; formal analysis, H.Z.; investigation, Y.J.; resources, K.Z. and J.Y.; data curation, Y.J.; writing—original draft preparation, Y.J.; writing—review and editing, H.Z. and L.Z.; visualization, Y.J.; supervision, K.Z.; project administration, K.Z.; funding acquisition, K.Z. and J.W. All authors have read and agreed to the published version of the manuscript.

Funding: This research was funded by the National Natural Science Foundation of China under Grant 51722406, 52074340, and 51874335, the Shandong Provincial Natural Science Foundation under Grant JQ201808, the Fundamental Research Funds for the Central Universities under Grant 18CX02097A, the Major Scientific and Technological Projects of CNPC under Grant ZD2019-183-008, the Science and Technology Support Plan for Youth Innovation of University in Shandong Province under Grant 2019KJH002, the National Science and Technology Major Project of China under Grant 2016ZX05025001-006, 111 Project under Grant B08028, the National Key Research and Development Program of China under Grant 2018AAA0100100, the Fundamental Research Funds for the Central Universities under Grant 20CX05002A and Grant 20CX05012A, and the Source Innovation Scientific and Incubation Project of Qingdao, China under Grant 2020-88.

Data Availability Statement: The data used in this paper are not publicly available due limitations of consent for the original study but could be obtained from Jiang upon the reasonable request.

Conflicts of Interest: The authors declare no conflict of interest. The funders had no role in the design of the study; in the collection, analyses, or interpretation of data; in the writing of the manuscript, or in the decision to publish the results.

Nomenclature

The nomenclature used in this paper is as follows:

Nomenclature	Explanations
C_t	total compressibility, bar^{-1}
i_k	water injection rate, m^3/Day
J	productivity index, $\text{m}^3/\text{Day}/\text{bar}$
M	number of injectors
N	number of producers
n	time-like variable
$\bar{p}$	average reservoir pressure, bar
p_{wf}	bottom hole pressure, bar
$\hat{q}$	estimated production rate, m^3/Day
q_j	liquid production rate, m^3/Day
t	time step, Day
V_p	drainage pore volume, m^3/Day
λ_{kj}	inter-well connectivity value
γ_{kj}	independent variable of inter-well connectivity of intelligent connectivity model
ρ	Pearson correlation coefficient
τ_i	time constant of capacitance resistance model, Day
Γ_j	comprehensive injection rate, m^3/day
k	injector index
j	producer index

References

1. Hashan, M.; Jahan, L.N.; Zaman, T.U.; Imtiaz, S.; Hossain, M.E. Modelling of fluid flow through porous media using memory approach: A review. *Math. Comput. Simul.* **2020**, *177*, 643–673. [CrossRef]
2. Mozolevski, I.; Murad, M.A.; Schuh, L.A. High order discontinuous Galerkin method for reduced flow models in fractured porous media. *Math. Comput. Simul.* **2021**, *190*, 1317–1341. [CrossRef]
3. Ma, X.; Zhang, K.; Zhang, L.; Yao, C.; Yao, J.; Wang, H.; Jian, W.; Yan, Y. Data-Driven Niching Differential Evolution with Adaptive Parameters Control for History Matching and Uncertainty Quantification. *SPE J.* **2021**, *26*, 993–1010. [CrossRef]
4. Xu, X.; Wang, C.; Zhou, P. GVRP considered oil-gas recovery in refined oil distribution: From an environmental perspective. *Int. J. Prod. Econ.* **2021**, *235*, 108078. [CrossRef]
5. Xu, X.; Lin, Z.; Li, X.; Shang, C.; Shen, Q. Multi-objective robust optimisation model for MDVRPLS in refined oil distribution. *Int. J. Prod. Res.* **2021**, *5*, 1–21. [CrossRef]
6. Yin, F.; Xue, X.; Zhang, C.; Zhang, K.; Han, J.; Liu, B.; Wang, J.; Yao, J. Multifidelity Genetic Transfer: An Efficient Framework for Production Optimization. *SPE J.* **2021**, *26*, 1614–1635. [CrossRef]
7. Zhang, K.; Zhang, J.; Ma, X.; Yao, C.; Zhang, L.; Yang, Y.; Wang, J.; Yao, J.; Zhao, H. History Matching of Naturally Fractured Reservoirs Using a Deep Sparse Autoencoder. *SPE J.* **2021**, *26*, 1700–1721. [CrossRef]
8. Xu, X.; Lin, Z.; Zhu, J. DVRP with limited supply and variable neighborhood region in refined oil distribution. *Ann. Oper. Res.* **2022**, *309*, 663–687. [CrossRef]
9. Heffer, K.J.; Fox, R.J.; McGill, C.A.; Koutsabeloulis, N.C. Novel Techniques Show Links between Reservoir Flow Directionality, Earth Stress, Fault Structure and Geomechanical Changes in Mature Waterfloods. *SPE J.* **1997**, *2*, 91–98. [CrossRef]
10. Tian, C.; Horne, R.N. Inferring Interwell Connectivity Using Production Data. In Proceedings of the SPE Annual Technical Conference and Exhibition, Dubai, United Arab Emirates, 26–28 September 2016. [CrossRef]
11. Unal, E.; Siddiqui, F.; Rezaei, A.; Eltaleb, I.; Kabir, S.; Soliman, M.Y.; Dindoruk, B. Use of Wavelet Transform and Signal Processing Techniques for Inferring Interwell Connectivity in Waterflooding Operations. In Proceedings of the SPE Annual Technical Conference and Exhibition, Calgary, AB, Canada, 30 September–2 October 2019. [CrossRef]
12. Wang, Y.; Kabir, C.S.; Reza, Z. Inferring Well Connectivity in Waterfloods Using Novel Signal Processing Techniques. In Proceedings of the SPE Annual Technical Conference and Exhibition, Dallas, TX, USA, 24–26 September 2018. [CrossRef]
13. Panda, M.N.; Chopra, A.K. An Integrated Approach to Estimate Well Interactions. In Proceedings of the SPE India Oil and Gas Conference and Exhibition, Society of Petroleum Engineers, New Delhi, India, 17–19 February 1998; p. SPE-39563-MS.
14. Artun, E. Characterizing interwell connectivity in waterflooded reservoirs using data-driven and reduced-physics models: A comparative study. *Neural Comput. Appl.* **2017**, *28*, 1729–1743. [CrossRef]
15. Jensen, J. Comment on "Characterizing interwell connectivity in waterflooded reservoirs using data-driven and reduced-physics models: A comparative study" by E. Artun. *Neural Comput. Appl.* **2016**, *28*, 1745–1746. [CrossRef]
16. Yousef, A.A.; Gentil, P.H.; Jensen, J.L.; Lake, L.W. A Capacitance Model To Infer Interwell Connectivity From Production and Injection Rate Fluctuations. *SPE Reserv. Eval. Eng.* **2006**, *9*, 630–646. [CrossRef]
17. Albertoni, A.; Lake, L.W. Inferring interwell connectivity only from well-rate fluctuations in waterfloods. *SPE Reserv. Eval. Eng.* **2003**, *6*, 6–16. [CrossRef]
18. Lake, L.W.; Liang, X.; Edgar, T.F.; Al Yousef, A.; Sayarpour, M.; Weber, D. Optimization Of Oil Production Based On A Capacitance Model Of Production And Injection Rates. In Proceedings of the Hydrocarbon Economics and Evaluation Symposium, Dallas, TX, USA, 1–3 April 2007.
19. Sayarpour, M.; Zuluaga, E.; Kabir, C.S.; Lake, L.W. The use of capacitance–resistance models for rapid estimation of waterflood performance and optimization. *J. Pet. Sci. Eng.* **2009**, *69*, 227–238. [CrossRef]
20. Sayarpour, M. *Development and Application of Capacitance-Resistive Models to Water/CO_2 Floods*; University of Texas at Austin: Austin, TX, USA, 2008.
21. Mamghaderi, A.; Bastami, A.; Pourafshary, P. Optimization of Waterflooding Performance in a Layered Reservoir Using a Combination of Capacitance-Resistive Model and Genetic Algorithm Method. *J. Energy Resour. Technol.* **2012**, *135*, 013102–013110. [CrossRef]
22. Zhao, H.; Kang, Z.; Zhang, X.; Sun, H.; Cao, L.; Reynolds, A.C. INSIM: A Data-Driven Model for History Matching and Prediction for Waterflooding Monitoring and Management with a Field Application. In Proceedings of the SPE Reservoir Simulation Symposium, Houston, TX, USA, 23–25 February 2015.
23. Guo, Z.; Reynolds, A.C. INSIM-FT in three-dimensions with gravity. *J. Comput. Phys.* **2019**, *380*, 143–169. [CrossRef]
24. Guo, Z.; Reynolds, A.C. INSIM-FT-3D: A Three-Dimensional Data-Driven Model for History Matching and Waterflooding Optimization. In Proceedings of the SPE Reservoir Simulation Conference, Society of Petroleum Engineers, Galveston, TX, USA, 10–11 April 2019; p. SPE-193841-MS. [CrossRef]
25. Zhao, H.; Xu, L.; Guo, Z.; Zhang, Q.; Liu, W.; Kang, X. Flow-Path Tracking Strategy in a Data-Driven Interwell Numerical Simulation Model for Waterflooding History Matching and Performance Prediction with Infill Wells. *SPE J.* **2020**, *25*, 1007–1025. [CrossRef]
26. Kansao, R.; Yrigoyen, A.; Haris, Z.; Saputelli, L. Waterflood Performance Diagnosis and Optimization Using Data-Driven Predictive Analytical Techniques from Capacitance Resistance Models CRM. In Proceedings of the SPE Europec Featured at 79th EAGE Conference and Exhibition, Paris, France, 12–15 June 2017. [CrossRef]

27. Olenchikov, D.; Posvyanskii, D. Application of CRM-Like Models for Express Forecasting and Optimizing Field Development. In Proceedings of the SPE Russian Petroleum Technology Conference, Moscow, Russia, 22–24 October 2019.
28. Nguyen, A.P.; Lasdon, L.S.; Lake, L.W.; Edgar, T.F. Capacitance Resistive Model Application to Optimize Waterflood in a West Texas Field. In Proceedings of the SPE Annual Technical Conference and Exhibition, Denver, CO, USA, 30 October–2 November 2011.
29. Guo, Z.; Reynolds, A.; Zhao, H. Waterflooding optimization with the INSIM-FT data-driven model. *Comput. Geosci.* **2018**, *22*, 745–761. [CrossRef]
30. Chen, B.; Pawar, R.J. Characterization of CO2 storage and enhanced oil recovery in residual oil zones. *Energy* **2019**, *183*, 291–304. [CrossRef]
31. Alimohammadi, H.; Rahmanifard, H.; Chen, N. Multivariate Time Series Modelling Approach for Production Forecasting in Unconventional Resources. In Proceedings of the SPE Annual Technical Conference and Exhibition, Virtual. 26–29 October 2020. [CrossRef]
32. Chen, B.; Harp, D.R.; Lin, Y.; Keating, E.H.; Pawar, R.J. Geologic CO_2 sequestration monitoring design: A machine learning and uncertainty quantification based approach. *Appl. Energy* **2018**, *225*, 332–345. [CrossRef]
33. Li, Y.; Wang, G.; McLellan, B.; Chen, S.-Y.; Zhang, Q. Study of the impacts of upstream natural gas market reform in China on infrastructure deployment and social welfare using an SVM-based rolling horizon stochastic game analysis. *Pet. Sci.* **2018**, *15*, 898–911. [CrossRef]
34. Boret, S.E.B.; Marin, O.R. Development of Surrogate models for CSI probabilistic production forecast of a heavy oil field. *Math. Comput. Simul.* **2019**, *164*, 63–77. [CrossRef]
35. Fumagalli, A.; Zonca, S.; Formaggia, L. Advances in computation of local problems for a flow-based upscaling in fractured reservoirs. *Math. Comput. Simul.* **2017**, *137*, 299–324. [CrossRef]
36. Xu, X.; Hao, J.; Zheng, Y. Multi-objective Artificial Bee Colony Algorithm for Multi-stage Resource Leveling Problem in Sharing Logistics Network. *Comput. Ind. Eng.* **2020**, *142*, 106338. [CrossRef]
37. Huang, D.S. Radial Basis Probabilistic Neural Networks: Model and Application. *Int. J. Pattern Recognit. Artif. Intell.* **1999**, *13*, 1083–1101. [CrossRef]
38. Huang, D.; Du, J. A Constructive Hybrid Structure Optimization Methodology for Radial Basis Probabilistic Neural Networks. *IEEE Trans. Neural Netw.* **2008**, *19*, 2099–2115. [CrossRef]
39. Karpatne, A.; Watkins, W.; Read, J.; Kumar, V. Physics-guided Neural Networks (PGNN): An Application in Lake Temperature Modeling. *arXiv* **2017**, arXiv:1710.11431.
40. Raissi, M.; Perdikaris, P.; Karniadakis, G.E. Physics-informed neural networks: A deep learning framework for solving forward and inverse problems involving nonlinear partial differential equations. *J. Comput. Phys.* **2019**, *378*, 686–707. [CrossRef]
41. Tartakovsky, A.M.; Marrero, C.O.; Perdikaris, P.; Tartakovsky, G.D.; Barajas-Solano, D. Physics-Informed Deep Neural Networks for Learning Parameters and Constitutive Relationships in Subsurface Flow Problems. *Water Resour. Res.* **2020**, *56*, e2019WR026731. [CrossRef]
42. Dehghani, H.; Zilian, A. A hybrid MGA-MSGD ANN training approach for approximate solution of linear elliptic PDEs. *Math. Comput. Simul.* **2021**, *190*, 398–417. [CrossRef]
43. Wang, N.; Zhang, D.; Chang, H.; Li, H. Deep learning of subsurface flow via theory-guided neural network. *J. Hydrol.* **2020**, *584*, 124700. [CrossRef]
44. Csiszár, O.; Csiszár, G.; Dombi, J. Interpretable neural networks based on continuous-valued logic and multicriteria decision operators. *Knowl.-Based Syst.* **2020**, *199*, 105972. [CrossRef]
45. Huang, C.; Xu, H.; Xu, Y.; Dai, P.; Xia, L.; Lu, M.; Bo, L.; Xing, H.; Lai, X.; Ye, Y. Knowledge-aware Coupled Graph Neural Network for Social Recommendation. In Proceedings of the 35th AAAI Conference on Artificial Intelligence (AAAI), Virtual. 2–9 February 2021. [CrossRef]
46. Zandvliet, M.J.; Bosgra, O.H.; Jansen, J.-D.; Van den Hof, P.; Kraaijevanger, J.B.F.M. Bang-bang control and singular arcs in reservoir flooding. *J. Pet. Sci. Eng.* **2007**, *58*, 186–200. [CrossRef]
47. Khan, Z.; Chaudhary, N.I.; Zubair, S. Fractional stochastic gradient descent for recommender systems. *Electron. Mark.* **2019**, *29*, 275–285. [CrossRef]

Article

Structural Balance under Weight Evolution of Dynamic Signed Network

Zhenpeng Li [1,†], Ling Ma [2,*,†], Simin Chi [2,†] and Xu Qian [2,†]

1 School of Electronics and Information Engineering, Taizhou University, Taizhou 318000, China; lizhenpeng@amss.ac.cn
2 School of Mathematics and Computer Science, Dali University, Dali 671000, China; 526845789@nit.zju.edu.cn (S.C.); qx@stu.dali.edu.cn (X.Q.)
* Correspondence: ml@stu.dali.edu.cn
† These authors contributed equally to this work.

Abstract: The mutual feedback mechanism between system structure and system function is the 'hot spot' of a complex network. In this paper, we propose an opinions–edges co-evolution model on a weighted signed network. By incorporating different social factors, five evolutionary scenarios were simulated to investigate the feedback effects. The scenarios included the variations of edges and signed weights and the variations of the proportions of positive and negative opinions. The level of balance achieved depends on the connection weight and the distribution of negative edges/opinions on the signed graph. This paper sheds light on the analysis of constraints and opportunities of social and cognitive processes, helping us understand the real-world opinions polarization process in depth. For example, the results serve as a confirmation of the imperfect balance theory, i.e., even if the system evolves to a stable state, the signed network still cannot achieve perfect structural balance.

Keywords: structural balance; feedback mechanism; opinions polarization

MSC: 91Cxx; 91Dxx; 91Exx

1. Introduction

Nodes in social networks represent individuals or organizations, and edges among nodes represent the interaction [1–6]. The signed network is a topology with positive and negative signs on the edges. The signed edge has abundant connotations in many real complex systems. For example, a negative edge usually means disagreement, hostility, opposition, and distrust; correspondingly, a positive edge represents agreement, friendship, support, and trust [7,8]. The investigations on the signed network can effectively improve our knowledge on signed complex systems, such as international relation [9], promoting and inhibiting neurons [1], trust prediction on social networks [10], consensus and polarization of online community [11], information diffusion [12], opinion dynamics [13,14].

The most basic theory in the field of the signed network is a structural balance theory [8], which was first put forward by Heider in 1946. This theory originated from the balanced model of the node's attitude towards things [15]. Cartright and Harry [16] extended the theory by combining the graph theory. Later, scholars made great extensions, for example, Kunegis et al. [17] suggested that the network structural balance is measured by counting the proportion of balanced triads in the whole signed network, Fachetti et al. [18] proposed an energy function definition to calculate the structural balance. Real-world signed networks rarely attain a perfectly balanced state. To quantify exactly how balanced they are, Aref et al. [19] formalized the concept of a measure of partial balance. Kirkley et al. [20] proposed two measures of structural balance based on hypothesized notions of "weak" and "strong" balance.

Indeed, since the seminal work of Heider, many fundamental concepts and significant theories have been proposed for the development of the social balance theory. The extension of the classic structure balance theory can be divided into four categories. They are the balance of nodes, the balance of triangles, the balance of complete networks, and the balance of arbitrary networks. See [21] for a comprehensive review of the variations, extensions, and calculating methods related to the classic social balance theory.

Although the structural balance theory in signed networks describes a stable signed system state, the system from imbalance to balance is a dynamic process [22,23]. For example, the formation of friend or enemy groups, the constantly changing international relation. In order to investigate the dynamics of structural balance, Wu et al. [24] set up a co-evolution model in the acyclic network and cycle network. Marvel et al. [25] proposed a continuous-time model of structural balance. He et al. [26] developed a new simulation model to study the impact of structural balance on the evolution of cooperation in signed networks. However, currently, the research of dynamic networks is mostly limited to non-signed nodes or signed networks without weights. The co-evolution models of nodes and edges based on weighted signed networks have not been deeply investigated because of their complexity.

2. Related Works

Social influence network and opinion change models, such as the French-DeGroot model [27], Friedkin–Johnsen model [28], formally entail the interpersonal influence on the formation of interpersonal agreements and polarization. Social influence and its induced homogeneous effect, however, do not fully interpret the global network structure, for example, the mounting two-polarization phenomenon in US political ecology that insulates democrats and republicans from opposing opinions about current events [29]. Social network influence theory entails the interpersonal influence on the formation of interpersonal agreements and polarization. From a complex network perspective, this influence process is the feedback effect of the network structure on network functions.

In the real world, most of the signed graphs are temporal, the nodes and edges vary over time, which makes the changing of the network structure, including the clustering and the structural balance of the network. Many researchers are interested in the dynamic processes over signed networks, i.e., the co-evolution between the signed edges and the nodes, such as the agreement and disagreement evolving over random dynamic networks [30–33]. However, most of these models lack the social mechanisms of opinion formation, evolution, and dissemination.

Real-world cases call for these two threads of research, opinion dynamics and structural balance dynamics, to be combined. Holme and Newman [34] presented a simple model of this combination without any theoretical analysis. Wang et al. [35], in the latest relevant research, proposed co-evolution models for both dynamics of opinions (people's views on a particular topic) and dynamics of social appraisals (the approval or disapproval towards each other). In their model, the system evolves as opinions and edge weights are updated over time by two rules: opinion dynamics, and appraisal dynamics. Both opinion and appraisal dynamics are governed by the evolution of the time-varying matrix of a dynamic system. The social–psychological mechanisms of the co-evolution model in [35] involve the structure balance theory and social influence network theory, i.e., the Friedkin–Johnsen model. Similar to [35], Kang and Li [36] proposed a co-evolution model of discrete-time opinion evolution vectors and appraisal signed networks. Social–psychological mechanisms of the co-evolution model in [36] involve structure balance and the social distancing theory. This paper, inspired by these works, provides a ruled-based node–edge co-evolution model. However, different from a dynamic system time-varying matrix method [35,36], our model is rule-based and similar to the agent-based modeling approach. In our model, the global structure balance index is used as judgment conditions for a simulation algorithm termination. Our model's social–psychological mechanisms involve the structure balance theory and bounded confidence model of opinion dynamics [37], since the bounded confidence model is more suitable for paired interactions in large groups for agent-based modeling.

Some empirical investigations show that the unbalanced triangles will evolve into balanced ones to make the network more stable [38], and that the global level of balance of very large online singed networks is indeed extremely balanced [18,20]. Related investigations show that the structural balance of signed networks in the real world is an increasing function of evolution time. The evidence of over-represented balanced triads is well above random expectations in the vast majority of real networks, such as the statistic observation in references [18,20,38,39].

These empirical conclusions confirm the validity of the classic Heider structure balance theory. However, we still find that the complete perfect balanced structure is rarely observed in the real-world signed networks [20]; there is almost no perfect intra-/inter-group structure balance.

Relevant reference analyses urge researchers to promote this kind of research in-depth. This paper is devoted toward investigating the dynamic structural balance of groups and the emerging macro polarization patterns of signed networks. However, the data sets on related opinions and signed edges are not easy to obtain, this is why we shifted to the model simulation approach. In order to explain real-world ubiquitous opinion polarization and limited structure balance, different influence parameter values are used to explore the influences of different social factors on structural balance and polarization.

3. Our Contribution

In this paper, based on structural balance and a co-evolution model, considering the dynamic mechanics of both opinions and relationships, we employed two evolution rules: opinion renewal and edge adjustment. In addition, we defined an influence matrix and two new neutral dyadic/triadic motifs. A new co-evolutionary mutual feedback algorithm is provided to simulate our proposed model under five evolutionary scenarios.

Our findings can explain the lack of the perfect Heider balance in many real-world systems. This work verifies that signed social networks are indeed limited-balanced, but the level of balance achieved depends on the connectivity of the graph, the percentage of positive edges, and the percentage of positive opinions, most of all, on the distributions of these negative edges/opinions on the signed graph.

Our computational analysis of balance in signed networks serves as a confirmation of the balance theory. Meanwhile, our simulation results suggest that the signed network in the real world is a dynamic equilibrium process, which cannot reach a perfect equilibrium state. The comprehensive numerical results suggest that values of balance at the micro-and macro-levels may match up to some extent, especially as the macro dynamic pattern of the signed network is closely related to its micro-structural balance.

Compared with the current investigations on opinion dynamics on static networks, the proposed co-evolution model in this paper characterizes the polarization of opinions in reality and predicts the existence of imperfect balance in the social context. Our model may also help predict the potential division of social groups and public opinion dynamics.

This paper sheds light on the analysis of constraints and opportunities of social and cognitive processes, helping us to understand the real-world opinion polarization process, in depth.

4. Structural Balance in Signed Network

The social network influence theory entails interpersonal influence on the formation of interpersonal agreements and polarization. From a complex network perspective, this influence process is the feedback effect of the network structure on network functions. In this section, based on the dynamic social influence network theory, we code the dynamic weight social influence matrix, and propose two new neutral dyadic, triadic motifs, as preparation for our co-evolution model.

4.1. Binary Structural Balance

In this investigation, we introduce an edge named neutral edge ("0"), which is a neutral status between positive and negative edges. It refers to a kind of edge without a clear position, which means that the connection between nodes is not clear or neutral. After introducing the neutral edge, we propose a binary motif in a signed network, firstly. Three types of the binary motif are shown in Figure 1. Specifically, two nodes share the same attitude; at the same time, the signed edge between the two nodes is positive; then, we say the binary motif is balanced. If two nodes share an opposite attitude, and the signed edge between i and j is positive, then the binary structure is unbalanced. Based on the above analysis, a binary group includes two parameters, one is the nodes' opinion and the other is the edge sign between the two nodes. A neutral edge ("0") means that there is no clear connection between two nodes. However, in the dynamic evolution process, the neutral edge has the opportunity to evolve into negative or positive, due to the constraints of structural balance.

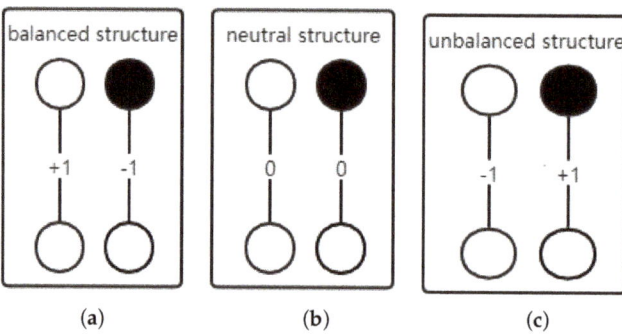

Figure 1. (a) Balanced binary groups, (b) neutral binary groups, (c) unbalanced binary groups.

4.2. Triad Structural Balance

Holland and Leinhardt [40] proposed the three basic binary motifs, reciprocity, asymmetric, and non-edge or null edge. It is worth noting that the null edge plays the same role as our proposed neutral edge ("0"). Since structural balance is defined on a triadic motif, which is constructed based on three basic binary motifs; binary balance is equal to triadic balance.

Figure 2a,b denote a balanced triadic structure, Figure 2c,d denote an unbalanced triadic structure [2]. If the product of signed edges in each cycle is positive, the signed graph is balanced [16]. If each triad in a signed complete graph is balanced, then the signed graph is balanced. Here, since we consider the chance of a tried with $edge = 0$, a "neutral triadic motif" is introduced, for the case, the product of three sides in a triad is 0.

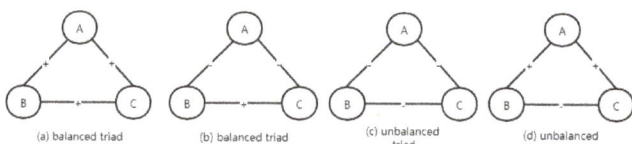

Figure 2. Triad structure in structural balance theory.

4.3. Global Structural Balance Index

Here, we use the global structural balance definition as formulated in Equation (1) [18], where $J_{ij} = +1$ denotes a positive edge between i and j, $J_{ij} = -1$, there is a negative edge between i and j, and $J_{ij} = 0$ implies a neutral edge between i and j. In the real world, a neutral edge might be considered a i and j have no influence on each other, or the two nodes remain neutral on an issue. s_i is a continuous real value, representing node i's opinion, and the range of s_i is $(-1,1)$; $1 > s_i > 0$ means node i holds a supportive attitude, $-1 < s_i < 0$ means node i holds a negative attitude, and $s_i = 0$ means node i hold an neutral attitude. It is worth noting that a triad-based structural balance is consistent with the global structural balance definition. A smaller value of h_s means a more balanced social structure.

$$h_s = \sum_{(i,j)} (1 - J_{ij} s_i s_j)/2 \tag{1}$$

4.4. Social Influence Matrix

The social influence network is a formal theory that forms attitudes and perspectives. It describes the influence processes of individuals on group attitudes in interpersonal networks. It allows the analysis of how the network structures of groups affect the formation of individual attitudes and group structures [41]. Based on this theory, we propose a social influence matrix, which provides a sociological perspective for the process of signed edge transformation. The type of edge will evolve according to the weight of the social influence matrix.

Friedkin and Johnsen's [41] social influence network theory is regarded as the cornerstone reference for social influence matrix consensus or polarization, as the important and regular group opinions dynamic pattern is generally observed in a group discussion and barging process. Friedkin and Johnsen's social influence network theory emphasizes that the interpersonal influence social structure, i.e., the social influence matrix is the underlying precondition for group consensus or opinion convergence [42]. In that model, the initial social influence structure of a group of actors is assumed to be fixed during the entire process of opinion formation. However, with the evolution of timestamps, considering both stubborn and susceptible effects, the interpersonal influence structure can be regarded as a dynamic recursive process. For this reason, the interpersonal influence structure in their model is also dynamic. Based on the dynamic social influence network theory, here we code the dynamic weight social influence matrix in Equation (2). In Equation (2), we set different influence weights to map to signed edges $-1, +1, 0$. To meet the needs of model simulation calculation, we set different weight ranges corresponding to different social influence intensities.

Within the framework of the social influence network theory, we set up three types of social influence, namely positive, negative, and neutral influence. Positive influence means that two individuals/nodes have homogeneous influence and a positive edge. Negative influence means that two individuals/nodes have opposite influence and a negative edge. Neutral influence means that two individuals/nodes do not influence each other. In this study, based on the adjacent matrix of the signed network, a social weighted influence matrix is randomly assigned to edges. With the assumption of strength difference—of mutual influence among individuals—we set three kinds of weights, w_{ij}, as shown in Figure 3 and Equation (2).

$$J_{ij}(t) = \begin{cases} -1, & \text{if } 0 < w_{ij} \leq 1 \\ 0, & \text{if } 1 < w_{ij} < 3 \\ +1, & \text{if } 3 \leq w_{ij} \end{cases} \tag{2}$$

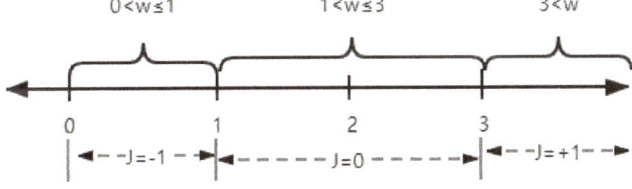

Figure 3. Mapping of weights and edges.

5. Co-Evolution Model of Opinions and Edges

The coupling effect of opinion propagation and network topology dynamics on networks leads to complex system behaviors. In order to study the propagation behavior and influencing factors in dynamic complex networks and the dynamic evolution process of the systems, we set up a co-evolution model of opinions and edges. In a social group, people are supposed to be motivated to keep a 'balanced edge' with others, when two people have the same attitude; if they have negative edges, they tend to change their edges or attitudes in order to maintain a balanced structure. The following is the evolution process introduced in detail.

5.1. Evolutionary Rule of Opinions

The Deffuant–Weisbuch (DW) model [37] is the most widely used continuous opinion dynamic model. The rule of this model is that two nodes change their opinions if the degree of disagreement is less than the threshold ϵ, i.e., $|s_i(t) - s_j(t)| \leq \epsilon$, $(i \neq j)$, the opinion is carried out as Equations (3) and (4). In this paper, we set the convergence parameter $\mu \in [0, 0.5]$, which indicates the strength of mutual influence among nodes.

$$s_i(t+1) = s_i(t) + \mu(s_j(t) - s_i(t)) \tag{3}$$

$$s_j(t+1) = s_j(t) + \mu(s_i(t) - s_j(t)) \tag{4}$$

The evolutionary rule of opinion follows Equation (5). To approach structural balance, the evolution of opinions will be based on the type of edge. By adjusting the proportion of initial positive and negative opinions, we can observe the evolution of group opinion. If i and j satisfy $\frac{J_{ij}}{s_i * s_j} \geq 0$, it means these two nodes follow the balanced binary conditions, and there is no need to change anyone's attitude. Considering the influence of the neighbor nodes, the opinion evolution will follow the DW model. On the contrary, if $\frac{J_{ij}}{s_i * s_j} < 0$, in the opinion evolution, the nodes will change their attitudes, and the attitudes in the next round will be opposite.

$$s_i(t+1) = \begin{cases} DW, & \text{if } \frac{J_{ij}}{s_i * s_j} \geq 0 \\ -s_i(t), & \text{if } \frac{J_{ij}}{s_i * s_j} < 0 \end{cases} \tag{5}$$

5.2. Evolutionary Rule of Edges

According to the different strengths of influence, we introduce three evolutionary rules of signed edges, respectively.

The rule for the evolution of the negative edge is illustrated in Figure 1, Equation (6), and Figure 4. When the edge is negative, it will change according to the opinion. If the attitudes of the two nodes are opposite, to achieve a balanced state, the negative edge will not change. If two nodes have the same attitude, the negative edge should evolve to a positive edge. According to the division of weight range, $w_{i,j}$ plus w_1 (the strength of $edge = -1$ change to $edge = +1$), and $w_1 \in (0,1)$, the negative edge evolves into the positive edge.

$$w_{ij}(t+1) = \begin{cases} w_{ij}(t), & \text{if } J_{ij} = -1 \text{ and } (s_i * s_j) < 0 \\ w_{ij}(t) + (w_1 + 2), & \text{if } J_{ij} = -1 \text{ and } (s_i * s_j) \geq 0 \end{cases} \tag{6}$$

The rule for the evolutionary of a positive edge is shown in Equation (7) and Figure 4. When the attitude of two nodes is the same, and the edge is positive, there is a balanced structure between them. If the attitudes of two nodes are opposite and the edge is positive, in order to make the approach a balanced structure, w_{ij} minus w_3 (the strength of $edge = +1$ change to $edge = -1$), and $w_3 \in (0,1)$, the positive edge evolves into negative.

$$w_{ij}(t+1) = \begin{cases} w_{ij}(t), & \text{if } J_{ij} = +1 \text{ and } (s_i * s_j) \geq 0 \\ w_{ij}(t) - (w_3 + 2), & \text{if } J_{ij} = +1 \text{ and } (s_i * s_j) < 0 \end{cases} \quad (7)$$

Figure 4. Evolutionary rules of $edge = +1$ and $edge = -1$.

The rule for the evolution of a neutral edge is formulated in Equation (8) and illustrated in Figure 5. No matter whether the attitudes of the two nodes are opposite or consistent, the neutral edge may evolve into a positive edge or a negative edge. When two nodes have the same attitude, to make the binary motif approach the balanced state, the neutral edge needs to evolve into a positive edge, which affects w_{ij} add w_2 (the strength of $edge = 0$ change to $edge = +1$). If two node opinions are opposite, in order to make the edge evolve into a negative edge, concerning the social influence weight w_{ij}, subtract w_2 (the strength of $edge = 0$ change to $edge = -1$). w_2 always falls into the range of $(0,1)$.

$$w_{ij}(t+1) = \begin{cases} w_{ij}(t) + w_2, & \text{if } J_{ij} = 0 \text{ and } (s_i * s_j) \geq 0 \\ w_{ij}(t) - w_2, & \text{if } J_{ij} = 0 \text{ and } (s_i * s_j) < 0 \end{cases} \quad (8)$$

Figure 5. Evolutionary rules of $edge = 0$.

5.3. Model Algorithm

In this section, we propose the algorithm realization of the provided model, in detail. Firstly, to consider the influence of the hub node on the network, we used the BA scale-free network [4]. We initialized an undirected BA network with 100 nodes, 1539 edges, and a network density equal to 0.3109. Moreover, the observation is based on the average results of 1000 realizations. We find that $|h_s(t+1) - h_s(t)| \leq 0.01$ after 30 rounds. The parameter assignment is shown in Table 1. The parameter $value = 0.5$ is used to control whether the opinion evolves or the edge evolves. The algorithm is defined as Algorithm 1. In each round, a random number will be generated; when the random number is greater than $value$, the opinion evolution will be carried out; when the random number is less than $value$, the edge evolution will be carried out.

Algorithm 1: Model implementation process

Input: $N, R_s+(0), R_s-(0), R_r+(0), R_r-(0), R_r0(0), \epsilon, \mu, value$.
Output: $round, h_s(round), R_s+(round), R_s-(round), R_r+(round),$
$R_r-(round), R_r0(round), tri+(round), tri-(round), tri0(round)$.

1 Scenario ← Selection scenario1, scenario2, scenario3, scenario4, scenario5;
2 Generate a social influence matrix A and a threshold $value$ according to the scenario;
3 $round \leftarrow 1$;
4 Compute $h_s(0), tri+(0), tri-(0), tri0(0)$;
5 $round \leftarrow 2$;
6 **repeat**
7   tcounter ← 1;
8     $h_s \leftarrow 0$;
9   According to the social influence matrix A, the signed matrix J is solved;
10   **for** *each node i from the node in turn* **do**
11   **for** *each node j from the node in turn* **do**
12   num=random();
13   **if** *num* **then**
14   **if** $J_{ij}(t) == -1$ *and* $(s_i * s_j) \geq 0$ **then**
15            $A[i][j] \leftarrow A[i][j] + (w_1 + 2)$
16   **else if** $J_{ij}(t) == 0$ *and* $(s_i * s_j) < 0$ **then**
17            $A[i][j] \leftarrow A[i][j] - w_2$
18   **else if** $J_{ij}(t) == 0$ *and* $(s_i * s_j) \geq 0$ **then**
19            $A[i][j] \leftarrow A[i][j] + w_2$
20   **else if** $J_{ij}(t) == +1$ *and* $(s_i * s_j) < 0$ **then**
21            $A[i][j] \leftarrow A[i][j] - (w_3 + 2)$
22   **else if** $num > value$ **then**
23   **if** $|s_i(t) - s_j(t)| \leq \epsilon$ *and* $\frac{J_{ij}}{(s_i * s_j)} \geq 0$ **then**
24            $s_i(t+1) \leftarrow s_i(t) + \mu(s_j(t) - s_i(t))$;
25   **else if** $|s_i(t) - s_j(t)| \leq \epsilon$ *and* $\frac{J_{ij}}{(s_i * s_j)} < 0$ **then**
26            $s_i(t+1) \leftarrow -s_i(t)$
27    $h_s(round) \leftarrow h_s(round) + (1 - J_{ij} * s_i * s_j)/2$;
28   tcounter ← tcounter+1;
29    $round \leftarrow round + 1$;
30 **until** *tcounter=30*;

Table 1. Initialization Parameters.

Symbols (Parameters)	Description
N	Network size
$round$	The number of iterations
ϵ	Difference of opinion
μ	Convergence of opinion
$value$	Judgment parameter
R_s-	The number of negative opinions
R_s+	The number of positive opinions
R_r+	The number of positive edges
R_r-	The number of negative edges
R_r0	The number of neutral edges
$tri+$	The number of balanced triads

Table 1. Cont.

Symbols (Parameters)	Description
$tri-$	The number of unbalanced triads
$tri0$	The number of neutral triads

6. Simulation Results

In this section, to explore the influence of different social factors on structural balance, we will integrate different social factors into the proposed co-evolution model, and simulate and discuss the simulation results, in detail. The parameters set in different scenarios are given in Table 2.

Table 2. Simulation scenarios.

Scenario	Changed Parameters	Changed Parameters
1	ϵ	The influence of parameter ϵ.
2	R_s-	The influence of negative opinions.
3	$value$	The relation between opinion evolution and edge evolution.
4	w_1, w_2, w_3	The influence of various weights.
5	R_r+, R_r-, R_r0	The influence of various edges.

6.1. Scenario 1, the Influence of Parameter ϵ

In this experiment, we discuss the influence of different ϵ on the structural balance weighted signed network. The ratio of $edge = +1$ is 0.2, the ratio of $edge = 0$ is 0.5, and the ratio of $edge = -1$ is 0.3. Meanwhile, the proportion of positive opinions is 0.7, the rest is negative. Moreover, convergence parameter $\mu = 0.3$. The same values are set for w_1, w_2 and w_3, i.e., $w_1 = w_2 = w_3 = 0.3$.

As shown in Figure 6a–c, when ϵ is large, the weighted signed network has the fast velocity to approach structural balance, the number of balanced triads and positive edges in the same round is the largest. The reason is that the larger ϵ promotes nodes interacting with others, thus promoting consensus. As shown in Figure 6d, all nodes hold the positive opinion, as long as $\epsilon > 0.1$. According to the binary structural balance, because all opinions are positive, all edges are positive in the end, and the proportion of balanced triads is also higher. Based on the above analysis, we can conclude that the larger the ϵ is, the faster the network approaches the structural balance.

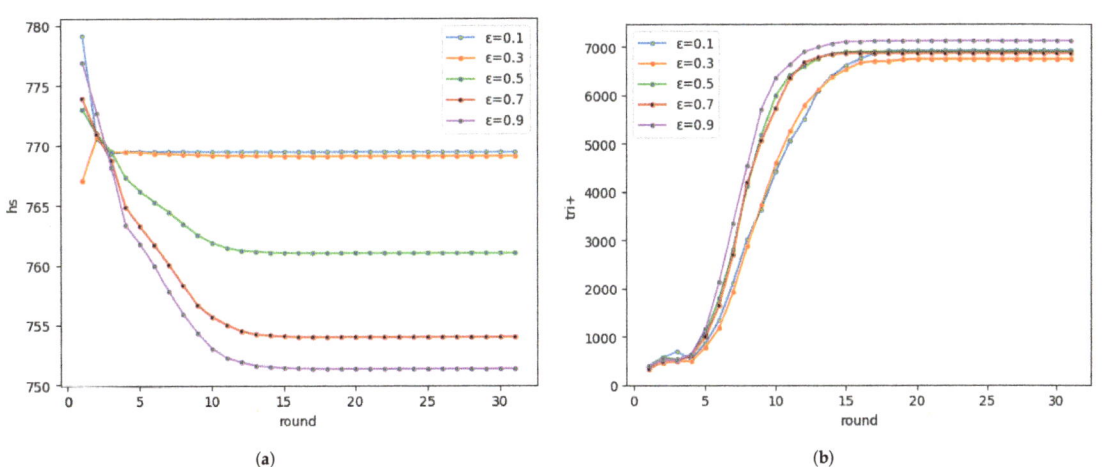

Figure 6. Cont.

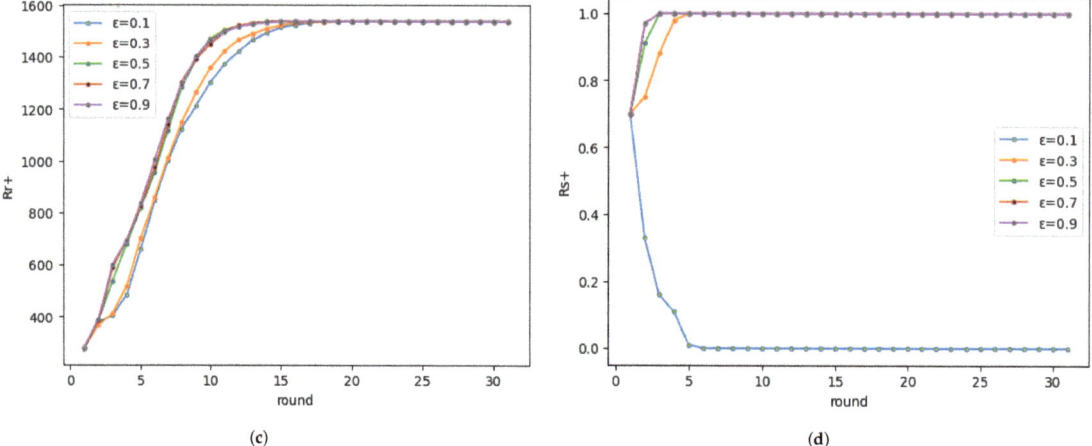

Figure 6. Effect of different ϵ: (**a**) h_s changes with time, (**b**) $tri+$ changes with time, (**c**) R_r+ changes with time, (**d**) R_s+ changes with time.

In conclusion, to accelerate the network to approach the structural balance, we can improve the tolerance of opinion differences by strengthening trust among nodes. In psychology, trust is a kind of stable belief, which maintains the common value and the stability of society.

6.2. Scenario 2, the Influence of Negative Opinions

This experiment discusses the influence of the initial number of negative opinions on the structural balance. Other parameter settings are the same as that in Scenario 2, the initial ratio of $edge = +1$ is 0.2, the ratio of $edge = 0$ is 0.5, and the ratio of $edge = -1$ is 0.3. Convergence parameter $\mu = 0.3$, and $\epsilon = 0.3$. The conversion strength between various edges are the same; that is, $w_1 = w_2 = w_3 = 0.3$. The parameter $value$ equals 0.7. To make our expression more compact, in the following scenarios, we focus on the change of h_s, since it is a key indicator for the evolution process of the signed networks. As shown in scenario 1, other indicators can be inferred from h_s.

The simulation results are shown in Figure 7. When all opinions are positive or negative, which is in the case of $R_s- = 0$ and $R_s- = 1$, the global structural balance index changes faster, and the network approaches structural balance faster. However, when the proportion of negative opinions is about 0.5, the global structural balance index does not change.

In scenario 1, because the positive opinions are in the majority at the beginning, the network can approach the balanced state under different ϵ. However, in this scenario, we set the same ϵ, when the positive or negative opinions occupy the majority, the network can approach the balanced state faster. Because the more nodes with the same attitude, according to the binary structural balance, the negative edge and neutral edge evolve to the positive edge, so the number of positive edges and balanced triads are the most. It can be concluded from scenario 2 that when there are many nodes with the same attitude in a network, the network can quickly approach the structural balance.

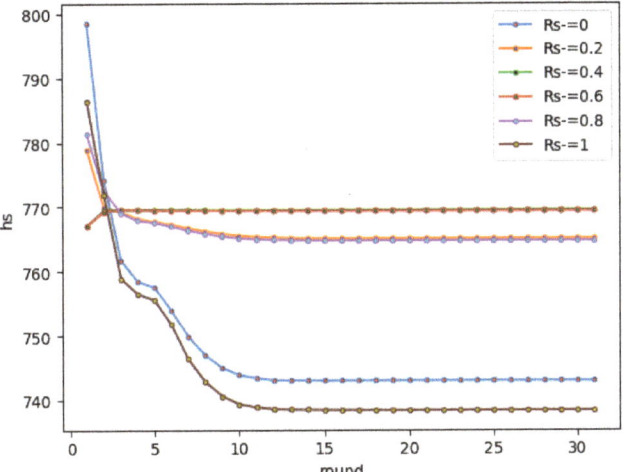

Figure 7. Effect of negative opinions on network.

6.3. Scenario 3, the Relation between Opinion Evolution and Edge Evolution

In this experiment, we discuss the influence of *value* on the structural balance. The initial conditions are as follows: negative edges account for 0.3, neutral edges account for 0.5, positive edges account for 0.2, and positive opinions account for 0.7. The conversion strength between various edges are the same, i.e., $w_1 = w_2 = w_3 = 0.3$. Moreover, we set $\mu = 0.3$, $\epsilon = 0.4$. Four experimental results are discussed as follows.

The first result of this experiment is the global structural balance index. As shown in Figure 8, the larger the *value* is, the faster the network approaches structural balance. When the *value* is terribly small, the network cannot approach a balanced state. It can be observed that the network approaches structural balance except for the case of *value* = 0.2.

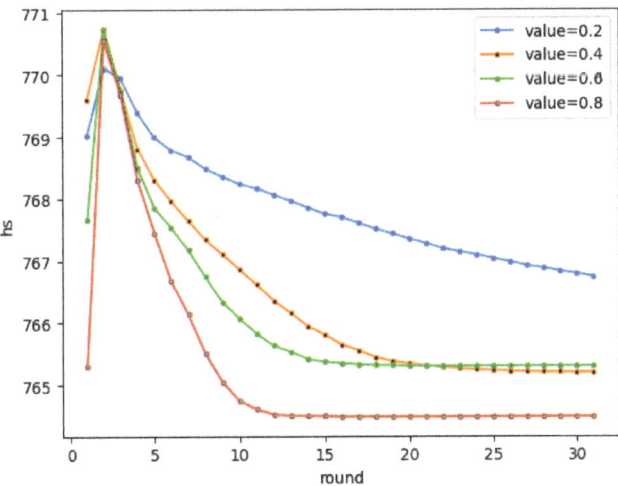

Figure 8. Effect of the parameter *value* on the global structural balance: h_s changes with time.

In Figure 9, we plot the impact of the control parameter *value* on the final network balanced triad and triad 0 (neutral triads). We observe that when *value* is larger, the number of balanced triads increase rapidly in Figure 9a. Moreover, neutral triads decrease rapidly in Figure 9b, When $value = 0.2$, a large number of neutral triads still exist after 30 rounds of evolution, it shows that the network has not reached structural balance. It can be concluded that in the process of approaching a balanced structure, it is more difficult to change the opinion than to change the edge.

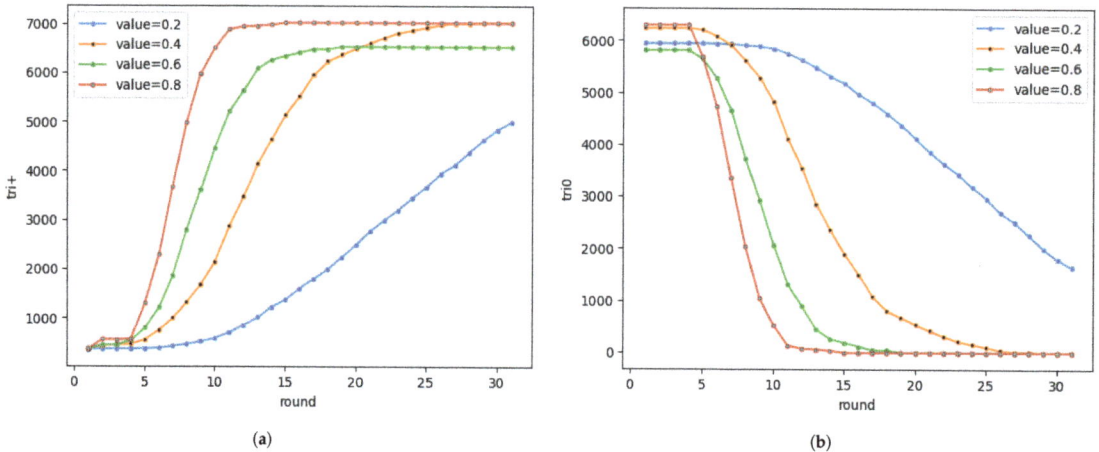

Figure 9. Effect of the parameter $value$ on the number of triads: (**a**) $tri+$ changes with time, (**b**) $tri0$ changes with time.

6.4. Scenario 4, the Influence of Various Strengths of Conversion

In this simulation, we explored the influence of the various strengths of conversion between various weighted edges. The strength of conversion represents the conversion level between different edges. The greater the strength is, the greater the connection strength between the nodes, and the more difficult the transformation of an edge is. In the initial network, we set the number of positive edges, negative edges, and neutral edges as equal, the convergence parameter $\mu = 0.3$, the degree of disagreement threshold was $\epsilon = 0.8$, the proportion of negative opinions was 0.3, the edge and node evolution control threshold parameter $value = 0.7$.

The first experiment involved observing the strength of the negative edge change to the positive edge. As seen in Figure 10, the experiment considered two cases, $w_1 = 0.5$ and $w_1 = 0.7$, respectively. When $w_1 = 0.7$, h_s reached a stable state quickly. This result shows that when w_1 is larger, i.e., the greater the strength of the negative edge change to the positive edge in the network, the network can approach a balanced structure more quickly. The result shows that it is difficult to change the negative edge to the positive.

The second experiment was to observe the transformation of neutral edges into negative and positive ones. As shown in Figure 11, when $w_2 = 0.5$ and $w_2 = 0.7$, the network approached a balanced state after 10 rounds. This experiment's results show that the strength of the neutral edge has a small influence on the structural balance. Because the neutral relationship implies that there is no clear relationship between two nodes, it is easier to convert the neutral edge to a positive edge or negative edge.

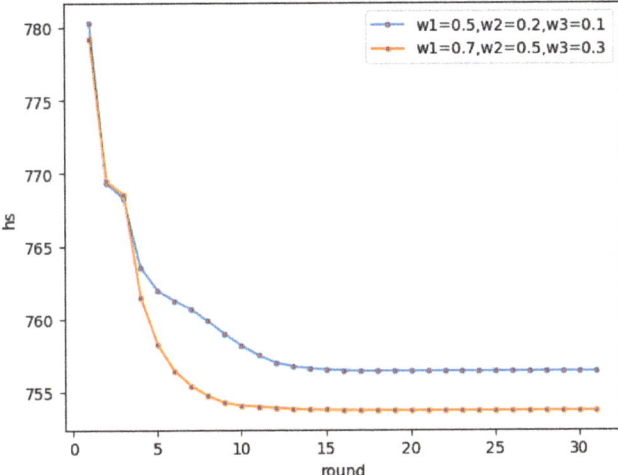

Figure 10. Effect of w_1: h_s changes with time.

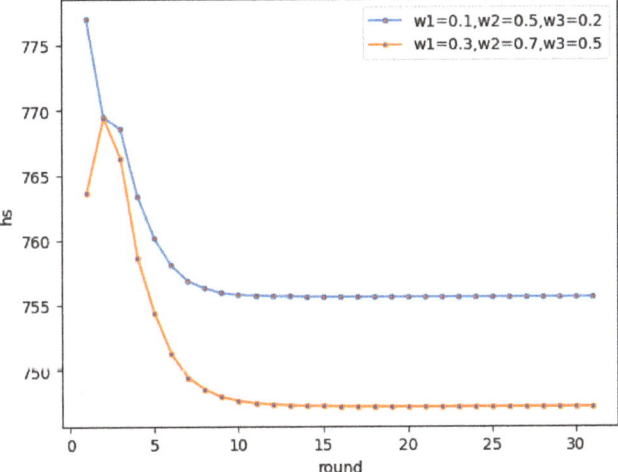

Figure 11. Effect of w_2: h_s changes with time.

The third experiment was to observe the strength of the positive edge change to the negative edge. As shown in Figure 12, after 10 rounds, h_s approached a stable state in the case of $w_3 = 0.7$; however, in the case of $w_3 = 0.5$, h_s was still evolving toward the structural balance. The result shows that it is difficult to convert the positive edge into the negative edge.

In conclusion, the various strengths of conversion have an effect on the final network structural balance. Increasing the strength of the negative edge and positive edge can promote the network to approach structural balance. We can conclude that it is easy to transform a neutral edge into a positive or negative edge; the contrary is difficult.

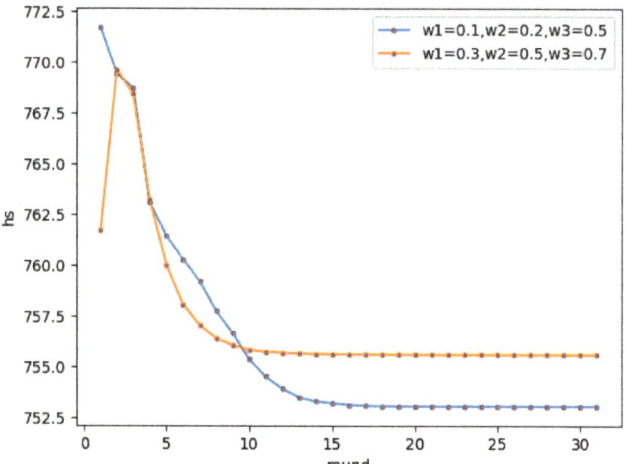

Figure 12. Effect of w_3: h_s changes with time.

6.5. Scenario 5, the Influence of Proportion of Positive and Negative Edges

In this experiment, we investigated the effects of different ratios of three types of edges on structural balance. We set the proportion of negative opinions as 0.3, $\mu = 0.7$, $\epsilon = 0.8$ and $value = 0.7$. The strength of conversion between various edges were the same; that is, $w_1 = w_2 = w_3 = 0.3$.

The influence of $edge = +1$ in the network is shown in Figure 13. It can be seen that the larger the ratio of R_r+, the faster h_s drops. By comparing with Figure 2, we can see that the proportion of positive edges in the balanced triads is $\frac{2}{3}$, and the proportion of the negative edges is $\frac{1}{3}$. Therefore, we conclude that the larger the number of initial R_r+ is, the faster the network approaches structural balance.

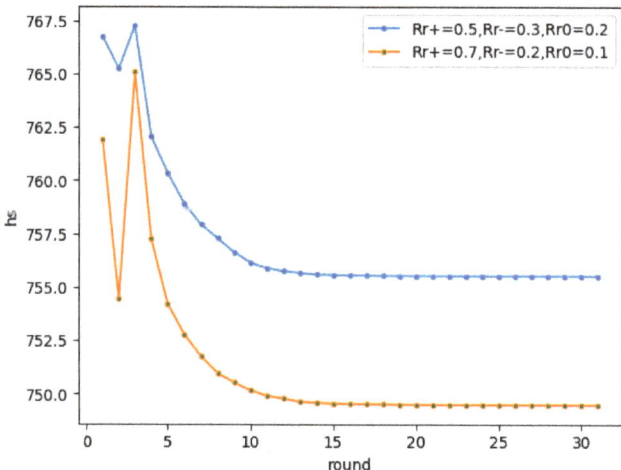

Figure 13. Effects of different initial ratios of positive edges: h_s changes with time.

Figure 14a,b show that positive edges are more likely to appear than negative and neutral edges. Therefore, the probability of a negative edge evolving into a positive edge is greater than that of a positive edge evolving into a negative edge within the framework of structural balance. The probability of structural transformation is illustrated in Figure 15, and the probability of structural transformation in Figure 15a is greater than that of Figure 15b.

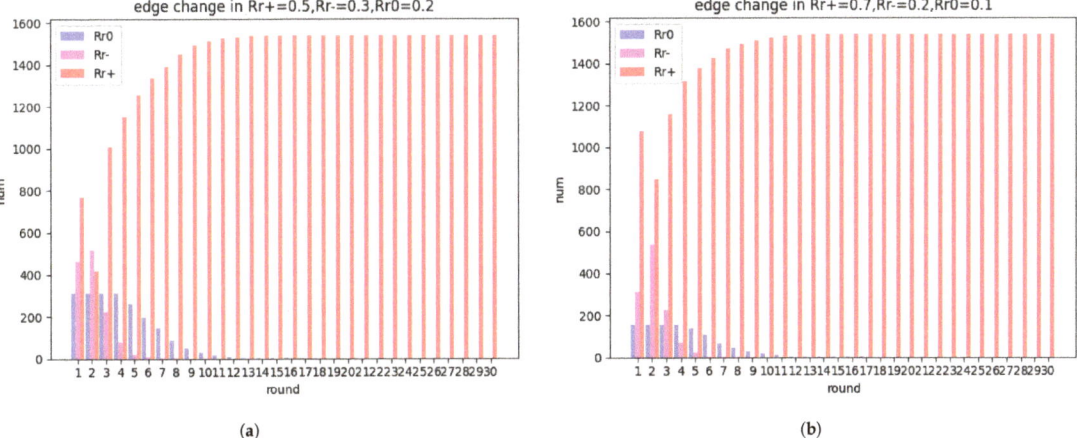

Figure 14. Changes in the number of various edges: (**a**) edges change in $R_r+ = 0.5$, $R_r- = 0.3$, $R_r0 = 0.2$; (**b**) edges change in $R_r+ = 0.7$, $R_r- = 0.2$, $R_r0 = 0.1$.

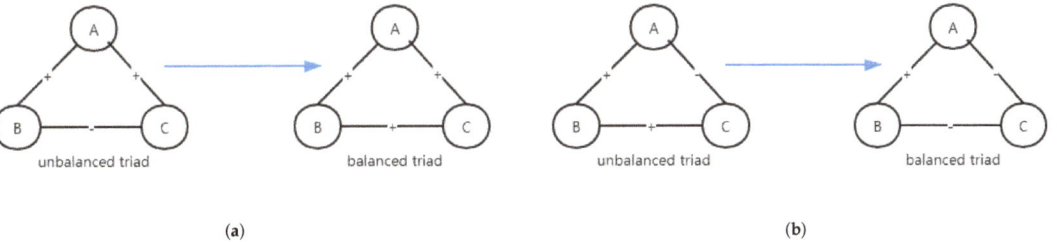

Figure 15. Changes of positive edge: (**a**) the edge between nodes B and C evolves from -1 to $+1$; (**b**) the edge between nodes B and C evolves from $+1$ to -1.

The influence of $edge = -1$ is shown in Figure 16. It can be observed that in the case of a low proportion of $R_r- = 0.5$, the network approaches structural balance faster. By analyzing Figure 2, we can see that the proportion of negative edges in the unbalanced triads is $\frac{2}{3}$, and the proportion of positive edges is $\frac{1}{3}$. Thus, the high proportion of negative edges will delay the network toward structural balance.

As shown in Figure 17a,b, we can see that the number of negative edges gradually decreased. The number of neutral edges remained unchanged in four rounds and then decreased, while the number of positive edges kept increasing until all edges became positive. Structural transformation is illustrated in Figure 18.

The influence of neutral edges on the final balanced state is shown in Figure 19. In Figure 19, it can be observed that after 20 rounds of evolution, a high number of neutral edges favor the network structural balance. The explanation is that the neutral edge may evolve to a positive edge and negative edge, and contribute to the increment of balanced triads.

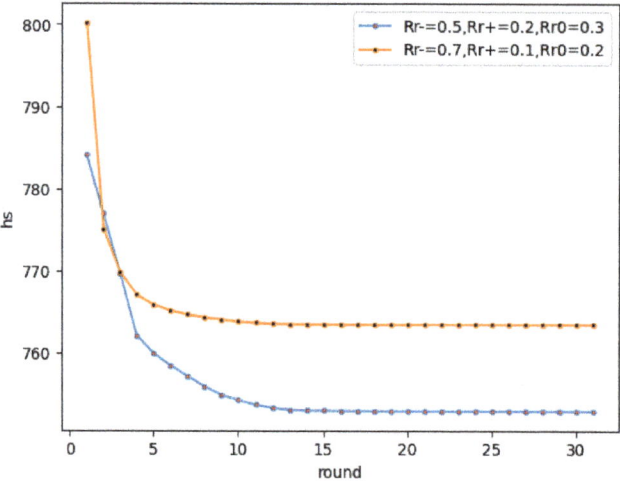

Figure 16. Effects of different initial ratios of negative edges: h_s changes with time.

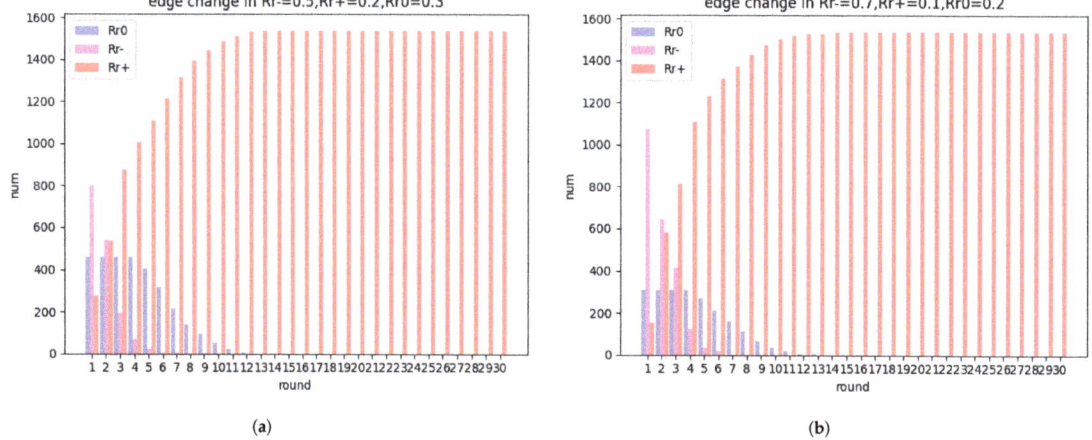

Figure 17. Changes in the number of various edges: (**a**) edges change in $R_r- = 0.5$, $R_r+ = 0.2$, $R_r0 = 0.3$; (**b**) edges change in $R_r- = 0.7$, $R_r+ = 0.1$, $R_r0 = 0.2$.

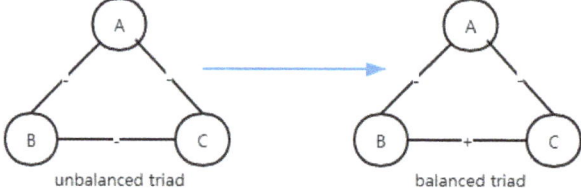

Figure 18. Negative edge changes: the edge between nodes B and C evolves from -1 to $+1$.

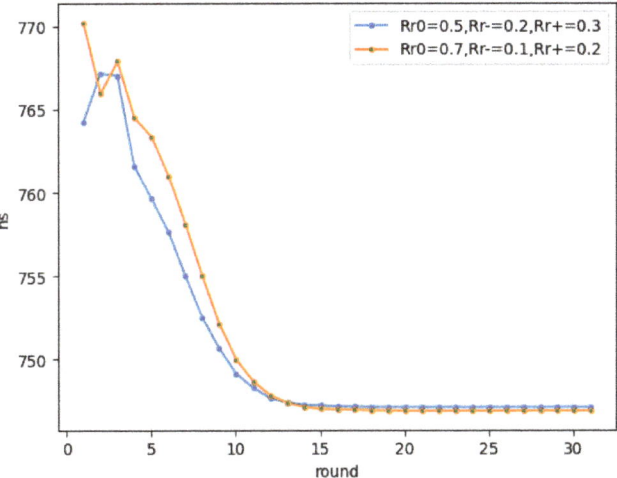

Figure 19. Effects of different initial ratios of the neutral edge: h_s changes with time.

By observing Figure 20a, we can see that both the number of neutral edges and negative edges decreased gradually before 10 rounds. This dynamic resulted in the gradual increase of positive edges. By observing Figure 20b, we can see that the number of neutral edges did not change in the first and second evolution rounds. However, from the third round, the negative and neutral edges began to decrease. These experimental results show that the probability of the neutral edge evolving into the positive edge was greater than that of the negative edge. The probability of structural transformation in Figure 21a is greater than that of Figure 21b. Since the network is toward a structural balance.

This scenario implies that we can increase the number of positive edges and neutral edges to make these edges become the main body, and reduce the negative edge to promote the harmonious development of the group. In a group, if there are more positive edges, the network will tend to be structurally balanced faster, while negative edges have a reverse effect.

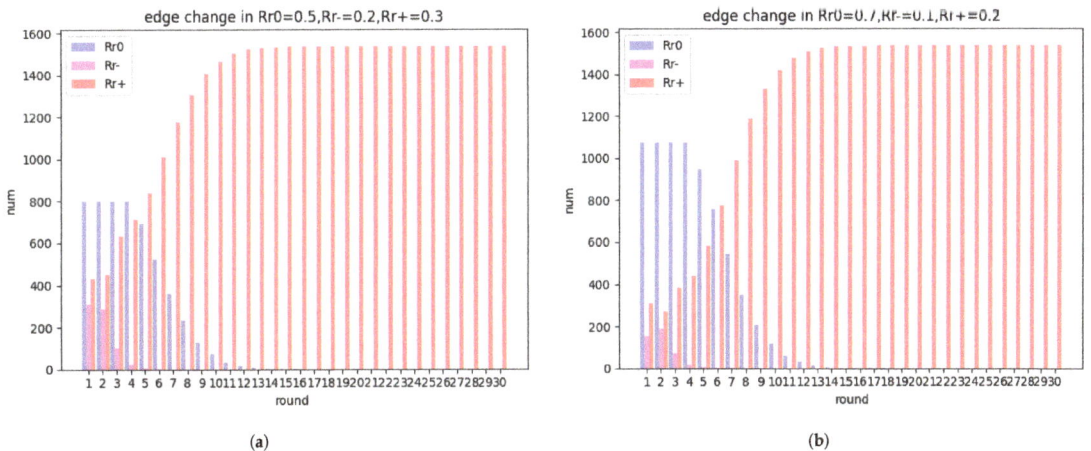

Figure 20. Changes in the number of various edges: (**a**) edges change in $R_r 0 = 0.5$, $R_r- = 0.2$, $R_r+ = 0.3$; (**b**) edges change in $R_r 0 = 0.7$, $R_r- = 0.1$, $R_r+ = 0.2$.

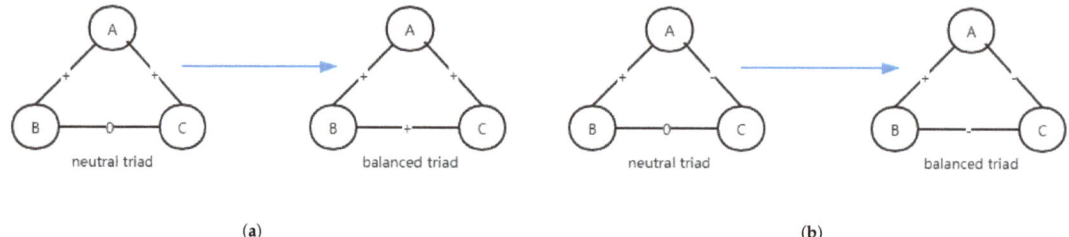

Figure 21. Changes of neutral edge: (**a**) the edge between nodes B and C evolves from 0 to +1; (**b**) the edge between nodes B and C evolves from 0 to −1.

7. Discussion

In our simulation, we also tested our proposed model on ER random graphs and WS small-world network structures. Our simulation suggests that final signed network evolution results are robust to different structures and sizes. The results only depend on the connection weight of the networks, the percentage of positive edges, and the percentage of positive opinions. We observed the same evolution trend on different signed networks.

In summary, five scenarios including variations of edges and signed weights and variations of the proportion of positive and negative opinions, were investigated to observe the final signed network stable state. Specifically, we performed extensive simulations to examine how different initial conditions affected the network evolution, i.e., the balance level of network structure and the opinion polarization pattern.

We observed that initial conditions, such as a high proportion of positive edges, positive opinions, and greater signed weights, could promote the signed network towards balance. Our simulation results suggest that the signed network in the real world is a dynamic equilibrium process, serving as confirmation of the imperfect balance theory, i.e., even if the system evolves to a stable state, the signed network still cannot achieve a perfect structural balance.

Importantly, the simulation results could explain the imperfect Heider balance of many real-world signed systems. Meanwhile, our computing model explains that the level of balance achieved depends on the connecting weight of the network, the percentage of positive edges, and the percentage of positive opinions, most of all, on the distributions of these positive edges/opinions and the weight on the signed network. The comprehensive numerical results suggest that values of balance at the micro-and macro-levels may match up to some extent; the macro dynamic pattern of the signed network is especially closely related to its microstructural balance.

Similar to the social influence network model, the proposed co-evolution model can be used to predict real-world signed network evolution on the final convergence state (structure balance level v.s. polarization pattern). However, the social influence network model (Friedkin, N.E. Johnsen, E.C., 1999) [28] and the co-evolution model of opinion and social tie dynamics (Wang, H.; Luo, F.; Gao J., 2021) [35] are based on rigorous time-varying matrix mathematical analyses. Our proposed model is a rule-based simulation, its effectiveness for large-scale signed social networks needs to be verified by an empirical data set. This is also the direction of our related work in the next step. In a follow-up to this study, we plan to conduct experiments based on real data sets to evaluate the effectiveness of the proposed social network evolution modeling. The basic idea is a rule-based model simulation and comparative analysis of a rule-based model adjustment with real-world empirical signed networks. Specifically, we will modify and estimate the key evolution parameters through the empirical process of edge-evolution and node-evolution of a real signed network G and then modify the rule-based model G^*. On the one hand, we can verify the effectiveness of our proposed model through the empirical evolution process of large-scale signed networks. On the other hand, we can refine our proposed model. Our ultimate expectation is that the refined model can achieve acceptable prediction accuracy and could be extended to the prediction and regulation of a real signed social system.

In our model, it is assumed that each node is homogeneous, and there is no special node, such as an opinion leader; in addition, final signed network evolution results only depend on different initial conditions, and are robust to different structures and sizes. Therefore, this model is also applicable to the case of having non-random distributions of opinions and edges.

8. Conclusions

In this investigation, based on the social influence network theory, we introduced a neutral binary motif and a triadic motif, and focused on the contributions of interpersonal influenced to the formation of interpersonal agreements and polarization. Our proposed edges–opinions co-evolution model entails a cognitive process when it deals with conflicting influential opinions and the signs and strengths of a social structure. This article extends the implications of the social structure balance theory and assesses the social influence theory in groups of dyads—triads with neutral relations.

Extensive simulations were performed in five cases. The results are summarized as follows: (1) the higher the tolerance for the difference of opinions, the faster the network can approach a balanced state. (2) The more nodes with the same attitude, the faster the network can reach structural balance. (3) When the edge evolution is faster than the opinion, the network can approach the balanced state faster. (4) The 'larger' the strengths of the positive and negative edges, the faster the network can approach the balanced state, while the strength of the neutral edge has a trivial effect. (5) The higher the proportion of positive and neutral edges, the faster the network can approach balance.

In particular, we showed that the persistent fluctuation of opinions is consistent with the minimal global energy function or a local triadic-signed structural balance emergence. This work verifies that signed social networks are indeed of limited balanced and could be used to explain the ubiquitous polarization phenomenon in online social networks. These results can provide us with a better understanding of the inherent mechanisms and key properties of signed networks.

Our model, however simple, should find further extensions and applications in social structures, where conditions of consistence are meaningful. For example, for a real signed network, in addition to structure and node attributes, the scale of the network will also change, such as the increase of nodes and the increase or deletion of edges. There may be other complex social mechanisms for the formation of real signed social networks, such as social status, social power theories, and combing with sentiment and behavioral data analysis [43–45]. The co-evolution feedback model we proposed can be further extended to such a case.

Next, we hope to collect real signed social network data to verify the effectiveness of several main conclusions obtained in this paper. We also hope to use the model and relevant conclusions proposed in this paper to empirically study collective action problems, such as information diffusion, cooperative evolution, and public opinion dissemination on signed social networks.

Author Contributions: Methodology, X.Q.; Visualization, S.C.; Writing—original draft, L.M.; Writing—review & editing, Z.L. All authors have read and agreed to the published version of the manuscript.

Funding: This research was supported by the National Natural Science Foundation of China under grant No. 71661001.

Data Availability Statement: All data included in this manuscript are available upon request by contacting with the corresponding author.

Acknowledgments: The authors thank the anonymous reviewers for their helpful comments on an earlier draft of this paper.

Conflicts of Interest: The authors declare no conflict of interest.

References

1. Brner, K.; Sanyal, S.; Vespignani A. Network science. *Annu. Rev. Inf. Sci. Technol.* **2010**, *41*, 537–607. [CrossRef]
2. Strogatz, S.H. Exploring complex networks. *Nature* **2001**, *410*, 268. [CrossRef] [PubMed]
3. Barabási, A.L. The New Science of Networks. *Phys. Today* **2003**, *6*.
4. Albert, R.; Barabasi, A.L. Statistical mechanics of complex networks. *Rev. Mod. Phys.* **2001**, *74*, xii. [CrossRef]
5. Boccaletti, S.; Latora, V.; Moreno, Y.; Chavez, M.; Hwang, D.U. Complex Networks: Structure and Dynamics. *Complex Syst. Complex. Sci.* **2006**, *424*, 175–308. [CrossRef]
6. Menache, I.; Ozdaglar, A.E. Network Games: Theory, Models, and Dynamics. *Synth. Lect. Commun. Netw.* **2011**, *4*, 159. [CrossRef]
7. Parisien, C.; Anderson, C.H.; Eliasmith, C. Solving the problem of negative synaptic weights in cortical models. *Neural Comput.* **2008**, *20*, 1473–1494. [CrossRef]
8. Heider, F. Attitudes and cognitive organization. *J. Psychol.* **1946**, *21*, 107–112. [CrossRef]
9. Ghosn, F.; Palmer, G.; Bremer, S.A. The MID3 data set, 1993–2001: Procedures, coding rules, and description. *Confl. Manag. Peace Sci.* **2004**, *21*, 133–154. [CrossRef]
10. DuBois, T.; Golbeck, J.; Srinivasan, A. Predicting trust and distrust in social networks. In Proceedings of the 2011 IEEE Third International Conference on Privacy, Security, Risk and Trust and 2011 IEEE Third International Conference on Social Computing, Boston, MA, USA, 9–11 October 2011; pp. 418–424.
11. Larusso, N.; Bogdanov, P.; Singh, A. Identifying communities with coherent and opposing views. In Proceeding of the 15th Annual Graduate Student Workshop in Computing, Santa Barbara, CA, USA, 28 September 2010; pp. 31–32.
12. Hosseini-Pozveh, M.; Zamanifar, K.; Naghsh-Nilchi, A.R. Assessing information diffusion models for influence maximization in signed social networks. *Expert Syst. Appl.* **2019**, *119*, 476–490 [CrossRef]
13. He, Q.; Sun, L.; Wang, X.; Wang, Z.; Huang, M.; Yi, B.; Wang, Y.; Ma, L. Positive Opinion Maximization in Signed Social Networks. *Inf. Sci.* **2021**, *558*, 34–49. [CrossRef]
14. Li, L.; Fan, Y.; Zeng, A.; Di, Z. Binary opinion dynamics on signed networks based on Ising model. *Physica A* **2019**, *525*, 433–442. [CrossRef]
15. Heider, F. Social perception and phenomenal causality. *Psychol. Reopinion* **1944**, *51*, 358–374. [CrossRef]
16. Cartwright, D.; Harary, F. A generalization of Heider's theory. *Psychol. Rev.* **1956**, *63*, 277–292. [CrossRef] [PubMed]
17. Kunegis, J.; Lommatzsch, A.; Bauckhage C. The slashdot zoo: Mining a social network with negative edges. In Proceedings of the 18th International Conference on World Wide Web, Madrid, Spain, 20–24 April 2009; pp. 741–750.
18. Facchetti, G.; Iacono, G.; Altafini C. Computing global structural balance in large-scale signed social networks. *Proc. Natl. Acad. Sci. USA* **2011**, *108*, 20953–20958. [CrossRef] [PubMed]
19. Aref, S.; Wilson, M.C. Measuring partial balance in signed networks. *J. Complex Netw.* **2018**, *6*, 566–595. [CrossRef]
20. Kirkley, A.; Cantwell, G.T.; Newman, M. Balance in signed networks. *Phys. Rev. E* **2019**, *99*, 012320. [CrossRef]
21. Zheng, X.; Zeng, D.; Wang, F.Y. Social balance in signed networks. *Inf. Syst. Front.* **2015**, *17*, 1077–1095. [CrossRef]
22. Hummon, N.P.; Doreian, P. Some dynamics of social balance processes: Bringing Heider back into balance theory. *Soc. Netw.* **2003**, *25*, 17–49. [CrossRef]
23. Antal, T.; Krapivsky, P.L.; Redner S. Dynamics of social balance on networks. *Phys. Rev. E* **2005**, *72*, 036121. [CrossRef]
24. Wu, Y.; Gao, L.; Zhang, Y.; Xiong, X. Structural balance and dynamics over signed BA scale-free network. *Physica A* **2019**, *525*, 866–877. [CrossRef]
25. Marvel, S.A.; Kleinberg, J.; Kleinberg, R.D.; Strogatz, S.H. Continuous-time model of structural balance. *Proc. Natl. Acad. Sci. USA* **2011**, *108*, 1771–1776. [CrossRef] [PubMed]
26. He, X.; Du, H.; Cai, M.; Feldman, M.W. The evolution of cooperation in signed networks under the impact of structural balance. *PLoS ONE* **2018**, *13*, e0205084.
27. French, J.R., Jr. A formal theory of social power. *Psychol. Rev.* **1956**, *63*, 181–194. [CrossRef] [PubMed]
28. Friedkin, N.E.; Johnsen, E.C. Social Influence Networks and Opinion Change. *Adv. Group Process.* **1999**, *16*, 1–29.
29. Conover, M.; Ratkiewicz, J.; Francisco, M.; Gonçalves, B.; Menczer, F.; Flammini, A. Political Polarization on Twitter. In Proceedings of the Fifth International Conference on Weblogs and Social Media, Barcelona, Spain, 17–21 July 2011.
30. Shi, G.; Johansson, M.; Johansson, K.H. How agreement and disagreement evolve over random dynamic networks. *IEEE J. Sel. Areas Commun.* **2013**, *31*, 1061–1071. [CrossRef]
31. Altafini, C. Consensus problems on networks with antagonistic interactions. *IEEE Trans. Autom. Control.* **2012**, *58*, 935–946. [CrossRef]
32. Shi, G.; Altafini, C.; Baras, J.S. Dynamics over signed networks. *SIAM Rev.* **2019**, *61*, 229–257. [CrossRef]
33. Altafini, C.; Lini, G. Predictable dynamics of opinion forming for networks with antagonistic interactions. *IEEE Trans. Autom. Control.* **2014**, *60*, 342–357. [CrossRef]
34. Holme, P.; Newman, M.E. Nonequilibrium phase transition in the coevolution of networks and opinions. *Phys. Rev. E* **2006**, *74*, 056108. [CrossRef]
35. Wang, H.; Luo, F.; Gao, J. Co-evolution of Opinion and Social Tie Dynamics towards Structural Balance. Available online: https://arxiv.org/abs/2107.05796 (accessed on 13 July 2021).

36. Kang, R.R.; Li, X. Coevolution of opinion dynamics on evolving signed appraisal networks. *Automatica* **2022**, *137*, 110138. [CrossRef]
37. Deffuant, G.; Neau, D.; Amblard, F.; Weisbuch, G. Mixing beliefs among interacting agents. *Adv. Complex Syst.* **2000**, *3*, 87–98. [CrossRef]
38. Liu, H.; Qu, C.; Niu Y, Wang, G. The evolution of structural balance in time-varying signed networks. *Future Gener. Comput. Syst.* **2020**, *102*, 403–408. [CrossRef]
39. Milo, R.; Shen-Orr, S.; Itzkovitz, S.; Kashtan, N.; Chklovskii, D.; Alon, U. Network motifs: Simple building blocks of complex networks. *Science* **2002**, *298*, 824–827. [CrossRef]
40. Holland, P.W.; Leinhardt, S . A Method for Detecting Structure in Sociometric Data. *Soc. Netw.* **1970**, *76*, 492–513. [CrossRef]
41. Friedkin, N.E.; Johnsen, E.C. *Social Influence Network Theory: A Sociological Examination of Small Group Dynamics*; Cambridge University Press: Cambridge, UK, 2011.
42. Li, Z.; Tang, X.; Chen, B.; Yang, J.; Su, P. Why continuous discussion can promote the consensus of opinions? *Comput. Soc. Netw.* **2016**, *3*, 9. [CrossRef]
43. Zhang, W.; Yan, S.S.; Li, J.; Tian, X.; Yoshida, T. Credit risk prediction of SMEs in supply chain finance by fusing demographic and behavioral data. *Transp. Res. Part E Logist. Transp. Rev.* **2022**, *158*, 102611. [CrossRef]
44. Wang, Q.; Zhang, W.; Li, J.; Mai, F.; Ma, Z. Effect of online review sentiment on product sales: The moderating role of review credibility perception. *Comput. Hum. Behav.* **2022**, *133*, 107272. [CrossRef]
45. Zhang, W.; Xie, R.; Wang, Q.; Yang, Y.; Li, J. A novel approach for fraudulent reviewer detection based on weighted topic modelling and nearest neighbors with asymmetric Kullback–Leibler divergence. *Decis. Support Syst.* **2022**, 113765. [CrossRef]

Article

The Sustainable Supply Chain Network Competition Based on Non-Cooperative Equilibrium under Carbon Emission Permits

Peiyue Cheng, Guitao Zhang * and Hao Sun

Departement of Management Science and Engineering, School of Business, Qingdao University, Qingdao 266071, China; 2019020339@qdu.edu.cn (P.C.); sunhao@qdu.edu.cn (H.S.)
* Correspondence: zhangguitao@qdu.edu.cn

Abstract: Under the background of a circular economy, this paper examines multi-tiered closed-loop supply chain network competition under carbon emission permits and discusses how stringent carbon regulations influence the network performance. We derive the governing equilibrium conditions for carbon-capped mathematical gaming models of each player and provide the equivalent variational inequality formulations, which are then solved by modified projection and contraction algorithms. The numerical examples empower us to investigate the effects of diverse carbon emission regulations (cap-and-trade regulation, mandatory cap policy, and cap-sharing scheme) on enterprises' decisions. The results reveal that the cap-sharing scheme is effective in coordinating the relationship between system profit and carbon emission abatement, while cap-and-trade regulation loses efficiency compared with the cap-sharing scheme. The government should allocate caps scientifically and encourage enterprises to adopt green production technologies, especially allowing large enterprises to share carbon quotas. This study can also contribute to the enterprises' decision-making and revenue management under different carbon emissions reduction regulations.

Keywords: non-cooperative equilibrium; complex supply chain network; environmental policies; circular economy

Citation: Cheng, P.; Zhang, G.; Sun, H. The Sustainable Supply Chain Network Competition Based on Non-Cooperative Equilibrium under Carbon Emission Permits. *Mathematics* **2022**, *10*, 1364. https://doi.org/10.3390/math10091364

Academic Editors: Wen Zhang, Xiaofeng Xu, Jun Wu and Kaijian He

Received: 26 February 2022
Accepted: 15 April 2022
Published: 19 April 2022

Publisher's Note: MDPI stays neutral with regard to jurisdictional claims in published maps and institutional affiliations.

Copyright: © 2022 by the authors. Licensee MDPI, Basel, Switzerland. This article is an open access article distributed under the terms and conditions of the Creative Commons Attribution (CC BY) license (https://creativecommons.org/licenses/by/4.0/).

1. Introduction

1.1. Background

As carbon emissions contribute to global warming through the greenhouse effect, the development of a circular economy has attracted the attention of many scholars [1–4]. Humans' industrial production continues to intensify, and carbon emissions are directly linked to supply chain activities, which include the production process, transportation, distribution, and end-of-life product disposal [5]. The production process is always accompanied by high emissions and environmental pollution, especially in industry. Therefore, sustainable supply chain development has become the focus of the *EU-ETS* and The Paris Agreement [6]. The European Commission announced that transportation has become the second-biggest greenhouse gas (GHG) emitter preceded only by energy, and accounts for almost a quarter of European GHG emissions. Especially, road transport has significant contributions to CO_2 emissions in addition to the contributions from the maritime and aviation sectors.

In reality, the supply chain has become more complex and rapidly evolved into supply chain networks along with globalization and specialization. In a complex supply chain network, firms face risks not only from variable demand but also from their competitors [7–9]. Therefore, pollution and sustainability issues should be highlighted because of their fierce effect on both supply chain networks and societies and countries.

As the main advocator of a low-carbon society, international organizations and governments have taken some actions at the macro level. For example, The Paris Agreement, which entered into force on 4 November 2016, made arrangements for global action on climate change after 2020. Many countries are facing unprecedented carbon emission stress and have thus set their abatement goals [10,11]. As the biggest developing country, the Chinese government promised that China's carbon emission intensity would be reduced by 60–65% in 2030, compared with that in 2005 [12]. The intensity of energy consumption would continue to decline, and the resource output efficiency would increase substantially. To achieve the promised emission reduction targets, governments have enacted several environmental policies which enforce firms to accomplish green transformation development.

On the other hand, the sustainable and circular economy also provides some opportunities for enterprises. The enterprises can build reverse channels or adopt green production technologies to undertake social responsibility. As a fast fashion brand, in 2016, Uniqlo established its R&D center called the Jeans Innovation Center (JIC) in California. Aiming at creating a more environmentally friendly production approach, JIC not only adopts ecological water washing materials but also develops laser-fading technology [10]. In the reverse flow, recycling and remanufacturing are efficient methods used to enhance resource utilization. The recycling process can be realized by two modes: original equipment manufacturers (OEMs) recycling and third-party recycling [13–15]. The latter mode is more efficient in dealing with the dramatically increased end-of-life (EOL) products and plays an important role in promoting a circular economy [16–18].

1.2. Practical Motivation

Our research investigates a real case of China's paper industrial supply chain network. The manufacturers are divided into two segments called eco manufacturers and non-eco manufacturers according to whether they employ advanced low-carbon production technology. In addition, the collection centers include online recycling platforms and third-party intelligent recycling systems.

According to survey data gathered by the China Paper Association, there were about 2700 large-scale paper-making enterprises in 2018, and there were about 500 emission control enterprises included in carbon trading. The paper and paperboard production capacity was 104.35 million tons, and the total amount of wastepaper recycling in China was 49.64 million tons.

In 2015, China's total carbon emissions were 9084.62×10^6 tons of carbon dioxide equivalent, of which the carbon emissions of the paper industry accounted for 1.67% of China's total emissions and ranked seventh among all industries. The carbon emission of a paper enterprise comprises three components: carbon emission from fossil fuel combustion, carbon emission from production, carbon emission from the net purchase of electricity and heat. According to the statistics, carbon emissions from fossil fuel combustion account for the majority, about 81.3%, and coal occupies the vast majority of fossil fuel combustion. Therefore, the use of coal can represent the carbon emissions of the paper industry. Through the above calculation, we can obtain the carbon dioxide produced per ton of paper and show this information in the form of labels; that is, make carbon labels and stick carbon labels on the products.

According to the statistics of most paper-making enterprises, the production of one ton of paper emits about 3000 kg of carbon dioxide, which is both directly produced in the production process and indirectly generated in the relevant links. In addition, the transport of paper products from manufacturers to consumers also produces carbon dioxide, especially in cases in which heavy vehicles are used for long-distance transportation. After it is used by consumers, paper can be recycled by a third-party recycler such as the Little Yellow Dog recycling system, which is widespread in some communities in China, and several online recycling platforms that also conduct wastepaper recycling. After cleaning and related treatment, about 800 kg of recycled paper can be obtained by recycling one ton of wastepaper; thus, this process can greatly reduce the use of raw materials and carbon emissions.

Paper enterprises are also constantly innovating their production technologies. Some manufacturers, such as Shanghai Oriental Champion Paper Co., Ltd., one of the leading thin paper manufacturers in China, Shanghai. have switched from off-site coal-fired power generation to on-site gas-fired power generation, which has improved energy efficiency, reduced the carbon footprint by 60%, and reduced power costs by one fifth.

1.3. Research Question and Contributions

On the basis of the above background, this paper tries to investigate three questions:

(1) There is always a conflict between environmental protection goals and economic development goals. As for the government, how to properly enact policy or combine the advantage of different policies? Moreover, what are the differences between each kind of polices?
(2) Carbon emission constraint incurs intense pressure on enterprises. They will face the choice of adjusting production planning passively or undertaking the social responsibility initiatively. Then, how should enterprises make operation decisions under different policies?
(3) What is the benefit of reverse logistics? Does it affect enterprise strategy? What are the related parameters that influence supply chain performance such as consumers' environmental awareness or recovery ratio?

To answer these questions, we first consider a strict carbon emission permits supply chain network in which the government sets an emission threshold. Then we extend the base model in two ways. First, we assume government adopts cap-and-trade regulation to stimulate enterprises' production enthusiasm. The government allocates enterprises free carbon caps before production begins, and firms should determine their strategy under certain caps. Second, we suppose caps flow among firms without transaction cost. This situation may occur among different enterprises within a large enterprise group and promote enterprises' collaboration.

Three CLSCN models were built based on practical cases. Using variational inequality theory, modified projection algorithms, and contraction algorithms, models can be transformed and solved. The equilibrium results under different situations are compared through numerical simulation.

The major contributions of this paper can be summarized as follows:

(1) We incorporate carbon trade regulations into the equilibrium model of a CLSCN to analyze the impacts of carbon trade behaviors of the two types of manufacturers on equilibrium decisions.
(2) We first propose the carbon trade subnet and the product transaction subnet in the SCN and introduce the carbon trade center as a place for carbon trading.
(3) By comparing three carbon reduction regulations, we illustrate the different laws of decision and profits and emission control and identify best practices for enterprises under different regulations.

We organized the remaining parts as follows. We provide a comparative discussion of the previous research highly related to our research in Section 2. Section 3 provides the notations and assumptions to accurately describe the decision models. In Section 4, the variational inequality models and the algorithm used to solve the models are described. Section 5 analyzes the results of numerical experiments to obtain the enlightenment of the management. Finally, we present the conclusions and suggestions in Section 6. The qualitative properties of the corresponding variational inequality models are presented in the Appendix C.

2. Literature Review

This paper focuses on sustainable supply chains, cap-and-trade regulations, non-cooperative equilibrium, and consumers' environmental awareness. To better highlight our research issue, we briefly reviewed some relevant studies on these subjects. We will also point out the difference between our study and previous ones.

2.1. Sustainable Supply Chain

Pressure from stakeholders for sustainable development is forcing top management to reconsider its supply chain management, and the pursuit of sustainability has evolved as a popular trend in supply chain management [10,19]. Motivated by international retailers (e.g., Walmart and H&M) cooperating with their suppliers to reduce carbon emissions across supply chains, [10] investigated information sharing and studied its effect on carbon emission reduction. Considering a supply chain consisting of two competing manufacturers and a retailer, [20] studied the optimal green technology investment strategy problem of upstream manufacturers. Guo et al. [21] established a fashion supply chain consisting of one manufacturer and two competing retailers and discussed how retailer competition and consumer returns affect the development of green products in the fashion industry.

Recently, remanufacturing has come into focus as an area of economic and environmental insight [22–25]. Savaskan et al. [22] were among the first to divide the CLSC recycling model into the manufacturer recycling model, vendor recycling model, and third-party recycling model. The results of their work illustrated that the vendor recycling model is the most effective approach. Taleizadeh et al. [26] analyzed the effects of the third-party recycler in a CLSC under deterministic demand. Zerang et al. [27] established a three-echelon closed-loop supply chain model, and the results showed that the manufacturer-Stackelberg case is often the most effective scenario in CLSC.

Although the above-mentioned papers investigate the closed-loop supply chain in depth, the cap-and-trade regulation has been neglected as an effective approach to reducing carbon emissions, and thus needs further discussion.

2.2. Cap-and-Trade Regulations

To stimulate enterprises to actively reduce their carbon emissions through economic incentives, the government launched carbon trading, which can also be called cap-and-trade regulations. The *European Union Emissions Trading Scheme (EU-ETS)* is a successful form of cap-and-trade regulations. China launched its first carbon trading pilot in 2013, which entered into force in 2019. Therefore, it is important to explore the impacts of cap-and-trade regulations on enterprises, and conducting a simulation study on global carbon emission rights trading can provide practical outcomes [28–35]. Zhang and Xu [36] provided a basis for decision making on the reasonable use or sale of carbon emission rights by manufacturers and made a comparative analysis of the effectiveness of carbon trading and carbon tax. Du et al. [37] analyzed the game between decision-makers on product pricing and output considering cap-and-trade regulations and obtained a unique Nash equilibrium based on the basic Newsboy model. Yang et al. [38] and Yang et al. [39] both explored the channel selection problems under cap-and-trade regulations. The former asserts that products' properties and consumers' channel preferences are key factors affecting manufacturers' channel selection. The latter highlights that both the level of carbon emissions reduction and the profits of manufacturers increase with the manufacturer's product promotion.

Unlike our research, the above studies do not combine cap-and-trade regulations with reverse logistics. Moreover, they ignore the fact that carbon trade volume should be a decision variable in decision making.

2.3. Supply Chain Network Based on Non-Cooperative Equilibrium

The business crosses and fierce competition among supply chain members present the supply chain as a hierarchical network structure, including various enterprises and demand markets. With the coexistence of a competition and cooperation relationship, according to the rational person assumption, the corporate goal is to maximize its profits. Non-cooperative competition among the same types of members in the network forms a Nash equilibrium. Our study is also related to the literature rooted in supply chain network equilibrium under different environmental policies. In this field, scholars have carried out several studies on decision-making problems with different network structures [5,38,39]. Nagurney et al. [40] first established the SCN equilibrium model, making a great contribution to the promotion and application of supply chain network theory, and applied it to diverse fields [41,42]. With the implementation of environmental protection policies, He et al. [43] studied the joint effect of the mandatory cap policy and operational decision mode on profitability and emissions. The results illustrate that the cap-sharing scheme can achieve Pareto improvement for chain players' profit and obtain a win-win situation for system profit and GHG emission reduction. Tao et al. [44] studied two types of mandatory cap policies under a multi-period scenario supply chain network and found that decision-makers can adjust their strategies under global carbon emissions constraints in most cases. He et al. [45] considered a supply chain super network constrained by a mandatory cap policy and examined the joint effect of stringent carbon regulations and operational decision modes on system performance.

2.4. Consumers' Environmental Awareness

Currently, consumers are increasingly concerned about the energy crisis and global warming and are focused on environmentally friendly and green products [34,46]. In 2014, the Eurobarometer Commission survey stated that 75% of Europeans tended to buy green products at a higher price [47,48], which promotes the development of eco-friendly products. In China, a report by the AliResearch Institute found that the total number of consumers who have environmental awareness increased by 14% during 2011~2015, and reached 65 million in 2015 [49]. Consumers' green preferences change their purchase behavior and promote low-carbon development [48]. Therefore, in this paper, the consumers' environmental awareness level is introduced to depict the social environment more realistically.

2.5. Research Gap

We highlight the contribution of the aforementioned studies in Table 1. The literature review has shown that most previous studies examine the optimization of the supply chain under the given emission regulations. When a carbon cap exists, most studies consider it as a given constant that constrains manufacturers' decision making. Most previous research related to carbon-constrained operations optimization only considers one or two kinds of carbon reduction policies. There is a lack of literature comparatively analyzing the impact of cap-and-trade regulations, mandatory cap policy, and cap-sharing schemes on multiple decision-makers under CLSCN.

Table 1. Comparison of related research papers in low-carbon regulations.

Literature	Consumer's Green Awareness	Low-Carbon Policy		Supply Chain Structure		Research Method	
		Carbon Tax	Cap-and-Trade	SC	Network	Empirical Analysis	Modeling Analysis
1. [1]							✓
2. [2]	✓		✓	✓			✓
3. [3]	✓	✓	✓		✓		✓
4. [4]	✓	✓			✓		✓
5. [5]	✓	✓			✓		✓
6. [7]		✓		✓			✓
7. [17]	✓		✓	✓			✓
8. [20]	✓			✓			✓
9. [21]	✓			✓			✓
10. [28]			✓	✓			✓
11. [31]						✓	
12. [32]						✓	
13. [35]	✓		✓	✓			✓
14. [39]					✓		✓
15. [48]	✓			✓			✓
16. [49]	✓		✓	✓			✓
This paper	✓	Cap-and-trade, mandatory cap, cap sharing			✓		✓

To fill this gap, our study focuses on how different regulations influence members' profits and carbon emissions in a CLSCN and investigate the remanufacturing's impact on members' equilibrium decisions. The results present meaningful information for the government to enact better carbon regulations and enterprises to adopt better operational policies.

3. Notations and Assumptions

3.1. Notations

The following parameters, decision variables, endogenous variables, and functions shown in Tables 2–5 are used throughout the remainder of this paper.

Table 2. Parameters of the model.

Parameters	Definition
i	A typical ecological manufacturer, $i = 1, 2, \cdots, I$.
j	A typical non − ecological manufacturer, $j = 1, 2, \cdots, J$.
k	A typical demand market, $k = 1, 2, \cdots, K$.
h	A typical collection center, $h = 1, 2, \cdots, H$.
ε	Unit carbon trading commission charged by carbon trading center.
ω	Unit carbon trading price between non-eco manufacturers and eco manufacturers.
ε_x	The recycling ratio of EOL products of manufacturers in demand markets, $x = i, j$.
δ	The proportion of reusable materials extracted from recycled products when collection centers dispose EOL products from demand markets.
β^x	$x = r$ denotes the raw material conversion ratio, $x = u$ denotes the reusable material conversion ratio.
σ	Consumer environmental awareness level.
cap_x	The carbon cap of manufacturers allocated by the government, $x = i, j$.
α_x^y	The carbon emission of unit product. $x = 1$ denotes non − eco product, $x = 2$ denotes eco product, $y = i, j$.
τ_t	Carbon emission factor of a truck.
x_s	The distance (in km) between two supply chain members. $s = jk, ik, hj, hi$.
t_x	The number of trucks serving different transactions in the CLSC network. $x = 1$ denotes the number of trucks between non-ecological manufacturers and demand markets; $x = 2$ denotes the number of trucks between non-ecological manufacturers and collection centers; $x = 3$ denotes the number of trucks between eco manufacturers and demand markets; $x = 4$ denotes the number of trucks between eco manufacturers and collection centers.
ρ	The total transport costs of unit product.

Table 3. Decision variables of the model.

Decision Variables	Notations
q_x^v	The amount of raw material used by manufacturers to produce new products, $x = i, j, \boldsymbol{q}_j^v = \left(q_j^v\right)_{J \times 1} \in R_+^J, \boldsymbol{q}_i^v = (q_i^v)_{I \times 1} \in R_+^I$.
q_x^u	The amount of reusable material used by manufacturers to remanufacture products, $x = i, j, \boldsymbol{q}_j^u = \left(q_j^u\right)_{J \times 1} \in R_+^J, \boldsymbol{q}_i^u = (q_i^u)_{I \times 1} \in R_+^I$.
q_{jk}	The amount of products that a non-ecological manufacturer j sells and transfers to demand market k, $\boldsymbol{Q}_1 = \left(q_{jk}\right)_{JK \times 1} \in R_+^{JK}$.
q_{hj}^u	The amount of reusable material from collection center h to non-ecological manufacturer j, $\boldsymbol{Q}_2 = \left(q_{hj}^u\right)_{HJ \times 1} \in R_+^{HJ}$.
q_{ik}	The amount of product that ecological manufacturer i sells and transfers to demand market k, $\boldsymbol{Q}_3 = (q_{ik})_{IK \times 1} \in R_+^{IK}$.
q_{hi}^u	The amount of reusable material from collection center h to ecological manufacturer i, $\boldsymbol{Q}_4 = \left(q_{hi}^u\right)_{HI \times 1} \in R_+^{HI}$.
q_{kh}^u	The amount of recycling EOL (end of life) product from demand market k to collection center h, $\boldsymbol{Q}_5 = \left(q_{kh}^u\right)_{KH \times 1} \in R_+^{KH}$.

Table 3. Cont.

Decision Variables	Notations
t_j	The carbon cap amount of non-ecological manufacturer j buying from carbon trade center, $T_1 = (t_j)_{J \times 1} \in R_+^J$.
t_i	The carbon cap amount of ecological manufacturer i selling to carbon trade center, $T_2 = (t_i)_{I \times 1} \in R_+^I$.
ρ_k^j	The price consumers paid for non-ecological products in demand market k, and $\rho^J = \left(\rho_k^j\right)_{K \times 1} \in R_+^K$.
ρ_k^i	The price consumers paid for ecological products in demand market k, and $\rho^I = \left(\rho_k^i\right)_{K \times 1} \in R_+^K$.

Table 4. Endogenous variables of the model.

Endogenous Variables	Notations
ρ_{xk}	The product price between manufacturers and demand market k, $x = i, j$.
ρ_{hk}	The EOL product recycling price paid by collection center h to consumers in demand market k.
ρ_{hj}	The reusable material price paid by non-ecological manufacturer j to collection center h.
ρ_{hi}	The reusable material price paid by ecological manufacturer i to collection center h.

Table 5. Functions of the model.

Functions	Notations
$f_x = f_x(\beta^r, q_x^v)$	The production cost function of manufacturers x, $x = i, j$.
$f_x^u = f_x^u(\beta^u, q_x^u)$	The remanufacturing cost function of manufacturers x, $x = i, j$.
$c_{xk} = c_{xk}(q_{xk})$	The transaction cost function from manufacturers x to demand market k, $x = i, j$.
$c_{xk}^K = c_{xk}^K(q_{xk})$	The transportation cost burden assumed by consumers to obtain the product.
$c_x^t = c_x^t(t_x)$	The carbon transaction cost undertaken by carbon trade center, $x = i, j$.
$c_{hx}^u = c_{hx}^u(q_{hx}^u)$	The transaction cost from collection center to manufacturers, $x = i, j$.
$c_h = c_h(q_{kh}^u)$	The disposal cost function of collection center h.
$c_{kh} = c_{kh}(q_{kh}^u)$	The transaction cost from demand market k to collection center h.
$\alpha_k^u(Q_5)$	Disutility to consumers due to collection of EOL product.
$d_k^l = d_k^l(\rho^I, \rho^J, \sigma)$	The demand function of ecological product.
$d_k^h = d_k^h(\rho^J, \rho^I)$	The demand function of non-ecological product.

3.2. Assumptions

To highlight the research question of the models developed later in Section 4, some assumptions need to be presented as follows.

Assumption 1. *The manufacturers are divided into two types called "non-eco manufacturer" and "eco manufacturer" according to whether they adopt green production technology. Eco manufacturers undertake higher production costs than non-eco manufacturers due to their possession of better production technology to decrease carbon emissions, and two products have a certain substitution relationship [50]. This assumption comes from reality (e.g., Huawei mobiles phones and Apple mobile phones). As it can be seen in the demand function:*

$$d_k^l = 250 - 2\rho_k^l - 1.5\rho_{3-k}^l + 0.5(\rho_k^h + \rho_{3-k}^h) + \sigma\psi \sum_{x=1}^{2}(1 - \alpha_x^l); d_k^h = 230 - 2\rho_k^h - 1.5\rho_{3-k}^h + 0.5(\rho_k^l + \rho_{3-k}^l) + \sigma\psi \sum_{x=1}^{2}(1 - \alpha_x^J)$$

the quantity of each kind of product is affected by both its own and another product's selling price, which represents the substitution relationship between them.

Assumption 2. *The new product and remanufactured product are homogeneous [51,52]. However, re-manufactured products have lower production costs and unit carbon emissions than the new ones. This assumption refers to the literature [22,53,54]. Savaskan et al. used the Eastman Kodak Company example to illustrate this relationship. Used cameras are typically upgraded to the quality of new ones, and both products can perfectly substitute each other. In this paper, we address the carbon emissions in the production process; thus, different types of products emit the same carbon dioxide when used.*

Assumption 3. *Carbon emissions are generated during both the production and transportation processes [50]. To avoid trivial cases and to focus on the goals of this research, we only consider the total carbon emissions of each truck and do not carry out further analyses on the distance covered by vehicles.*

Assumption 4. *The carbon quota allocation mechanism is based on "Benchmarking," which can be more effective in pushing facilities to reduce carbon emissions [2,55]. Under cap-and-trade regulations, caps can be sold or bought to satisfy the target production [2].*

Assumption 5. *The consumers' environmental awareness level is reflected in the demand function [56,57].*

Assumption 6. *The cost functions in this paper are all continuous differentiable convex functions [40,58].*

4. Model

In this paper, we consider three scenarios of carbon reduction regulations. The mandatory cap policy requires manufacturers not to emit more than a specific quota. Otherwise, the firm will face heavy penalties that force it to comply with the policy. As for the cap sharing policy, the total carbon emissions of different firms cannot exceed the aggregate quota of these firms; the carbon quotas can be transferred freely between two types of manufacturers. The cap-and-trade policy requires a carbon trade market that charges a certain commission from the enterprises participating in the carbon transaction and seeks maximum profit.

In addition, the European Commission is willing to regulate heavy-duty vehicles' carbon emissions; this willingness is modeled in this paper. Trucks are only supposed to be used in the main logistics phases: (1) forward logistics: transferring products from manufacturers to customers; (2) reverse logistics: transferring reusable raw materials from collection centers to manufacturers. As assumed in [59], transferring EOL products from demand markets to collection centers is undertaken by smaller dimension vans that are not regulated strictly.

In the following, we construct three equilibrium models according to different policies, and the different closed-loop supply chain network structures are shown in Figure 1.

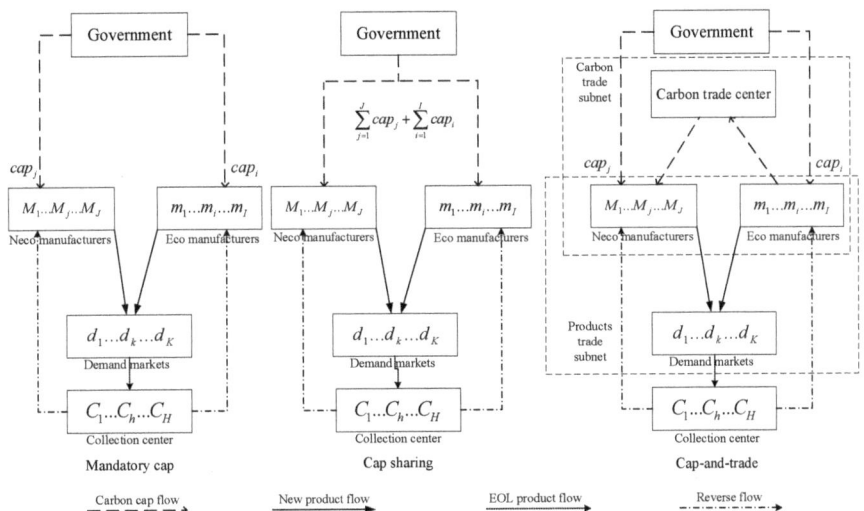

Figure 1. Closed-loop supply chain network structures.

4.1. Demand Market Decisions

Demand markets are the final demand points of product transaction in forward flow and are also the source of EOL products in reverse flow. In a forward transaction, consumers of each demand market decide the quantity of non-eco products and eco products that they want to buy according to the prices charged by manufacturers and transaction costs. In a reverse transaction, consumers sell the EOL products to collection centers when the recycling prices are reasonable and can compensate for the loss of consumers caused by recycling.

According to the previous functions and notations definition, for the non-eco products in demand market k, we have the following complementary relationships:

$$\rho_{jk}^* + c_{jk}^{K*} \begin{cases} = \rho_k^{h*}, & \text{if } q_{jk}^* > 0 \\ \geq \rho_k^{h*}, & \text{if } q_{jk}^* = 0 \end{cases} \tag{1}$$

$$d_k^h \begin{cases} = \sum_{j=1}^{J} q_{jk}^*, & \text{if } \rho_k^{h*} > 0 \\ \leq \sum_{j=1}^{J} q_{jk}^*, & \text{if } \rho_k^{h*} = 0 \end{cases} \tag{2}$$

When the transactions between non-eco manufacturers and demand markets occur, $q_{jk}^* > 0$ and $\rho_k^{h*} > 0$ hold simultaneously, and the demand and supply are equal. Otherwise, the transactions cannot occur.

Similarly, for the eco products, we have:

$$\rho_{ik}^* + c_{ik}^{K*} \begin{cases} = \rho_k^{l*}, & \text{if } q_{ik}^* > 0 \\ \geq \rho_k^{l*}, & \text{if } q_{ik}^* = 0 \end{cases} \tag{3}$$

$$d_k^l \begin{cases} = \sum_{i=1}^{I} q_{ik}^*, & \text{if } \rho_k^{l*} > 0 \\ \leq \sum_{i=1}^{I} q_{ik}^*, & \text{if } \rho_k^{l*} = 0 \end{cases} \tag{4}$$

In the reverse logistics, after the consumption process, part of the products become EOL products that have no use value and can be recycled. When these EOL products are sent to collection centers, it will bring disutility to consumers. We assume $\alpha_k^u(Q_5)$ is a monotonically increasing function that depends on the collected volume vector Q_5, which means more EOL products collection brings higher consumers' disutility. Further, the more recycling products are recycled by collection centers, the higher the buy-back prices are. If the buy-back price ρ_{kh}^{u*} can compensate the disutility of consumers, that is, $\rho_{kh}^{u*} = \alpha_k^u(Q_5^*)$, then recycling transactions will occur; otherwise, recycling transactions will not occur. This relationship can be described as the following complementary form:

$$\alpha_k^u(Q_5^*) \begin{cases} = \rho_{kh}^{u*}, & \text{if } q_{kh}^{u*} > 0 \\ \geq \rho_{kh}^{u*}, & \text{if } q_{kh}^{u*} = 0 \end{cases} \tag{5}$$

$$s.t. \sum_{h=1}^{H} q_{kh}^u \leq \varepsilon_j \sum_{j=1}^{J} q_{jk} + \varepsilon_i \sum_{i=1}^{I} q_{ik} \tag{6}$$

Constraint (6) indicates that the products in reverse logistics are always less than those in forward logistics.

Integrating the forward and reverse behavior of consumers, the optimality conditions of demand markets can be defined as follows: determine the optimal solution $(Q_1^*, Q_3^*, \rho^{J*}, \rho^{I*}, Q_5^*, \gamma^*) \in \Omega_k$, satisfying:

$$\sum_{j=1}^{J} \sum_{k=1}^{K} \left[\rho_{jk}^* + c_{jk}^{K*} - \rho_k^{h*} - \varepsilon_j \gamma_k^*\right] \times \left[q_{jk} - q_{jk}^*\right] + \sum_{i=1}^{I} \sum_{k=1}^{K} \left[\rho_{ik}^* + c_{ik}^{K*} - \rho_k^{l*} - \varepsilon_i \gamma_k^*\right] \times \left[q_{ik} - q_{ik}^*\right] +$$
$$\sum_{k=1}^{K} \left[\sum_{j=1}^{J} q_{jk}^* - d_k^{h*}\right] \times \left[\rho_k^h - \rho_k^{h*}\right] + \sum_{k=1}^{K} \left[\sum_{i=1}^{I} q_{ik}^* - d_k^{l*}\right] \times \left[\rho_k^l - \rho_k^{l*}\right] + \tag{7}$$
$$\sum_{h=1}^{H} \sum_{k=1}^{K} \left[\alpha_k^u(Q_5^*) - \rho_{kh}^{u*} + \gamma_k^*\right] \times \left[q_{kh}^u - q_{kh}^{u*}\right] + \sum_{k=1}^{K} \left[\varepsilon_j \sum_{j=1}^{J} q_{jk}^* + \varepsilon_i \sum_{i=1}^{I} q_{ik}^* - \sum_{k=1}^{K} q_{kh}^{u*}\right] \times \left[\gamma_k - \gamma_k^*\right] \geq 0.$$
$$\forall (Q_1, Q_3, \rho^J, \rho^I, Q_5, \gamma) \in \Omega_k$$

where $\Omega_k = R_+^{JK+IK+J+I+KH+K}$, γ_k is the Lagrangian multiplier corresponding to Constraint (6), and $\gamma = (\gamma_k)_{K \times 1} \in R_+^K$.

4.2. Collection Centers' Decisions

In the reverse logistics, the collection center h recycles these EOL products by paying price ρ_{kh}^u to consumers in demand markets. After separating, detecting, and other treatments, these EOL products are transformed to various reusable materials and then are sold to manufacturers at price ρ_{hj}^u and ρ_{hi}^u, respectively. Therefore, the collection center h needs to decide the recycling quantity of EOL products and the sold quantity of reusable materials. Collection center h seeks to maximize its profit that can be described as:

$$\max \left[\sum_{j=1}^{J} \rho_{hj}^{u*} q_{hj}^u + \sum_{i=1}^{I} \rho_{hi}^{u*} q_{hi}^u - \sum_{k=1}^{K} (\rho_{kh}^{u*} q_{kh}^u + c_{kh}) - c_h\right] \tag{8}$$

$$s.t. \sum_{j=1}^{J} q_{hj}^u + \sum_{i=1}^{I} q_{hi}^u \leq \delta \sum_{k=1}^{K} q_{kh}^u \tag{9}$$

The objective function is the difference of the revenues and costs. The revenues are $\sum_{j=1}^{J} \rho_{hj}^{u*} q_{hj}^u + \sum_{i=1}^{I} \rho_{hi}^{u*} q_{hi}^u$ resulting from selling reusable materials to non-eco manufacturers and eco manufacturers at prices ρ_{hj}^{u*} and ρ_{hi}^{u*}, respectively. The costs include the buy-back price $\sum_{k=1}^{K} \rho_{kh}^{u*} q_{kh}^u$ paid for consumers in demand markets, the disposal cost c_h, and the transaction cost c_{kh}. Constraint (9) ensures the trade-off between manufacturing and re-manufacturing. Finally, all decision variables are non-negative.

All collection centers compete in a non-cooperative manner, and all functions related are assumed continuous and convex. The optimal conditions of all collection centers can be expressed as following variational inequality: determine the optimal solution $(Q_2^*, Q_4^*, Q_5^*, \lambda^*) \in \Omega_h$, satisfying:

$$\sum_{j=1}^{J}\sum_{h=1}^{H}\left[\lambda_h^* - \rho_{hj}^{u*}\right] \times \left[q_{hj}^u - q_{hj}^{u*}\right] + \sum_{i=1}^{I}\sum_{h=1}^{H}\left[\lambda_h^* - \rho_{hi}^{u*}\right] \times \left[q_{hi}^u - q_{hi}^{u*}\right] + \\ \sum_{h=1}^{H}\sum_{k=1}^{K}\left[\frac{\partial c_{kh}^*}{\partial q_{kh}^u} + \frac{\partial c_h^*}{\partial q_{kh}^u} + \rho_{kh}^{u*} - \delta\lambda_h^*\right] \times \left[q_{kh}^u - q_{kh}^{u*}\right] + \sum_{h=1}^{H}\left[\delta\sum_{k=1}^{K}q_{kh}^{u*} - \sum_{j=1}^{J}q_{hj}^{u*} - \sum_{i=1}^{I}q_{hi}^{u*}\right] \times \left[\lambda_h - \lambda_h^*\right] \geq 0. \quad (10)$$

$$\forall (Q_2, Q_4, Q_5, \lambda) \in \Omega_h$$

where $\Omega_h = R_+^{HJ+HI+KH+H}$, λ_h is the Lagrangian multiplier corresponding to constraint (9), and $\lambda = (\lambda_h)_{H \times 1} \in R_+^H$.

4.3. The Supply Chain Network under Cap-and-Trade (CT) Policy

Under the cap-and-trade policy, we assume that the unit carbon quota price is exogenous and remains unchanged.

4.3.1. Non-Ecological Manufacturers' Decisions

We first study non-eco manufacturers' decisions. According to the previous Assumption 4, the non-eco manufacturer j needs to buy the quota that can be expressed as $t_j = \alpha_1^J \beta^r q_j^v + \alpha_2^J \beta^u q_j^u + t_1 \tau_t \sum_{k=1}^{K} x_{jk} q_{jk} + t_2 \tau_t \sum_{h=1}^{H} x_{hj} q_{hj}^u - cap_j$, the corresponding payment is $\varepsilon t_j + \omega t_j$. When manufacturer j pursues the maximization of profit, the objective function can be represented as:

$$\max \left[\sum_{k=1}^{K}\left(\rho_{jk}^* q_{jk} - c_{jk}\right) - \sum_{h=1}^{H}\left(\rho_{hj}^{u*} q_{hj}^u + c_{hj}\right) - f_j - f_j^u - \rho\left(t_1 \sum_{k=1}^{K} x_{jk} q_{jk} + t_2 \sum_{h=1}^{H} x_{hj} q_{hj}^u\right) - \varepsilon t_j - \omega t_j\right] \quad (11)$$

$$s.t.\ q_j^u \leq \sum_{h=1}^{H} q_{hj}^u \quad (12)$$

$$\sum_{k=1}^{K} q_{jk} \leq \beta^r q_j^v + \beta^u q_j^u \quad (13)$$

$$\alpha_1^J \beta^r q_j^v + \alpha_2^J \beta^u q_j^u + t_1 \tau_t \sum_{k=1}^{K} x_{jk} q_{jk} + t_2 \tau_t \sum_{h=1}^{H} x_{hj} q_{hj}^u - cap_j - t_j = 0 \quad (14)$$

Constraint (14) ensures that the manufacturer j's total carbon emissions are equal to the sum of cap_j and t_j.

Based on the CT model, in this case, manufacturer j needs to make an additional decision regarding the carbon transaction amount t_j. Hence, the optimum solution of the above objective function is characterized by the following variational inequality with $(q_j^{v*}, q_j^{u*}, Q_1^*, Q_2^*, T_1^*, \varphi_1^*, \varphi_2^*, \varphi_3^*) \in \Omega_j^1$, such that:

$$\sum_{j=1}^{J}\left[\frac{\partial f_j^*}{\partial q_j^v}-\beta^r\varphi_j^{2*}-\alpha_1^I\beta^r\varphi_j^{3*}\right]\times\left[q_j^v-q_j^{v*}\right]+$$

$$\sum_{j=1}^{J}\left[\frac{\partial f_j^{u*}}{\partial q_j^u}+\varphi_j^{1*}-\beta^u\varphi_j^{2*}-\alpha_2^I\beta^u\varphi_j^{3*}\right]\times\left[q_j^u-q_j^{u*}\right]+$$

$$\sum_{j=1}^{J}\sum_{k=1}^{K}\left[\frac{\partial c_{jk}^*}{\partial q_{jk}}-\rho_{jk}^*+\rho t_1 x_{jk}+\varphi_j^{2*}-t_1\tau_t x_{jk}\varphi_j^{3*}\right]\times\left[q_{jk}-q_{jk}^*\right]+$$

$$\sum_{j=1}^{J}\sum_{h=1}^{H}\left[\frac{\partial c_{hj}^{u*}}{\partial q_{hj}^u}+\rho_{hj}^{u*}+\rho t_2 x_{hj}-\varphi_j^{1*}-t_2\tau_t x_{hj}\varphi_j^{3*}\right]\times\left[q_{hj}^u-q_{hj}^{u*}\right]+ \quad (15)$$

$$\sum_{j=1}^{J}\left[\varepsilon+\omega+\varphi_j^{3*}\right]\times\left[t_j-t_j^*\right]+\sum_{j=1}^{J}\left[\sum_{h=1}^{H}q_{hj}^{u*}-q_j^{u*}\right]\times\left[\varphi_j^1-\varphi_j^{1*}\right]+$$

$$\sum_{j=1}^{J}\left[\beta^r q_j^{v*}+\beta^u q_j^{u*}-\sum_{k=1}^{K}q_{jk}^*\right]\times\left[\varphi_j^2-\varphi_j^{2*}\right]+$$

$$\sum_{j=1}^{J}\left[\alpha_1^I\beta^r q_j^{v*}+\alpha_2^I\beta^u q_j^{u*}+t_1\tau_t\sum_{k=1}^{K}x_{jk}q_{jk}^*+t_2\tau_t\sum_{h=1}^{H}x_{hj}q_{hj}^{u*}-cap_j-t_j^*\right]\times\left[\varphi_j^3-\varphi_j^{3*}\right]\geq 0.$$

$$\forall(q_j^v,q_j^u,Q_1,Q_2,T_1,\varphi_1,\varphi_2,\varphi_3)\in\Omega_j^1$$

where $\Omega_j^1=R_+^{2J+JK+HJ+3J}\times R^J$. Note that φ_j^1, φ_j^2, and φ_j^3 are the Lagrangian multiplier associated with Constraint (12), Constraint (13), and Constraint (14), respectively, while $\varphi_1=\left(\varphi_j^1\right)_{J\times 1}\in R_+^J$, $\varphi_2=\left(\varphi_j^2\right)_{J\times 1}\in R_+^J$, $\varphi_3=\left(\varphi_j^3\right)_{J\times 1}\in R^J$.

To explore the significance of management, we give some explanations for VI (15). From the 3rd term of VI (15), we have $\rho_{jk}^*=\frac{\partial c_{jk}^*}{\partial q_{jk}}+\rho t_1 x_{jk}+\varphi_j^{2*}-t_1\tau_t x_{jk}\varphi_j^{3*}$ when $q_{jk}^*>0$; in other words, the transaction price between non-ecological manufacturer j and demand market k comprises a marginal transaction cost, unit truck transportation cost, and related carbon emission factor. From the 1st term of VI (15), we have $\varphi_j^{2*}=\frac{1}{\beta^r}\left(\frac{\partial f_j^*}{\partial q_j^v}-\alpha_1^I\beta^r\varphi_j^{3*}\right)$ when $q_j^{v*}>0$, and are mainly marginal production costs. Therefore, the previous stage cost transmits to the next stage by the transaction price.

A point that is necessary to show is that the corresponding Lagrangian multipliers of Constraint (14) may be negative because Constraint (14) is an equation. In addition, t_j^* is affected by the sum of ε and ω.

4.3.2. Ecological Manufacturers' Decisions

Similarly, the surplus carbon quotas of the eco manufacturer can be expressed as $t_i=cap_i-\alpha_1^I\beta^r q_i^v-\alpha_2^I\beta^u q_i^u-t_3\tau_t\sum_{k=1}^{K}x_{ik}q_{ik}-t_4\tau_t\sum_{h=1}^{H}x_{hi}q_{hi}^u$. We, therefore, obtain the manufacturer i's objective below to maximize its profit through aggregate revenue minus costs:

$$\max\left[\sum_{k=1}^{K}(\rho_{ik}^*q_{ik}-c_{ik})-\sum_{h=1}^{H}(\rho_{hi}^*q_{hi}^u+c_{hi})-f_i-f_i^u-\rho\left(t_3\sum_{k=1}^{K}x_{ik}q_{ik}+t_4\sum_{h=1}^{H}x_{hi}q_{hi}^u\right)-\varepsilon t_i+\omega t_i\right] \quad (16)$$

$$s.t. \quad q_i^u\leq\sum_{h=1}^{H}q_{hi}^u \quad (17)$$

$$\sum_{k=1}^{K}q_{ik}\leq\beta^r q_i^v+\beta^u q_i^u \quad (18)$$

$$cap_i-\alpha_1^I\beta^r q_i^v-\alpha_2^I\beta^u q_i^u-t_3\tau_t\sum_{k=1}^{K}x_{ik}q_{ik}-t_4\tau_t\sum_{h=1}^{H}x_{hi}q_{hi}^u=t_i \quad (19)$$

The last item of objective function ωt_i denotes the manufacturer i's extra revenue. Constraint (19) ensures that the total carbon emissions of manufacturer i plus t_i equals cap_i. In this case, manufacturer i needs to make an additional decision on the carbon transaction amount t_i. Therefore, the optimum solution of the above objective function can be characterized by the following variational inequality with $(q_i^{v*}, q_i^{u*}, Q_3^*, Q_4^*, T_2^*, \phi_1^*, \phi_2^*, \phi_3^*) \in \Omega_I^1$:

$$\sum_{i=1}^{I}\sum_{k=1}^{K}\left[\frac{\partial c_{ik}^*}{\partial q_{ik}} - \rho_{ik}^* + \rho t_3 x_{ik} + \phi_i^{2*} + t_3 \tau_t x_{ik} \phi_i^{3*}\right] \times [q_{ik} - q_{ik}^*] +$$
$$\sum_{i=1}^{I}\sum_{h=1}^{H}\left[\frac{\partial c_{hi}^{u*}}{\partial q_{hi}^u} + \rho_{hi}^{u*} + \rho t_4 x_{hi} - \phi_i^{1*} + t_4 \tau_t x_{hi} \phi_i^{3*}\right] \times [q_{hi}^u - q_{hi}^{u*}] +$$
$$\sum_{i=1}^{I}\left[\varepsilon - \omega + \phi_i^{3*}\right] \times [t_i - t_i^*] + \sum_{i=1}^{I}\left[\sum_{h=1}^{H} q_{hi}^{u*} - q_i^{u*}\right] \times [\phi_i^1 - \phi_i^{1*}] + \quad (20)$$
$$\sum_{i=1}^{I}\left[\beta^r q_i^{v*} + \beta^u q_i^{u*} - \sum_{k=1}^{K} q_{ik}^*\right] \times [\phi_i^2 - \phi_i^{2*}] +$$
$$\sum_{i=1}^{I}\left[cap_i - \alpha_1^I \beta^r q_i^v - \alpha_2^I \beta^u q_i^u - t_3 \tau_t \sum_{k=1}^{K} x_{ik} q_{ik} - t_4 \tau_t \sum_{h=1}^{H} x_{hi} q_{hi}^u - t_i\right] \times [\phi_i^3 - \phi_i^{3*}] \geq 0.$$

$$\forall (q_i^v, q_i^u, Q_3, Q_4, T_2, \phi_1, \phi_2, \phi_3) \in \Omega_I^1$$

where $\Omega_I^1 = R_+^{2I+IK+HI+2I} \times R^I$. Note that ϕ_i^1, ϕ_i^2 and ϕ_i^3 are the Lagrangian multipliers associated with Constraint (17), Constraint (18), and Constraint (19), respectively, while $\phi_1 = (\phi_i^1)_{I \times 1} \in R_+^I$, $\phi_2 = (\phi_i^2)_{I \times 1} \in R_+^I$, $\phi_3 = (\phi_i^3)_{I \times 1} \in R^I$.

4.3.3. Carbon Trade Center's Decisions

Carbon trade centers charge a certain fee ε for unit carbon trade volume. Simultaneously, carbon trade centers should undertake associated cost $\sum_{j=1}^{J} c_j^t + \sum_{i=1}^{I} c_i^t$. The carbon trade center also pursues profit maximization, which can be described as:

$$\max\left[\sum_{j=1}^{J}(\varepsilon t_j^* - c_j^t(t_j^*)) + \sum_{i=1}^{I}(\varepsilon t_i^* - c_i^t(t_i^*))\right] \quad (21)$$

$$\text{s.t.} \sum_{j=1}^{J} t_j \leq \sum_{i=1}^{I} t_i \quad (22)$$

Constraint (22) shows the balance between the demand supply of the carbon quota. The profit of the carbon trade center seeking to maximize can be transformed into the following variational inequality: determine the optimal solution $\forall (T_1^*, T_2^*, \zeta_c^*) \in \Omega_c$, satisfying:

$$\sum_{j=1}^{J}\left[\frac{\partial c_j^{t*}}{\partial t_j} + \lambda_c^* - \varepsilon\right] \times [t_j - t_j^*] + \sum_{i=1}^{I}\left[\frac{\partial c_i^{t*}}{\partial t_i} - \varepsilon - \lambda_c^*\right] \times [t_i - t_i^*] + \left[\sum_{i=1}^{I} t_i^* - \sum_{j=1}^{J} t_j^*\right] \times [\lambda_c - \lambda_c^*] \geq 0. \quad (23)$$

$$\forall (T_1, T_2, \zeta_c) \in \Omega_c$$

where $\Omega_c = R_+^{J+I+1}$. Note that ζ_c is the Lagrangian multiplier associated with Constraint (22) and $\zeta_c \in R_+$.

4.3.4. The Equilibrium Conditions of Closed-Loop Supply Chain Network in the CT Model

Under the cap-and-trade regulations, for the closed-loop supply chain network, the Nash equilibrium (Nash 1950) conditions of VI (7), VI (10), VI (15), VI (20), and VI (23) must hold simultaneously, and no one gains more from altering the current strategies.

Definition 1. *The equilibrium of the CLSCN under cap-and-trade regulation occurs when the sum of the left-hand side (L.H.S.) of (7), L.H.S. of (10), L.H.S. of (15), L.H.S. of (20), and L.H.S. of (23) is non-negative.*

Theorem 1. The equilibrium conditions of the CLSCN under cap-and-trade regulations are equivalent to the solutions of VI as follows: determine the optimal solution $(q_j^{v*}, q_j^{u*}, q_i^{v*}, q_i^{u*}, Q_1^*, Q_2^*, Q_3^*, Q_4^*, Q_5^*, T_1^*, T_2^*, \rho^{J*}, \rho^{I*}, \varphi_1^*, \varphi_2^*, \varphi_3^*, \phi_1^*, \phi_2^*, \phi_3^*, \zeta_c, \lambda^*, \gamma^*) \in \Omega^1$, satisfying:

$$\sum_{j=1}^{J}\left[\frac{\partial f_j^*}{\partial q_j^v} - \beta^r \varphi_j^{2*} - \alpha_1^I \beta^r \varphi_j^{3*}\right] \times \left[q_j^v - q_j^{v*}\right] + \sum_{j=1}^{J}\left[\frac{\partial f_j^{u*}}{\partial q_j^u} + \varphi_j^{1*} - \beta^u \varphi_j^{2*} - \alpha_2^I \beta^u \varphi_j^{3*}\right] \times \left[q_j^u - q_j^{u*}\right] +$$

$$\sum_{i=1}^{I}\left[\frac{\partial f_i^*}{\partial q_i^v} - \beta^r \phi_i^{2*} + \alpha_1^I \beta^r \phi_i^{3*}\right] \times \left[q_i^v - q_i^{v*}\right] + \sum_{i=1}^{I}\left[\frac{\partial f_i^{u*}}{\partial q_i^u} + \phi_i^{1*} - \beta^u \phi_i^{2*} + \alpha_2^I \beta^u \phi_i^{3*}\right] \times \left[q_i^u - q_i^{u*}\right] +$$

$$\sum_{j=1}^{J}\sum_{k=1}^{K}\left[\frac{\partial c_{jk}^*}{\partial q_{jk}} + c_{jk}^{K*} - \rho_k^{h*} - \varepsilon_j \gamma_k^* + \rho t_1 x_{jk} + \varphi_j^{2*} - t_1 \tau_t x_{jk} \varphi_j^{3*}\right] \times \left[q_{jk} - q_{jk}^*\right] +$$

$$\sum_{i=1}^{I}\sum_{k=1}^{K}\left[\frac{\partial c_{ik}^*}{\partial q_{ik}} + c_{ik}^{K*} - \rho_k^{l*} - \varepsilon_i \gamma_k^* + \rho t_3 x_{ik} + \phi_i^{2*} + t_3 \tau_t x_{ik} \phi_i^{3*}\right] \times \left[q_{ik} - q_{ik}^*\right] +$$

$$\sum_{j=1}^{J}\sum_{h=1}^{H}\left[\frac{\partial c_{hj}^{u*}}{\partial q_{hj}^u} + \rho t_2 x_{hj} - \varphi_j^{1*} + t_2 \tau_t x_{hj} \varphi_j^{3*} + \lambda_h^*\right] \times \left[q_{hj}^u - q_{hj}^{u*}\right] +$$

$$\sum_{i=1}^{I}\sum_{h=1}^{H}\left[\frac{\partial c_{hi}^{u*}}{\partial q_{hi}^u} + \rho t_4 x_{hi} - \phi_i^{1*} + t_4 \tau_t x_{hi} \phi_i^{3*} + \lambda_h^*\right] \times \left[q_{hi}^u - q_{hi}^{u*}\right] +$$

$$\sum_{j=1}^{J}\left[\frac{\partial c_j^{t*}}{\partial t_j} + \lambda_c^* + \omega + \varphi_j^{3*}\right] \times \left[t_j - t_j^*\right] + \sum_{i=1}^{I}\left[\frac{\partial c_i^{t*}}{\partial t_i} - \lambda_c^* - \omega + \phi_i^{3*}\right] \times \left[t_i - t_i^*\right] +$$

$$\sum_{k=1}^{K}\left[\sum_{j=1}^{J} q_{jk}^* - d_k^{h*}\right] \times \left[\rho_k^h - \rho_k^{h*}\right] + \sum_{k=1}^{K}\left[\sum_{i=1}^{I} q_{ik}^* - d_k^{l*}\right] \times \left[\rho_k^l - \rho_k^{l*}\right] +$$

$$\sum_{h=1}^{H}\sum_{k=1}^{K}\left[\alpha_k^u(Q_5^*) + \gamma_k^* + \frac{\partial c_{kh}^*}{\partial q_{kh}^u} + \frac{\partial c_{kh}^{t*}}{\partial q_{kh}} - \delta \lambda_h^*\right] \times \left[q_{kh}^u - q_{kh}^{u*}\right] +$$

$$\sum_{j=1}^{J}\left[\sum_{h=1}^{H} q_{hj}^{u*} - q_j^{u*}\right] \times \left[\varphi_j^1 - \varphi_j^{1*}\right] + \sum_{j=1}^{J}\left[\beta^r q_j^{v*} + \beta^u q_j^{u*} - \sum_{k=1}^{K} q_{jk}^*\right] \times \left[\varphi_j^2 - \varphi_j^{2*}\right] +$$

$$\sum_{j=1}^{J}\left[\alpha_1^I \beta^r q_j^{v*} + \alpha_2^I \beta^u q_j^{u*} + t_1 \tau_t \sum_{k=1}^{K} x_{jk} q_{jk}^* + t_2 \tau_t \sum_{h=1}^{H} x_{hj} q_{hj}^{u*} - cap_j - t_j^*\right] \times \left[\varphi_j^3 - \varphi_j^{3*}\right] +$$

$$\sum_{i=1}^{I}\left[\sum_{h=1}^{H} q_{hi}^{u*} - q_i^{u*}\right] \times \left[\phi_i^1 - \phi_i^{1*}\right] + \sum_{i=1}^{I}\left[\beta^r q_i^{v*} + \beta^u q_i^{u*} - \sum_{k=1}^{K} q_{ik}^*\right] \times \left[\phi_i^2 - \phi_i^{2*}\right] +$$

$$\sum_{i=1}^{I}\left[cap_i - \alpha_1^I \beta^r q_i^{v*} - \alpha_2^I \beta^u q_i^{u*} - t_3 \tau_t \sum_{k=1}^{K} x_{ik} q_{ik}^* - t_4 \tau_t \sum_{h=1}^{H} x_{hi} q_{hi}^{u*} - t_i\right] \times \left[\phi_i^3 - \phi_i^{3*}\right] +$$

$$\left[\sum_{i=1}^{I} t_i^* - \sum_{j=1}^{J} t_j^*\right] \times [\lambda_c - \lambda_c^*] + \sum_{h=1}^{H}\left[\delta \sum_{k=1}^{K} q_{kh}^{u*} - \sum_{j=1}^{J} q_{hj}^{u*} - \sum_{i=1}^{I} q_{hi}^{u*}\right] \times [\lambda_h - \lambda_h^*] +$$

$$\sum_{k=1}^{K}\left[\varepsilon_j \sum_{j=1}^{J} q_{jk}^* + \varepsilon_i \sum_{i=1}^{I} q_{ik}^* - \sum_{k=1}^{K} q_{kh}^{u*}\right] \times [\gamma_k - \gamma_k^*] \geq 0. \tag{24}$$

$$\forall (q_j^v, q_j^u, q_i^v, q_i^u, Q_1, Q_2, Q_3, Q_4, Q_5, T_1, T_2, \rho^J, \rho^I, \varphi_1, \varphi_2, \varphi_3, \phi_1, \phi_2, \phi_3, \zeta_c, \lambda, \gamma) \in \Omega^1$$

where $\Omega^1 = \Omega_J^1 \times \Omega_I^1 \times \Omega_c \times \Omega_k \times \Omega_h$.

Proof. Adding VI (7), VI (10), VI (15), VI (20), and VI (23) together, we can obtain VI (24). At the same time, when VI (24) holds, then VI (7), VI (10), VI (15), VI (20), and VI (23) are also satisfied, respectively. □

Let $X_1 \equiv (q_j^v, q_j^u, q_i^v, q_i^u, Q_1, Q_2, Q_3, Q_4, Q_5, T_1, T_2, \rho^J, \rho^I, \varphi_1, \varphi_2, \varphi_3, \phi_1, \phi_2, \phi_3, \zeta_c, \lambda, \gamma)$, $F(X_1) \equiv (F_x(X_1))_{22 \times 1}$, the specific parts $F_x(X_1)$ $(x = 1, \cdots, 22)$ of $F(X_1)$ are given by the terms proceeding the multiplication signs in VI (24). Then, we can rewrite the VI (24) in standard form of VI following: determine the optimal vector $X_1^* \in \Omega^1$, satisfying:

$$\langle F(X_1^*), X_1^* \rangle \geq 0, \forall X_1 \in \Omega^1 \tag{25}$$

The notation $\langle \cdot, \cdot \rangle$ denotes the inner product in M_1—dimensional Euclidean space, where $M_1 = 2J + 2I + JK + HJ + IK + HI + KH + J + I + 2K + 3J + 3I + 1 + H + K$.

4.4. The Supply Chain Network under Mandatory Cap Policy (MC)

In this section, we characterize how the exogenously given strict cap policy affects the supply chain members' decisions.

4.4.1. Non-Ecological Manufacturers' Decisions

We describe the decision making and operational characteristics of non-eco manufacturers and provide optimal conditions. Hence, considering the transaction between manufacturer j and other supply chain members, we give the manufacturer j's objective function as follows:

$$max\left[\sum_{k=1}^{K}\left(\rho_{jk}^{*}q_{jk}-c_{jk}\right)-\sum_{h=1}^{H}\left(\rho_{hj}^{u*}q_{hj}^{u}+c_{hj}\right)-f_{j}-f_{j}^{u}-\rho\left(t_{1}\sum_{k=1}^{K}x_{jk}q_{jk}+t_{2}\sum_{h=1}^{H}x_{hj}q_{hj}^{u}\right)\right] \quad (26)$$

$$s.t. \; q_{j}^{u} \leq \sum_{h=1}^{H} q_{hj}^{u} \quad (27)$$

$$\sum_{k=1}^{K} q_{jk} \leq \beta^{r}q_{j}^{v} + \beta^{u}q_{j}^{u} \quad (28)$$

$$\alpha_{1}^{J}\beta^{r}q_{j}^{v} + \alpha_{2}^{J}\beta^{u}q_{j}^{u} + t_{1}\tau_{t}\sum_{k=1}^{K}x_{jk}q_{jk} + t_{2}\tau_{t}\sum_{h=1}^{H}x_{hj}q_{hj}^{u} \leq cap_{j} \quad (29)$$

Constraint (28) can be called the production balance constraint; Constraint (29) ensures the total carbon emissions generated by manufacturer j cannot exceed its quota cap_j.

According to the previous Assumption 6, the objective functions of manufacturers are continuously concave. All decision variables are non-negative. In this situation, non-ecological manufacturer j determines the amount of raw materials and recycled EOL products, the output and transaction amount of the new product, and the remanufactured product.

All non-eco manufacturers compete in a non-cooperative fashion, and the profits of each non-eco manufacturer seeking to maximize can be transformed simultaneously into the following variational inequality: determine the optimal solution $(q_{j}^{v*}, q_{j}^{u*}, Q_{1}^{*}, Q_{2}^{*}, \mu_{1}^{*}, \mu_{2}^{*}, \mu_{3}^{*})$ $\in \Omega_{j}^{2}$, satisfying:

$$\sum_{j=1}^{J}\left[\frac{\partial f_{j}^{*}}{\partial q_{j}^{v}} - \beta^{r}\mu_{j}^{2*} + \alpha_{1}^{J}\beta^{r}\mu_{j}^{3*}\right] \times \left[q_{j}^{v} - q_{j}^{v*}\right] + \sum_{j=1}^{J}\left[\frac{\partial f_{j}^{u*}}{\partial q_{j}^{u}} + \mu_{j}^{1*} - \beta^{u}\mu_{j}^{2*} + \alpha_{2}^{J}\beta^{u}\mu_{j}^{3*}\right] \times \left[q_{j}^{u} - q_{j}^{u*}\right] +$$

$$\sum_{j=1}^{J}\sum_{k=1}^{K}\left[\frac{\partial c_{jk}^{*}}{\partial q_{jk}} - \rho_{jk}^{*} + \rho t_{1}x_{jk} + \mu_{j}^{2*} + t_{1}\tau_{t}x_{jk}\mu_{j}^{3*}\right] \times \left[q_{jk} - q_{jk}^{*}\right] +$$

$$\sum_{j=1}^{J}\sum_{h=1}^{H}\left[\frac{\partial c_{hj}^{u*}}{\partial q_{hj}^{u}} + \rho_{hj}^{u*} + \rho t_{2}x_{hj} - \mu_{j}^{1*} + t_{2}\tau_{t}x_{hj}\mu_{j}^{3*}\right] \times \left[q_{hj}^{u} - q_{hj}^{u*}\right] + \quad (30)$$

$$\sum_{j=1}^{J}\left[\sum_{h=1}^{H}q_{hj}^{u*} - q_{j}^{u*}\right] \times \left[\mu_{j}^{1} - \mu_{j}^{1*}\right] + \sum_{j=1}^{J}\left[\beta^{r}q_{j}^{v*} + \beta^{u}q_{j}^{u*} - \sum_{k=1}^{K}q_{jk}^{*}\right] \times \left[\mu_{j}^{2} - \mu_{j}^{2*}\right] +$$

$$\sum_{j=1}^{J}\left[cap_{j} - \alpha_{1}^{J}\beta^{r}q_{j}^{v*} - \alpha_{2}^{J}\beta^{u}q_{j}^{u*} - t_{1}\tau_{t}\sum_{k=1}^{K}x_{jk}q_{jk}^{*} - t_{2}\tau_{t}\sum_{h=1}^{H}x_{hj}q_{hj}^{u*}\right] \times \left[\mu_{j}^{3} - \mu_{j}^{3*}\right] \geq 0.$$

$$\forall (q_{j}^{v}, q_{j}^{u}, Q_{1}, Q_{2}, \mu_{1}, \mu_{2}, \mu_{3}) \in \Omega_{j}^{2}$$

where $\Omega_{j}^{2} = R_{+}^{2J+JK+HJ+3J}$. Note that μ_{j}^{1}, μ_{j}^{2}, and μ_{j}^{3} are the Lagrangian multipliers associated with Constraint (27), Constraint (28), and Constraint (29), respectively, while $\mu_{1} = \left(\mu_{j}^{1}\right)_{J\times 1} \in R_{+}^{J}$, $\mu_{2} = \left(\mu_{j}^{2}\right)_{J\times 1} \in R_{+}^{J}$, $\mu_{3} = \left(\mu_{j}^{3}\right)_{J\times 1} \in R_{+}^{J}$.

Similar to the CT model, we can give the economic interpretation of VI (30). From the 3rd term of VI (30), we have $\rho_{jk}^{*} = \frac{\partial c_{jk}^{*}}{\partial q_{jk}} + \rho t_{1}x_{jk} + \mu_{j}^{2*} + t_{1}\tau_{t}x_{jk}\mu_{j}^{3*}$ when $q_{jk}^{*} > 0$; that is, the transaction price between non-ecological manufacturer j and demand market k

comprises the marginal transaction cost, unit truck transportation cost, and the factor of carbon emission. From the 1st term of VI (30), we have $\mu_j^{2*} = \frac{1}{\beta^r}\left(\frac{\partial f_j^*}{\partial q_j^v} + \alpha_1^I \beta^r \mu_j^{3*}\right)$ when $q_j^{v*} > 0$, which is mainly affected by the production marginal cost and conversion rate. Therefore, we can determine that the costs of the previous stage are transmitted to the next stage through the product transaction.

4.4.2. Ecological Manufacturers' Decisions

Similarly, we describe the manufacturer i's objective function as follows:

$$\max \left[\sum_{k=1}^{K}(\rho_{ik}^* q_{ik} - c_{ik}) - \sum_{h=1}^{H}(\rho_{hi}^* q_{hi}^u + c_{hi}) - f_i - f_i^u - \rho\left(t_3 \sum_{k=1}^{K} x_{ik} q_{ik} + t_4 \sum_{h=1}^{H} x_{hi} q_{hi}^u\right)\right] \quad (31)$$

$$s.t. \quad q_i^u \leq \sum_{h=1}^{H} q_{hi}^u \quad (32)$$

$$\sum_{k=1}^{K} q_{ik} \leq \beta^r q_i^v + \beta^u q_i^u \quad (33)$$

$$\alpha_1^I \beta^r q_i^v + \alpha_2^I \beta^u q_i^u + t_3 \tau_t \sum_{k=1}^{K} x_{ik} q_{ik} + t_4 \tau_t \sum_{h=1}^{H} x_{hi} q_{hi}^u \leq cap_i \quad (34)$$

In this situation, eco manufacturer i determines the amount of raw materials and recycled EOL products, the output and transaction amount of the new product, and the remanufactured product.

All eco manufacturers compete in a non-cooperation fashion, and the optimality conditions of all eco manufacturers can be described simultaneously as variational inequality: determine the optimal solution $(q_i^{v*}, q_i^{u*}, Q_3^*, Q_4^*, \eta_1^*, \eta_2^*, \eta_3^*) \in \Omega_I^2$, satisfying:

$$\sum_{i=1}^{I}\left[\frac{\partial f_i^*}{\partial q_i^v} - \beta^r \eta_i^{2*} + \alpha_1^I \beta^r \eta_i^{3*}\right] \times [q_i^v - q_i^{v*}] + \sum_{i=1}^{I}\left[\frac{\partial f_i^{u*}}{\partial q_i^u} + \eta_i^{1*} - \beta^u \eta_i^{2*} + \alpha_2^I \beta^u \eta_i^{3*}\right] \times [q_i^u - q_i^{u*}] +$$

$$\sum_{i=1}^{I}\sum_{k=1}^{K}\left[\frac{\partial c_{ik}^*}{\partial q_{ik}} - \rho_{ik}^* + \rho t_3 x_{ik} + \eta_i^{2*} + t_3 \tau_t x_{ik} \eta_i^{3*}\right] \times [q_{ik} - q_{ik}^*] +$$

$$\sum_{i=1}^{I}\sum_{h=1}^{H}\left[\frac{\partial c_{hi}^{u*}}{\partial q_{hi}^u} + \rho_{hi}^* + \rho t_4 x_{hi} - \eta_i^{1*} + t_4 \tau_t x_{hi} \eta_i^{3*}\right] \times [q_{hi}^u - q_{hi}^{u*}] + \quad (35)$$

$$\sum_{i=1}^{I}\left[\sum_{h=1}^{H} q_{hi}^{u*} - q_i^{u*}\right] \times [\eta_i^1 - \eta_i^{1*}] + \sum_{i=1}^{I}\left[\beta^r q_i^{v*} + \beta^u q_i^{u*} - \sum_{k=1}^{K} q_{ik}^*\right] \times [\eta_i^2 - \eta_i^{2*}] +$$

$$\sum_{i=1}^{I}\left[cap_i - \alpha_1^I \beta^r q_i^{v*} - \alpha_2^I \beta^u q_i^{u*} - t_3 \tau_t \sum_{k=1}^{K} x_{ik} q_{ik}^* - t_4 \tau_t \sum_{h=1}^{H} x_{hi} q_{hi}^{u*}\right] \times [\eta_i^3 - \eta_i^{3*}] \geq 0.$$

$$\forall (q_i^v, q_i^u, Q_3, Q_4, \eta_1, \eta_2, \eta_3) \in \Omega_I^2$$

where $\Omega_I^2 = R_+^{2I+IK+HI+3I}$. Note that η_i^1, η_i^2, and η_i^3 are the Lagrangian multipliers associated with Constraint (32), Constraint (33), and Constraint (34), respectively, while $\eta_1 = (\eta_i^1)_{I \times 1} \in R_+^I$, $\eta_2 = (\eta_i^2)_{I \times 1} \in R_+^I$, $\eta_3 = (\eta_i^3)_{I \times 1} \in R_+^I$.

The equilibrium conditions of the closed-loop supply chain network in the mandatory cap model can be obtained in the same way with the CT model, so this part is presented in Appendix A.

4.5. The Supply Chain Network under Cap-Sharing Scheme (CS)

The government examines the total emissions of a typical industry in a certain period according to the national emission reduction plan. In this section, we examine a setting in which two types of manufacturers make decisions centralized, and the carbon caps are permitted to be transferred freely, which is therefore called the cap-sharing scheme. From the perspective of the whole industry, the total carbon emissions of manufacturers do not exceed the government's regulations.

Manufacturers' Decisions

In this case, manufacturer j and manufacturer i need to decide the amount of raw materials and recycled EOL products, the transaction amount, and the EOL product transaction amount, respectively. For convenience, let $A_x = \sum_{k=1}^{K}\left(\rho_{xk}^{*}q_{xk} - c_{xk}\right) - \sum_{h=1}^{H}\left(\rho_{hx}^{u*}q_{hx}^{u} + c_{hx}^{u}\right) - f_x - f_x^{u}$ ($x = i, j$), $B_1 = t_1 \sum_{k=1}^{K} x_{jk}q_{jk} + t_2 \sum_{h=1}^{H} x_{hj}q_{hj}^{u}$, $B_2 = t_3 \sum_{k=1}^{K} x_{ik}q_{ik} + t_4 \sum_{h=1}^{H} x_{hi}q_{hi}^{u}$, then we can describe the typical manufacturer objective function as follows:

$$\max\left[A_x - \rho B_y\right] \tag{36}$$

$$\text{s.t. } q_x^u \leq \sum_{h=1}^{H} q_{hx}^u \tag{37}$$

$$\sum_{k=1}^{K} q_{xk} \leq \beta^r q_x^v + \beta^u q_x^u \tag{38}$$

$$\left[\begin{array}{l} \sum_{j=1}^{J}\left[\alpha_1^I \beta^r q_j^v + \alpha_2^I \beta^u q_j^u + t_1 \tau_t \sum_{k=1}^{K} x_{jk} q_{jk} + t_2 \tau_t \sum_{h=1}^{H} x_{hj} q_{hj}^u\right] \\ + \sum_{i=1}^{I}\left[\alpha_1^I \beta^r q_i^v + \alpha_2^I \beta^u q_i^u + t_3 \tau_t \sum_{k=1}^{K} x_{ik} q_{ik} + t_4 \tau_t \sum_{h=1}^{H} x_{hi} q_{hi}^u\right] \end{array}\right] \leq \sum_{j=1}^{J} cap_j + \sum_{i=1}^{I} cap_i \tag{39}$$

When $x = i$ and $y = 1$, Equation (36) denotes the profit of ecological manufacturer i; when $x = j$ and $y = 2$, Equation (36) denotes the profit of non-ecological manufacturer j. Constraint (39) can be called the carbon emissions constraint. All decision variables are non-negative; in addition, all manufacturers of the same type compete in a non-cooperation fashion, and the profits of each manufacturer seeking maximization can be transformed simultaneously into the following variational inequality to determine the optimal solution $(q_j^{v*}, q_j^{u*}, q_i^{v*}, q_i^{u*}, Q_1^*, Q_2^*, Q_3^*, Q_4^*, \theta_1^*, \theta_2^*, \theta_3^*, \theta_4^*, \theta^{5*}) \in \Omega_{JI}^3$, satisfying:

$$\begin{aligned}
&\sum_{j=1}^{J}\left[\frac{\partial f_j^*}{\partial q_j^v} - \beta^r \theta_j^{2*} + \alpha_1^I \beta^r \theta^{5*}\right] \times \left[q_j^v - q_j^{v*}\right] + \sum_{j=1}^{J}\left[\frac{\partial f_j^{u*}}{\partial q_j^u} + \theta_j^{1*} - \beta^u \theta_j^{2*} + \alpha_2^I \beta^u \theta^{5*}\right] \times \left[q_j^u - q_j^{u*}\right] + \\
&\sum_{i=1}^{I}\left[\frac{\partial f_i^*}{\partial q_i^v} - \beta^r \theta_i^{4*} + \alpha_1^I \beta^r \theta^{5*}\right] \times \left[q_i^v - q_i^{v*}\right] + \sum_{i=1}^{I}\left[\frac{\partial f_i^{u*}}{\partial q_i^u} + \theta_i^{3*} - \beta^u \theta_i^{4*} + \alpha_2^I \beta^u \theta^{5*}\right] \times \left[q_i^u - q_i^{u*}\right] + \\
&\sum_{j=1}^{J}\sum_{k=1}^{K}\left[\frac{\partial c_{jk}^*}{\partial q_{jk}} - \rho_{jk}^* + \rho t_1 x_{jk} + \theta_j^{2*} + t_1 \tau_t x_{jk}\theta^{5*}\right] \times \left[q_{jk} - q_{jk}^*\right] + \\
&\sum_{j=1}^{J}\sum_{h=1}^{H}\left[\frac{\partial c_{hj}^{u*}}{\partial q_{hj}^u} + \rho_{hj}^{u*} + \rho t_2 x_{hj} - \theta_j^{1*} + t_2 \tau_t x_{hj}\theta^{5*}\right] \times \left[q_{hj}^u - q_{hj}^{u*}\right] + \\
&\sum_{i=1}^{I}\sum_{k=1}^{K}\left[\frac{\partial c_{ik}^*}{\partial q_{ik}} - \rho_{ik}^* + \rho t_3 x_{ik} + \theta_i^{4*} + t_3 \tau_t x_{ik}\theta^{5*}\right] \times \left[q_{ik} - q_{ik}^*\right] + \\
&\sum_{i=1}^{I}\sum_{h=1}^{H}\left[\frac{\partial c_{hi}^{u*}}{\partial q_{hi}^u} + \rho_{hi}^{u*} + \rho t_4 x_{hi} - \theta_i^{3*} + t_4 \tau_t x_{hi}\theta^{5*}\right] \times \left[q_{hi}^u - q_{hi}^{u*}\right] + \\
&\sum_{j=1}^{J}\left[\sum_{h=1}^{H} q_{hj}^{u*} - q_j^{u*}\right] \times \left[\theta_j^1 - \theta_j^{1*}\right] + \sum_{j=1}^{J}\left[\beta^r q_j^{v*} + \beta^u q_j^{u*} - \sum_{k=1}^{K} q_{jk}^*\right] \times \left[\theta_j^2 - \theta_j^{2*}\right] + \\
&\sum_{i=1}^{I}\left[\sum_{h=1}^{H} q_{hi}^{u*} - q_i^{u*}\right] \times \left[\theta_i^3 - \theta_i^{3*}\right] + \sum_{i=1}^{I}\left[\beta^r q_i^{v*} + \beta^u q_i^{u*} - \sum_{k=1}^{K} q_{ik}^*\right] \times \left[\theta_i^4 - \theta_i^{4*}\right] + \\
&\left[\left[\begin{array}{l}\sum_{j=1}^{J} cap_j \\ +\sum_{i=1}^{I} cap_i\end{array}\right] - \left[\begin{array}{l}\sum_{j=1}^{J}\left[\alpha_1^I \beta^r q_j^{v*} + \alpha_2^I \beta^u q_j^{u*} + t_1 \tau_t \sum_{k=1}^{K} x_{jk} q_{jk}^* + t_2 \tau_t \sum_{h=1}^{H} x_{hj} q_{hj}^{u*}\right] \\ +\sum_{i=1}^{I}\left[\alpha_1^I \beta^r q_i^{v*} + \alpha_2^I \beta^u q_i^{u*} + t_3 \tau_t \sum_{k=1}^{K} x_{ik} q_{ik}^* + t_4 \tau_t \sum_{h=1}^{H} x_{hi} q_{hi}^{u*}\right]\end{array}\right]\right] \times \left[\theta^5 - \theta^{5*}\right] \geq 0.
\end{aligned} \tag{40}$$

$$\forall (q_j^v, q_j^u, q_i^v, q_i^u, Q_1, Q_2, Q_3, Q_4, \theta_1, \theta_2, \theta_3, \theta_4, \theta^5) \in \Omega_{JI}^3$$

where $\Omega_{JI}^3 = R_+^{2J+2I+JK+HJ+IK+HI+2J+2I+1}$.

Note that θ_j^1, θ_j^2, θ_j^3, and θ_j^4 are the Lagrangian multipliers associated with Constraint (37), Constraint (38) for $x = j, i$, respectively, and θ_j^5 is the Lagrangian multiplier associated with Constraint (39), $\boldsymbol{\theta}_1 = \left(\theta_j^1\right)_{J\times 1} \in R_+^J$, $\boldsymbol{\theta}_2 = \left(\theta_j^2\right)_{J\times 1} \in R_+^J$, $\boldsymbol{\theta}_3 = \left(\theta_i^3\right)_{I\times 1} \in R_+^I$, $\boldsymbol{\theta}_4 = \left(\theta_i^4\right)_{I\times 1} \in R_+^I$.

The equilibrium conditions of the closed-loop supply chain network in the CS model are shown in Appendix B.

The qualitative properties of VI. (24), VI. (40), and VI. (41) are presented in Appendix C.

5. Discussion

In this section, we provide several numerical examples to verify the foregoing theoretical results and present a further comparison of the decisions and profits with three carbon reduction regulations. In reality, the cap from the government may change with the changing of emission reduction targets; similarly, consumers' low-carbon preferences will also change with social development. Therefore, we will analyze the parameters of cap_j, cap_i, ε_j, ε_i and σ.

Consider a closed-loop supply chain network comprising two non-ecological manufacturers, two ecological manufacturers, two demand markets, and two collection centers; when considering the cap-and-trade regulation, there also exists a carbon trade center.

Because the design is simple and easy to implement, the decision variables and Lagrange multipliers can be obtained at the same time. Like [40], we select a modified projection and contraction algorithm with a fixed step length to solve VI (24), VI (40), and VI (A1), and design the program with MATLAB. The convergence criterion is that the absolute value of the difference between the values of the two iterations is no more than 10^{-8}. The selection of the function form refers to [40,58], the related parameters are set as: $\beta^r = 0.95$, $\beta^u = 0.9$, $\rho = 1$, $t_1 = t_2 = t_3 = t_4 = 2$, $x_{jk} = x_{ik} = x_{hj} = x_{hi} = 1$, $\tau_t = 1$, $\varepsilon_j = 0.3$, $\varepsilon_i = 0.2$, $\delta = 1$, $\alpha_1^J = 0.6$, $\alpha_1^I = 0.8$, $\alpha_2^J = 0.3$, $\alpha_2^I = 0.5$. Referring to related literature [38–40,50,60], the functions are set as follows: $f_i = 8.5(\beta^r q_i^v)^2 + \beta^{r2} q_i^v q_{3-i}^v + 2\beta^r q_i^v$, $f_i^u = 3(\beta^u q_i^u)^2 + 1.5\beta^u q_i^u + 1$, $f_j = 8.0(\beta^r q_i^v)^2 + \beta^{r2} q_i^v q_{3-i}^v + 2\beta^r q_i^v$, $f_j^u = 0.5(\beta^u q_j^u)^2 + 0.5\beta^u q_j^u + 1$, $c_{jk} = 0.2t_1 q_{jk} + 1$, $c_{ik} = 0.2t_3 q_{ik} + 1$, $c_{jk}^K = 0.2q_{jk} + 0.1$, $c_{ik}^K = 0.2q_{ik} + 0.1$, $c_{kh} = 0.1q_{kh}^u + 0.5$, $c_{hj}^u = 0.1t_2 q_{hj}^u + 1$, $c_{hi}^u = 0.1t_4 q_{hi}^u + 1$, $c_h = 2.5\left(\sum_{k=1}^{2} q_{kh}^u\right)^2 + 2\sum_{k=1}^{2} q_{kh}^u$, $\alpha_k^u(Q_5) = 0.5\sum_{k=1}^{2}\sum_{k=1}^{2} q_{kh}^u + 5$, $c_x^t = 0.1t_x^2$, $d_k^l = 250 - 2\rho_k^l - 1.5\rho_{3-k}^l + 0.5(\rho_k^h + \rho_{3-k}^h) + \sigma\psi \sum_{x=1}^{2}(1 - \alpha_x^I)$, $d_k^h = 230 - 2\rho_k^h - 1.5\rho_{3-k}^h + 0.5(\rho_k^l + \rho_{3-k}^l) + \sigma\psi \sum_{x=1}^{2}(1 - \alpha_x^J)$.

The demand functions are associated with the price of two types of products; due to the consumer's low carbon preference, there is also a relationship between demand and the product's unit carbon emission amount. We assume the low-carbon factor $\psi = 10$. Refs. [40,50] used a similar form of demand function in their numerical examples.

It is obvious that all the functions listed above are convex and continuously differentiable. Then, the solutions of VI (24), VI (40), and VI (41) satisfy Theorem A3, Theorem A4, and Theorem A6 in Appendix C. The detailed values and formula construction basis can be seen in Appendix D.

5.1. Analyzing the Effects of Cap on Optimal Decisions and Profits

We assume that cap_j and cap_i change from 9 to 26, respectively, then group the related equilibrium results into several matrixes corresponding to three carbon reduction regulations. We select data from the matrixes including the profits of manufacturers and recyclers and calculate the carbon emissions and the total profits of the supply chain based on the relevant data. The relevant results are illustrated in Figures 2–7.

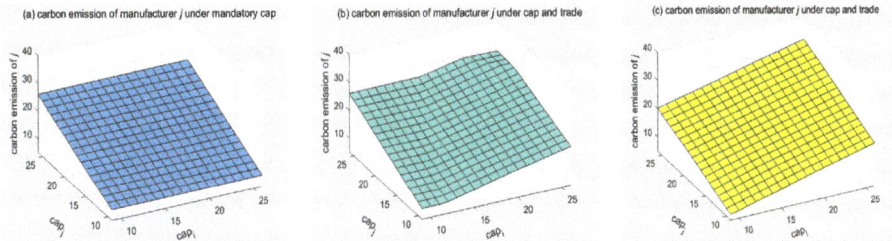

Figure 2. Carbon emissions of non-eco manufacturer.

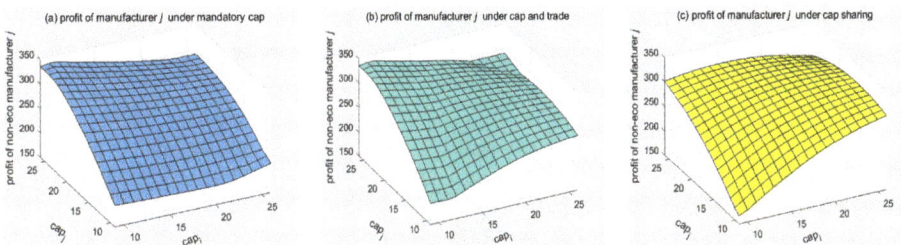

Figure 3. Profits of non-eco manufacturer.

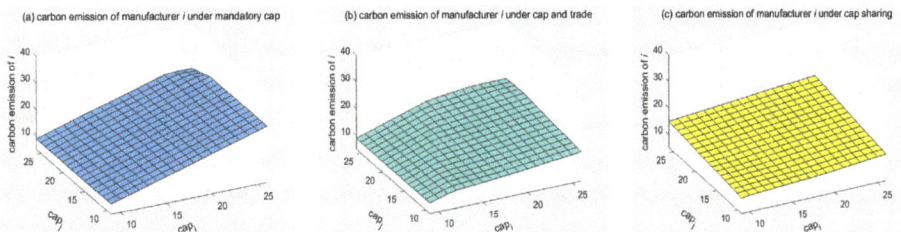

Figure 4. Carbon emissions of eco manufacturer.

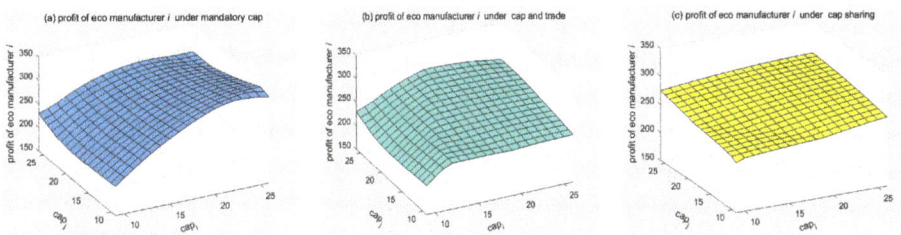

Figure 5. Profits of eco manufacturer.

Figures 2 and 4 illustrate the carbon emissions of two types of manufacturers under three carbon emission reduction regulations, respectively. Figures 3 and 5 illustrate the profits of two types of manufacturers under three policies. Figures 6 and 7 show the network performance.

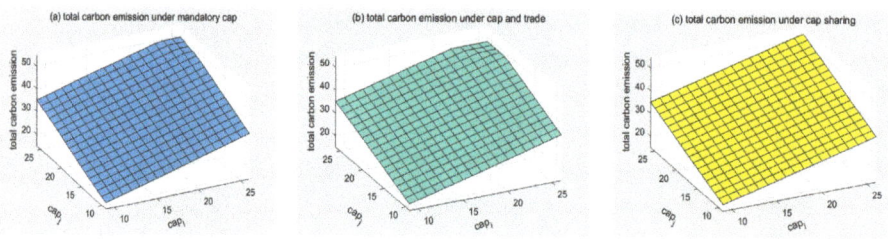

Figure 6. Total carbon emissions.

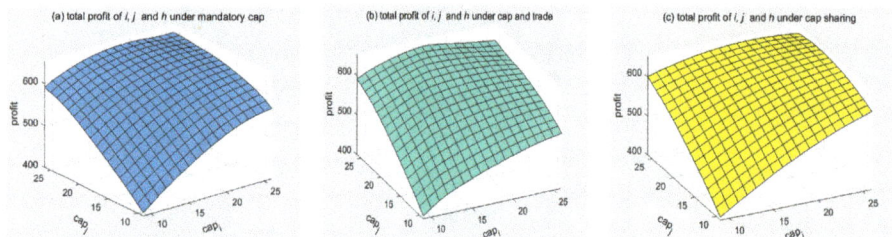

Figure 7. Total profits.

5.1.1. The Effects on Non-Ecological Manufacturer

As it can be seen from Figure 2, the trends are similar under the three regulations. Overall, the larger cap_j or cap_i incurs more carbon emissions. In Figure 2a, we can see that the carbon emission under MC is only affected by cap_j, Figure 2b shows that the carbon emission under CT is greatly affected by cap_j, and Figure 2c shows that the carbon emission under CS is affected by cap_j and cap_i simultaneously. The maximum value and minimum value appear in Figure 2c.

Comparing the three subfigures in Figure 2, the results show its carbon emissions and profits under policy MC are always lower than the other two policies, which means policy MC limits the enterprise's production activity and injures its profit. However, there is a special interval: when cap_i is less than 14, policy CS is conductive to decrease carbon emissions because the lower cap cannot activate the recycling process. Policy CT and Constraint (6) are invalid. In addition, there is no cap trade between two manufacturers, manufacturers only use the allocated cap to produce, and policy MC and CT have the same effects on the equilibrium results.

When cap_i is larger than 14, policy CS and CT are valid. Under policy CS, carbon caps are transferred freely from eco manufacturers to non-eco manufacturers. When caps transaction exists, policy CT promotes the effective allocation of carbon caps and benefits social-economic development. The maximum profit appears in the region when cap_i is relatively small while cap_j is large under policy CT. This can be explained by the adequacy caps reducing its carbon trade activities.

In Figure 3, the trends are also similar under three regulations. The maximum values appear in Figure 3a,b, while the minimum value appears in Figure 3c. Figure 3a states that the profit is mainly affected by cap_j and is slightly affected by cap_i. This phenomenon is different from carbon emissions. The reason can be explained by: the increasing caps will stimulate production activities, more customers turn to buy eco-products, and eco manufacturers' profits increase. Figure 3c illustrates cap_j and cap_i have the same effects on non-eco manufacturers' profit, and the profit is only influenced by caps.

The comparison of these three subfigures shows policy CT is a cost-effective carbon reduction policy. Particularly, when cap_i is lower, the profit in Figure 3b is similar to that in Figure 3a; when cap_i is higher, the profit in Figure 3b is similar to that in Figure 3c.

In addition, it should be noted that when cap_j and cap_i are large enough, the changing carbon emission trend is not exactly with that of the profit under policy CS, because the transportation cost increases rapidly with the intense production and recycling activities.

5.1.2. The Effects on Ecological Manufacturer

The analysis of eco manufacturers is similar to that of non-ecological manufacturers.

According to Figure 4, the equilibrium results of eco manufacturers are opposite to non-eco manufacturers in Figure 2. In Figure 4a, its carbon emission is only affected by cap_i in most ranges, which is similar to Figure 2a. In Figure 4b, when cap_i is at a relatively low level, it has no extra caps for sale, and policy CT is the same as MC. When cap_i gradually increases, the extra carbon quotas bring cap transactions. In Figure 4c, due to the adoption of ecological production technology, its carbon emission changes slightly.

Comparing the three subfigures of Figure 4, policy CS is the most effective method to reduce carbon emissions. Particularly, when cap_i is relatively small, carbon quotas are not transferred from eco manufacturers to non-eco manufacturers. Combined with Figure 5b, the carbon emissions and profits are identical under policy MC and CT. Policy MC is always beneficial for the eco manufacturer to obtain higher profits when cap_i is large. This phenomenon occurs because carbon quotas are adequate for it to produce more products, while policy CT and CS may force carbon caps to transfer to non-eco manufacturers.

5.1.3. The Effects on Supply Chain Performance

In this subsection, we focus on the impact of different policies on the whole supply chain performance. Total carbon emission and profit are given in Figure 6. From the environmental perspective, total carbon emissions are equal in three scenarios. From the economic perspective, according to Figure 7, we can clearly see that the best policy is cap sharing, but the difference between each policy is small. Combined with the previous figures, when caps increase, policy CS also perform well in reducing manufacturers' carbon emissions and promoting their profits. From the view of the government, the carbon trade model sacrifices part of the efficiency of the supply chain in exchange for government control and supervision of the carbon trading market. Although policy CS is an ideal regulation, if it lowers the carbon trade cost, policy CT may have a similar performance to policy CS, which makes it easier for the government to achieve the emissions reduction target.

Policy CT is conducive to the government to control the carbon emissions of enterprises; at the same time, the government may permit cap sharing within a large enterprise when there are different levels of low carbon technology applied in production.

5.2. Analyzing Effects of ε_j and ε_i on Optimal Decisions and Profits

Figure 8 illustrates the impacts of parameter ε_j and ε_i in the interval $[0, 0.3]$ on carbon emission amount and EOL product quantity, while Figure 9 shows the impacts on decision-makers' profits.

From Figure 8, we can see that manufacturers' carbon emission curves remain unchanged in policy MC. In policy CT and CS, manufacturer j's carbon emission curve almost decreases, then increases, and finally stays invariant, while manufacturer i's curve has an opposite trend, and $\varepsilon_i = \varepsilon_j = 0.09$ is the turning point. The observed phenomenon can be explained in the following manner. From the equilibrium decision value, we can see that the use of raw materials has been in a downward trend; thus, the emissions from raw materials continue to decrease. At first, non-eco manufacturer j's carbon emissions are higher due to the higher unit emission factor. For EOL products, the point at which manufacturer i begins to have EOL is 0, while the point at which manufacturer j begins to have EOL is 0.6. Therefore, the carbon emissions of j decreases at the beginning, and when $\varepsilon_i = \varepsilon_j = 0.09$, carbon emissions are minimum. After this point, the emission increased by the production and transportation of EOL remanufacturing is higher than the decrease in raw materials, and the emissions increase again. For eco manufacturer i, the same explanation can be made.

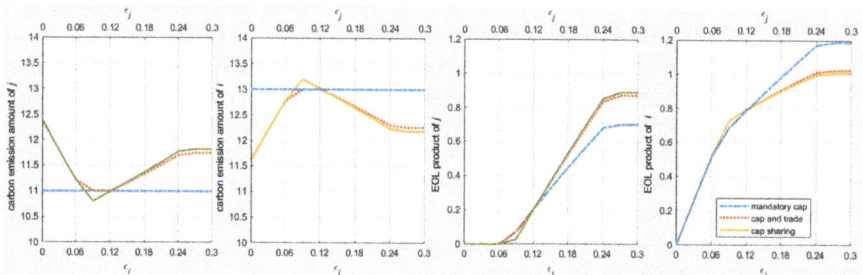

Figure 8. The effects on carbon emission amount and EOL product quantity.

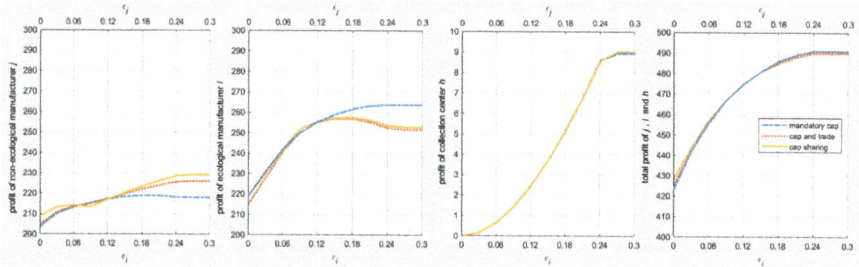

Figure 9. The effects on decision-makers' profits.

As for EOL product quantity, it is worth noting that when $\varepsilon_i = \varepsilon_j > 0$, the manufacturer i's EOL product quantity increases gradually, when ε_j and ε_i are in the interval (0.06,0.09), the manufacturer j's EOL product quantity becomes positive, and there is a turning point at 0.09 for manufacturer i under policy CS. When $\varepsilon_i = \varepsilon_j > 0.24$, these curves in three scenarios gradually stabilize. In this scenario, Constraint (6) does not hold, which means that the collection center is unable to recycle at a specified proportion.

According to Figure 9, manufacturer i always obtains more profit than manufacturer j. Overall, there is little difference in the total profits of the three cases; in particular, the total profits of all decision-makers in the policy CS are always higher than that in the other two cases. As for the collection center, the profit is almost the same under different regulations. For government, the recycling ratio should be set in an appropriate range. When it is too high, the enterprise will not comply with it, and it is meaningless. When the recycling ratio is set too low, it will fail to achieve the goal of resource utilization.

5.3. Analysis Effects of σ on Optimal Decisions and Profits

Figure 10 illuminates the impacts of parameter σ in the interval [0,1] on the product transaction amount and the carbon emissions amount, while Figure 11 shows the impacts on decision-makers' profits.

In CS policy, increasing σ has positive effects on the manufacturer i's products transaction amount, whereas for manufacturer j, the situation is reversed. In the other two scenarios, the products transaction amounts stay unchanged. The carbon emission curve has a synchronous changing trend with the product transaction.

As can be seen from Figure 11, the profit of non-ecological manufacturer j maintains stability in policy CS and increases a little in policy CT and MC. However, the profit of ecological manufacturer i increases rapidly under the three regulations. The change in profits shows that this situation is more favorable to ecological manufacturers. For the total profit of the two types of manufacturers, there are almost no differences in these three cases. Similar to the analysis of previous examples, the profit of collection center h is mainly affected by the EOL collection amount; thus, it maintains stability at first and decreases later. Therefore, the increasement of σ will promote the development and impacts little on carbon emission.

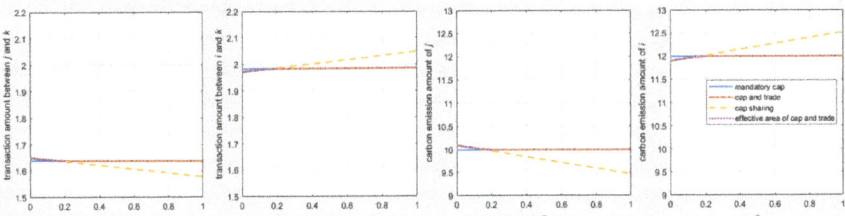

Figure 10. The effects on products transaction amount and carbon emission amount.

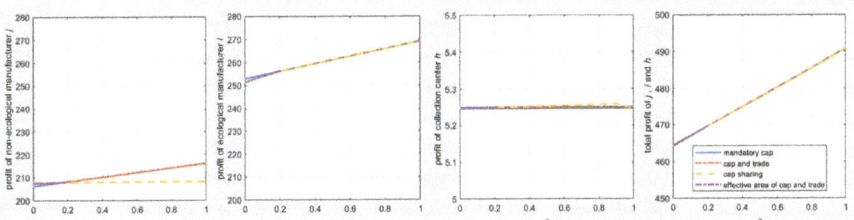

Figure 11. The effects on decision-makers' profits.

5.4. Managerial Insights

Compared with the literature [3], this research highlights the difference between carbon emission reduction policies, and based on numerical examples and analysis, we present several managerial insights as follows. This may facilitate the government and enterprises to refer to when issuing policies and enterprises making operation decisions.

- Firstly, by comparing the three carbon emission policies, even though cap-and-trade regulations are more flexible than mandatory cap policy, it still loses a little efficiency than cap-sharing schemes. Both cap-and-trade regulations and cap-sharing schemes can encourage firms to adjust their production and pricing strategies. Governments should allocate caps properly and implement cap-sharing schemes in some pilot enterprises.
- Secondly, the proposed model proves that investment in green production technology helps ecological manufacturers gain lower carbon emissions and high profits. The technologies work both in forward and reverse channels. For wise enterprise leadership, correct decisions should be made on when and how to adopt cleaner production technology.
- Thirdly, the reverse supply chain should be valued at a strategic level because of its essential role in promoting a circular economy and sustainable development. Especially high-emission enterprises can complete green transformation and reduce emissions through recycling and remanufacturing processes.
- Finally, consumers are increasingly concerned about the impact of the production process on the environment. On the one hand, governments can reward manufacturers for producing more environmentally friendly products. On the other hand, the information or technology can be shared between enterprises.

6. Conclusions

In this paper, we expand the previous research to a CLSC network based on non-cooperative equilibrium. This paper provides a research framework for a series of Nash game problems of low-carbon supply chain networks with complex relationships between horizontal and vertical competitive members. The profit maximum problem with nonlinear constraints can be transformed into variational inequality, and the equilibrium results can be obtained through a modified projection and contraction algorithm.

In the forward flow, we suppose three different environmental regulations, namely mandatory cap, cap-and-trade, and cap sharing. The collection and remanufacturing of EOL products are taken into consideration in the reverse flow. The effects of policies on network performance are discussed in detail. The results show that:

(1) Policy CS is effective in coordinating the relationship between economic development and environmental protection. In practice, the government may permit carbon cap sharing among enterprises, especially within a large enterprise to achieve a win-win situation. In other situations, CS policy may act as the ideal goal to measure the performance of MC and CT regulations.
(2) Policy MC is easy to implement for governments, and the carbon reduction goal can be reached either. However, the carbon quotas cannot be converted to revenue, even if there are excess quotas for manufacturers.
(3) Additionally, policy CT may lose a little efficiency compared with cap-sharing schemes, but it benefits government regulations. If governments can adjust cap transaction costs or relax carbon quotas, policy CT may show better performance. Moreover, policy CT can promote manufacturers adopting green technology to reduce carbon emissions, and the carbon emission rights have the nature of assets and create extra revenue.
(4) It should be noted that in all scenarios, ecological manufacturers always show better performances, which means the green technology innovation can benefit firms both in sustainable development and economic development.
(5) Consumers' environmental protection awareness has a positive effect on ecological manufacturers but hurts non-eco manufacturers, especially in cap-sharing schemes. Moreover, when the recycling rate is at a relatively high level, it effectively helps eco manufacturers to use more reusable materials and reduce carbon emissions, whereas when it exceeds a certain value, the change has almost no influence on equilibrium results.

This study mainly contributes to the enterprises' decision making and revenue management under three carbon emissions reduction regulations. Through numerical simulations, we verified the validity of each policy. For future research, possible extensions can be as follows:

(1) Information sharing can be considered, especially the production cost for different manufacturers.
(2) The model can include irrational behavior factors of decision-makers, such as free-riding behavior.
(3) The online transaction fashion can be incorporated into the model, especially in the post-COVID-19 era.
(4) Some practical constraints, such as financial constraints and capacity constraints, can be considered in the model in future research.

Author Contributions: Conceptualization, P.C. and G.Z.; methodology and model, P.C. and G.Z.; software, P.C.; validation, P.C., G.Z. and H.S.; numerical analysis, G.Z.; investigation, P.C.; resources, P.C.; data curation, P.C.; writing—original draft preparation, P.C.; writing—review and editing, P.C.; visualization, G.Z.; supervision, G.Z.; project administration, H.S.; funding acquisition, G.Z. All authors have read and agreed to the published version of the manuscript.

Funding: This research was funded by the National Social Science Foundation of China [grant number 19BGL091].

Institutional Review Board Statement: Not applicable.

Informed Consent Statement: Not applicable.

Data Availability Statement: Not applicable.

Acknowledgments: We greatly appreciate the associate editor and the anonymous reviewers for their insightful comments and constructive suggestions, which have greatly helped us to improve the manuscript and guide us forward to the future research.

Conflicts of Interest: The authors declare no conflict of interest. The funders had no role in the design of the study; in the collection, analyses, or interpretation of data; in the writing of the manuscript, or in the decision to publish the results.

Appendix A

The equilibrium conditions of the closed-loop supply chain network in the MC model

Under the government's mandatory cap regulation, at equilibrium conditions of the supply chain network, the Nash equilibrium (Nash 1950) conditions of VI (7), VI (10), VI (30), and VI (35) must hold simultaneously, and no one gains more from altering strategies.

Definition A1. *The equilibrium of the CLSCN under mandatory cap occurs when the sum of the L.H.S. of (7), L.H.S. of (10), L.H.S. of (30), and L.H.S. of (35) is non-negative.*

Theorem A1. *The equilibrium conditions of the CLSCN under mandatory cap are equivalent to the solutions of the VI as follows: determine the optimal solution* $(q_j^{v*}, q_j^{u*}, q_i^{v*}, q_i^{u*}, Q_1^*, Q_2^*, Q_3^*, Q_4^*, Q_5^*, \rho^{J*}, \rho^{I*}, \mu_1^*, \mu_2^*, \mu_3^*, \eta_1^*, \eta_2^*, \eta_3^*, \lambda^*, \gamma^*) \in \Omega^2$, *satisfying:*

$$\sum_{j=1}^{J}\left[\frac{\partial f_j^*}{\partial q_j^v} - \beta^r\mu_j^{2*} + \alpha_1^J\beta^r\mu_j^{3*}\right] \times \left[q_j^v - q_j^{v*}\right] + \sum_{j=1}^{J}\left[\frac{\partial f_j^{u*}}{\partial q_j^u} + \mu_j^{1*} - \beta^u\mu_j^{2*} + \alpha_2^J\beta^u\mu_j^{3*}\right] \times \left[q_j^u - q_j^{u*}\right] +$$
$$\sum_{i=1}^{I}\left[\frac{\partial f_i^*}{\partial q_i^v} - \beta^r\mu_i^{2*} + \alpha_1^J\beta^r\eta_i^{3*}\right] \times \left[q_i^v - q_i^{v*}\right] + \sum_{i=1}^{I}\left[\frac{\partial f_i^{u*}}{\partial q_i^u} + \eta_i^{1*} - \beta^u\mu_i^{2*} + \alpha_2^J\beta^u\eta_i^{3*}\right] \times \left[q_i^u - q_i^{u*}\right] +$$
$$\sum_{j=1}^{J}\sum_{k=1}^{K}\left[\frac{\partial c_{jk}^*}{\partial q_{jk}} + \rho t_1 x_{jk} + \mu_j^{2*} + t_1\tau_t x_{jk}\mu_j^{3*} + c_{jk}^{K*} - \rho_k^{h*} - \varepsilon_j\gamma_k^*\right] \times \left[q_{jk} - q_{jk}^*\right] +$$
$$\sum_{j=1}^{J}\sum_{h=1}^{H}\left[\frac{\partial c_{hj}^{u*}}{\partial q_{hj}^u} + \rho t_2 x_{hj} - \mu_j^{1*} + t_2\tau_t x_{hj}\mu_j^{3*} + \lambda_h^*\right] \times \left[q_{hj}^u - q_{hj}^{u*}\right] +$$
$$\sum_{i=1}^{I}\sum_{k=1}^{K}\left[\frac{\partial c_{ik}^*}{\partial q_{ik}} + \rho t_3 x_{ik} + \eta_i^{2*} + t_3\tau_t x_{ik}\eta_i^{3*} + c_{ik}^{K*} - \rho_k^{I*} - \varepsilon_i\gamma_k^*\right] \times \left[q_{ik} - q_{ik}^*\right] +$$
$$\sum_{i=1}^{I}\sum_{h=1}^{H}\left[\frac{\partial c_{hi}^{u*}}{\partial q_{hi}^u} + \rho t_4 x_{hi} - \eta_i^{1*} + t_4\tau_t x_{hi}\eta_i^{3*} + \lambda_h^*\right] \times \left[q_{hi}^u - q_{hi}^{u*}\right] +$$
$$\sum_{h=1}^{H}\sum_{k=1}^{K}\left[\frac{\partial c_{kh}^{u*}}{\partial q_{kh}^u} + \frac{\partial c_h^*}{\partial q_{kh}} - \delta\lambda_h^* + \alpha_k^u(Q_5^*) + \gamma_k^*\right] \times \left[q_{kh}^u - q_{kh}^{u*}\right] + \quad \text{(A1)}$$
$$\sum_{k=1}^{K}\left[\sum_{j=1}^{J}q_{jk}^* - d_k^{h*}\right] \times \left[\rho_k^h - \rho_k^{h*}\right] + \sum_{k=1}^{K}\left[\sum_{i=1}^{I}q_{ik}^* - d_k^{l*}\right] \times \left[\rho_k^I - \rho_k^{I*}\right] +$$
$$\sum_{j=1}^{J}\left[\sum_{h=1}^{H}q_{hj}^{u*} - q_j^{u*}\right] \times \left[\mu_j^1 - \mu_j^{1*}\right] + \sum_{j=1}^{J}\left[\beta^r q_j^{v*} + \beta^u q_j^{u*} - \sum_{k=1}^{K}q_{jk}^*\right] \times \left[\mu_j^2 - \mu_j^{2*}\right] +$$
$$\sum_{j=1}^{J}\left[cap_j - \alpha_1^J\beta^r q_j^{v*} - \alpha_2^J\beta^u q_j^{u*} - t_1\tau_t\sum_{k=1}^{K}x_{jk}q_{jk}^* - t_2\tau_t\sum_{h=1}^{H}x_{hj}q_{hj}^{u*}\right] \times \left[\mu_j^3 - \mu_j^{3*}\right] +$$
$$\sum_{i=1}^{I}\left[\sum_{h=1}^{H}q_{hi}^{u*} - q_i^{u*}\right] \times \left[\eta_i^1 - \eta_i^{1*}\right] + \sum_{i=1}^{I}\left[\beta^r q_i^{v*} + \beta^u q_i^{u*} - \sum_{k=1}^{K}q_{ik}^*\right] \times \left[\eta_i^2 - \eta_i^{2*}\right] +$$
$$\sum_{i=1}^{I}\left[cap_i - \alpha_1^J\beta^r q_i^{v*} - \alpha_2^J\beta^u q_i^{u*} - t_3\tau_t\sum_{k=1}^{K}x_{ik}q_{ik}^* - t_4\tau_t\sum_{h=1}^{H}x_{hi}q_{hi}^{u*}\right] \times \left[\eta_i^3 - \eta_i^{3*}\right] +$$
$$\sum_{h=1}^{H}\left[\delta\sum_{k=1}^{K}q_{kh}^{u*} - \sum_{j=1}^{J}q_{hj}^{u*} - \sum_{i=1}^{I}q_{hi}^{u*}\right] \times \left[\lambda_h - \lambda_h^*\right] + \sum_{k=1}^{K}\left[\varepsilon_j\sum_{j=1}^{J}q_{jk}^* + \varepsilon_i\sum_{i=1}^{I}q_{ik}^* - \sum_{h=1}^{H}q_{kh}^{u*}\right] \times \left[\gamma_k - \gamma_k^*\right] > 0.$$

$$\forall (q_j^v, q_j^u, q_i^v, q_i^u, Q_1, Q_2, Q_3, Q_4, Q_5, \rho^J, \rho^I, \mu_1, \mu_2, \mu_3, \eta_1, \eta_2, \eta_3, \lambda, \gamma) \in \Omega^2$$

where $\Omega^2 = \Omega_j^2 \times \Omega_I^2 \times \Omega_k \times \Omega_h$.

Proof. Adding VI (7), VI (10), VI (30), and VI (35) together, we can obtain VI (A1). Meanwhile, when VI (A1) holds, then VI (7), VI (10), VI (30), and VI (35) are also satisfied, respectively. □

Let $X_2 \equiv (q_j^v, q_j^u, q_i^v, q_i^u, Q_1, Q_2, Q_3, Q_4, Q_5, \rho^J, \rho^I, \mu_1, \mu_2, \mu_3, \eta_1, \eta_2, \eta_3, \lambda, \gamma)$, $F(X_2) \equiv (F_x(X_2))_{19 \times 1}$, The specific parts $F_x(X_2)$ ($x = 1, \cdots, 19$) of $F(X_2)$ are given by the terms proceeding the multiplication signs in VI (A1). Then, we can rewrite the VI (A1) in the standard form of VI following: determine the optimal vector $X_2^* \in \Omega^2$, satisfying: $\langle F(X_2^*), X_2^* \rangle \geq 0, \forall X_2 \in \Omega^2$.

The notation $\langle \cdot, \cdot \rangle$ denotes the inner product in M_2—dimensional Euclidean space, where $M_2 = 2J + 2I + JK + HJ + IK + HI + KH + 2K + 3J + 3I + H + K$.

Appendix B

The equilibrium conditions of closed-loop supply chain network in CS model

Under the government's cap-sharing regulations, for the closed-loop supply chain network, the Nash equilibrium (Nash 1950) conditions of VI (7), VI (10), and VI (40) must hold simultaneously, and no one gains more from altering current strategies.

Definition A2. *The equilibrium of the CLSCN under cap-sharing regulations occurs when the sum of the L.H.S. of (7), L.H.S. of (10), and L.H.S. of (40) is non-negative.*

Theorem A2. *The equilibrium conditions of the CLSCN under cap-sharing regulations are equivalent to the solutions of the VI as follows, determine the optimal solution* $(q_j^{v*}, q_j^{u*}, q_i^{v*}, q_i^{u*}, Q_1^*, Q_2^*, Q_3^*, Q_4^*, Q_5^*, \rho^{J*}, \rho^{I*}, \theta_1^*, \theta_2^*, \theta_3^*, \theta_4^*, \theta^{5*}, \lambda^*, \gamma^*) \in \Omega^3$, *satisfying:*

$$\sum_{j=1}^{J} \left[\frac{\partial f_j^*}{\partial q_j^v} - \beta^r \theta_j^{2*} + \alpha_1^J \beta^r \theta^{5*} \right] \times \left[q_j^v - q_j^{v*} \right] + \sum_{j=1}^{J} \left[\frac{\partial f_j^{u*}}{\partial q_j^u} + \theta_j^{1*} - \beta^u \theta_j^{2*} + \alpha_2^J \beta^u \theta^{5*} \right] \times \left[q_j^u - q_j^{u*} \right] +$$

$$\sum_{i=1}^{I} \left[\frac{\partial f_i^*}{\partial q_i^v} - \beta^r \theta_i^{4*} + \alpha_1^I \beta^r \theta^{5*} \right] \times \left[q_i^v - q_i^{v*} \right] + \sum_{i=1}^{I} \left[\frac{\partial f_i^{u*}}{\partial q_i^u} + \theta_i^{3*} - \beta^u \theta_i^{4*} + \alpha_2^I \beta^u \theta^{5*} \right] \times \left[q_i^u - q_i^{u*} \right] +$$

$$\sum_{j=1}^{J} \sum_{k=1}^{K} \left[\frac{\partial c_{jk}^*}{\partial q_{jk}} + \rho t_1 x_{jk} + \theta_j^{2*} + t_1 \tau_t x_{jk} \theta^{5*} + c_{jk}^{K*} - \rho_k^{h*} - \varepsilon_j \gamma_k^* \right] \times \left[q_{jk} - q_{jk}^* \right] +$$

$$\sum_{j=1}^{J} \sum_{h=1}^{H} \left[\frac{\partial c_{hj}^{u*}}{\partial q_{hj}^u} + \rho t_2 x_{hj} - \theta_j^{1*} + t_2 \tau_t x_{hj} \theta^{5*} + \lambda_h^* \right] \times \left[q_{hj}^u - q_{hj}^{u*} \right] +$$

$$\sum_{i=1}^{I} \sum_{k=1}^{K} \left[\frac{\partial c_{ik}^*}{\partial q_{ik}} + \rho t_3 x_{ik} + \theta_i^{4*} + t_3 \tau_t x_{ik} \theta^{5*} + c_{ik}^{K*} - \rho_k^{l*} - \varepsilon_i \gamma_k^* \right] \times \left[q_{ik} - q_{ik}^* \right] +$$

$$\sum_{i=1}^{I} \sum_{h=1}^{H} \left[\frac{\partial c_{hi}^{u*}}{\partial q_{hi}^u} + \rho t_4 x_{hi} - \theta_i^{3*} + t_4 \tau_t x_{hi} \theta^{5*} + \lambda_h^* \right] \times \left[q_{hi}^u - q_{hi}^{u*} \right] +$$

$$\sum_{h=1}^{H} \sum_{k=1}^{K} \left[\alpha_k^u (Q_5^*) + \gamma_k^* + \frac{\partial c_{kh}^*}{\partial q_{kh}^u} + \frac{\partial c_h^*}{\partial q_{kh}^u} - \delta \lambda_h^* \right] \times \left[q_{kh}^u - q_{kh}^{u*} \right] + \qquad (A2)$$

$$\sum_{k=1}^{K} \left[\sum_{j=1}^{J} q_{jk}^* - d_k^{h*} \right] \times \left[\rho_k^h - \rho_k^{h*} \right] + \sum_{k=1}^{K} \left[\sum_{i=1}^{I} q_{ik}^* - d_k^{l*} \right] \times \left[\rho_k^l - \rho_k^{l*} \right] +$$

$$\sum_{j=1}^{J} \left[\sum_{h=1}^{H} q_{hj}^{u*} - q_j^{u*} \right] \times \left[\theta_j^1 - \theta_j^{1*} \right] + \sum_{j=1}^{J} \left[\beta^r q_j^{v*} + \beta^u q_j^{u*} - \sum_{k=1}^{K} q_{jk}^* \right] \times \left[\theta_j^2 - \theta_j^{2*} \right] +$$

$$\sum_{i=1}^{I} \left[\sum_{h=1}^{H} q_{hi}^{u*} - q_i^{u*} \right] \times \left[\theta_i^3 - \theta_i^{3*} \right] + \sum_{i=1}^{I} \left[\beta^r q_i^{v*} + \beta^u q_i^{u*} - \sum_{k=1}^{K} q_{ik}^* \right] \times \left[\theta_i^4 - \theta_i^{4*} \right] +$$

$$\left[\left[\sum_{j=1}^{J} cap_j + \sum_{i=1}^{I} cap_i \right] - \left[\sum_{j=1}^{J} \left[\alpha_1^J \beta^r q_j^{v*} + \alpha_2^J \beta^u q_j^{u*} + t_1 \tau_t \sum_{k=1}^{K} x_{jk} q_{jk}^* + t_2 \tau_t \sum_{h=1}^{H} x_{hj} q_{hj}^{u*} \right] + \sum_{i=1}^{I} \left[\alpha_1^I \beta^r q_i^{v*} + \alpha_2^I \beta^u q_i^{u*} + t_3 \tau_t \sum_{k=1}^{K} x_{ik} q_{ik}^* + t_4 \tau_t \sum_{h=1}^{H} x_{hi} q_{hi}^{u*} \right] \right] \right] \times \left[\theta^5 - \theta^{5*} \right] +$$

$$\sum_{k=1}^{K} \left[\varepsilon_j \sum_{j=1}^{J} q_{jk}^* + \varepsilon_i \sum_{i=1}^{I} q_{ik}^* - \sum_{k=1}^{K} q_{kh}^{u*} \right] \times \left[\gamma_k - \gamma_k^* \right] + \sum_{h=1}^{H} \left[\delta \sum_{k=1}^{K} q_{kh}^{u*} - \sum_{j=1}^{J} q_{hj}^{u*} - \sum_{i=1}^{I} q_{hi}^{u*} \right] \times \left[\lambda_h - \lambda_h^* \right] \geq 0$$

$$\forall (q_j^v, q_j^u, q_i^v, q_i^u, Q_1, Q_2, Q_3, Q_4, Q_5, \rho^J, \rho^I, \theta_1, \theta_2, \theta_3, \theta_4, \theta^5, \lambda, \gamma) \in \Omega^3$$

where $\Omega^3 = \Omega_{JI}^3 \times \Omega_k \times \Omega_h$.

Proof. Adding VI (7), VI (10), and VI (40) together, we can obtain VI (A2). At the same time, when VI (A2) holds, then VI (7), VI (10), and VI (40) are also satisfied, respectively. □

Let $X_3 \equiv (q_j^v, q_j^u, q_i^v, q_i^u, Q_1, Q_2, Q_3, Q_4, Q_5, \rho^J, \rho^I, \theta_1, \theta_2, \theta_3, \theta_4, \theta^5, \lambda, \gamma)$, $F(X_3) \equiv (F_x(X_3))_{18 \times 1}$, the specific parts $F_3(X_3)$ ($x = 1, \cdots, 18$) of $F(X_3)$ are given by the terms proceeding the multiplication signs in VI (A2). Then, we can rewrite the VI (A2) in standard form of VI following: determine the optimal vector $X_3^* \in \Omega^3$, satisfying: $\langle F(X_3^*), X_3^* \rangle \geq 0$, $\forall X_3 \in \Omega^3$.

The notation $\langle \cdot, \cdot \rangle$ denotes the inner product in M_3—dimensional Euclidean space, where $M_3 = 2J + 2I + JK + HJ + IK + HI + KH + 2K + 2J + 2I + 1 + H + K$.

Appendix C

Qualitative Properties

In this appendix, we provide the existence and uniqueness results of VI (24), VI (40), and VI (A1), and prove that the solutions of these VIs are the equilibriums of the closed-loop supply chain network under different regulations. Because the process and steps of the proof are basically the same, we only give the proof process of VI (24). Similar to [39,40], we give the following theorems, a variational inequality admits at least one solution if the entering function $F(X_1)$ is continuous and the feasible region is compact. Obviously, $F(X_1)$ is continuous, while the feasible region Ω^1 is not compact; thus, we impose a weak condition on Ω^1 to guarantee the solution existence of VI (24).

Similar with [58], let $\Omega =$
$\{ (q_j^v, q_j^u, q_i^v, q_i^u, Q_1, Q_2 Q_3, Q_4, Q_5, \rho^J, \rho^I, \mu_1, \mu_2, \mu_3, \eta_1, \eta_2, \eta_3, \lambda, \gamma) \,|\, 0 \leq q_j^v \leq r_1; 0 \leq q_j^u \leq r_2; 0 \leq q_i^v \leq r_3; 0 \leq q_i^u \leq r_4;$
$0 \leq Q_1 \leq r_5; 0 \leq Q_2 \leq r_6; 0 \leq Q_3 \leq r_7; 0 \leq Q_4 \leq r_8; 0 \leq Q_5 \leq r_9; 0 \leq T_1 \leq r_{10}; 0 \leq T_2 \leq r_{11}; 0 \leq \rho^J \leq r_{12}; 0 \leq \rho^I \leq r_{13};$
$0 \leq \varphi_1 \leq r_{14}; 0 \leq \varphi_2 \leq r_{15}; 0 \leq \varphi_3 \leq r_{16}; 0 \leq \phi_1 \leq r_{17}; 0 \leq \phi_2 \leq r_{18}; 0 \leq \phi_3 \leq r_{19}; 0 \leq \zeta_c \leq r_{20}; 0 \leq \lambda \leq r_{21}; 0 \leq \gamma \leq r_{22} \}$,

where $r = (r_1, r_2, r_3, r_4, r_5, r_6, r_7, r_8, r_9, r_{10}, r_{11}, r_{12}, r_{13}, r_{14}, r_{15}, r_{16}, r_{17}, r_{18}, r_{19}, r_{20}, r_{21}, r_{22}) \geq 0$, and $q_j^v \leq r_1$ means $q_j^v \leq r_1$ for all $j = 1, \cdots, J$, and other notations can be interpreted in the same manner. Obviously, Ω is a bounded, closed convex set, and $\Omega \in \Omega^1$. From Hammond et al. [58], the following VI $\langle F(X_1^*), X_1^* \rangle \geq 0$, $\forall X_1 \in \Omega$, admits at least one solution. We have the following theorem.

Theorem A3. *(Existence) Variational inequality (24) admits a solution if and only if there is an $r > 0$, such that variational inequality (41) admits at least one solution in Ω with $q_j^v < r_1$, $q_j^u < r_2$, $q_i^v < r_3$, $q_i^u < r_4$, $Q_1 < r_5$, $Q_2 < r_6$, $Q_3 < r_7$, $Q_4 < r_8$, $Q_5 < r_9$, $T_1 \leq r_{10}$, $0 \leq T_2 \leq r_{11}, \rho^J < r_{12}, \rho^I < r_{13}, \varphi_1 < r_{14}, \varphi_2 < r_{15}, \varphi_3 < r_{16}, \phi_1 < r_{17}, \phi_2 < r_{18}, \phi_3 < r_{19}, \zeta_c < r_{20}, \lambda < r_{21}, \gamma < r_{22}$.*

Proof. The proof of this theorem follows from Theorem 2. □

Theorem A4. *(Monotonicity) When the cost functions and demand functions in VI (24) are convex, then the vector function $F(X_1)$ in VI (25) is monotone.*

Proof. Let $X_1^1 \in \Omega$ and $X_1^2 \in \Omega$, $\nabla H(X_1) = F(X_1)$, according to Assumption 5 in Section 2, all functions in this paper are convex, then we have $H(X_1^1) \geq H(X_1^2) + \nabla H(X_1^2)^T (X_1^1 - X_1^2)$ and $H(X_1^2) \geq H(X_1^1) + \nabla H(X_1^1)^T (X_1^2 - X_1^1)$, adding two formulas, $[\nabla H(X_1^1) - \nabla H(X_1^2)]^T (X_1^1 - X_1^2) \geq 0$, that is, $\langle F(X_1) - F(X_2), X_1 - X_2 \rangle \geq 0$. Thus, we conclude that VI (25) is monotone. □

Theorem A5. *(Strict monotonicity) When one of the cost functions and demand functions in VI (24) is strictly convex, then VI (25) is strictly monotone.*

Proof. Let $X_1^1, X_1^2 \in \Omega$, and $X_1^1 \neq X_1^2$, we can know at least one element in the vector X_1^1 and X_1^2 is not equal. No loss generality, let us suppose $q_j^{v1} \neq q_j^{v2}$. At the same time, we also suppose the production cost function f_j is strictly convex. Thus, we have $\langle F(X_1) - F(X_2), X_1 - X_2 \rangle > 0$; that is, VI (25) is strictly monotone. □

Theorem A6. *(Uniqueness) When VI (25) is strictly monotone, VI (24) has a unique solution in Ω.*

Proof. The proof of uniqueness of solution follows easily from Kinderlehrer and Stampacchia [61]. □

Theorem A7. *(Lipschitz continuity) Suppose that $f_j, f_j^u, f_i, f_i^u, c_{jk}, c_{hj}^u, c_{ik}, c_{hi}^u, c_{kh}^u$ and c_h have bounded second-order derivatives. Suppose that $c_{jk}^K, c_{ik}^K, \alpha_k^u(Q_5), -d_k^h$ and $-d_k^l$ have bounded first-order derivatives. The VI (24) is Lipschitz continuous. That is $\|F(X_1^1) - F(X_1^2)\| \leq L\|X_1^1 - X_1^2\|$, $X_1^1, X_1^2 \in \Omega$, with $L > 0$.*

Proof. Applying the mean value theorem of integrals to vector function $F(X_1)$ can immediately demonstrate Theorem A7. □

Appendix D

$\alpha_1^I = 0.6$ is lower than $\alpha_1^J = 0.8$ and $\alpha_2^I = 0.3$ is lower than $\alpha_2^J = 0.5$, which illustrates the result of the eco manufacturers' adoption of green technology. The selection of t_i and x_{xy} refers to Allevi et al. [50]. The other parameters are decided from the operation of paper industry enterprises.

The production cost of eco manufacturer i: $f_i = 8.5(\beta^r q_i^v)^2 + \beta^{r2} q_i^v q_{3-i}^v + 2\beta^r q_i^v$, $i = 1, 2$.

The production cost depends on the amount of raw materials used by both eco manufacturers, so it reflects the competitive relationship between eco manufacturers. In the numerical examples of the SCN equilibrium model, Nagurney et al. [40] first used this production cost function form, then other researchers such as [38,39] adopted this production cost function form.

The remanufacturing cost of eco manufacturer i: $f_i^u = 3(\beta^u q_i^u)^2 + 1.5\beta^u q_i^u + 1$, $i = 1, 2$.

Similarly, the production cost function and remanufacturing cost function of non-eco manufacturer j can be described as:

$$f_j^u = 0.5(\beta^u q_j^u)^2 + 0.5\beta^u q_j^u + 1, \ j = 1, 2; \ f_i = 8.0(\beta^r q_i^v)^2 + \beta^{r2} q_i^v q_{3-i}^v + 2\beta^r q_i^v, \ i = 1, 2.$$

We need to point out that the production cost and remanufacturing cost of the eco manufacturer is higher than that of non-eco manufacturer j, which is consistent with the previous Assumption 1.

The transaction cost functions between manufacturers and demand markets: $c_{jk} = 0.2t_1 q_{jk} + 1$, $c_{ik} = 0.2t_3 q_{ik} + 1$, $c_{jk}^K = 0.2q_{jk} + 0.1$, $c_{ik}^K = 0.2q_{ik} + 0.1$, $j = 1, 2, i = 1, 2, k = 1, 2$.

The transaction cost burdened by manufacturers and consumers comprises two parts: variable cost, which is associated with product quantity, and fixed cost, which is associated with the transaction action; whereas the cost burdened by manufacturers is also associated with the truck number.

The transaction cost functions between the collection center and demand market, and between the collection center and manufacturers: $c_{kh} = 0.1q_{kh}^u + 0.5$, $c_{hj}^u = 0.1t_2 q_{hj}^u + 1$, $c_{hi}^u = 0.1t_4 q_{hi}^u + 1$, $i = 1, 2, h = 1, 2, k = 1, 2, j = 1, 2$.

Similar to [50], c_{hj}^u and c_{hi}^u include the number of trucks, which shows the transport effect. The disposal cost function of the collection center: $c_h = 2.5 \left(\sum_{k=1}^{2} q_{kh}^u \right)^2 + 2 \sum_{k=1}^{2} q_{kh}^u$, $h = 1, 2$, the disutility function of consumers: $\alpha_k^u(Q_5) = 0.5 \sum_{k=1}^{2} \sum_{k=1}^{2} q_{kh}^u + 5, k = 1, 2$.

According to carbon trading data related to the paper industry and related study [60], the carbon trade cost of manufacturers: $c_x^t = 0.1 t_x^2, x = i, j, i = 1, 2, j = 1, 2$.

The demand functions:

$$d_k^l = 250 - 2\rho_k^l - 1.5\rho_{3-k}^l + 0.5(\rho_k^h + \rho_{3-k}^h) + \sigma \psi \sum_{x=1}^{2} (1 - \alpha_x^l), \ k = 1, 2;$$

$$d_k^h = 230 - 2\rho_k^h - 1.5\rho_{3-k}^h + 0.5(\rho_k^l + \rho_{3-k}^l) + \sigma \psi \sum_{x=1}^{2} (1 - \alpha_x^l), \ k = 1, 2.$$

The manufacturers' production functions indicate that competition exists between the same types of manufacturers, and there is no competition between different types of manufacturers. The demand functions are associated with the price of two types of products; due to the consumer's low carbon preference, there is also a relationship between demand and the product's unit carbon emission amount. We assume the low carbon factor $\psi = 10$.

It is obvious that all the functions listed above are convex and continuously differentiable. Then, the solutions of VI (24), VI (40), and VI (A1) satisfy Theorem A3, Theorem A4, and Theorem A6.

References

1. Liu, P.T.; Liu, L.Y.; Xu, X. Carbon footprint and carbon emission intensity of grassland wind farms in Inner Mongolia. *J. Clean. Prod.* **2021**, *313*, 127878. [CrossRef]
2. Liu, M.L.; Li, Z.H.; Anwar, S. Supply chain carbon emission reductions and coordination when consumers have a strong preference for low-carbon products. *Environ. Sci. Pollut. Res.* **2021**, *28*, 19969–19983. [CrossRef] [PubMed]
3. Cheng, P.Y.; Ji, G.X.; Zhang, G.T. A closed-loop supply chain network considering consumer's low carbon preference and carbon tax under the cap-and-trade regulation. *Sustain. Prod. Consum.* **2022**, *29*, 614–635. [CrossRef]
4. Zhang, G.T.; Cheng, P.Y.; Sun, H. Carbon reduction decisions under progressive carbon tax regulations: A new dual-channel supply chain network equilibrium model. *Sustain. Prod. Consum.* **2021**, *27*, 1077–1092. [CrossRef]
5. Yu, M.; Cruz, J.M.; Li, M.D. The sustainable supply chain network competition with environmental tax policies. *Int. J. Prod. Econ.* **2019**, *217*, 218–231. [CrossRef]
6. Guchhait, R.; Sakar, B. Economic and environmental assessment of an unreliable supply chain management. *RAIRO-Oper. Res.* **2021**, *55*, 3153–3170. [CrossRef]
7. Xu, X.F.; He, Y.Y. Blockchain application in modern logistics information sharing: A review and case study analysis. *Prod. Plan. Control* **2022**, 1–15. [CrossRef]
8. Zhang, W.; Yan, S.; Li, J. Credit risk prediction of SMEs in supply chain finance by fusing demographic and behavioral data. *Transport. Res. E Logist. Transport. Rev.* **2022**, *158*, 102611. [CrossRef]
9. Guchhait, R.; Pareek, S.; Sakar, B. How Does a Radio Frequency Identification Optimize the Profit in an Unreliable Supply Chain Management? *Mathematics* **2019**, *7*, 490. [CrossRef]
10. Wu, Y.S.; Lu, R.H.; Yang, J. Government-led low carbon incentive model of the online shopping supply chain considering the O2O model. *J. Clean. Prod.* **2021**, *279*, 123271. [CrossRef]
11. He, L.; Hu, C.; Zhao, D. Carbon emission mitigation through regulatory policies and operations adaptation in supply chains: Theoretic developments and extensions. *Nat. Hazards* **2016**, *84*, 179–207. [CrossRef]
12. Dinan, T. *Policy Options for Reducing CO_2 Emissions*; Congress of the U.S. Congressional Budget Office: Washington, DC, USA, 2008.
13. Yu, Y.G.; Zhou, S.J.; Shi, Y. Information sharing or not across the supply chain: The role of carbon emission reduction. *Transport. Res. E Logist. Transport. Rev.* **2020**, *137*, 101915. [CrossRef]
14. Xu, X.F.; Wang, C.L.; Zhou, P. GVRP considered oil-gas recovery in refined oil distribution: From an environmental perspective. *Int. J. Prod. Econ.* **2021**, *235*, 108078. [CrossRef]
15. Cao, J.; Chen, X.H.; Zhang, X.M. Overview of remanufacturing industry in China: Government policies, enterprise, and public awareness. *J. Clean. Prod.* **2020**, *242*, 1–17. [CrossRef]
16. Cai, J.Y.; Cai, Z. Renewable resource industry's international experience and enlightenment. *Econ. Geogr.* **2010**, *30*, 2044–2049.

17. Xing, E.F.; Shi, C.D.; Zhang, J.X. Double third-party recycling closed-loop supply chain decision under the perspective of carbon trading. *J. Clean. Prod.* **2020**, *259*, 1–11. [CrossRef]
18. Patel, G.S. A Stochastic Production Cost Model for Remanufacturing Systems. Master's Thesis, The University of Texas-Pan American, Edinburg, TX, USA, 2006.
19. Gregorio, R.S.; Sofía, E.M.; Carlos, R.A. Multivariable Supplier Segmentation in Sustainable Supply Chain Management. *Sustainability* **2020**, *12*, 4556.
20. Zhang, X.X.; Ji, Y.N.; Shen, C.L. Manufacturers' green investment in a competitive market with a common retailer. *J. Clean. Prod.* **2020**, *276*, 123164. [CrossRef]
21. Guo, S.; Choi, T.M.; Shen, B. Green product development under competition: A study of the fashion apparel industry. *Eur. J. Oper. Res.* **2020**, *280*, 523–538. [CrossRef]
22. Savaskan, R.C.; Bhattacharya, S.; Van Wassenhove, L.N. Closed-loop supply chain models with product remanufacturing. *Manag. Sci.* **2004**, *50*, 239–252. [CrossRef]
23. Chen, C.K.; Ulya, M.A. Analyses of the reward-penalty mechanism in green closed-loop supply chains with product remanufacturing. *Int. J. Prod. Econ.* **2019**, *210*, 211–223. [CrossRef]
24. Taleizadeh, A.A.; Alizadeh-Basban, N.; Niaki, S.T.A. A closed-loop supply chain considering carbon reduction, quality improvement effort, and return policy under two remanufacturing scenarios. *J. Clean. Prod.* **2019**, *232*, 1230–1250. [CrossRef]
25. Yang, Y.; Xu, X. A differential game model for closed-loop supply chain participants under carbon emission permits. *Comput. Ind. Eng.* **2019**, *135*, 1077–1090. [CrossRef]
26. Taleizadeh, A.A.; Moshtagh, M.S.; Moon, I. Optimal decisions of price, quality, effort level and return policy in a three-level closed-loop supply chain based on different game theory approaches. *Eur. J. Int. Eng.* **2017**, *11*, 486–525. [CrossRef]
27. Zerang, E.S.; Taleizadeh, A.A.; Razmj, J. Analytical comparisons in a three-echelon closed-loop supply chain with price and marketing effort-dependent demand: Game theory approaches. *Environ. Dev. Sustain.* **2018**, *20*, 451–478. [CrossRef]
28. Chu, J.F.; Shao, C.F.; Ali, E. Performance evaluation of organizations considering economic incentives for emission reduction: A carbon emission permit trading approach. *Energy Econ.* **2021**, *101*, 105398. [CrossRef]
29. Wang, Y.J.; Chen, W.D.; Liu, B.Y. Manufacturing/remanufacturing decisions for a capital-constrained manufacturer considering carbon emission cap and trade. *J. Prod. Clean.* **2017**, *140*, 1118–1128. [CrossRef]
30. Xu, L.; Wang, C. Sustainable manufacturing in a closed-loop supply chain considering emission reduction and remanufacturing. *Resour. Conserv. Recycl.* **2018**, *131*, 297–304. [CrossRef]
31. Wang, C.; Miao, Z.; Chen, X. Factors affecting changes of greenhouse gas emissions in belt and road countries. *Renew. Sust. Energ. Rev.* **2021**, *147*, 111220. [CrossRef]
32. Zhu, Q.; Li, X.; Li, F. Analyzing the sustainability of China's industrial sectors: A data-driven approach with total energy consumption constraint. *Ecol. Indic.* **2021**, *122*, 107235. [CrossRef]
33. Chai, Q.F.; Xiao, Z.D.; Lai, K.H. Can carbon cap and trade mechanism be beneficial for remanufacturing? *Int. J. Prod. Econ.* **2018**, *203*, 311–321. [CrossRef]
34. Si, M.X.; Bai, L.; Du, K. Fuel consumption analysis and cap and trade system evaluation for Canadian in situ oil sands extraction. *Renew. Sustain. Energy Rev.* **2021**, *146*, 111145. [CrossRef]
35. Ji, J.N.; Zhang, Z.Y.; Yang, L. Comparisons of initial carbon allowance allocation rules in an O2O retail supply chain with the cap-and-trade regulation. *Int. J. Prod. Econ.* **2017**, *187*, 68–84. [CrossRef]
36. Zhang, B.; Xu, L. Multi-item production planning with carbon cap and trade mechanism. *Int. J. Prod. Econ.* **2013**, *144*, 118–127. [CrossRef]
37. Du, S.; Ma, F.; Fu, Z. Game-theoretic analysis for an emission-dependent supply chain in a 'cap-and-trade' system. *Ann. Oper. Res.* **2015**, *228*, 135–149. [CrossRef]
38. Yang, G.F.; Wang, Z.P.; Li, X.Q. The optimization of the closed-loop supply chain network. *Transport. Res. E Logist. Transport. Rev.* **2008**, *45*, 16–28. [CrossRef]
39. Xu, X.F.; He, J.; Zheng, Y. Multi-objective artificial bee colony algorithm for multi-stage resource leveling problem in sharing logistics network. *Comput. Ind. Eng.* **2020**, *142*, 106338. [CrossRef]
40. Nagurney, A.; Dong, J.; Zhang, D. A supply chain network equilibrium model. *Transp. Res. Part E Logist. Transp. Rev.* **2002**, *38*, 281–303. [CrossRef]
41. Nagurney, A.; Daniele, P.; Shukla, S. A supply chain network game theory model of cybersecurity investments with nonlinear budget constraints. *Ann. Oper. Res.* **2017**, *248*, 405–427. [CrossRef]
42. Nagurney, A.; Yu, M. Sustainable fashion supply chain management under oligopolistic competition and brand differentiation. *Int. J. Prod. Econ.* **2012**, *135*, 532–540. [CrossRef]
43. He, L.F.; Xu, Z.G.; Niu, Z.W. Joint optimal production planning for complex supply chains constrained by carbon emission abatement policies. *Discrete Dyn. Nat. Soc.* **2014**, *2014*, 361923. [CrossRef]
44. Tao, Z.G.; Zhong, Y.G.; Sun, H. Multi-period closed-loop supply chain network equilibrium with carbon emission constrains. *Resour. Conserv. Recycl.* **2015**, *104*, 354–365. [CrossRef]
45. He, L.F.; Mao, J.; Hu, C.L. Carbon emission regulation and operations in the supply chain network under stringent carbon policy. *J. Clean. Prod.* **2019**, *238*, 1–18. [CrossRef]

46. Li, Q.; Long, R.; Chen, H. Empirical study of the willingness of consumers to purchase low-carbon products by considering carbon labels: A case study. *J. Clean. Prod.* **2017**, *161*, 1237–1250. [CrossRef]
47. Hong, Z.; Wang, H.; Yu, Y. Green product pricing with non-green product reference. *Transp. Res. Part E Logist. Transp. Rev.* **2018**, *115*, 1–15. [CrossRef]
48. Ma, S.G.; He, Y.; Gu, R.; Li, S.S. Sustainable supply chain management considering technology investments and government intervention. *Transp. Res. Part E Logist. Transp. Rev.* **2021**, *149*, 102290. [CrossRef]
49. Tong, W.; Mu, D.; Zhao, F. The impact of cap-and-trade mechanism and consumers' environmental preferences on a retailer-led supply chain. *Resour. Conserv. Recycl.* **2019**, *142*, 88–100. [CrossRef]
50. Allevi, E.; Gnudi, A.; Konnov, I.V. Evaluating the effect of environmental regulations on a closed-loop supply chain network: A variational inequality approach. *Ecol. Environ. Conserv.* **2018**, *261*, 1–43. [CrossRef]
51. Gao, J.; Han, H.; Hou, L. Pricing and effort decisions in a closed-loop supply chain under different channel power structures. *J. Clean. Prod.* **2016**, *112*, 2043–2205. [CrossRef]
52. Hong, X.; Govindan, K.; Xu, L. Quantity and collection decisions in a closed-loop supply chain with technology licensing. *Eur. J. Oper. Res.* **2017**, *3*, 820–829. [CrossRef]
53. Huang, Y.; Wang, Z. Values of information sharing: A comparison of supplier-remanufacturing and manufacturer-remanufacturing scenarios. *Transport. Res. Part E* **2017**, *106*, 20–44. [CrossRef]
54. Huang, Y.; Wang, Z. Closed-loop supply chain models with product take-back and hybrid remanufacturing under technology licensing. *J. Clean. Prod.* **2017**, *142*, 3917–3927. [CrossRef]
55. Liao, Z.; Zhu, X.; Shi, J. Case study on initial allocation of Shanghai carbon emission trading based on Shapley value. *J. Clean. Prod.* **2015**, *103*, 338–344. [CrossRef]
56. Ray, S.; Jewkes, E.M. Customer lead time management when both demand and price are lead time sensitive. *Eur. J. Oper. Res.* **2004**, *153*, 769–781. [CrossRef]
57. Liu, Z.G.; Anderson, T.D.; Cruz, J.M. Consumer environmental awareness and competition in two-stage supply chains. *Eur. J. Oper. Res.* **2012**, *218*, 602–613. [CrossRef]
58. Hammond, D.; Beullens, P. Closed-loop supply chain network equilibrium under legislation. *Eur. J. Oper. Res.* **2007**, *183*, 895–908. [CrossRef]
59. Paksoy, T.; Özceylan, E.; Weber, G.W. A multi objective model for optimization of a green supply chain network. *Glob. J. Technol. Optim.* **2011**, *2*, 84–96. [CrossRef]
60. Cheng, F.L.; Sue, J.L.; Charles, L. Analysis of the impacts of combining carbon taxation and emission trading on different industry sectors. *Energy Policy* **2008**, *36*, 722–729.
61. Kinderlehrer, D.; Stampacchia, G. *An Introduction to Variational Inequalities and their Applications*; Society for Industrial Mathematics: Philadelphia, PA, USA, 1987.

Article

Mining Campus Big Data: Prediction of Career Choice Using Interpretable Machine Learning Method

Yuan Wang [1,2], Liping Yang [2], Jun Wu [2,*], Zisheng Song [3] and Li Shi [4]

1. College of Humanities and Law, Beijing University of Chemical Technology, Beijing 100029, China; wangyuan@mail.buct.edu.cn
2. School of Economics and Management, Beijing University of Chemical Technology, Beijing 100029, China; lipingphd@163.com
3. Department of International Exchange and Cooperation, Beijing University of Chemical Technology, Beijing 100029, China; zishengsong@163.com
4. China Information Communication Technology Group Corporation, Beijing 100191, China; simon_shl@126.com
* Correspondence: wujun@mail.buct.edu.cn

Abstract: The issue of students' career choice is the common concern of students themselves, parents, and educators. However, students' behavioral data have not been thoroughly studied for understanding their career choice. In this study, we used eXtreme Gradient Boosting (XGBoost), a machine learning (ML) technique, to predict the career choice of college students using a real-world dataset collected in a specific college. Specifically, the data include information on the education and career choice of 18,000 graduates during their college years. In addition, SHAP (Shapley Additive exPlanation) was employed to interpret the results and analyze the importance of individual features. The results show that XGBoost can predict students' career choice robustly with a precision, recall rate, and an $F1$ value of 89.1%, 85.4%, and 0.872, respectively. Furthermore, the interaction of features among four different choices of students (i.e., choose to study in China, choose to work, difficulty in finding a job, and choose to study aboard) were also explored. Several educational features, especially differences in grade point average (GPA) during their college studying, are found to have relatively larger impact on the final choice of career. These results can be of help in the planning, design, and implementation of higher educational institutions' (HEIs) events.

Keywords: career choice; prediction; machine learning; college students

MSC: 68T09

1. Introduction

Educational data mining (EDM) is the application of data mining technology in the educational environment. With the development of modern information technologies, large amounts of educational data are stored in higher educational institutions (HEIs) even at the smallest granularity, such as daily attendance records. However, data storage alone is not sufficient for administrators and managers to make decisions. In response, colleges and universities actively promote the deep integration of artificial intelligence and education, fueling educational reform and innovation, which has become an inevitable trend to meet the development needs [1–3].

The decisions of HEIs include administrative or academic nature. Furthermore, the new goal of education in China requires universities to deeply grasp the patterns of students' daily behavior, innovating the mode and methods involved in talent training, which is also a political task of promoting the deep integration of artificial intelligence and education and propelling educational reform as well as innovation. To achieve this goal, more efficient and user-friendly information-processing methods are needed to enable modern-day decision-making processes in HEIs [4].

Citation: Wang, Y.; Yang, L.; Wu, J.; Song, Z.; Shi, L. Mining Campus Big Data: Prediction of Career Choice Using Interpretable Machine Learning Method. *Mathematics* 2022, 10, 1289. https://doi.org/10.3390/math10081289

Academic Editor: Catalin Stoean

Received: 24 March 2022
Accepted: 11 April 2022
Published: 13 April 2022

Publisher's Note: MDPI stays neutral with regard to jurisdictional claims in published maps and institutional affiliations.

Copyright: © 2022 by the authors. Licensee MDPI, Basel, Switzerland. This article is an open access article distributed under the terms and conditions of the Creative Commons Attribution (CC BY) license (https://creativecommons.org/licenses/by/4.0/).

Identity development primarily relates to career identity, which is mainly developed during adolescence [5]. A student's professional identity may be shaped by adequate career exploration and continuous commitment in their college life [6]. Therefore, it is of great importance for universities to develop appropriate career counseling centers. The career counseling center will teach students some career planning methods or give some guidance according to students' development needs. However, as we know, it is difficult for students to clearly determine their postgraduation destinations. From a psychological point of view, personal ideas and minds may vary greatly. This makes it difficult for HEIs to offer relevant services. With the development of information technology, in modern universities, the campus big data can be recorded through the campus information system. This means that all behavioral data of students on campus can be recorded in real time. Such behavior data can reflect the students' learning process, unique habits, experiences, preferences, and state of mind. Therefore, analyzing campus big data through data mining technology can help students better understand themselves and solve the problem of employment difficulties.

Aiming to provide a practical insight into understanding students' graduation decisions and their effect, we exploited machine learning techniques in a specific Chinese college. Specifically, we first constructed an optimal forecasting model based on an optimization method called Tree-structured Parzen Estimator (TPE) and XGBoost algorithm. Then, we used the Shapley Additivity explanation (SHAP) to explain the result obtained by the forecasting model. The main research work can be summarized as follows:

(1) We use the supervised machine learning method, specifically XGBoost, to support decision making for HEIs based on real data analysis.
(2) We performed a model optimization process to mitigate classification errors and to make complex ML models understandable.
(3) We further put forward some policy to improve the operations of the education system and better serve students' career choice.

Contribution

In our contributions, we have:

1. Proposed a novel framework using interpretable machine learning method to identify the significant factors that affecting the students' career choice;
2. Obtained a real-world educational dataset containing four years of education records of 18,000 undergraduates in a specific college;
3. Compared the performance of the proposed framework through state-of-the-art methods to validate the findings and further explored the obtained results to obtain a deep insight for students' career choice;
4. Proposed framework and policy suggestions to help HEIs and their managers for better understand their current world.

The rest of this paper is organized as follows. Section 2 reviews the literature, which presents the previous work related to EDM and reviews the literature about ML methods and conventional statistical techniques to approach high-dimensional educational data. Section 3 explains the materials and methods, including dataset collection, data cleaning, and modeling. Section 4 describes the obtained results using the interpretable machine learning method. Section 5 concludes the paper and highlights future work in this area of research.

2. Literature Review
2.1. Educational Data Mining

There are many methods and applications of EDM, and these studies can not only follow the application goal, such as improving learning quality, but also reach the theoretical goal, that is, to improve people's understanding of the learning process. In addition, EDM applications can categorize end-users by targets. EDM can be applied to any stakeholders involved in the education system, such as students, teachers, managers, and researchers [7], also providing feedback, personalization, and recommendation, improving students' learning process [8]. The application of EDM can also discover and provide a decision-support system that can help educators plan courses to improve teaching performance [9], providing administrators with resources and tools for decision making and organization [10]. Educational findings can help researchers better understand educational structures and assess learning effectiveness.

2.2. Machine Learning in Educational Area

Machine learning (ML) is a powerful approach for data mining and decision support among information technologies [11]. In terms of the education system, some notable examples include Accounting Systems [12], Enterprise Resource Planning [13,14], academic management [15], and prediction [16–18]. As a novel approach to improving schooling quality, HEIs need to predict and understand students' graduation destination by analyzing students' daily behavior.

Several studies used campus big data to predict students' future. However, most of them focus on predicting/evaluating academic performance. Shaukat et al. [19–21] attempted to evaluate the students' performance in a data mining perspective, and the performance of HEIs were found to be of importance in students' performance. Amez and Baert elaborated on smartphone use and academic performance [22]. Though the existing methods used mainstream data mining techniques, the collection and appropriate exploration of educational data remains a common concern of students themselves, parents, and educators. Further, it is important to know what and more importantly why; thus, it is necessary to not only predict but also interpret the results. In our study, a state-of-the-art method is used to explain the obtained predictions, which fills the research gap mentioned above.

Previous studies have shown that tree-based supervised machine learning algorithms are among the best candidates to apply to educational data sets because of their clear structure ability to explain [12,23]. As a powerful tree-based ML method, eXtreme Gradient Boosting (XGBoost) was proposed by Chen and Guestrin in 2017 [24]. Since its introduction, it has been applied in many research areas, such as energy forecasting [21] and financial forecasting [25,26]. In addition, it is noteworthy that the application of machine learning needs to be fully understood, and such interventions may have a potentially long-lasting impact on people's learning, development, and life-long functioning [27]. Considering the powerful predictive ability of XGBoost in the EDM area, we choose to use it as a predictor to identify the features that influence college students' career choices.

3. Materials and Methods

Figure 1 is the flow chart of methods used in this paper. We first collected the data and sorted it out to form a data set with students' labels of choices and characteristics. Then, we used a hyperparametric optimization method called Tree-structured Parzen Estimator to obtain the optimal XGBoost model's structure. Then, we further discussed the optimal predicted result to discover the factors that impact the students' decisions. Specifically, the Shapley Additivity explanation method was employed to determine the impact of students' basic information, academic characteristics, rewards, and honors on their decisions of final career choice. Finally, we summarized our research and put forward relevant policy suggestions.

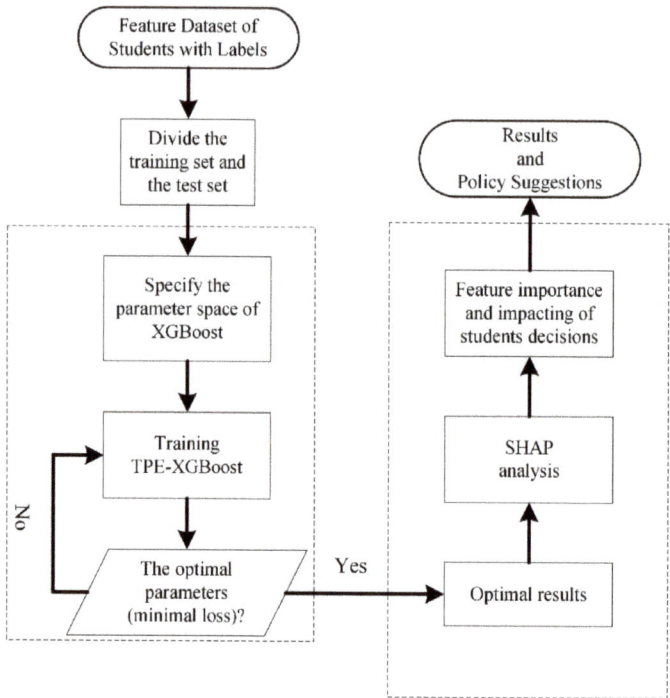

Figure 1. Research Framework.

3.1. XGBoost Algorithm

XGBoost, developed by Chen and Guestrin [24], is a powerful boosting algorithm that supports parallel computing. Recently, it has been utilized in various disciplines, such as energy forecasting [25,28] and the financial sector [26,29]. Its basic components are classification and regression trees (CARTs) and can be described as:

$$\hat{y}_i = \sum_{k=1}^{K} f_k(x_i), \quad f_k \in F, \tag{1}$$

where $i = 1, 2, \ldots, n$. n is number of samples, F is the set of all CARTs in the model, and f_k is the function of F.

The objective function of XGBoost, as shown in Equation (2), is to minimize error term $L(\theta)$ and regularization item $\Omega(\theta)$, which measures prediction error and complexity, respectively.

$$f_{obj}(\theta) = L(\theta) + \Omega(\theta), \tag{2}$$

where $L(\theta) = l(y_i, \hat{y}_i) = \sum_{i=1}^{n}(y_i - \hat{y}_i)^2$, $\Omega(\theta) = \sum_{k=1}^{K} \Omega(f_k)$. That is, the first term is loss function, which evaluates the loss or error between the model's predicted value and the true value. This function must be differentiable and convex; the second regularization term is used to control model complexity and tends to choose simple models to avoid over-fitting problems.

During the iterative training period, a new function f that does not affect the original model will be added in the time t to observe the objective function. If the newly added f can minimize the objective function as much as possible, it will be added, as shown in Equation (3).

$$f_{obj}^{(t)} = \sum_{i=1}^{n}(y_i - (\hat{y}_i + f_t(x_i)))^2 + \Omega(f_t) + C, \tag{3}$$

where $f_t(x_i)$ denotes the newly added f in time t, and C is a constant term.

Next, we introduce the Taylor formula to expand the objective function $f_{obj}{}^{(t)}$ to achieve the purpose of approximation and simplification. The approximate objective function is shown as follows:

$$f_{obj}{}^{(t)} \approx \sum_{i=1}^{n}[l(y_i, \hat{y}_i^{(t-1)}) + g_i f_t(x_i) + \frac{1}{2}h_i f_t^2(x_i)] + \Omega(f_t) + C, \tag{4}$$

where g_i is the first step statistics of the loss function; h_i is the second. $g_i = \partial_{\hat{y}^{(t-1)}} l(y_i, \hat{y}^{(t-1)})$, $h_i = \partial^2_{\hat{y}^{(t-1)}} l(y_i, \hat{y}^{(t-1)})$.

Suppose q represents tree structure, and w represents leaf weight; the compacity of model can be expressed as:

$$f_t(x) = w_{q(x)}, w \in R^T, q : R^T \rightarrow \{1, 2, \ldots, T\}. \tag{5}$$

Define the complexity as the sum of the number of leaves and squares of fraction value corresponding to leaf nodes in each tree, as shown in Equation (6):

$$\Omega(f_t) = \gamma T + \frac{1}{2}\lambda \sum_{j=1}^{T} w_j^2, \tag{6}$$

where γ, λ are adjusted parameters to prevent over-fitting. Let $I_j = \{i|q(x_i) = j\}$ denote the set of leaf samples in the j-th tree, and $G_j = \sum_{i \in I_j} g_i$, $H_j = \sum_{i \in I_j} h_i$; we obtain:

$$f_{obj}{}^{(t)} = \sum_{j=1}^{T}\left[G_j w_j + \frac{1}{2}(H_j + \lambda)w_j^2\right] + \gamma T. \tag{7}$$

Solve Equation (7); it is simple to obtain the following:

$$w_j^* = \frac{-G_j}{H_j + \lambda}, \tag{8}$$

$$f_{obj} = -\frac{1}{2}\sum_{j=1}^{T}\frac{G_j}{H_j + \lambda} + \gamma T, \tag{9}$$

where f_{obj} is a scoring function that measures the model performance. A smaller f_{obj} means a better predictive model. The pseudocodes for split finding in XGBoost are shown in Algorithm 1:

Algorithm 1: Exact Greedy Algorithm for Split Finding

Input: I, instance set of current node
Input: d, feature dimension
gain$\leftarrow 0$
$G \leftarrow \sum_{i \in I} g_i, H \leftarrow \sum_{i \in I} h_i$
for $k = 1$ to m do
    $G_L \leftarrow 0, H_L \leftarrow 0$
    for j in sorted (I, by x_{jk}) do
        $G_L \leftarrow G_L + g_j, H_L \leftarrow H_L + h_j$
        $G_R \leftarrow G - G_L, H_R \leftarrow H - H_L$
        score $\leftarrow \max(score, \frac{G_L^2}{H_L + \lambda} + \frac{G_R^2}{H_R + \lambda} - \frac{G^2}{H + \lambda})$
    end
end
Output: Split with max score

Thus, for CART algorithm, the computation complexity is $O(NMD)$, where N is the number of samples, M is the feature number, and D denotes the depth of generated trees. When using CART as a base classifier, XGBoost explicitly adds regularization terms to control the complexity of the model, which helps prevent overfitting and thus improves the generalization of the model. Thus, the computation complexity of XGBoost is between $O(NlogN)$ and $O(log2k)$.

3.2. Tree-Structured Parzen Estimator for Model Optimization

Generally, hyperparameters refers to a set of parameters in which their values should be set before training starts (e.g., the number of CARTs and learning rate). They define the model architecture and control the learning process, playing a fundamental role in the development of machine learning models. Hyperparameter optimization is the process of adjusting hyperparameters to approximate the optimal prediction result. Compared with other methods (i.e., random search and grid search), automatic hyperparameter tuning can form the knowledge between parameters and models to reduce the number of tests and thus improve the efficiency of the tuning process. In this study, we implemented a variant of Bayesian optimization (BO), called Tree-structured Parzen Estimator, to automatically optimize the hyperparameters of the XGBoost model.

TPE converts superparameter space to a nonparametric density distribution to model the process of $p(x|y)$. There are three conversion modes: uniform distribution to truncated Gaussian mixture distribution, logarithmic uniform distribution to exponential-phase Gaussian mixture distribution, and discrete distribution to heavy-weighted discrete distribution. Then, the hyperparameter space is divided into two groups, namely good and bad samples, based on their fitness values and a predefined value y^* (usually set to 15%), as described in Equation (10):

$$p(x|y) = \begin{cases} l(x), if\ y < y^* \\ g(x), if\ y \geq y^* \end{cases}, \quad (10)$$

where $l(x), g(x)$ represents the probabilities that the hyperparameter set $\{x^i\}$ is in the good and bad groups, respectively. Then, we can summarize expected improvement (EI) as:

$$EI_{y^*}(x) = \int_{-\infty}^{\infty}(y^* - y)p(y|x)dy = \int_{-\infty}^{y^*}(y^* - y)\frac{p(x|y)p(y)}{p(x)}dy. \quad (11)$$

At last, let $\gamma = p(y < y^*)$, and $p(x) = \int p(x|y)p(y)dy = \gamma l(x) + (1-\gamma)g(x)$; we can thus easily obtain:

$$EI_{y^*}(x) = \left(r + \frac{g(x)}{l(x)}(1-\gamma)\right)^{-1}. \quad (12)$$

Hence, each iteration returns an x^* that obtains the maximum EI value.

3.3. Shapley Additivity exPlanation

Model interpretability is the main challenge in the application of machine learning methods, but the field of educational big data prediction using machine learning has not been paid enough attention. In order to improve the interpretation of machine learning model, this paper uses the SHAP method to assign a value to each input variable to reflect its importance to the predictor [30].

For students' feature subset $S \subseteq F$ (where F stands for the set of all factors), two models were trained to extract the effect of factor i. The first model $f_{S \cup \{i\}}(x_{S \cup \{i\}})$ was trained with factor I, while the other one $f_S(x_S)$ was trained without it, where $x_{S \cup \{i\}}$ and x_S are the values of input features. Then, $f_{S \cup \{i\}}(x_{S \cup \{i\}}) - f_S(x_S)$ was computed for each possible subset $S \subseteq F \setminus \{i\}$. The Shapley value of a risk factor i is calculated using Equation (13).

$$\phi_i = \sum_{S \subseteq F \setminus \{i\}} \frac{|S|!(|F| - |S| - 1)!}{|F|!}(f_{S \cup \{i\}}(x_{S \cup \{i\}}) - f_S(x_S)) \quad (13)$$

However, a major limitation of Equation (13) is that as the number of features increases, the computation cost will grow exponentially. To solve this problem, Lundberg et al. [20] proposed a computation-tractable explanation method, i.e., TreeExplainer, for decision tree-based ML models such as RF. The TreeExplainer method makes it much more efficient to calculate a risk factor's SHAP value both locally and globally [31].

The SHAP combines optimal allocation with local explanations using the classic Shapley values. It would help users to trust the predictive models in not only what the prediction is but also why and how the prediction is made [32]. Thus, the SHAP interaction values can be calculated as the difference between the Shapley values of factor i with and without factor j in Equation (14):

$$\phi_{i,j} = \sum_{S \subseteq F \setminus \{i,j\}} \frac{|S|!(|F|-|S|-2)!}{|F|!} (f_{S \cup \{i,j\}}(x_{S \cup \{i,j\}}) - f_{S \cup \{i\}}(x_{S \cup \{i\}}) - f_{S \cup \{j\}}(x_{S \cup \{j\}}) - f_S(x_S)). \tag{14}$$

Based on this advantage, we can use it to explain the XGBoost model according to Decision Tree in order to find the impact of predicting student' different characteristics on their final destination. Therefore, compared with existing methods (such as feature importance in Random Forests), SHAP can not only sort the feature importance but also show the positive and negative effects of features on the results so as to improve the interpretation ability of model output.

3.4. Data and Preprocess Methods

3.4.1. Data Source

This study obtained first-hand data through collection, investigation and other methods and conducted strict declassification at the beginning of data collection and integration. The data contain about 18,000 undergraduates in the class of 2018, 2019, and 2020 in a certain university, mainly including the initial data at the beginning of enrollment; students' participation in scientific research, academic development, award, and excellence evaluation; the appointment of student leaders; student' financial difficulties, loans, and repayment; student' graduation status, etc. More details can be found in Appendix A.1. The data collected are changeable and traceable during their undergraduate period. Student behavior characteristics and growth patterns can be deeply mined through artificial intelligence methods such as data mining and association analysis.

3.4.2. Data Description

Based on the original data set, we further eliminated the data that are invalid and missing (see Appendix A.2). Finally, we secured a data set containing 10,292 students and 20 features, as shown in Table 1. Further graduation choices were divided finely into four categories, as shown in Table 2.

Table 1. Dataset description.

	Classification	Description	Symbol
Input	Essential Data	Gender	X1
		National	X2
		Political Landscape	X3
		Examinee Category	X4
		Score of college entrance examination	X5
		Note	X6
		Category of students with difficulty	X7
	Honors	Scholarship awarded by university	X8
		Scholarship awarded by provincial	X9
		Total amount of money	X10
	GPA Data	GPA of First Term	X11
		GPA of Second Term	X12
		GPA of Third Term	X13
		GPA of Fourth Term	X14
		GPA of Fifth Term	X15
		GPA of Sixth Term	X16
		GPA of Seventh Term	X17
		GPA of Eighth Term	X18
		Overall GPA	X19
Output	Destination	Final Employment	Y

Table 2. Breakdown of students' graduation destination.

Classification	Content	Alphabetize	Population
Further Study in China	Master's Doctorate Preparing for the Entrance Exam Second Bachelor's Degree	Y1	4264
Employment	Sign Labor Contract Sign an Employment Agreement Certificate of Employment Self-employed Freelance Work Joined the Army Volunteer in the West	Y2	4372
Difficulties in Employment	Waiting for Employment in Beijing Return to Hometown for Employment Apply for Non-Employment Delay	Y3	617
Study Abroad	Has Gone Abroad Plans to Go Abroad	Y4	1038

4. Results and Discussion

4.1. Feature Selection

In the machine learning method, it is easy to deal with highly correlated independent variables that may lead to over-fitting [33]. Therefore, detecting the correlation of related variables through correlation analysis is not that important. However, the variables (noise variables) that are not important to the model prediction results will not only increase the model redundancy, causing training interference, but are also not conducive to the interpretation of the model output. Hence, before starting model training, we first used Recursive Feature Elimination (RFE) for feature selection. RFE is a simple adverse selection method, which uses repeated multi-fold verification method to fit the model. See [34] for more details about RFE. Figure 2 illustrates the results of Recursive Feature Elimination in this paper.

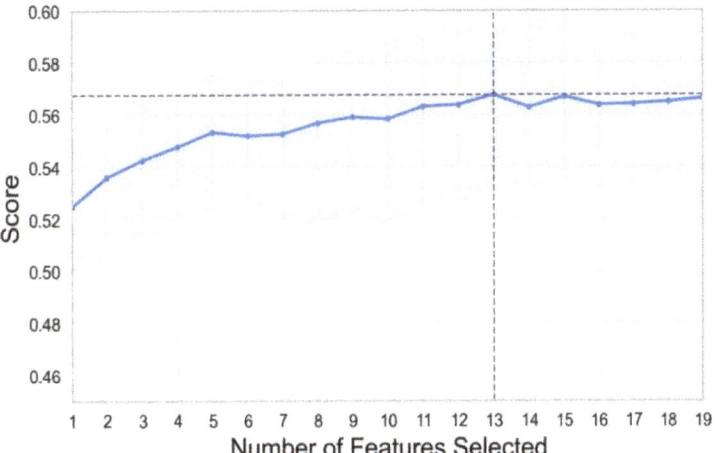

Figure 2. RFE feature selection results of XGBoost.

As can be seen from Figure 2, when the input feature number is less than 13, the prediction score of the model increases along with the rising input features; when the parameter is higher than 13, with the increasing of input features, the prediction score of the model does not go up but down, indicating that noise variables have appeared in the model at this time. Therefore, we are sure that the optimal number of input variables of the model is 13. The best variable set is: X1, X4, X5, X7, X10, X11, X12, X14, X15, X16, X17, X18, X19.

4.2. Evaluation Metrics

On the basis of the above optimal variable set, the model was adjusted by TPE method by considering the importance of hyperparameters. Each type of sample was divided into four types: true positive (*TP*), false positive (*FP*), true negative (*TN*), and false negative (*FN*) according to the real category and prediction category of the sample. The F1-Score method is used to evaluate the model performance, as shown in Equation (15). The score of the final model is the average of F1 values of all categories. With the number of iterations set to 30, the parameter selection process is shown in Figure 2.

$$F1 = \frac{2 \times P \times R}{P + R}, \quad (15)$$

where *P* denotes precision measuring the accuracy of the model, as shown in Equation (16); *R* is recall ratio representing the comprehensiveness of the model, as shown in Equation (17) [35,36]. Generally speaking, when the *p*-value is high, *R* value is usually low and vice versa. F1 value is proposed to comprehensively consider these two measurements and better indicate the prediction performance of the predictive model.

$$P = \frac{TP}{TP + FP}. \quad (16)$$

$$R = \frac{TP}{TP + FN}. \quad (17)$$

4.3. Comparison of Model's Performance

In general, the larger the F1 value of the model, the better the prediction performance of the model. On the contrary, the smaller the F1 value is, it indicates that the constructed model cannot well adapt to the research problem in this paper. We need to consider rebuilding the feature input or change a more suitable model. In the following section, we further conduct 10-fold cross validation and paired *t*-test [37] to compare our model with other mainstream methods.

As shown in Figure 3, the best *F*1 value in hyperparameter optimization process is 0.872, showing that the model constructed in this paper can better predict the decisions of college students. The combination of hyperparameters corresponding to the optimal *F*1 value is shown in Table 3. In addition, to provide more numerical insights, we compared the proposed method with the state-of-the-art methods [38], as shown in Table 4.

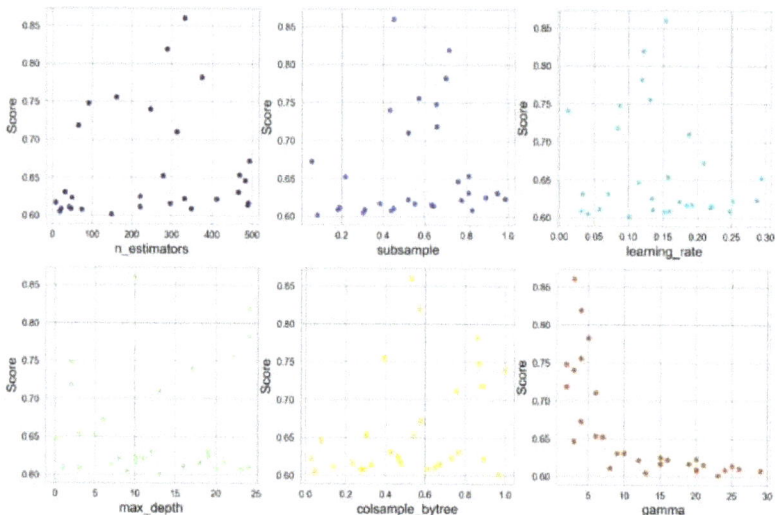

Figure 3. TPE optimization process.

Table 3. Hyper-parameters of XGBoost.

Hyperparameters	Value	Meaning
n_estimators	331	Number of trees
subsample	0.4494	Percentage of random sample
max_depth	10	Maximum depth of each tree
colsample_bytree	0.5294	Random sampling characteristics
gamma	3	Penalty term for complexity
learning_rate	0.1533	Learning rate

Table 4. Comparisons of proposed method with other mainstream methods (10-fold average).

Model	p	R	F1	Performance Comparison (%)
Decision Tree	0.803	0.812	0.807	−7.454% ** (0.035)
SVM	0.791	0.788	0.789	−9.518% * (0.072)
Random Forest	0.847	0.824	0.835	−4.243% *** (0.001)
Light GBM	0.889	0.846	0.866	−0.689% (0.301)
XGBoost	0.891	0.854	0.872	/

Note: XGBoost is the benchmark for paired *t*-test. Negative performance of *F*1 indicates that the method presents worse performance than XGBoost. * At the 10% level. ** At the 5% level. *** At the 1% level. *p*-Values are in parentheses.

4.4. SHAP Approach for Results Interpretation

Under the structure of the optimal model above, the SHAP summary diagram is used in this section to explain the overall prediction results of the model. This paper explains the model of students studying in China, at work, under difficult circumstance, and studying overseas, respectively, so as to explore the predictive role of different characteristics in the final direction of students.

Choose to study in China: students studying in China account for a large proportion of the students studied, and the output of their prediction results is shown in Figure 4.

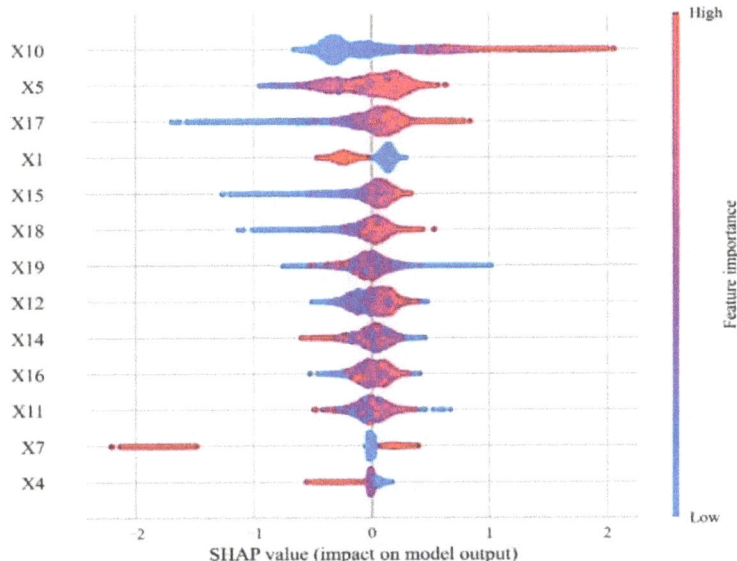

Figure 4. SHAP summary diagram of domestic advanced students.

In Figure 4, the closer the color of sample points to red, the larger the value of sample points it shows and vice versa. For those students, features X10, X5, X17, X1, and X15 are the five most important variables for prediction, i.e., total amount of scholarship, college entrance examination score, GPA of the seventh semester, gender, and GPA of the fifth semester. Among them, in terms of X10, the red sample points are mainly distributed in the positive area, suggesting that the larger the total amount of scholarships, the higher the SHAP value of the model, indicating that students with more scholarships tend to choose domestic education.

For X5, although a small number of red sample points are distributed in the negative area of SHAP, most of the red sample points are distributed near the positive area of SHAP, showcasing that students with high grades in college entrance examination also tend to study in China; the grade points of the seventh semester (X17) and the fifth semester (X15) are the same, and the red sample points tend to be distributed in the area with positive SHAP value, indicating that students with higher eigenvalues also tend to choose domestic education. Interestingly, in terms of gender (X1), the red dots (i.e., females) are mainly distributed in the negative area of SHAP, while the blue dots (males) are mostly distributed in the positive area of SHAP, suggesting that boys in school are more likely to choose domestic education than girls.

Choose to work: According to Figure 5, we can see that for students who are predicted to work, the features X10, X17, X12, X11, and X14 are the five most important variables for the prediction, which are the total amount of scholarships, GPA in the seventh semester, GPA in the second semester, GPA in the first semester, and GPA in the fourth semester. By analyzing feature X10, it is found that most of the red sample points are distributed in the area with negative SHAP value, indicating that the more scholarship students win, the less they will choose to work, which is consistent with the analysis above, which is to say that students who win more scholarships prefer to study in China. The remaining four variables are academic variables, and most of the blue dots are distributed in the area where the SHAP value is positive, showing that students with unremarkableGPA in the seventh, second, first, and fourth semester will prefer to work.

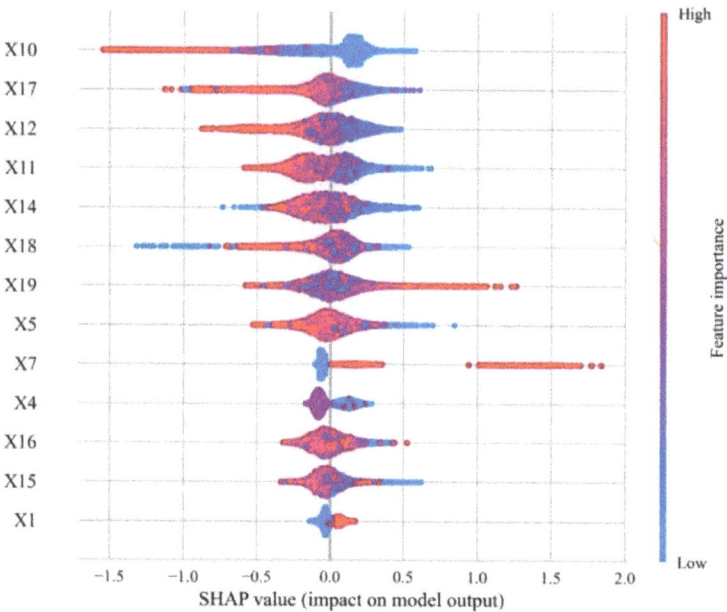

Figure 5. SHAP summary diagram of successful employment students.

Difficult to find a job: from Figure 6, we can see that for students whose decisions are hard to predict, the features X10, X5, X19, X11, and X15 are the five most important variables for prediction, which equal to the total amount of scholarships, score of college entrance examination, average GPA during college, GPA in the first semester, and GPA in the fifth semester.

By analyzing the feature X10, we can find that most of the red sample points are distributed in the area with negative SHAP value, indicating that the more scholarships students win, the less they will be distributed in this category; that is, students who obtain more scholarships generally will not face the pressure of delayed graduation or employment difficulties. It is worth noting that the second variable that is more important for prediction is the score of college entrance examination (X5). In terms of analyzing this score, it can be found that the red sample points are distributed in both areas where the SHAP value is positive and negative, but the higher scores (shown as red sample points) are generally distributed in the areas where the SHAP value is negative, and the general scores (color near purple) are more distributed in the areas where the SHAP value is positive. It demonstrates that students with high grades tend to maintain excellent learning habits and will not face the problems of delayed graduation or employment difficulties during college years or graduation, while students with medium grades have a certain probability of facing the above problems. The remaining three variables are academic variables, and most of the blue dots are distributed in the area with positive SHAP value, indicating that students with poor academic performance often face certain employment and graduation difficulties.

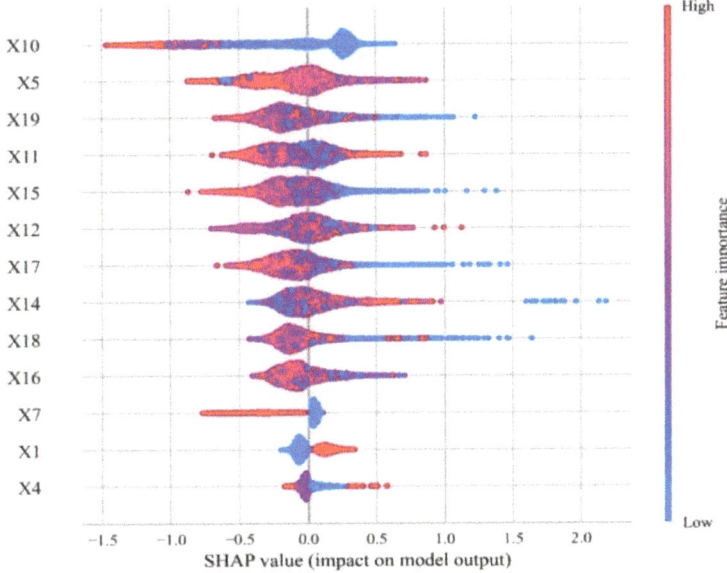

Figure 6. SHAP summary diagram of difficult students.

Choose to study aboard: according to Figure 7, for the prediction of students studying abroad, feature X4, X7, X11, X5, and X17 are the five most crucial variables for the prediction, i.e., category of exam taker, category of difficult student, GPA in the first semester, score of college entrance examination, and GPA in the seventh semester. By analyzing feature X4, it is found that most of the blue dot (i.e., students in rural areas) students are distributed in the negative area of SHAP, indicating that most of these students will not choose to study abroad. For feature X7, the category of students with difficulties (family difficulties, family difficulties, and disabilities), samples with large numbers are mostly distributed in areas with negative number of SHAP, indicating that most students with difficulties will not choose to study abroad. Compared with other students, those in rural areas and students with difficulties are not able to afford to go abroad, so they are not likely to study abroad. The finding above is consistent with the actual situation. For feature X11, we may find that most of blue points are distributed in the area with negative value of SHAP, indicating that low GPA in the first semester will have negative effect on their intention of studying abroad. The features X5 and X17 are less obvious, which means that the score of college entrance examination and GPA in the seventh semester have little impact on studying abroad.

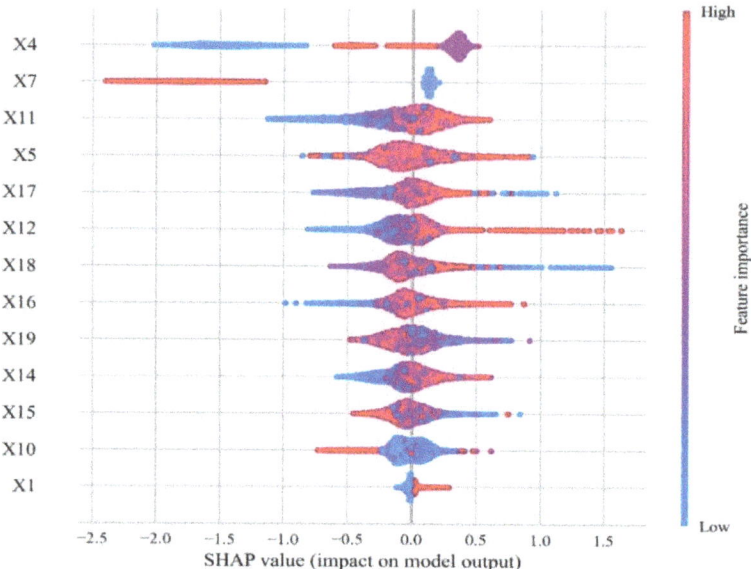

Figure 7. SHAP summary diagram of students studying abroad.

5. Conclusions

In this study, we used machine learning tools such as XGBoost, TPE, and SHAP to perform prediction of college students' career choice. The methods are supported by using data from one college located in Beijing. Based on the analysis above, we may draw the following conclusions:

(1) Within students' basic information, the score of college entrance examination plays an important role in predicting graduates' career choice. The results of empirical analysis show that students with high scores tend to choose further education in China, and the higher their scores, the less likely they are to face employment and graduation problems. However, it is worth noting that more students with an intermediate score suffer in employment and graduation compared with those students achieving low scores.

(2) Total amount of scholarships has an important impact on the final academic direction. Students with a higher amount tend to choose domestic postgraduate education rather than employment because they have better learning ability and make clear academic plans. At the same time, it should be noted that the evaluation of scholarship is based on the comprehensive achievements rather than GPA solely, so it is necessary to remind students of the importance of comprehensive development in their lower grade.

(3) In terms of academic data, GPA in the first semester has a vital impact on students' future choice, which is quite obvious among students taking up further education. Most students with low GPA in the first semester will not consider studying abroad or further education in China. Most of them go to job market directly, or some of them face problems in employment or graduation.

Limitations and Future Directions

The limitations of this work could be the heterogeneity of the dataset and its quantity, such as the lack of more detailed personal characteristics (e.g., the education level of their parents). Future studies should undertake surveys to collect more data of different schools and more personal characteristics to supplement or verify the algorithm. Thus, the ML algorithm for predicting students' career choice can be updated and re-trained to achieve more reliable and accurate results.

Author Contributions: Conceptualization, Y.W.; methodology, J.W., Y.W., Z.S. and L.S.; validation, L.Y.; investigation, Y.W.; data curation, Y.W. and L.Y; writing—original draft preparation, L.Y., Y.W., Z.S. and L.S.; supervision, J.W.; project administration, J.W.; funding acquisition, Y.W. All authors have read and agreed to the published version of the manuscript.

Funding: This research was funded by the Humanities and Social sciences of the Ministry of Education (grant numbers ZS20210038) and Research Project of Ideological and Political work in colleges and universities in Beijing (grant numbers BJSZ2021ZC25), and BUCT Fund for (2021BHDSQYR06).

Institutional Review Board Statement: Not applicable.

Informed Consent Statement: Not applicable.

Data Availability Statement: Data sharing is not applicable to this article.

Conflicts of Interest: The authors declare no conflict of interest.

Appendix A

Appendix A.1. Data Information

Table A1. Data Attributes and Characteristics.

New State Attribute	Data Attributes and Characteristics (2014–2018, 2015–2019, 2016–2020)										
	Comprehensive Quality			Scientific Research		Academic Achievement		Awards obtained during university	Grant	Repayment of National Student Loans	Attribute of Employment Status
	Student Cadre Position	Situation of Winning Awards	Outstanding Graduate of Beijing	Participation in Innovation Credits	Participation in the Scientific research "Meng Ya"	GPA Throughout College	Scholar-ship Award				
Initial Data at the Beginning of Enrollment	Organization Name	Time	Yes	Participate in or Not	Level	First Term	Time	Time	Grants received during university	On Time	Graduation Information
Sex	Position	Category	No	Win an Award or Not	Rank	Second Term	Name and Level	Name and Level	Time	Over Time	Graduating Year
Political Status				Time		Third Term		Total	Name and Level		Political Status
Nation						Fourth Term			Total		Type of Registration Card Issued
Students Birth Place						Fifth Term					Reasons for not Being Employed
School						Sixth Term					Job Category
Major						Seven Term					Graduated or Not
Examinee Category						Eighth Term					Implementation Channels
Subject											Graduate Destination
College Entrance Examination Results						Overall GPA					Forms of Employment
Date of Birth						Total Credits					Channel and Time
Grade											Category of Difficult Students

Appendix A.2. Data Processing and Coding

Table A2. Data Processing and Coding.

Features	Gender	Coding
Gender	Male	0
	Female	1
National	Han	0
	Ethnic Minorities	1
Political Landscape	Masses	0
	The Communist Youth League	1
	Probationary Party Member	2
Examinee Category	Rural Fresh Graduates	0
	Urban Fresh Graduates	1
	Former Rural Graduates	2
	Former Urban Graduates	3
	Rural to Urban Fresh Graduates	4
Note	No	0
	Highest Score in the Major	1
	Special Talents in Arts	2
	High Level Athletes	3
	Directed student	4
	Poverty Alleviation Program	5
	Independent Recruitment	6
Difficult Students	Non-Difficult Students	0
	Family Difficulties and Physical Disability	1
	Former Urban Graduates	2
Provincial and Municipal Outstanding Graduates or Not	No	0
	Yes	1
Awarded at the School Level above or Not	No	0
	Yes	1
Total Amount of Scholarships Awarded during University	Total Amount of Scholarships Awarded during University	Total Amount of Scholarships Awarded during University

References

1. Jordan, M.I.; Mitchell, T.M. Machine learning: Trends, perspectives, and prospects. *Science* **2008**, *349*, 255–260. [CrossRef] [PubMed]
2. Olaya, D.; Vásquez, J.; Maldonado, S.; Miranda, J.; Verbeke, W. Uplift Modeling for preventing student dropout in higher education. *Decis. Support Syst.* **2020**, *134*, 113320. [CrossRef]
3. Maldonado, S.; Miranda, J.; Olaya, D.; Vásquez, J.; Verbeke, W. Redefining profit metrics for boosting student retention in higher education. *Decis. Support Syst.* **2021**, *143*, 113493. [CrossRef]
4. Nauman, M.; Akhtar, N.; Alhudhaif, A.; Alothaim, A. Guaranteeing correctness of machine learning based decision making at higher educational institutions. *IEEE Access* **2021**, *9*, 92864–92880. [CrossRef]
5. Erikson, E.H. *Identity: Youth and Crisis*; WW Norton & Company: Manhattan, NY, USA, 1994; pp. 176–200.
6. Marcia, J.E.; Waterman, A.S.; Matteson, D.R.; Archer, S.L. *Ego Identity. A Handbook for Psychosocial Research*; Springer Science and Business Media: New York, NY, USA, 2012.
7. Chrysafiadi, K.; Virvou, M. Student modeling approaches: A literature review for the last decade. *Expert Syst. Appl.* **2013**, *40*, 4715–4729. [CrossRef]
8. Wan, S.; Niu, Z. An e-learning recommendation approach based on the self-organization of learning resource. *Knowl.-Based Syst.* **2018**, *160*, 71–87. [CrossRef]
9. Hsia, T.C.; Shie, A.J.; Chen, L.C. Course planning of extension education to meet market demand by using data mining techniques—An example of Chinkuo technology university in Taiwan. *Expert Syst. Appl.* **2008**, *34*, 596–602. [CrossRef]
10. Injadat, M.; Moubayed, A.; Nassif, A.B.; Shami, A. Systematic ensemble model selection approach for educational data mining. *Knowl.-Based Syst.* **2020**, *200*, 105992. [CrossRef]
11. Alam, T.M.; Shaukat, K.; Hameed, I.A.; Khan, W.A.; Sarwar, M.U.; Iqbal, F.; Luo, S. A novel framework for prognostic factors identification of malignant mesothelioma through association rule mining. *Biomed. Signal Process. Control* **2021**, *68*, 102726. [CrossRef]
12. Shuhidan, S.M.; Nori, W.M. Accounting information system and decision useful information fit towards cost conscious strategy in Malaysian higher education institutions. *Procedia Econ. Financ.* **2015**, *31*, 885–895. [CrossRef]
13. Noaman, A.Y.; Ahmed, F.F. ERP systems functionalities in higher education. *Procedia Comput. Sci.* **2015**, *65*, 385–395. [CrossRef]
14. Wen, Z.; Qiang, W.; Ye, Y.; Yoshida, T. A 2020 perspective on "DeRec: A data-driven approach to accurate recommendation with deep learning and weighted loss function". *Electron. Commer. Res. Appl.* **2021**, *48*, 101064.
15. Anastasios, T.; Cleo, S.; Effie, P.; Olivier, J.; George, M. Institutional research management using an integrated information system. *Procedia-Soc. Behav. Sci.* **2013**, *73*, 518–525. [CrossRef]
16. Wen, Z.; Shaoshan, Y.; Jian, L.; Xin, T.; Yoshida, T. Credit risk prediction of SMEs in supply chain finance by fusing demographic and behavioral data. *Transp. Res. Part E*, **2022**; *in press*.

17. Wen, Z.; Wang, Q.; Yoshida, T.; Jian, L. RP-LGMC: Rating prediction based on local and global information with matrix clustering. *Comput. Oper. Res.* **2021**, *129*, 105228.
18. Wen, Z.; Li, X.; Li, J.; Yang, Y. Two-stage Rating Prediction Approach Based on Matrix Clustering on Implicit Information. *IEEE Trans. Comput. Soc. Syst.* **2020**, *7*, 517–535.
19. Shaukat, K.; Nawaz, I.; Aslam, S.; Zaheer, S.; Shaukat, U. Student's performance in the context of data mining. In Proceedings of the 2016 19th International Multi-Topic Conference (INMIC), Islamabad, Pakistan, 1–8 December 2016; IEEE: Piscataway, NJ, USA, 2016.
20. Shaukat, K.; Nawaz, I.; Aslam, S.; Zaheer, S.; Shaukat, U. *Student's Performance: A Data Mining Perspective*; LAP Lambert Academic Publishing: Saarbrücken, Germany, 2017.
21. Alam, T.M.; Mushtaq, M.; Shaukat, K.; Hameed, I.A.; Sarwar, M.U.; Luo, S. A Novel Method for Performance Measurement of Public Educational Institutions Using Machine Learning Models. *Appl. Sci.* **2021**, *11*, 9296. [CrossRef]
22. Amez, S.; Baert, S. Smartphone use and academic performance: A literature review. *Int. J. Educ. Res.* **2020**, *103*, 101618. [CrossRef]
23. Nieto, Y.; Gacía-Díaz, V.; Montenegro, C.; González, C.C.; Crespo, R.G. Usage of machine learning for strategic decision making at higher educational institutions. *IEEE Access* **2019**, *7*, 75007–75017. [CrossRef]
24. Chen, T.; Guestrin, C. Xgboost: A scalable tree boosting system. In Proceedings of the 22nd ACM Sigkdd International Conference on Knowledge Discovery and Data Mining, San Francisco, CA, USA, 24–27 August 2016; pp. 785–794.
25. Yang, L.; Zhao, Y.; Niu, X.; Song, Z.; Gao, Q.; Wu, J. Municipal Solid Waste Forecasting in China Based on Machine Learning Models. *Front. Energy Res.* **2021**, *9*, 763977. [CrossRef]
26. Jabeur, S.B.; Mefteh-Wali, S.; Viviani, J.L. Forecasting gold price with the XGBoost algorithm and SHAP interaction values. *Ann. Oper. Res.* **2021**, 1–21. [CrossRef]
27. Varshney, K.R.; Alemzadeh, H. On the safety of machine learning: Cyber-physical systems, decision sciences, and data products. *Big Data* **2017**, *5*, 246–255. [CrossRef] [PubMed]
28. De Clercq, D.; Wen, Z.; Fei, F.; Caicedo, L.; Yuan, K.; Shang, R. Interpretable machine learning for predicting biomethane production in industrial-scale anaerobic co-digestion. *Sci. Total Environ.* **2020**, *712*, 134574. [CrossRef] [PubMed]
29. Jiang, C.; Wang, Z.; Zhao, H. A prediction-driven mixture cure model and its application in credit scoring. *Eur. J. Oper. Res.* **2019**, *277*, 20–31. [CrossRef]
30. Lundberg, S.M.; Lee, S.I. A unified approach to interpreting model predictions. In Proceedings of the 31st International Conference on Neural Information Processing Systems 2017, Los Angeles, CA, USA, 4–7 December 2017; pp. 4768–4777.
31. Lundberg, S.M.; Erion, G.; Chen, H.; DeGrave, A.; Prutkin, J.M.; Nair, B.; Lee, S.I. From local explanations to global understanding with explainable AI for trees. *Nat. Mach. Intell.* **2020**, *2*, 56–67. [CrossRef]
32. Ayoub, J.; Yang, X.J.; Zhou, F. Combat COVID-19 infodemic using explainable natural language processing models. *Inf. Processing Manag.* **2021**, *58*, 102569. [CrossRef]
33. Shaukat, K.; Luo, S.; Varadharajan, V.; Hameed, I.A.; Xu, M. A survey on machine learning techniques for cyber security in the last decade. *IEEE Access* **2020**, *8*, 222310–222354. [CrossRef]
34. Shieh, M.D.; Yang, C.C. Multiclass SVM-RFE for product form feature selection. *Expert Syst. Appl.* **2008**, *35*, 531–541. [CrossRef]
35. Shaukat, K.; Luo, S.; Varadharajan, V.; Hameed, I.A.; Chen, S.; Liu, D.; Li, J. Performance comparison and current challenges of using machine learning techniques in cybersecurity. *Energies* **2020**, *13*, 2509. [CrossRef]
36. Shaukat, K.; Luo, S.; Chen, S.; Liu, D. Cyber threat detection using machine learning techniques: A performance evaluation perspective. In Proceedings of the 2020 International Conference on Cyber Warfare and Security (ICCWS), Norfolk, VA, USA, 1–6 October 2020; IEEE: Piscataway, NJ, USA, 2020.
37. Kim, T.K. T-test as a parametric statistic. *Korean J. Anesthesiol.* **2015**, *68*, 540. [CrossRef]
38. Nie, M.; Xiong, Z.; Zhong, R.; Deng, W.; Yang, G. Career Choice Prediction Based on Campus Big Data—Mining the Potential Behavior of College Students. *Appl. Sci.* **2020**, *10*, 2841. [CrossRef]

Article

Information Acquisition for Product Design in a Green Supply Chain

Mengli Fan [1,*], Yi Huang [2] and Wei Xing [2,*]

1. School of Economics, Shandong University of Finance and Economics, Jinan 250014, China
2. School of Economics and Management, China University of Petroleum (Huadong), Qingdao 266580, China; garry2008@gmail.com
* Correspondence: realhyi@163.com (M.F.); xingweimail@gmail.com (W.X.)

Abstract: This paper studies the interaction between the product development mode and the acquisition of consumers' environmental awareness (CEA) information in a two-echelon green supply chain. Our study shows that when the downstream manufacturer achieves the CEA information superiority, the in-house mode improves the total environmental quality and is better for supply chain members than the outsourcing mode. In contrast, when the upstream supplier achieves the information advantage, the green product development modes affect neither the decisions nor the performance of supply chain members because the supplier discloses its CEA information through pricing and/or green level decisions. We further find that under the outsourcing mode, the supplier has more incentive to achieve CEA information superiority, which always improves the total environmental quality and may benefit the manufacturer; however, under the in-house mode, the supplier's superior information benefits the manufacturer and itself as well as total environmental quality only under certain conditions. Finally, we show that the downstream CEA information disclosure under the outsourcing mode helps supply chain members achieve a Pareto improvement and increases the total environmental quality; this finding is contrary to the extant literature that focuses on demand intercept information disclosure.

Keywords: green supply chain; environmental awareness; information acquisition; outsourcing; in-house

MSC: 91A05

1. Introduction

The public interest in environmental issues has increased significantly in recent years. The improved consumers' environmental awareness (CEA), the premium that consumers would be willing to pay for environmental improvement, motivated firms to design and introduce a variety of green products into consumer markets [1–3]. For instance, the development of green vehicles has been an area of strong interest since the transport sector accounts for approximately 14% of worldwide greenhouse gas emissions [4]. Automakers are making significant efforts to go green, introducing various fuel-efficient and low-emission vehicles, including hybrids and fuel-cell cars, into markets [5]. Meanwhile, component suppliers also strive to design green vehicle components for both profits and social responsibilities. Mitsubishi, a major engine supplier, has designed and provided the MIVEC engine with Auto Stop and Go (AS&G) idle-stop technology, which can achieve a 12% improvement in fuel efficiency.

When a firm plans to develop a green product or introduce a green function into a conventional product, it usually faces two challenges. First, the firm needs to choose green product development strategies, namely, the outsourcing mode and in-house mode. Under the outsourcing mode, the firm does not design the green function by itself but directly procures a key component with a green function from a supplier. In contrast, under the in-house mode, the firm develops the green function on its own, although it still procures other components from its supplier. For instance, Great Wall Motor Company (GWM), an auto maker in China, typically procures engines from its suppliers. To develop an eco-friendly vehicle, one option for the auto maker is to procure a fuel-saving engine (such as an engine with AS&G idle-stop technology) from the engine supplier. The alternative option is to procure a conventional engine without the green function but design an energy-saving component, such as a braking energy recovery system, on its own. To provide a clear understanding of the green product development modes, this paper considers the situation when only one party, the supplier or manufacturer, introduces one green function into a product. This is practically reasonable because it could be too costly and add reliability risks when multiple green technologies are introduced at the same time.

The second challenge is a higher demand uncertainty when introducing a green product into markets. When General Motors first introduced eAssist, a hybrid system, into Buick LaCrosse, a major concern is the unfamiliarity of the traditional customer segment towards the hybrid technology, which would hurt the sales of the new model [6]. If the CEA level is low, a high green level of a product will not attract more consumers, and the high production cost of the green function may even dampen the demand for the green product. In contrast, if the CEA level is high, a lower green level may be less attractive. Therefore, it is necessary for firms to obtain accurate CEA information and design appropriate green levels to better meet consumers' needs.

In reality, information acquisition capabilities of firms are quite different, leading to information asymmetry. In a two-echelon supply chain, two information asymmetry scenarios exist. One is that the manufacturer has a better CEA information acquisition capability than the supplier. For instance, GWM is located in China and knows its consumers' CEA level better than its engine supplier, and thus has the CEA information superiority. The other is that the supplier has an information advantage compared with the manufacturer. This situation typically occurs for new products or products with short life cycles [7].

The green supply chain has been an important topic in the operations management literature [3,8–10]. However, few papers have studied the effect of green product development strategies on the total environmental quality. Moreover, CEA information, a critical factor affecting green product designs, has received little attention in the information acquisition literature. Therefore, the main purpose of this study is to fill the above research gaps. In particular, we seek to address the following research questions: (1) Who should develop the green function of a product under different CEA information asymmetries: suppliers or manufacturers, and why? (2) How does the superior CEA information of the manufacturer or supplier affect the performance of supply chain members under the outsourcing or in-house mode? (3) Which green product development mode and what CEA information structure are better for improving total environmental quality?

To answer these questions, we consider a supply chain where a manufacturer procures a key component from a supplier and uses it to produce a green product. According to the green product development mode and CEA information structure, there exist four scenarios: OS (IS), the green function is developed under the outsourcing (in-house) mode while the supplier possesses the superior CEA information; OM (IM), the green function is developed under the outsourcing (in-house) mode whereas the manufacturer has the CEA information advantage. We draw the following findings and insights that are novel to the literature. First, we focus on information acquisition on consumers' green preference rather than demand intercept. We find that the CEA information creates the *green match effect*, which helps firms design a more appropriate green level to better meet the consumers' green preference. Due to such effect, the CEA information affects the decisions of the supply chain members in a quite different way compared with the demand intercept information. Second, we explicitly investigate how the CEA information affects the green product development strategies (outsourcing vs. in-housing) and the total environmental quality. We find that when the manufacturer possesses superior CEA information, the in-house mode always benefits both the supplier and the manufacturer, and also improves the total environmental quality, compared with the outsourcing strategy. However, when the supplier achieves the CEA information advantage, the green product development mode does not affect the decisions and performance of the supply chain members because the supplier discloses its private CEA information through the pricing and/or green level decisions. In summary, our study complements the existing literature by revealing that the CEA information also affects the outsourcing decision and total environmental quality.

The rest of this paper is organized as follows. Section 2 reviews the literature and Section 3 describes the model. Section 4 derives the equilibria of different scenarios and Section 5 presents the major insights. Finally, Section 6 offers the concluding remarks. All the proofs are provided in Appendix A.

2. Literature Review

The environmental issue has received growing attention in the operations management literature in recent years. To develop and introduce a green product, a firm should not only maximize its profit but also consider the consumers' preference and government regulation; hence, a number of new research issues are emerging. For instance, some researchers investigate how to coordinate a green supply chain [8–12]. Xie studied how green supply chain structures affect energy saving [13]. Several studies on the product design decisions are related to product recovery strategies, such as lease strategies [14], remanufacturing [15], and modular design [16]. Krishnan and Lacourbe, and Yenipazarli and Vakharia studied situations in which a monopolist designs a green product and a conventional product to meet two market segments [17,18]. Rahmani and Yavari, and Zhang et al. focus on how consumer environmental concern affects pricing strategies in a competitive setting [19,20]. Liu et al. examine the interaction of CEA and competition intensity [3]. How sharing logistics and product recovery affect the environment is a hot research topic in recent years [21–23]. The aforementioned papers ignore the outsourcing modes and CEA information; in contrast, this paper reveals how these two factors affect environmental issues.

Information acquisition and disclosure play a critical role in supply chain management and the extant literature focuses on the effect of information acquisition and disclosure on demand intercept. For instance, Guo analyzed the efficiency effect of information acquisition in a sequential decision setting [24]. Vertical information sharing under different supply chain structures was investigated as well [7,25–29]. Fu et al. explored the interaction between information system and network design [30]. Recently, how to obtain information through data has become a research hotspot [31–33]. Different from the aforementioned studies, which focus on demand intercept information, CEA information affects not only demand but also product design. Thus, the main findings in this work are significantly different from those in the aforementioned literature.

This study is also related to the literature on outsourcing decisions. A supply chain consisting of an original equipment manufacturer (OEM) and a contract manufacturer (CM) is investigated, in which the CM is also a competitor of the OEM [34–38]. Chen et al. and Esmaeili-Najafabadi et al. studied outsourcing strategies by considering multi-dimensional uncertainties [39,40]. The aforementioned literature does not consider environmental issues and the effect of CEA information asymmetry. In contrast, this paper reveals the critical role played by the CEA information in the firms' outsourcing decisions; this is a new reason for firms to change their outsourcing decisions. To our knowledge, this study is the first in the literature aiming at understanding how the outsourcing decision affects total environmental quality. We summarize the related literature in Table 1.

Table 1. Classification of recent literature.

Literature Streams	Related Literature	This Paper
Green Supply Chain Design and Environment	[3,8–23]	✓
Information Acquisition and Disclosure	[7,24–33]	✓
Outsourcing Decisions	[34–40]	✓

3. Model

Consider a two-echelon supply chain that consists of a supplier (she) and a manufacturer (he); and both are profit maximizers. The manufacturer procures a key component from the supplier as a one-to-one input to produce a green product and sells it in a consumer market. The demand function for the green product is $D = a + \tau e - p$, where a is the demand intercept, p represents the selling price, e stands for the green level, and τ measures the CEA level. This type of demand function reflects the common understanding that the improvement of the CEA and/or green level can increase the market demand for the green product; it has been commonly adopted in the existing literature [3,12]. To focus on the interaction of CEA information acquisition with green product development strategy, we assume that the demand intercept a is deterministic but the CEA level τ is a random variable, which captures the demand uncertainty of the green product. This assumption is practically reasonable because one of the main challenges for new product designs comes from customers' acceptance of the new feature [37]. Specifically, we assume that $\tau \sim N(\mu, \sigma^2)$ with $\mu > 0$. To avoid triviality, the standard deviation σ is assumed to be sufficiently smaller than the mean μ [25–27]. The normal distribution is commonly used in the information acquisition and sharing literature [29].

As mentioned in Section 1, information acquisition capabilities of the supply chain members may be quite different, thereby leading to two information asymmetry scenarios. When the manufacturer is more capable of acquiring the CEA information than the supplier (i.e., OM and IM scenarios), they observe a signal $f_m = \tau + \varepsilon_m$ of the CEA level. Conversely, when the supplier has the superior CEA information (i.e., OS and IS scenarios), they obtain a signal $f_s = \tau + \varepsilon_s$. We adopt the common assumption that $\varepsilon_i \sim N(0, \sigma_i^2)$, $i \in \{m, s\}$, and ε_i is independent of τ [29]. Denote $\lambda_m \equiv \sigma^2/(\sigma^2 + \sigma_m^2)$ and $\lambda_s \equiv \sigma^2/(\sigma^2 + \sigma_s^2)$ as the CEA information accuracies of the manufacturer and supplier, respectively. The larger the value of λ_m (λ_s) is the more accurate the CEA information possessed by the manufacturer (supplier) than their counterpart. In the limiting case in which $\lambda_i = 1, i = s, m$, the signal perfectly reveals the exact CEA. In the opposite limiting case in which $\lambda_i = 0$, the signal lacks valuable information on the CEA uncertainty, and the posterior distribution is identical to the previous CEA distribution. We exclude these two extreme cases and restrict our scope to $\lambda_i \in (0,1)$. To capture the CEA information asymmetry without complicating our analyses, we assume that the player with poor acquisition capability does not have any CEA information. This is practically reasonable because the CEA information possessed by the firm with poor acquisition capability is typically known by the firm who achieves CEA information superiority [25]. We note that acquiring information typically requires a fixed investment, including buying ERP systems and advanced data analytical technologies, or purchasing information service from consultants. However, as a kind of sunk cost (fixed payment), it cannot change the main insights. Thus, ignoring information acquisition cost is commonly adopted in the extant literature [25]. The supplier and manufacturer have common knowledge about other parameters except for the CEA signals [27].

There are two green product development strategies (modes) from which the manufacturer can choose: outsoucing and in-house. The green function can play the same role in the green product whether developed under the outsourcing mode or the in-house mode, and needs the same product cost per unit. For example, although the engine and braking system have different functions in a vehicle, their effects on environmental improvement are the same, which can be measured by energy saving [7]. This assumption also allows us to show whether the manufacturer adopts the outsourcing or if the in-house mode is driven solely by the CEA information rather than by other reasons [38]. We use he^2 to measure the unit green function cost, where h is a positive cost coefficient. This quadratic cost function reflects that environmental improvement requires an increasing marginal cost, including more expensive materials, energy sources, as well as production and logistic operations, and it is commonly used to describe the production cost related to the product's environmental improvement [3,17]. The assembling cost per unit for the manufacturer is a constant under both modes; we normalize it to zero, which will not affect our findings [13].

Under the in-house mode, the manufacturer procures a conventional component from the supplier and designs the green function on their own. The profit of the supplier is $\pi_s = (w_c - c)D$, where w_c and c stand for the wholesale price and the unit regular cost of the conventional component, respectively. As the leader in the Stackelberg game, the supplier only needs to set the wholesale price of the conventional component based on her CEA information. However, the manufacturer needs to decide the selling price p as well as the green level e of the green product. His profit is given by $\pi_m = (p - w_c - he^2)D$.

Under the outsourcing mode, the manufacturer does not design the green function but procures a green component directly from the supplier. In such a case, the supplier's profit is given by $\pi_s = (w_g - c - he^2)D$, where w_g is the wholesale price of the green component. The unit cost of the green component includes the regular cost c and the green function cost he^2. As the Stackelberg leader, the supplier determines the wholesale price w_g and the green level e of the green component to maximize their expected profit under different CEA information structures; as the follower, the manufacturer sets the selling price p of the green product to maximize their expected profit based on their own CEA information, and the profit is given by $\pi_m = (p - w_g)D$.

In the following analyses, we use superscripts *om*, *im*, *os*, and *is* to denote the equilibrium results under the OM, IM, OS, and IS scenarios, respectively. For instance, Π_s^{om} denotes the ex ante expected profit (performance) of the supplier under the OM scenario where the manufacturer adopts the outsourcing mode and has the superior CEA information compared with the supplier. Moreover, we use $\Pi_{SC}^i \equiv \Pi_m^i + \Pi_s^i, i \in \{im, om, is, os\}$, to measure the performance of the whole supply chain under different scenarios, and denote $TG^i \equiv E_\tau[e^i D^i]$ as the total environmental quality, where $E_\tau[\cdot]$ is the expectation operator with respective to the random τ. Agrawal et al. gives detailed definitions of total environmental quality [14].

For future comparison, we first investigate two non-information scenarios in which neither the supplier nor the manufacturer acquires the CEA information. The decision problems of the supplier and manufacturer are respectively given by $\max_{w_g,e} E_\tau[(w_g - c - he^2)D]$ and $\max_p E_\tau[(p - w_g)D]$ under the outsourcing mode, and by $\max_{w_c} E_\tau[(w_c - c)D]$ and $\max_{p,e} E_\tau[(p - w_c - he^2)D]$ under the in-house mode. Solving these two Stackelberg games yields the following findings.

Proposition 1. *Without CEA information, the following properties hold: (1) The green product development strategy does not affect the equilibrium green level, the equilibrium selling price of the green product, and the equilibrium expected profits of the supplier and manufacturer. (2) The green development strategy does not affect the total environmental quality.*

Hence, we only use superscripts B to denote the equilibrium results under the non-information scenarios. The equilibrium decisions are $e^B = \mu/2h$,

$$w_c^B = \frac{a+c}{2} + \frac{\mu^2}{8h}, \quad w_g^B = \frac{a+c}{2} + \frac{3\mu^2}{8h}, \quad p^B = \frac{3a+c}{4} + \frac{7\mu^2}{16h}.$$

The equilibrium expected profits of the manufacturer and supplier are given by:

$$\Pi_m^B = \left(\frac{a-c}{4} + \frac{\mu^2}{16h}\right)^2,$$

and $\Pi_s^B = 2\Pi_m^B$, respectively. In equilibrium, the total environmental quality is:

$$TG^B = \frac{\mu(a-c)}{8h} + \frac{\mu^3}{32h^2}.$$

Although the wholesale price of the green component is higher than that of the conventional component, the price difference (i.e., $w_g^B - w_c^B = \frac{\mu^2}{4h}$) just compensates the green function cost per unit (i.e., he^2). This implies that without CEA information, going green does not help the supplier achieve an additional marginal profit. Therefore, the green product development mode does not affect the equilibrium expected profits of the supplier and manufacturer, neither does it influence the total environmental quality. In the following sections, we will show how the CEA information changes the results in Proposition 1.

4. Equilibrium Analysis

In this section, we derive the equilibria of the OM, IM, OS, and IS scenarios. Comparing the equilibria with those of the non-information cases, we identify three effects of the CEA information on the decisions of the supply chain members.

4.1. Equilibrium of OM Scenario

Under the OM scenario, the manufacturer achieves the CEA information superiority and adopts the outsourcing mode. The supplier does not have any CEA information and her decision problem is still $\max_{w_g,e} E_\tau[(w_g - c - he^2)D]$. However, the manufacturer acquires the CEA information and uses the signal f_m to update his new belief on the CEA level; hence, his decision problem is given by $\max_p E_\tau[(p - w_g)D|f_m]$.

Proposition 2. *Under the OM scenario, the unique equilibrium decisions are given by $w_g^{om} = w_g^B$, $e^{om} = e^B$, and:*

$$p^{om} = \frac{3a+c}{4} + \frac{3\mu^2 + 4\mu[(1-\lambda_m)\mu + \lambda_m f_m]}{16h}.$$

The product development and information sharing decisions are typically long-term strategies, which take place before the signal f_m is observed. To examine these two decisions, we need to compute the ex ante profits of the supply chain members by taking expectation with respect to the signal f_m. For example, the manufacturer's expected profit is $E_\tau[\pi_m|f_m] = \frac{a-c}{4} + \frac{\mu^2 + 4\mu\lambda_m(f_m-\mu)}{16h}$. We can obtain the manufacturer's ex ante profit by $E_{f_m}[E_\tau[\pi_m|f_m]]$; that is, $\Pi_m^{om} = \Pi_m^B + \frac{\lambda_m \mu^2 \sigma^2}{16h^2}$. Similarly, we obtain the ex ante profits of the supplier and total environmental quality: $\Pi_s^{om} = \Pi_s^B$ and $TG^{om} = TG^B$.

Compared with the non-information case, the manufacturer under the OM scenario benefits from the CEA information acquisition, and the benefit decreases in the cost coefficient h, but increases in the information accuracy λ_m and the standard deviation σ of the CEA level. This is due to the well-known efficiency effect [24]. That is, the manufacturer can adjust the selling price according to the CEA signal they obtain. If the CEA signal f_m is higher (lower) than the expected value of the CEA level μ, the manufacturer sets the selling price higher (lower) than in the non-information case because his perceived demand for the green product would be higher (lower) than in the non-information case. However, the supplier does not have any CEA information; hence, she charges the same wholesale price and designs the same green level as those under the non-information case. Therefore, the supplier's performance is not affected by the manufacturer's CEA information acquisition. This finding is similar to the insights in Guo [24], which focuses on information acquisition in demand intercept. We further find that the manufacturer's CEA information acquisition cannot improve the total environmental quality compared with the non-information case because the supplier does not have further CEA information and cannot adjust the green level to better meet the consumers' green preference.

4.2. Equilibrium of IM Scenario

Under the IM scenario, the manufacturer achieves the CEA information superiority and is also able to develop the green function in house. In this case, the supplier's decision problem is given by $\max_{w_c} E_\tau[(w_c - c)D]$. However, the manufacturer acquires the CEA information and uses the signal f_m to decide the green level and the selling price of the green product. The manufacturer's decision problem is thus $\max_{p,e} E_\tau[(p - w_c - he^2)D|f_m]$.

Proposition 3. *Under the IM scenario, the unique equilibrium decisions are given by:*

$$w_c^{im} = \frac{a+c}{2} + \frac{\mu^2 + \lambda_m \sigma^2}{8h}, \quad e^{im} = \frac{(1-\lambda_m)\mu + \lambda_m f_m}{2h},$$

and:

$$p^{im} = \frac{3a+c}{4} + \frac{\mu^2 + \lambda_m \sigma^2 + 6[(1-\lambda_m)\mu + \lambda_m f_m]^2}{16h}.$$

Similar to the OM scenario, we take expectation with respect to the signal f_m, based on the equilibrium pricing decisions, to obtain the ex ante profits of the supply chain members. We have:

$$\Pi_m^{im} = \Pi_m^B + \frac{\lambda_m \sigma^2[8h(a-c) + 18\mu^2 + 9\lambda_m \sigma^2]}{16^2 h^2}, \quad \Pi_s^{im} = \Pi_s^B + \frac{\lambda_m \sigma^2[16h(a-c) + 4\mu^2 + 2\lambda_m \sigma^2]}{16^2 h^2}.$$

Furthermore, the total environmental quality is computed as $TG^{im} = TG^B + \frac{5\lambda_m \mu \sigma^2}{32h^2}$.

Proposition 3 shows that the manufacturer can fine-tune the green level and the selling price according to the CEA signal. Therefore, both the efficiency and green match effects occur. The latter effect enables the manufacturer to adjust the green level according to the updated CEA information, while the former helps him set an appropriate selling price of the green product. These two effects directly benefit the manufacturer in contrast to the non-information case. Knowing this, the supplier always sets a higher wholesale price than in the non-information case. Hence, the supplier benefits from the wholesale price premium (i.e., $w_c^{im} - w_c^{in} = \frac{\lambda_m \sigma^2}{8h}$), which increases the accuracy of the manufacturer's CEA information as well as the standard deviation of the CEA. This finding is different from the insight in the literature on demand intercept information and the OM case, and complements the existing literature by revealing that the efficiency and green match effects together can induce the strategic effect, which enables the supplier to increase their wholesale price and share part of the benefit of the CEA information acquisition. We can verify that when $h > \frac{14\mu^2 + 7\lambda_m \sigma^2}{8(a-c)}$, the manufacturer's CEA information provides more value to the supplier than to themself (i.e., $\Pi_s^{im} - \Pi_s^B > \Pi_m^{im} - \Pi_m^B$). Furthermore, the total environmental quality is also improved by the green match and efficiency effects compared with the non-information case.

4.3. Equilibria of OS and IS Scenarios

Under the IS scenario, the supplier obtains a CEA signal f_s and their decision problem is $\max_{w_c} E_\tau[(w_c - c)D|f_s]$. As the Stackelberg leader, the supplier reveals the signal f_s to the manufacturer through an announcement of the wholesale price w_c. That is, the manufacturer can infer the signal f_s through the wholesale price charged by the supplier. The information leakage is widely observed in various two-echelon supply chains [7]. Furthermore, the supplier cannot use w_c to signal any forecast other than the true forecast. The reason is that if the supplier sets a higher w_c to signal a forecast higher than the true forecast and the manufacturer believes the supplier, the manufacturer will set a higher selling price, which results in a lower expected demand, compared with the case where the supplier sets w_c based on true information. The tradeoff between a higher w_c and lower demand enables the supplier to find that it is not optimal to make the manufacturer believe a higher forecast than the actual. The manufacturer then uses the signal f_s to set the green level and selling price of the green product, i.e., $\max_{p,e} E_\tau[(p - w_c - he^2)D|f_s]$. Under the OS scenario, the supplier's decision problem is $\max_{w_g,e} E_\tau[(w_g - c - he^2)D|f_s]$. Similar to the IS scenario, the supplier reveals the signal f_s through their announcement of the wholesale price and green level. The manufacturer then uses the signal f_s to solve their pricing decision problem, i.e., $\max_p E_\tau[(p - w_g)D|f_s]$. We, therefore, refer to these two cases as the symmetric information scenario.

Proposition 4. *Under the OS and IS scenarios, the unique equilibrium decisions are given by:*

$$w_g^{os} = \frac{a+c}{2} + \frac{3[(1-\lambda_s)\mu + \lambda_s f_s]^2}{16h}, \quad w_c^{is} = \frac{a+c}{2} + \frac{[(1-\lambda_s)\mu + \lambda_s f_s]^2}{16h},$$

$$e^{os} = e^{is} = \frac{(1-\lambda_s)\mu + \lambda_s f_s}{2h}, \quad p^{os} = p^{is} = \frac{3a+c}{4} + \frac{7[(1-\lambda_s)\mu + \lambda_s f_s]^2}{16h}.$$

Based on the equilibrium pricing decisions, we take expectation with respect to signal f_s to obtain the ex ante profits of the supply chain members. We have:

$$\Pi_m^{os} = \Pi_m^{is} = \Pi_m^B + \frac{\lambda_s \sigma^2[8h(a-c) + 6\mu^2 + 3\lambda_s \sigma^2]}{256h^2}$$

and $\Pi_s^{os} = \Pi_s^{is} = 2\Pi_m^{is}$; and the total environmental quality is given by:

$$TG^{os} = TG^{is} = TG^B + \frac{3\lambda_s \mu \sigma^2}{32h^2}.$$

We make the following observations. First, under the symmetric information scenario, the green product development strategy does not affect the equilibrium green level, the equilibrium selling price of the green product, the ex ante equilibrium expected profits of the players, and the total environmental quality. Second, both the supplier and manufacturer can adjust the wholesale price and the selling price according to the signal under both the IS and OS scenarios. Third, the supplier's CEA information acquisition can improve the ex ante equilibrium profits of the players and the total environmental quality compared with the non-information cases.

5. The Value of CEA Information

If the supply chain has been operating under the outsourcing or in-house mode, who should be the one in each case to acquire the CEA information: the supplier or the manufacturer?

5.1. Outsourcing Mode

Proposition 5 shows that if the supply chain has been operating under the outsourcing mode, the supplier's superior CEA information is always more valuable for herself than the manufacturer's. This is because the supplier can design the green level and make the wholesale pricing decision according to their updated CEA information. Intuitively, the manufacturer should benefit more from their own superior CEA information (i.e., in the OM case) than the supplier's (i.e., in the OS case). However, this intuition is not correct. Proposition 5(2) states that the manufacturer benefits more from the supplier's information acquisition than from $\lambda_m < \lambda_m^O$, i.e., in region Ω_L in Figure 1. This result indicates that when the manufacturer has a relatively poor capacity for CEA information acquisition, they should encourage the supplier to take the initiative to acquire the CEA information; otherwise, they should acquire the CEA information themself. Although the supplier's CEA information helps the manufacturer set an appropriate selling price, it also helps the supplier fine-tune the green level as well as the wholesale price. Furthermore, the expected wholesale price in the OS case is higher than that in the OM case; i.e., the strategic effect occurs. When $\lambda_m < \lambda_m^O$, the supply chain members agree that the supplier should take the initiative to acquire the CEA information, in which the manufacturer benefits from the efficiency effect whereas the supplier benefits from both the green match and strategic effects.

Proposition 5. *Under the outsourcing mode, (1) $\Pi_s^{os} > \Pi_s^{om}$; (2) $\Pi_m^{os} > \Pi_m^{om}$ iff $\lambda_m < \lambda_m^O$; (3) $\Pi_{SC}^{os} > \Pi_{SC}^{om}$ iff $\lambda_m < 3\lambda_m^O$; and (4) $TG^{os} > TG^{om}$, where:*

$$\lambda_m^O \equiv \frac{[8h(a-c) + 6\mu^2 + 3\lambda_s \sigma^2]\lambda_s}{16\mu^2}.$$

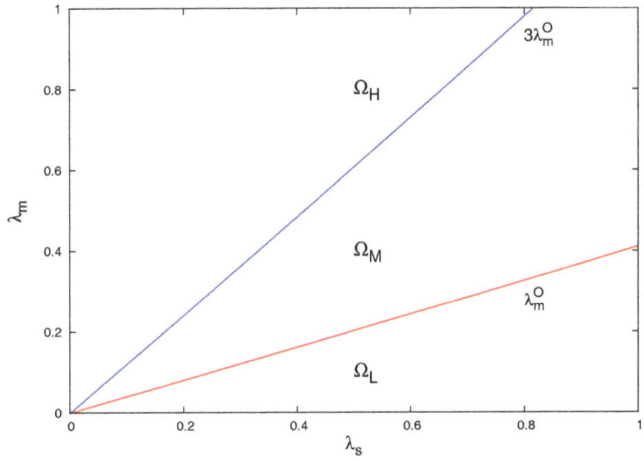

Figure 1. Effect of CEA information accuracies under outsourcing mode.

In the medium region (i.e., region Ω_M in Figure 1) where the manufacturer has a reasonable capability of CEA information acquisition, the supplier's superior CEA information benefits the whole supply chain but not the manufacturer, in contrast to the manufacturer's CEA superior information case. However, when the manufacturer has a very good capability of CEA information acquisition, i.e., in region Ω_H, both the manufacturer and the whole supply chain can benefit more from the manufacturer's CEA information acquisition than from the supplier's.

Proposition 5(4) indicates that the total environmental quality is always improved more by the supplier's superior CEA information than by the manufacturer's under the outsourcing mode. The more accurate the CEA information is, the more improvement of the total environmental quality. This is because that the supplier will set an appropriate green level and an appropriate level of wholesale price when equipped with the superior CEA information, which in turn allows the green product design to meet the consumer demand better. This result implies that environmental associations and government agencies should help or encourage the supplier to obtain more accurate CEA information when the manufacturer outsources the green component to the supplier.

5.2. In-House Mode

When the supply chain has been operating under the in-house mode, should the manufacturer or the supplier take the initiative to acquire CEA information?

Proposition 6. *Under the in-house mode, there exist three positive thresholds, λ_m^M, λ_m^S, and λ_m^{SC}, such that, (1) $\Pi_s^{is} > \Pi_s^{im}$ iff $\lambda_m < \lambda_m^S$; (2) $\Pi_m^{is} > \Pi_m^{im}$ iff $\lambda_m < \lambda_m^M$; (3) $\Pi_{SC}^{is} > \Pi_{SC}^{im}$ iff $\lambda_m < \lambda_m^{SC}$; and (4) $TG^{is} > TG^{im}$ iff $\lambda_m/\lambda_s < 0.6$.*

When the manufacturer's CEA information accuracy is smaller than λ_m^S, which is a function of the supplier's CEA information accuracy, the supplier prefers to acquire the CEA information on her own. When the manufacturer's CEA information accuracy is greater than λ_m^M, the manufacturer is better off acquiring CEA information themself. There is also a threshold at which the whole supply chain is better off with the manufacturer's information acquisition if it is accurate enough.

To illustrate, we plot Figure 2 with $a = 50, \mu = 50, \sigma = 15, c = 20$, and $h = 2$. In region Ω_1, the supplier's superior CEA information benefits both the supplier and manufacturer more than the manufacturer's. Therefore, if the manufacturer is less capable of acquiring the CEA information, it is optimal for them to depend on the supplier's CEA information. However, the opposite is true in region Ω_3, where the manufacturer's CEA information is relatively more accurate, and both players prefer the manufacturer's superior CEA information. In region Ω_{21}, where $\lambda_m^M < \lambda_m < \lambda_m^{SC}$, the manufacturer prefers to acquire the CEA information themself, but the supplier disagrees with them, and the entire supply chain suffers from this. In the region of Ω_{22} where $\lambda_m^{SC} < \lambda_m < \lambda_m^S$, the manufacturer still prefers to acquire the CEA information themself and the whole supply chain benefits from this, but not the supplier.

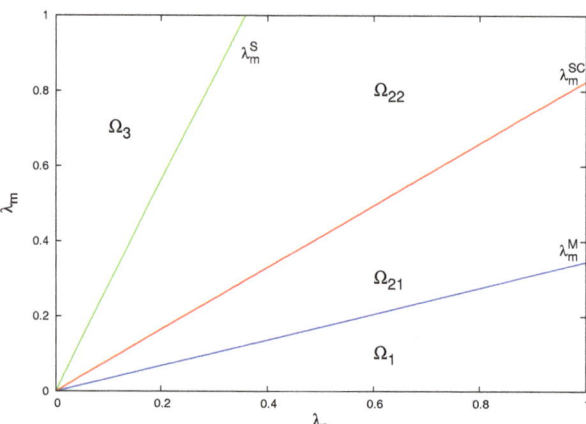

Figure 2. Effect of CEA information accuracies under in-house mode.

Recall from Section 4 that the green match effect improves the total environmental quality under the IM and IS scenarios. Proposition 6(4) shows that the manufacturer's CEA information is more effective in improving the total environmental quality than the supplier's. Hence, the manufacturer under the in-house mode should be encouraged to acquire CEA information, although they may be less capable of acquiring CEA information than the supplier.

5.3. The Effect of Downstream Information Disclosure

We can obtain some insights from the downstream information disclosure perspective by setting $\lambda_m = \lambda_s = \lambda$. In particular, given that the supply chain has adopted the outsourcing strategy, the OM scenario represents the non-information-disclosure case, whereas the OS scenario represents the case where the manufacturer requires and reveals information to the supplier voluntarily. We also analyze this question from the information sharing perspective: suppose the supplier cannot acquire any useful information, while the manufacturer can. Then, the OM scenario represents the setting without information sharing, while the OS scenario represents the CEA information sharing case.

Proposition 7. (1) *The downstream CEA information disclosure always benefits the supplier under both the outsourcing and in-house modes;* (2) *the downstream CEA information disclosure* benefits the manufacturer iff $\lambda > [10\mu^2 - 8h(a-c)]/(3\sigma^2)$ under the outsourcing mode, and always hurts them under the in-house mode; (3) the downstream CEA information disclosure always improves the whole supply chain's performance under the outsourcing mode, but always hurts it under the in-house mode; and (4) the downstream CEA information disclosure always improves the total environmental quality under the outsourcing mode, but always hurts it under the in-house mode.

The extant literature find that downstream information disclosure (sharing) on the demand intercept always benefits the upstream firm but hurts the downstream firm and the entire supply chain [24]. As a result, the downstream firm will not share demand intercept information with the upstream firm voluntarily. This is also true with the CEA information under the in-house mode. However, we find that under the outsourcing mode, the supply chain members can achieve a Pareto improvement through the downstream CEA information disclosure. When the manufacturer is more capable of acquiring CEA information and/or the CEA uncertainty is relatively large, it is better for them to disclose the CEA information to the upstream supplier. This is also due to the green match effect; that is, the manufacturer's CEA information helps the supplier design a more appropriate green level to better meet the consumers' preference than without CEA information.

6. Outsourcing or In-House?

We note from Propositions 1 and 4 that under symmetric CEA information, the green product development strategy does not affect the decisions and performance of the supply chain members and total environmental quality. In contrast, when the manufacturer has superior CEA information, the asymmetric information occurs, the impact of the green product development on the supply chain is quite different.

Proposition 8. *If the manufacturer achieves the CEA superiority, (1) $\Pi_s^{im} > \Pi_s^{om}$; (2) $\Pi_m^{im} > \Pi_m^{om}$; and (3) $TG^{im} > TG^{om}$.*

Proposition 8 states that when the manufacturer has superior CEA information, keeping green design and production in-house benefits both the supplier and manufacturer, and thus improves the performance of the whole supply chain. Both the efficiency and green match effects provide more value for the manufacturer under the IM scenario than the benefit from the efficiency effect solely under the OM scenario. By anticipating that the more appropriate green level attracts more expected potential demand in the market, i.e., $E[a + \tau e^{im}] > E[a + \tau e^{om}]$, the supplier then has the opportunity to use the strategic effect to share part of the benefit from the manufacturer's CEA information acquisition. Therefore, when the manufacturer possesses the superior CEA information, switching from an outsourcing strategy to an in-house strategy can help the supply chain members achieve a Pareto improvement.

We further find that under the CEA information asymmetry, the green product development strategies do not affect the expected green level, i.e., $E[e^{im}] = E[e^{om}]$. However, the green match effect under the IM scenario helps the manufacturer design a product with a more appropriate green level to better meet the consumers' preference and also improve the total environmental quality. Therefore, when the manufacturer achieves superior CEA information, the government agencies or green organizations should encourage firms to develop the green component in house.

7. Conclusions

This paper studies the interaction between the CEA information acquisition and green product development strategies in a two-echelon supply chain. The main findings and managerial insights from this paper can be summarized as follows.

First, without CEA information, the green product development mode does not affect the performance of the supply chain members and total environmental quality. In contrast, with CEA information, the findings are quite different. When the supplier achieves the CEA information advantage, the green product development strategies do not affect the decisions and performance of the supply chain members because the supplier reveals its private CEA information through pricing and/or green level decisions. However, when the manufacturer possesses superior CEA information, the in-house strategy can benefit the supplier and manufacturer. The reason is that the efficiency and green match effects provide more value for the manufacturer in the IM case than the benefit from the efficiency effect solely in the OM case; knowing this, the supplier has the opportunity to use the strategic effect to share part of the benefit of the manufacturer's CEA information acquisition.

Second, under the outsourcing mode, the supplier's CEA information superiority always benefits themselves. However, the manufacturer prefers the supplier's information superiority only when they have a weaker/lower information acquisition capacity. Under the in-house mode, the CEA information superiority of either the supplier or the manufacturer benefits the supply chain members and total environmental quality under some conditions.

Third, under the outsourcing mode, the manufacturer's CEA information disclosure may also benefit themselves and increase the performance of the entire supply chain. This finding is different from the extant literature that focuses on demand information without considering product development strategies. Moreover, the CEA information disclosure always improves the total environmental quality because the better match between green products and consumers' green preference leads to better outcomes for environment. These results suggest that overly green products induced by government subsidies or NGO pressure might not be ideal. The key message to policy makers is that the firm with superior CEA information should be encouraged to undertake the green product design.

This paper takes an initial step to explore the interaction between product development and CEA information acquisition in a green supply chain. More specifically, we reveal that the effects of CEA information, which has attracted less attention from researchers and practitioners, are also related to the environmental issues. Our study also highlights an interesting finding that the CEA information sharing may help supply chain members achieve a Pareto improvement, and can improve the total environmental quality. This finding also suggests that managers should pay attention to who achieves the CEA information advantage and the product development mode when going green.

There are several limitations to this study. First, we only examine the effect of CEA information. In practice, there exist other types of information, such as on-demand and input cost, and these different types of information interact with each other. It will be interesting to study the effect of multi-dimensional information on product development. Second, we do not consider upstream and downstream competitions. How competition affects green product development under asymmetric information is worth exploring.

Author Contributions: Conceptualization, M.F. and W.X.; methodology, Y.H.; formal analysis, M.F.; investigation, Y.H.; writing—original draft preparation, M.F. and Y.H.; writing—review and editing, W.X.; supervision, W.X.; project administration, W.X.; funding acquisition, W.X. All authors have read and agreed to the published version of the manuscript.

Funding: This work has been supported by the Natural Science Foundation of Shandong Province under Grant ZR2020MG009.

Institutional Review Board Statement: Not applicable.

Informed Consent Statement: Not applicable.

Data Availability Statement: Not applicable.

Conflicts of Interest: The authors declare no conflict of interest.

Appendix A

Proof of Proposition 1. (1) Liu et al. provide the more detailed proof of the outsourcing case without CEA information acquisition [3]. We rewrite it here for convenience. The manufacturer's decision problem is given by $\max_p E[\pi_m] = E[(p - w_g)(a + \tau e - p)]$. Given a pair of w_g and e, the unique response function to this problem is $p^*(w,e) = \frac{a+w_g+\mu e}{2}$. The supplier's decision problem is given by $\max_{w_g,e} E[\pi_s] = E[(w_g - c - he^2)(a + \tau e - p)]$. Plug $p^*(w,e)$ into $E[\pi_s]$ and solve the first order conditions. There are three solutions that satisfy the necessary condition for the optimal solution. However, if $a > c$, only one solution ($w_g^* = \frac{a+c}{2} + \frac{3\mu^2}{8h}, e^* = \frac{\mu}{2h}$) guarantees a positive demand and non-negative profits of the supply chain members. Since the objective function of the supplier is not concave, we cannot simply check the second condition. Instead, using the method provided by Liu et al. (2012), we then verify that w_g^* and e^* also satisfy the following sufficient condition: $E[\pi_s(w_g^*, e^*)] > E[\pi_s(w_g, e)]$, for all w_g and e that satisfy a positive demand and non-negative profits. Therefore, (w_g^*, e^*) is the unique optimal solution for the supplier. Plug w_g^* and e^* back to $p^*(w,e)$, we have $p^* = \frac{3a+c}{4} + \frac{7\mu^2}{16h}$. Note that we have verified that the demand of the product is positive. In addition, it is easy to verify that the value of the manufacturer's expected profit is non-negative. We can further obtain the expected profits of the supply chain members $\Pi_m^* = E[\pi_m] = (\frac{a-c}{4} + \frac{\mu^2}{16h})^2$ and $\Pi_s^* = E[\pi_s] = 2(\frac{a-c}{4} + \frac{\mu^2}{16h})^2$. The total environmental quality is $TG^* = \frac{\mu(a-c)}{8h} + \frac{\mu^3}{32h^2}$.

(2) Under the in-house scenario, the decision problems of the manufacturer and supplier are given by $\max_{p,e} E[\pi_m] = E[(p - w_c - he^2)(a + \tau e - p)]$ and $\max_{w_c} E[\pi_s] = E[(w_c - c)(a + \tau e - p)]$, respectively. We have $\partial E[\pi_m]/\partial p = a + \mu e - 2p + w + he^2$ and $\partial E[\pi_m]/\partial e = -2he(a + \mu e - p) + \mu(p - w_c - he^2)$. Let $\partial E[\pi_m]/\partial p = 0$, we have $p^*(e) = (a + \mu e + w + he^2)/2$. Plugging $p^*(e)$ into $\partial E[\pi_m]/\partial e$ and let $\partial E[\pi_m]/\partial e = 0$, we have $(\mu - 2he)(a + \mu e - w - he^2) = 0$. There are three solutions that satisfy the above equation (the necessary condition for the optimal solution). However, if $a > c$, only one solution ($p^* = \frac{a+w}{2} + \frac{3\mu^2}{8h}, e^* = \frac{\mu}{2h}$) guarantees a positive demand and non-negative profits of the supply chain members. Using the method provided by Liu et al. (2012), we then verify that p^* and e^* also satisfy the following sufficient condition for the optimal solution: $E[\pi_m(p^*, e^*)] > E[\pi_m(p, e)]$ for all p and e that satisfy a positive demand and non-negative profits. Therefore, (p^*, e^*) is the unique optimal solution for the manufacturer. Plugging p^* and e^* into $E[\pi_s]$ and solving $\max_{w_c} E[\pi_s]$, we obtain the unique equilibrium wholesale price $w_c^* = \frac{a+c}{2} + \frac{\mu^2}{8h}$. Plugging w_c^* back into $p^* = \frac{a+w}{2} + \frac{3\mu^2}{8h}$, we obtain $p^* = \frac{3a+c}{4} + \frac{7\mu^2}{16h}$. Finally, we can obtain the expected profits of the manufacturer and the supplier $\Pi_m^* = E[\pi_m] = (\frac{a-c}{4} + \frac{\mu^2}{16h})^2$ and $\Pi_s^* = E[\pi_s] = 2(\frac{a-c}{4} + \frac{\mu^2}{16h})^2$. The total environmental quality is $TG^* = \frac{\mu(a-c)}{8h} + \frac{\mu^3}{32h^2}$.

(3) Comparing the equilibrium resolutions under the outsourcing mode with those under the in-house mode, we obtain the results in Proposition 1. □

Proof of Proposition 2. Under the OM scenario, the manufacturer's decision problem is $\max_p E[\pi_m|f_m] = E[(p - w_g)(a + \tau e - p)|f_m]$. The unique response function to the manufacturer's problem is $p^*(w,e) = \frac{a+w_g+E[\tau|f_m]e}{2}$, given a (w,e). The supplier's decision problem is $\max_{w_g,e} E[\pi_s] = E[(w_g - c - he^2)(a + \tau e - p)]$. Plug $p^*(w,e)$ into $E[\pi_s]$ and solve the first order conditions. Similar to the outsourcing mode in the proof of Proposition 1, there are three solutions that satisfy the first order conditions. However, only one solution ($e^{om} = \frac{\mu}{2h}, w_g^{om} = \frac{a+c}{2} + \frac{3\mu^2}{8h}$) guarantees a positive demand and non-negative profits of the players. Using the method of Liu et al. (2012), we then verify that e^{om} and w_g^{om} is the unique optimal solution for the supplier. Plug e^{om} and w_g^{om} to $p^*(w,e)$, we have $p^{om} = \frac{3a+c}{4} + \frac{3\mu^2+4\mu[(1-\lambda_m)\mu+\lambda_m f_m]}{16h}$. We can further obtain $\Pi_m^{om} = E[E[\pi_m|f_m]] = (\frac{a-c}{4} + \frac{\mu^2}{16h})^2 + \frac{\lambda_m\mu^2\sigma^2}{16h^2}$, $\Pi_s^{om} = 2(\frac{a-c}{4} + \frac{\mu^2}{16h})^2$, and $TG^{om} = \frac{\mu(a-c)}{8h} + \frac{\mu^3}{32h^2}$. □

Proof of Proposition 3. Under the IM scenario, the manufacturer's decision problem is $\max_{p,e} E[\pi_m|f_m] = E[(p - w_c - he^2)(a + \tau e - p)|f_m]$. For a given w_c, we have $\partial E[\pi_m|f_m]/\partial p = a + E[\tau|f_m]e - 2p + w + he^2$ and $\partial E[\pi_m|f_m]/\partial e = -2he(a + E[\tau|f_m]e - p) + E[\tau|f_m]$

$(p - w - he^2)$. Let $\partial E[\pi_m|f_m]/\partial p = 0$, we have $p^*(e) = (a + E[\tau|f_m]e + w + he^2)/2$. Plugging $p^*(e)$ into $\partial E[\pi_m|f_m]/\partial e$ and let $\partial E[\pi_m|f_m]/\partial e = 0$, we have $(E[\tau|f_m] - 2he)(a + E[\tau|f_m]e - w - he^2) = 0$. There are three solutions that satisfy the above equation (the necessary condition for the optimal solution). The following analysis is similar to the proof of Proposition 1. If $a > c$, we can verify that only (e^{im}, p^{im}) are the equilibrium solutions, where $e^{im} = \frac{E[\tau|f_m]}{2h} = \frac{(1-\lambda_m)\mu + \lambda_m f_m}{2h}$ and $p^{im} = \frac{a+w_c}{2} + \frac{3(E[\tau|f_m])^2}{8h} = \frac{a+w_c}{2} + \frac{3[(1-\lambda_m)\mu + \lambda_m f_m]^2}{8h}$. The supplier's decision problem is $\max_{w_c} E[\pi_s] = E[(w_c - c)(a + \tau e - p)]$. Plug e^{im} and p^{im} into $E[\pi_s]$, we have $E[\pi_s] = (w_c - c)(\frac{a-w_c}{2}) + \frac{\mu^2 + \lambda_m \sigma^2}{8h}$. Then, we can get the equilibrium wholesale price $w^{im} = \frac{a+c}{2} + \frac{\mu^2 + \lambda_m \sigma^2}{8h}$. Plug w^{im} back into p^{im}, we have $p^{im} = \frac{3a+c}{4} + \frac{\mu^2 + \lambda_m \sigma^2 + 6((1-\lambda_m)\mu + \lambda_m f_m)^2}{16h}$. Finally, we have $\Pi_m^{im} = E[E[\pi_M|f_m]] = (\frac{a-c}{4} + \frac{\mu^2}{16h})^2 + \frac{\lambda_m \sigma^2[8h(a-c) + 18\mu^2 + 9\lambda_m \sigma^2]}{16^2 h^2}$, $\Pi_s^{im} = 2(\frac{a-c}{4} + \frac{\mu^2}{16h})^2 + \frac{\lambda_m \sigma^2[16h(a-c) + 4\mu^2 + 2\lambda_m \sigma^2]}{16^2 h^2}$, and $TG^{im} = \frac{\mu(a-c)}{8h} + \frac{\mu^3}{32h^2} + \frac{5\lambda_m \mu \sigma^2}{32h^2}$.

The above computation uses the following equations: $E[X] = \mu$, $E[X^2] = \mu^2 + \sigma^2$, $E[X^3] = \mu^3 + 3\mu\sigma^2$, $E[X^4] = \mu^4 + 6\mu^2\sigma^2 + 3\sigma^4$, and $Var[aX + bX^2] = \sigma^2[a^2 + 4ab\mu + 4b^2\mu^2 + 2b^2\sigma^2]$, for $X \sim N[\mu, \sigma^2]$. □

Proof of Proposition 4. (1) Under the OS scenario, the manufacturer's decision problem is $\max_p E[\pi_m|f_s] = E[(p - w_g)(a + \tau e - p)|f_s]$. The unique response function is $p^*(w_g, e) = \frac{a + w_g + E[\tau|f_s]e}{2}$. The supplier's decision problem is $\max_{w_g, e} E[\pi_s|f_s] = E[(w_g - c - he^2)(a + \tau e - p)|f_s]$. Plug $p^*(w_g, e)$ into $E[\pi_s|f_s]$ and solve the first order conditions. There are three solutions that satisfy the first conditions (the necessary condition for the optimal solution). We can verify that the solution $(e^{os} = \frac{(1-\lambda_s)\mu + \lambda_s f_s}{2h}, w_g^{os} = \frac{a+c}{2} + \frac{3[(1-\lambda_s)\mu + \lambda_s f_s]^2}{8h})$ is the unique optimal solution for the supplier's decision. Plug e^{os} and w_g^{os} back to $p^*(w_g, e)$, we have $p^{os} = \frac{3a+c}{4} + \frac{7[(1-\lambda_s)\mu + \lambda_s f_s]^2}{16h}$. Finally, we obtain $\Pi_m^{os} = E[E[\pi_m^{os}|f_s]] = (\frac{a-c}{4} + \frac{\mu^2}{16h})^2 + \frac{\lambda_s \sigma^2(8h(a-c) + 6\mu^2 + 3\lambda_s \sigma^2)}{16^2 h^2}$, $\Pi_s^{os} = E[E[\pi_s^{os}|f_s]] = 2(\frac{a-c}{4} + \frac{\mu^2}{16h})^2 + \frac{2\lambda_s \sigma^2(8h(a-c) + 6\mu^2 + 3\lambda_s \sigma^2)}{16^2 h^2}$, and $TG^{os} = \frac{\mu(a-c)}{8h} + \frac{\mu^3}{32h^2} + \frac{3\lambda_s \mu \sigma^2}{32h^2}$.

(2) Under the IS scenario, the manufacturer's and the supplier's decision problems are $\max_{p,e} E[\pi_m|f_s] = E[(p - w_c - he^2)(a + \tau e - p)|f_s]$ and $\max_{w_c} E[\pi_s|f_s] = E[(w_c - c)(a + \tau e - p)|f_s]$. Using the similar method, we obtain the results in the above part of proof.

(3) Comparing the equilibrium resolutions under the IS scenario with those under the OS case, we obtain Proposition 4. □

Proof of Proposition 5. We can verify that $\Pi_s^{os} - \Pi_s^{om} = \frac{2\lambda_s \sigma^2[8h(a-c) + 6\mu^2 + 3\lambda_s \sigma^2]}{16^2 h^2} > 0$, $\Pi_m^{os} - \Pi_m^{om} = \frac{\sigma^2[-16\lambda_m \mu^2 + \lambda_s(8h(a-c) + 6\mu^2 + 3\lambda_s \sigma^2)]}{16^2 h^2}$, and $\Pi_{SC}^{os} - \Pi_{SC}^{om} = \frac{\sigma^2[-16\lambda_m \mu^2 + 3\lambda_s(8h(a-c) + 6\mu^2 + 3\lambda_s \sigma^2)]}{16^2 h^2}$. Therefore, $\Pi_m^{os} > \Pi_m^{om}$ if and only if $\lambda_m < \lambda_m^O$, and $\Pi_{SC}^{os} > \Pi_{SC}^{om}$ if and only if $\lambda_m < 3\lambda_m^O$, where $\lambda_m^O \equiv \lambda_s[8h(a-c) + 6\mu^2 + 3\lambda_s \sigma^2]/(16\mu^2)$. We also obtain $TG^{os} - TG^{om} = \frac{3\lambda_s \mu \sigma^2}{32h^2} > 0$. □

Proof of Proposition 6. We have $\Pi_s^{im} - \Pi_s^{is} = \frac{\sigma^2[2\sigma^2 \lambda_m^2 + (16h(a-c) + 4\mu^2)\lambda_m - (16h(a-c) + 12\mu^2)\lambda_s - 6\sigma^2 \lambda_s^2]}{16^2}$. The equation $2\sigma^2 \lambda_m^2 + (16h(a-c) + 4\mu^2)\lambda_m - (16h(a-c) + 12\mu^2)\lambda_s - 6\sigma^2 \lambda_s^2 = 0$ has two roots, however, there is only one positive root: $\lambda_m^S \equiv \frac{-16h(a-c) - 4\mu^2 + \sqrt{(16h(a-c) + 4\mu^2)^2 + 8\sigma^2((16h(a-c) + 12\mu^2)\lambda_s + 6\sigma^2 \lambda_s^2)}}{4\sigma^2} > 0$. Then we can verify that if $\lambda_m < \lambda_m^S$, $\Pi_s^{im} - \Pi_s^{is} < 0$, and otherwise, $\Pi_s^{im} - \Pi_s^{is} \geq 0$. Similarly, we have obtained the results in Proposition 6(2) and 6(3), where $\lambda_m^M = \frac{-8h(a-c) - 18\mu^2 + \sqrt{(8h(a-c) + 18\mu^2)^2 + 36\sigma^2((8h(a-c) + 6\mu^2)\lambda_s + 3\lambda_s^2 \sigma^2)}}{18\sigma^2} > 0$ and $\lambda_m^{SC} = \frac{-24h(a-c) - 22\mu^2 + \sqrt{(24h(a-c) + 22\mu^2)^2 + 44\sigma^2((24h(a-c) + 18\mu^2)\lambda_s + 9\sigma^2 \lambda_s^2)}}{22\sigma^2} > 0$. Comparing TG^{is} and TG^{im}, we can show that if $\lambda_m/\lambda_s < 0.6$, $TG^{im} < TG^{is}$, and otherwise, $TG^{im} \geq TG^{is}$. □

Proof of Proposition 7. Let $\lambda_m = \lambda_s = \lambda$, we obtain the results from Propositions 5 and 6. □

Proof of Proposition 8. We can verify that $\Pi_m^{om} - \Pi_m^{im} = -\frac{\lambda_m \sigma^2 [8h(a-c) + 2\mu^2 + 9\lambda_m \sigma^2]}{16^2 h^2} < 0$ and $\Pi_s^{om} - \Pi_s^{im} = -\frac{\lambda_m \sigma^2 [16h(a-c) + 4\mu^2 + 2\lambda_m \sigma^2]}{16^2 h^2} < 0$. We have $TG^{im} - TG^{om} = \frac{5\lambda_m \mu \sigma^2}{32h^2} > 0$. □

References

1. Wu, Z.; Pagell, M. Balancing proiorities: Decision-making in sustainbale supply chain. *J. Oper. Manag.* **2011**, *29*, 577–590. [CrossRef]
2. Barbarossa, C.; Pelsmacker, P.D.; Moons, I. Personal values, green self-identity and electric car adoption. *Ecol. Econ.* **2017**, *140*, 190–200. [CrossRef]
3. Liu, Z.; Anderson, T.D.; Cruz, J.M. Consumer environmental awareness and compettition in two-stage supply chains. *Eur. J. Oper. Res.* **2012**, *218*, 602–613. [CrossRef]
4. IEA. World Energy Outlook: Summary and Conclusions. 2007. Available online: https://www.iea.org/reports/world-energy-outlook-2007 (accessed on 1 November 2007).
5. Flakus, G. Automakers Show off Green, Fuel Efficient Vehicles. 2009. Available online: https://voa-story.com/2008-01-15-automakers-show-off-green-fuel-efficient-vehicles/ (accessed on 15 January 2008).
6. Migliore, G.; Vaughn, M.L.A. Auto Show: Buick Gives the Lacrosse an Electric Assist. *Auto Week*, 2010. Available online: http://www.autoweek.com/article/20101115/LOSANGELES/101119954 (accessed on 14 November 2010).
7. Jiang, B.; Tian, L.; Xu, Y.; Zhang, F. To share or not to share: Demand forecast sharing in a distribution channel. *Mark. Sci.* **2016**, *35*, 800–809. [CrossRef]
8. Zhang, L.; Wang, J.; You, J. Consumer environmental awareness and channel coordination with two substitutable products. *Eur. J. Oper. Res.* **2015**, *241*, 63–73. [CrossRef]
9. Taleizadeh, A.A.; Alizadeh-Basban, N.; Sarker, B.R. Coordinated contracts in a two-echelon green supply chain considering pricing strategy. *Comput. Ind. Eng.* **2018**, *124*, 249–275. [CrossRef]
10. Gao, J.; Xiao, Z.; Wei, H. Competition and coordination in a dual-channel green supply chain with an eco-label policy. *Comput. Ind. Eng.* **2021**, *153*, 1–16. [CrossRef]
11. Ghosh, D.; Shah, J. A comparative analysis of greening policies across supply chain structures. *Comput. Ind. Eng.* **2012**, *135*, 568–583. [CrossRef]
12. Swami, S.; Shah, J.D. Channel coordination in green supply chain management. *J. Oper. Res. Soc.* **2013**, *64*, 336–351. [CrossRef]
13. Xie, G. Modeling decision processes of a green supply chain with regulation on energy saving level. *Comput. Oper. Res.* **2015**, *54*, 266–273. [CrossRef]
14. Agrawal, V.V.; Ferguson, M.; Toktay, L.B.; Thomas, V.M. Is leasing greener than selling. *Manag. Sci.* **2012**, *58*, 523–533. [CrossRef]
15. Subramanian, R.; Ferguson, M.; Toktay, L.B. Remanufacturing and the component commonality decision. *Prod. Oper. Manag.* **2013**, *22*, 36–53. [CrossRef]
16. Agrawal, V.V.; Ülkü, S. The role of modular upgradability as a green design strategy. *Manuf. Serv. Oper. Manag.* **2013**, *15*, 640–648. [CrossRef]
17. Krishnan, V.V.; Lacourbe, P. Designing Product Lines with Higher Aggregate Environmental Quality. 2011. SSRN 1744301. Available online: https://papers.ssrn.com/sol3/papers.cfm?abstract_id=1744301 (accessed on 22 January 2011)
18. Yenipazarli, A.; Vakharia, A. Pricing, market coverage and capapcity: Can green and brow products co-exist? *Eur. J. Oper. Res.* **2015**, *242*, 304–315. [CrossRef]
19. Rahmani, K.; Yavari, M. Pricing policies for a dual-channel supply chain under demand disruption. *Comput. Ind. Eng.* **2019**, *127*, 493–510. [CrossRef]
20. Zhang, C.; Liu, Y.; Han, G. Two-stage pricing strategies of a dual-channel supply chain considering public green preference. *Comput. Ind. Eng.* **2021**, *151*, 106988. [CrossRef]
21. Xu, X.; Lin, Z.; Xing, L. Multi-objective robust optimisation model for MDVRPLS in refined oil distribution. *Int. J. Prod. Res.* **2021**, *5*, 1–21. [CrossRef]
22. Xu, X.; Wang, C.; Zhou, P. GVRP considered oil-gas recovery in refined oil distribution: From an environmental perspective. *Internat. J. Prod. Econom.* **2021**, *235*, 108078. [CrossRef]
23. Xu, X.; Hao, J.; Zheng, Y. Multi-objective artificial bee colony algorithm for multi-stage resource leveling problem in sharing logistics network. *Comput. Ind. Eng.* **2020**, *142*, 106338. [CrossRef]
24. Guo, L. The benefits of downstream information acquisition. *Mark. Sci.* **2009**, *28*, 457–471. [CrossRef]
25. Shang, W.; Ha, A.Y.; Tong, S. Information sharing in a supply chain with a common retailer. *Manag. Sci.* **2016**, *62*, 245–263. [CrossRef]
26. Wang, Y.; Tang, W.; Zhao, R. Information sharing and information concealment in the presence of a dominant retailer. *Comput. Ind. Eng.* **2018**, *121*, 36–50. [CrossRef]
27. Huang, S.; Chen, S.; Guan, X. Retailer information sharing under endogenous channel structure with investment spillovers. *Comput. Ind. Eng.* **2020**, *142*, 106346. [CrossRef]

28. Wang, J.; Zhuo, W. Strategic information sharing in a supply chain under potential supplier encroachment. *Comput. Ind. Eng.* **2020**, *150*, 106880. [CrossRef]
29. Chen, Y.J.; Tang, C.S. The economic value of market information for farmers in developing economies. *Prod. Oper. Manag.* **2015**, *24*, 1441–1452. [CrossRef]
30. Fu, Q.; Abdul Rahman, A.A.; Jiang, H.; Abbas, J.; Comite, U. Sustainable supply chain and business performance: The impact of strategy, network design, information systems, and organizational structure. *Sustainability* **2022**, *14*, 1080. [CrossRef]
31. Zhang, W.; Yan, S.; Li, J.; Tian, X.; Yoshida, T. Credit risk prediction of SMEs in supply chain finance by fusing demographic and behavioral data. *Transp. Res. Part E* **2022**, *158*, 102611. [CrossRef]
32. Wang, Q.; Zhang, W.; Li, J.; Mai, F.; Ma, Z. Effect of online review sentiment on product sales: The moderating role of review credibility perception. *Comput. Hum. Behav.* **2022**, *133*, 107272. [CrossRef]
33. Zhang, W.; Xie, R.; Wang, Q.; Yang, Y.; Li, J. A novel approach for fraudulent reviewer detection based on weighted topic modelling and nearest neighbors with asymmetric Kullback-Leibler divergence. *Decis. Support. Syst.* **2022**, 113765. [CrossRef]
34. Wang, Y.; Niu, B.; Guo, P. On the advantage of quantity leadership when outsourcing production to a competitive contract manufacturer. *Prod. Oper. Manag.* **2013**, *22*, 104–119. [CrossRef]
35. Niu, B.; Wang, Y.; Guo, P. Equilibrium pricing sequence in a co-opetitive supply chain with the ODM as a downstream rival of its OEM. *Omega* **2015**, *57*, 249–270. [CrossRef]
36. Shi, J. Contract manufacturer's encroachment strategy and quality decision with different channel leadership structures. *Comput. Ind. Eng.* **2019**, *137*, 106078. [CrossRef]
37. Lee, H.; Schmidt, G. Using value chains to enhance innovation. *Prod. Oper. Manag.* **2017**, *26*, 617–632. [CrossRef]
38. Zhu, X. Management the risks of outsourcing: Time, quality and correlated costs. *Transp. Res. Part E* **2016**, *90*, 121–133. [CrossRef]
39. Chen, K.; Zhao, H.; Xiao, T. Outsourcing contracts and ordering decisions of a supply chain under multi-dimensional uncertainties. *Comput. Ind. Eng.* **2019**, *130*, 127–141. [CrossRef]
40. Esmaeili-Najafabadi, E.; Azad, N.; Pourmohammadi, H.; Nezhad, M. Risk-averse outsourcing strategy in the presence of demand and supply uncertainties. *Comput. Ind. Eng.* **2021**, *151*, 106906. [CrossRef]

Article

Lightweight Image Super-Resolution Based on Local Interaction of Multi-Scale Features and Global Fusion

Zhiqing Meng [1,*], Jing Zhang [1], Xiangjun Li [2,*] and Lingyin Zhang [1]

1 School of Management, Zhejiang University of Technology, Hangzhou 310023, China; 2112004010@zjut.edu.cn (J.Z.); 2112104208@zjut.edu.cn (L.Z.)
2 School of Information Engineering, Xi'an University, Xi'an 710061, China
* Correspondence: mengzhiqing@zjut.edu.cn (Z.M.); leelindass@xawl.edu.cn (X.L.)

Abstract: In recent years, computer vision technology has been widely applied in various fields, making super-resolution (SR), a low-level visual task, a research hotspot. Although deep convolutional neural network has made good progress in the field of single-image super-resolution (SISR), its adaptability to real-time interactive devices that require fast response is poor due to the excessive amount of network model parameters, the long inference image time, and the complex training model. To solve this problem, we propose a lightweight image reconstruction network (MSFN) for multi-scale feature local interaction based on global connection of the local feature channel. Then, we develop a multi-scale feature interaction block (FIB) in MSFN to fully extract spatial information of different regions of the original image by using convolution layers of different scales. On this basis, we use the channel stripping operation to compress the model, and reduce the number of model parameters as much as possible on the premise of ensuring the reconstructed image quality. Finally, we test the proposed MSFN model with the benchmark datasets. The experimental results show that the MSFN model is better than the other state-of-the-art SR methods in reconstruction effect, computational complexity, and inference time.

Keywords: multi-scale; local interaction; lightweight image reconstruction network; global fusion

MSC: 68T01; 68T07

Citation: Meng, Z.; Zhang, J.; Li, X.; Zhang, L. Lightweight Image Super-Resolution Based on Local Interaction of Multi-Scale Features and Global Fusion. *Mathematics* 2022, 10, 1096. https://doi.org/10.3390/math10071096

Academic Editor: Jakub Nalepa

Received: 21 February 2022
Accepted: 25 March 2022
Published: 29 March 2022

Publisher's Note: MDPI stays neutral with regard to jurisdictional claims in published maps and institutional affiliations.

Copyright: © 2022 by the authors. Licensee MDPI, Basel, Switzerland. This article is an open access article distributed under the terms and conditions of the Creative Commons Attribution (CC BY) license (https://creativecommons.org/licenses/by/4.0/).

1. Introduction

Single-image super-resolution (SISR) refers to the process of recovering a natural and clear high-resolution (HR) image from a low-resolution (LR) image. SISR has a wide range of applications in the real world, which are often used to improve the visual quality of images [1] and the performance of other high-level vision tasks [2], especially in the fields of satellite and aerial imaging [3–5], medical imaging [6–8], ultrasound imaging [9], and face recognition [10] etc. However, since different HR images can be downsampled to the same LR image, as a result, the incompatibility makes SISR still a challenging task.

In recent years, with the continuous improvement of computer learning capabilities, deep neural networks, especially methods based on convolutional neural networks, have been widely used in SISR, which has greatly promoted the development of image reconstructions. Dong et al. [11] first introduced a convolutional neural network (CNN) into the field of SR images, and proposed a super-resolution convolutional neural network (SRCNN). However, as the input LR image needs to be preprocessed by bicubic interpolation, the computational complexity is increased, and the high-frequency details in the original image are lost, which limit the efficiency of image reconstruction. Shi et al. [12] proposed an efficient sub-pixel convolutional neural network (ESPCN), which effectively replaces the bicubic interpolation preprocessing with a sub-pixel convolutional algorithm for upsampling operation, thereby reducing the overall computational complexity and avoiding the checkerboard effect caused by the deconvolution layer. In pursuit of better model performance, Zhang et al. [13] proposed the very deep residual channel attention network (RCAN) based on ESPCN, which stacks a large number of residual blocks and local connections to obtain better reconstruction quality.

It is found that increasing the network depth can improve the quality of image reconstruction, but it also leads to a substantial increase in the number of model parameters, and it also makes the training model more complicated. To solve this problem, Tai et al. [14] added a recursive block to the neural network to reduce model parameters, constructed a deep recursive residual network (DRRN), and transmitted the residual information through a combination of global learning and local learning to reduce the difficulty of training. DRRN uses a shared parameter strategy to reduce the parameters, but, in fact, it requires a huge amount of calculation to reconstruct the image. Hui et al. [15] proposed an information distillation network (IDN) which divides the features into two parts, with one part retained and the other part continuing to be used to extract information; thus, the model parameters are reduced under the premise of ensuring the quality of reconstruction quantity. Liu et al. [16] proposed a residual feature distillation network (RFDN) based on residual learning. The network retains the original features of the image without introducing additional parameters through residual connection, but the obtained feature map lacks related information of local features. Based on RFDN, this paper strips the channels with rich information features in the model, and pays more attention to the multi-scale channel information of the original image and the associated information of the local area. The main work of this paper is as follows:

- We propose a lightweight image super-resolution reconstruction network based on local feature channels and global connection mechanism, which separates the channels in the model and retains the channel features with rich spatial information. Our model significantly reduces the number of model parameters.
- We construct a feature fusion block based on local interaction of multi-scale features, which includes channel attention mechanism and multi-scale local feature interaction mechanism. The multi-scale local feature interaction mechanism is mainly composed of feature interaction blocks, through which local attention and interaction can effectively improve the authenticity of the reconstructed image compared with the original image, and realize the connection and fusion of multi-scale features.
- We use residual learning and global connection to fuse local features and global features, retain the high-frequency information and edge details of the original image, and improve the quality of the reconstructed image. As shown in Figure 1, on the Urban100 test set with scaling factor ×4, the PSNR of the reconstructed image of the MSFN model reaches 26.34 dB. Compared with the models CARN and SRMDNF of the same size, the reconstruction effect of our model is greatly improved.

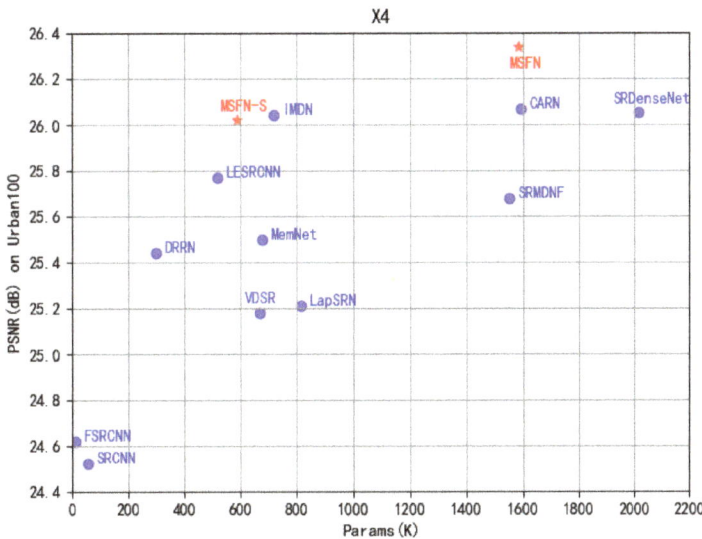

Figure 1. Trade-off between reconstruction performance and parameters on Urban100 with scaling factor ×4.

2. Related Work

In recent years, the super-resolution of single image has been studied extensively [17–19]. We present an overview of the deep CNN for image super-resolution in Section 2.1. In order to reduce model parameters and speed up image reasoning, lightweight image super-resolution models have been widely studied. We will elaborate on this part in Section 2.2.

2.1. Deep CNN for Image Super-Resolution

Dong et al. [11] used end-to-end convolutional neural network (SRCNN) for the first time to extract, map, and reconstruct image features, and found that the reconstruction effect exceeded the traditional image super-resolution (SR) method. However, the network structure is simple and the correlation between low-resolution (LR) image and original image is not considered. Some researchers started with the depth of the network, hoping to fully extract the relevant information between images through the deep network model. Kim et al. [20] proposed a very deep super-resolution (VDSR) convolutional network based on the global residual learning method, which not only improves the reconstruction effect, but also accelerates the network convergence speed. Haris et al. [21] proposed a deep back-projection network (DBPN) for super-resolution with iterative up–down sampling, which provides timely feedback of the error mapping at each stage, and performs better, especially in large-scale images. Yang et al. [22] used skip connections to increase the number of network layers, which enhanced the feature expression ability of the network and made the reconstructed image closer to the real image. Lim et al. [23] removed the batch specification layers that affected the reconstruction effect in an enhanced deep super-resolution network (EDSR), and stacked more convolutional layers to achieve better performance of the model. In order to improve the visual effect of reconstructed images, Yang et al. [24] constructed a multi-level feature extraction module using dense connections, which can obtain richer hierarchical feature images. With the deepening of the network structure, the number of parameters and the computational complexity of this type of model increase greatly, limiting its application in the real world.

2.2. Lightweight CNN for Image Super-Resolution

In order to reduce the number of model parameters, the complexity, and training difficulty of network calculation, researchers began to improve the deep network, compressing the model by sharing parameters, residual learning, attention mechanism, and information distillation, and proposed a lightweight image reconstruction network based on CNN. Kim et al. [25] used a deep recursive structure in the deep recursive convolutional network (DRCN) to share parameters, but the model performance was degraded compared with VDSR in some test sets, and the actual amount of computation of the model did not decrease accordingly. Tai et al. [14] proposed a deep recursive residual network (DRRN)-based DRCN, which reduces storage cost and computational complexity by global connection of multipath residual information. Li et al. [26] added an adaptive weighted block in residual learning to fully extract image features and effectively limit the number of model parameters. Hu et al. [27] introduced channel attention mechanism into a deep neural network, and added weight to the features of each output channel in the convolution operation to reasonably allocate limited computer resources, so as to obtain a wide application in the lightweight network architecture. Hui et al. [28] proposed an information distillation network, which uses a combination of embedding loss and information distillation to solve the problem of image recognition. They used a small-size convolution kernel to compress network parameters and reduce the computational cost and complexity of the training model. Tian et al. [29] proposed heterogeneous structure in information extraction and enhancement blocks, which greatly reduced the computational cost and memory consumption. Hui et al. [15] used convolution kernels with sizes of 1×1 and 3×3 to enhance the extracted features, which made the model have better image reconstruction performance and inference speed. Jiang et al. [30] constructed a sparse perceptive attention module based on pruning, which can reduce the model size without a noticeable drop in performance. However, these methods cannot make full use of the associated information between the original image and the low-resolution (LR) image, and the interaction of information between different regions has not been paid enough attention. Based on this, we adopt a fusion block based on multi-scale feature local interaction to fully extract the feature information in the original image. In addition, we strip and compress the channels, and make a trade-off between the performance and the inference speed, which effectively improves the comprehensive performance of the model.

3. Proposed Method

3.1. Network Architecture

In this paper, we propose a lightweight image reconstruction network based on local interaction of multi-scale features, and use local interaction of multi-scale features and the global connection of comparative residuals to learn second-order feature statistics in order to obtain more representative features. The network structure we propose mainly includes five parts: shallow feature extraction block, deep feature extraction block based on multi-scale interaction mechanism, global feature fusion block, upsampling block, and image reconstruction block, as shown in Figure 2.

As shown in Equation (1), I_{LR} represents the input image, and the network uses a convolution layer to extract the shallow features of the input image I_{LR}. The shallow feature extraction block can be expressed as follows:

$$X_{SF} = F_{SF}(I_{LR}) \qquad (1)$$

where $F_{SF}(\cdot)$ represents a simple single-layer convolution mapping, which aims to achieve shallow feature extraction. The shallow feature X_{SF} is extracted through single-layer convolution, and then X_{SF} is input into the deep feature extraction block based on multi-scale interaction mechanism to obtain the high-dimensional feature X_{PF} after feature mapping, which is expressed as Equation (2):

$$X_{PF} = F_{DPAM}(X_{SF}) \qquad (2)$$

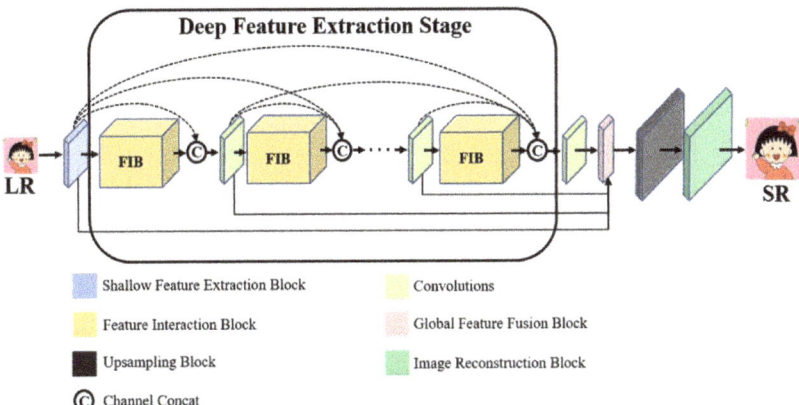

Figure 2. The architecture of our proposed lightweight image reconstruction network (MSFN).

The deep feature extraction block is composed of M feature interaction blocks (FIBs) and M skip connections, where $F_{DPAM}(\cdot)$ represents the mapping function corresponding to the deep feature extraction block, and X_{SF} represents extracted feature maps with deep receptive fields. The features extracted from each FIB are first concatenated in the channel dimension in series to form new high-dimensional features, and then a single-convolution layer is used to reduce the dimensionality of the obtained high-dimensional features. Compared with the existing SISR methods, our feature extraction block based on the multi-scale feature interaction mechanism proposed in this paper can make the network more effectively use the extracted features and suppress invalid features. Moreover, this block can compare and fuse the receptive field information of different scales in the original image, fully retain the texture information of the low-resolution (LR) image, and effectively improve the quality of the reconstructed image. The features extracted from FIB are input into the global feature fusion block, and the feature information extracted at different stages is retained to the maximum extent by means of global connection. The fused feature X_{GF} is shown in Equation (3):

$$X_{GF} = F_{GFF}([X_{PF_1}, X_{PF_2} \cdots X_{PF_m}]) \tag{3}$$

where X_{PF_m} represents the high-dimensional feature extracted by the M-th FID. The feature information extracted by the M FIBs is input into the mapping function $F_{GFF}(\cdot)$ corresponding to the feature fusion block, and the feature information is spliced in the channel dimension to obtain the global feature X_{GF} based on the entire network.

Then, the features after fusion and transformation are used as the input of upsampling block, and the input is upsampled by using the method of sub-pixel convolution [12] to obtain a high-resolution (HR) feature mapping. The features after upsampling are shown in Equation (4):

$$X_{SR} = F_{UP}^L(X_{GF}) = PS(X_{GF}) \tag{4}$$

$$PS(T_{x,y,c \cdot r^2}) = T_{rx,ry,c} \tag{5}$$

In the above Equation, $F_{UP}^L(\cdot)$ represents the upsampling operation based on sub-pixel convolution, and X_{SR} represents the high-resolution (HR) feature map output after upsampling. At present, the commonly used upsampling methods in the field of super-resolution (SR) reconstruction include interpolation operation, transposed convolution operation, and sub-pixel convolution operation. The sub-pixel convolution operation achieves upsampling by rearranging pixels, reducing the amount of model parameters. Therefore, in order to make the network achieve better results in terms of reconstruction rate and accuracy, we choose to implement upsampling through sub-pixel convolution operation. In Equation (4), $PS(\cdot)$ represents a periodic sorting operator, which rearranges the feature map with a size of $H \times W \times C \cdot r^2$ into a feature map with a shape of $rH \times rW \times C$. Equation (5) mathematically describes the subpixel upsampling operation, the effect of which is shown in Figure 3.

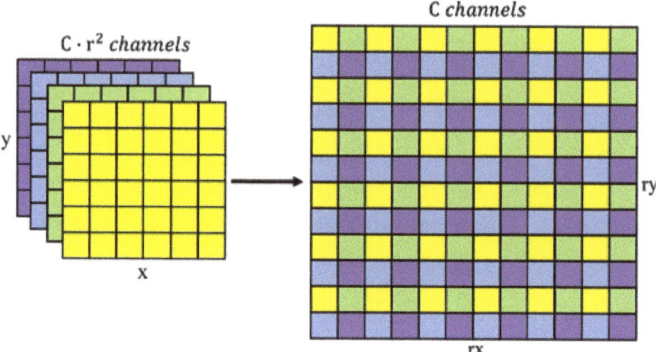

Figure 3. Sub-pixel sample operation.

3.2. Multi-Scale Feature Interaction Block

In this section, we provide more details on the multi-scale FIB. The FIB is the main structure for feature mapping and local fusion in the network, which constructs N multi-scale feature interaction components (MSCs) and N channel attention blocks (CABs) for pixel information of different scales. The FIB structure is shown in Figure 4.

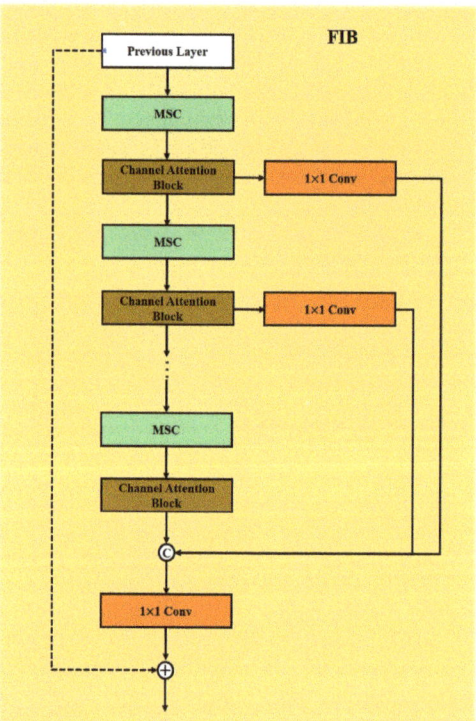

Figure 4. Multi-scale feature interaction block (FIB).

The input of each FIB needs to pass through the MSC to extract the feature information under the condition of multiple receptive fields. As shown in Equation (6), the output feature X_{out}^{i-1} of the $i-1$th MSC is the input feature X_{in}^{i} of the i-th MSC. $F_{MSC}^{i}(\cdot)$ is the mapping relationship corresponding to the i-th MSC, through which we can extract the interaction and spatial information of the regional features of X_{in}^{i} at different scales, so that the high-frequency information and edge texture details of the input image relatively can be completely preserved by the feature X_{out}^{i}.

$$X_{out}^{i} = F_{MSC}^{i}(X_{in}^{i}) \quad (X_{in}^{i} = X_{out}^{i-1}) \qquad (6)$$

The specific architecture of the MSC is shown in Figure 5. It can be seen that the MSC is mainly composed of three filters of different scales, and the convolution kernel sizes of the filter are 1×1, 3×3, and 5×5, respectively. MSCs enrich spatial information by expanding receptive fields, in which the large-scale filters are mainly used to extract feature attention information in different regions, and the small-scale filters are used to enhance the correlation degree between local regions. We pad the edge of the feature map with elements with zero pixel value to ensure that the size of the feature map remains unchanged after the convolution operation. When the size of the convolution kernel of the filter is 3×3 and 5×5, the corresponding edge filling scale is 1 and 2, respectively. When the size of the convolution kernel of the filter is 1×1, no edge filling is performed in the feature map.

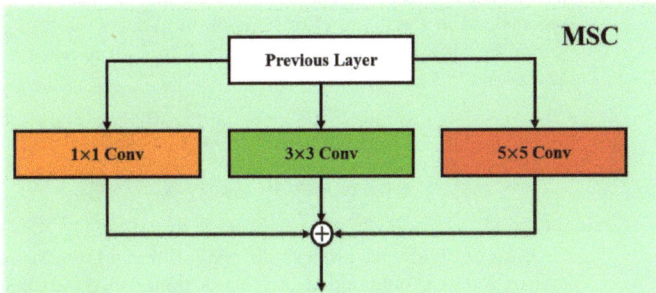

Figure 5. Multi-scale feature extraction component.

The MSC uses filters of different scales to extract and enhance feature information, and the enhanced features are added pixel by pixel according to their weights to obtain a new feature map with rich spatial elements, as shown in Equations (7) [31], (8), and (9):

$$X_i = b_i + \sum_{j=0}^{C_{in}-1} W_i \times X_{pre} \quad (i = 1,2,3) \qquad (7)$$

$$X_{MF} = \sum_{i=1}^{3} k_i \times C_i \times X_i \quad (k_i = 1, i = 1,2,3) \qquad (8)$$

$$C_i = \frac{1}{|X_i|} \quad (i = 1,2,3) \qquad (9)$$

In Equation (7), W_1, W_2, and W_3 represent the weight coefficients corresponding to filters with convolution kernel sizes 1×1, 3×3, and 5×5, respectively. As shown in Figure 6, convolution kernels of different scales focus on the correlation information between different regions of the same object, and then perform weighted summation for the extracted feature information. In Equation (9), C_i represents the two-norm value of each feature vector, and each feature map is normalized by this value. In Figure 6, k_1, k_2, and k_3 represent the corresponding weight coefficients of feature information extracted from each convolution kernel, respectively. In this paper, $k_1 = k_2 = k_3 = 1$, which makes the extracted feature map X_{MF} have rich spatial information features and regional interactions, and is helpful for the restoration and construction of key features and edge information in subsequent image reconstruction.

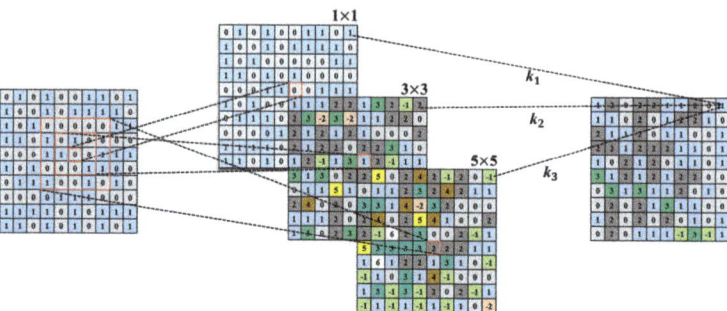

Figure 6. Multi-scale convolution operation.

The features extracted by the feature interaction component are firstly input into the channel attention component, then the output result is input into the remaining $N-1$ MSCs and CABs for iterative optimization; finally, the features obtained at each stage are spliced in the channel dimension, and then the high-dimensional feature X^i is obtained by residual connection with the initial input feature X_{pre}. Specifically, as shown in Equations (10) and (11):

$$X^i = F^i_{CAB}(F^i_{MSC}(\cdots F^1_{CAB}(F^1_{MSC}(X_{pre})))) \quad (i=1,2,\cdots,N) \tag{10}$$

$$X_t = F_{conv1}(Concat[F^i_{conv1}(X^1),\cdots,F^{N-1}_{conv1}(X^{N-1})] + X^N) + X_{pre} \tag{11}$$

where $F^i_{MSC}(\cdot)$ and $F^i_{CAB}(\cdot)$ represent the relationship corresponding to the i-th MSC and CAB, respectively. We use a single convolutional layer to reduce the dimensionality of the feature maps X^i obtained at each stage, then splice the dimension-reduced features in the channel dimension, and finally add the original feature X_{pre} on the pixel-level dimension to obtain the final feature map X_t.

4. Experiments

In this section, we firstly test the influence of the number of FIBs and channels on the quality of the reconstructed image; secondly, we perform test experiments on SR benchmark datasets such as Set5 [32], Set14 [33], Urban100 [34], BSD100 [35], and Manga109 [36]; and then we use the peak signal-to-noise ratio (PSNR) and structural similarity (SSIM) of the Y-channel in YCbCr as quantitative indicators to compare the experimental data with other excellent super-resolution (SR) methods. Finally, we visualize the reconstruction results and analyze the reconstruction effects from a subjective visual perspective.

4.1. Training Settings

In order to compare with existing network algorithms, such as DRRN [14], CARN [37], MemNet [38], and IMDN [28], we use the same training dataset—the DIV2K dataset [39]. The dataset used in this paper includes a total of 800 training images, 100 validation images, and 100 test images, and contains rich scenes with rich edge and texture details. Meanwhile, we perform data enhancement on the training images [40] by using random rotation, horizontal flip, and small window slice to make the training data expand to eight times the original one, so that it can adapt to image reconstruction problems with different tilt angles.

In the training phase, we set batch size to 16, LR input size to 64 × 64, and the number of channels in the convolution layer to 48. The deep feature extraction block based on multi-scale feature interaction mechanism contains six FIBs, and each FIB contains four MSCs and four CABs. Among them, the selection of the number of channels and the numbers of FIBs will be explained in detail in Section 4.2 of this paper. Meanwhile, the model parameters are optimized using the Adam [41] algorithm, which are set to $\beta_1 = 0.9$, $\beta_2 = 0.999$, and $\varepsilon = 10^{-8}$. The learning rate is initially set to 10^{-3} by using weight normalization and then decreased to half each 200 epoch of back-propagation. All the experiments were completed on a computer with the following specifications: Intel i7-9700, 32 GB RAM, and NVIDIA GeForce RTX2080Ti 12 GB GPU.

4.2. Ablation Experiment

We first study the influence of the number of multi-scale feature interaction blocks (FIBs) in the model on the final experimental results, taking the DIK2K dataset as the training object, and then we test the quantitative indicators of the model on the Set14 dataset. The experimental results are shown in Table 1 and Figure 7.

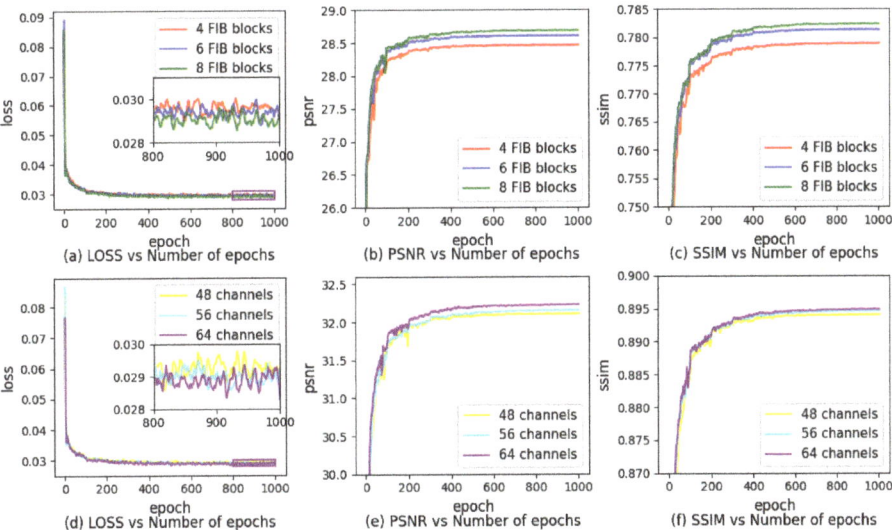

Figure 7. The influence of the number of FIBs on the model reconstruction effect. (a) LOSS vs. number of epochs; (b) PSNR vs. number of epochs; (c) SSIM vs. number of epochs. The influence of the number of channels in the FIB on the model reconstruction effect. (d) LOSS vs. number of epochs; (e) PSNR vs. number of epochs; (f) SSIM vs. number of epochs.

Table 1. The influence of the number of FIBs on the model reconstruction effect.

Scale	Number of FIBs	Number of Channels	Params (K)	Set14	
				PSNR (dB)	SSIM
4×	4	48	395	28.47	0.7789
	6		571	28.61	0.7814
	8		747	28.69	0.7824

In order to better understand the relationship between the number of FIBs and the quality of image reconstruction, we set the number of channels to 48, control the number, and keep parameters of other components in the model unchanged, and only change the number of FIBs. It can be seen from Table 1 that the image reconstruction quality is positively correlated with the number of FIBs. Here we set the scaling factor to four: it shows that when the number of FIBs increases from four to six, the model parameters are relatively increased by 176 K, and the PSNR of reconstructed images is relatively increased by 0.14, which indicates that the reconstruction quality has been significantly improved. When the number of FIBs increases from six to eight, the SSIM value of the reconstructed image is improved to 0.7824. The influence curves of the number of FIBs on the LOSS value, PSNR value, and SSIM value of reconstruction results are shown in Figure 7a–c. As the number of FIBs increases, the LOSS value of reconstructed image relative to the original image decreases, while the value of quantitative indicators such as PSNR and SSIM increases.

In order to verify the influence of the number of channels in the FIB on the reconstruction quality of the model, we perform comparative experiments on models with different numbers of channels. It can be seen from Table 2 that as the number of channels increases, the reconstruction quality of the model for the Urban100 dataset increases, but the number of model parameters also increases sharply. When the number of channels is adjusted from 48 to 64, the number of the entire model parameters is greatly increased from 571 K to 1004 K, while the SSIM value is only increased by 0.0009. Figure 7d–f show the comparison of LOSS value, PSNR value, and SSIM value of models based on different number of channels on Set5 dataset, respectively. It can be found that although the image reconstruction quality can be improved by increasing the number of channels in FIB, the number of model parameters also increases sharply, as shown in Table 2. Therefore, from the perspective of model lightweight, the larger number of channels is not the better one, and it needs to be considered comprehensively in combination with the number of model parameters. As can be seen from Tables 1 and 2 and Figure 7, when we set the number of FIBs to six and the number of channels to 48 after considering comprehensively, the model has the best comprehensive performance in terms of parameter number and reconstruction effect.

Table 2. The influence of the number of channels in the FIB on the model reconstruction effect.

Scale	Number of FIBs	Number of Channels	Params (K)	Set5	
				PSNR (dB)	SSIM
4×	6	48	571	32.12	0.8941
		56	772	32.16	0.8947
		64	1004	32.23	0.8950

In order to further explore the operation mechanism of feature extraction from different-sized convolution kernels and their influence on reconstructed images, we stripped the feature map extracted from convolution layers of the first MSC at different scales in the second FIB and performed visual analysis on the separated features. Figure 8b shows that the small-scale convolution kernel pays more attention to the pixel information of the shallow layer, focusing on extracting the small-resolution features in the original image. By analyzing Figure 8c,d, we can find that the larger the size of the convolution kernel, the more global the extracted information, and the more attention is given to the relevance of local information. Therefore, using convolution kernels of different scales to extract and pay attention to spatial information of different levels has theoretical significance and practical effect in terms of visualized results.

4.3. Quantitative Analysis

We compared the proposed MSFN with commonly used baseline SR models with ×2, ×3, and ×4 scales, including SRCNN [11], FSRCNN [42], VDSR [20], LapSRN [43], DRRN [14], MemNet [38], LESRCNN [29], SRMDNF [44], SRDenseNet [45], CARN [37], and IMDN [28], and here we use PSNR and SSIM [46] as quantitative evaluation metrics. PSNR evaluates the distortion level between the image and the target image based on the error between the corresponding pixels. PSNR is the most common and widely used objective evaluation metric of images. In order to compare the reconstruction performance with the mainstream super-resolution algorithm, PSNR is selected as one of the quantitative evaluation metrics. However, since PSNR does not take into account the visual characteristics of human eyes, the evaluation results are often inconsistent with people's subjective feeling. Therefore, we compare the reconstruction results of each algorithm on SSIM metric.

SSIM is a full-reference image quality evaluation metric, which measures image similarity from the three aspects of brightness, contrast, and structure. SSIM is more consistent with the characteristics of human eye observation images in the objective world.

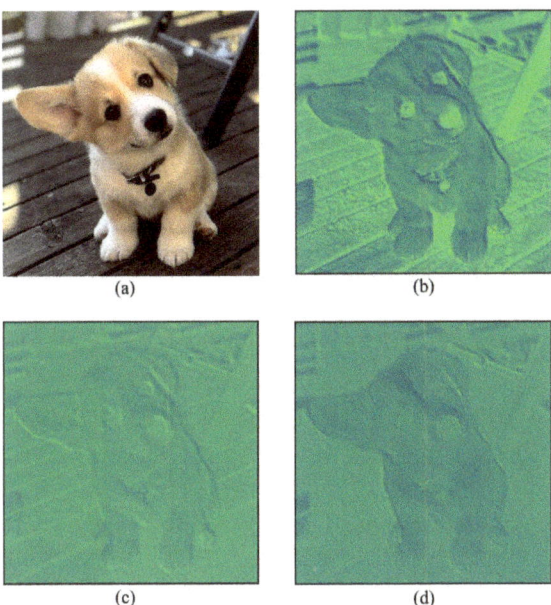

Figure 8. Feature map visualization: (**a**) input image; (**b**) feature map output by the convolution kernel with a size of 1×1; (**c**) feature map output by the convolution kernel with a size of 3×3; (**d**) feature map output by the convolution kernel with a size of 5×5.

The specific results are shown in Table 3 (the red text font represents the optimal results, the number of FIBs in the MSFN model and the MSFN-S model is set to six, the number of channels is set to 48, and the convolution kernel of MSC in the MSFN-S model is set to 1×1, 3×3, and 1×1, respectively)

It can be seen from Table 3 that when the scaling factor is 2, the PSNR value of the MSFN model proposed in this paper is increased by 0.25 dB, 0.25 dB, 0.15 dB, 0.32 dB, and 0.61 dB on the five datasets, respectively, compared with the CARN model of the same parameter scale; it also can be seen that the MSFN model is superior to the CARN model in reconstruction effect. When the scaling factor is 3, the number of parameters of the small-scale MSFN-S model is similar to that of the LESRCNN model, but the image reconstruction quality is much higher than that of the LESRCNN model. The test result on the BSD100 dataset is increased by 0.2 dB, which greatly improves the quality of the reconstructed image, so that the reconstructed image contains rich original information and texture details. When the scaling factor is 4, we screened out the model whose reconstruction quality exceeds 32.10 dB on Set5, among which the MSFN-S model has the smallest number of parameters, and the MSFN-S model obtains better results in the reconstruction tests of other datasets. With Manga109 as the test dataset, the SSIM value of the MSFN reconstructed image is the best in the larger model structure with more than 1000 K parameters, and the optimal value is 0.9089, which is improved by 0.0065 compared with the SRMDNF model of the same scale.

Table 3. Average PSNR/SSIM value for scale factor ×2, ×3, and ×4 on datasets Set5, Set14, BSD100, Urban100, and Manga109.

Method	Scale	Params	Set5 PSNR/SSIM	Set14 PSNR/SSIM	BSD100 PSNR/SSIM	Urban100 PSNR/SSIM	Manga109 PSNR/SSIM
Bicubic		-	33.66/0.9299	30.24/0.8688	29.56/0.8431	26.88/0.8403	30.80/0.9339
SRCNN		57 K	36.66/0.9542	32.45/0.9067	31.36/0.8879	29.50/0.8946	35.60/0.9663
FSRCNN		13 K	37.05/0.9560	32.66/0.9090	31.53/0.8920	29.88/0.9020	36.67/0.9710
VDSR		666 K	37.53/0.9590	33.05/0.9130	31.90/0.8960	30.77/0.9140	37.22/0.9750
LapSRN		813 K	37.52/0.9591	33.08/0.9130	31.08/0.8950	30.41/0.9101	37.27/0.9740
DRRN		297 K	37.74/0.9591	33.23/0.9136	32.05/0.8973	31.23/0.9188	37.60/0.9736
MemNet	2×	678 K	37.78/0.9597	33.28/0.9142	32.08/0.8978	31.31/0.9195	37.72/0.9740
LESRCNN		516 K	37.65/0.9586	33.32/0.9148	31.95/0.8964	31.45/0.9206	-/-
SRMDNF		1511 K	37.79/0.9601	33.32/0.9159	32.05/0.8985	31.33/0.9204	38.07/0.9761
CARN		1592 K	37.76/0.9590	33.52/0.9166	32.09/0.8978	31.92/0.9256	38.36/0.9764
IDN		715 K	37.83/0.9600	33.30/0.9148	32.08/0.8985	31.27/0.9196	-/-
IMDN		694 K	38.00/0.9605	33.63/0.9177	32.19/0.8996	32.17/0.9283	38.88/0.9774
MSFN-S		555 K	37.96/0.9603	33.61/0.9181	32.15/0.8988	32.14/0.9272	38.85/0.9772
MSFN		1568 K	38.01/0.9606	33.77/0.9193	32.24/0.9000	32.24/0.9286	38.97/0.9776
Bicubic		-	30.39/0.8682	27.55/0.7742	27.21/0.7385	24.46/0.7349	26.95/0.8556
SRCNN		8 K	32.75/0.9090	29.30/0.8215	28.41/0.7863	26.24/0.7989	30.48/0.9117
FSRCNN		13 K	33.18/0.9140	29.37/0.8240	28.53/0.7910	26.43/0.8080	31.10/0.9210
VDSR		666 K	33.67/0.9210	29.78/0.8320	28.83/0.7990	27.14/0.8290	32.01/0.9340
LapSRN		813 K	33.82/0.9227	29.87/0.8230	28.82/0.7980	27.07/0.8280	32.31/0.9350
DRRN		297 K	34.03/0.9244	29.96/0.8349	28.95/0.8004	27.53/0.8378	32.42/0.9359
MemNet	3×	678 K	34.09/0.9248	30.00/0.8350	28.96/0.8001	27.56/0.8376	32.51/0.9369
LESRCNN		516 K	33.93/0.9231	30.12/0.8380	28.91/0.8005	27.70/0.8415	-/-
SRMDNF		1528 K	34.12/0.9254	30.04/0.8382	28.97/0.8025	27.57/0.8398	33.00/0.9403
CARN		1592 K	34.29/0.9255	30.29/0.8407	29.06/0.8034	28.06/0.8493	33.49/0.9440
IDN		715 K	34.11/0.9253	29.99/0.8354	28.95/0.8013	27.42/0.8359	-/-
IMDN		703 K	34.36/0.9270	30.32/0.8417	29.09/0.8046	28.17/0.8519	33.61/0.9445
MSFN-S		562 K	34.31/0.9265	30.33/0.8421	29.11/0.8053	28.22/0.8531	33.65/0.9451
MSFN		1574 K	34.47/0.9275	30.38/0.8428	29.20/0.8082	28.55/0.8549	33.71/0.9463
Bicubic		-	28.42/0.8104	26.00/0.7027	25.96/0.6675	23.14/0.6577	24.89/0.7866
SRCNN		8 K	30.48/0.8628	27.50/0.7513	26.90/0.7101	24.52/0.7221	27.58/0.8555
FSRCNN		13 K	30.72/0.8660	27.61/0.7550	26.98/0.7150	24.62/0.7280	27.90/0.8610
VDSR		666 K	31.35/0.8830	28.02/0.7680	27.29/0.7260	25.18/0.7540	28.83/0.8870
LapSRN		813 K	31.54/0.8850	28.19/0.7720	27.32/0.7270	25.21/0.7560	29.09/0.8900
DRRN		297 K	31.68/0.8888	28.21/0.7720	27.38/0.7284	25.44/0.7638	29.18/0.8914
MemNet		678 K	31.74/0.8893	28.26/0.7723	27.40/0.7281	25.50/0.7630	29.42/0.8942
LESRCNN	4×	516 K	31.88/0.8903	28.44/0.7772	27.45/0.7313	25.77/0.7732	-/-
SRMDNF		1552 K	31.96/0.8925	28.35/0.7787	27.49/0.7337	25.68/0.7731	30.09/0.9024
SRDenocNet		2015 K	32.02/0.8934	28.50/0.7782	27.53/0.7337	26.05/0.7819	-/-
CARN		1592 K	32.13/0.8937	28.60/0.7806	27.58/0.7349	26.07/0.7837	30.40/0.9082
IDN		715 K	31.82/0.8903	28.25/0.7730	27.41/0.7297	25.41/0.7632	-/-
IMDN		715 K	32.21/0.8948	28.58/0.7811	27.56/0.7353	26.04/0.7838	30.42/0.9074
MSFN-S		571 K	32.12/0.8941	28.61/0.7814	27.56/0.7348	26.02/0.7834	30.45/0.9075
MSFN		1583 K	32.26/0.8946	28.65/0.7815	27.62/0.7364	26.34/0.7906	30.58/0.9089

Red color indicates the best performance.

In order to understand the comprehensive performance of each model, we compare the amount of computational complexity required in the image reconstruction process, the inference time, and the PSNR value of the reconstruction result with those of the models such as LESRCNN [29], CARN [37], IMDN [28], and MSFN-S.

FLOPs stands for floating point operands and can be used to measure the complexity of algorithms and models. Equation (12) describes the theoretical concept of FLOPs mathematically [47]:

$$FLOPs = (2 \times C_i \times K^2 - 1) \times H \times W \times C_o \quad (12)$$

C_i and C_o represent the input and output channels, respectively, K represents the size of the convolution kernel, and H and W represent the size of the output feature map. We randomly select an image from the Set14 dataset with a resolution of 528 × 656 as the test image. We input the image into each reconstruction model, and calculate the computational complexity required by the convolution layer in each model according to Equation (12). Meanwhile, we record the inference time and reconstruction effect in Table 4. From the perspective of inference time, MSFN-S inference test image only takes 31 ms, while IMDN and CARN model need 37 ms and 62 ms to complete inference, respectively. From the perspective of image reconstruction quality, MSFN-S has the highest image quality, with which the value of PSNR reaches 26.67 dB. Therefore, the MSFN-S model is more efficient than the other three models in terms of information timeliness and reconstruction capability.

Table 4. Complexity of five networks for SISR.

Method	FLOPs (G)	Time (ms)	PSNR (dB)
LESRCNN	77	44	26.37
CARN	41	62	26.57
IMDN	21	37	26.62
MSFN-S	18	31	26.67

4.4. Qualitative Visual Analysis

Since quantitative indicators such as PSNR and SSIM do not pay attention to the continuity of local details and cannot fully reflect the image quality, we make a visual analysis of the reconstructed images of each model. Here, we use img005 in the Set14 dataset, img019 in the BSD100 dataset, img026 in the Urban100 dataset, and img093 in the Manga109 dataset for the analysis of visualization, with the results shown in Figure 9, from which we can see that the models SRCNN, DRRN, MemNet, and LESRCNN have weak ability to reconstruct edge information and lack relatively clear line information. For example, in the reconstruction result of the img005 image, the edge lines of the headwear are blurry, and the contours of small objects cannot be restored well, while the reconstructed image of the MSFN model has better line information. From the reconstructed image of img019 by MSFN, it can be seen that MSFN can better restore the details of the bifurcation in the upper left corner of the original image, while models such as CARN cannot. Compared with IMDN and other models, the MSFN model has improved its ability to recover key information of the original image. In the original image of img093, there is a black spot in the lower left corner of the eye. Only the MSFN model pays attention to the continuity of the global information and local details of the original image, so that the detailed information of the black spot is better reconstructed. By comparing the visualization results, it can be seen that the MSFN model has a certain improvement in image reconstruction effect compared with the existing models.

In order to verify the correctness more accurately of the subjective judgments of various reconstruction methods, we designed an image definition questionnaire that requires respondents to score the definition of the reconstruction results of each model according to their subjective feelings and select the best restored image given the original image. A total of 108 valid questionnaires were collected in this survey, and the final results are shown in Figure 10, where the y-axis label of the line graph in Figure 10 is the score, which indicates the respondent's definition score of the reconstructed image. Scores range from 0 to 10, with higher scores indicating clearer images to respondents. The y-axis of the bar chart is labeled as frequency, which indicates the number of times interviewees select the reconstructed image as the best restored image. Figure 10c is a subjective analysis of the reconstruction results of img093. It can be seen that the sharpness scores of the reconstruction results of MSFN and MSFN-S are higher than the reconstruction results of the other algorithms. Since MSFN better restores the eye details of the img093, such as the outline of the eye edge and black spots, the number of people who think that the MSFN reconstruction result is closest to the original image is the largest. From Figure 10b,d, it can be found that people think that the reconstructed images of MSFN are more realistic and have higher definition. Therefore, from the perspective of subjective visualization, we can conclude that the reconstruction effect of the MSFN model is better, and the reconstructed image has more local details.

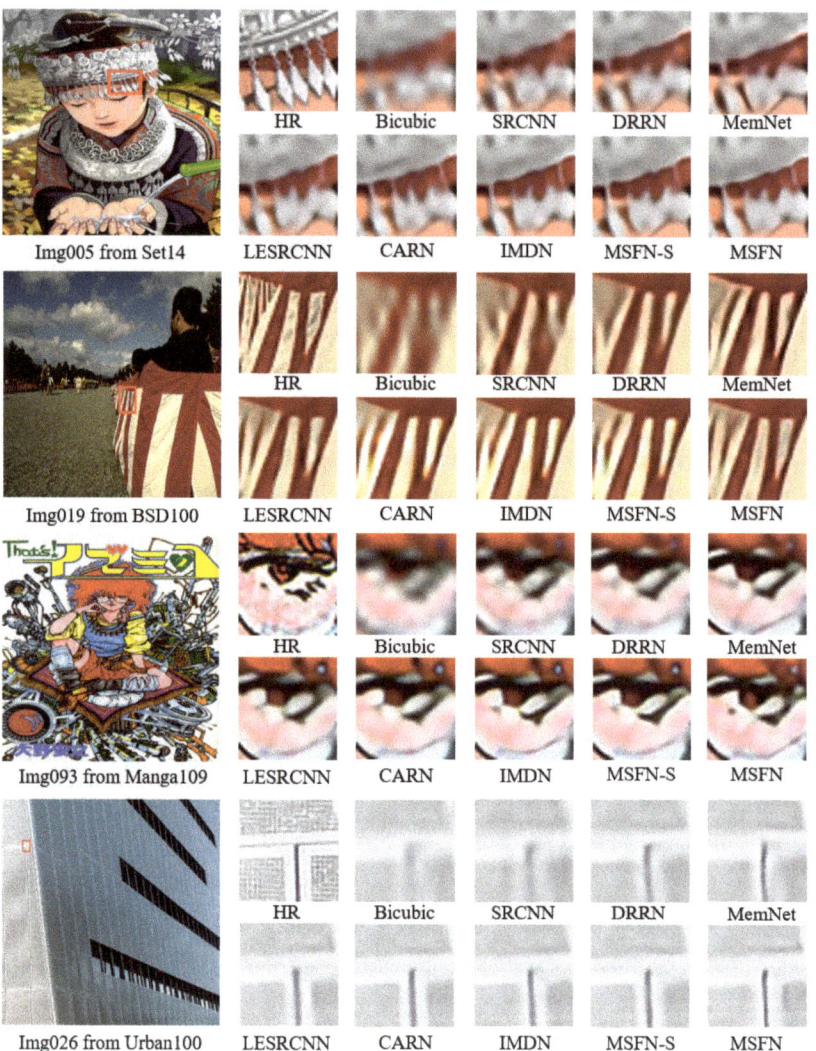

Figure 9. Comparison of reconstructed HR images of img005, img019, img026, and img093 by different SR algorithms with the scale factor ×4.

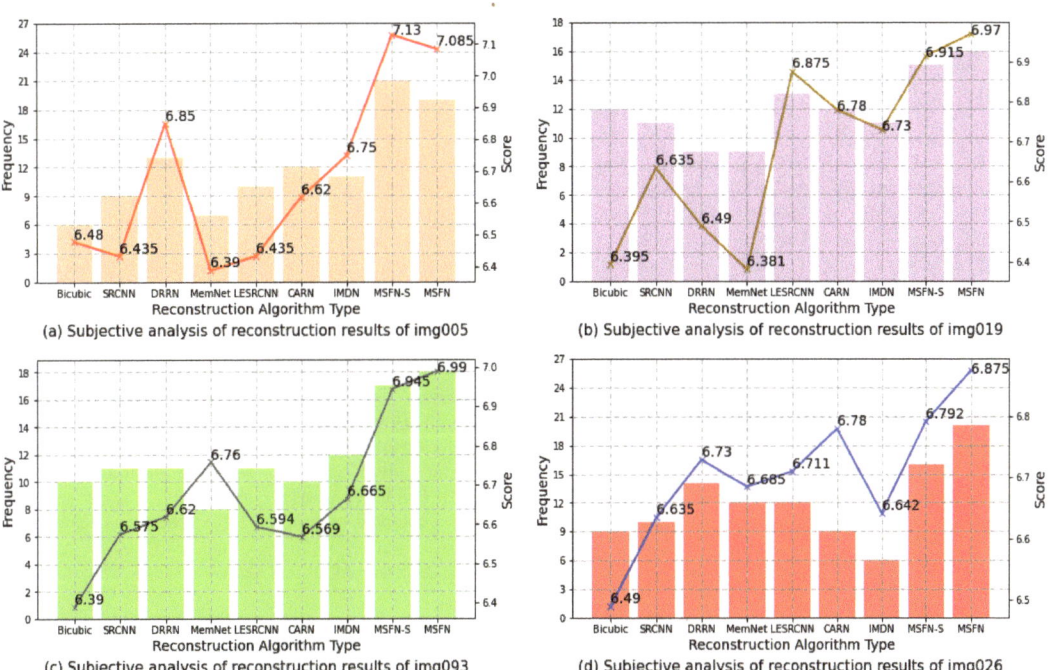

Figure 10. Subjective analysis of different reconstructed images. (**a**) Subjective analysis of reconstruction results of img005; (**b**) subjective analysis of reconstruction results of img019; (**c**) subjective analysis of reconstruction results of img093; (**d**) subjective analysis of reconstruction results of img026.

5. Conclusions

We propose a lightweight image reconstruction network based on multi-scale local interaction and global fusion mechanism. The network uses filters of different sizes to pay attention to the interactive information and correlation degree of different regions of the same pixel, so that the convolution kernels of the same level have different sizes of receptive fields, and retain the rich spatial information of the original image under the condition of fewer parameters. Therefore, our proposed model is superior to other image super-resolution (SR) models of the same level in both subjective visual effects and quantitative indicators. Although the effectiveness of the proposed method has been verified in this paper, we will carry out further study in other applications (such as image denoising and blur reduction) in the future. Besides this, our proposed method is only applied to the models with magnification factor of 2, 3, and 4, and the customization of magnification factor is very important for practical application scenarios. Therefore, the customization of magnification factor of this model needs to be further studied.

Author Contributions: Conceptualization, Z.M. and J.Z.; methodology, Z.M. and X.L.; investigation, L.Z.; writing—original draft preparation, J.Z. and L.Z.; writing—review and editing, X.L. and L.Z.; supervision, Z.M.; funding acquisition, Z.M. All authors have read and agreed to the published version of the manuscript.

Funding: This research is funded by National Natural Science Foundation of China (No. 11871434).

Institutional Review Board Statement: Not applicable.

Informed Consent Statement: Not applicable.

Data Availability Statement: Not applicable.

Conflicts of Interest: The authors declare no conflict of interest.

References

1. Zhou, W.J.; Lin, X.Y.; Zhou, X.; Lei, J.S.; Yu, L.; Luo, T. Multi-layer fusion network for blind stereoscopic 3D visual quality prediction. *Signal Process.-Image Commun.* **2021**, *91*, 116095. [CrossRef]
2. Lu, B.; Chen, J.; Chellappa, R. UID-GAN: Unsupervised Image Deblurring via Disentangled Representations. *IEEE Trans. Biom. Behav. Identity Sci.* **2020**, *2*, 26–39. [CrossRef]
3. Lei, S.; Shi, Z.W.; Zou, Z.X. Super-Resolution for Remote Sensing Images via Local-Global Combined Network. *IEEE Geosci. Remote Sens. Lett.* **2017**, *14*, 1243–1247. [CrossRef]
4. Shermeyer, J.; Van Etten, A. The effects of super-resolution on object detection performance in satellite imagery. In Proceedings of the CVPR, Long Beach, CA, USA, 16–20 June 2019.
5. Yoo, S.; Lee, J.; Bae, J.; Jang, H.; Sohn, H.-G. Automatic generation of aerial orthoimages using sentinel-2 satellite imagery with a context-based deep learning approach. *Appl. Sci.* **2021**, *11*, 1089. [CrossRef]
6. Ren, S.; Jain, D.K.; Guo, K.H.; Xu, T.; Chi, T. Towards efficient medical lesion image super-resolution based on deep residual networks. *Signal Process.-Image Commun.* **2019**, *75*, 1–10. [CrossRef]
7. Shafiei, F.; Fekri-Ershad, S. Detection of Lung Cancer Tumor in CT Scan Images Using Novel Combination of Super Pixel and Active Contour Algorithms. *Trait. Du Signal* **2020**, *37*, 1029–1035. [CrossRef]
8. Mahapatra, D.; Bozorgtabar, B.; Garnavi, R.J.C.M.I. Image super-resolution using progressive generative adversarial networks for medical image analysis. *Comput. Med. Imaging Graph.* **2019**, *71*, 30–39. [CrossRef] [PubMed]
9. Wu, M.-J.; Karls, J.; Duenwald-Kuehl, S.; Vanderby, R., Jr.; Sethares, W. Spatial and frequency-based super-resolution of ultrasound images. *Comput. Methods Biomech. Biomed. Eng. Imaging Vis.* **2014**, *2*, 146–156. [CrossRef] [PubMed]
10. Kwon, O. Face recognition Based on Super-resolution Method Using Sparse Representation and Deep Learning. *J. Korea Multimed. Soc.* **2018**, *21*, 173–180. [CrossRef]
11. Dong, C.; Loy, C.C.; He, K.M.; Tang, X.O. Image Super-Resolution Using Deep Convolutional Networks. *IEEE Trans. Pattern Anal. Mach. Intell.* **2016**, *38*, 295–307. [CrossRef]
12. Shi, W.; Caballero, J.; Huszár, F.; Totz, J.; Aitken, A.P.; Bishop, R.; Rueckert, D.; Wang, Z. Real-time single image and video super-resolution using an efficient sub-pixel convolutional neural network. In Proceedings of the CVPR, Las Vegas, NV, USA, 27–30 June 2016; pp. 1874–1883.
13. Zhang, Y.; Li, K.; Li, K.; Wang, L.; Zhong, B.; Fu, Y. Image super-resolution using very deep residual channel attention networks. In Proceedings of the ECCV, Munich, Germany, 8–14 September 2018; pp. 286–301.
14. Tai, Y.; Yang, J.; Liu, X. Image super-resolution via deep recursive residual network. In Proceedings of the CVPR, Honolulu, HI, USA, 21–26 July 2017; pp. 3147–3155.
15. Hui, Z.; Wang, X.; Gao, X. Fast and accurate single image super-resolution via information distillation network. In Proceedings of the CVPR, Salt Lake City, UT, USA, 18–22 June 2018; pp. 723–731.
16. Liu, J.; Tang, J.; Wu, G. Residual feature distillation network for lightweight image super-resolution. In Proceedings of the ECCV, Glasgow, UK, 23–28 August 2020; pp. 41–55.
17. Chen, H.; He, X.; Qing, L.; Wu, Y.; Ren, C.; Sheriff, R.E.; Zhu, C. Real-world single image super-resolution: A brief review. *Inf. Fusion* **2022**, *79*, 124–145. [CrossRef]
18. Dun, Y.; Da, Z.; Yang, S.; Xue, Y.; Qian, X. Kernel-attended residual network for single image super-resolution. *Knowl.-Based Syst.* **2021**, *213*, 106663. [CrossRef]
19. Tao, Y.; Conway, S.J.; Muller, J.-P.; Putri, A.R.; Thomas, N.; Cremonese, G. Single image super-resolution restoration of TGO CaSSIS colour images: Demonstration with perseverance rover landing site and Mars science targets. *Remote Sens.* **2021**, *13*, 1777. [CrossRef]
20. Kim, J.; Lee, J.K.; Lee, K.M. Accurate image super-resolution using very deep convolutional networks. In Proceedings of the CVPR, Las Vegas, NV, USA, 27–30 June 2016; pp. 1646–1654.
21. Haris, M.; Shakhnarovich, G.; Ukita, N. Deep back-projection networks for super-resolution. In Proceedings of the CVPR, Salt Lake City, UT, USA, 18–22 June 2018; pp. 1664–1673.
22. Yang, X.; Li, X.; Li, Z.; Zhou, D. Image super-resolution based on deep neural network of multiple attention mechanism. *J. Vis. Commun. Image Represent.* **2021**, *75*, 103019. [CrossRef]
23. Lim, B.; Son, S.; Kim, H.; Nah, S.; Mu Lee, K. Enhanced deep residual networks for single image super-resolution. In Proceedings of the CVPR, Honolulu, HI, USA, 21–26 July 2017; pp. 136–144.
24. Yang, X.; Zhang, Y.; Guo, Y.; Zhou, D. An image super-resolution deep learning network based on multi-level feature extraction module. *Multimed. Tools Appl.* **2021**, *80*, 7063–7075. [CrossRef]
25. Kim, J.; Lee, J.K.; Lee, K.M. Deeply-recursive convolutional network for image super-resolution. In Proceedings of the CVPR, Las Vegas, NV, USA, 27–30 June 2016; pp. 1637–1645.
26. Li, Z.; Wang, C.; Wang, J.; Ying, S.; Shi, J. Lightweight adaptive weighted network for single image super-resolution. *Comput. Vis. Image Underst.* **2021**, *211*, 103254. [CrossRef]
27. Hu, J.; Shen, L.; Sun, G. Squeeze-and-excitation networks. In Proceedings of the CVPR, Salt Lake City, UT, USA, 18–22 June 2018; pp. 7132–7141.
28. Hui, Z.; Gao, X.; Yang, Y.; Wang, X. Lightweight image super-resolution with information multi-distillation network. In Proceedings of the 27th ACM International Conference on Multimedia, Nice, France, 21–25 October 2019; pp. 2024–2032.

29. Tian, C.; Zhuge, R.; Wu, Z.; Xu, Y.; Zuo, W.; Chen, C.; Lin, C.-W. Lightweight image super-resolution with enhanced CNN. *Knowl.-Based Syst.* **2020**, *205*, 106235. [CrossRef]
30. Jiang, X.; Wang, N.; Xin, J.; Xia, X.; Yang, X.; Gao, X. Learning lightweight super-resolution networks with weight pruning. *Neural Netw.* **2021**, *144*, 21–32. [CrossRef] [PubMed]
31. Bouvrie, J. Notes on Convolutional Neural Networks. 2006. Available online: https://web-archive.southampton.ac.uk/cogprints.org/5869/ (accessed on 1 February 2022).
32. Bevilacqua, M.; Roumy, A.; Guillemot, C.; Alberi-Morel, M.L. Low-complexity single-image super-resolution based on nonnegative neighbor embedding. In Proceedings of the 23rd British Machine Vision Conference Location (BMVC), Guildford, UK, 3–7 September 2012.
33. Zeyde, R.; Elad, M.; Protter, M. On single image scale-up using sparse-representations. In Proceedings of the International Conference on Curves and Surfaces, Avignon, France, 24–30 June 2010; pp. 711–730.
34. Huang, J.-B.; Singh, A.; Ahuja, N. Single image super-resolution from transformed self-exemplars. In Proceedings of the CVPR, Boston, MA, USA, 7–12 June 2015; pp. 5197–5206.
35. Martin, D.; Fowlkes, C.; Tal, D.; Malik, J. A database of human segmented natural images and its application to evaluating segmentation algorithms and measuring ecological statistics. In Proceedings of the ICCV, Vancouver, BC, Canada, 7–14 July 2001; pp. 416–423.
36. Matsui, Y.; Ito, K.; Aramaki, Y.; Fujimoto, A.; Ogawa, T.; Yamasaki, T.; Aizawa, K. Sketch-based manga retrieval using manga109 dataset. *Multimed. Tools Appl.* **2017**, *76*, 21811–21838. [CrossRef]
37. Ahn, N.; Kang, B.; Sohn, K.-A. Fast, accurate, and lightweight super-resolution with cascading residual network. In Proceedings of the ECCV, Munich, Germany, 8–14 September 2018; pp. 252–268.
38. Tai, Y.; Yang, J.; Liu, X.; Xu, C. Memnet: A persistent memory network for image restoration. In Proceedings of the CVPR, Honolulu, HI, USA, 21–26 July 2017; pp. 4539–4547.
39. Agustsson, E.; Timofte, R. Ntire 2017 challenge on single image super-resolution: Dataset and study. In Proceedings of the CVPR Workshops, Honolulu, HI, USA, 21–26 July 2017; pp. 126–135.
40. Namozov, A.; Im Cho, Y. An improvement for medical image analysis using data enhancement techniques in deep learning. In Proceedings of the 2018 International Conference on Information and Communication Technology Robotics (ICT-ROBOT), Busan, Korea, 6–8 September 2018; pp. 1–3.
41. Kingma, D.P.; Ba, J. Adam: A method for stochastic optimization. In Proceedings of the 3rd International Conference for Learning Representations, San Diego, CA, USA, 7–9 May 2015.
42. Dong, C.; Loy, C.C.; Tang, X. Accelerating the super-resolution convolutional neural network. In Proceedings of the ECCV, Amsterdam, The Netherlands, 11–14 October 2016; pp. 391–407.
43. Lai, W.-S.; Huang, J.-B.; Ahuja, N.; Yang, M.-H. Deep laplacian pyramid networks for fast and accurate super-resolution. In Proceedings of the CVPR, Honolulu, HI, USA, 21–26 July 2017; pp. 624–632.
44. Zhang, K.; Zuo, W.; Zhang, L. Learning a single convolutional super-resolution network for multiple degradations. In Proceedings of the CVPR, Salt Lake City, UT, USA, 18–22 June 2018; pp. 3262–3271.
45. Tong, T.; Li, G.; Liu, X.; Gao, Q. Image super-resolution using dense skip connections. In Proceedings of the CVPR, Honolulu, HI, USA, 21–26 July 2017; pp. 4799–4807.
46. Wang, Z.; Bovik, A.C.; Sheikh, H.R.; Simoncelli, E.P. Image quality assessment: From error visibility to structural similarity. *IEEE Trans. Image Process.* **2004**, *13*, 600–612. [CrossRef] [PubMed]
47. Molchanov, P.; Tyree, S.; Karras, T.; Aila, T.; Kautz, J. Pruning convolutional neural networks for resource efficient inference. *arXiv* **2016**, arXiv:1611.06440.

MDPI
St. Alban-Anlage 66
4052 Basel
Switzerland
www.mdpi.com

Mathematics Editorial Office
E-mail: mathematics@mdpi.com
www.mdpi.com/journal/mathematics

Disclaimer/Publisher's Note: The statements, opinions and data contained in all publications are solely those of the individual author(s) and contributor(s) and not of MDPI and/or the editor(s). MDPI and/or the editor(s) disclaim responsibility for any injury to people or property resulting from any ideas, methods, instructions or products referred to in the content.

www.ingramcontent.com/pod-product-compliance
Lightning Source LLC
LaVergne TN
LVHW070249100526
838202LV00015B/2195